Dodge Caravan
Plymouth
Voyager &
Chrysler
Town & Country
Automotive
Repair
Manual

**by L. Alan LeDoux
and John H Haynes**

Member of the Guild of Motoring Writers

Models covered:

Dodge Caravan, Plymouth Voyager and
Chrysler Town & Country
1996 through 2002

*Does not include information on All-Wheel drive (AWD) and
alternative fuel models*

(30011 - 7T19)

ABCDE
FGHIJ
KLMNO
P   3

Haynes Publishing Group
Sparkford Nr Yeovil
Somerset BA22 7JJ England

Haynes North America, Inc
861 Lawrence Drive
Newbury Park
California 91320 USA

Acknowledgements

Wiring diagrams provided exclusively for Haynes North America, Inc. by Valley Forge Technical Communications. Technical consultants who contributed to this project include Steven Von Eschen and Walter Visnisky.

© **Haynes North America, Inc. 1998, 1999, 2002**

With permission from J.H. Haynes & Co. Ltd.

A book in the Haynes Automotive Repair Manual Series

Printed in the U.S.A.

ISBN 1 56392 469 2

Library of Congress Control Number 2002105216

While every attempt is made to ensure that the information in this manual is correct, no liability can be accepted by the authors or publishers for loss, damage or injury caused by any errors in, or omissions from, the information given.

Contents

Introductory pages

About this manual   0-5
Introduction to the Chrysler Mini-Van models   0-5
Vehicle identification numbers   0-6
Buying parts   0-8
Maintenance techniques, tools and working facilities   0-8
Booster battery (jump) starting   0-16
Jacking and towing   0-16
Automotive chemicals and lubricants   0-17
Conversion factors   0-18
Fraction, decimal and millimeter equivalents   0-19
Safety first!   0-20
Troubleshooting   0-21

Chapter 1
Tune-up and routine maintenance   **1-1**

Chapter 2   Part A
Four-cylinder engine   **2A-1**

Chapter 2   Part B
3.0L V6 engine   **2B-1**

Chapter 2   Part C
3.3L and 3.8L V6 engines   **2C-1**

Chapter 2   Part D
General engine overhaul procedures   **2D-1**

Chapter 3
Cooling, heating and air conditioning systems   **3-1**

Chapter 4
Fuel and exhaust systems   **4-1**

Chapter 5
Engine electrical systems   **5-1**

Chapter 6
Emissions and engine control systems   **6-1**

Chapter 7
Automatic transaxle   **7-1**

Chapter 8
Driveaxles   **8-1**

Chapter 9
Brakes   **9-1**

Chapter 10
Suspension and steering systems   **10-1**

Chapter 11
Body   **11-1**

Chapter 12
Chassis electrical system   **12-1**

Wiring diagrams   **12-23**

Index   **IND-1**

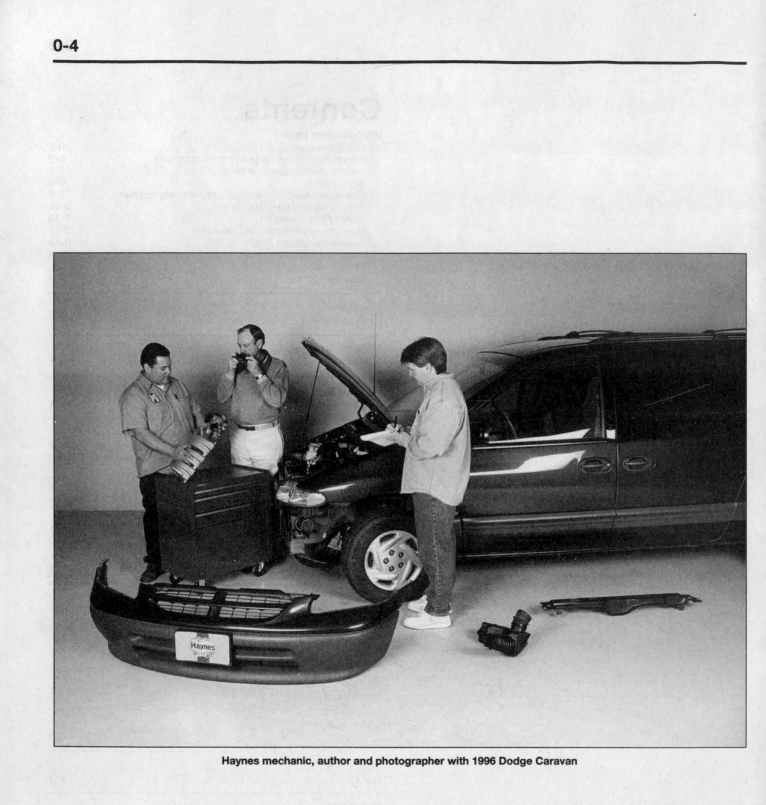

Haynes mechanic, author and photographer with 1996 Dodge Caravan

About this manual

Its purpose

The purpose of this manual is to help you get the best value from your vehicle. It can do so in several ways. It can help you decide what work must be done, even if you choose to have it done by a dealer service department or a repair shop; it provides information and procedures for routine maintenance and servicing; and it offers diagnostic and repair procedures to follow when trouble occurs.

We hope you use the manual to tackle the work yourself. For many simpler jobs, doing it yourself may be quicker than arranging an appointment to get the vehicle into a shop and making the trips to leave it and pick it up. More importantly, a lot of money can be saved by avoiding the expense the shop must pass on to you to cover its labor and overhead costs. An added benefit is the sense of satisfaction and accomplishment that you feel after doing the job yourself.

Using the manual

The manual is divided into Chapters. Each Chapter is divided into numbered Sections, which are headed in bold type between horizontal lines. Each Section consists of consecutively numbered paragraphs.

At the beginning of each numbered Section you will be referred to any illustrations which apply to the procedures in that Section. The reference numbers used in illustration captions pinpoint the pertinent Section and the Step within that Section. That is, illustration 3.2 means the illustration refers to Section 3 and Step (or paragraph) 2 within that Section.

Procedures, once described in the text, are not normally repeated. When it's necessary to refer to another Chapter, the reference will be given as Chapter and Section number. Cross references given without use of the word "Chapter" apply to Sections and/or paragraphs in the same Chapter. For example, "see Section 8" means in the same Chapter.

References to the left or right side of the vehicle assume you are sitting in the driver's seat, facing forward.

Even though we have prepared this manual with extreme care, neither the publisher nor the author can accept responsibility for any errors in, or omissions from, the information given.

NOTE

A **Note** provides information necessary to properly complete a procedure or information which will make the procedure easier to understand.

CAUTION

A **Caution** provides a special procedure or special steps which must be taken while completing the procedure where the Caution is found. Not heeding a Caution can result in damage to the assembly being worked on.

WARNING

A **Warning** provides a special procedure or special steps which must be taken while completing the procedure where the Warning is found. Not heeding a Warning can result in personal injury.

Introduction to the Dodge Caravan, Plymouth Voyager and Chrysler Town & Country

The Dodge Caravan, Plymouth Voyager, and Chrysler Town & Country are front engine, front wheel drive mini-van models. These models are available in either standard length and long length bodies, are equipped with a standard rear liftgate door and a sliding side door on the curb side (passenger side) of the vehicle, and an optional sliding side door on the driver's side. They feature transversely mounted four-cylinder or V6 engines, equipped with electronic multi-port fuel injection. The engine drives the front wheels through a four-speed automatic transaxle via independent driveaxles.

The fully-independent front suspension consists of coil spring/strut units, lower control arms with stabilizer bar links connecting the stabilizer bar. The rear suspension uses a beam axle and spindle/hub units supported by leaf springs. A lateral bar called a panhard rod locates the beam axle, and is connected between the beam axle unit and the vehicle body. A rear stabilizer bar is equipped on some models.

The power-assisted rack-and-pinion steering unit is mounted behind the engine.

Front brakes are discs; the rear brakes are either drum or optional disc-type. Power brake assist is standard with an Antilock Brake System (ABS) optional.

Vehicle identification numbers

Vehicle identification numbers

Modifications are a continuing and unpublicized process in vehicle manufacturing. Since spare parts manuals and lists are compiled on a numerical basis, the individual vehicle numbers are essential to correctly identify the component required.

Vehicle Identification Number (VIN)

The Vehicle Identification Number (VIN), which appears on the Vehicle Certificate of Title and Registration, is also embossed on a gray plate located on the upper left (driver's side) corner of the dashboard, near the windshield (see illustration). The VIN tells you when and where a vehicle was manufactured, its country of origin, make, type, passenger safety system, line, series, body style, engine and assembly plant.

VIN engine and model year codes

Two particularly important pieces of information found in the VIN are the engine code and the model year code. counting from the left, the engine code designation is the 8th digit and the model year code designation is the 10th digit.

On the models covered by this manual the engine codes are:

B	2.4L 4-cyl
3	3.0L V6
R	3.3L V6
L	3.8L V6

On the models covered by this manual the model year codes are:

T	1996
V	1997
W	1998
X	1999
Y	2000
1	2001
2	2002

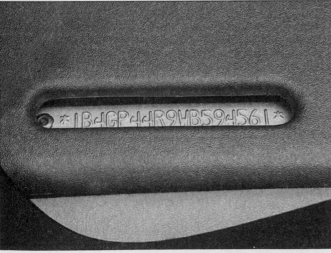

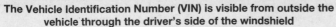

The Vehicle Identification Number (VIN) is visible from outside the vehicle through the driver's side of the windshield

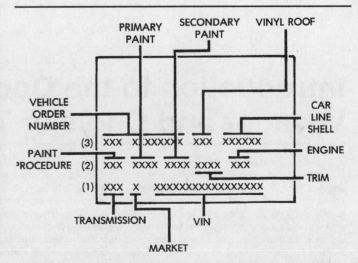

The manufacturer's Body Code Plate is located on the radiator closure panel crossmember in the engine compartment

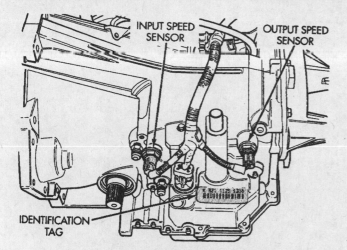

The transaxle identification number is located on a sticker at the left (driver's side) end of the transaxle

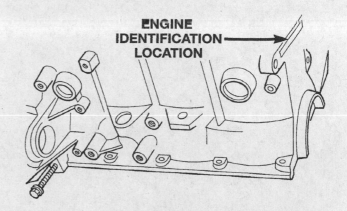

The 2.4L four-cylinder engine identification number is located at the rear of the cylinder block

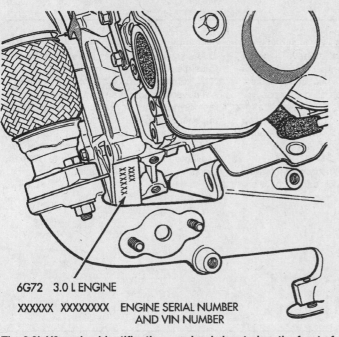

6G72 3.0 L ENGINE

XXXXX XXXXXXXX ENGINE SERIAL NUMBER AND VIN NUMBER

The 3.0L V6 engine identification number is located on the front of the engine near the exhaust crossover pipe, below the cylinder head

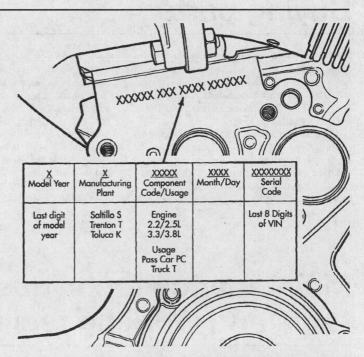

X Model Year	X Manufacturing Plant	XXXXX Component Code/Usage	XXXX Month/Day	XXXXXXXX Serial Code
Last digit of model year	Saltillo S Trenton T Toluca K	Engine 2.2/2.5L 3.3/3.8L Usage Pass Car PC Truck T		Last 8 Digits of VIN

The 3.3L and 3.8L V6 engine identification number is located on the rear of the cylinder block below the cylinder head

Body Code Plate

The body code plate, which is located in the engine compartment on the radiator support crossmember, provides more specific information about the vehicle - type of engine, transaxle, paint, etc. (see illustration).

Transaxle Identification Number

The Transaxle Identification Number is located on a sticker on top of the left end of transaxle housing (see illustration).

Engine Identification Number

The Engine Identification Number is stamped into the rear of the engine block (see illustrations).

Buying parts

Replacement parts are available from many sources, which generally fall into one of two categories - authorized dealer parts departments and independent retail auto parts stores. Our advice concerning these parts is as follows:

Retail auto parts stores: Good auto parts stores will stock frequently needed components which wear out relatively fast, such as clutch components, exhaust systems, brake parts, tune-up parts, etc. These stores often supply new or reconditioned parts on an exchange basis, which can save a considerable amount of money. Discount auto parts stores are often very good places to buy materials and parts needed for general vehicle maintenance such as oil, grease, filters, spark plugs, belts, touch-up paint, bulbs, etc. They also usually sell tools and general accessories, have convenient hours, charge lower prices and can often be found not far from home.

Authorized dealer parts department: This is the best source for parts which are unique to the vehicle and not generally available elsewhere (such as major engine parts, transmission parts, trim pieces, etc.).

Warranty information: If the vehicle is still covered under warranty, be sure that any replacement parts purchased - regardless of the source - do not invalidate the warranty!

To be sure of obtaining the correct parts, have engine and chassis numbers available and, if possible, take the old parts along for positive identification.

Maintenance techniques, tools and working facilities

Maintenance techniques

There are a number of techniques involved in maintenance and repair that will be referred to throughout this manual. Application of these techniques will enable the home mechanic to be more efficient, better organized and capable of performing the various tasks properly, which will ensure that the repair job is thorough and complete.

Fasteners

Fasteners are nuts, bolts, studs and screws used to hold two or more parts together. There are a few things to keep in mind when working with fasteners. Almost all of them use a locking device of some type, either a lockwasher, locknut, locking tab or thread adhesive. All threaded fasteners should be clean and straight, with undamaged threads and undamaged corners on the hex head where the wrench fits. Develop the habit of replacing all damaged nuts and bolts with new ones. Special locknuts with nylon or fiber inserts can only be used once. If they are removed, they lose their locking ability and must be replaced with new ones.

Rusted nuts and bolts should be treated with a penetrating fluid to ease removal and prevent breakage. Some mechanics use turpentine in a spout-type oil can, which works quite well. After applying the rust penetrant, let it work for a few minutes before trying to loosen the nut or bolt. Badly rusted fasteners may have to be chiseled or sawed off or removed with a special nut breaker, available at tool stores.

If a bolt or stud breaks off in an assembly, it can be drilled and removed with a special tool commonly available for this purpose. Most automotive machine shops can perform this task, as well as other repair procedures, such as the repair of threaded holes that have been stripped out.

Flat washers and lockwashers, when removed from an assembly, should always be replaced exactly as removed. Replace any damaged washers with new ones. Never use a lockwasher on any soft metal surface (such as aluminum), thin sheet metal or plastic.

Fastener sizes

For a number of reasons, automobile manufacturers are making wider and wider use of metric fasteners. Therefore, it is important to be able to tell the difference between standard (sometimes called U.S. or SAE) and metric hardware, since they cannot be interchanged.

All bolts, whether standard or metric, are sized according to diameter, thread pitch and length. For example, a standard 1/2 - 13 x 1 bolt is 1/2 inch in diameter, has 13 threads per inch and is 1 inch long. An M12 - 1.75 x 25 metric bolt is 12 mm in diameter, has a thread pitch of 1.75 mm (the distance between threads) and is 25 mm long. The two bolts are nearly identical, and easily confused, but they are not interchangeable.

In addition to the differences in diameter, thread pitch and length, metric and standard bolts can also be distinguished by examining the bolt heads. To begin with, the distance across the flats on a standard bolt head is measured in inches, while the same dimension on a metric bolt is sized in millimeters (the same is true for nuts). As a result, a standard wrench should not be used on a metric bolt and a metric wrench should not be used on a standard bolt. Also, most standard bolts have slashes radiating out from the center of the head to denote the grade or strength of the bolt, which is an indication of the amount of torque that can be applied to it. The greater the number of slashes, the greater the strength of the bolt. Grades 0 through 5 are commonly used on automobiles. Metric bolts have a property class (grade) number, rather than a slash, molded into their heads to indicate bolt strength. In this case, the higher the number, the stronger the bolt. Property class numbers 8.8, 9.8 and 10.9 are commonly used on automobiles.

Strength markings can also be used to distinguish standard hex nuts from metric hex nuts. Many standard nuts have dots stamped into one side, while metric nuts are marked with a number. The greater the number of dots, or the higher the number, the greater the strength of the nut.

Metric studs are also marked on their ends according to property class (grade). Larger studs are numbered (the same as metric bolts), while smaller studs carry a geometric code to denote grade.

It should be noted that many fasteners, especially Grades 0 through 2, have no distinguishing marks on them. When such is the case, the only way to determine whether it is standard or metric is to measure the thread pitch or compare it to a known fastener of the same size.

Standard fasteners are often referred to as SAE, as opposed to metric. However, it should be noted that SAE technically refers to a non-metric fine thread fastener only. Coarse thread non-metric fasteners are referred to as USS sizes.

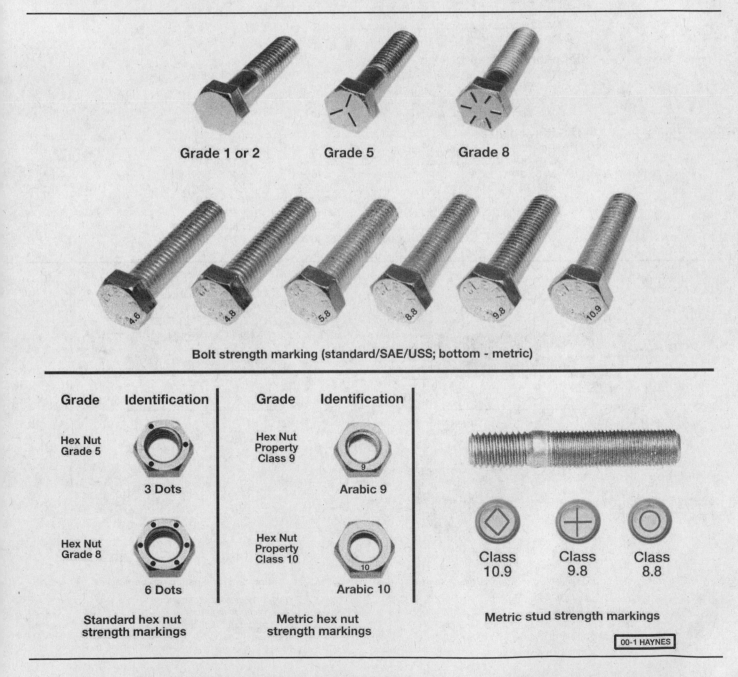

Grade 1 or 2   Grade 5   Grade 8

Bolt strength marking (standard/SAE/USS; bottom - metric)

Grade	Identification		Grade	Identification
Hex Nut Grade 5	3 Dots		Hex Nut Property Class 9	Arabic 9
Hex Nut Grade 8	6 Dots		Hex Nut Property Class 10	Arabic 10

Standard hex nut strength markings

Metric hex nut strength markings

Class 10.9   Class 9.8   Class 8.8

Metric stud strength markings

Since fasteners of the same size (both standard and metric) may have different strength ratings, be sure to reinstall any bolts, studs or nuts removed from your vehicle in their original locations. Also, when replacing a fastener with a new one, make sure that the new one has a strength rating equal to or greater than the original.

Tightening sequences and procedures

Most threaded fasteners should be tightened to a specific torque value (torque is the twisting force applied to a threaded component such as a nut or bolt). Overtightening the fastener can weaken it and cause it to break, while undertightening can cause it to eventually come loose. Bolts, screws and studs, depending on the material they are made of and their thread diameters, have specific torque values, many of which are noted in the Specifications at the beginning of each Chapter. Be sure to follow the torque recommendations closely. For fasteners not assigned a specific torque, a general torque value chart is presented here as a guide. These torque values are for dry (unlubricated) fasteners threaded into steel or cast iron (not aluminum). As was previously mentioned, the size and grade of a fastener determine the amount of torque that can safely be applied to it. The figures listed here are approximate for Grade 2 and Grade 3 fasteners. Higher grades can tolerate higher torque values.

Fasteners laid out in a pattern, such as cylinder head bolts, oil pan bolts, differential cover bolts, etc., must be loosened or tightened in sequence to avoid warping the component. This sequence will normally be shown in the appropriate Chapter. If a specific pattern is not given, the following procedures can be used to prevent warping.

Metric thread sizes	Ft-lbs	Nm
M-6	6 to 9	9 to 12
M-8	14 to 21	19 to 28
M-10	28 to 40	38 to 54
M-12	50 to 71	68 to 96
M-14	80 to 140	109 to 154

Pipe thread sizes		
1/8	5 to 8	7 to 10
1/4	12 to 18	17 to 24
3/8	22 to 33	30 to 44
1/2	25 to 35	34 to 47

U.S. thread sizes		
1/4 - 20	6 to 9	9 to 12
5/16 - 18	12 to 18	17 to 24
5/16 - 24	14 to 20	19 to 27
3/8 - 16	22 to 32	30 to 43
3/8 - 24	27 to 38	37 to 51
7/16 - 14	40 to 55	55 to 74
7/16 - 20	40 to 60	55 to 81
1/2 - 13	55 to 80	75 to 108

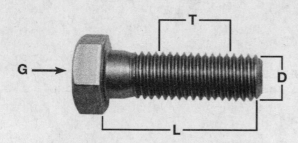
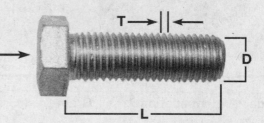

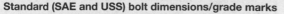

00-2 HAYNES

Standard (SAE and USS) bolt dimensions/grade marks

G   *Grade marks (bolt strength)*
L   *Length (in inches)*
T   *Thread pitch (number of threads per inch)*
D   *Nominal diameter (in inches)*

Metric bolt dimensions/grade marks

P   *Property class (bolt strength)*
L   *Length (in millimeters)*
T   *Thread pitch (distance between threads in millimeters)*
D   *Diameter*

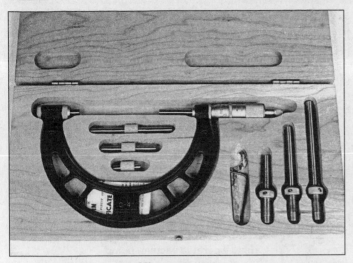
Micrometer set

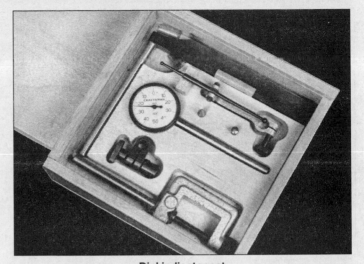
Dial indicator set

Initially, the bolts or nuts should be assembled finger-tight only. Next, they should be tightened one full turn each, in a criss-cross or diagonal pattern. After each one has been tightened one full turn, return to the first one and tighten them all one-half turn, following the same pattern. Finally, tighten each of them one-quarter turn at a time until each fastener has been tightened to the proper torque. To loosen and remove the fasteners, the procedure would be reversed.

Component disassembly

Component disassembly should be done with care and purpose to help ensure that the parts go back together properly. Always keep track of the sequence in which parts are removed. Make note of special characteristics or marks on parts that can be installed more than one way, such as a grooved thrust washer on a shaft. It is a good idea to lay the disassembled parts out on a clean surface in the order that they were removed. It may also be helpful to make sketches or take instant photos of components before removal.

When removing fasteners from a component, keep track of their locations. Sometimes threading a bolt back in a part, or putting the washers and nut back on a stud, can prevent mix-ups later. If nuts and bolts cannot be returned to their original locations, they should be kept in a compartmented box or a series of small boxes. A cupcake or muffin tin is ideal for this purpose, since each cavity can hold the bolts and nuts from a particular area (i.e. oil pan bolts, valve cover bolts, engine mount bolts, etc.). A pan of this type is especially helpful when working on assemblies with very small parts, such as the carburetor, alternator, valve train or interior dash and trim pieces. The cavities can be marked with paint or tape to identify the contents.

Whenever wiring looms, harnesses or connectors are separated, it is a good idea to identify the two halves with numbered pieces of masking tape so they can be easily reconnected.

Gasket sealing surfaces

Throughout any vehicle, gaskets are used to seal the mating surfaces between two parts and keep lubricants, fluids, vacuum or pressure contained in an assembly.

Many times these gaskets are coated with a liquid or paste-type gasket sealing compound before assembly. Age, heat and pressure can sometimes cause the two parts to stick together so tightly that they are very difficult to separate. Often, the assembly can be loosened by striking it with a soft-face hammer near the mating surfaces. A regular hammer can be used if a block of wood is placed between the hammer and the part. Do not hammer on cast parts or parts that could be easily damaged. With any particularly stubborn part, always recheck to make sure that every fastener has been removed.

Avoid using a screwdriver or bar to pry apart an assembly, as they can easily mar the gasket sealing surfaces of the parts, which must remain smooth. If prying is absolutely necessary, use an old broom handle, but keep in mind that extra clean up will be necessary if the wood splinters.

After the parts are separated, the old gasket must be carefully scraped off and the gasket surfaces cleaned. Stubborn gasket material can be soaked with rust penetrant or treated with a special chemical to soften it so it can be easily scraped off. A scraper can be fashioned from a piece of copper tubing by flattening and sharpening one end. Copper is recommended because it is usually softer than the surfaces to be scraped, which reduces the chance of gouging the part. Some gaskets can be removed with a wire brush, but regardless of the method used, the mating surfaces must be left clean and smooth. If for some reason the gasket surface is gouged, then a gasket sealer thick enough to fill scratches will have to be used during reassembly of the components. For most applications, a non-drying (or semi-drying) gasket sealer should be used.

Hose removal tips

Warning: *If the vehicle is equipped with air conditioning, do not disconnect any of the A/C hoses without first having the system depressurized by a dealer service department or a service station.*

Hose removal precautions closely parallel gasket removal precautions. Avoid scratching or gouging the surface that the hose mates against or the connection may leak. This is especially true for radiator hoses. Because of various chemical reactions, the rubber in hoses can bond itself to the metal spigot that the hose fits over. To remove a hose, first loosen the hose clamps that secure it to the spigot. Then, with slip-joint pliers, grab the hose at the clamp and rotate it around the spigot. Work it back and forth until it is completely free, then pull it off. Silicone or other lubricants will ease removal if they can be applied between the hose and the outside of the spigot. Apply the same lubricant to the inside of the hose and the outside of the spigot to simplify installation.

As a last resort (and if the hose is to be replaced with a new one anyway), the rubber can be slit with a knife and the hose peeled from the spigot. If this must be done, be careful that the metal connection is not damaged.

If a hose clamp is broken or damaged, do not reuse it. Wire-type clamps usually weaken with age, so it is a good idea to replace them with screw-type clamps whenever a hose is removed.

Tools

A selection of good tools is a basic requirement for anyone who plans to maintain and repair his or her own vehicle. For the owner who has few tools, the initial investment might seem high, but when compared to the spiraling costs of professional auto maintenance and repair, it is a wise one.

To help the owner decide which tools are needed to perform the tasks detailed in this manual, the following tool lists are offered: *Maintenance and minor repair,*

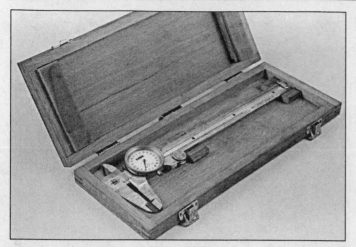

Dial caliper

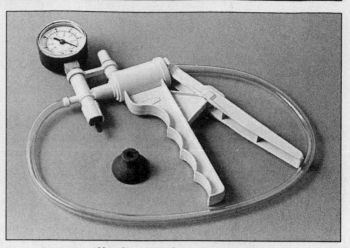

Hand-operated vacuum pump

Timing light

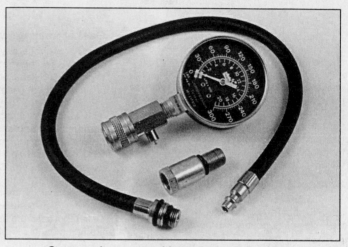

Compression gauge with spark plug hole adapter

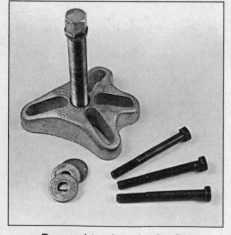

Damper/steering wheel puller

General purpose puller

Hydraulic lifter removal tool

Repair/overhaul and *Special.*

The newcomer to practical mechanics should start off with the *maintenance and minor repair* tool kit, which is adequate for the simpler jobs performed on a vehicle. Then, as confidence and experience grow, the owner can tackle more difficult tasks, buying additional tools as they are needed.

Eventually the basic kit will be expanded into the *repair and overhaul* tool set. Over a period of time, the experienced do-it-yourselfer will assemble a tool set complete enough for most repair and overhaul procedures and will add tools from the special category when it is felt that the expense is justified by the frequency of use.

Maintenance and minor repair tool kit

The tools in this list should be considered the minimum required for performance of routine maintenance, servicing and minor repair work. We recommend the purchase of combination wrenches (box-end and open-

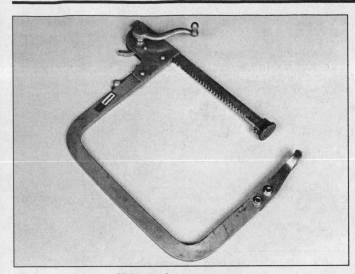

Valve spring compressor

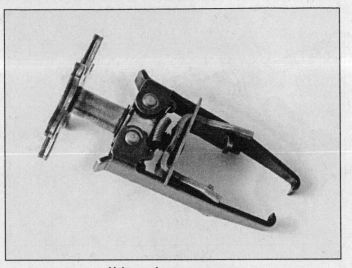

Valve spring compressor

Ridge reamer

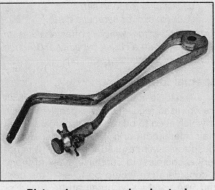

Piston ring groove cleaning tool

Ring removal/installation tool

end combined in one wrench). While more expensive than open end wrenches, they offer the advantages of both types of wrench.

> Combination wrench set (1/4-inch to
> 1 inch or 6 mm to 19 mm)
> Adjustable wrench, 8 inch
> Spark plug wrench with rubber insert
> Spark plug gap adjusting tool
> Feeler gauge set
> Brake bleeder wrench
> Standard screwdriver (5/16-inch x
> 6 inch)
> Phillips screwdriver (No. 2 x 6 inch)
> Combination pliers - 6 inch
> Hacksaw and assortment of blades
> Tire pressure gauge
> Grease gun
> Oil can
> Fine emery cloth
> Wire brush
> Battery post and cable cleaning tool
> Oil filter wrench
> Funnel (medium size)
> Safety goggles
> Jackstands (2)
> Drain pan

Note: *If basic tune-ups are going to be part of routine maintenance, it will be necessary to purchase a good quality stroboscopic timing*

light and combination tachometer/dwell meter. Although they are included in the list of special tools, it is mentioned here because they are absolutely necessary for tuning most vehicles properly.

Repair and overhaul tool set

These tools are essential for anyone who plans to perform major repairs and are in addition to those in the maintenance and minor repair tool kit. Included is a comprehensive set of sockets which, though expensive, are invaluable because of their versatility, especially when various extensions and drives are available. We recommend the 1/2-inch drive over the 3/8-inch drive. Although the larger drive is bulky and more expensive, it has the capacity of accepting a very wide range of large sockets. Ideally, however, the mechanic should have a 3/8-inch drive set and a 1/2-inch drive set.

> Socket set(s)
> Reversible ratchet
> Extension - 10 inch
> Universal joint
> Torque wrench (same size drive as
> sockets)
> Ball peen hammer - 8 ounce
> Soft-face hammer (plastic/rubber)

Ring compressor

> Standard screwdriver (1/4-inch x 6 inch)
> Standard screwdriver (stubby -
> 5/16-inch)
> Phillips screwdriver (No. 3 x 8 inch)
> Phillips screwdriver (stubby - No. 2)
> Pliers - vise grip
> Pliers - lineman's
> Pliers - needle nose
> Pliers - snap-ring (internal and external)
> Cold chisel - 1/2-inch

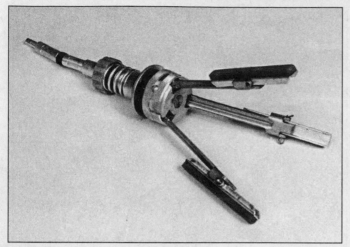

Cylinder hone

Brake hold-down spring tool

Scribe
Scraper (made from flattened copper tubing)
Centerpunch
Pin punches (1/16, 1/8, 3/16-inch)
Steel rule/straightedge - 12 inch
Allen wrench set (1/8 to 3/8-inch or 4 mm to 10 mm)
A selection of files

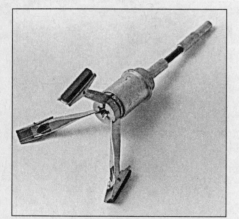

Brake cylinder hone

Wire brush (large)
Jackstands (second set)
Jack (scissor or hydraulic type)

Note: Another tool which is often useful is an electric drill with a chuck capacity of 3/8-inch and a set of good quality drill bits.

Special tools

The tools in this list include those which are not used regularly, are expensive to buy, or which need to be used in accordance with their manufacturer's instructions. Unless these tools will be used frequently, it is not very economical to purchase many of them. A consideration would be to split the cost and use between yourself and a friend or friends. In addition, most of these tools can be obtained from a tool rental shop on a temporary basis.

This list primarily contains only those tools and instruments widely available to the public, and not those special tools produced by the vehicle manufacturer for distribution to dealer service departments. Occasionally, references to the manufacturer's special tools are included in the text of this manual. Generally, an alternative method of doing the job without the special tool is offered. How-

ever, sometimes there is no alternative to their use. Where this is the case, and the tool cannot be purchased or borrowed, the work should be turned over to the dealer service department or an automotive repair shop.

Valve spring compressor
Piston ring groove cleaning tool
Piston ring compressor
Piston ring installation tool
Cylinder compression gauge
Cylinder ridge reamer
Cylinder surfacing hone
Cylinder bore gauge
Micrometers and/or dial calipers
Hydraulic lifter removal tool
Balljoint separator
Universal-type puller
Impact screwdriver
Dial indicator set
Stroboscopic timing light (inductive pick-up)
Hand operated vacuum/pressure pump
Tachometer/dwell meter
Universal electrical multimeter
Cable hoist
Brake spring removal and installation tools
Floor jack

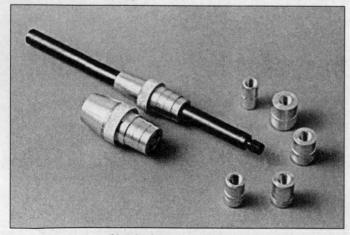

Clutch plate alignment tool

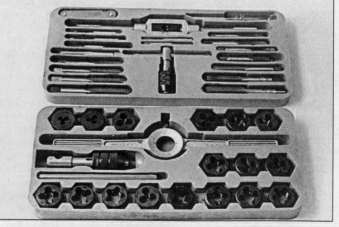

Tap and die set

Buying tools

For the do-it-yourselfer who is just starting to get involved in vehicle maintenance and repair, there are a number of options available when purchasing tools. If maintenance and minor repair is the extent of the work to be done, the purchase of individual tools is satisfactory. If, on the other hand, extensive work is planned, it would be a good idea to purchase a modest tool set from one of the large retail chain stores. A set can usually be bought at a substantial savings over the individual tool prices, and they often come with a tool box. As additional tools are needed, add-on sets, individual tools and a larger tool box can be purchased to expand the tool selection. Building a tool set gradually allows the cost of the tools to be spread over a longer period of time and gives the mechanic the freedom to choose only those tools that will actually be used.

Tool stores will often be the only source of some of the special tools that are needed, but regardless of where tools are bought, try to avoid cheap ones, especially when buying screwdrivers and sockets, because they won't last very long. The expense involved in replacing cheap tools will eventually be greater than the initial cost of quality tools.

Care and maintenance of tools

Good tools are expensive, so it makes sense to treat them with respect. Keep them clean and in usable condition and store them properly when not in use. Always wipe off any dirt, grease or metal chips before putting them away. Never leave tools lying around in the work area. Upon completion of a job, always check closely under the hood for tools that may have been left there so they won't get lost during a test drive.

Some tools, such as screwdrivers, pliers, wrenches and sockets, can be hung on a panel mounted on the garage or workshop wall, while others should be kept in a tool box or tray. Measuring instruments, gauges, meters, etc. must be carefully stored where they cannot be damaged by weather or impact from other tools.

When tools are used with care and stored properly, they will last a very long time. Even with the best of care, though, tools will wear out if used frequently. When a tool is damaged or worn out, replace it. Subsequent jobs will be safer and more enjoyable if you do.

How to repair damaged threads

Sometimes, the internal threads of a nut or bolt hole can become stripped, usually from overtightening. Stripping threads is an all-too-common occurrence, especially when working with aluminum parts, because aluminum is so soft that it easily strips out.

Usually, external or internal threads are only partially stripped. After they've been cleaned up with a tap or die, they'll still work. Sometimes, however, threads are badly damaged. When this happens, you've got three choices:

1) Drill and tap the hole to the next suitable oversize and install a larger diameter bolt, screw or stud.

2) Drill and tap the hole to accept a threaded plug, then drill and tap the plug to the original screw size. You can also buy a plug already threaded to the original size. Then you simply drill a hole to the specified size, then run the threaded plug into the hole with a bolt and jam nut. Once the plug is fully seated, remove the jam nut and bolt.

3) The third method uses a patented thread repair kit like Heli-Coil or Slimsert. These easy-to-use kits are designed to repair damaged threads in straight-through holes and blind holes. Both are available as kits which can handle a variety of sizes and thread patterns. Drill the hole, then tap it with the special included tap. Install the Heli-Coil and the hole is back to its original diameter and thread pitch.

Regardless of which method you use, be sure to proceed calmly and carefully. A little impatience or carelessness during one of these relatively simple procedures can ruin your whole day's work and cost you a bundle if you wreck an expensive part.

Working facilities

Not to be overlooked when discussing tools is the workshop. If anything more than routine maintenance is to be carried out, some sort of suitable work area is essential.

It is understood, and appreciated, that many home mechanics do not have a good workshop or garage available, and end up removing an engine or doing major repairs outside. It is recommended, however, that the overhaul or repair be completed under the cover of a roof.

A clean, flat workbench or table of comfortable working height is an absolute necessity. The workbench should be equipped with a vise that has a jaw opening of at least four inches.

As mentioned previously, some clean, dry storage space is also required for tools, as well as the lubricants, fluids, cleaning solvents, etc. which soon become necessary.

Sometimes waste oil and fluids, drained from the engine or cooling system during normal maintenance or repairs, present a disposal problem. To avoid pouring them on the ground or into a sewage system, pour the used fluids into large containers, seal them with caps and take them to an authorized disposal site or recycling center. Plastic jugs, such as old antifreeze containers, are ideal for this purpose.

Always keep a supply of old newspapers and clean rags available. Old towels are excellent for mopping up spills. Many mechanics use rolls of paper towels for most work because they are readily available and disposable. To help keep the area under the vehicle clean, a large cardboard box can be cut open and flattened to protect the garage or shop floor.

Whenever working over a painted surface, such as when leaning over a fender to service something under the hood, always cover it with an old blanket or bedspread to protect the finish. Vinyl covered pads, made especially for this purpose, are available at auto parts stores.

Booster battery (jump) starting

Observe the following precautions when using a booster battery to start a vehicle:

a) *Before connecting the booster battery, make sure the ignition switch is in the Off position.*

b) *Ensure that all electrical equipment (lights, heater, wipers etc.) are switched off.*

c) *Make sure that the booster battery is the same voltage as the discharged battery in the vehicle.*

d) *If the battery is being jump started from the battery in another vehicle, the two vehicles MUST NOT TOUCH each other.*

e) *Make sure the transaxle is in Neutral (manual transaxle) or Park (automatic transaxle).*

f) *Wear eye protection when jump starting a vehicle.*

Connect one jumper lead between the positive (+) terminals of the two batteries. Connect the other jumper lead first to the negative (-) terminal of the booster battery, then to a good engine ground on the vehicle to be started (see illustration). Attach the lead at least 18 inches from the battery, if possible. Make sure that the jumper leads will not contact the fan, drivebelt of other moving parts of the engine.

Start the engine using the booster battery and allow the engine idle speed to stabilize. Disconnect the jumper leads in the reverse order of connection.

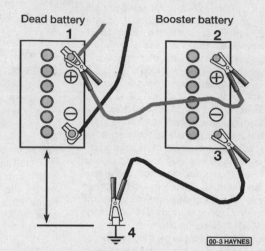

Make the booster battery cable connections in the numerical order shown (note that the negative cable of the booster battery is NOT attached to the negative terminal of the dead battery)

Jacking and towing

Jacking

The jack supplied with the vehicle should be used only for raising the vehicle when changing a tire or placing jackstands under the frame. **Warning:** *Never work under the vehicle or start the engine when this jack is being used as the only means of support.*

The vehicle should be on firm, level ground with the wheels blocked and the transaxle in Park (automatic transaxle). If a tire is being changed, first loosen the lug nuts one-half turn only to initially loosen the lug nuts before jacking the vehicle - then leave the lug nuts them in place until jacking the vehicle to raise the wheel off the ground. Make sure no passengers are inside the vehicle as it's being raised off the ground.

Place the jack under the side of the vehicle at the jacking point nearest the wheel to be changed (see illustration). **Caution:** *Never place the jack under the rear springs themselves.* If you're using a floor jack, place it beneath the unibody frame jacking point at the front or rear as shown in the illustration. **Note:** *If your van is equipped with optional factory-installed ground effects panels around the bottom exterior side sills of the vehicle, special hoisting pads are to be used - they are labeled HOIST POINT.* Operate the jack with a slow, smooth motion until the wheel is raised off the ground. If you're using jackstands, position them at the support points.

Remove the lug nuts, pull off the wheel, install the spare and thread the lug nuts back on with the beveled sides facing in. Tighten them snugly, but wait until the vehicle is lowered to tighten them completely.

Lower the vehicle, remove the jack and tighten the lug nuts (if loosened or removed) in a criss-cross pattern. If possible, tighten them with a torque wrench (see Chapter 1 for the torque figures). If you don't have access to a torque wrench, have the nuts checked by a service station or repair shop as soon as possible. Retighten the lug nuts after 500 miles.

If the vehicle is equipped with a temporary spare tire, remember that it is intended only for temporary use until the regular tire can be repaired. Do not exceed the maximum speed that the tire is rated for.

Towing

It is recommended the vehicle be towed with the front (drive) wheels off the ground or carried on a flatbed truck to prevent damage to the transaxle. A wheel lift or towing dolly is recommended. If absolutely necessary, the vehicle may be towed from the rear with the front wheels on the ground or from the front using a tow bar with all four wheels on the ground, providing that speed don't exceed 25 mph and the distance is less than 15 miles; the transaxle can be damaged if these limitations are exceeded.

While towing, the parking brake must be released. Do not exceed 50 mph (35 mph on rough roads). For complete safety, in the event that the front wheels were to touch the ground, the transaxle must be in Neutral and the steering must be unlocked (ignition switch in the OFF position).

Safety is a major consideration while towing and all applicable state and local laws must be obeyed. A safety chain system must be used at all times. Remember that power steering and power brakes will not work with the engine off.

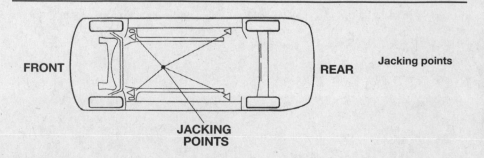

FRONT   **REAR**   **Jacking points**

JACKING POINTS

Automotive chemicals and lubricants

A number of automotive chemicals and lubricants are available for use during vehicle maintenance and repair. They include a wide variety of products ranging from cleaning solvents and degreasers to lubricants and protective sprays for rubber, plastic and vinyl.

Cleaners

Carburetor cleaner and choke cleaner is a strong solvent for gum, varnish and carbon. Most carburetor cleaners leave a dry-type lubricant film which will not harden or gum up. Because of this film it is not recommended for use on electrical components.

Brake system cleaner is used to remove grease and brake fluid from the brake system, where clean surfaces are absolutely necessary. It leaves no residue and often eliminates brake squeal caused by contaminants.

Electrical cleaner removes oxidation, corrosion and carbon deposits from electrical contacts, restoring full current flow. It can also be used to clean spark plugs, carburetor jets, voltage regulators and other parts where an oil-free surface is desired.

Demoisturants remove water and moisture from electrical components such as alternators, voltage regulators, electrical connectors and fuse blocks. They are non-conductive, non-corrosive and non-flammable.

Degreasers are heavy-duty solvents used to remove grease from the outside of the engine and from chassis components. They can be sprayed or brushed on and, depending on the type, are rinsed off either with water or solvent.

Lubricants

Motor oil is the lubricant formulated for use in engines. It normally contains a wide variety of additives to prevent corrosion and reduce foaming and wear. Motor oil comes in various weights (viscosity ratings) from 0 to 50. The recommended weight of the oil depends on the season, temperature and the demands on the engine. Light oil is used in cold climates and under light load conditions. Heavy oil is used in hot climates and where high loads are encountered. Multi-viscosity oils are designed to have characteristics of both light and heavy oils and are available in a number of weights from 5W-20 to 20W-50.

Gear oil is designed to be used in differentials, manual transmissions and other areas where high-temperature lubrication is required.

Chassis and wheel bearing grease is a heavy grease used where increased loads and friction are encountered, such as for wheel bearings, balljoints, tie-rod ends and universal joints.

High-temperature wheel bearing grease is designed to withstand the extreme temperatures encountered by wheel bearings

in disc brake equipped vehicles. It usually contains molybdenum disulfide (moly), which is a dry-type lubricant.

White grease is a heavy grease for metal-to-metal applications where water is a problem. White grease stays soft under both low and high temperatures (usually from -100 to +190-degrees F), and will not wash off or dilute in the presence of water.

Assembly lube is a special extreme pressure lubricant, usually containing moly, used to lubricate high-load parts (such as main and rod bearings and cam lobes) for initial start-up of a new engine. The assembly lube lubricates the parts without being squeezed out or washed away until the engine oiling system begins to function.

Silicone lubricants are used to protect rubber, plastic, vinyl and nylon parts.

Graphite lubricants are used where oils cannot be used due to contamination problems, such as in locks. The dry graphite will lubricate metal parts while remaining uncontaminated by dirt, water, oil or acids. It is electrically conductive and will not foul electrical contacts in locks such as the ignition switch.

Moly penetrants loosen and lubricate frozen, rusted and corroded fasteners and prevent future rusting or freezing.

Heat-sink grease is a special electrically non-conductive grease that is used for mounting electronic ignition modules where it is essential that heat is transferred away from the module.

Sealants

RTV sealant is one of the most widely used gasket compounds. Made from silicone, RTV is air curing, it seals, bonds, waterproofs, fills surface irregularities, remains flexible, doesn't shrink, is relatively easy to remove, and is used as a supplementary sealer with almost all low and medium temperature gaskets.

Anaerobic sealant is much like RTV in that it can be used either to seal gaskets or to form gaskets by itself. It remains flexible, is solvent resistant and fills surface imperfections. The difference between an anaerobic sealant and an RTV-type sealant is in the curing. RTV cures when exposed to air, while an anaerobic sealant cures only in the absence of air. This means that an anaerobic sealant cures only after the assembly of parts, sealing them together.

Thread and pipe sealant is used for sealing hydraulic and pneumatic fittings and vacuum lines. It is usually made from a Teflon compound, and comes in a spray, a paint-on liquid and as a wrap-around tape.

Chemicals

Anti-seize compound prevents seizing,

galling, cold welding, rust and corrosion in fasteners. High-temperature ant-seize, usually made with copper and graphite lubricants, is used for exhaust system and exhaust manifold bolts.

Anaerobic locking compounds are used to keep fasteners from vibrating or working loose and cure only after installation, in the absence of air. Medium strength locking compound is used for small nuts, bolts and screws that may be removed later. High-strength locking compound is for large nuts, bolts and studs which aren't removed on a regular basis.

Oil additives range from viscosity index improvers to chemical treatments that claim to reduce internal engine friction. It should be noted that most oil manufacturers caution against using additives with their oils.

Gas additives perform several functions, depending on their chemical makeup. They usually contain solvents that help dissolve gum and varnish that build up on carburetor, fuel injection and intake parts. They also serve to break down carbon deposits that form on the inside surfaces of the combustion chambers. Some additives contain upper cylinder lubricants for valves and piston rings, and others contain chemicals to remove condensation from the gas tank.

Miscellaneous

Brake fluid is specially formulated hydraulic fluid that can withstand the heat and pressure encountered in brake systems. Care must be taken so this fluid does not come in contact with painted surfaces or plastics. An opened container should always be resealed to prevent contamination by water or dirt.

Weatherstrip adhesive is used to bond weatherstripping around doors, windows and trunk lids. It is sometimes used to attach trim pieces.

Undercoating is a petroleum-based, tar-like substance that is designed to protect metal surfaces on the underside of the vehicle from corrosion. It also acts as a sound-deadening agent by insulating the bottom of the vehicle.

Waxes and polishes are used to help protect painted and plated surfaces from the weather. Different types of paint may require the use of different types of wax and polish. Some polishes utilize a chemical or abrasive cleaner to help remove the top layer of oxidized (dull) paint on older vehicles. In recent years many non-wax polishes that contain a wide variety of chemicals such as polymers and silicones have been introduced. These non-wax polishes are usually easier to apply and last longer than conventional waxes and polishes.

Conversion factors

Length (distance)

Inches (in)	X	25.4	= Millimeters (mm)	X	0.0394	= Inches (in)
Feet (ft)	X	0.305	= Meters (m)	X	3.281	= Feet (ft)
Miles	X	1.609	= Kilometers (km)	X	0.621	= Miles

Volume (capacity)

Cubic inches (cu in; in³)	X	16.387	= Cubic centimeters (cc; cm³)	X	0.061	= Cubic inches (cu in; in³)
Imperial pints (Imp pt)	X	0.568	= Liters (l)	X	1.76	= Imperial pints (Imp pt)
Imperial quarts (Imp qt)	X	1.137	= Liters (l)	X	0.88	= Imperial quarts (Imp qt)
Imperial quarts (Imp qt)	X	1.201	= US quarts (US qt)	X	0.833	= Imperial quarts (Imp qt)
US quarts (US qt)	X	0.946	= Liters (l)	X	1.057	= US quarts (US qt)
Imperial gallons (Imp gal)	X	4.546	= Liters (l)	X	0.22	= Imperial gallons (Imp gal)
Imperial gallons (Imp gal)	X	1.201	= US gallons (US gal)	X	0.833	= Imperial gallons (Imp gal)
US gallons (US gal)	X	3.785	= Liters (l)	X	0.264	= US gallons (US gal)

Mass (weight)

Ounces (oz)	X	28.35	= Grams (g)	X	0.035	= Ounces (oz)
Pounds (lb)	X	0.454	= Kilograms (kg)	X	2.205	= Pounds (lb)

Force

Ounces-force (ozf; oz)	X	0.278	= Newtons (N)	X	3.6	= Ounces-force (ozf; oz)
Pounds-force (lbf; lb)	X	4.448	= Newtons (N)	X	0.225	= Pounds-force (lbf; lb)
Newtons (N)	X	0.1	= Kilograms-force (kgf; kg)	X	9.81	= Newtons (N)

Pressure

Pounds-force per square inch (psi; lbf/in²; lb/in²)	X	0.070	= Kilograms-force per square centimeter (kgf/cm²; kg/cm²)	X	14.223	= Pounds-force per square inch (psi; lbf/in²; lb/in²)
Pounds-force per square inch (psi; lbf/in²; lb/in²)	X	0.068	= Atmospheres (atm)	X	14.696	= Pounds-force per square inch (psi; lbf/in²; lb/in²)
Pounds-force per square inch (psi; lbf/in²; lb/in²)	X	0.069	= Bars	X	14.5	= Pounds-force per square inch (psi; lbf/in²; lb/in²)
Pounds-force per square inch (psi; lbf/in²; lb/in²)	X	6.895	= Kilopascals (kPa)	X	0.145	= Pounds-force per square inch (psi; lbf/in²; lb/in²)
Kilopascals (kPa)	X	0.01	= Kilograms-force per square centimeter (kgf/cm²; kg/cm²)	X	98.1	= Kilopascals (kPa)

Torque (moment of force)

Pounds-force inches (lbf in; lb in)	X	1.152	= Kilograms-force centimeter (kgf cm; kg cm)	X	0.868	= Pounds-force inches (lbf in; lb in)
Pounds-force inches (lbf in; lb in)	X	0.113	= Newton meters (Nm)	X	8.85	= Pounds-force inches (lbf in; lb in)
Pounds-force inches (lbf in; lb in)	X	0.083	= Pounds-force feet (lbf ft; lb ft)	X	12	= Pounds-force inches (lbf in; lb in)
Pounds-force feet (lbf ft; lb ft)	X	0.138	= Kilograms-force meters (kgf m; kg m)	X	7.233	= Pounds-force feet (lbf ft; lb ft)
Pounds-force feet (lbf ft; lb ft)	X	1.356	= Newton meters (Nm)	X	0.738	= Pounds-force feet (lbf ft; lb ft)
Newton meters (Nm)	X	0.102	= Kilograms-force meters (kgf m; kg m)	X	9.804	= Newton meters (Nm)

Vacuum

Inches mercury (in. Hg)	X	3.377	= Kilopascals (kPa)	X	0.2961	= Inches mercury
Inches mercury (in. Hg)	X	25.4	= Millimeters mercury (mm Hg)	X	0.0394	= Inches mercury

Power

Horsepower (hp)	X	745.7	= Watts (W)	X	0.0013	= Horsepower (hp)

Velocity (speed)

Miles per hour (miles/hr; mph)	X	1.609	= Kilometers per hour (km/hr; kph)	X	0.621	= Miles per hour (miles/hr; mph)

Fuel consumption*

Miles per gallon, Imperial (mpg)	X	0.354	= Kilometers per liter (km/l)	X	2.825	= Miles per gallon, Imperial (mpg)
Miles per gallon, US (mpg)	X	0.425	= Kilometers per liter (km/l)	X	2.352	= Miles per gallon, US (mpg)

Temperature

Degrees Fahrenheit = (°C x 1.8) + 32

Degrees Celsius (Degrees Centigrade; °C) = (°F - 32) x 0.56

*It is common practice to convert from miles per gallon (mpg) to liters/100 kilometers (l/100km), where mpg (Imperial) x l/100 km = 282 and mpg (US) x l/100 km = 235

DECIMALS to MILLIMETERS

Decimal	mm	Decimal	mm
0.001	0.0254	0.500	12.7000
0.002	0.0508	0.510	12.9540
0.003	0.0762	0.520	13.2080
0.004	0.1016	0.530	13.4620
0.005	0.1270	0.540	13.7160
0.006	0.1524	0.550	13.9700
0.007	0.1778	0.560	14.2240
0.008	0.2032	0.570	14.4780
0.009	0.2286	0.580	14.7320
0.010	0.2540	0.590	14.9860
0.020	0.5080		
0.030	0.7620		
0.040	1.0160	0.600	15.2400
0.050	1.2700	0.610	15.4940
0.060	1.5240	0.620	15.7480
0.070	1.7780	0.630	16.0020
0.080	2.0320	0.640	16.2560
0.090	2.2860	0.650	16.5100
0.100	2.5400	0.660	16.7640
0.110	2.7940	0.670	17.0180
0.120	3.0480	0.680	17.2720
0.130	3.3020	0.690	17.5260
0.140	3.5560		
0.150	3.8100		
0.160	4.0640	0.700	17.7800
0.170	4.3180	0.710	18.0340
0.180	4.5720	0.720	18.2880
0.190	4.8260	0.730	18.5420
0.200	5.0800	0.740	18.7960
0.210	5.3340	0.750	19.0500
0.220	5.5880	0.760	19.3040
0.230	5.8420	0.770	19.5580
0.240	6.0960	0.780	19.8120
0.250	6.3500	0.790	20.0660
0.260	6.6040		
0.270	6.8580	0.800	20.3200
0.280	7.1120	0.810	20.5740
0.290	7.3660	0.820	21.8280
0.300	7.6200	0.830	21.0820
0.310	7.8740	0.840	21.3360
0.320	8.1280	0.850	21.5900
0.330	8.3820	0.860	21.8440
0.340	8.6360	0.870	22.0980
0.350	8.8900	0.880	22.3520
0.360	9.1440	0.890	22.6060
0.370	9.3980		
0.380	9.6520		
0.390	9.9060	0.900	22.8600
0.400	10.1600	0.910	23.1140
0.410	10.4140	0.920	23.3680
0.420	10.6680	0.930	23.6220
0.430	10.9220	0.940	23.8760
0.440	11.1760	0.950	24.1300
0.450	11.4300	0.960	24.3840
0.460	11.6840	0.970	24.6380
0.470	11.9380	0.980	24.8920
0.480	12.1920	0.990	25.1460
0.490	12.4460	1.000	25.4000

FRACTIONS to DECIMALS to MILLIMETERS

Fraction	Decimal	mm	Fraction	Decimal	mm
1/64	0.0156	0.3969	33/64	0.5156	13.0969
1/32	0.0312	0.7938	17/32	0.5312	13.4938
3/64	0.0469	1.1906	35/64	0.5469	13.8906
1/16	0.0625	1.5875	9/16	0.5625	14.2875
5/64	0.0781	1.9844	37/64	0.5781	14.6844
3/32	0.0938	2.3812	19/32	0.5938	15.0812
7/64	0.1094	2.7781	39/64	0.6094	15.4781
1/8	0.1250	3.1750	5/8	0.6250	15.8750
9/64	0.1406	3.5719	41/64	0.6406	16.2719
5/32	0.1562	3.9688	21/32	0.6562	16.6688
11/64	0.1719	4.3656	43/64	0.6719	17.0656
3/16	0.1875	4.7625	11/16	0.6875	17.4625
13/64	0.2031	5.1594	45/64	0.7031	17.8594
7/32	0.2188	5.5562	23/32	0.7188	18.2562
15/64	0.2344	5.9531	47/64	0.7344	18.6531
1/4	0.2500	6.3500	3/4	0.7500	19.0500
17/64	0.2656	6.7469	49/64	0.7656	19.4469
9/32	0.2812	7.1438	25/32	0.7812	19.8438
19/64	0.2969	7.5406	51/64	0.7969	20.2406
5/16	0.3125	7.9375	13/16	0.8125	20.6375
21/64	0.3281	8.3344	53/64	0.8281	21.0344
11/32	0.3438	8.7312	27/32	0.8438	21.4312
23/64	0.3594	9.1281	55/64	0.8594	21.8281
3/8	0.3750	9.5250	7/8	0.8750	22.2250
25/64	0.3906	9.9219	57/64	0.8906	22.6219
13/32	0.4062	10.3188	29/32	0.9062	23.0188
27/64	0.4219	10.7156	59/64	0.9219	23.4156
7/16	0.4375	11.1125	15/16	0.9375	23.8125
29/64	0.4531	11.5094	61/64	0.9531	24.2094
15/32	0.4688	11.9062	31/32	0.9688	24.6062
31/64	0.4844	12.3031	63/64	0.9844	25.0031
1/2	0.5000	12.7000	1	1.0000	25.4000

Safety first!

Regardless of how enthusiastic you may be about getting on with the job at hand, take the time to ensure that your safety is not jeopardized. A moment's lack of attention can result in an accident, as can failure to observe certain simple safety precautions. The possibility of an accident will always exist, and the following points should not be considered a comprehensive list of all dangers. Rather, they are intended to make you aware of the risks and to encourage a safety conscious approach to all work you carry out on your vehicle.

Essential DOs and DON'Ts

DON'T rely on a jack when working under the vehicle. Always use approved jackstands to support the weight of the vehicle and place them under the recommended lift or support points.

DON'T attempt to loosen extremely tight fasteners (i.e. wheel lug nuts) while the vehicle is on a jack - it may fall.

DON'T start the engine without first making sure that the transmission is in Neutral (or Park where applicable) and the parking brake is set.

DON'T remove the radiator cap from a hot cooling system - let it cool or cover it with a cloth and release the pressure gradually.

DON'T attempt to drain the engine oil until you are sure it has cooled to the point that it will not burn you.

DON'T touch any part of the engine or exhaust system until it has cooled sufficiently to avoid burns.

DON'T siphon toxic liquids such as gasoline, antifreeze and brake fluid by mouth, or allow them to remain on your skin.

DON'T inhale brake lining dust - it is potentially hazardous (see *Asbestos* below).

DON'T allow spilled oil or grease to remain on the floor - wipe it up before someone slips on it.

DON'T use loose fitting wrenches or other tools which may slip and cause injury.

DON'T push on wrenches when loosening or tightening nuts or bolts. Always try to pull the wrench toward you. If the situation calls for pushing the wrench away, push with an open hand to avoid scraped knuckles if the wrench should slip.

DON'T attempt to lift a heavy component alone - get someone to help you.

DON'T rush or take unsafe shortcuts to finish a job.

DON'T allow children or animals in or around the vehicle while you are working on it.

DO wear eye protection when using power tools such as a drill, sander, bench grinder, etc. and when working under a vehicle.

DO keep loose clothing and long hair well out of the way of moving parts.

DO make sure that any hoist used has a safe working load rating adequate for the job.

DO get someone to check on you periodically when working alone on a vehicle.

DO carry out work in a logical sequence and make sure that everything is correctly assembled and tightened.

DO keep chemicals and fluids tightly capped and out of the reach of children and pets.

DO remember that your vehicle's safety affects that of yourself and others. If in doubt on any point, get professional advice.

Asbestos

Certain friction, insulating, sealing, and other products - such as brake linings, brake bands, clutch linings, torque converters, gaskets, etc. - may contain asbestos. Extreme care must be taken to avoid inhalation of dust from such products, since it is hazardous to health. If in doubt, assume that they do contain asbestos.

Fire

Remember at all times that gasoline is highly flammable. Never smoke or have any kind of open flame around when working on a vehicle. But the risk does not end there. A spark caused by an electrical short circuit, by two metal surfaces contacting each other, or even by static electricity built up in your body under certain conditions, can ignite gasoline vapors, which in a confined space are highly explosive. Do not, under any circumstances, use gasoline for cleaning parts. Use an approved safety solvent.

Always disconnect the battery ground (-) cable at the battery before working on any part of the fuel system or electrical system. Never risk spilling fuel on a hot engine or exhaust component. It is strongly recommended that a fire extinguisher suitable for use on fuel and electrical fires be kept handy in the garage or workshop at all times. Never try to extinguish a fuel or electrical fire with water.

Fumes

Certain fumes are highly toxic and can quickly cause unconsciousness and even death if inhaled to any extent. Gasoline vapor falls into this category, as do the vapors from some cleaning solvents. Any draining or pouring of such volatile fluids should be done in a well ventilated area.

When using cleaning fluids and solvents, read the instructions on the container carefully. Never use materials from unmarked containers.

Never run the engine in an enclosed space, such as a garage. Exhaust fumes contain carbon monoxide, which is extremely poisonous. If you need to run the engine, always do so in the open air, or at least have the rear of the vehicle outside the work area.

If you are fortunate enough to have the use of an inspection pit, never drain or pour gasoline and never run the engine while the vehicle is over the pit. The fumes, being heavier than air, will concentrate in the pit with possibly lethal results.

The battery

Never create a spark or allow a bare light bulb near a battery. They normally give off a certain amount of hydrogen gas, which is highly explosive.

Always disconnect the battery ground (-) cable at the battery before working on the fuel or electrical systems.

If possible, loosen the filler caps or cover when charging the battery from an external source (this does not apply to sealed or maintenance-free batteries). Do not charge at an excessive rate or the battery may burst.

Take care when adding water to a non maintenance-free battery and when carrying a battery. The electrolyte, even when diluted, is very corrosive and should not be allowed to contact clothing or skin.

Always wear eye protection when cleaning the battery to prevent the caustic deposits from entering your eyes.

Household current

When using an electric power tool, inspection light, etc., which operates on household current, always make sure that the tool is correctly connected to its plug and that, where necessary, it is properly grounded. Do not use such items in damp conditions and, again, do not create a spark or apply excessive heat in the vicinity of fuel or fuel vapor.

Secondary ignition system voltage

A severe electric shock can result from touching certain parts of the ignition system (such as the spark plug wires) when the engine is running or being cranked, particularly if components are damp or the insulation is defective. In the case of an electronic ignition system, the secondary system voltage is much higher and could prove fatal.

Troubleshooting

Contents

Symptom — **Section**

Engine
Engine backfires ... 15
Engine diesels (continues to run) after switching off ... 18
Engine hard to start when cold ... 3
Engine hard to start when hot ... 4
Engine lacks power ... 14
Engine lopes while idling or idles erratically ... 8
Engine misses at idle speed ... 9
Engine misses throughout driving speed range ... 10
Engine rotates but will not start ... 2
Engine runs with oil pressure light on ... 17
Engine stalls ... 13
Engine starts but stops immediately ... 6
Engine stumbles on acceleration ... 11
Engine surges while holding accelerator steady ... 12
Engine will not rotate when attempting to start ... 1
Oil puddle under engine ... 7
Pinging or knocking engine sounds during acceleration or uphill ... 16
Starter motor noisy or excessively rough in engagement ... 5

Engine electrical system
Alternator light fails to come on when key is turned on ... 21
Alternator light fails to go out ... 20
Battery will not hold a charge ... 19

Fuel system
Excessive fuel consumption ... 22
Fuel leakage and/or fuel odor ... 23

Cooling system
Coolant loss ... 28
External coolant leakage ... 26
Internal coolant leakage ... 27
Overcooling ... 25
Overheating ... 24
Poor coolant circulation ... 29

Automatic transaxle
Engine will start in gears other than Park or Neutral ... 34
Fluid leakage ... 30
General shift mechanism problems ... 32

Transaxle fluid brown or has burned smell ... 31
Transaxle slips, shifts roughly, is noisy or has no drive in forward or reverse gears ... 35
Transaxle will not downshift with accelerator pedal pressed to the floor ... 33

Driveaxles
Clicking noise in turns ... 36
Shudder or vibration during acceleration ... 37
Vibration at highway speeds ... 38

Brakes
Brake pedal feels spongy when depressed ... 46
Brake pedal travels to the floor with little resistance ... 47
Brake roughness or chatter (pedal pulsates) ... 41
Dragging brakes ... 44
Excessive brake pedal travel ... 43
Excessive pedal effort required to stop vehicle ... 42
Grabbing or uneven braking action ... 45
Noise (high-pitched squeal with brakes applied) ... 40
Parking brake does not hold ... 48
Vehicle pulls to one side during braking ... 39

Suspension and steering systems
Abnormal or excessive tire wear ... 50
Abnormal noise at the front end ... 55
Cupped tires ... 60
Erratic steering when braking ... 57
Excessive pitching and/or rolling around corners or during braking ... 58
Excessive play or looseness in steering system ... 64
Excessive tire wear on inside edge ... 62
Excessive tire wear on outside edge ... 61
Hard steering ... 53
Poor returnability of steering to center ... 54
Rattling or clicking noise in steering gear ... 65
Shimmy, shake or vibration ... 52
Suspension bottoms ... 59
Tire tread worn in one place ... 63
Vehicle pulls to one side ... 49
Wander or poor steering stability ... 56
Wheel makes a thumping noise ... 51

This Section provides an easy reference guide to the more common problems which may occur during the operation of your vehicle. These problems and their possible causes are grouped under headings denoting various components or systems, such as Engine, Cooling system, etc. They also refer you to the Chapter and/or Section which deals with the problem.

Remember that successful troubleshooting is not a mysterious art practiced only by professional mechanics. It is simply the result of the right knowledge combined with an intelligent, systematic approach to the problem. Always work by a process of elimination, starting with the simplest solution and working through to the most complex - and never overlook the obvious. Anyone can run the gas tank dry or leave the lights on overnight, so don't assume that you are exempt from such oversights.

Finally, always establish a clear idea of why a problem has occurred and take steps to ensure that it doesn't happen again. If the electrical system fails because of a poor connection, check the other connections in the system to make sure that they don't fail as well. If a particular fuse continues to blow, find out why - don't just replace one fuse after another. Remember, failure of a small component can often be indicative of potential failure or incorrect functioning of a more important component or system.

Engine

1 Engine will not rotate when attempting to start

1 Battery terminal connections loose or corroded (Chapter 1).
2 Battery discharged or faulty (Chapter 1).
3 Automatic transaxle not completely engaged in Park (Chapter 7).
4 Broken, loose or disconnected wiring in the starting circuit (Chapters 5 and 12).
5 Starter motor pinion jammed in flywheel ring gear (Chapter 5).
6 Starter solenoid faulty (Chapter 5).
7 Starter motor faulty (Chapter 5).
8 Ignition switch faulty (Chapter 12).
9 Starter pinion or flywheel teeth worn or broken (Chapter 5).
10 Engine seized.

2 Engine rotates but will not start

1 Fuel tank empty.
2 Battery discharged (engine rotates slowly) (Chapter 5).
3 Battery terminal connections loose or corroded (Chapter 1).
4 Leaking fuel injector(s), fuel pump, pressure regulator, etc. (Chapter 4).

5 Fuel not reaching fuel injection system (Chapter 4).
6 Ignition components damp or damaged (Chapter 5).
7 Worn, faulty or incorrectly gapped spark plugs (Chapter 1).
8 Broken, loose or disconnected wiring in the starting circuit (Chapter 5).
9 Broken, loose or disconnected wires at the ignition coil or faulty coil (Chapter 5).
10 Broken or stripped timing belt or chain (Chapter 2).

3 Engine hard to start when cold

1 Battery discharged or low (Chapter 1).
2 Malfunctioning fuel system (Chapter 4).
3 Fuel injector(s) leaking (Chapter 4).
4 Malfunctioning engine control system (Chapter 6).

4 Engine hard to start when hot

1 Air filter clogged (Chapter 1).
2 Fuel not reaching the fuel injection system (Chapter 4).
3 Malfunctioning engine control system (Chapter 6).
4 Corroded battery connections, especially ground (Chapter 1).

5 Starter motor noisy or excessively rough in engagement

1 Pinion or flywheel gear teeth worn or broken (Chapter 5).
2 Starter motor mounting bolts loose or missing (Chapter 5).

6 Engine starts but stops immediately

1 Loose or faulty electrical connections at distributor, coil or alternator (Chapter 5).
2 Insufficient fuel reaching the fuel injector(s) (Chapters 1 and 4).
3 Vacuum leak at the gasket between the intake plenum/fuel injection throttle body (Chapters 1 and 4).
4 Malfunctioning engine control system (Chapter 6).

7 Oil puddle under engine

1 Oil pan gasket and/or oil pan drain bolt washer leaking (Chapter 2).
2 Oil pressure sending unit leaking (Chapter 2).
3 Valve covers leaking (Chapter 2).
4 Engine oil seals leaking (Chapter 2).
5 Oil pump housing leaking (Chapter 2).

8 Engine lopes while idling or idles erratically

1 Vacuum leakage (Chapters 2 and 4).
2 Leaking EGR valve (Chapter 6).
3 Air filter clogged (Chapter 1).
4 Fuel pump not delivering sufficient fuel to the fuel injection system (Chapter 4).
5 Leaking head gasket (Chapter 2).
6 Timing chain/belt and/or sprockets worn (Chapter 2).
7 Camshaft lobes worn (Chapter 2).
8 Malfunctioning engine control system (Chapter 6).

9 Engine misses at idle speed

1 Spark plugs worn or not gapped properly (Chapter 1).
2 Faulty spark plug wires (Chapter 1).
3 Vacuum leaks (Chapter 1).
4 Uneven or low compression (Chapter 2).
5 Defective fuel injector (Chapter 4).
6 Malfunctioning engine control system (Chapter 6).
7 Camshaft lobe or valve train component worn (Chapter 2).

10 Engine misses throughout driving speed range

1 Fuel filter clogged and/or impurities in the fuel system (Chapter 1).
2 Low fuel output at the injector(s), injector defective (Chapter 4).
3 Faulty or incorrectly gapped spark plugs (Chapter 1).
4 Incorrect ignition timing (Chapter 5).
5 Spark plug wire defective (Chapters 1 or 5).
6 Faulty engine control/emission system components (Chapter 6).
7 Low or uneven cylinder compression pressures (Chapter 2).
8 Weak or faulty ignition system (Chapter 5).
9 Vacuum leak at the fuel injection throttle body, intake manifold, or vacuum hoses (Chapter 4).
10 Camshaft lobe or valve train component worn (Chapter 2).

11 Engine stumbles on acceleration

1 Spark plugs fouled (Chapter 1).
2 Fuel filter clogged (Chapter 1).
3 Malfunctioning fuel supply or fuel injection system (Chapter 4).
4 Malfunctioning engine control system (Chapter 6).
5 EVAP system leaking or malfunctioning (Chapter 6).
6 Alternator output low or excessive (Chapter 5).

12 Engine surges while holding accelerator steady

1 Intake air leak (Chapter 4).
2 Malfunctioning Torque Converter Clutch/Solenoid (TCC) (Chapter 6).
3 Malfunctioning fuel supply or fuel injection system (Chapter 4).
4 Malfunctioning engine control system (Chapter 6).
5 Contaminated or defective oxygen sensors (Chapter 6).
6 Malfunctioning EGR system (Chapter 6).

13 Engine stalls

1 Accelerator cable linkage binding or sticking (Chapter 4).
2 Idle air control system malfunctioning (Chapter 4).
3 Fuel filter clogged and/or water and impurities in the fuel system (Chapters 1 and 4).
4 Malfunctioning fuel supply or fuel injection system (Chapter 4).
5 Malfunctioning engine control system (Chapter 6).
6 Malfunctioning EGR system (Chapter 6).

14 Engine lacks power

1 Incorrect ignition timing.
2 Faulty or incorrectly gapped spark plugs (Chapter 1).
3 Faulty ignition coil (Chapter 5).
4 Rear brakes binding (Chapter 9).
5 Automatic transmission fluid level incorrect (Chapter 1 and 7).
6 Malfunctioning fuel supply or fuel injection system (Chapter 4).
7 Malfunctioning engine control system (Chapter 6).
8 Low cylinder compression (Chapter 2C).
9 Restriction in the catalytic converter or exhaust system (Chapter 4).

15 Engine backfires

1 Emission control system not functioning properly (Chapter 6).
2 Ignition timing incorrect (Chapter 5).
3 Faulty secondary ignition system; cracked spark plug insulator, faulty plug wires (Chapters 1 and 5).
4 Fuel injection system malfunction (Chapter 4).
5 Vacuum leak at fuel injectors, intake manifold or vacuum hoses (Chapter 4).
6 EGR stuck open all the time (Chapter 6).
7 Malfunctioning engine control system (Chapter 6).

16 Pinging or knocking engine sounds during acceleration or uphill

1 Incorrect grade (octane) of fuel.
2 Fuel injection system faulty (Chapter 4).
3 Improper or damaged spark plugs or wires (Chapter 1).
4 Faulty or incorrect thermostat (Chapter 3).
5 Low coolant levels (Chapter 1).
6 Knock sensor system faulty (Chapter 6).
7 Vacuum leak (Chapter 2C and 4).
8 EGR system not functioning properly (Chapter 6).
9 Malfunctioning engine control system (Chapter 6).

17 Engine runs with oil pressure light on

1 Low oil level (Chapter 1).
2 Short in wiring circuit (Chapter 12).
3 Faulty oil pressure sender (Chapter 2).
4 Worn engine bearings and/or oil pump (Chapter 2).

18 Engine diesels (continues to run) after switching off

1 Excessive engine operating temperature (Chapter 3).
2 Idle speed to high (Chapter 4).

Engine electrical system

19 Battery will not hold a charge

1 Alternator drivebelt defective or not tightened properly (Chapter 1).
2 Battery electrolyte level low (Chapter 1).
3 Battery terminals loose or corroded (Chapter 1).
4 Alternator not charging properly (Chapter 5).
5 Loose, broken or faulty wiring in the charging circuit (Chapter 5).
6 Short in vehicle wiring (Chapter 12).
7 Internally defective battery (Chapters 1 and 5).

20 Alternator light fails to go out

1 Faulty alternator or charging circuit (Chapter 5).
2 Alternator drivebelt defective or out of adjustment (Chapter 1).
3 Alternator voltage regulator inoperative (Chapter 5).

21 Alternator light fails to come on when key is turned on

1 Warning light bulb defective (Chapter 12).
2 Fault in the printed circuit, dash wiring or bulb holder (Chapter 12).

Fuel system

22 Excessive fuel consumption

1 Dirty or clogged air filter element (Chapter 1).
2 Restriction in the catalytic converter or exhaust system (Chapter 4).
3 Emissions or engine control system not functioning properly (Chapter 6).
4 Fuel injection system malfunction (Chapter 4).
5 Low tire pressure or incorrect tire size (Chapter 1).

23 Fuel leakage and/or fuel odor

1 Leaking fuel feed or return line (Chapters 1 and 4).
2 Tank overfilled.
3 Evaporative canister filter clogged (Chapters 1 and 6).
4 Fuel injection system malfunction (Chapter 4).

Cooling system

24 Overheating

1 Insufficient coolant in system (Chapter 1).
2 Water pump drivebelt defective or out of adjustment (Chapter 1).
3 Radiator core blocked or grille restricted (Chapter 3).
4 Thermostat faulty (Chapter 3).
5 Electric radiator fan inoperative or blades broken or cracked (Chapter 3).
6 Radiator cap not maintaining proper pressure (Chapter 3).

25 Overcooling

1 Faulty thermostat (Chapter 3).
2 Inaccurate temperature gauge sending unit (Chapter 3)

26 External coolant leakage

1 Deteriorated/damaged hoses; loose

clamps (Chapters 1 and 3).
2   Water pump seal defective (Chapter 3).
3   Leakage from radiator core or coolant reservoir bottle (Chapter 3).
4   Engine drain or water jacket core plugs leaking (Chapter 2).

27 Internal coolant leakage

1   Leaking cylinder head gasket (Chapter 2).
2   Cracked cylinder bore or cylinder head (Chapter 2).

28 Coolant loss

1   Too much coolant in system (Chapter 1).
2   Coolant boiling away because of over-heating (Chapter 3).
3   Internal or external leakage (Chapter 3).
4   Faulty radiator cap (Chapter 3).

29 Poor coolant circulation

1   Inoperative water pump (Chapter 3).
2   Restriction in cooling system (Chapters 1 and 3).
3   Water pump drivebelt defective/out of adjustment (Chapter 1).
4   Thermostat sticking (Chapter 3).

Automatic transaxle

Note: *Due to the complexity of the automatic transaxle, it is difficult for the home mechanic to properly diagnose and service this component. For problems other than the following, the vehicle should be taken to a dealer or transmission shop.*

30 Fluid leakage

1   Automatic transmission fluid is a deep red color. Fluid leaks should not be confused with engine oil, which can easily be blown onto the transaxle by air flow.
2   To pinpoint a leak, first remove all built-up dirt and grime from the transaxle housing with degreasing agents and/or steam cleaning. Then drive the vehicle at low speeds so air flow will not blow the leak far from its source. Raise the vehicle and determine where the leak is coming from. Common areas of leakage are:
a) *Pan (Chapters 1 and 7)*
b) *Dipstick tube (Chapters 1 and 7)*
c) *Transaxle oil lines (Chapters 3 and 7)*

31 Transaxle fluid brown or has a burned smell

Transaxle fluid burned (Chapter 1).

32 General shift mechanism problems

1   Chapter 7 deals with checking and adjusting the shift linkage on automatic transaxles. Common problems which may be attributed to poorly adjusted linkage are:
a) *Engine starting in gears other than Park or Neutral.*
b) *Indicator on shifter pointing to a gear other than the one actually being used.*
c) *Vehicle moves when in Park.*
2   Refer to Chapter 7 for the shift linkage adjustment procedure.

33 Transaxle will not downshift with accelerator pedal pressed to the floor

Fault in the transaxle electronic controls.

34 Engine will start in gears other than Park or Neutral

Shift linkage out of adjustment (Chapter 7).

35 Transaxle slips, shifts roughly, is noisy or has no drive in forward or reverse gears

There are many probable causes for the above problems, but the home mechanic should be concerned with only one possibility - fluid level. Before taking the vehicle to a repair shop, check the level and condition of the fluid as described in Chapter 1. Correct the fluid level as necessary or change the fluid and filter if needed. If the problem persists, have a professional diagnose the cause.

Driveaxles

36 Clicking noise in turns

Worn or damaged outboard CV joint (Chapter 8).

37 Shudder or vibration during acceleration

1   Excessive toe-in (Chapter 10).
2   Worn or damaged inboard or outboard CV joints (Chapter 8).
3   Sticking or worn inboard CV joint assembly (Chapter 8).

38 Vibration at highway speeds

1   Out-of-balance front wheels and/or tires (Chapters 1 and 10).
2   Out-of-round front tires (Chapters 1 and 10).
3   Worn CV joint(s) (Chapter 8).

Brakes

Note: *Before assuming that a brake problem exists, make sure that:*
a) *The tires are in good condition and properly inflated (Chapter 1).*
b) *The front end alignment is correct (Chapter 10).*
c) *The vehicle is not loaded with weight in an unequal manner.*

39 Vehicle pulls to one side during braking

1   Incorrect tire pressures (Chapter 1).
2   Front end out of line (have the front end aligned).
3   Front or rear tires not matched to one another.
4   Restricted brake lines or hoses (Chapter 9).
5   Malfunctioning caliper or drum brake assembly (Chapter 9).
6   Loose suspension parts (Chapter 10).
7   Loose calipers (Chapter 9).
8   Excessive wear of brake shoe or pad material or disc/drum on one side (Chapter 9).

40 Noise (high-pitched squeal when the brakes are applied)

1   Front disc brake pads worn out. The noise comes from the wear sensor rubbing against the disc (does not apply to all vehicles). Replace pads with new ones immediately (Chapter 9).
2   Incorrectly installed new pads (many require an anti-squeal compound on the backing plates).

41 Brake roughness or chatter (pedal pulsates)

1   Excessive lateral runout of brake disc (Chapter 9).
2   Rear brake drum out-of-round (Chapter 9).
3   Uneven pad wear (Chapter 9).
4   Defective disc (Chapter 9).

42 Excessive brake pedal effort required to stop vehicle

1   Malfunctioning power brake booster (Chapter 9).
2   Partial system failure (Chapter 9).
3   Excessively worn pads or shoes (Chapter 9).
4   Piston in caliper or wheel cylinder stuck or sluggish (Chapter 9).
5   Brake pads or shoes contaminated with oil or grease (Chapter 9).
6   New pads or shoes installed and not yet seated. It will take a while for the new material to seat against the disc or drum.

43 Excessive brake pedal travel

1   Partial brake system failure (Chapter 9).
2   Insufficient fluid in master cylinder (Chapters 1 and 9).
3   Air trapped in system (Chapters 1 and 9).

44 Dragging brakes

1   Incorrect adjustment of brake light switch (Chapter 9).
2   Master cylinder pistons not returning correctly (Chapter 9).
3   Restricted brake lines or hoses (Chapters 1 and 9).
4   Incorrect parking brake adjustment (Chapter 9).
5   Caliper piston sticking (Chapter 9).

45 Grabbing or uneven braking action

1   Malfunction of proportioning valve (Chapter 9).
2   Malfunction of power brake booster unit (Chapter 9).
3   Binding brake pedal mechanism (Chapter 9).
4   Brake fluid, grease or oil on brake pads or shoes (Chapter 9).

46 Brake pedal feels spongy when depressed

1   Air in hydraulic lines (Chapter 9).
2   Master cylinder mounting bolts loose (Chapter 9).
3   Master cylinder defective (Chapter 9).

47 Brake pedal travels to the floor with little resistance

1   Little or no fluid in the master cylinder reservoir caused by leaking caliper or wheel cylinder piston(s) (Chapter 9).
2   Loose, damaged or disconnected brake lines (Chapter 9).

48 Parking brake does not hold

Parking brake linkage improperly adjusted (Chapters 1 and 9).

Suspension and steering systems

Note: *Before attempting to diagnose the suspension and steering systems, perform the following preliminary checks:*
a) *Tires for wrong pressure and uneven wear.*
b) *Steering universal joints from the column to the steering gear for loose connectors or wear.*
c) *Front and rear suspension and the steering gear assembly for loose or damaged parts.*
d) *Out-of-round or out-of-balance tires, bent rims and loose and/or rough wheel bearings.*

49 Vehicle pulls to one side

1   Mismatched or uneven tires (Chapter 10).
2   Broken or sagging springs (Chapter 10).
3   Wheels in need of alignment (Chapter 10).
4   Front brake dragging (Chapter 9).

50 Abnormal or excessive tire wear

1   Wheel alignment (Chapter 10).
2   Sagging or broken springs (Chapter 10).
3   Tire out of balance (Chapter 10).
4   Worn strut damper (Chapter 10).
5   Overloaded vehicle.
6   Tires not rotated regularly.
7   Tire pressure not correct (Chapter 1).

51 Wheel makes a thumping noise

1   Blister or bump on tire (Chapter 10).
2   Improper strut damper action (Chapter 10).

52 Shimmy, shake or vibration

1   Tire or wheel out-of-balance or out-of-round (Chapter 10).
2   Loose or worn wheel bearings (Chapters 1, 8 and 10).
3   Worn tie-rod ends (Chapter 10).
4   Worn lower balljoints (Chapters 1 and 10).
5   Excessive wheel runout (Chapter 10).
6   Blister or bump on tire (Chapter 10).
7   Steering gear mounting bolts loose (Chapter 10).

53 Hard steering

1   Lack of lubrication at balljoints, tie-rod ends and steering gear assembly (Chapter 10).
2   Front wheel alignment (Chapter 10).
3   Low tire pressure(s) (Chapters 1 and 10).
4   Power steering fluid low (Chapter 1).
5   Power steering pump or steering gear defective (Chapter 10).

54 Poor returnability of steering to center

1   Lack of lubrication at balljoints and tie-rod ends (Chapter 10).
2   Binding in balljoints (Chapter 10).
3   Binding in steering column (Chapter 10).
4   Lack of lubricant in steering gear assembly (Chapter 10).
5   Front wheels in need of alignment or front suspension components bent (Chapter 10).

55 Abnormal noise at the front end

1   Lack of lubrication at balljoints and tie-rod ends (Chapters 1 and 10).
2   Damaged strut mounting (Chapter 10).
3   Worn control arm bushings or tie-rod ends (Chapter 10).
4   Loose stabilizer bar (Chapter 10).
5   Loose wheel nuts (Chapters 1 and 10).
6   Loose suspension bolts (Chapter 10).

56 Wander or poor steering stability

1   Mismatched or uneven tires (Chapter 10).
2   Lack of lubrication at balljoints and tie-rod ends (Chapters 1 and 10).
3   Worn strut assemblies (Chapter 10).
4   Loose stabilizer bar (Chapter 10).
5   Broken or sagging springs (Chapter 10).
6   Wheel alignment (Chapter 10).

57 Erratic steering when braking

1   Wheel bearings worn (Chapter 10).
2   Broken or sagging springs (Chapter 10).
3   Leaking wheel cylinder or caliper (Chapter 9).
4   Warped brake discs (Chapter 9).

58 Excessive pitching and/or rolling around corners or during braking

1   Loose stabilizer bar (Chapter 10).

2   Worn strut dampers or mountings (Chapter 10).
3   Broken or sagging springs (Chapter 10).
4   Overloaded vehicle.

59   Suspension bottoms

1   Overloaded vehicle.
2   Worn strut dampers (Chapter 10).
3   Incorrect, broken or sagging springs (Chapter 10).

60   Cupped tires

1   Front wheel or rear wheel alignment (Chapter 10).
2   Worn strut dampers (Chapter 10).
3   Wheel bearings worn (Chapter 10).
4   Excessive tire or wheel runout (Chapter 10).
5   Worn balljoints (Chapter 10).

61   Excessive tire wear on outside edge

1   Inflation pressures incorrect (Chapter 1).
2   Excessive speed in turns.
3   Front end alignment incorrect (excessive toe-in). Have professionally aligned.
4   Suspension arm bent or twisted (Chapter 10).

62   Excessive tire wear on inside edge

1   Inflation pressures incorrect (Chapter 1).
2   Front end alignment incorrect (toe-out). Have professionally aligned.
3   Loose or damaged steering components (Chapter 10).

63   Tire tread worn in one place

1   Tires out of balance.

2   Damaged or buckled wheel. Inspect and replace if necessary.
3   Defective tire (Chapter 1).

64   Excessive play or looseness in steering system

1   Wheel bearing(s) worn (Chapter 10).
2   Tie-rod end loose (Chapter 10).
3   Steering gear loose (Chapter 10).
4   Worn or loose steering intermediate shaft (Chapter 10).

65   Rattling or clicking noise in steering gear

1   Insufficient or improper lubricant in steering gear assembly (Chapter 10).
2   Steering gear attachment loose (Chapter 10).

Chapter 1
Tune-up and routine maintenance

Contents

	Section			Section
Air filter replacement	21		Fluid level checks	4
Automatic transaxle fluid and filter change	22		Fuel filter replacement	31
Automatic transaxle fluid level check	6		Fuel system check	19
Battery check, maintenance and charging	9		Introduction	2
Brake system check	18		Maintenance schedule	1
Chassis lubrication	17		Positive Crankcase Ventilation (PCV) valve check	
Cooling system check	10		and replacement	26
Cooling system servicing			Power steering fluid level check	7
(draining, flushing and refilling)	25		Seat belt check	30
Differential lubricant change	24		Spark plug check and replacement	28
Differential lubricant level check	16		Spark plug wire check and replacement	29
Driveshaft boot check	23		Steering and suspension check	14
Drivebelt check, adjustment and replacement	20		Tire and tire pressure checks	5
Engine oil and filter change	8		Tire rotation	13
Evaporative emissions control system check	27		Tune-up general information	3
Exhaust Gas Recirculation (EGR) system test	32		Underhood hose check and replacement	11
Exhaust system check	15		Wiper blade inspection and replacement	12

Specifications

Recommended lubricants and fluids

Note: *Listed here are manufacturer recommendations at the time this manual was written. Manufacturers occasionally upgrade their fluid and lubricant specifications, so check with your local auto parts store for current recommendations.*

Engine oil

Type	API SG SH or SG/CD multigrade and fuel efficient oil
Viscosity	See accompanying chart

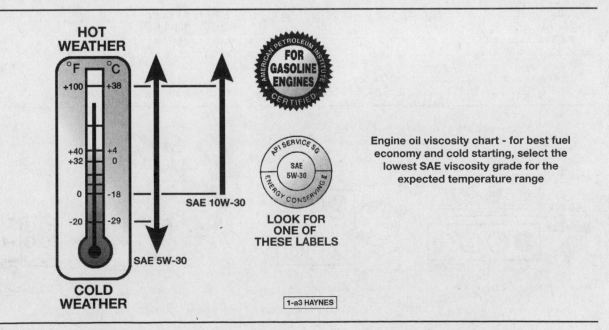

Engine oil viscosity chart - for best fuel economy and cold starting, select the lowest SAE viscosity grade for the expected temperature range

Recommended lubricants and fluids (continued)

Automatic transaxle fluid	
1996 through 1999	Mopar ATF plus 3 or ATF plus 3 Type 7176
2000 and later	Mopar ATF plus 4 or ATF plus 4 Type 9602
Differential oil	Common sump with the automatic transaxle
Power steering fluid	Mopar power steering fluid or equivalent
Brake fluid..	DOT 3 specifications and SAE J1703 standards
Engine coolant	50/50 mixture of ethylene glycol-based antifreeze and water
Parking brake mechanism grease	White lithium-based grease NLGI no. 2
Chassis lubrication grease	NLGI no. 2 multi-purpose chassis grease
Hood, door and trunk/liftgate hinge lubricant	Engine oil
Door hinge and check spring grease................................	NLGI no. 2 multi-purpose chassis grease
Key lock cylinder lubricant...	Graphite spray
Hood latch assembly lubricant	Mopar Lubriplate or equivalent
Door latch striker lubricant	Mopar Door Ease no. 3744859 or equivalent

Capacities*

Engine oil (including filter)	
2.4L engine	
1996 through 1998..	4.5 qts
1999 and later	5.0 qts
3.0L engine	4.0 qts
3.3/3.8L engine	
1996 through 1998..	4.0 qts
1999 and later	4.5 qts
Automatic transaxle	
31TH/O-haul Fill	8.5 qts
41TE/O-haul Fill...	9.1 qts
Cooling system	
2.4L engine	9.5 qts
3.0L engine	10.5 qts
3.3/3.8L engine..	10.5 qts

*All capacities approximate. Add as necessary to bring to appropriate level.

Brakes

Disc brake pad wear limit (including metal shoe)	5/16 inch
Drum brake shoe wear limit...	1/16 inch

Ignition system

Spark plug type	
2.4L (1999 through 2000)	Champion RC12YC5 or equivalent
2.4L (2001 and later)...	Champion RE14CC5 or equivalent
3.0L	Champion RN11YC4 or equivalent
3.3/3.8L	Champion RN14PMP5 or equivalent
Spark plug gap	
2.4L	0.048 to 0.053 inch
3.0L	0.039 to 0.044 inch
3.3/3.8L	0.048 to 0.053 inch
Spark plug wire resistance	
2.4L	
#1 & #4	4.2 K ohms
#2 & #3	4.2 K ohms

The blackened terminal shown on the distributor cap indicates the Number One spark plug wire position

2.0 and 2.4 L engine

3.0L V6 engine

3.0L V6 engine

3.3L and 3.8L V6 engine

Engine cylinder and coil terminal locations

3.0L
#1 .... 14.0 K ohms
#2 .... 10.4 K ohms
#3 .... 14.9 K ohms
#4 .... 11.5 K ohms
#5 .... 17.5 K ohms
#6 .... 10.3 K ohms
3.3/3.8L (1996 through 2000)
#1 .... 18.5 K ohms
#2 .... 15.5 K ohms
#3 .... 20.4 K ohms
#4 .... 21.2 K ohms
#5 .... 27.7 K ohms
#6 .... 26.7 K ohms
3.3/3.8L (2001 and later)
#1 .... 22.5 K ohms
#2 .... 22.8 K ohms
#3 .... 19.3 K ohms
#4 .... 19.3 K ohms
#5 .... 13.6 K ohms
#6 .... 16.4 K ohms
Firing order
2.4L 1-3-4-2
3.0/3.3/3.8L 1-2-3-4-5-6

Torque specifications   **Ft-lbs** (unless otherwise indicated)

Spark plugs... 20
Wheel lug nuts 100
Automatic transaxle
  Pan bolts 15
  Filter-to-valve body screws..................................... 45 in-lbs

Typical 3.3/3.8L engine compartment layout (1996 through 2000 models)

1 Automatic transaxle dipstick
2 Brake master cylinder reservoir
3 Windshield washer fluid reservoir
4 Battery
5 Power steering fluid reservoir
6 Engine oil dipstick
7 Upper radiator hose
8 Engine oil filler cap
9 Air filter housing
10 Engine coolant reservoir

Typical 3.3/3.8L engine compartment (2001 and later models)

1	Automatic transaxle dipstick	5	Power steering fluid reservoir	9	Air filter housing
2	Brake master cylinder reservoir	6	Engine oil dipstick	10	Engine coolant reservoir
3	Windshield washer fluid reservoir	7	Upper radiator hose		
4	Battery	8	Engine oil filler cap		

Typical 3.3/3.8L engine compartment underside components

1	Front brake caliper	3	Inner CV joint boot	6	Outer CV joint boot	9	Tie rod end
2	Spring and shock absorber strut	4	Engine oil drain plug	7	Steering gear	10	Stabilizer bar
		5	Automatic transaxle	8	Suspension cradle		

Typical rear underside components (1996 through 2000 models)

1	Resonator/tailpipe	4	Leaf spring	7	Track bar
2	Fuel tank	5	Muffler	8	Axle assembly
3	Fuel filler hose	6	Rear drum brake	9	Shock absorber

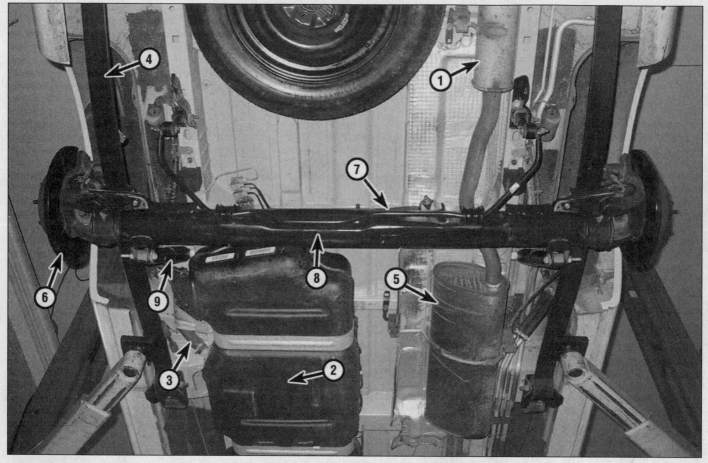

Typical rear underside components (2001 and later models)

1	Resonator/tailpipe	4	Leaf spring	7	Track bar
2	Fuel tank	5	Muffler	8	Axle assembly
3	Fuel filler hose	6	Rear disc or drum brake	9	Shock absorber

1 Chrysler, Dodge and Plymouth minivans Maintenance schedule

The following maintenance intervals are based on the assumption that the vehicle owner will be doing the maintenance or service work, not the dealer service department. Time and mileage intervals are loosely based on factory recommendations, although most have been shortened to ensure that lubricants and fluids are checked/changed at intervals that promote maximum engine/driveline service life. To keep vehicles in peak operating condition, and maximize the vehicle's resale value, maintenance procedures may be performed more often than recommended in the following schedule. Owner initiative is encouraged.

When the vehicle is new it should be serviced initially by a factory authorized dealer service department to protect the factory warranty. In many cases the initial maintenance check is done at no cost to the owner (check with your dealer service department for more information).

Every 250 miles or weekly, whichever comes first

Check the engine oil level; add oil as necessary (see Section 4)
Check the engine coolant level; add coolant as necessary (see Section 4)
Check the windshield washer fluid level (see Section 4)
Check the battery electrolyte level (see Section 4)
Check the brake fluid level (see Section 4)
Check the tires and tire pressures (see Section 5)
Check the automatic transaxle fluid level (see Section 6)
Check the power steering fluid level (see Section 7)
Check the operation of all lights
Check the horn operation

Every 3000 miles or 3 months, whichever comes first

Change the engine oil and filter (see Section 8)*

Every 7,500 miles or 6 months, whichever comes first

Check and clean the battery (see Section 9)
Check the cooling system hoses and connections for leaks and damage (see Section 10)
Check the condition of all vacuum hoses and connections (see Section 11)
Check the wiper blade condition (see Section 12)
Rotate the tires (see Section 13)
Check for freeplay in the steering linkage and balljoints (see Section 14)
Check the exhaust pipes and hangers (see Section 15)

Every 15,000 miles or 12 months, whichever comes first

Lubricate the front suspension steering balljoints (see Section 17)*
Check the brakes (see Section 18)*
Check the fuel system hoses and connections for leaks and damage (see Section 19)
Check the drivebelts (see Section 20)

Every 30,000 miles or 24 months, whichever comes first

Replace the air filter element (see Section 21)*
Change the automatic transaxle fluid and filter (see Section 22)*
Check the driveaxle boots (see Section 23)*
Drain and replace the engine coolant (see Section 25)
Check and replace if necessary, the PCV valve (see Section 26)
Check the fuel evaporative emission system hoses (see Section 27)
Replace the spark plugs (see Section 28)
Check the condition of the primary ignition wires and spark plug wires (see Section 29)
Check the operation of the seat belts (see Section 30)

Every 60,000 miles or 48 months, whichever comes first

Replace the fuel filter (see Section 31)
* This item is affected by "severe" operating conditions described below. If the vehicle is operated under "severe" conditions, perform all maintenance procedures marked with an asterisk (*) at the following intervals:
Consider the conditions "severe" if most driving is done . . .
In dusty areas
Towing a trailer
Idling for extended periods and/or low-speed operation
When temperatures remain below freezing and most trips are less than four miles
In heavy traffic where temperatures regularly reach 90-degrees F or higher

Every 2,000 miles

Change the engine oil and filter

Every 9,000 miles

Check the driveaxle, suspension and steering boots
Check the brakes
Lubricate the tie-rod ends

Every 15,000 miles

Replace the air filter element
Change the automatic transaxle fluid and filter

2   Introduction

This Chapter is designed to help the home mechanic maintain Chrysler, Dodge and Plymouth minivans. Primary goals are maximum performance, economy, safety, and reliability.

A master maintenance schedule is included, followed by procedures dealing with each item on the schedule. Visual checks, adjustments, component replacement and other helpful items are included. See the illustrations of the engine compartment and the underside of the vehicle for the location of components.

Follow the mileage/time maintenance schedule and the step-by-step procedures, which are a preventive maintenance program, to maximize reliability and vehicle service life. It's a comprehensive program - maintaining some items at the specified intervals, but not others will not produce the same results.

You'll discover that procedures can - and should - be grouped together because of the nature of the procedure you're performing or because of the proximity of components.

If the vehicle is raised, you should inspect the exhaust, suspension, steering and fuel systems while you're under the vehicle. When you rotate the tires, it makes sense to check the brakes while the wheels are removed. Finally, if you rent or borrow a torque wrench, even if you only need to tighten the spark plugs, you might as well check the torque of as many critical fasteners as time allows.

The first step in this maintenance program is to prepare yourself before the actual work begins. Read through the procedures you're planning to do, then gather the parts and tools required. If you run into problems, seek advice from a mechanic or an experienced do-it-yourselfer. **Note:** *Because of the lack of space in the engine compartment, it may be of benefit to remove the engine cowl (see Chapter 11) to perform some of the maintenance procedures.*

3   Tune-up general information

The term "tune-up" represents a combination of individual operations rather than one specific procedure.

If a routine maintenance schedule is followed, and frequent checks are made of fluid levels and high wear items, from the time the vehicle is new, the engine will stay in relatively good running condition and the need for additional work will be minimal.

There will be times when the engine runs poorly due to lack of regular maintenance. This is likely if a used vehicle is purchased, which hasn't received regular and frequent maintenance checks. In this case, an engine tune-up will be necessary to establish routine maintenance intervals.

The first step in any tune-up or diagnostic procedure is a cylinder compression check. A compression check (see Chapter 2A) will help determine the condition of internal engine components and can be used as a guide for tune-up and repair procedures. If a compression check indicates serious internal engine wear, a conventional tune-up will not improve engine performance, and would be a waste of time and money. The compression check should be done by someone with the right equipment and the knowledge to use it properly.

The following procedures are required to properly tune a poor running engine:

Minor tune-up

Check all engine related fluids (see Section 4)

Clean, inspect and test the battery (see Section 9)

Replace the spark plugs (see Section 28)

Inspect the spark plug wires (see Section 29)

Check and adjust the drivebelts (see Section 20)

Check the air filter (see Section 21)

Check the PCV valve (see Section 26)

Check all underhood hoses (see Section 11)

Service the cooling system (see Section 25)

Major tune-up

All items listed under Minor tune-up plus . . .

Replace the air filter (see Section 21)

Check the fuel system (see Section 19)

Replace the fuel filter (see Section 31)

Check the charging system (see Chapter 5)

4   Fluid level checks (every 250 miles or weekly)

Note: *The following fluid level checks are to be done on a 250 mile or weekly basis. Additional fluid level checks can be found in specific maintenance procedures which follow. Regardless of the intervals, check under the vehicle periodically for fluid leaks.*

1   Fluids are an essential part of the lubrication, cooling, brake, and window washer systems. Fluids gradually become depleted and/or contaminated during normal vehicle operation and must be replenished periodically. Before adding fluid to any of the following components, see *Recommended lubricants and fluids* at the beginning of this Chapter. **Note:** *The vehicle must be level when fluid levels are checked.*

Engine oil

Refer to illustrations 4.4a, 4.4b and 4.5

2   Engine oil level is checked with the dipstick located at the front left (driver's) side of the engine. The dipstick extends through a tube and into the oil pan at the bottom of the engine.

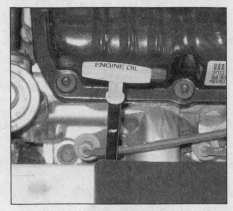

4.4a   The engine oil dipstick is located at the front of the engine

3   The oil level should be checked before the vehicle has been driven, or 15 minutes after the engine has been shut off. If the oil is checked immediately after driving the vehicle, oil will remain in the upper engine components, resulting in an inaccurate reading.

4   Pull the dipstick from the tube **(see illustration)** and wipe the oil off the end with a clean rag or paper towel. Insert the dipstick all the way back into the tube, then pull it out again. Note the oil level at the end of the dipstick. Add oil if required to keep the level at the Max mark **(see illustration)**.

5   Remove the oil cap (clearly marked) located on the valve cover **(see illustration)** and add oil. A funnel may reduce spills when oil is added.

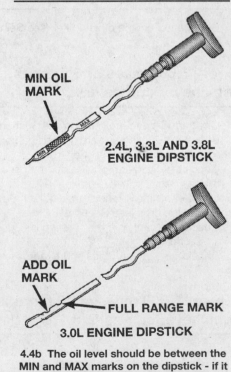

4.4b   The oil level should be between the MIN and MAX marks on the dipstick - if it isn't, add enough oil to bring the level up to or near the MAX mark (it takes one quart to raise the level from the MIN to MAX mark)

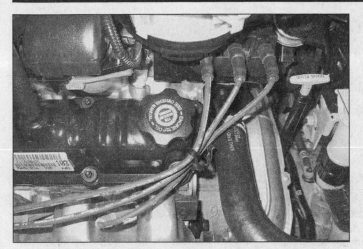

4.5 Turn the oil fill cap counterclockwise to remove it

4.8 Make sure the coolant level in the reservoir is at or near the MAX mark - if it's below the MIN mark, add more coolant

6   Don't let the oil level drop below the MIN mark or engine damage may occur, and don't overfill the engine by adding too much oil - it may result in fouled spark plugs, oil leaks or seal failures.

7   Checking the oil level is an important preventive maintenance step. A consistently low oil level indicates leakage through damaged seals, defective gaskets, past worn rings or valve guides. If the oil is milky in color or contains water droplets, the block may be cracked and should be checked immediately. The condition of the oil should be checked each time you check the oil level. Slide your thumb and index finger up the dipstick before wiping off the oil. If you see small dirt or metal particles on the dipstick, the oil should be changed (see Section 8).

Engine coolant

Refer to illustration 4.8

Warning: *Do not allow antifreeze to contact your skin or painted surfaces of the vehicle. Flush contaminated areas immediately with plenty of water. Don't store new coolant or leave old coolant lying where it's accessible to children or pets - they're attracted by its sweet smell. Ingestion of a small amount of coolant can be fatal! Wipe up garage floor and drip pan spills immediately. Keep antifreeze containers covered and repair cooling system leaks immediately.*

8   Vehicles covered by this manual are equipped with a pressurized coolant recovery system, making coolant level checks easy. A coolant recovery system reservoir attached to the inner fender panel or the radiator is connected by a hose to the radiator filler neck **(see illustration)**. As the engine warms up, coolant escapes through a valve in the radiator cap and travels through the hose into the reservoir. As the engine cools, the coolant is automatically drawn back into the coolant recovery system reservoir to maintain the correct level.

9   Coolant level should be checked when the engine is at normal operating temperature. The fluid level should be maintained

above the Cold Fill mark.

10   If a small amount of coolant is required to bring the system to the proper level, regular water can be used. If a large amount of coolant is required, high-quality antifreeze/coolant should be mixed with water in the proportion specified on the antifreeze container and added to the reservoir. This will keep the solution from getting diluted.

11   Remove reservoir cap to add coolant. **Warning:** *Don't remove the cap when the engine is warm!* When the engine has cooled, wrap a thick cloth around the cap and turn it to the first stop. If steam escapes from the cap, allow the engine to cool, then remove the cap.

12   Check the condition of the coolant when the coolant level is checked. It should be relatively clear. If it's brown or rust colored, the system should be drained, flushed, and refilled (see Section 25).

13   If the coolant level drops frequently, there may be a leak in the system. Check the radiator, hoses, filler cap, drain plugs, and water pump (see Section 25). If no leaks are found, have the filler cap pressure tested by a service station.

Windshield washer fluid

Refer to illustration 4.14

14   Windshield and rear window washer fluid is stored in the plastic reservoir in the engine compartment **(see illustration)**. Maintain the fluid level in the reservoir about one inch below the filler cap.

15   In mild climates, plain water can be used in the reservoirs, but they should be kept no more than two-thirds full to allow for expansion if the water freezes. In colder climates, use windshield washer antifreeze, available at auto parts stores, to lower the freezing point of the fluid. Mix the antifreeze with water according to the directions on the container. **Caution:** *Don't use cooling system antifreeze - it'll damage the vehicle's paint. To prevent icing in cold weather, warm the windshield with the defroster before using the washer.*

Battery electrolyte

Warning: *Precautions must be followed when checking or servicing a battery. Hydrogen gas, which is highly flammable, is produced in the cells. Keep lighted tobacco, open flames, bare light bulbs, and sparks away from the battery. The battery electrolyte is dilute sulfuric acid, which can burn skin and cause serious injury if splashed in your eyes (wear safety glasses). It'll ruin clothes and painted surfaces. When working around the battery, remove metal jewelry which could contact the positive battery terminal and a ground, causing a direct short.*

16   Vehicles equipped with a maintenance-free battery require no maintenance - the battery is sealed and has no removable caps for adding water.

17   If a maintenance-type battery is used, the caps on top of the battery should be removed periodically to check the electrolyte level. This check is even more critical during warm summer months.

18   Remove each of the caps and add distilled water to bring the level in each cell to the split ring in the filler opening.

19   Check the overall condition of the battery, and related components when the battery water level is checked. See Section 9 for complete battery check and maintenance procedures.

4.14 Flip up the cap to add more fluid to the windshield washer reservoir

Brake fluid

Refer to illustration 4.21

20   The master cylinder is located on the driver's side of the engine compartment firewall.

21   The brake fluid level should be maintained at the MAX mark on the reservoir **(see illustration)**.

22   If the fluid level is low, use a rag to clean the top of the reservoir. Foreign matter entering the master cylinder when the cap is removed may block brake system lines. Cover painted surfaces around the master cylinder; brake fluid will ruin paint. Carefully pour new brake fluid into the master cylinder. Use the brake fluid specified by the manufacturer, found in the *Recommended lubricants and fluids* section at the beginning of this Chapter. Mixing different types of brake fluid can damage the system.

23   Inspect the fluid and the master cylinder for contamination. The brake hydraulic system doesn't normally need periodic draining and refilling, but if rust deposits, dirt particles, or water droplets are in the fluid, the system should be dismantled, cleaned, and refilled with fresh fluid.

24   Reinstall the master cylinder cap.

25   The brake fluid level in the master cylinder drops slightly as the brake shoes or pads wear. If the master cylinder needs to be topped-off frequently, it's an indication of leaks in the brake system which should be corrected immediately. Check all brake lines, connections, wheel cylinders, and the power

4.21 The brake fluid level on the translucent white plastic brake fluid reservoir should be kept at the MAX mark (arrow)

brake booster (see Chapter 9).

26   If you find the reservoir empty or nearly empty, the brake system should be bled (see Chapter 9).

5   Tire and tire pressure checks (every 250 miles or weekly)

Refer to illustrations 5.2, 5.3, 5.4a, 5.4b and 5.8

1   Periodic tire inspection may spare you the inconvenience of being stranded with a flat tire. It provides you with important infor-

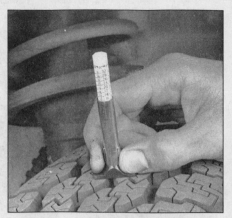

5.2 Use a tire tread depth indicator to monitor tire wear - they are available at auto parts stores and service stations and cost very little

mation about potential problems in the steering and suspension systems.

2   The original tires on these vehicles have 1/2-inch wide bands that appear when tread depth reaches 1/16-inch, indicating that the tires are worn out. Monitor tread wear with a simple, inexpensive device known as a tread depth indicator **(see illustration)**.

3   Note abnormal tread wear **(see illustration)**. Tread pattern irregularities such as cupping, flat spots, and uneven wear from one side to the other indicates front end alignment and/or balance problems. Take the vehicle to a tire shop or service station if any

UNDERINFLATION

INCORRECT TOE-IN OR EXTREME CAMBER

CUPPING

Cupping may be caused by:

- Underinflation and/or mechanical irregularities such as out-of-balance condition of wheel and/or tire, and bent or damaged wheel.
- Loose or worn steering tie-rod or steering idler arm.
- Loose, damaged or worn front suspension parts.

OVERINFLATION

FEATHERING DUE TO MISALIGNMENT

5.3 This chart will help you determine the condition of the tires, the probable cause(s) of abnormal wear and the corrective action necessary

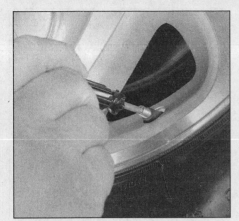

5.4a If a tire loses air on a steady basis, check the valve core first to make sure it's snug (special inexpensive wrenches are commonly available at auto parts stores)

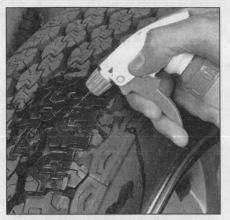

5.4b If the valve core is tight, raise the corner of the vehicle with the low tire and spray a soapy water solution onto the tread as the tire is turned slowly - leaks will cause small bubbles to appear

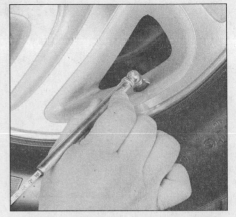

5.8 To extend the life of the tires, check the air pressure at least once a week with an accurate gauge (don't forget the spare!)

of these conditions appear.

4   Inspect for cuts, punctures and nails or tacks. A tire may hold air pressure for a short time or leak down very slowly after it has been punctured. If a slow leak persists, check the valve stem core to make sure its tight **(see illustration)**. Check the tread for an object embedded in the tire or for a "plug" that may have begun to leak (radial tire punctures are repaired with a plug). If a puncture is suspected, it can be verified by spraying a solution of soapy water onto the puncture area **(see illustration)**. The soapy solution will bubble if there's a leak. Unless the puncture is very large, a tire shop or service station can usually repair the tire.

5   Carefully inspect the inner sidewall of each tire for brake fluid leakage. If you see any, inspect the brakes immediately.

6   Correct air pressure adds miles to the lifespan of tires, improves mileage and enhances overall ride quality. Tire pressure cannot be accurately estimated by looking at a tire, especially if it's a radial. A tire pressure gauge is essential. Keep an accurate gauge in the vehicle or in your garage. Gauges on the nozzles of air hoses at gas stations are often inaccurate.

7   Check tire pressure when the tires are cold, which means the vehicle has not been driven over a mile in the previous three hours. A pressure rise of four to eight pounds is not uncommon after the tires are warm.

8   Unscrew the valve cap and push the gauge firmly onto the valve stem **(see illustration)**. Compare the pressure to the recommended tire pressure shown on the placard on the driver's side door pillar. Be sure to reinstall the valve cap to keep dirt and moisture out of the valve stem. Check all four tires and, if necessary, add enough air to bring them up to the recommended pressure.

9   Keep the spare tire inflated to the specified pressure (refer to your owner's manual or the tire sidewall). Note that the pressure recommended for the compact spare is higher than for the tires on the vehicle.

6   Automatic transaxle fluid level check (every 250 miles or weekly)

Refer to illustrations 6.3 and 6.4

1   The transaxle fluid should be at normal operating temperature for an accurate dipstick reading. Drive the vehicle for several miles, making frequent starts and stops to allow the transmission to shift through all gears.

2   Park the vehicle on a level surface, put the transaxle in Park and let the engine idle.

3   Remove the transaxle dipstick **(see illustration)** and wipe it thoroughly with a clean rag.

4   Replace the dipstick in the transaxle until the cap seats completely. Remove the dipstick and note the fluid level. The fluid level should be in the area marked Hot (between the two upper holes in the dipstick) **(see illustration)**. If the fluid isn't hot (temperature about 100-degrees F), the level should be in the area marked Warm (between the two lower holes).

5   If the fluid level is at or below the Add mark on the dipstick, add enough fluid to raise the level within the marks indicated for the appropriate temperature. Add fluid directly into the dipstick hole, and use a funnel to prevent spills.

6   Do not overfill the transaxle - allow the fluid level above the upper hole on the dipstick - it could cause internal transmission damage. To prevent overfilling, add fluid a little at a time, driving the vehicle and check-

6.3 The automatic transaxle fluid dipstick is located on the left side of the engine compartment on early models, or on later models behind the lower right side of the radiator

ing the level between additions.

7   Use the transaxle fluid specified by the manufacturer, found in the *Recommended lubricants and fluids* section at the beginning of this Chapter.

8   Fluid condition should be checked along with the level. If it's a dark reddish-brown color, or smells burned, it should be changed. If you're in doubt about the condition of the fluid, purchase new fluid and compare the two for color and smell.

9   If the transaxle needs to be topped-off frequently, there is probably a leak which should be found and corrected before it becomes serious.

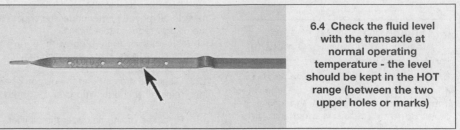

6.4 Check the fluid level with the transaxle at normal operating temperature - the level should be kept in the HOT range (between the two upper holes or marks)

7.2 The power steering reservoir dipstick is located on the right side of the engine compartment on early models, or on the left side of the intake manifold on later models

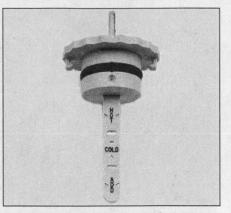

7.5 The power steering fluid dipstick (earlier models) is marked for checking the fluid cold (as shown) or hot

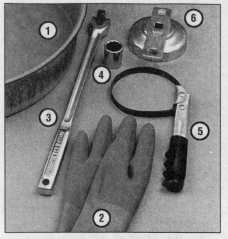

8.3 These tools are required when changing the engine oil and filter

1   **Drain pan** - It should be fairly shallow in depth, but wide to prevent spills
2   **Rubber gloves** - When removing the drain plug and filter, you will get oil on your hands (the gloves will prevent burns)
3   **Breaker bar** - Sometimes the oil drain plug is tight, and a long breaker bar is needed to loosen it
4   **Socket** - To be used with the breaker bar or a ratchet (must be the correct size to fit the drain plug - six-point preferred)
5   **Filter wrench** - This is a metal band-type wrench, which requires clearance around the filter to be effective
6   **Filter wrench** - This type fits on the bottom of the filter and can be turned with a ratchet or breaker bar (different-size wrenches are available for different types of filters)

7   Power steering fluid level check (every 250 miles or weekly)

Refer to illustrations 7.2 and 7.5

1   Power steering systems may require occasional fluid replenishment.
2   The reservoir for the power steering pump is in the engine compartment **(see illustration)**.
3   The power steering fluid level can be checked with the engine hot or cold.
4   With the engine off, check the fluid level visually through the translucent reservoir if possible. For a more accurate reading, the dipstick can be checked on earlier models. Wipe the reservoir cap and the area around the cap with a rag. This will prevent foreign material from falling into the reservoir when the cap is removed.
5   Turn and pull out the reservoir cap, which has a dipstick attached to it. Wipe the fluid from the bottom of the dipstick with a clean rag. Reinstall the cap and then remove it again to get a fluid level check. The fluid should be at the Full Cold mark on the dipstick **(see illustration)**. If the engine is warm, the fluid level can be checked on the other side of the dipstick.
6   If additional fluid is required, use a funnel to pour power steering fluid directly into the reservoir. The correct type of fluid can be found in the *Recommended lubricants and fluids* section at the beginning of this Chapter.
7   If the reservoir needs to be topped-off frequently, check power steering hoses, hose connections, the power steering pump, and the steering box for leaks.

8   Engine oil and filter change (every 3,000 miles or 3 months)

Refer to illustrations 8.3, 8.9, 8.14 and 8.19

1   Frequent oil changes are the most important preventive maintenance procedures done by the home mechanic. When engine oil ages, it gets diluted and contaminated, which ultimately leads to premature engine wear.
2   A new filter should be installed every time the oil is changed.
3   Gather tools, materials, and a supply of clean rags and newspapers (to clean up spills) before beginning this procedure **(see illustration)**. **Note:** *To avoid rounding off the corners of the drain plug, use a six-point wrench or socket.*
4   The job is a lot easier if the vehicle is lifted on a hoist, driven onto ramps, or supported by jackstands. **Warning:** *Don't work under a vehicle that is supported only by a jack!*
5   Crawl underneath the vehicle to familiarize yourself with the location of the oil drain plug and the oil filter. Engine and exhaust components will be hot, it's a good idea to figure out potential problems before starting.
6   Warm the engine to normal operating temperature. Use the warm-up time to gather everything necessary for the job. The correct type of oil can be found in the *Recommended lubricants and fluids* section at the beginning of this Chapter.
7   When the oil is warm (warm oil will drain better and sludge will flow easier), raise the vehicle and support it securely on jackstands (see *Jacking and towing* at the front of this manual).
8   Put all tools, rags, and newspapers under the vehicle. Place the drain pan under the drain plug. The oil will initially spurt from the engine, so position the pan carefully.
9   Do not to touch hot exhaust components. Remove the drain plug at the bottom of the oil pan **(see illustration)**. If the oil is very hot, you may need to wear gloves while unscrewing the plug.
10   Drain the oil into the pan. The pan may have to be moved further under the engine as the oil flow reduces to a trickle.
11   Clean the drain plug with a rag to remove small metal particles which may contaminate the new oil.
12   Clean the area around the oil pan opening, reinstall the drain plug, and tighten it securely.
13   Place the drain pan under the oil filter.

14   Loosen the oil filter with an oil filter wrench **(see illustration)**. Chain or metal band filter wrenches may distort the filter canister, but don't worry - the filter should be discarded.
15   The oil filter may be too tight to be loosened, or inaccessible with a conventional filter wrench. Tools that fit over the end of the

8.9 To avoid rounding off the corners, use the correct size box-end wrench or a socket to remove the engine oil drain plug

8.14 The oil filter is usually on very tight and normally will require a special wrench for removal - DO NOT use a wrench to tighten the oil filter!

8.19 Lubricate the oil filter gasket with clean engine oil before installing the filter on the engine

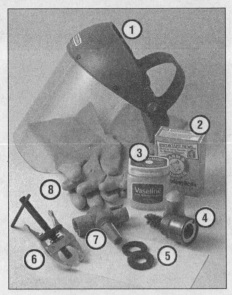

9.1 Tools and materials required for battery maintenance

filter, and can be turned with a ratchet or breaker bar are available, and may be better suited for removing the filter. If the filter is extremely tight, place the wrench near the threaded end of the filter, next to the engine.

16 Unscrew the old filter - be careful, it's full of oil - and empty the filter into the drain pan.

17 Compare the old and new filter to make sure they're identical.

18 Remove all oil, dirt, and sludge from the oil filter mount area with a clean rag. Check the old filter to make sure the rubber gasket isn't stuck to the engine.

19 Apply a light coat of oil to the rubber gasket on the new oil filter **(see Illustration)**.

20 Tighten the new filter following directions on the filter canister or packing box. Most manufacturers recommend that filters be installed hand-tight - avoid over tightening.

21 Remove tools and materials from under the vehicle, be careful not to spill the oil in the drain pan. Jack up the vehicle, remove the jackstands, and lower the vehicle.

22 Find the oil filler cap in the engine compartment.

23 Use a funnel when adding oil if the filler opening is obstructed.

24 Add the specified amount of new oil. Wait a few minutes to allow the oil to drain into the pan, then check the dipstick (see Section 4). If the oil level is at or above the Add mark, start the engine and allow the oil to circulate.

25 Run the engine for about a minute, then shut it off. Look under the vehicle for leaks at the oil pan drain plug and around the oil filter. If they are leaking, retighten them.

26 After the oil has circulated and the filter has filled, recheck the oil level. If necessary, add oil to bring the level to the Full mark on the dipstick.

27 Check for leaks and keep a close watch on the oil level during the first few trips after an oil change.

28 Old engine oil cannot be reused and should be disposed of properly. Oil reclamation centers, auto repair shops, and gas stations will normally accept used oil. After the

9.5 On some models, the battery is secured by a clamp at the base - make sure the nut is tight (arrow)

oil has cooled, it should be poured into containers (plastic bottles with screw-on tops) prior to transport to a disposal site or reclamation center.

9 Battery check, maintenance and charging (every 7,500 miles or 6 months)

Refer to illustrations 9.1, 9.5, 9.6a, 9.6b, 9.7a and 9.7b

1 Routine preventive maintenance of the battery is the only way to ensure quick and reliable starts. Before performing battery maintenance, make sure that you have the required equipment **(see illustration)**.

2 Precautions should be taken when battery maintenance is performed. Turn the engine and accessories off and disconnect the negative battery terminal cable before servicing the battery.

3 The battery produces hydrogen gas, which is flammable and explosive. Never smoke, light a match, or create a spark around the battery, and always charge the battery in a ventilated area.

4 Electrolyte contains poisonous, corrosive sulfuric acid. Do not ingest it, or allow it to get in your eyes or on your skin or clothes.

1 *Face shield/safety goggles* - When removing corrosion with a brush, the acidic particles can easily fly up into your eyes

2 *Baking soda* - A solution of baking soda and water can be used to neutralize corrosion

3 *Petroleum jelly* - A layer of this on the battery posts will help prevent corrosion

4 *Battery post/cable cleaner* - This wire brush cleaning tool will remove all traces of corrosion from the battery posts and cable clamps

5 *Treated felt washers* - Placing one of these on each post, directly under the cable clamps, will help prevent corrosion

6 *Puller* - Sometimes the cable clamps are very difficult to pull off the posts, even after the nut/bolt has been completely loosened. This tool pulls the clamp straight up and off the post without damage

7 *Battery post/cable cleaner* - Here is another cleaning tool which is a slightly different version of Number 4 above, but it does the same thing

8 *Rubber gloves* - Another safety item to consider when servicing the battery; remember that's acid inside the battery!

Wear safety glasses when working near the battery.

5 Check the condition of the battery. If the positive terminal and cable clamp on your vehicle's battery has a rubber protector, make sure that it's not torn or damaged. It should completely cover the terminal. Look for corroded or loose connections, cracks in the case or cover, and loose hold-down clamps **(see illustration)**. Check the entire length of each cable for cracks and frayed conductors.

9.6a Battery terminal corrosion usually appears as light, fluffy powder

9.6b Remove the cable from a battery post with a wrench - sometimes special battery pliers are required for this procedure if corrosion has caused deterioration of the nut hex (always remove the ground cable first and hook it up last!)

6   If there is corrosion (white, fluffy deposits) **(see illustration)**, around the terminals, the battery should be removed and cleaned. Loosen the cable clamp nuts with a wrench. Remove the negative cable clamp first and then the positive cable clamp, and slide them off the terminals **(see illustration)**. Disconnect the hold-down clamp nuts, remove the clamp, and lift the battery from the engine compartment.

7   Clean the cable clamps with a battery brush or a terminal cleaner and a solution of warm water and baking soda **(see illustrations)**. Wash the terminals and the top of the battery case with the same solution making sure that the solution doesn't get into the battery. Wear safety goggles and rubber gloves when cleaning the cables, terminals, and battery top, to prevent any solution from coming in contact with your eyes or hands. Wear old clothes - even diluted, sulfuric acid will burn holes in clothing. Thoroughly wash all cleaned areas with plain water.

8   Before reinstalling the battery, inspect the plastic battery carrier. If it's dirty or corroded, remove and clean it with warm water and baking soda. Inspect the metal brackets that support the carrier. If they are corroded, wash them off. If corrosion is extensive, sand the brackets down to bare metal and spray them with a zinc-based primer (available at auto paint and body supply stores).

9   Reinstall the battery carrier and the battery in the engine compartment. Make sure that no parts or wires are laying on the carrier during battery installation.

10   Install treated felt washers around the terminals (available at auto parts stores), then coat the terminals and the cable clamps with petroleum jelly or grease to prevent further corrosion. Install the cable clamps and tighten the nuts. Install the negative cable last.

11   Install the hold-down clamp and nuts. Tighten the nut only enough to hold the battery firmly in place. Overtightening this nut can crack the battery case.

Charging

12   Remove all of the cell caps (if equipped) and cover the holes with a clean cloth to prevent spattering electrolyte. Disconnect the negative battery cable and hook the battery charger leads to the battery posts (positive to positive, negative to negative). Plug in the charger making sure it is set at 12 volts.

13   If you're using a charger rated higher than two amps, check the battery regularly to make sure it doesn't overheat. If you're using a trickle charger, you can let the battery charge overnight after checking it regularly for the first couple of hours.

14   Measure the specific gravity with a hydrometer every hour during the last few hours of the charging cycle if the battery has removable cell caps. Hydrometers are inexpensive and available at auto parts stores. Follow the instructions that come with the hydrometer. The battery is charged when

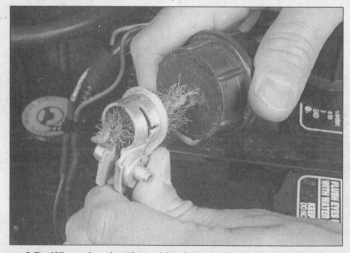

9.7a When cleaning the cable clamps, all corrosion must be removed (the inside of the clamp is tapered to match the taper on the post, so don't remove too much material)

9.7b Regardless of the type of tool used on the battery posts, a clean, shiny surface should be the result

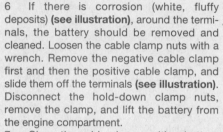

Check for a chafed area that could fail prematurely.

Check for a soft area indicating the hose has deteriorated inside.

Overtightening the clamp on a hardened hose will damage the hose and cause a leak.

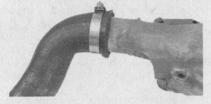

Check each hose for swelling and oil-soaked ends. Cracks and breaks can be located by squeezing the hose.

10.4 Hoses, like drivebelts, have a habit of failing at the worst possible time - to prevent the inconvenience of a blown radiator or heater hose, inspect them carefully as shown here

there's no change in the specific gravity reading for two hours and the electrolyte in the cells is gassing (bubbling) freely. The specific gravity reading in each cell should be very close to the others. If not, the battery probably has a bad cell(s).

15   Batteries with sealed tops may have built-in hydrometers on the top that indicate the charge by the color displayed in the hydrometer window. Normally, a bright-colored hydrometer indicates a full charge and a dark hydrometer indicates the battery needs charging. Check the battery manufacturer's instructions to be sure you know what the colors mean.

16   If the battery is sealed and has no hydrometer, you can hook up a digital voltmeter across the battery terminals to check the charge. A fully charged battery should read 12.6 volts or more.

17   Further information on the battery and jump starting can be found in Chapter 5 and at the front of this manual.

10   Cooling system check (every 7,500 miles or 6 months)

Refer to illustration 10.4
Warning: *The electric cooling fan may start any time the ignition switch is On. Make sure the ignition is Off when working near the fan.*

1   Many major engine failures are caused by a faulty cooling system. If the vehicle has an automatic transmission, the cooling system also cools the transmission fluid.

2   The cooling system should be checked with the engine cold. Do this before the vehicle has been driven or after it has been shut off for three or four hours.

3   Remove the radiator cap and clean the cap (inside and out) with water. Clean the filler neck on the radiator and remove all traces of corrosion.

4   Carefully check the entire length of the upper and lower radiator hoses and the smaller heater hoses, and replace any that are cracked, swollen, or deteriorated. Cracks are easier to see if the hose is squeezed **(see illustration)**.

5   Make sure that all hose connections are tight. A cooling system leak usually shows up as white or rust-colored deposits around the leak.

6   Use compressed air or a soft brush to remove bugs, leaves, and other debris from the front of the radiator or air conditioning condenser. Do not damage the delicate cooling fins, or cut yourself on them.

7   Have the cap and system pressure tested. Most gas stations and repair shops will do this for a minimal charge If you don't have a pressure tester.

11   Underhood hose check and replacement (every 7,500 miles or 6 months)

Warning: *Replacement of air conditioning hoses must be left to a dealer service department or an air conditioning shop equipped to safely depressurize the system. Never remove air conditioning components or hoses until the system has been depressurized.*

General

1   High temperatures under the hood can cause rubber and plastic hoses used for engine, accessories, and emission systems to deteriorate. Inspections for cracks, loose clamps, material hardening, and leaks should be done periodically.

2   Cooling system hose information can be found in Section 25.

3   Some hoses are secured with clamps. Make sure they are tight and do not allow the hose to leak. If clamps are not used, make sure the hose hasn't expanded and/or hardened where it slips over the fitting, allowing it to leak.

Vacuum hoses

4   Vacuum hoses, especially those in the emissions system, are often color coded or identified by colored stripes molded into the hose. Different systems require hoses with different wall thickness, and collapse and temperature resistance. When replacing hoses, make sure the new ones are identical to the old ones.

5   If more than one hose is removed at a time, be sure to label the hoses and attach points to insure proper replacement.

6   When checking vacuum hoses, be sure to include plastic T-fittings. Check the fittings for cracks and the hose where it fits over the fitting for enlargement, which could cause leakage.

7   A small piece of vacuum hose (1/4-inch inside diameter) can be used as a stethoscope to find vacuum leaks. Hold one end of the hose to your ear and probe around vacuum hoses and fittings, listening for the "hissing" sound of a vacuum leak. **Warning:** *When probing with the vacuum hose stethoscope, be careful not to allow your body or the hose to come into contact with moving engine components such as the drivebelt, cooling fan, etc.*

Fuel hose

Warning: *Gasoline is extremely flammable; take extra precautions when working on any part of the fuel system. Don't smoke or allow open flames or bare light bulbs near the work area, and don't work in a garage where a natural gas-type appliance (such as a water heater or clothes dryer) with a pilot light is present. If you spill fuel on your skin, rinse it off immediately with soap and water. When you work on the fuel system, wear safety glasses and have a Class B type fire extinguisher handy. Relieve the fuel system pressure (see Chapter 4) before working on any part of the fuel system.*

8   Check rubber fuel hoses for damage and deterioration. Examine for cracks where the hose bends and just before clamping points, such as the fuel injection unit.

9   High quality fuel line, designed for fuel injection systems, should be used for fuel line replacement. **Warning:** *Never use vacuum line, clear plastic tubing or water hose for fuel lines.*

Metal lines

10   Metal lines are often used for fuel lines between the fuel tank and fuel injection unit. Check to ensure the line is not bent, crimped, or cracked.

11   Seamless steel tubing should be used If a section of metal fuel line must be replaced. Copper and aluminum tubing does not have the strength to withstand normal engine vibration.

12   Check the metal brake lines at the master cylinder and brake proportioning or ABS

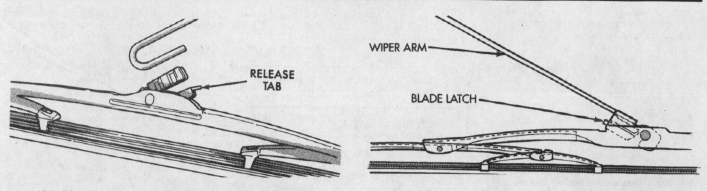

12.4 Disengage the release tab holding the wiper blade to the wiper arm

12.8 Release the latch holding the blade to the wiper arm

unit (if used) for cracks or loose fittings. Brake fluid leakage requires immediate inspection and repair.

12   Wiper blade inspection and replacement (every 7,500 miles or 6 months)

Windshield wipers

Refer to illustrations 12.4

Note: *Before replacing windshield or rear wiper blades, make sure the new blades are exact replacements for those being removed.*

1   The windshield and rear wiper blades should be checked periodically for cracks and deterioration.
2   Turn on the ignition switch and cycle the wipers to a position parallel to the A-pillar, then turn off the ignition.
3   Lift the wiper blade assembly away from the windshield.
4   Disengage the release tab holding the wiper blade to the wiper arm **(see illustration)**.
5   Remove the wiper blade from the wiper arm.
6   Installation is the reverse of removal.

Rear wiper

Refer to illustration 12.8

7   Lift the wiper blade away from the rear window.
8   Release the latch holding the blade to the wiper arm **(see illustration)**.
9   Installation is the reverse of removal.

13   Tire rotation (every 7,500 miles or 6 months)

Refer to illustration 13.2

1   Tires should be rotated at specified intervals and when uneven wear is noticed. Since the vehicle will be raised and the tires removed, this is a good time to check the brakes (see Section 18). Read the appropriate Section if other work is to be done at the same time.

2   Radial tires must be rotated in a specific pattern depending upon whether or not the spare is included in the rotation **(see illustration)**.
3   See *Jacking and towing* in the front of this manual for procedures to follow when raising the vehicle and changing a tire. If the brakes are to be checked, don't apply the parking brake and make sure at least two tires are blocked to prevent the vehicle from rolling.
4   The entire vehicle should be raised. This can be done on a hoist or by jacking up each corner of the vehicle and lowering it onto jackstands. Use four jackstands and double-check the vehicle stability.
5   After tire rotation, check and adjust tire pressures and wheel lug nut tightness.

14   Steering and suspension check (every 7,500 miles or 6 months)

1   When the front of the vehicle is raised for service it is a good idea to check suspension and steering components for wear and damage.
2   Indications of wear and damage include: excessive play in the steering wheel, excessive lean in corners, body movement on rough roads, or binding in the steering wheel.
3   Before the vehicle is raised, test the shock absorbers. Push down (or rock) the vehicle at each corner. If it does not return to level within one or two bounces, the shocks are worn and should be replaced. At the same time, check for squeaks and unusual noises in the suspension. Check the shock absorbers for leakage. Shock absorbers and suspension information can be found in Chapter 10.
4   Raise the front of the vehicle and support it securely with jackstands (see *Jacking and towing* at the front of this manual).
5   Check the front wheel hub nuts (in the center of each wheel) for tightness and make sure they're properly crimped.
6   Crawl under the vehicle and check for loose bolts, broken or disconnected parts, and deteriorated rubber bushings on all suspension and steering components. Look for grease or fluid leaks around the steering gear boots. Check the power steering hoses and connections for leaks and the steering joints for wear.
7   Have a helper turn the steering wheel from side-to-side and check steering components for looseness, chafing and binding. If the wheels don't respond to steering wheel movement, find where the slack is located.

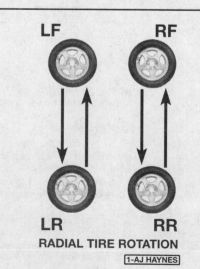

13.2 The recommended tire rotation pattern for these models

15.2 Check the exhaust system mounting bolts, brackets and hangers for damage

15 Exhaust system check (every 7,500 or 6 months)

Refer to illustration 15.2

1   With the engine cold (at least three hours after the vehicle has been driven), check the exhaust system from the exhaust manifold to the end of the tailpipe. This should be done on a hoist for unrestricted access.

2   Check pipes and connections for leakage and/or corrosion indicating a potential failure. Make sure that all brackets and hangers are tight and in good condition **(see illustration)**.

3   Inspect the underside of the vehicle for holes, corrosion, and open seams which may allow exhaust gases to enter the passenger compartment. Seal all openings with silicone sealant or body putty.

4   Rattles and other noises may be traced to the exhaust system, especially the mounts and hangers. Try to move the pipes, muffler, and catalytic converter. If the components contact the body, secure them with new mounts.

5   This is an ideal time to check the condition of the engine by inspecting the end of the tailpipe. Exhaust deposits indicate the engine state-of-tune. If the pipe is black and sooty or coated with white deposits, the engine may need a tune-up (including a thorough fuel injection system inspection).

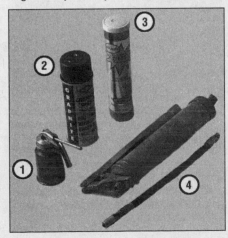

16 Differential lubricant level check

The differential oil pan is common with the transaxle oil pan. Separate fluid level checks and filling of the differential is **not** necessary.

17 Chassis lubrication (every 15,000 miles or 12 months)

Refer to illustration 17.1

1   A grease gun and a cartridge filled with the proper grease (see *Recommended lubricants and fluids*), graphite spray, and an oil can filled with engine oil are required to lubricate chassis components **(see illustration)**. If plugs are used instead of grease fittings, grease fittings have to be purchased and installed.

2   Raise the vehicle and support it securely on jackstands (see *Jacking and towing* at the front of this manual).

3   Before using the grease gun, pump a little grease from the nozzle to remove dirt from the end of the gun. Wipe the nozzle clean with a rag.

4   Crawl under the vehicle and lubricate the components (take plenty of rags).

5   Wipe grease fittings clean and push the nozzle firmly over them. Pump the lever on the grease gun to pump grease into the fitting until it oozes out between the two components. If grease escapes around the grease gun nozzle, the fitting is clogged or the nozzle is not completely seated on the fitting. Re-seat the gun nozzle on the fitting and try again. Replace the fitting with a new one If necessary.

6   Lubricate the sliding contact and pivot points of the parking brake cable and the cable guides and levers. Smear chassis grease on the cable and related parts with your fingers.

7   Lower the vehicle to the ground.

8   Open the hood and smear chassis grease on the hood latch mechanism. Have a helper pull the hood release lever inside the vehicle as you lubricate the cable at the latch.

9   Lubricate all the hinges (door, hood, etc.) with the recommended lubricant to keep them in proper working order.

17.1 Materials required for chassis and body lubrication

1   *Engine oil - Light engine oil in a can like this can be used for door and hood hinges*

2   *Graphite spray - Used to lubricate lock cylinders*

3   *Grease - Grease, in a variety of types and weights, is available for use in a grease gun. Check the Specifications for your requirements*

4   *Grease gun - A common grease gun, shown here with a detachable hose and nozzle, is needed for chassis lubrication. After use, clean it thoroughly*

10   Key lock cylinders can be lubricated with spray-on graphite or silicone lubricant available at auto parts stores.

11   Lubricate the door weather stripping with silicone spray. This will reduce chafing and retard wear.

18 Brake system check (every 15,000 miles or 12 months)

Refer to illustrations 18.5, 18.14 and 18.16

Warning: *Dust created by the brake system may contain asbestos, which is harmful to your health. Never blow it out with compressed air and don't inhale it. An approved filtering mask should be worn when working on brakes. Do not use petroleum-based solvents to clean brake parts. Use brake system cleaner only!*

1   Brakes should be inspected every time the wheels are removed or a defect is suspected. Indications of potential brake system problems include: the vehicle pulling to one side when braking, unusual noises from the brakes, excessive brake pedal travel, pulsating pedal, and fluid leakage - usually seen on the inside of the tire or wheel.

Disc brakes (front and rear)

2   Disc brakes can be visually checked by removing the wheels.

3   Raise the vehicle and place it securely on jackstands. Remove the wheels (see *Jacking and towing* at the front of this manual).

4   The disc brake caliper which contains the pads is now visible. There is an outer brake pad and an inner pad. Both should be checked for wear.

5   Note the pad thickness by looking at each end of the caliper and through the inspection hole in the caliper body **(see illustration)**. If the combined thickness of the pad lining and the metal backing is 5/16-inch or less, the pads should be replaced.

6   If you're in doubt about the condition of the pads, remove them for closer inspection or replacement (see Chapter 9).

7   Before installing the wheels, check for leakage around the brake hose connections

18.5 By looking at the end of the caliper, you can determine the thickness of the remaining friction material on both the inner and outer pads

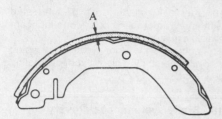

18.14 If the lining is bonded to the brake shoe, measure the lining thickness from the outer surface to the metal shoe, as shown here; if the lining is riveted to the shoe, measure from the lining outer surface to the rivet head

at the caliper and for damaged brake hoses (cracks, leaks, chafed areas, etc.). Replace hoses or fittings as necessary (see Chapter 9).

8   Check the discs for score marks, wear, and burned spots. If these conditions exist, the hub/disc assembly should be removed for servicing (see Chapter 9).

Drum brakes

9   Raise the vehicle and support it securely on jackstands (see *Jacking and towing* at the front of this manual). Block the front tires to prevent the vehicle from rolling. Don't apply the parking brake or it will lock the drums.
10   Remove the rear wheels.
11   Mark the hub so it can be reinstalled in the same position. Use a scribe, chalk, etc. on the drum, hub and backing plate.
12   Remove the brake drum (see Chapter 9).
13   With the drum removed, clean off dirt and dust using brake cleaner. **Warning:** *Don't blow the out dust with compressed air and don't inhale it (it may contain asbestos, which is harmful to your health).*
14   Note the thickness of the lining on the front and rear brake shoes. If the material is within 1/16-inch of the recessed rivets or metal backing, the shoes should be replaced **(see illustration)**. The shoes should also be replaced if they're cracked, glazed (shiny areas), or covered with brake fluid.

15   Make sure the brake springs are connected and in good condition.
16   Check brake components (including hoses and connections) for fluid leakage. Carefully pry back the rubber cups on the wheel cylinder located at the top of the brake shoes **(see illustration)**. Leakage indicates that the wheel cylinders should be overhauled (see Chapter 9).
17   Wipe the inside of the drum with a clean rag and denatured alcohol or brake cleaner. Be careful not to inhale asbestos dust.
18   Check the inside of the drum for cracks, score marks, deep scratches, and "hard spots" which appear as small discolored areas. If imperfections cannot be removed with fine emery cloth, the drum must be taken to an automotive machine shop to be "turned".
19   Repeat the procedure on the remaining wheel. If the inspection reveals that all parts are in good condition, reinstall the brake drums, and the wheels, and lower the vehicle to the ground.

Parking brake

20   The parking brake is operated by a foot pedal and locks the rear brakes. The easiest way to check the parking brake is to park the vehicle on a steep hill, set the parking brake, and shift the transmission to Neutral. If the parking brake does not keep the vehicle from rolling, it needs adjustment (see Chapter 9).

---

19   Fuel system check (every 15,000 miles or 12 months)

Refer to illustration 19.6
Warning: *Gasoline is extremely flammable. Take extra precautions when working on any part of the fuel system. Don't smoke or allow open flames or bare light bulbs near the work area, and don't work in a garage where a natural gas-type appliance (such as a water heater or clothes dryer) with a pilot light is present. If you spill fuel on your skin, rinse it off immediately with soap and water. When you work on the fuel system, wear safety glasses and have a Class B type fire extinguisher handy.*

1   The fuel system on fuel injected vehicles is pressurized even when the engine is off and must be depressurized before servicing (see Chapter 4). After depressurization; be prepared to catch fuel spurting from lines disconnected for servicing. Plug all disconnected fuel lines to prevent the fuel tank from siphoning out.
2   The fuel system is most accessible with the vehicle on a hoist so components on the underside are visible. If a hoist is not available, raise the vehicle and support it securely on jackstands.
3   If the gasoline can be smelled while driving, or after the vehicle has been parked in the sun, the fuel system should be inspected immediately.
4   Remove the gas cap and check for damage, corrosion, and proper seal imprint on the gasket. Replace the cap with a new one if necessary.
5   Inspect the gas tank and filler neck for punctures, cracks, or other damage. The connection between the filler neck and the tank is critical. A rubber filler neck can leak due to loose clamps or deteriorated rubber; problems a home mechanic can fix easily. **Warning:** *Do not try to repair a fuel tank yourself (except to replace rubber components). A welding torch or open flame can cause fuel vapors to explode if the proper precautions are not taken.*
6   Check all rubber hoses and metal lines leading from the fuel tank for loose connections, deteriorated hoses, crimped lines, or other damage **(see illustration)**. Inspect the lines all the way to the front of the vehicle and repair or replace damaged sections as necessary (see Chapter 4).

---

20   Drivebelt check, adjustment and replacement (every 15,000 miles or 12 months)

Refer to illustrations 20.2a, 20.2b, 20.2c, 20.2d, 20.2e, 20.3a, 20.3b, 20.4 and 20.8
Warning: *The electric cooling fan may start any time the ignition switch is On. Make sure the ignition is Off when working near the fan.*

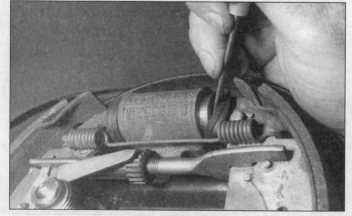

18.16   Use a small screwdriver to carefully pry the boot away from the cylinder and check for fluid leakage

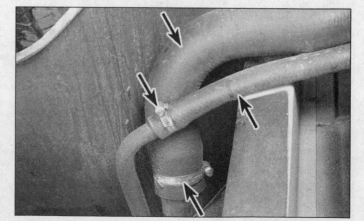

19.6   Check the fuel tank hoses and clamps (arrows) for damage and deterioration

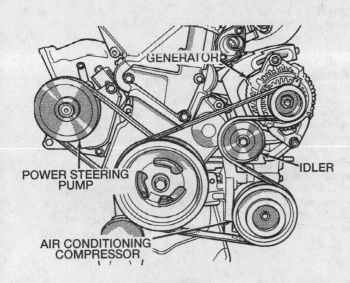

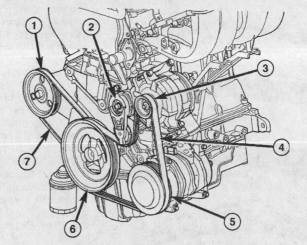

20.2a 2.4L engine drivebelt layout (1996 through 2000)

20.2b 2.4L engine drivebelt layout (2001 and later models)

1	Power steering pump pulley	5	Air conditioning compressor pulley
2	Belt tensioner	6	Crankshaft pulley
3	Generator pulley	7	Power steering belt
4	Serpentine belt		

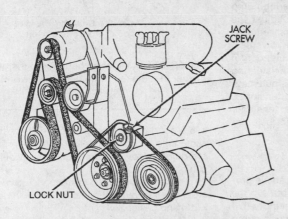

20.2c 3.0L engine drivebelt layout

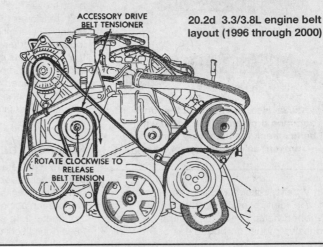

20.2d 3.3/3.8L engine belt layout (1996 through 2000)

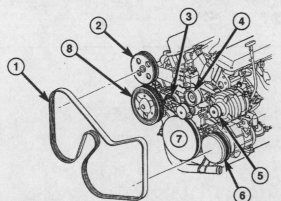

20.2e 3.3/3.8L engine drivebelt layout (2001 and later models)

1	Serpentine belt	5	Generator pulley
2	Power steering pump pulley	6	Air conditioning compressor pulley
3	Belt tensioner	7	Crankshaft pulley
4	Idler pulley	8	Water pump pulley

1   The drivebelts, or V-belts at the front of the engine, play a vital role in the overall operation of the vehicle and its components. Belts are prone to failure after a period of time and should be inspected and adjusted periodically to prevent major damage.

2   The number of belts used depends on the engine accessories. On the 2.4L engine, two drivebelts are used: a serpentine belt to turn the air conditioning compressor and the alternator and a V-belt to turn the power steering pump. The 3.0L engine uses two belts: a serpentine belt to turn the alternator and power steering pump and a V-belt to turn the air conditioner. The 3.3/3.8L engine uses a single serpentine (V-ribbed) belt to drive all components **(see illustrations)**.

3   With the engine off, open the hood and locate the drivebelts at the front of the engine. Use a flashlight to check each belt.

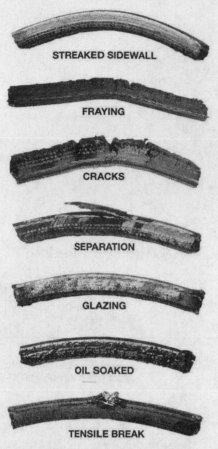

20.3a Here are some of the more common problems associated with V-belts (check the belts very carefully to prevent an untimely breakdown)

STREAKED SIDEWALL

FRAYING

CRACKS

SEPARATION

GLAZING

OIL SOAKED

TENSILE BREAK

On V-belts, check for cracks and separation of the belt plies **(see illustration)**. On V-ribbed belts, check for separation of the adhesive rubber on both sides of the core, core separation from the belt side, a severed core, separation of the ribs from the adhesive rubber, cracking or separation of the ribs,

and torn or worn ribs or cracks in the inner ridges of the ribs **(see illustration)**. On either belt, check for fraying and glazing, which gives the belt a shiny appearance. Both sides of the belt should be inspected. You will have to twist the belt to check the underside. Use your fingers to feel the belt where you can't see it. If any of the above conditions are evident, replace the belt (go to Step 6).

4   The tightness of each belt is checked by pushing on it halfway between the pulleys. Apply about 10 pounds of force with your thumb and see how much the belt moves (deflects). Measure the deflection with a ruler **(see illustration)**. The belt should deflect about 1/4-inch if the distance between pulleys is between 7 and 11 inches and around 1/2-inch if the distance is between 12 and 16 inches.

Adjustment

5   If adjustment is required on the 1996 through 2000 2.4L engine alternator or air conditioning compressor belt, loosen the upper locking nut and adjust the belt tensioner. To adjust the power steering pump belt, loosen the pivot bolt and adjust the belt tensioner. If adjustment is required on the 3.0L engine air conditioner drive belt, loosen the idler pulley lock nut and turn the adjustment screw. The power steering and alternator drive belt tension is automatically maintained with a dynamic tensioner. On 3.3/3.8L engines, a dynamic tensioner automatically maintains the correct belt tension.

Replacement

6   To replace a belt, follow the above procedures for drivebelt adjustment but slip the belt off the crankshaft pulley and remove it. If you are replacing the power steering pump belt on the 2.4L engine, you have to remove the air conditioning compressor and alternator belts first because of the way they are arranged on the crankshaft pulley. Because belts tend to wear out more or less together,

ACCEPTABLE

Cracks Running Across "V" Portions of Belt

UNACCEPTABLE

1/2" Missing Two or More Adjacent Ribs 13 mm or longer

Cracks Running Parallel to "V" Portions of Belt

20.3b Check V-ribbed belts for signs of wear like these - if the belt looks worn, replace it

it is a good idea to replace both belts at the same time. Mark each belt and its appropriate pulley groove so the replacement belts can be installed correctly.

7   Take the old belt(s) to the parts store in order to make a direct comparison for length, width and design.

8   After replacing a V-ribbed drivebelt, make sure it fits properly in the ribbed grooves in the pulleys **(see illustration)**. It is essential that the belt be properly centered.

9   Adjust the belt(s) in accordance with the procedure outlined above.

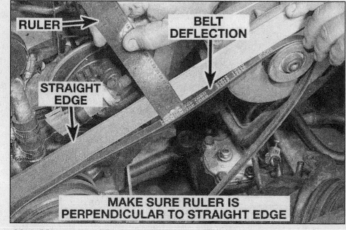

RULER

BELT DEFLECTION

STRAIGHT EDGE

MAKE SURE RULER IS PERPENDICULAR TO STRAIGHT EDGE

20.4 Measuring drivebelt deflection with a straightedge and ruler

CORRECT

WRONG   WRONG

20.8 When installing the V-ribbed belt, make sure it is centered on the pulley - it must not overlap either edge of the pulley

21 Air filter replacement (every 30,000 miles or 24 months)

Refer to illustrations 21.2 and 21.3

1 The air filter is located in a housing in the left front corner of the engine compartment and should be replaced at specified intervals.
2 Remove the housing screws and lift off the cover **(see illustration)**.
3 Lift out the filter **(see illustration)**.
4 Clean the inside of the housing with a rag. Be careful not to drop anything into the air cleaner assembly.
5 Place the new air filter in the housing and install the cover. Be sure to tighten hose clamps that were loosened or removed.

22 Automatic transaxle fluid and filter change (every 30,000 miles or 24 months)

Refer to illustration 22.3

1 The automatic transmission fluid and filter should be changed and the magnet cleaned at the recommended intervals.
2 Raise the front of the vehicle, support it securely on jackstands, and apply the parking brake.
3 Place a container under the transaxle pan and loosen the pan bolts **(see illustration)**. Completely remove the bolts along the rear of the pan. Tap the corner of the pan to break the seal and allow the fluid to drain into the container (the remaining bolts will prevent the pan from separating from the transmission). Remove the remaining bolts and detach the pan.
4 Install a new filter and gasket, clean the magnet(s), and re-tighten the filter screws.
5 Remove the old sealant from the pan and transmission body (don't nick or gouge the sealing surfaces) and clean the pan magnet with a clean, lint-free cloth.
6 Apply a 1/8-inch bead of RTV to the pan sealing surface and position it on the trans-

21.2 Use a socket and remove the air cleaner housing bolts

21.3 Remove or lift up on the air filter housing and remove the element

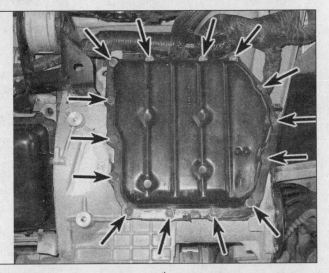
22.3 Use a socket and extension to remove the transaxle pan bolts

mission. Install the bolts and tighten them to the torque in this Chapter's *Specifications* using a criss-cross pattern. Work up to the final torque in three or four steps.
7 Lower the vehicle and add four quarts of the specified transaxle fluid (see *Recommended lubricants and fluids* at the beginning of this Chapter). Start the engine and allow it to idle for a minute, then move the shift lever through each gear position, ending in Park or Neutral. Check for fluid leaks around the pan.
8 If necessary, add more fluid (a little at a time) until the level is between the Add and Full marks (be careful not to overfill it).
9 Make sure the dipstick is completely seated or dirt could get into the transaxle.

23 Driveaxle boot check (every 30,000 miles or 24 months)

Refer to illustration 23.3

If the driveaxle boots are damaged or deteriorated, serious and costly damage can occur to the CV joints. The boots should be inspected carefully at the recommended intervals.

Raise the front of vehicle, support it

securely on jackstands, and apply the parking brake.

Crawl under the vehicle and check the four driveaxle boots (two on each driveaxle) carefully for cracks, tears, holes, deteriorated rubber and loose or missing clamps **(see illustration)**. If the boots are dirty, wipe them clean before beginning the inspection.

If damage or deterioration is present, replace the boots with new ones and check the CV joints for damage (see Chapter 8).

24 Differential lubricant change

The differential oil pan is common with the transaxle oil pan. Separate fluid level checks and filling of the differential is **not** necessary.

25 Cooling system servicing - draining, flushing, and refilling (every 30,000 miles or 24 months)

Refer to illustrations 25.4, 25.6 and 25.7
Warning: *Do not allow engine coolant (antifreeze) to contact your skin or painted*

23.3 Push on the boot to check for damage and signs of leaking grease

25.4 The drain fitting is located at the bottom of the radiator (arrow) (typical)

surfaces of the vehicle. Rinse off spills immediately with water. Antifreeze is highly toxic if ingested. Never leave antifreeze in an open container or in puddles on the floor. Children and pets are attracted by it's sweet smell and may drink it. Check with local authorities about antifreeze disposal. Many communities have collection centers which can dispose of antifreeze safely.

1   The cooling system should be drained, flushed, and refilled periodically to replenish the antifreeze mixture. This will prevent rust formation and corrosion, which can impair cooling system performance and cause engine damage. When the cooling system is serviced, the hoses and radiator cap should be inspected and replaced, if necessary (see Section 10).

Draining

2   With the engine running, move the heater control to maximum heat.
3   Place a large container under the radiator to catch the coolant mixture as it's drained.
4   Without removing the radiator pressure cap and with the system not under pressure,

shut off the engine and open the drain cock **(see illustration)**.
5   The coolant reservoir tank should empty first, then remove the radiator pressure cap.
6   To vent the 2.4L engine, remove the coolant temperature sensor located above the water outlet housing **(see illustration)**.
7   To vent the 3.3/3.8L engines, remove the vent plug **(see illustration)**.

Flushing

8   If the radiator is severely contaminated or clogged, remove (see Chapter 3) and reverse flush it. Insert a hose in the bottom radiator outlet and force clean water backwards through the radiator and out through the top. A radiator repair shop should be consulted if further cleaning or repair is necessary.
9   If the coolant is regularly drained and the system refilled with the correct antifreeze mixture, there should be no need to use chemical cleaners.

Refilling

10   Fill the system to 50% of it's capacity with antifreeze, then finish filling the system with water.
11   The 2.4L engine requires venting by removal of the coolant sensor on top of the water outlet connector **(see illustration 25.6)**.
12   1996 and 1997 3.3/3.8L engines require the removal of the plug on the front cylinder head **(see illustration 25.7)**.
13   When the coolant reaches the coolant sensor hole (2.4L engine), or the vent plug hole (3.3/3.8 engines), install the coolant sensor or the vent plug.
14   Run the engine until it reaches normal operating temperature and, with the engine idling, add water to the correct level and install the radiator cap.
15   Keep a close watch on the coolant level and the cooling system hoses during the first few miles of driving. Tighten the hose clamps and add more coolant if required.

26   Positive Crankcase Ventilation (PCV) valve check and replacement (every 30,000 miles or 24 months)

Refer to illustrations 26.1a, 26.1b, 26.1c and 26.1d

1   The PCV valves for the 2.4L, 3.0L, and 3.3/3.8 engines are located near the intake manifold **(see illustrations)**.
2   With the engine idling at normal operating temperature, remove the PCV valve from it's attaching point.
3   A hissing sound should be heard. Place your finger over the valve opening. If there's no vacuum at the valve, check for a plugged hose, plenum port, or valve. Replace plugged or deteriorated hoses.
4   Turn the engine off and shake the valve. The valve should rattle freely. Replace it if it does not operate properly. **Warning:** *Do not attempt to clean the PCV valve.*
5   Replace the PCV valve with the correct one for your specific vehicle and engine size. Compare the old and new valves to make sure they're identical.
6   Installation is the reverse of removal.

27   Evaporative emissions control system check (every 30,000 miles or 24 months)

Refer to illustration 27.2

1   The evaporative emissions control system draws fuel vapors from the gas tank and fuel system, stores them in a charcoal canister and routes them to the intake manifold during normal engine operation.
2   The most common symptom of a defective evaporative emission system is a strong fuel odor in the engine compartment or from underneath the vehicle. If a fuel odor is detected, inspect the charcoal canister(s) located under the driver's seat. On models

25.6 2.4L engine temperature sensor   **25.7 3.3/3.8L engine vent plug**

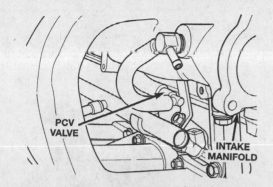

26.1a 2.4L engine PCV valve

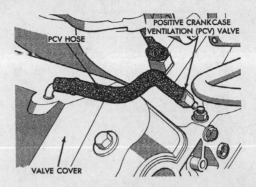

26.1b 3.0L engine PCV valve

26.1c 3.3/3.8L engine PCV valve on rear valve cover . . .

26.1d . . . and the fresh air hose on the front valve cover

since 2001, there are two charcoal canisters in the system. Check the canister(s) and all hoses for damage and deterioration.

3   The evaporative emissions control system, inspection, and canister removal/renewal is explained in detail in Chapter 6.

28   Spark plug check and replacement (every 30,000 miles or 24 months)

Refer to illustrations 28.2, 28.5a, 28.5b, 28.5c, 28.7, 28.11, 28.17 and 28.18

1   On 2.4L engines, the spark plugs are located on the top of the engine. On 3.0L and 3.3/3.8L engines, the spark plugs are located on the sides of the engine.

2   Tools required for spark plug replacement include a ratchet, a spark plug socket (padded inside to protect the porcelain insulators on new plugs), extensions, and a feeler gauge to check and adjust the spark plug gap (see illustration). A plug wire removal tool is available for pulling the spark plug wire boot from the spark plug, but it isn't mandatory. A torque wrench should be used to tighten the spark plugs because these engines have aluminum cylinder heads.

3   When replacing spark plugs, purchase new spark plugs ahead of time, check and

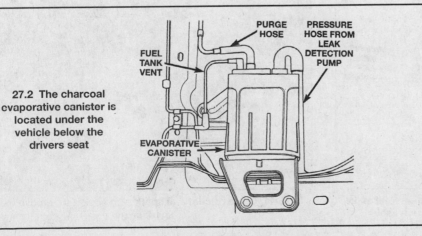

27.2 The charcoal evaporative canister is located under the vehicle below the drivers seat

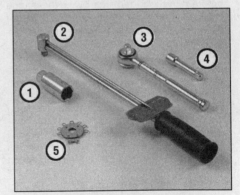

28.2 Tools required for changing spark plugs

1   Spark plug socket - This will have special padding inside to protect the spark plug's porcelain insulator

2   Torque wrench - Although not mandatory, using this tool is the best way to ensure the plugs are tightened properly

3   Ratchet - Standard hand tool to fit the spark plug socket

4   Extension - Depending on model and accessories, you may need special extensions and universal joints to reach one or more of the plugs

5   Spark plug gap gauge - This gauge for checking the gap comes in a variety of styles. Make sure the gap for your engine is included

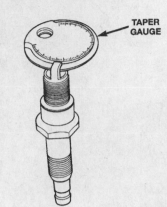

28.5a Spark plug manufacturers recommend using a wire-type gauge when checking the gap - if the wire does not slide between the electrodes with a slight drag, adjustment is required

28.5b To avoid damage to the platinum tips on the electrodes, use only a taper gauge to check plug gap

28.5c To change the gap, bend the side electrode only, as indicated by the arrows, and be very careful not to crack or chip the porcelain insulator surrounding the center electrode

adjust the gap, and replace them one at a time. Be sure to purchase the correct plug for your specific engine. This information can be found in the *Specifications* at the front of this Chapter, in the factory owner's manual, or on the Vehicle Emissions Control Information label located under the hood. If the sources do not agree, purchase the spark plug specified on the VECI label, it was printed for your specific engine.

4   Allow the engine to cool completely before removing the plugs. While the engine is cooling off, inspect the new spark plugs for defects and regap them if necessary.

5   On non-platinum tipped spark plugs, check the gap by inserting the proper thickness gauge between the electrodes at the tip of the plug (see illustration). On platinum tipped spark plugs check the gap by inserting a taper gauge between the platinum pads on the electrodes at the tip of the plug (see illustration). Spark plug gap is listed on the VECI label in the engine compartment and in this Chapter's *Specifications*. The gauge should

touch each of the electrodes. If the gap is incorrect, the adjuster on the thickness gauge can be used to bend the curved side electrode to the proper gap (see illustration). Check for cracks in the spark plug body (if any are found, the plug should not be used). If the side electrode is not exactly over the center electrode, use the adjuster to align them.

Removal - V6 engines

6   Cover the fender to prevent paint damage.

7   When the engine is cool, remove the spark plug wire from one spark plug. Pull only on the boot at the end of the wire; don't pull the wire. Twist the boot gently and pull it off the plug (see illustration).

8   Use compressed air to blow dirt or foreign material away from the spark plug area. A bicycle pump can also be used if air is not available. The idea is to keep foreign matter from falling into the cylinder through the spark plug hole when the spark plug is removed.

Spark plug #1

9   Remove the drivebelt (see Section 20).

10   Remove the four alternator alternator bracket bolts (see Chapter 5) and push the alternator rearward.

11   Remove the spark plug with the spark plug socket and ratchet (see illustration).

Spark plugs # 3 and 5

12   Remove the resonator and the intake strut bolt at the cylinder head.

13   Remove the intake strut bolt at the intake manifold and swing the strut out of the way.

14   Remove the spark plugs with the spark plug socket and ratchet.

Spark plugs # 2, 4, and 6

15   Spark plugs 2, 4, and 5 are easily accessible.

16   Compare the spark plugs with the chart on the inside back cover of this manual to get an indication of the overall condition of the engine.

Installation

17   Lightly coat the threads of the spark plugs with anti-seize compound (see illus-

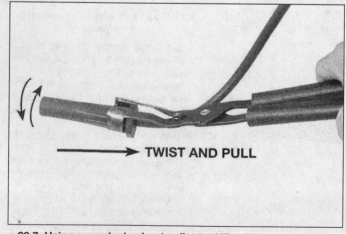

28.7 Using a spark plug boot puller tool like this one will make the job of removing the spark plug boots much easier

28.11 Use a ratchet and spark plug socket to remove the spark plugs

28.17 Apply a thin coat of anti-seize compound to the spark plug threads

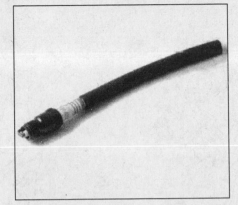

28.18 A length of 3/8-inch ID rubber hose will save time and prevent damaged threads when installing the spark plugs

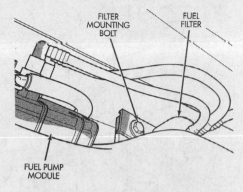

31.2 The fuel filter is located under the vehicle, on top of the fuel tank

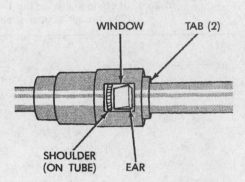

31.4 Squeeze the retainer tabs and pull the quick connect fitting off the fuel tube (typical)

tration) to keep the spark plugs from seizing in the aluminum cylinder head.

18   It's difficult to install spark plugs into their holes without cross-threading them. Fit a piece of 3/8-inch ID rubber hose over the end of the spark plug (see illustration). The flexible hose acts as a universal joint to align the plug with the spark plug hole. If the spark plug begins to cross-thread, the hose will slip on the spark plug and prevent thread damage. Tighten the spark plug to the torque listed in this Chapter's *Specifications*.

19   Attach the plug wire to the new spark plug by gently twisting the boot and pushing until it firmly seats on the spark plug.

20   Repeat the above procedure for the remaining spark plugs. Replace them one at a time to prevent mixing spark plug wires.

29 Spark plug wire check and replacement (every 30,000 miles or 24 months)

1   Spark plug wires should be checked at recommended intervals or when new spark plugs are installed.

2   The wires should be inspected one at a time to prevent mixing them up, which is essential for proper engine operation. **Note:** *Access to spark plugs in V-6 engines that are difficult to reach is described in Section 28.*

3   Disconnect the spark plug wire from the spark plug. A spark plug wire removal tool can be used, or you can grab the rubber boot, twist gently, and pull the wire free. Pull on the rubber boot, not on the spark plug wire.

4   Check inside the boot for corrosion, which is a white, crusty powder (don't mistake the white dielectric grease used on spark plug wire boots for corrosion).

5   Push the spark plug wire and boot back onto the spark plug. It should fit tightly on the spark plug. If it doesn't, remove the spark plug wire and use a pair of pliers to crimp the metal connector inside the wire boot until the fit is snug.

6   Clean built-up dirt and grease along the entire length of each wire with a clean cloth.

Inspect the wires for burned areas, cracks, and other damage. Bend the wires in several places to make sure that the inside conductor hasn't hardened. Repeat the procedure for the rest of the wires.

7   If new spark plug wires are necessary, buy a complete set, pre-cut for your particular engine. Terminals and rubber boots should already be installed on the wires. Replace the wires one at a time to avoid mixing up the firing order. Make sure the terminals are securely seated in the coil pack and on the spark plugs.

30 Seat belt check (every 30,000 miles or 24 months)

1   Check the seat belts, buckles, latch plates, and guide loops for damage and signs of wear.

2   Make sure the seat belt reminder light comes on when the key is turned to the Run or Start positions. A chime should also sound.

3   Seat belts are designed to lock up during a sudden stop or impact, but allow free movement during normal driving. Make sure the retractors hold the belt against your chest when driving and rewind the belt all the way when the buckle is unlatched.

4   If the above checks reveal problems with the seat belt system, replace parts as necessary.

31 Fuel filter replacement (every 60,000 miles or 48 months)

Refer to illustrations 31.2 and 31.4
Warning: *Gasoline is extremely flammable. Take extra precautions when you work on any part of the fuel system. Don't smoke or allow open flames or bare light bulbs near the work area, and don't work in a garage where a natural gas-type appliance (such as a water heater or clothes dryer) with a pilot light is present. If you spill fuel on your skin, rinse it off immediately with soap and water. When*

you work on the fuel system, wear safety glasses and have a Class B type fire extinguisher handy.

1   Depressurize the fuel system (see Chapter 4).

2   The fuel filter is a disposable canister located in the rear of the vehicle, on top of the fuel tank (see illustration).

3   Raise the rear of the vehicle, support it securely on jackstands, and block the front tires. The fuel tank must be lowered down to allow access to the filter and lines (see Chapter 4, Section 7).

4   Wrap a cloth around the fuel filter to catch residual fuel (which may still be under pressure) and disconnect the quick-connect fittings from the fuel pump module and chassis fuel supply tube. Squeeze the retainer tabs together (see illustration) and pull the fuel tube/quick disconnect fitting assembly from the fuel tube nipple. The retainer will remain on the fuel tube.

5   Remove the mounting bolt and detach the bracket and filter from the vehicle (see illustration 31.2).

6   Place the new filter in position, install the mounting bolt, and tighten it securely.

7   Lubricate the fittings with clean engine oil and insert the quick-connect fittings until they lock in place.

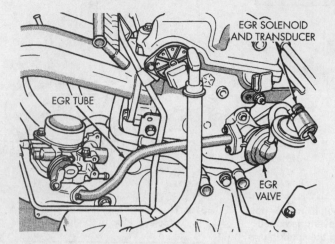

**32.2a EGR components on the 2.4L engine
(1996 through 2000 models)**

**32.2b EGR tube (1) and valve (2) on the 2.4L engine
(2001 and later models)**

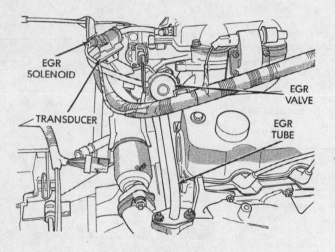

32.2c EGR components on the 3.0L engine

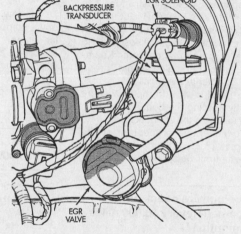

**32.2d EGR components on the 3.3/3.8L engine
(1996 through 2000 models)**

8   Start the engine and check for leaks at the hose connections.

32 Exhaust Gas Recirculation (EGR) system test (every 30,000 miles or 24 months)

Refer to illustrations 32.2a, 32.2b, 32.2c, 32.2d and 32.2e

1   A malfunctioning EGR system can causes engine knock, hesitation, rough idle, and stalling.

2   Inspect hoses and connections between the throttle body, intake manifold, EGR solenoid and transducer, and the EGR valve **(see illustrations)**. Replace hardened, cracked or melted hoses, and faulty connectors.

3   Check the EGR control system and EGR valve with the engine warm and idling.

4   Shift the transmission into neutral and

allow the engine to idle for about a minute. Rev the engine to about 2,000 rpm, but not over 3,000.

5   The EGR valve stem should move when accelerating the engine (the position of the groove on the EGR valve stem should

change). Repeat the test several times to confirm movement.

6   If the EGR valve stem moves, the control system is operating normally.

7   If the control system is not operating normally (see Chapter 6).

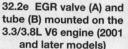
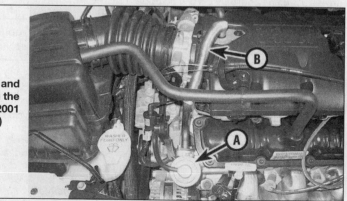

32.2e EGR valve (A) and tube (B) mounted on the 3.3/3.8L V6 engine (2001 and later models)

Chapter 2 Part A
Four-cylinder engine

Contents

	Section		Section
Camshafts - removal, inspection and installation	10	Intake manifold - removal, inspection and installation	4
Camshaft oil seal - replacement	8	Oil pan - removal and installation	13
CHECK ENGINE light	See Chapter 6	Oil pump - removal, inspection and installation	14
Crankshaft front oil seal - replacement	7	Rear main oil seal - replacement	16
Cylinder compression check	See Chapter 2D	Repair operations possible with the	
Cylinder head - removal and installation	12	engine in the vehicle	2
Drivebelt check, adjustment, and		Rocker arm and hydraulic valve lash adjuster - removal,	
replacement	See Chapter 1	inspection and installation	9
Driveplate - removal and installation	15	Spark plug replacement	See Chapter 1
Engine mounts - check and replacement	17	Timing belt and covers - removal, inspection and installation	6
Engine oil and filter change	See Chapter 1	Top dead center (TDC) for	
Engine overhaul - general		number one piston - locating	See Chapter 2D
information	See Chapter 2D	Vacuum gauge diagnostics checks	See Chapter 2D
Engine - removal and installation	See Chapter 2D	Valve cover - removal and installation	3
Exhaust manifold - removal and installation	5	Valve springs, retainers and seals - replacement	11
General information	1	Water pump replacement	See Chapter 3

Specifications

General

Bore	3.4446 to 3.4452 inches
Stroke	3.976 inches
Compression ratio	9.4:1
Compression pressure	170 to 225 psi
Displacement	148 cubic inches
Firing order	1-3-4-2
Oil pressure	
At idle speed	4 psi (minimum)
At 3000 rpm	25 to 80 psi

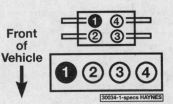

Cylinder and coil terminal locations

Camshaft

Bearing journal diameter	1.021 to 1.022 inches
Bearing bore diameter	1.024 to 1.025 inches
Bearing clearance	0.0027 to 0.003 inch
End play	0.0019 to 0.0066 inch
Lobe lift	
Intake	0.324 inch
Exhaust	0.256 inch
Cylinder head warpage	
Head gasket surface	0.004 inch maximum
Exhaust manifold mounting surfaces	0.006 inch maximum (per foot)

Intake and exhaust manifolds

Warpage limit	0.006 inch maximum (per foot)

Oil pump

Cover warpage limit	0.003 inch
Inner rotor thickness	0.370 inch (minimum)
Outer rotor thickness	0.370 inch (minimum)
Outer rotor diameter	3.148 inches (minimum)
Rotor-to-pump cover clearance	0.004 inch
Outer rotor-to-housing clearance	0.015 inch (maximum)
Inner rotor-to-outer rotor lobe clearance	0.008 inch (maximum)
Pressure relief spring free length	2.39 inches (approximate)

Torque Specifications

	Ft-lbs (unless otherwise indicated)
Camshaft bearing cap bolts	
M6 bolts	105 in-lbs
M8 bolts	21
Camshaft position sensor bolts	20
Camshaft sprocket bolt	75
Crankshaft pulley bolt	100
Cylinder head bolts	
First pass	25
Second pass	50
Third pass	50
Final pass	Tighten an additional 90-degrees (1/4 turn)
Driveplate-to-crankshaft bolts	70
Engine mounts	
Front mount **(see illustration 17.9)**	
Bolts 2, 3 and 4	80
Bolts 1 and 5	40
Left mount	
Mount-to-transmission bolts	40
Through bolt	55
Right mount	
Engine mount to rail fasteners	50
Horizontal fastener	111
Vertical engine fastener	75
Rear mount	
Through bolt	55
Strut and structural collar bolts **(see illustration 13.13)**	
Bolts 1 through 3	75
Bolts 4 through 8	45
Exhaust manifold-to-cylinder head bolts	
1996 through 2000	17
2001 and later	14
Exhaust manifold-to-exhaust pipe bolts	20
Exhaust manifold heat shield	105 in-lbs
Intake manifold-to-cylinder head bolts	
1996 through 2000	17
2001 and later	21
Oil filter adapter fastener	60
Oil pan bolts	105 in-lbs
Oil pump	
Attaching bolts	21
Cover screws	105 in-lbs
Pick-up tube bolt	21
Relief valve cap bolt	30
Thermostat housing bolts	17
Timing belt	
Cover bolts	
Outer-to-inner attaching bolts	40 in-lbs
Inner cover-to-head/oil pump bolts	105 in-lbs
Tensioner bolts (mechanical type)	21
Tensioner pulley bolt	30
Timing belt idler pulley bolt	
1996 through 1998	45
1999	40
Valve cover bolts	105 in-lbs

Refer to Part C for additional torque Specification Section

1   General information

Chapter 2A covers in-vehicle engine repair procedures on the 2.4 liter four-cylinder engine. Information concerning engine removal and installation and engine block and cylinder head overhaul can be found in Chapter 2D.

The following repair procedures are based on the assumption that the engine is installed in the vehicle. If the engine has been removed from the vehicle and mounted on a stand, many of the steps outlined in Chapter 2A will not apply.

The specifications included in Chapter 2A apply only to the procedures contained in Chapter 2A. Chapter 2D contains the specifi-

cations necessary for cylinder head and engine block rebuilding.

The four-cylinder 2.4L Double Overhead Camshaft (DOHC) engine covered in this Chapter features four valves per cylinder arranged in two inline banks. The cylinder block is the closed deck design used for cooling and weight reduction and has the water pump molded into the block. The 2.4L

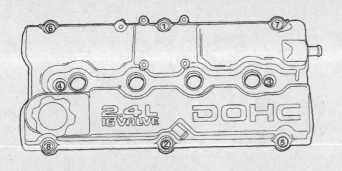

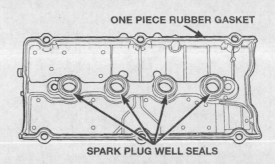
ONE PIECE RUBBER GASKET

SPARK PLUG WELL SEALS

3.6 Remove the valve cover mounting bolts

3.8 Install new valve cover gaskets and spark plug seals

engine has two balance shafts installed at the crankshaft end of the engine. For more information on the balance shafts refer to Chapter 2D.

2   Repair operations possible with the engine in the vehicle

Many repair operations can be accomplished without removing the engine from the vehicle.

Clean the engine compartment and the exterior of the engine with degreaser before any work is done. It will make the job easier and help keep dirt out of the internal parts of the engine.

It may be helpful to remove the hood to improve access to the engine when repairs are performed (see Chapter 11). Cover the fenders to prevent damage to the paint. Special pads are available, but an old bedspread or blanket will also work.

If vacuum, exhaust, oil, or coolant leaks develop, indicating a need for gasket or seal replacement, the repairs can generally be made with the engine in the vehicle. The intake and exhaust manifold gaskets, oil pan gasket, camshaft, and crankshaft oil seals

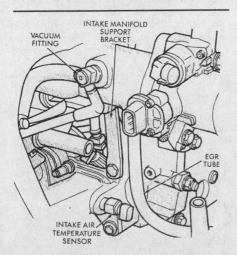

4.4 Disconnect the vacuum hoses from the fittings and the electrical connector from the intake air temperature sensor

and cylinder head gasket are all accessible with the engine in place.

Exterior engine components, such as the intake and exhaust manifolds, the oil pan, the oil pump, the water pump, the starter motor, the alternator, the distributor, and fuel system components can be removed for repair with the engine in place.

The camshafts and the cylinder head can be removed without pulling the engine and valve component servicing can also be accomplished with the engine in the vehicle. Timing belt and sprockets replacement is also possible with the engine in the vehicle.

Repair or replacement of piston rings, pistons, connecting rods, and rod bearings is possible with the engine in the vehicle. However, this practice is not recommended because of the cleaning and preparation work that must be done to the components involved.

3   Valve cover - removal and installation

Removal

Refer to illustration 3.6

1   Disconnect the cable from the negative terminal of the battery.
2   Remove the spark plug wires (see Chapter 1) and the ignition coil pack (see Chapter 5).
3   Disconnect the ground strap from the valve cover.
4   Label and disconnect emission hoses and electrical cables which connect to or cross over the valve cover.
5   Remove the nuts holding the front and rear intake manifold supports from the cylinder head cover studs.
6   Remove the valve cover bolts and lift the cover off **(see illustration)**. If the cover sticks to the cylinder head, tap on it with a soft-faced hammer or place a wood block against the cover and tap on the wood with a hammer. **Caution:** *If you pry between the valve cover and the cylinder head, be careful not to gouge or nick the gasket surfaces of either part. A leak could develop after reassembly.*
7   Remove the valve cover gasket 1/2 round seal. Thoroughly clean the valve cover

and remove all traces of old gasket material. Gasket removal solvents are available from auto parts stores and may prove helpful. After cleaning the surfaces, degrease them with a rag soaked in lacquer thinner or acetone.

Installation

Refer to illustration 3.8

8   Install new valve cover gaskets and spark plug seals **(see illustration)**.
9   Install the 1/2 round seal and apply anaerobic RTV sealant to the camshaft cap corners and at the top edges of the 1/2 round seal.
10   Place the valve cover on the engine and install the cover bolts. Tighten the valve cover bolts in 3 steps to the torque listed in this Chapter's Specifications using a criss-cross pattern. Start in the middle of the cover and work outwards.
11   Installation of the remaining components is the reverse of removal.
12   When installation is complete, start the engine and check for oil leaks.

4   Intake manifold - removal, inspection and installation

Warning: *Allow the engine to cool completely before beginning this procedure.*

Removal (1996 through 2000 models)

Refer to illustrations 4.4, 4.5, 4.8, 4.11a, 4.11b, 4.11c and 4.14

1   Relieve the fuel system pressure (see Chapter 4).
2   Disconnect the cable from the negative terminal of the battery.
3   Remove the air intake duct and resonator from the throttle body and disconnect the accelerator cable and cruise control cable (if equipped). Disconnect the electrical connectors from the throttle position sensor and idle air control valve (see Chapter 4).
4   Remove the vacuum hoses from the vacuum fittings and disconnect the electrical connector from the intake air temperature sensor **(see illustration)**. Remove the EGR tube from the EGR valve.
5   Refer to Chapter 4 and remove the fuel

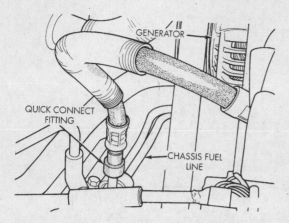

4.5 Disconnect the fuel line quick-connect fitting

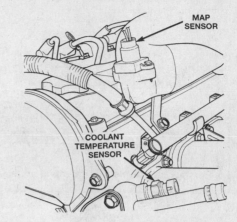

4.8 Disconnect the electrical connectors from the MAP sensor and coolant temperature sensor

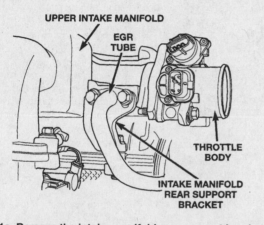

4.11a Remove the intake manifold rear support bracket

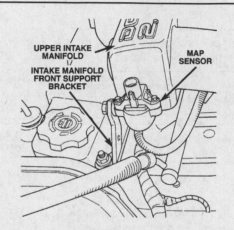

4.11b Remove the intake manifold front support bracket

hose quick connect fitting from the chassis fuel line **(see illustration)**.

6   Withdraw the dipstick and remove the dipstick tube from the engine block.

7   Drain the cooling system (see Chapter 1). Remove the heater, and upper radiator hoses at the intake manifold.

8   Disconnect the electrical connectors from the MAP sensor and coolant tempera-

ture sensor **(see illustration)**.

9   Remove the accessory drive belts (see Chapter 1).

10   Remove the generator and the generator bracket (see Chapter 5).

11   Remove the rear support bracket bolts, the front support bracket and the center support bracket bolts **(see illustrations)**.

12   Label and disconnect any remaining

vacuum hoses, wire harness connectors, brackets, and emission hoses connected to the throttle body or intake manifold.

13   Label and disconnect the electrical connectors from the fuel injectors and lay the fuel injector harness aside (see Chapter 4).

14   Remove the nuts/bolts from the intake manifold and remove it from the engine **(see illustration)**. If it sticks, lightly tap the mani-

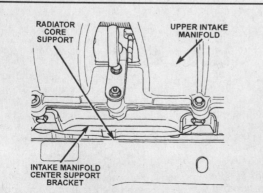

4.11c Remove the intake manifold center support bracket

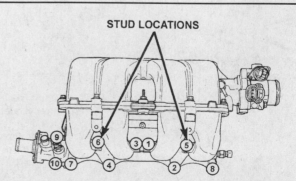

4.14 Locations of the intake manifold nuts/bolts and bolt tightening sequence

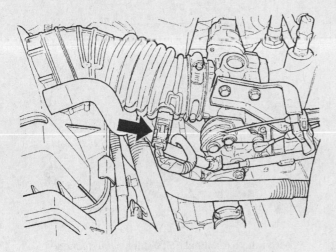

4.21 Disconnect the intake air temperature (IAT) sensor

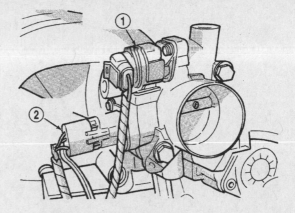

4.23 Throttle body electrical connector locations (typical)

1   *Idle air control electrical connector*
2   *Throttle position sensor (TPS) connector*

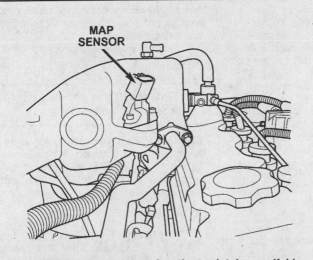

4.24 MAP sensor connector location on intake manifold

4.29 Upper intake manifold support bracket assembly

1   *Bracket to cylinder head cover nut*
2   *Bracket to upper intake manifold bolt*
3   *Upper intake manifold bracket*

fold with a soft-face hammer or carefully pry it from the cylinder head. **Caution:** *Do not pry between the gasket sealing surfaces.*

Inspection (all years)

15   Remove the intake manifold gasket by carefully scraping all traces of gasket material from both the cylinder head and the intake manifold. **Caution:** *The cylinder head and intake manifold are made of aluminum and are easily nicked or gouged. Don't damage the gasket surfaces or a leak may result after the work is complete. Gasket removal solvents are available from auto parts stores and may prove helpful.*

16   Use a straightedge and feeler gauge to check the intake manifold mating surface for warpage. Check the intake manifold surface on the cylinder head also. If warpage on any surface exceeds the limits listed in this Chapter's Specifications, the intake manifold and/or cylinder head must be replaced or resurfaced by an automotive machine shop.

Installation (1996 through 2000 models)

17   Install the intake manifold, using a new gasket. Tighten the nuts/bolts in three stages, following the recommended tightening sequence **(see illustration 4.14)**, to the torque listed in this Chapter's Specifications.
18   Installation of the remaining components is the reverse of removal.

Removal (2001 and later models)

Refer to illustrations 4.21, 4.23, 4.24, 4.29, 4.34 and 4.38

19   Relieve the system pressure (see Chapter 4).
20   Disconnect the cable from the negative terminal of the battery.
21   Disconnect the connector from the inlet air temperature sensor **(see illustration)**.
22   Disconnect the air intake tube from the

throttle body and remove the upper air cleaner housing.
23   Disconnect the connector from the throttle position sensor **(see illustration)**.
24   Disconnect the connector from the MAP sensor **(see illustration)**.
25   Disconnect the vacuum lines for the purge solenoid and PCV valve from the intake manifold.
26   Label and disconnect the vacuum lines for the power brake booster, LDP, EGR transducer and speed control vacuum reservoir (models so equipped) from the fittings on the intake manifold.
27   Disconnect the throttle, the speed control (model so equipped) and the transaxle control (3-speed automatic transaxle models) cables from the throttle lever and bracket (see Chapter 4).
28   Disconnect the EGR tube from the EGR valve.
29   Remove the upper manifold support bracket bolts **(see illustration)**.

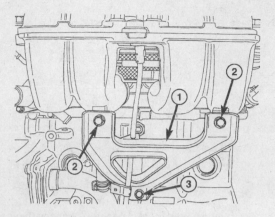

4.34 Lower intake manifold support bracket assembly

1   *Support bracket*
2   *Bracket to upper intake manifold bolts*
3   *Bracket to lower engine block bolt*

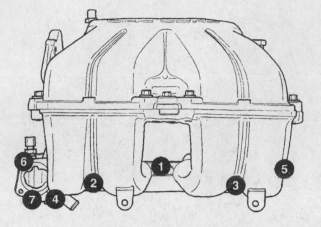

4.38 Intake manifold bolt tightening sequence

30   Withdraw the dipstick from the tube.
31   Refer to Chapter 4 and disconnect the fuel hose quick disconnect fitting.
32   Drain the cooling system (see Chapter 1). Remove the heater supply and radiator upper hoses at the intake manifold.
33   Disconnect the coolant temperature sensor/fuel injector wire harness connector.
34   Remove the lower intake manifold support bracket upper bolts **(see illustration)**.
35   Disconnect the fuel injector electrical harness connector.
36   Remove the power steering reservoir bolts and set the reservoir aside. Do not disconnect the fluid line from the reservoir.
37   Remove the lower intake manifold support bracket lower bolts **(see illustration 4.34)** and remove the intake manifold assembly. If it sticks, lightly tap the manifold with a soft-face hammer or carefully pry it from the cylinder head. **Caution:** *Do not pry between the gasket sealing surfaces.*

Installation (2001 and later models)

38   Install the intake manifold, using a new gasket. Tighten the bolts in three stages, following the recommended tightening sequence **(see illustration)**, to the torque listed in this Chapter's Specifications.
39   Installation of the remaining components is the reverse of removal.

5   Exhaust manifold - removal, inspection and installation

Warning: *Allow the engine to cool completely before beginning this procedure.*

Removal

1   Disconnect the cable from the negative terminal of the battery.
2   Set the parking brake and block the rear wheels.
3   Raise the front of the vehicle and sup-

port it securely on jackstands.
4   Working under the vehicle, apply penetrating oil to the exhaust pipe-to-manifold fasteners to make removal easier. Remove the exhaust pipe from the exhaust manifold at the flex-joint.
5   Disconnect the wiring harness from the upstream oxygen sensor (see Chapter 6).
6   Remove the exhaust manifold bolts, and the exhaust manifold. **Note:** *The exhaust pipe may have to be removed from the vehicle to ease manifold removal (see Chapter 4).*

Inspection

7   Use a wire brush to clean the exhaust manifold bolts. Replace any that have thread damage.
8   Use a scraper to remove all traces of gasket material from the exhaust flange mating surfaces and inspect them for wear and cracks. **Caution:** *When removing gasket material, be very careful not to scratch or gouge the sealing surface. Any damage to the surface may cause a leak after reassembly. Gasket removal solvents are available from auto parts stores and may prove helpful.*
9   Use a straightedge and feeler gauge to check the exhaust manifold-to-cylinder head mating surface for warpage. Check the surface on the cylinder head also. If warpage exceeds the limits listed in this Chapter's Specifications, the exhaust manifold and/or cylinder head must be replaced or resurfaced by an automotive machine shop.

Installation

Refer to illustrations 5.11a and 5.11b
10   Apply Loctite No. 271 to the mounting bolt threads prior to installation.
11   Install the new gasket (dry - use no sealant), manifold, and bolts. Tighten the bolts in several stages, following the recommended tightening sequence **(see illustration)**, to the torque listed in this Chapter's Specifications.
12   Installation of the remaining compo-

nents is the reverse of removal. **Note:** *Install a new gasket between the exhaust manifold and exhaust pipe.*
13   Run the engine and check for exhaust leaks.

6   Timing belt and covers - removal, inspection and installation

Caution: *If the timing belt failed with the engine operating, damage to the valves may have occurred. Perform an engine compression check after belt replacement to determine if any valve damage is present.*

Removal

> **** CAUTION ****
>
> The timing system is complex. Severe engine damage will occur if you make any mistakes. Do not attempt this procedure unless you are highly experienced with this type of repair. If you are at all unsure of your abilities, consult an expert. Double-check all your work and be sure everything is correct before you attempt to start the engine.

Refer to illustrations 6.5, 6.6, 6.7, 6.11, and 6.12
Caution: *Do not turn the crankshaft or camshafts after the timing belt has been removed. This will damage the valves from contact with the pistons. Do not try to turn the crankshaft with the camshaft sprocket bolts and do not rotate the crankshaft counterclockwise.*
1   Disconnect the cable from the negative terminal of the battery.
2   Raise the vehicle and support it securely on jack stands.
3   Remove the right inner splash shield (see Chapter 11).
4   Remove the accessory drive belts (see Chapter 1).

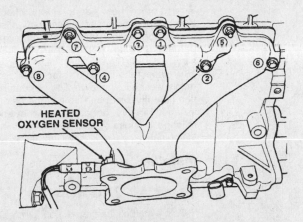

5.11a Exhaust manifold bolt tightening sequence (1996 through 2000 models)

HEATED OXYGEN SENSOR

5.11b Exhaust manifold bolt tightening sequence (2001 and later models)

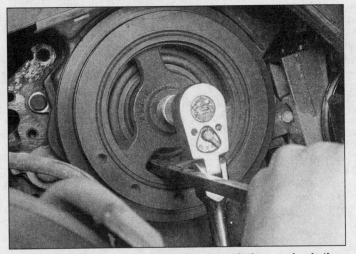

6.5 Insert a large screwdriver or bar through the opening in the crankshaft pulley and wedge it against the engine block, then loosen the bolt with a socket and breaker bar

6.6 Install a three-jaw puller onto the pulley, position the center post of the puller on the crankshaft end (use the proper insert to keep from damaging the crankshaft threads), and remove the pulley from the crankshaft

5   Loosen the center bolt in the crankshaft pulley. If it is tight, break it loose by inserting a large screwdriver or bar through the opening in the pulley, to hold the pulley stationary. Loosen the bolt with a socket and breaker bar **(see illustration)**.

6   Install a three-jaw puller on center hub of the pulley and remove the pulley from the crankshaft **(see illustration)**. Use the proper insert to keep the puller from damaging the crankshaft bolt threads. If the pulley is difficult to remove, tap the center bolt of the puller with a brass mallet to break it loose. **Caution:** *Do not use a puller that has jaws which grip the outer diameter of the pulley. The pulley damper and hub may separate. Use only the type shown in the illustration.*

7   Remove the lower timing belt cover fasteners, and the cover **(see illustration)**.

8   Lower the vehicle and remove the upper timing belt fasteners, and the cover **(see illustration 6.7)**.

9   Reinstall the crankshaft bolt using an appropriate spacer (this will enable you to turn the crankshaft later).

10   Remove the right (passenger side)

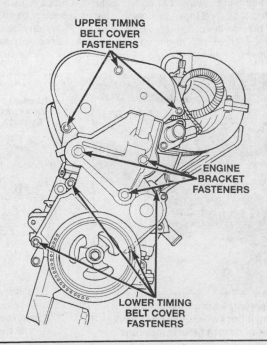

UPPER TIMING BELT COVER FASTENERS

ENGINE BRACKET FASTENERS

LOWER TIMING BELT COVER FASTENERS

6.7 Timing belt outer cover fastener locations

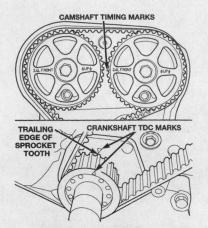

6.11 Before removing the timing belt, make sure the camshaft sprockets and crankshaft timing marks align with their respective marks - rotate the engine (clockwise only as viewed from the crankshaft end) as required to align both sets of timing marks. The crankshaft sprocket timing mark is aligned on the trailing edge of the sprocket tooth

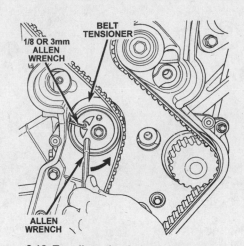

6.12 To relieve the timing belt tension, place the appropriate size Allen wrench in the pulley and apply torque in a counterclockwise direction until the retaining pin holes align and insert a 1/8 inch drill bit to hold the pulley in place

engine mount and mounting bracket (see Section 17). Make sure the engine is supported with a floor jack placed under the oil pan. Place a wood block on the jack head to prevent the floor jack from denting or damaging the oil pan.

11   Align the camshaft sprocket(s) and crankshaft timing marks before removing the timing belt **(see illustration)**. If necessary, align the timing marks by rotating the crankshaft - clockwise only! If you plan to reuse the timing belt, paint an arrow on it to indicate the direction of rotation (clockwise).

12   Insert a 6 mm Allen wrench in the hexagon fitting in the tensioner pulley. Insert a 1/8 inch drill bit (or 3 mm Allen wrench) into the small hole on the pulley. Apply light pressure to the Allen wrench and rotate the tensioner pulley counterclockwise until the drill

bit slides into the locking hole **(see illustration)**.

13   Slip the timing belt off the sprockets and set it aside. If you plan to reuse the timing belt, store it in a plastic bag - do not allow the belt to come in contact with oil or water, this will greatly shorten belt life.

14   If it's necessary to remove the camshaft sprocket(s), and/or timing belt rear cover (for camshaft seal replacement), (see Section 8).

Inspection

Refer to illustration 6.18

15   Inspect the crankshaft front oil seal for leaks. Replace it, if necessary (see Section 7).

16   Inspect the water pump for evidence of leakage (usually indicated by a trail of wet or dried coolant). Check the pulley for excessive play and bearing roughness. Replace it, if necessary (see Chapter 3).

17   Rotate the tensioner pulley and idler pul-

ley and move them side-to-side to check for bearing roughness and excess play. Visually inspect timing belt sprockets for signs of damage or wear. Replace parts as necessary.

18   Inspect the timing belt for cracks, separation, wear missing teeth, and oil contamination **(see illustration)**. Replace the belt if it's in questionable condition or the engine mileage is close to that referenced in the *Maintenance schedule* (see Chapter 1).

Installation

> ** ** CAUTION ** **
>
> Before starting the engine, carefully rotate the crankshaft by hand through at least two full revolutions (use a socket and breaker bar on the crankshaft pulley center bolt). If you feel any resistance, STOP! There is something wrong - most likely, valves are contacting the pistons. You must find the problem before proceeding. Check your work and see if any updated repair information is available.

Refer to illustration 6.20

19   Confirm that the timing marks on the camshaft sprockets are aligned **(see illustration 6.11)**.

20   Rotate the exhaust camshaft sprocket clockwise so the timing mark is 1/2 notch below the intake camshaft timing mark **(see illustration)**.

21   Align the crankshaft sprocket timing mark with the arrow mark on the oil pump housing **(see illustration 6.11)**.

22   Install the timing belt as follows: Place the belt on the crankshaft sprocket; maintaining tension on the belt, wrap it around the water pump sprocket, idler pulley, camshaft sprockets, and the tensioner pulley. To take up belt slack, rotate the exhaust camshaft counterclockwise until the timing marks on both sprockets align.

23   Pull the drill bit from the tensioner pulley.

24   Use the bolt in the center of the crankshaft sprocket to turn the crankshaft clockwise two complete revolutions. **Caution:** *If you feel resistance while turning the crankshaft - STOP, the valves may be hitting the pistons do to incorrect valve timing. Recheck the valve timing.* **Note:** *The camshaft and crankshaft sprocket marks will align every two revolutions of the crankshaft.*

25   Recheck the alignment of the timing marks **(see illustrations 6.11)**. If the marks do not align properly, loosen the tensioner, slip the belt off the camshaft sprocket, realign the marks, reinstall the belt, and recheck the alignment.

26   Installation of the remaining components is the reverse of removal. Tighten the crankshaft pulley bolt to the torque listed in this Chapter's Specifications.

27   Start the engine and road test the vehicle.

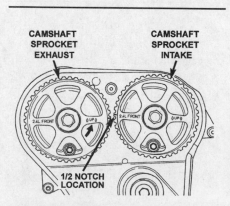

6.18 Carefully inspect the timing belt - bending it backwards will often make wear or damage more apparent

6.20 Rotate the exhaust camshaft sprocket clockwise so the timing mark is 1/2 notch below the timing mark on the intake camshaft sprocket

7.2 Attach a bolt-type gear puller to the crankshaft sprocket and remove the sprocket from the crankshaft

7.3 Use a screwdriver to carefully pry the front crankshaft seal from its bore

7.5 Lubricate the new front crankshaft seal with engine oil and, using a hammer and socket, drive the seal into the bore until it's flush with the oil pump housing

7.6 Position the crankshaft sprocket with the word FRONT (arrow) facing out and install it onto the crankshaft

7 Crankshaft front oil seal - replacement

Refer to illustrations 7.2, 7.3, 7.5 and 7.6
Caution: *Do not rotate the camshaft(s) or crankshaft when the timing belt is removed or damage to the engine may occur.*

1 Remove the timing belt (see Section 6).
2 Remove the crankshaft timing belt sprocket from the crankshaft with a bolt-type gear puller **(see illustration)**. Remove the Woodruff key from the crankshaft keyway.
3 Wrap the tip of a small screwdriver with tape. Work from below the right inner fender, and use the screwdriver to carefully pry the seal out of its bore **(see illustration)**. Take care to prevent damaging the oil pump assembly, the crankshaft, and the seal bore.
4 Clean and inspect the seal bore and sealing surface on the crankshaft. Minor imperfections can be removed with emery cloth. If there is a groove worn in the

crankshaft sealing surface (from contact with the seal), installing a new seal will probably not stop the leak.
5 Lubricate the new seal with engine oil and use a hammer and the appropriate size socket, to drive the seal into the bore until it's flush with the oil pump housing **(see illustration)**.
6 Install the Woodruff key and the crankshaft timing belt sprocket with the word FRONT facing out on the crankshaft **(see illustration)**.
7 Installation of the remaining components is the reverse of removal. Tighten the crankshaft pulley bolt to the torque listed in this Chapter's Specifications.
8 Start the engine and check for oil leaks.

8 Camshaft oil seal - replacement

Refer to illustrations 8.5a, 8.5b, 8.6, 8.8a, 8.8b and 8.10
Caution: *Do not rotate the camshaft(s) or crankshaft when the timing belt is removed or damage to the engine may occur.*

1 Remove the timing belt (see Section 6).
2 Rotate the crankshaft counterclockwise until the crankshaft sprocket is three notches BTDC **(see illustration 6.11)**. This will prevent engine damage if the camshaft sprocket rotates during sprocket bolt removal.
3 Hold the camshaft sprocket and remove the camshaft sprocket bolt. **Note:** *To hold the camshaft/sprocket while loosening the bolt, a strap-type pulley holder tool is recommended and is available at most auto parts stores.* Use two large screwdrivers to pry the sprocket off the camshaft. If the strap wrench is unavailable, remove the valve cover and access the camshaft wrenching flats.
4 Remove the idler pulley.
5 Remove the bolts holding the rear cover to the engine block and cylinder head. Remove the rear cover **(see illustrations)**.

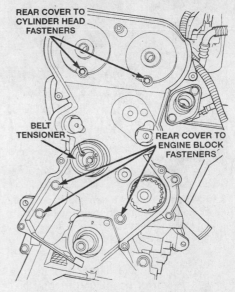

8.5a Rear timing belt cover fasteners

REAR COVER TO CYLINDER HEAD FASTENERS

BELT TENSIONER

REAR COVER TO ENGINE BLOCK FASTENERS

8.5b Remove the rear timing belt cover

8.6 Carefully pry the camshaft seal out of the bore - DO NOT nick or scratch the camshaft or seal bore

8.8a Using a hammer and socket, gently tap the new seal into place with the spring side facing inward

8.8b If space is limited and you can't use a hammer and socket to install the seal, a seal installer can be made from a section of pipe (of appropriate diameter), a bolt and washer. Place the pipe over the seal and press it into place by tightening the bolt

8.10 When installing a camshaft sprocket, make sure the pin in the camshaft is aligned with the hole in the sprocket (arrows)

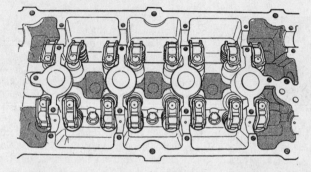

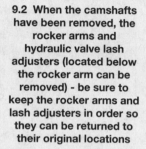

9.2 When the camshafts have been removed, the rocker arms and hydraulic valve lash adjusters (located below the rocker arm can be removed) - be sure to keep the rocker arms and lash adjusters in order so they can be returned to their original locations

6   Pry out the camshaft oil seal using a small screwdriver (see illustration). Don't scratch the bore or damage the camshaft in the process (if the camshaft is damaged, the new seal will leak).
7   Clean the bore and coat the outer edge of the new seal with engine oil or multi-purpose grease. Lubricate the seal lip.
8   Use a socket (with an outside diameter slightly smaller than the outside diameter of the seal) and a hammer (see illustration). Carefully drive the new seal into the cylinder head until it's flush with the face of the cylinder head. If a socket isn't available, a short section of pipe will work. Note: *If engine location makes it difficult to use a hammer to install the camshaft seal, fabricate a seal installation tool from a piece of pipe cut to the appropriate length, a bolt, and a large washer (see illustration). Place the pipe over the seal and thread the bolt into the camshaft. The seal can now be pressed into the bore by tightening the bolt.*
9   Install the rear timing belt cover and idler pulley.

10   Install the camshaft sprocket, aligning the pin in the camshaft with the hole in the sprocket (see illustration). Hold the camshaft sprocket (see Step 2) and tighten the sprocket bolt to the torque listed in this Chapter's Specifications.
11   Reinstall the timing belt (see Section 6).
12   Run the engine and check for oil leaks at the camshaft seal.

9   Rocker arm and hydraulic valve lash adjuster - removal, inspection and installation

Removal

Refer to illustration 9.2
1   Remove the camshafts (see Section 10).
2   After the camshafts have been removed; the rocker arms (a.k.a. cam followers) can be lifted off (see illustration). Caution: *Each rocker arm and valve lash adjuster must be returned to it's original location, so mark them or place them in a marked container (such as an egg carton or cupcake tray) so they won't get mixed up.*
3   Remove the rocker arms and hydraulic valve lash adjusters from the cylinder head.

Inspection

Refer to illustration 9.4
4   Visually check the rocker arm tip, roller,

and lash adjuster pocket for wear (see illustration). Replace them if wear or damage is found.
5   Inspect each adjuster carefully for signs of wear and damage particularly on the ball tip that contacts the rocker arm. Lash adjusters frequently become clogged, we recommend replacing them if you're concerned about their condition or if the engine is exhibiting valve "tapping" noises.

Installation

6   Prior to installation, the lash adjusters must be partially full of engine oil - indicated by little or no plunger action when the

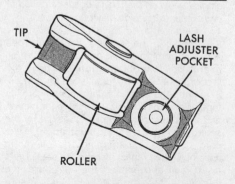

9.4 Inspect the rocker arm tip, roller, and lash adjuster pocket for wear

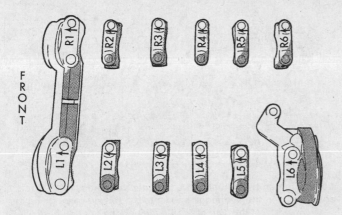

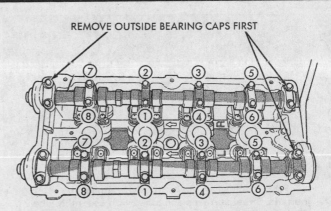

10.4 The camshaft bearing caps are numbered - they must be reinstalled in the same locations

10.5 Remove the outside bearing caps first, then loosen the remaining bearing cap bolts in the sequence shown - 1/4 turn at a time until they can be removed by hand

---

adjuster is depressed. If there is excessive plunger travel, place the rocker arm assembly in clean engine oil and pump the plunger until the plunger travel is eliminated. **Note:** *If the plunger still travels within the rocker arm when full of oil, it's defective and the rocker arm assembly must be replaced.*

7   Install the hydraulic lash adjusters and rocker arms in their original locations on the cylinder head.

8   Install the camshafts (see Section 10).

9   When re-starting the engine after replacing the rocker arm/lash adjusters, the adjusters will normally make "tapping" noises. After warming-up the engine, slowly increase the engine speed from idle to 3,000 rpm and back to idle over one minute period. If the adjuster(s) do not become quiet, they should be replaced.

---

10 Camshaft(s) - removal, inspection and installation

Removal

Refer to illustrations 10.4, and 10.5

1   Remove the valve cover (see Section 3).

2   Remove the timing belt (see Section 6).

3   Remove the camshaft sprockets and the rear timing belt cover (see Section 8).

4   The camshaft bearing caps are identified with their numbered location in the cylinder head **(see illustration).**

5   Remove the outside bearing caps at each end of the camshafts, Remove the remaining camshaft bearing caps. Loosen the bolts a little at a time to prevent distorting the camshafts, in the sequence shown **(see illustration).** When the bearing caps have all been loosened enough for removal, they may still be difficult to remove. Use the bearing cap bolts for leverage and move the cap back and forth to loosen the cap from the cylinder head. If they are still difficult to remove you can tap them gently with a soft face mallet until they can be lifted off. **Caution:** *Store them in order so they can be returned to their original locations, with the*

same side facing forward.

6   Carefully lift the camshafts out of the cylinder head. Mark the camshafts INTAKE and EXHAUST. They cannot be mixed-up.

7   Remove the front seal from each camshaft. **Note:** I*t would be prudent to inspect the rocker arms and lash adjusters at this time* (see Section 9).

Inspection

Refer to illustration 10.9

8   Clean the camshaft(s) and the gasket surface. Inspect the camshaft for wear and/or damage to the lobe surfaces, bearing journals, and seal contact surfaces. Inspect the camshaft bearing surfaces in the cylinder head and bearing caps for scoring and other damage.

9   Measure the camshaft bearing journal diameters **(see illustration).** Measure the inside diameter of the camshaft bearing surfaces in the cylinder head, using a telescoping gauge (temporarily install the bearing caps). Subtract the journal measurement from the bearing measurement to obtain the camshaft bearing oil clearance. Compare this

clearance with the value listed this Chapter's Specifications. Replace worn components as required.

10   Replace the camshaft if it fails any of the above inspections. **Note:** *If the lobes are worn, replace the rocker arms and lash adjusters along with the camshaft. The cylinder head may need to be replaced, if the camshaft bearing surfaces in the head are damaged or excessively worn.*

11   Clean and inspect the cylinder head (see Chapter 2D).

Camshaft end play measurement

Refer to illustration 10.14

12   Lubricate the camshaft(s) and cylinder head bearing journals with clean engine oil.

13   Place the camshaft in its original location in the cylinder head. **Note:** *Do not install the rocker arms for this check.* Install the rear bearing cap and tighten the bolts to the torque listed in this Chapter's Specifications.

14   Install a dial indicator on the cylinder head and place the indicator tip on the camshaft at the sprocket end **(see illustration).**

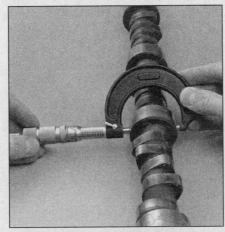

10.9 Measure the camshaft bearing journal diameters with a micrometer and compare the measurements to the dimensions given in this Chapter's Specifications

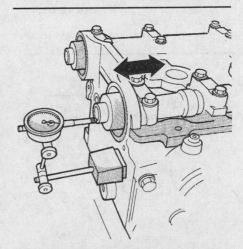

10.14 Measure the camshaft endplay with a dial indicator positioned on the sprocket end of the camshaft as shown

10.17 Prior to installing the camshaft, lubricate the bearing journals, thrust surfaces and lobes with assembly lube or clean engine oil

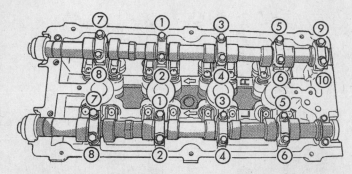

10.19 Tighten the camshaft bearing caps progressing in three equal steps in the sequence shown to the torque value given in this Chapter's Specifications

15   Use a screwdriver to carefully pry the camshaft to the fully to the rear (toward the camshaft position sensor) until it stops. Zero the dial indicator and pry the camshaft fully to the front (toward the dial indicator end). The amount of indicator travel is the camshaft endplay. Compare the endplay with the tolerance given in this Chapter's Specifications. If the endplay is excessive, check the camshaft and cylinder head bearing journals for wear. Replace as necessary.

Installation

Refer to illustrations 10.17, 10.19 and 10.20

16   Install the valve lash adjusters and rocker arms (see Section 9).
17   Clean the camshaft and bearing journals and caps. Liberally coat the journals, lobes, and thrust portions of the camshaft with assembly lube or engine oil **(see illustration)**.
18   Carefully install the camshafts in the cylinder head in their original location. Temporarily install the camshaft sprockets and rotate the camshafts so their timing marks align **(see illustration 6.11)**. Make sure the crankshaft is positioned with the crankshaft sprocket timing mark at three notches BTDC. **Caution:** *If the pistons are at TDC when tightening the camshaft bearing caps, damage to the engine may occur.*
19   Install the bearing caps, except for the

No. 1 and No. 6 (left side) end caps **(see illustration 10.4)**. Tighten the bolts in several steps, in the sequence shown to the torque listed in this Chapter's Specifications **(see illustration)**.
20   Apply a small bead of anaerobic sealant (approximately 1/8 inch) to the No. 1 and No. 6 (left side) bearing caps **(see illustration)**. Install the bearing caps and tighten the bolts to the torque listed in this Chapter's Specifications.
21   Install new camshaft oil seals (see Section 8).
22   Install the timing belt, covers, and related components (see Section 6).
23   Run the engine and check for oil leaks.

11   Valve springs, retainers and seals - replacement

Refer to illustrations 11.4, 11.7, 11.8, 11.13 and 11.15
Note: *Broken valve springs and defective valve stem seals can be replaced without removing the cylinder heads. Two special tools and a compressed air source are normally required to perform this operation, so*

read through this Section carefully and rent or buy the tools before attempting the job.
1   Remove the valve cover (see Section 3).
2   Remove the spark plug from the cylinder having the defective component. If all of the valve stem seals are being replaced, all of the spark plugs should be removed.
3   Turn the crankshaft until the piston in the affected cylinder is at top dead center on the compression stroke (see Chapter 2D). If you're replacing all of the valve stem seals, begin with cylinder number one and work on the valves for one cylinder at a time. Move from cylinder-to-cylinder following the firing order sequence shown in this Chapter's Specifications.
4   Thread an adapter into the spark plug hole **(see illustration)** and connect an air hose from a compressed air source to it. Most auto parts stores can supply the air hose adapter. **Note:** *Many cylinder compression gauges utilize a screw-in fitting that may work with your air hose quick-disconnect fitting.*
5   Remove the rocker arms (see Section 9).
6   Apply compressed air to the cylinder. **Warning:** *The piston may be forced down by compressed air, causing the crankshaft to turn suddenly. If the wrench used to position the number one piston at TDC is still attached*

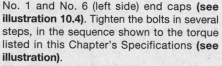

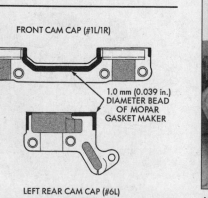

10.20 Apply a small bead of anaerobic sealant to the No. 1 and left side No. 6 bearing caps as shown

11.4 This is what the air hose adapter that threads into the spark plug hole looks like - they're usually available from auto parts stores

11.7 Use needle-nose pliers (shown) or a small magnet to remove the valve spring keepers - be careful not to drop them down into the engine!

11.8 Remove the valve guide seal/spring seat assembly with a pair of pliers

11.13 Gently tap the new seal into place with a hammer and a deep socket

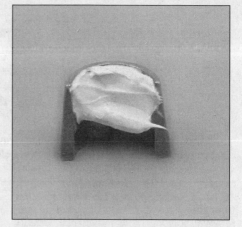

11.15 Apply a small dab of grease to each keeper before installation to hold it in place on the valve stem until the spring is released

to the crankshaft bolt, it could cause damage or injury when the crankshaft moves.

7   Stuff clean shop rags into the cylinder head holes above and below the valves to prevent parts and tools from falling into the engine. Use a valve spring compressor to compress the spring and remove the keepers with small needle-nose pliers or a magnet **(see illustration)**.

8   Remove the spring retainer and valve spring, then remove the valve guide seal/spring seat assembly **(see illustration)**. **Caution:** *If air pressure fails to hold the valve in the closed position during this operation, the valve face and/or seat is probably damaged. The cylinder head will have to be removed for additional repair operations.*

9   Wrap a rubber band or tape around the top of the valve stem so the valve won't fall into the combustion chamber, then release the air pressure.

10   Inspect the valve stem for damage. Rotate the valve in the guide and check the end for eccentric movement, which indicates the valve is bent and needs to be replaced.

11   Move the valve up-and-down in the guide. If the valve stem binds, either the valve is bent or the guide is damaged. In either case, the head will have to be removed for repair.

12   Pull up on the valve stem to close the valve, reapply air pressure to the cylinder to retain the valve in the closed position, then remove the tape or rubber band from the valve stem.

13   Lubricate the valve stem with engine oil and install a new valve guide seal/spring seat assembly. Tap it into place with deep socket **(see illustration)**.

14   Install the spring in position over the valve.

15   Install the valve spring retainer. Compress the valve spring and carefully position the keepers in the groove. Apply a small dab of grease to the inside of each keeper to hold it in place **(see illustration)**.

16   Remove the pressure from the spring tool and make sure the keepers are seated.

17   Disconnect the air hose and remove the

adapter from the spark plug hole.

18   Install the rocker arms (see Section 9).

19   Install the spark plug(s) and connect the wire(s).

20   Install the valve cover (see Section 3).

21   Start and run the engine.

22   Check for oil leaks and unusual sounds coming from the valve cover area.

---

12   Cylinder head - removal and installation

Caution: *Allow the engine to cool completely before beginning this procedure.*

Removal

Refer to illustrations 12.14 and 12.15

1   Position the number one piston at Top Dead Center (see Chapter 2D).

2   Disconnect the cable from the negative terminal of the battery.

3   Relieve the fuel system pressure (see Chapter 4). Drain the cooling system (see Chapter 1).

4   Remove the coil packs, spark plug wires and spark plugs (see Chapters 1 and 5).

5   Remove the intake manifold (see Section 4). Cover the intake ports on the manifold and cylinder head with duct tape to keep out debris and contamination.

6   Remove the power steering reservoir and hoses and place them out of the way (see Chapter 10).

7   Remove the exhaust manifold (see Section 5). **Note:** *The exhaust manifold is easier to remove after the cylinder head is removed. If possible, leave it attached.*

8   Disconnect the upper radiator hose from the thermostat housing (see Chapter 3).

9   Disconnect the electrical connector from the camshaft position sensor (see Chapter 5). Disconnect the electrical connectors from the fuel injectors and lay the harness aside (see Chapter 4).

10   Remove the timing belt (see Section 6).

11   Remove the camshaft sprockets, idler pulley and rear timing belt cover (see Section 8).

12   Remove the camshafts, rocker arms and valve lash adjusters (see Sections 9 and 10).

13   Loosen the cylinder head bolts, 1/4-turn at a time, in the *reverse* order of the tightening sequence **(see illustration 12.19)** until they can be removed by hand. **Note:** *Write down the location of the different length bolts so they can be reinstalled in their original locations.*

14   Carefully lift the cylinder head straight up and place it on wood blocks to prevent damage to the sealing surfaces. If the head sticks to the engine block, dislodge it by placing a wood block against the head casting and tapping the wood with a hammer or by prying the head with a prybar placed carefully on a casting protrusion **(see illustration)**. **Note:** *Cylinder head disassembly and inspection procedures are covered in Chapter 2D. It's also a good idea to have the head checked for warpage, even if you're just replacing the gasket.*

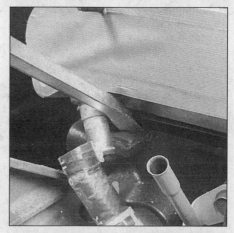

12.14 If the head is stuck to the engine block, dislodge it by placing a wood block against the head casting and tapping the wood with a hammer or by prying the head with a prybar placed carefully on a casting protrusion

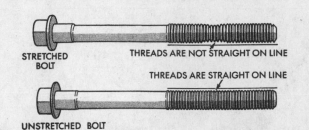

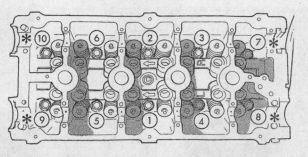

12.15 Place a precision straightedge along the cylinder head bolt thread profile as shown; if any part of the bolt threads are not on the straightedge, the bolt must be replaced

12.19 Cylinder head bolt TIGHTENING sequence

15   Remove all traces of old gasket material from the block and head. Special gasket removal solvents that soften gaskets and make removal much easier are available at auto parts stores. **Caution:** *The cylinder head is aluminum. Be very careful not to gouge the sealing surfaces.* Place clean shop rags into the cylinders to help keep out debris when working on the block. Use a vacuum to remove contamination from the engine. Use a tap of the correct size to chase the threads in the engine block. Clean and inspect all threaded fasteners for damage. Inspect the cylinder head bolt threads for "necking," where the diameter of threads narrow due to bolt stretching **(see illustration)**. If a cylinder head bolt exhibits damage or necking, it must be replaced. **Note:** *If further cylinder head disassembly is required, refer to Chapter 2D.*
16   Refer to Chapter 2D for cleaning and inspection of the cylinder head.

Installation

Refer to illustrations 12.19
17   Place a new gasket and the cylinder head in position on the engine block.
18   Apply clean engine oil to the cylinder head bolt threads and install them in their original locations.
19   Tighten the cylinder head bolts in the sequence shown, **(see illustration)** progressing in three stages to the torque listed in this Chapter's Specifications. After the third pass, tighten the bolts an additional 90-degrees (1/4 turn). **Note:** *A torque wrench is not required for the final step. Mark the bolts in relation to the cylinder head and place another mark 90 degrees clockwise from the starting mark. Using a socket and breaker bar, tighten the bolts in sequence, the additional 90-degrees.*
20   Install the rocker arms and hydraulic valve lash adjusters (see Section 9).
21   Install the rear timing belt cover, camshafts, and camshaft sprockets (see Section 10).
22   Install the timing belt (see Section 6). After installation, slowly rotate the crankshaft manually, clockwise through two complete revolutions. Recheck the camshaft timing marks.

23   Installation of the remaining components is the reverse of removal.
24   Refill the cooling system and check fluid levels (see Chapter 1).
25   Start the engine and run it until normal operating temperature is reached. Check for leaks and proper operation.

13   Oil pan - removal and installation

Removal

Refer to illustrations 13.7a, 13.7b, 13.8a and 13.8b
1   Disconnect the cable from the negative terminal of the battery.
2   Raise the vehicle and support it securely on jackstands.
3   Remove the accessory drivebelt splash shield (see Chapter 11).
4   Drain the engine oil (see Chapter 1).
5   On 1998 and later models, remove the front engine mount bracket (see Section 17). Remove the bolts attaching the strut to the engine and transaxle **(see illustration 13.13)**.
6   Remove the bolts attaching the structural collar to the engine, the oil pan, and the transaxle **(see illustration 13.13)**.
7   Use a criss-cross pattern to loosen and remove the mounting bolts, then lower the oil pan from the vehicle. If the pan is stuck, tap it with a soft-faced hammer **(see illustrations)** or place a wood block against the pan and tap the wood block with a hammer. **Caution:**

13.7a If the oil pan is stuck to the block, tap it with a soft faced mallet to break it loose

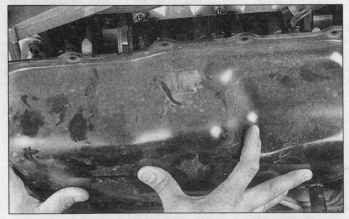

13.7b Remove the oil pan from the block - be careful not to spill any residual oil that may be inside

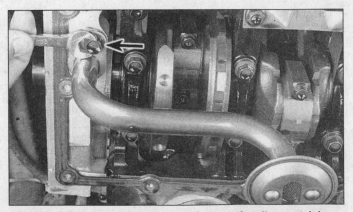

13.8a Unscrew the bolt (arrow) and remove the oil pump pick-up tube assembly - clean both the tube and screen thoroughly and inspect for damage or foreign debris

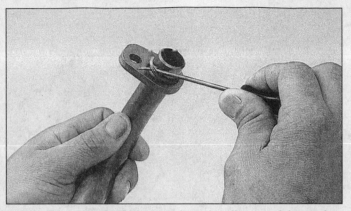

13.8b Removing the O-ring seal from the oil pump pick-up tube

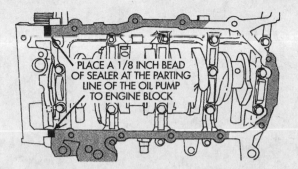

PLACE A 1/8 INCH BEAD OF SEALER AT THE PARTING LINE OF THE OIL PUMP TO ENGINE BLOCK

13.11 Apply a 1/8-inch bead of RTV sealant to the cylinder block-to-oil pump assembly joint on the oil pan flange

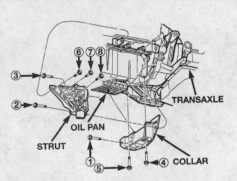

TRANSAXLE

OIL PAN

STRUT

COLLAR

13.13 Oil pan-to-transmission structural collar and strut installation details - 1998 models

If you're wedging something between the oil pan and the engine block to separate the two, be extremely careful not to gouge or nick the gasket surface of either part; an oil leak could result.

8   Remove the oil pump pick-up tube and screen assembly **(see illustration)**. Remove the O-ring seal from the oil pick-up tube and discard it **(see illustration)**. Thoroughly clean the tube and screen.

9   Clean the sealing surfaces on the oil pan and block. Use a scraper to remove all traces of old gasket material. Gasket removal solvents are available at auto parts stores and may prove helpful. Check the oil pan sealing surface for distortion. Straighten or replace as necessary. After cleaning and straightening (if necessary), wipe the gasket surfaces of the pan and block clean with a rag soaked in lacquer thinner or acetone.

Installation

Refer to illustrations 13.11 and 13.13

10   Place a new O-ring on the oil pick-up tube and install it on the oil pump housing. Tighten the bolt to the torque listed in this Chapter's Specifications.

11   Apply a 1/8-inch bead of RTV sealant at the cylinder block-to-oil pump assembly joint at the oil pan flange **(see illustration)**. Install a new oil pan gasket.

12   Place the oil pan in position and install

the bolts finger tight. Working side-to-side from the center out, tighten the bolts to the torque listed in this Chapter's Specifications.

13   On 1998 models, install the strut and structural collar using the following procedure **(see illustration)**: **Caution:** *The strut and structural collar must be installed as described or damage to the strut, collar or oil pan could occur.*

a) *Place the collar into position and install bolt 1, hand-tight only.*
b) *Install bolt 4, hand-tight only.*
c) *Place the strut into position and install bolt 3, hand-tight only.*
d) *Install bolt 2, hand-tight only.*
e) *Install bolt 6, hand-tight only.*
f) *Install bolt 5, hand-tight only.*
g) *Tighten bolts 1, 2 and 3 to the torque listed in this Chapter's Specifications.*
h) *Install bolts 7 and 8, hand-tight only.*
i) *Tighten bolts 4 through 8 to the torque listed in this Chapter's Specifications.*

14   Install the front engine mount bracket.

15   The remaining installation steps are the reverse of removal.

16   Refill the crankcase with the proper quantity and grade of oil (see *Recommended*

lubricants and fluids Section in Chapter 1).

17   Run the engine and check for leaks.

18   Road test the vehicle and recheck for leaks.

14 Oil pump - removal, inspection and installation

Note: *The oil pump pressure relief valve can be serviced without removing the oil pan and oil pick-up tube.*

Removal

Refer to illustrations 14.5a, 14.5b, 14.6a, 14.6b, 14.6c, 14.8 and 14.9

1   Disconnect the cable from the negative terminal of the battery.

2   Remove the timing belt (see Section 6).

3   Remove the oil pan and pick-up tube assembly (see Section 13).

4   Remove the crankshaft sprocket (see Section 7).

5   Remove the bolts and detach the oil pump assembly from the engine **(see illustration)**. **Caution:** *If the pump doesn't come off by hand, tap it gently with a soft-faced*

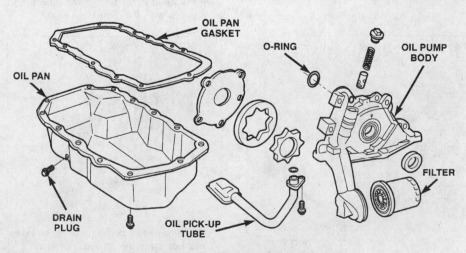

OIL PAN GASKET

O-RING

OIL PUMP BODY

OIL PAN

FILTER

DRAIN PLUG

OIL PICK-UP TUBE

14.5a Oil pump and related components

14.5b If the pump will not come off by hand, tap it gently with a soft-faced hammer or pry gently on a casting protrusion

14.6a Remove the rotor cover mounting screws (arrows) . . .

14.6b . . . and lift off the rotor cover

hammer or pry on a casting boss **(see illustration).**

6   Remove the mounting screws and the rotor assembly cover from the oil pump housing. Pull the inner and outer rotors from the body **(see illustrations). Caution:** *Be very careful with these components. Close tolerances are critical in creating the correct oil pressure. Nicks or other damage will require replacement of the complete pump assembly.*

7   Use a hammer and brass drift to remove the crankshaft front seal from the oil pump housing, then discard it.

8   Remove the O-ring seal from the oil pump housing discharge port and discard it **(see illustration).**

9   Disassemble the relief valve assembly; take note of the way the relief valve piston is installed. Remove the cap bolt, and the bolt, washer, spring, and relief valve **(see illustration).**

Inspection

Refer to illustrations 14.12a, 14.12b, 14.12c, 14.12d and 14.12e

10   Clean all components, including the

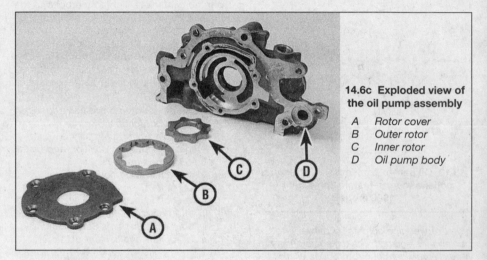

14.6c Exploded view of the oil pump assembly

A   Rotor cover
B   Outer rotor
C   Inner rotor
D   Oil pump body

block surfaces and oil pan, with solvent. Inspect all surfaces for excessive wear and/or damage.

11   Inspect the oil pressure relief valve piston sliding surface and valve spring for damage. If either the spring or the valve is damaged, they must be replaced as a set. Measure the relief valve spring free length and compare it with the dimension listed in this

Chapter's Specifications. Replace the spring if it's out of tolerance by more than 1/8 of an inch.

12   Check the oil pump rotor dimensions and clearances with a micrometer or vernier calipers and a feeler gauge **(see illustrations)** and compare the results to the values listed in this Chapter's Specifications. Replace both rotors if any dimension is out of tolerance.

14.8 Remove the discharge port O-ring seal from the oil pump body - apply clean engine oil to the new seal at installation

14.9 Remove the oil pressure relief valve cap bolt from the oil pump body and withdraw the spring and the relief valve piston

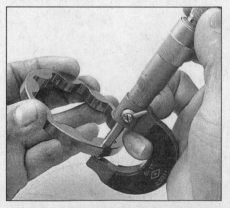

14.12a Measure the outer rotor thickness at four locations equally spaced and calculate the average

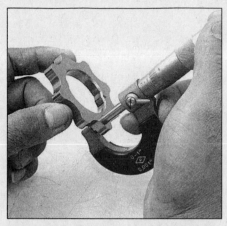

14.12b Measure the inner rotor thickness with a micrometer or caliper

14.12c Measure the outer rotor's outer diameter with a micrometer or caliper

14.12d Use a flat feeler gauge to measure the outer rotor-to-oil pump body clearance

14.12e With the rotors installed, place a precision straightedge across the rotor cover surface and measure the clearance between the rotors and the rotor cover surface

14.16 Apply a bead of anaerobic sealant to the oil pump housing sealing surface as shown

Installation

Refer to illustration 14.16

13   Lubricate the relief valve piston, piston bore, and spring with clean engine oil. Install the relief valve piston in the bore with the grooved end going in first, followed by the spring and cap bolt. Tighten the cap bolt to the torque listed in this Chapter's Specifications. **Note:** *If the relief valve piston is installed incorrectly, serious engine damage could occur.*

14   Lubricate the oil pump rotor recess in the housing and the inner and outer rotors with clean engine oil and install both rotors in the body. If the inner rotor has a chamfer, install it with the chamfer facing the rotor cover. Fill the rotor cavity with clean engine oil and install the cover. Tighten the cover screws to the torque listed in this Chapter's Specifications.

15   Install a new O-ring in the oil discharge passage.

16   Apply anaerobic sealant to the oil pump body sealing surface **(see illustration)** and position the pump assembly on the block, aligning the inner rotor and crankshaft drive flats. Tighten the oil pump bolts to the torque listed in this Chapter's Specifications.

17   Install the new crankshaft front seal in the oil pump housing (see Section 7).

18   Install the crankshaft sprocket (see Section 7) and timing belt (see Section 6).

19   Install the oil pump pick-up tube assembly and oil pan (see Section 13).

20   Install a new oil filter (see Chapter 1) and lower the vehicle.

21   Fill the crankcase with the proper quantity and grade of oil (see *Recommended lubricants and fluids* Section in Chapter 1).

22   Connect the negative battery cable.

23   After the sealant has cured, per the manufacturer's directions, start the engine and check for leaks.

15   Driveplate - removal and installation

Removal

Refer to illustration 15.4

1   Raise the vehicle and support it securely on jackstands.

2   Remove the transaxle (see Chapter 7).

3   To ensure correct alignment during reinstallation, match-mark the driveplate and

15.4 Match-mark the position of the driveplate and backing plate to the crankshaft and, using an appropriate tool to hold the driveplate, remove the bolts

backing plate to the crankshaft so they can be reassembled in the same position.

4   Remove the bolts that hold the driveplate to the crankshaft **(see illustration)**. A special tool is available at most auto parts stores to hold the driveplate while loosening

16.3 Using a 3/16 inch flat blade screwdriver, very carefully pry the crankshaft rear main seal out of it's bore - DO NOT nick or scratch the sealing surfaces on the crankshaft or seal bore

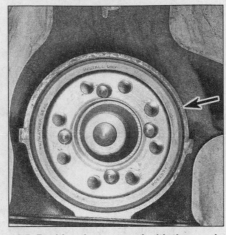

16.5 Position the new seal with the words THIS SIDE OUT facing out. Install this seal DRY! DO NOT lubricate! Gently and evenly drive the seal into the cylinder block until it is FLUSH with the outer surface of the block. DO NOT drive it past flush or there will be an oil leak - the seal must be FLUSH!

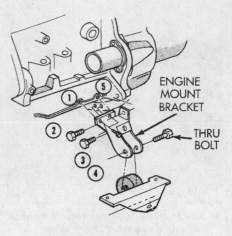

17.9 Front engine mount installation details

the bolts. If the tool is not available, wedge a screwdriver in the starter ring gear teeth to jam the driveplate.

5   Remove the driveplate from the crankshaft. The driveplate is fairly heavy, be sure to support it while removing the last bolt.

6   Clean the driveplate to remove grease and oil. Inspect the driveplate for damage or other defects (see Chapter 2A).

7   Clean and inspect the mating surfaces of the driveplate and the crankshaft.

8   If the crankshaft rear main seal is leaking, replace it before reinstalling the driveplate (see Section 16).

Installation

9   Position the driveplate and backing plate against the crankshaft. Align the previously applied match marks. Before installing the bolts, apply thread-locking compound to the threads.

10   Hold the driveplate with the holding tool, or wedge a screwdriver in the starter ring gear teeth to keep the driveplate from turning. Tighten the bolts to the torque listed in this Chapter's Specifications.

11   The remaining installation steps are the reverse of removal.

16   Rear main oil seal - replacement

Refer to illustrations 16.3 and 16.5

1   The rear main oil seal is pressed into a bore machined into the rear main bearing cap and engine block.

2   Remove the driveplate (see Section 15).

3   **Note:** *Verify that the oil seal is installed flush with the outer surface of the block.* Pry out the old seal with a 3/16-inch flat blade screwdriver **(see illustration)**. **Caution:** *To prevent an oil leak, be careful not to scratch or damage the crankshaft sealing surface or the seal bore in the engine block.*

4   Clean the crankshaft and seal bore in the block thoroughly and de-grease them by wiping them with a rag soaked in lacquer thinner or acetone. DO NOT lubricate the lip or outer diameter of the new seal - it must be installed like it comes from the manufacturer - DRY.

5   Position the new seal on the crankshaft. **Note:** *When installing the new seal, the words THIS SIDE OUT on the seal must face out.* Use an appropriate size driver and pilot tool to drive the seal into the cylinder block until it is flush with the outer surface of the block. If the seal is driven in past flush, there will be an oil leak. Make sure that the seal is flush **(see illustration)**.

6   Installation of the remaining components is the reverse of removal.

17   Engine mounts - check and replacement

1   Engine mounts seldom require attention, but broken or deteriorated mounts should be replaced immediately or the added strain placed on driveline components may cause damage or accelerated wear.

Check

2   The engine must be raised slightly to remove the weight from the mounts.

3   Raise the vehicle and support it securely on jackstands, then position a jack under the engine oil pan. Place a large wood block between the jack head and the oil pan to prevent oil pan damage. Carefully raise the engine just enough to take the weight off the mounts. **Warning:** *DO NOT place any part of your body under the engine when only a jack supports it!*

4   Check the mounts to see if the rubber is cracked, hardened, or separated from the metal backing. Sometimes the rubber will split right down the center.

5   Check for movement between the mount plates and the engine or frame (use a large screwdriver or pry bar to attempt to move the mounts). If no movement is noted, lower the engine and tighten the mount fasteners.

6   Rubber preservative may be applied to the mounts to help slow deterioration.

Replacement

Refer to illustrations 17.9, 17.17, 17.20 and 17.27

Front Mount

7   Raise the front of the vehicle and support it securely on jackstands.

8   Place a floorjack under the engine (with a wood block between the jack head and oil pan) and raise the engine slightly to relieve the weight from the mounts.

9   Remove the front engine mount through bolt from the insulator and front crossmember-mounting bracket **(see illustration)**.

10   Remove six screws from the air dam to all access to the front mount screws.

11   Remove the front engine mount screws and remove the insulator assembly.

12   Install the new mount and tighten the bolts to the torque listed in this Chapter's Specifications **(see illustration 17.9)**.

Left Mount

13   Raise the front of the vehicle and support it securely on jackstands.

14   Remove the left front wheel.

15   Place a floorjack under the engine (with a wood block between the jack head and oil pan) and raise the engine slightly to relieve the weight from the mounts.

16   Remove the insulator through bolt from the mount.

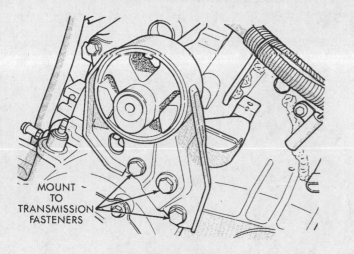

17.17 Typical left engine mount

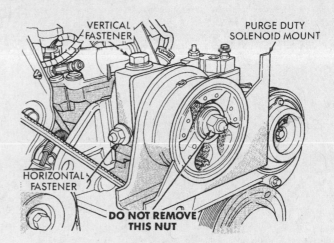

17.20 Typical right engine mount

17   Remove the transmission mount fasteners and remove the mount **(see illustration)**.
18   Install the new mount and tighten the bolts to the torque listed in this Chapter's Specifications.

Right Mount

19   Raise the front of the vehicle and support it securely on jackstands. Remove the purge duty solenoid and wiring harness from the engine mount bracket.
20   Remove the two right engine mount insulator vertical fasteners from the frame rail and loosen the one horizontal fastener. **Note:** *Do not remove the large nut located at the*

end of the core **(see illustration)**.
21   Place a floorjack under the engine (with a wood block between the jack head and oil pan) and raise the engine slightly to relieve the weight from the mounts.
22   Remove the vertical and horizontal fasteners from the engine side bracket. Remove the mount assembly.
23   Install the new mount and tighten the bolts to the torque listed in this Chapter's Specifications.

Rear Mount

24   Raise the front of the vehicle and sup-

port it securely on jackstands. Remove the left front wheel.
25   Place a floor jack under the engine (with a wood block between the jack head and oil pan) and raise the engine slightly to relieve the weight from the mounts.
26   Remove the insulator through bolt from the mount and rear suspension crossmember.
27   Remove the four mount fasteners and remove the mount **(see illustration)**.
28   Install the new mount and tighten the bolts to the torque listed in this Chapter's Specifications.

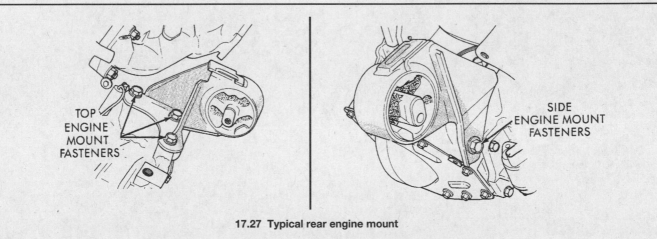

17.27 Typical rear engine mount

Notes

Chapter 2 Part B
3.0L V6 engine

Contents

	Section
Camshaft oil seal - replacement	9
Camshaft(s) - removal, inspection, and installation	11
CHECK ENGINE light	See Chapter 6
Crankshaft front oil seal - replacement	8
Crankshaft pulley/vibration damper - removal and installation	6
Cylinder compression check	See Chapter 2D
Cylinder heads - removal and installation	13
Drivebelt check, adjustment and replacement	See Chapter 1
Driveplate - removal and installation	16
Engine mounts - check and replacement	18
Engine oil and filter change	See Chapter 1
Engine overhaul - general information	See Chapter 2D
Engine - removal and installation	See Chapter 2D
Exhaust manifolds - removal and installation	5
General information	1

	Section
Intake manifold - removal and installation	4
Oil pan - removal and installation	14
Oil pump - removal, inspection and installation	15
Rear main oil seal - replacement	17
Repair operations possible with the engine in the vehicle	2
Rocker arms and hydraulic lash adjusters - check, removal, inspection, and installation	10
Spark plug replacement	See Chapter 1
Timing belt - removal, installation, and adjustment	7
Top Dead Center (TDC) for number one piston	See Chapter 2D
Vacuum gauge diagnostic checks	See Chapter 2D
Valve covers - removal and installation	3
Valve spring, retainer, and seals - replacement	12
Water pump - removal and installation	See Chapter 3

Specifications

General
Bore	3.587 inches
Stroke	2.992 inches
Compression ratio	8.85:1
Compression pressure	178 psi
Displacement	181 cubic inches
Firing order	1-2-3-4-5-6
Oil pressure	
At idle speed	10 psi
At 3000 rpm	45 to 75 psi
Cylinder numbers (drivebelt end-to-transaxle end)	
Rear (firewall side)	1-3-5
Front (radiator side)	2-4-6

Camshaft
Camshaft runout limit	0.004 inch
Lobe height	1.624 inches
Lobe wear limit	0.020 inch

Oil pump
Cover warpage limit	0.003 inch
Inner rotor thickness	0.744 inch
Outer rotor thickness	0.744 inch
Outer rotor diameter	3.246 inches
Rotor-to-pump cover clearance	0.003 inch
Case-to-outer rotor clearance	0.007 inch
Inner rotor-to-outer rotor lobe clearance	0.0068 inch
Case-to-inner rotor clearance	0.003 inch

The blackened terminal shown on the distributor cap indicates the Number One spark plug wire position

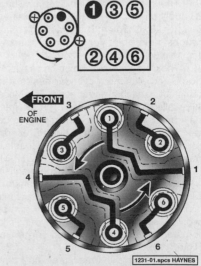

Cylinder numbering, distributor rotation and spark plug wire terminal locations

Torque specifications

	Ft-lbs (unless otherwise indicated)
Camshaft sprocket bolt	70
Camshaft position sensor bolt...	20
Crankshaft vibration damper bolt	100
Cylinder head bolts	
Step 1	50
Step 2	65
Step 3	80
Distributor drive adapter bolts	130 in-lbs
Driveplate mounting bolts..	75*
Exhaust manifold nuts...	175 in-lbs
Exhaust manifold heat shield bolts......................................	105 in-lbs
Exhaust pipe-to-manifold bolts...	21
Exhaust crossover pipe bolts...	51
Intake manifold nuts/bolts	20
Oil pan bolts	105 in-lbs
Oil pick-up tube-to-pump bolts	21
Oil pump assembly mounting bolts	130 in-lbs
Oil pump relief plug	36
Oil pump cover bolts	104 in-lbs
Rocker arm shaft bolts	180 in-lbs
Thermostat housing bolts	17
Timing belt cover bolts	115 in-lbs
Timing belt tensioner locking bolt..	20
Timing belt tensioner pulley assembly	30
Valve cover bolts	88 in-lbs

Apply a thread locking compound to the threads prior to installation

1   General information

Chapter 2B covers in-vehicle repair procedures for the 3.0L V6 engine. Information concerning engine removal and installation, and engine block and cylinder head overhaul can be found in Chapter 2D.

The following repair procedures are based on the assumption that the engine is installed in the vehicle. If the engine has been removed from the vehicle and mounted on a stand, many of the steps outlined in Chapter 2B will not apply.

The specifications included in Chapter 2B apply only to the procedures contained in Chapter 2B. Chapter 2D contains the specifications necessary for cylinder head and engine block rebuilding.

The 60-degree V6 engine has a cast iron block, and aluminum cylinder heads with a camshaft in each cylinder head. The block is thin-walled for light weight. A "cradle frame" main bearing casting - the main bearing caps are cast as a unit, with a bridge, or truss, connecting them - supports the cast iron crankshaft.

Camshafts are driven by the crankshaft timing belt. A spring loaded tensioner, adjusted by an eccentric type locknut, maintains belt tension. Each camshaft actuates two valves per cylinder through hydraulic lash adjusters and shaft-mounted forged aluminum rocker arms.

Each cast aluminum three-ring piston has two compression rings and a three-piece oil control ring. The piston pins are pressed into forged steel connecting rods.

The distributor, mounted on the drivebelt end of the front cylinder head, is driven by a helical gear on the camshaft. The water pump, on the timing belt end of the block, is driven off the crankshaft by a drivebelt and pulley. The gear type oil pump is mounted in the oil pump case, attached to the timing belt cover, and is driven by the crankshaft.

Oil travels from the oil pump, through the filter, to the main oil gallery. It is then routed to the main bearings, the crankshaft, the connecting rod bearings and pistons, and cylinder walls, or the cylinder heads.

2   Repair operations possible with the engine in the vehicle

Many major repair operations can be accomplished without removing the engine from the vehicle.

Clean the engine compartment and the exterior of the engine with degreaser before any work is done. It will make the job easier and help keep dirt out of the internal parts of the engine.

It may be helpful to remove the hood to improve access to the engine when repairs are performed (see Chapter 11). Cover the fenders to prevent damage to the paint. Special pads are available, but an old bedspread or blanket will also work.

If vacuum, exhaust, oil, or coolant leaks develop, indicating a need for gasket or seal replacement, the repairs can generally be made with the engine in the vehicle. The intake and exhaust manifold gaskets, oil pan gasket, camshaft, and crankshaft oil seals and cylinder head gaskets are all accessible with the engine in the vehicle.

Exterior engine components, such as the intake and exhaust manifolds, the oil pan (and the oil pump), the water pump, the starter motor, the alternator, the distributor, and fuel system components can be removed for repair with the engine in the vehicle.

The camshaft and the cylinder heads can be removed without pulling the engine and valve component servicing can also be accomplished with the engine in the vehicle. Timing belt and sprockets replacement is also possible with the engine in the vehicle.

Repair or replacement of piston rings, pistons, connecting rods, and rod bearings is possible with the engine in the vehicle, however, this practice is not recommended because of the cleaning and preparation work that must be done to the components involved.

3   Valve covers - removal and installation

1   Relieve the fuel system pressure (see Chapter 4).
2   Disconnect the cable from the negative terminal of the battery.

Removal

Front (radiator side) valve cover

Refer to illustrations 3.3 and 3.7

3   Remove the breather hose by sliding the hose clamp back and pulling the hose off the

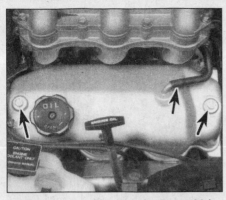

3.3 To remove the front (radiator side) valve cover, remove the breather hose and the spark plug wires, then remove the two cover retaining bolts and washers

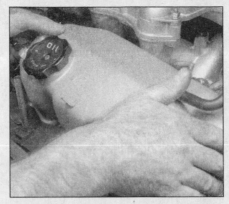

3.7 Remove the valve cover - if it's stuck to the cylinder head, try to jar it loose with a block of wood and a hammer or slip a flexible putty knife between the cylinder head and cover to break the gasket seal; don't pry at the cover-to-cylinder head joint or you may damage the sealing surfaces

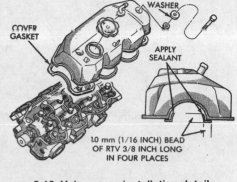

3.19 Valve cover installation details - apply a 1/16-inch bead of RTV to the areas shown

valve cover fitting **(see illustration)**.
4   Remove the spark plug wires from the spark plugs. Label them with masking tape to prevent confusion during installation. Label and remove wires and hoses attached to the valve cover.
5   Withdraw the dipstick and remove the dipstick tube from the engine block (follow the tube down the front of the block and you'll find a single bracket bolt holding the tube to the block).
6   Remove the valve cover bolts and washers.
7   Detach the valve cover **(see illustration)**. **Caution:** *If the cover is stuck to the cylinder head, tap one end with a block of wood and a hammer to jar it loose. If that doesn't work, slip a flexible putty knife between the cylinder head and cover to break the gasket seal. Don't pry at the cover-to-cylinder head joint or damage to the sealing surfaces may occur (leading to future oil leaks).*

Rear (firewall side) valve cover

8   Remove the breather hose from the cover **(see illustration 3.3)**.
9   Label and remove the spark plug wires.
10   Release the wiring retainers, then label and remove the wiring and hoses.
11   Remove the air cleaner and the air cleaner assembly (see Chapter 4).
12   Remove the air inlet duct and resonator from the throttle body.
13   Remove the windshield wiper motor (see Chapter 12).
14   Remove the accessory drivebelt (see Chapter 1).
15   Remove the alternator (see Chapter 5).
16   Remove the valve cover bolts and washers and lift off the valve cover. Read the **Caution** in Step 7.

Installation

Refer to illustration 3.19
17   The mating surfaces of each cylinder head and valve cover must be perfectly clean when the covers are installed. Use a gasket scraper to remove all traces of sealant and

old gasket material, then clean the mating surfaces with lacquer thinner or acetone. If there's sealant or oil on the mating surfaces when the cover is installed, oil leaks may develop.
18   Clean the mounting screw threads with a die if necessary, to remove corrosion and restore damaged threads. Make sure the threaded holes in the cylinder head are clean - run a tap into them to remove corrosion and restore damaged threads.
19   Gaskets should be mated to the covers before the covers are installed. Apply a bead of RTV sealant to the cover in the areas indicated **(see illustration)**, then place the gasket inside the cover and allow the sealant to set up so the gasket adheres to the cover. If the sealant isn't allowed to set, the gasket may fall out of the cover when it's installed on the engine.
20   Carefully position the cover on the cylinder head and install the bolts.
21   Tighten the bolts in three or four steps to the torque listed in this Chapter's Specifications.

22   Installation of the remaining components is the reverse of removal.
23   Start the engine and check for oil leaks after the engine is warm.

4   Intake manifold - removal and installation

Removal

Refer to illustrations 4.4, 4.5 and 4.7
1   Relieve the fuel pressure (see Chapter 4).
2   Disconnect the cable from the negative battery terminal.
3   Drain the cooling system (see Chapter 1). Remove the radiator hose from the thermostat housing and the heater hose from the heater pipe.
4   Remove the air intake plenum **(see illustration)** (see Chapter 4). Cover the intake manifold ports to prevent parts/tools from falling into the engine.
5   Disconnect the fuel injector wiring harness from the engine wiring harness. Remove the vacuum connections from the fuel rail and the fuel pressure regulator **(see illustration)**.

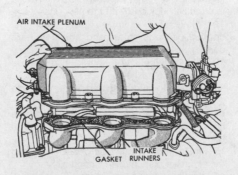

4.4 Remove the air intake plenum

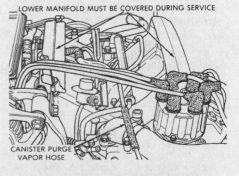

4.5 Remove the vacuum connections from the fuel rail and fuel pressure regulator

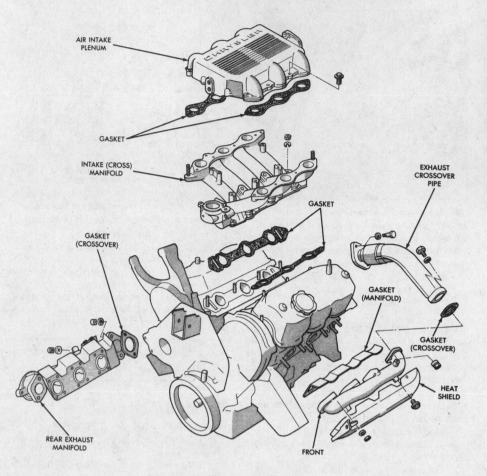

4.7 An exploded view of the intake and exhaust manifold assemblies

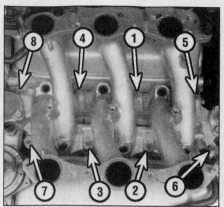

4.14 Nut tightening sequence for the intake manifold

5   Exhaust manifolds - removal and installation

Warning: *Let the engine cool completely before starting this procedure.*

Removal

Refer to illustrations 5.6, 5.7, 5.9, 5.10a, 5.10b and 5.10c

1   Disconnect the cable from the negative terminal of the battery.

2   Raise the vehicle and support it securely on jackstands.

3   Spray penetrating oil on the exhaust manifold fasteners and allow it to soak in.

4   To remove the front exhaust manifold, remove the coolant reservoir (see Chapter 3) and the dipstick tube (follow the tube down the front of the block and you'll find a single bracket bolt holding the tube to the block) **(see illustration 5.10a)**.

5   To remove the rear exhaust manifold, remove the air cleaner assembly, the air intake duct and the oxygen sensor lead wire.

6   Remove the bolts and nuts that attach the flange(s) of the crossover pipe to the front and/or rear exhaust manifold(s) **(see illustration)**.

5.6 Remove the exhaust crossover pipe flange nuts/bolts (arrows) (only the upper flange bolts are visible)

6   Disconnect the fuel inlet hose from the fuel rail. Remove the fuel rail bolts and lift the fuel rail/injector assembly from the intake manifold (see Chapter 4).

7   Remove the nuts/washers and the intake manifold **(see illustration)**.

8   The manifold will probably stick to the cylinder heads and may require force to break the gasket seal. **Caution:** *Don't pry between the manifold and the cylinder heads or damage to the gasket sealing surfaces may occur, leading to vacuum leaks.*

Installation

Refer to illustration 4.14

Note: *The mating surfaces of the cylinder heads and manifold must be perfectly clean when the manifold is installed. Gasket removal solvents are available at most auto parts stores and may be helpful when removing old gasket material. Cylinder heads are made of aluminum, aggressive scraping can cause damage. Be sure to follow the directions printed on the container.*

9   Use a gasket scraper to remove all traces of sealant and old gasket material, then clean the mating surfaces with lacquer thinner or acetone. If there's old sealant or oil on the mating surfaces when the manifold is

installed, oil or vacuum leaks may develop. Use a vacuum cleaner to remove material that falls into the intake ports in the cylinder heads.

10   Use a tap of the correct size to chase the threads in the bolt holes, then use compressed air (if available) to remove debris from the holes. **Warning:** *Wear safety glasses or a face shield to protect your eyes when using compressed air!*

11   Place the gaskets on the cylinder heads. No sealant is required; however, follow the instructions included with the new gaskets.

12   Make sure all intake port openings, coolant passage holes, and bolt holes are correctly aligned.

13   Carefully set the manifold in place, do not disturb the gaskets.

14   Install the nuts/bolts and tighten them to the torque listed in this Chapter's Specifications in the recommended sequence **(see illustration)**. Work up to the final torque in two steps.

15   Install the fuel rail/injector assembly and the air intake plenum (see Chapter 4).

16   Installation of the remaining components is the reverse of removal.

17   Start the engine and check for oil and coolant leaks at the intake manifold joints.

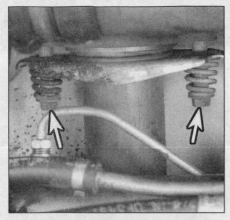

5.7 Remove the exhaust pipe flange bolts (arrows) from the front and rear exhaust manifold

7   Remove the front and rear exhaust manifold exhaust pipe flange bolts (see illustration).
8   To remove the rear exhaust manifold, disconnect the EGR tube (see Chapter 6).
9   To remove the front exhaust manifold,

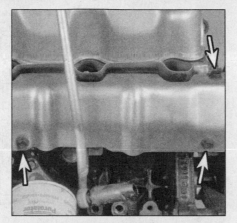

5.9 To remove the front exhaust manifold, remove the dipstick tube (see next illustration) and the heat shield bolts (arrows)

remove the three heat shield bolts (see illustration) and the heat shield.
10   Remove the exhaust manifold(s) and gasket(s) (see illustrations).
11   Carefully inspect the manifold(s) and

fasteners for cracks and damage.
12   Use a scraper to remove all traces of old gasket material and carbon deposits from the manifold and cylinder head mating surfaces. If the gasket was leaking, have the manifold checked for warpage at an automotive machine shop. Resurface it if necessary.

Installation

Refer to illustrations 5.13a and 5.13b

13   Position the new gasket(s) over the cylinder head studs. **Note:** *Install the gasket with the numbers 1-3-5 on the top on the rear bank and install the gasket with the numbers 2-4-6 on the front bank* (see illustrations).
14   Install the manifold and tighten the nuts finger-tight.
15   Working from the center out, tighten the nuts to the torque in this Chapter's Specifications in three or four equal steps.
16   Installation of the remaining components is the reverse of removal. Use new gaskets when connecting the exhaust crossover pipe to the exhaust manifolds.
17   Start the engine and check for exhaust leaks.

5.10a Front exhaust manifold bolts and dipstick tube bracket bolt (arrows)

5.10b Rear exhaust manifold lower bolts (arrows) . . .

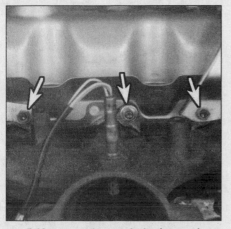

5.10c . . . and upper bolts (arrows)

5.13a Install a new steel exhaust manifold gasket onto the manifold studs (rear gasket shown, front gasket similar)

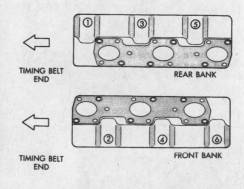

5.13b Be sure to install the correct exhaust manifold gasket onto the corresponding cylinder head

6.5a To remove the two-piece pulley from the vibration damper, remove these bolts (arrows)

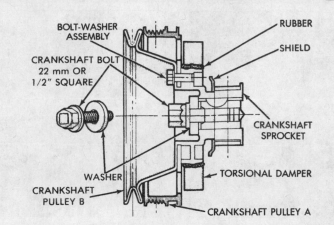

6.5b This cross-section view shows the relationship between the two pulley halves and the vibration damper - note the keyway which locks the damper onto the nose of the crankshaft

6.6a If you don't have a chain wrench, you can fabricate a crankshaft holding tool with a piece of angle iron and a couple of bolts of the same thread pitch and diameter as the holes in the crankshaft pulley . . .

6 Crankshaft pulley/vibration damper - removal and installation

Removal

Refer to illustrations 6.5a, 6.5b, 6.6a and 6.6b

1 Disconnect the cable from the negative terminal of the battery.

2 Loosen the lug nuts of the right front wheel, raise the front of the vehicle and support it securely on jackstands.

3 Remove the wheel and the inner splash shield.

4 Remove the accessory drivebelts (see Chapter 1).

5 Remove the bolts attaching the pulley to the vibration damper and remove the pulley **(see illustration)**. **Note:** *The crankshaft pulley is actually a two-piece design* **(see illustration)**.

6 Wrap a cloth and a chain wrench around the vibration damper. Hold the crankshaft from turning and use a socket wrench to loosen the damper bolt. If you don't have a chain wrench, make a crank holding tool with a piece of angle iron and a couple of bolts of the correct diameter and thread pitch. Drill a couple of holes in the angle iron the same distance apart as any two holes in the crank pulley, insert the bolts through the angle iron and thread them into the pulley holes **(see illustration)**. Or, remove the driveplate cover **(see illustration)** and lock the crank by jamming a screwdriver between the ring gear teeth and the bellhousing.

7 Remove the vibration damper. If it's stuck, install a vibration damper/steering wheel puller that bolts onto the damper hub and pull it off the nose of the crankshaft. **Caution:** *Do not attempt to remove it using a jaw-type puller that grips the outer edge of the damper or damage to the damper will occur.*

Installation

8 Lightly lubricate the seal contact surface with engine oil and position it on the nose of the crankshaft. Align the keyway in the pulley

6.6b . . . or remove the flywheel/driveplate cover and immobilize the crank by jamming a large screwdriver between the ring gear and the bellhousing

7.5 Remove the bolts (arrows) and remove the tensioner pulley assembly for the serpentine belt

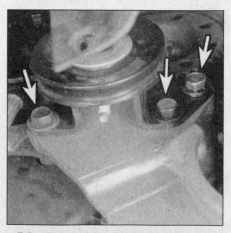

7.6a Remove these bolts (arrows) and remove the tensioner pulley assembly for the air conditioning compressor drivebelt

with the key in the crankshaft and push the pulley into place by hand. If necessary, tap lightly on the damper using a block of wood and a hammer.

9 Hold the crankshaft as described in Step 6, then install the bolt and tighten it to the torque in this Chapter's Specifications.

10 Installation of the remaining components is the reverse of removal.

7 Timing belt - removal, installation and adjustment

Removal

** CAUTION **

The timing system is complex. Severe engine damage will occur if you make any mistakes. Do not attempt this procedure unless you are highly experienced with this type of repair. If you are at all unsure of your abilities, consult an expert. Double-check all your work and be sure everything is correct before you attempt to start the engine.

Refer to illustrations 7.5, 7.6a, 7.6b, 7.6c, 7.7, 7.8, 7.10, 7.11, 7.12a, 7.12b, 7.13a, 7.13b, 7.13c, 7.14 and 7.16

1 Disconnect the cable from the negative terminal of the battery.

2 Loosen the lug nuts on the right front wheel, raise the front of the vehicle and support it securely on jackstands. Remove the right front wheel and the inner splash shield.

3 Position the number one piston at TDC on the compression stroke (see Chapter 2D).

4 Remove the drivebelt for the air conditioning compressor and the serpentine belt for the alternator and power steering pump (see Chapter 1).

5 Remove the tensioner pulley assembly for the serpentine belt **(see illustration)**.

6 Remove the tensioner pulley assembly for the compressor drivebelt **(see illustrations)** and the compressor mounting bracket.

7 Remove the bolts from the power steering pump mounting bracket and set the pump and bracket aside **(see illustration)**.

8 Remove the crankshaft pulley and vibration damper (see Section 6). Remove the crankshaft sprocket flange **(see illustration)**. **Note:** *Don't allow the crankshaft to rotate during removal of the pulley. If the crankshaft moves, the number one piston won't be at TDC.*

9 Place a floorjack and a block of wood under the engine oil pan for support.

10 Scribe or mark the relationship of the engine support assembly to the engine bracket, then remove the right engine mount **(see illustration)**.

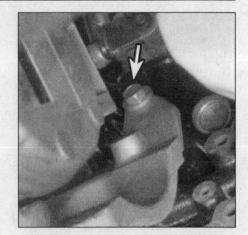

7.6b Remove this compressor bracket bolt (arrow), push the compressor and bracket assembly aside and support it with a piece of wire

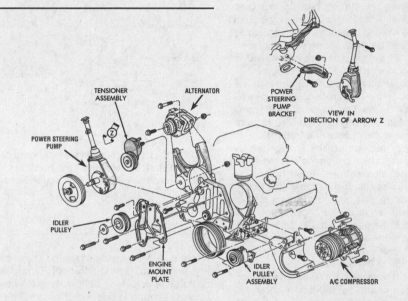

7.6c Installation details of the accessory brackets and pulleys

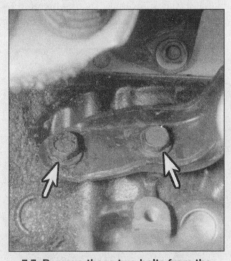

7.7 Remove these two bolts from the power steering pump bracket, swing the pump and bracket assembly aside and support it with a piece of wire

7.8 After you've removed the crankshaft pulley and vibration damper, remove this crankshaft sprocket flange

7.10 To remove the right engine mount, remove the bolts from the engine mount bracket and the vehicle body (arrows)

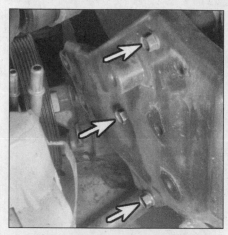

7.11 Remove the bolts (arrows) and remove the engine mount bracket

7.12a Remove the bolts (arrows) and remove the three timing belt covers (not all the bolts are visible in this photo)

11   Remove the engine mount bracket **(see illustration)**.
12   Remove the timing belt covers **(see illustrations)**. Note the various type and sizes of bolts by making a diagram or taking careful notes while the timing belt cover is being removed. The bolts must be reinstalled in their original locations.
13   Make sure that the number one piston is still at TDC on the compression stroke by verifying that the timing marks on all three timing belt sprockets are aligned with their respective alignment marks **(see illustrations)**.
14   Relieve tension on the timing belt by loosening the nut on the timing belt tensioner pulley **(see illustration)**. Push the pulley towards the firewall, then retighten the bolt.
15   Check to see that the timing belt is marked with an arrow to show which side faces out. If there isn't a mark, paint one on (only if the same belt will be reinstalled). Slide the timing belt off the sprockets and check the condition of the tensioner.
16   Inspect the timing belt **(see illustration)**. Look at the backside (the side without the teeth): If it's cracked or peeling, or it's hard, glossy and inflexible, and leaves no indentation when pressed with your fingernail, replace the belt. Look at the drive side: If teeth are missing, cracked or excessively worn, replace the belt.

Installation

> ** ** CAUTION ** **
>
> Before starting the engine, carefully rotate the crankshaft by hand through at least two full revolutions (use a socket and breaker bar on the crankshaft pulley center bolt). If you feel any resistance, STOP! There is something wrong - most likely, valves are contacting the pistons. You must find the problem before proceeding. Check your work and see if any updated repair information is available.

Refer to illustrations 7.17a and 7.17b
17   Install the timing belt by prying the ten-

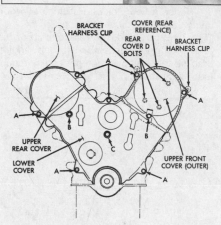

7.12b There are four different lengths of timing belt cover bolts - the bolts are designated as A, B, C and D, according to their size

A	M6X20	C	M6X25
B	M6X55	D	M6X10

sioner away from the spring to the end of the adjustment slot **(see illustration)**. Temporarily tighten the locking bolt, making sure the tensioner spring is positioned properly **(see illustration)**.

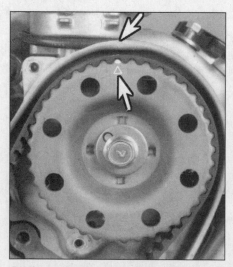

7.13b . . . the front camshaft sprocket . . .

7.13a To confirm that the number one piston is still at TDC on the compression stroke, verify that the timing marks on the rear camshaft sprocket . . .

18   *Install the belt on the crankshaft sprocket first, and keep the belt tight on the tension side.*
19   *Install the belt on the front (radiator side) camshaft sprocket, the water pump pulley, and the rear camshaft sprocket and timing belt tensioner. Be careful not to nudge the camshaft sprocket(s) or*

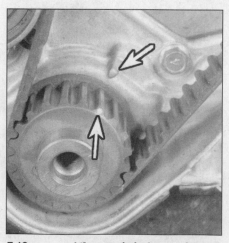

7.13c . . . and the crankshaft sprocket are aligned with their respective stationary alignment marks

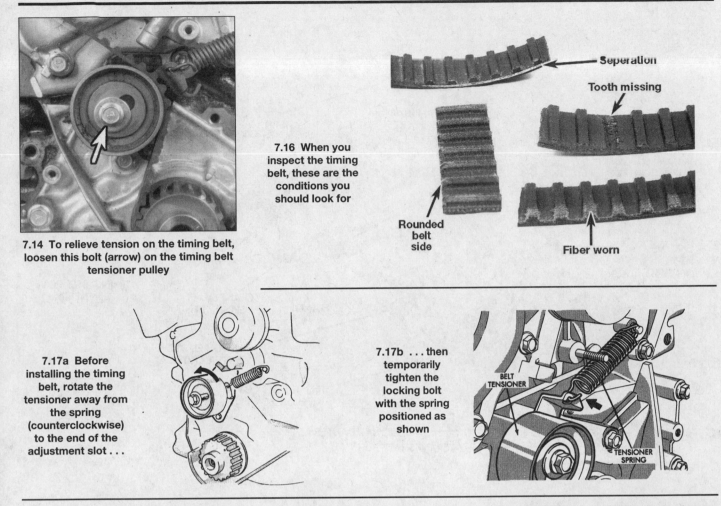

7.14 To relieve tension on the timing belt, loosen this bolt (arrow) on the timing belt tensioner pulley

7.16 When you inspect the timing belt, these are the conditions you should look for

Seperation

Tooth missing

Rounded belt side

Fiber worn

7.17a Before installing the timing belt, rotate the tensioner away from the spring (counterclockwise) to the end of the adjustment slot . . .

7.17b . . . then temporarily tighten the locking bolt with the spring positioned as shown

BELT TENSIONER

TENSIONER SPRING

crankshaft gear off the timing marks. Install the timing belt with the arrow pointing away from the engine.

20   Align the factory-made white lines on the timing belt with the punch mark on each of the camshaft sprockets and the crankshaft sprocket. Make sure all three sets of timing marks are properly aligned (**see illustration 7.23**). **Note:** *Be sure to install the*

crankshaft sprocket flange on the crankshaft gear (**see illustration 7.8**).

Adjustment

Refer to illustrations 7.23 and 7.25

21   Loosen the tensioner nut and let the tensioner assembly spring toward the belt - the spring tensioner will automatically apply the proper amount of tension to the belt.

22   Slowly turn the crankshaft clockwise

two full revolutions, returning the number one piston to TDC on the compression stroke. **Caution:** *If excessive resistance is felt while turning the crankshaft, it's an indication that the pistons are coming into contact with the valves. Go back over the procedure to correct the situation before going on.*

23   Make sure all the timing marks are still aligned properly (**see illustration**). Tighten

7.23 After turning the crankshaft two full revolutions and returning the number one piston to TDC, the timing belt and marks should look like this - if they don't, loosen the tensioner pulley, remove the belt, realign the marks and reinstall the belt

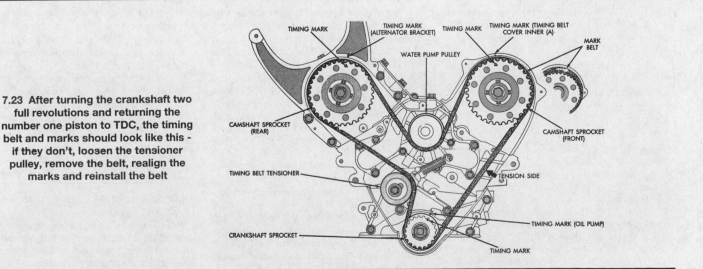

TIMING MARK

TIMING MARK (ALTERNATOR BRACKET)

TIMING MARK

TIMING MARK (TIMING BELT COVER INNER (A))

MARK BELT

WATER PUMP PULLEY

CAMSHAFT SPROCKET (REAR)

CAMSHAFT SPROCKET (FRONT)

TIMING BELT TENSIONER

TENSION SIDE

TIMING MARK (OIL PUMP)

CRANKSHAFT SPROCKET

TIMING MARK

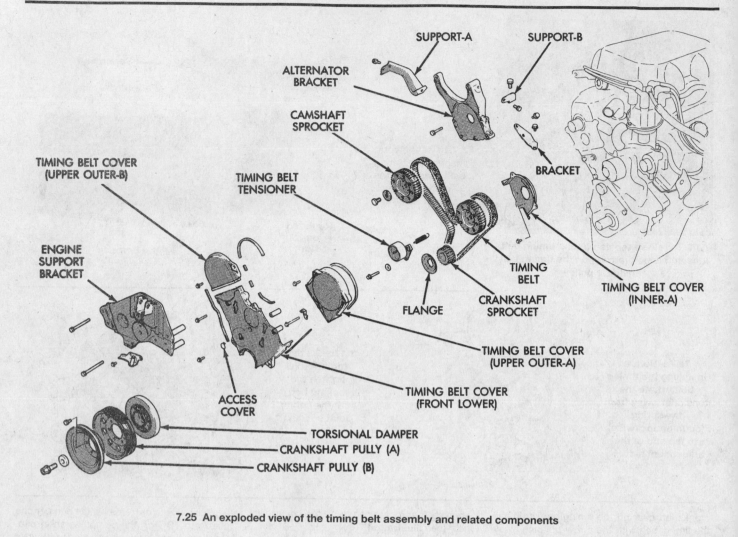

7.25 An exploded view of the timing belt assembly and related components

the tensioner bolt to the torque in this Chapter's Specifications while keeping the tensioner steady with your hand.

24   Check the deflection of the timing belt by observing the force the tensioner pulley applies to the timing belt. If the belt seems loose, replace the tensioner spring.

25   Installation of the remaining components is the reverse of removal. Refer to the appropriate sections **(see illustration)**.

8   Crankshaft front oil seal - replacement

Refer to illustrations 8.3, 8.4, 8.7, 8.8a and 8.8b

1   Disconnect the cable from the negative terminal of the battery.

2   Remove the drivebelts (see Chapter 1), crankshaft pulley (see Section 6) and timing belt (see Section 7).

3   You should be able to slide the crankshaft sprocket **(see illustration)** off by hand. If the sprocket is stuck, wedge two screwdrivers behind the crankshaft sprocket and carefully pry the sprocket off the crankshaft. Some crankshaft sprockets can be pried off easily with screwdrivers. Others are more difficult to remove because corrosion fuses them onto the crankshaft. If the sprocket on your engine is difficult to pry off, be very careful not to damage the oil pump with the screwdrivers.

4   If the sprocket won't come loose, drill and tap two holes into the face of the sprocket and use a bolt-type puller to pull it off the crankshaft **(see illustration)**. **Caution:** *Do not reuse a drilled sprocket - replace it.*

5   Remove the timing belt guide plate.

6   Carefully pry the oil seal out with a screwdriver or seal removal tool. Don't scratch or nick the crankshaft in the process!

7   Before installation, apply a coat of multi-purpose grease to the inside of the seal **(see illustration)**.

8   Fabricate a seal installation tool with a short length of pipe of equal or slightly smaller than the outside diameter of the seal itself. File the end of the pipe that will bear down on the seal until it's free of sharp edges. You'll also need a large washer, slightly larger in diameter than the pipe, on which the bolt head can seat **(see illustra-tion)**. Install the oil seal by pressing it into position with the seal installation tool **(see illustration)**. When you see and feel the seal stop moving, don't turn the bolt any more, you'll damage the seal.

9   Slide the timing belt guide plate onto the nose of the crankshaft.

10   Make sure the Woodruff key is in place in the crankshaft.

11   Apply a thin coat of assembly lube to the inside of the timing belt sprocket and slide it onto the crankshaft.

12   Installation of the remaining components is the reverse of removal. See Section 7 for the timing belt installation and adjustment procedure. Tighten all bolts to the torque in this Chapter's Specifications.

9   Camshaft oil seal - replacement

Refer to illustrations 9.3, 9.4a, 9.4b, 9.5a, 9.5b, 9.6, 9.7a and 9.7b

Note: *The 3.0L engine is equipped with two camshaft oil seals on the front (timing belt end) as well as two camshaft oil plugs on the rear (transaxle end) of the engine.*

8.3 If you are unable to pull the crankshaft sprocket off by hand, try to lever it off with a pair of small prybars

8.4 If the crankshaft sprocket is drilled and tapped with two holes, remove the sprocket with a bolt-type puller

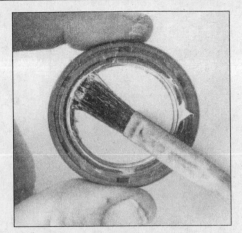

8.7 Apply a film of grease to the lips of the new seal before installing it - if you apply a small amount of grease to the outer edge, it will be easier to push into the bore

8.8a Fabricate a seal installation tool from a piece of pipe and a large washer . . .

8.8b . . . and press the seal into the bore - the pipe must bear against the outer edge of the seal as the bolt is tightened

9.3 Fabricate a sprocket holding tool from a piece of angle iron and a couple of bolts to lock the camshaft sprocket in place while you loosen the retaining bolt

1   Disconnect the cable from the negative terminal of the battery.
2   Remove the drivebelts (see Chapter 1), crankshaft pulley (see Section 6) and timing belt (see Section 7).
3   Fabricate a camshaft sprocket holding tool from a piece of angle iron and a couple of large bolts that will fit through the holes in the sprocket. Lock the camshaft sprocket in place and loosen the sprocket retaining bolt **(see illustration)**. When the bolt is out, the sprocket can be removed by hand. **Note:** *Don't mix up the camshaft sprockets. If you're removing both sprockets, mark each one with an "F" (front, radiator side) or an "R" (rear, firewall side). They must be installed on the same cam from which they were removed.*
4   To replace the seal for the front camshaft, remove the inner timing belt cover **(see illustration)**. To remove the seal for the rear camshaft, remove the alternator bracket **(see illustration)**.

9.4a To replace the seal on the front camshaft, remove the inner timing cover bolts (arrows) and remove the cover

9.4b To remove the seal on the rear camshaft, remove the camshaft sprocket, the alternator bracket bolts (arrows) and remove the bracket

9.5a To remove the distributor drive adapter, remove the distributor hold-down nut (upper arrow), remove the distributor and remove the three adapter retaining bolts (arrows)

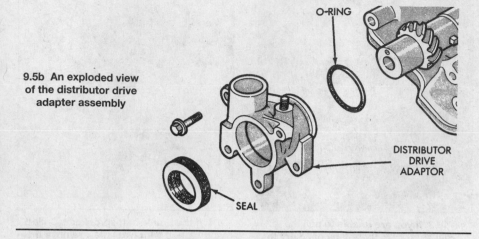

9.5b An exploded view of the distributor drive adapter assembly

O-RING

DISTRIBUTOR DRIVE ADAPTOR

SEAL

9.6 To extract a camshaft seal, drill a couple of small holes in the old seal, thread a pair of sheetmetal screws into the holes and pry the seal out with a screwdriver and a claw hammer

5   To replace the seal on the front camshaft, it's a good idea to replace the O-ring between the distributor drive adapter and the cylinder head. Remove the distributor (see Chapter 5) and the adapter **(see illustrations)**. **Note:** *If you remove the adapter, skip the following Steps describing on-vehicle seal replacement.* Pry out the old seal, install a new seal with the adapter on the bench, reattach the adapter, tighten the bolts securely, and install the distributor.

6   If you're replacing a rear seal or you do not want to remove the distributor drive adapter, drill a couple of small holes in the old seal, thread a pair of sheetmetal screws into the holes, then carefully remove the old oil seal with a screwdriver and a claw hammer **(see illustration)**. Don't nick or scratch the camshaft in the process.

7   There are several ways to install the new seal. Fabricate a seal installation tool as described in Section 8 or use a very large socket with an inside diameter large enough to clear the nose of the camshaft and carefully drive the seal into place **(see illustrations)**. Remove the sprocket positioning pin from the nose of the cam, if necessary, to

prevent damaging the pin.

8   If you replaced the front cam seal, reinstall the inner timing belt cover.

9   When you install the sprocket, make sure the R or F mark faces out! The side of the pulley with the deep recess must face the engine, which means the shallow recess must face out.

10   Use your sprocket holding tool to tighten the bolt to the torque in this Chapter's Specifications.

11   Installation of the remaining components is the reverse of removal.

10   Rocker arm and hydraulic valve lash adjusters - check, removal, inspection, and installation

Check

Refer to illustration 10.1

1   Check the hydraulic lash adjusters for freeplay by inserting a small wire through the air bleed hole in the rocker arm while lightly pushing the check ball down **(see illustration)**.

9.7a You can press a new seal into place with a section of pipe and a bolt of the proper size and thread pitch (don't let the camshaft turn as the bolt is tightened)

9.7b As a last resort, you can also drive a cam seal into place with a hammer and a large socket, but make sure you don't damage the sprocket positioning pin on the end of the camshaft

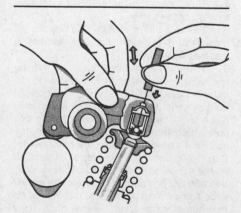

10.1 When performing the freeplay test, make sure the adjuster that's being tested has the corresponding camshaft lobe pointing away from the rocker arm (closed valve)

10.4 Loosen the bolts for the rocker arm shafts a little at a time in the sequence shown

10.6a Before you lift the rocker assembly off the cylinder head, make sure you tape the hydraulic lash adjusters into their bores in the tips of the rocker arms, or they'll fall out

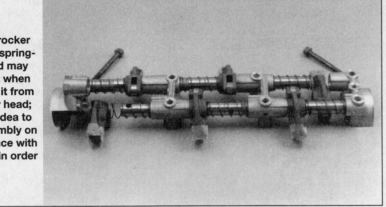

10.6b The rocker assembly is spring-loaded, and may come apart when you remove it from the cylinder head; it's a good idea to set the assembly on a clean surface with all the parts in order

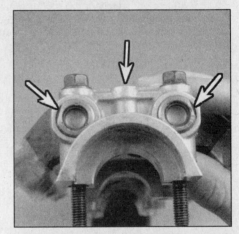

10.6c Each bearing cap should be marked ("1,""2", etc.) listing its position on the cylinder head (center arrow), if the number is missing, make one with a scribe or punch - also note the flat space (left and right arrows); when you reassemble the rocker assembly, position the flats as shown

2   Lightly hold the check ball down and move the rocker arm up and down to check for freeplay. There should be a small amount of movement. If there is no freeplay, replace the adjuster with a new unit.

Removal

Refer to illustrations 10.4, 10.6a, 10.6b and 10.6c

3   Position the engine at TDC for the number 1 cylinder (see Chapter 2D). Remove the valve cover (see Section 3).
4   Loosen the rocker arm shaft bolts **(see illustration)** in two or three stages, working from the ends toward the middle of the shafts. **Caution:** *Some of the valves will be open when you loosen the rocker arm shaft bolts and the rocker arm shafts will be under a certain amount of valve spring pressure. The bolts must be loosened gradually. Loosening a bolt all at once near a rocker arm under spring pressure could bend or break the rocker arm shaft.*
5   Prior to removal, scribe or paint identifying marks on the rocker arms to ensure they will be installed in their original locations.
6   Remove the bolts and lift off the rocker arm shaft assemblies and hydraulic valve lash adjusters one at a time. Lay them down

on a workbench in the same relationship to each other that they're in when installed. They must be reinstalled on the same cylinder head. Note the location of the stamped bearing cap number and the position of the notches **(see illustrations)**.

Inspection

Refer to illustration 10.8

7   Check the rocker arm tip, roller, and lash adjuster pocket for wear. Replace them if wear or damage is found.
8   Inspect each lash adjuster **(see illustration)** carefully for signs of wear and damage, particularly on the ball tip that contacts the rocker arm. The hydraulic lash adjusters frequently become clogged. Replace them if you're concerned about their condition or if the engine is exhibiting valve "tapping" noises.

Installation

Refer to illustrations 10.10a, 10.10b and 10.10c

9   The lash adjusters must be partially full of engine oil - indicated by little or no plunger action when the adjuster is depressed. If there's excessive plunger travel, place the rocker assembly into clean engine oil and

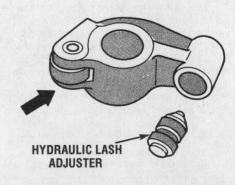

HYDRAULIC LASH ADJUSTER

10.8 The hydraulic lash adjusters are precision units installed in the machined opening in the rocker arm assemblies

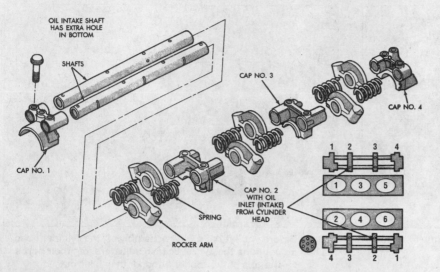

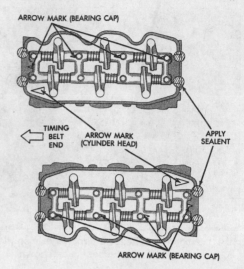

10.10a An exploded view of the rocker arm assembly - note that bearing cap No. 2 on each cylinder head must be in the proper position to ensure that the rocker assembly receives oil from the cylinder head oil galley directly below the No. 2 cap

10.10b The arrows on the bearing caps should point in the same direction as the arrows on the cylinder heads

10.10c Using an inch-pound torque wrench, tighten the rocker arm assembly bolt pairs in the exact opposite order in which you loosened them

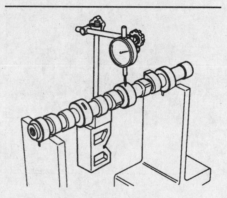

11.7 You'll need a dial indicator and a set of V-blocks to measure the camshaft runout

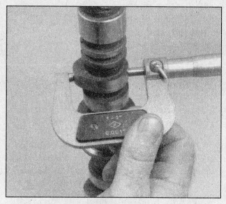

11.8 Use a micrometer to measure cam lobe height

pump the plunger until the plunger travel is eliminated. **Note:** *If the plunger still travels with the rocker arm when full of oil, it's defective, and the rocker arm assembly must be replaced.*

10   Installation of the remaining components is the reverse of removal. **Note:** Be sure the arrows stamped into the cylinder head and the bearing caps **(see illustrations)** are pointing in the same direction. Tighten the rocker arm shaft bolts, in several steps, to the torque in this Chapter's Specifications following the reverse of the loosening sequence **(see illustration 10.4)**.

11   Camshaft(s) - removal, inspection, and installation

Removal

1   Disconnect the cable from the negative battery terminal. Position the engine at TDC for the number 1 cylinder (see Chapter 2D).

2   Remove the timing belt and camshaft sprocket(s) (see Section 7). If you're removing the rear (firewall side) camshaft, remove the alternator and alternator bracket. If you're removing the front (radiator side) camshaft, remove the inner timing belt cover and the distributor drive adapter (see Section 9).

3   Remove the rocker arm assembly (see Section 10).

4   Carefully pry the camshaft plugs from the rear section (transaxle end) of the cylinder head. Don't scratch or nick the camshaft in the process!

5   Carefully lift the camshaft from the cylinder head.

Inspection

Refer to illustrations 11.7 and 11.8

6   Check the camshaft bearing surfaces for pitting, score marks, galling, and abnormal wear. If the bearing surfaces are damaged, the cylinder head will have to be replaced.

7   Check camshaft runout by placing the

camshaft between two V-blocks and set up a dial indicator on the center journal **(see illustration)**. Zero the dial indicator. Turn the camshaft slowly and note the total indicator reading. Record your readings and compare them with the runout in this Chapter's Specifications. If the runout exceeds the specified runout, replace the camshaft.

8   Check the camshaft lobe height by measuring each lobe with a micrometer **(see illustration)**. Compare the measurement to the cam lobe height in this Chapter's Specifications. Subtract the measured cam lobe height from the specified height to compute wear on the cam lobes. Compare it to the specified wear limit. If it's greater than the specified wear limit, replace the camshaft.

9   Inspect the contact and sliding surfaces of each hydraulic lash adjuster for scoring or damage (see Section 10). Replace defective parts.

10   Check the rocker arms and shafts for abnormal wear, pits, galling, score marks, and rough spots. Don't attempt to restore rocker arms by grinding the pad surfaces. Replace defective parts.

Installation

11   Lubricate the camshaft bearing journals and lobes with moly-base grease or engine assembly lube, then install it carefully in the cylinder head. Don't scratch the bearing surfaces with the cam lobes!

12   Install the alternator bracket.

13   Install the distributor drive adapter bolts and tighten them to the torque in this Chapter's Specifications.

14   Install the inner timing belt cover.

15   Make sure the mark on the crankshaft sprocket is still aligned with its mark on the oil pump. Slide the camshaft sprockets onto the camshafts and align the marks on the sprockets with their corresponding marks on the cylinder heads. Install the bolts and tighten them to the torque listed in this Chapter's Specifications.

16   Install the timing belt (see Section 7).

17   Installation of the remaining components is the reverse of removal.

12   Valve spring, retainer and seals - replacement

This procedure is essentially the same as for the 2.4 liter four-cylinder engines. Refer to Chapter 2A, Section 11, and follow the procedure outlined there.

13   Cylinder heads - removal and installation

Note: *Allow the engine to cool completely before beginning this procedure.*

Removal

1   Position the engine at TDC for the number 1 cylinder (see Chapter 2D). Drain the engine coolant (see Chapter 1).

2   Remove the timing belt cover, timing belt (see Section 7), and the camshaft sprockets (see Section 9).

3   Remove the intake manifold (see Section 4).

4   Remove the rocker arms components and hydraulic lash adjusters (see Section 10).

5   Remove the exhaust manifolds (see Section 5). **Note:** *If desired, each manifold may remain attached to the cylinder head until after the cylinder head is removed from the engine. However, the manifold must be disconnected from the exhaust system and/or crossover pipe.*

Front (radiator side) cylinder head

6   Remove the distributor (see Chapter 5).

7   Remove the air conditioning compressor from the bracket without disconnecting any hoses (see Chapter 3) and set it aside. It may be helpful to secure the compressor to the vehicle with rope or wire to make sure it doesn't hang by its hoses.

8   Remove the air conditioning compressor bracket (see Chapter 3).

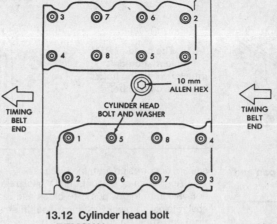

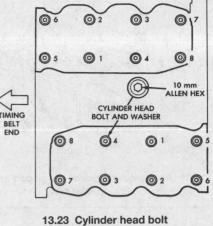

13.12 Cylinder head bolt REMOVAL sequence

13.23 Cylinder head bolt TIGHTENING sequence

Rear (firewall side) cylinder head

9   Remove the heater hoses and brackets from the transaxle end of the cylinder head.

10   Remove the air cleaner housing from the engine compartment (see Chapter 4).

11   Remove the alternator (see Chapter 5) and bracket from the cylinder head.

Both cylinder heads

Refer to illustration 13.12

12   Loosen the cylinder head bolts with a 10 mm Allen hex-bit in 1/4-turn increments until they can be removed by hand. Follow the proper numerical sequence for removal **(see illustration)**.

13   Cylinder head bolts must be reinstalled in their original locations. To keep them from getting mixed up, store them in cardboard holders marked to indicate the bolt pattern. Mark the holders F (front) and R (rear) and indicate the timing belt end of the engine.

14   Lift the cylinder head off the block. If resistance is felt, dislodge the cylinder head by striking it with a wood block and hammer. If prying is required, pry only on a casting protrusion - be very careful not to damage the cylinder head or block!

15   If necessary, remove the camshafts (see Section 11).

Installation

Refer to illustration 13.23

16   Remove all traces of old gasket material from the cylinder heads and the engine block. The mating surfaces of the cylinder heads and block must be perfectly clean when the cylinder heads are installed.

17   Use a gasket scraper to remove all traces of carbon and old gasket material, then clean the mating surfaces with lacquer thinner or acetone. If there's oil on the mating surfaces when the cylinder heads are installed, the gaskets may not seal correctly and leaks may develop. Use a vacuum cleaner to remove debris that falls into the cylinders.

18   Check the block and cylinder head mating surfaces for nicks, deep scratches, and

other damage. If damage is slight, it can be removed with a file - if it's excessive, machining may be the only alternative.

19   Use a tap of the correct size to chase the threads in the cylinder head bolt holes. Mount each bolt in a vise and run a die down the threads to remove corrosion and restore the threads. Dirt, corrosion, sealant, and damaged threads will affect torque readings. Ensure that the threaded holes in the block are clean and dry.

20   Position the new gaskets over the dowel pins on the block.

21   Carefully position the cylinder heads on the block without disturbing the gaskets.

22   Lightly oil the threads and install the bolts in their original locations. Tighten them finger tight.

23   Tighten the bolts in three steps, in the proper sequence **(see illustration)**, to the torque in this Chapter's Specifications.

24   Installation of the remaining components is the reverse of removal.

25   Add coolant and change the engine oil and filter (see Chapter 1).

26   Start the engine and check carefully for oil and coolant leaks.

14   Oil pan - removal and installation

Removal

Refer to illustration 14.11

1   Disconnect the cable from the negative terminal of the battery.

2   Raise the vehicle and support it securely on jackstands.

3   Remove the vehicle splash pan.

4   Drain the engine oil and install a new oil filter (see Chapter 1).

5   Unbolt the exhaust pipe from the rear manifold (see Section 5).

6   Support the engine/transaxle securely from above with an engine hoist or preferably, a three-bar engine support fixture (available at most automotive retail parts stores or equipment rental yards). **Warning:** *Be abso-*

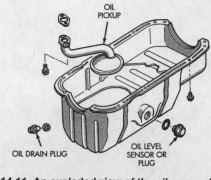

14.11 An exploded view of the oil pan and oil pick-up assembly

14.14 The bead of RTV sealant shouldn't interfere with the holes for the oil pan bolts

lutely certain the engine/transaxle is securely supported! DO NOT place any part of your body under the engine/transaxle - it could crush you if the means of support fails!

7   Unbolt the engine mounts (see Section 18). Raise the engine/transaxle assembly to provide clearance for oil pan removal.

8   Remove the oil pan bolts.

9   Remove the oil pan. Don't pry between the pan and block or damage to the sealing surfaces may result and oil leaks could develop. If the pan is stuck, dislodge it with a hammer and a block of wood.

10   Use a gasket scraper to remove all traces of old gasket material and sealant from the block and pan. Clean the mating surfaces with lacquer thinner or acetone.

11   Unbolt the oil pick-up tube and screen assembly **(see illustration)**.

Installation

Refer to illustrations 14.14 and 14.15

12   Replace the gasket on the flange of the oil pick-up tube and reinstall the tube. Tighten the pick-up tube bolts to the torque in this Chapter's Specifications.

13   Ensure that the threaded holes in the block are clean (use a tap to remove any sealant or corrosion from the threads).

14   Apply a small amount of RTV sealant (or equivalent) to the oil pump-to-block and rear seal retainer-to-block junctions **(see illustration)** and apply a thin continuous bead along the circumference of the oil pan flange. **Note:** *Allow the sealant to "set-up" (slightly harden) before installing the gasket.*

15   Install the oil pan and tighten the bolts in three or four steps, in the sequence shown **(see illustration)**, to the torque in this Chapter's Specifications.

16   Installation of the remaining components is the reverse of removal.

17   Allow at least 30 minutes for the sealant to dry.

18   Fill the crankcase with oil (see Chapter 1), start the engine, and check for oil pressure and leaks.

15   Oil pump - removal, inspection and installation

Removal

Refer to illustration 15.3

1   Remove the timing belt (see Section 7) and the crankshaft sprocket (see Section 8). Remove the oil pan and pick-up tube (see Section 14).

2   Unbolt the power steering pump (see Chapter 10) without disconnecting the hoses.

Remove the power steering pump bracket.

3   Remove the oil pump bolts from the front of the engine **(see illustration)**.

4   Use a block of wood and a hammer to break the oil pump loose.

5   Pull out on the oil pump to remove it from the engine block.

6   Use a scraper to remove old gasket material and sealant from the oil pump and engine block mating surfaces. Clean the mating surfaces with lacquer thinner or acetone.

Inspection

Refer to illustrations 15.7, 15.9, 15.10a, 15.10b, 15.10c, 15.10d, 15.10e and 15.10f

7   Remove the screws holding the rear cover to the oil pump **(see illustration)**.

8   Clean all components with solvent, then inspect them for wear and damage.

9   Remove the oil pressure relief valve plug, washer, spring, and valve (plunger) **(see illustration)**. Check the oil pressure relief valve sliding surface and valve spring. If either the spring or the valve is damaged, they must be replaced as a set.

10   Check the following clearances with a feeler gauge **(see illustrations)** and compare the measurements to the clearances in this Chapter's Specifications:

   a) *Case-to-outer rotor*
   b) *Rotor end clearance*
   c) *Case-to-inner rotor*

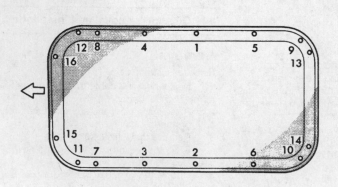

14.15 Oil pan bolt tightening sequence

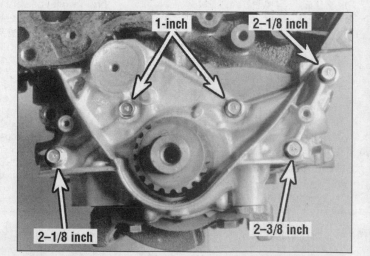

15.3 To remove the oil pump assembly from the engine, detach the camshaft sprocket, then remove these bolts (arrows) - note the correct locations for the different length bolts for reassembly

15.7 The screws retaining the pump cover are screwed on tightly at the factory - you'll probably need to use an impact driver to break them loose (otherwise, you'll strip out the heads)

15.9 An exploded view of the oil pump assembly

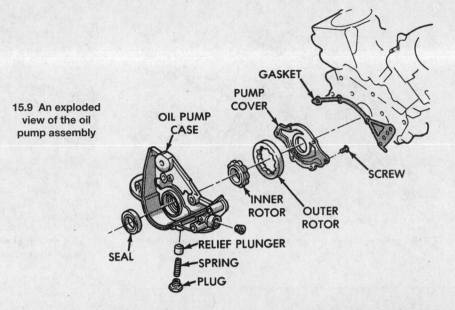

GASKET

PUMP COVER

OIL PUMP CASE

SCREW

INNER ROTOR

OUTER ROTOR

RELIEF PLUNGER

SEAL

SPRING

PLUG

15.10a Use a feeler gauge to determine the clearance between the outer rotor and the case

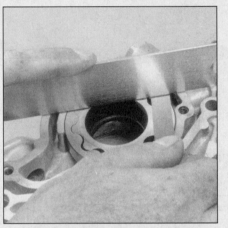

15.10b Use a straightedge and a feeler gauge to determine the rotor end clearance (the clearance between the rotor face and the pump cover)

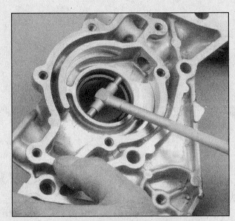

15.10c Determining the third measurement, the clearance between the inner rotor and the case, is trickier: First, measure the inside diameter of the inner rotor bore in the case with a bore gauge . . .

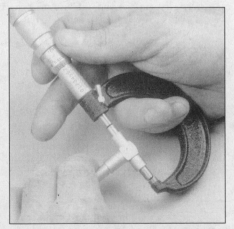

15.10d . . . measure the bore gauge with a micrometer . . .

15.10e . . . measure the diameter of the inner rotor with a micrometer . . .

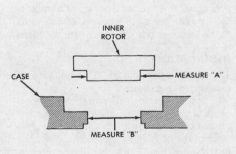

INNER ROTOR

CASE

MEASURE "A"

MEASURE "B"

15.10f . . . and subtract measurement "A" from measurement "B" (I.D. of the rotor bore in the case minus the O.D. of the inner rotor)

17.3 To remove the rear main oil seal retainer, remove these five bolts

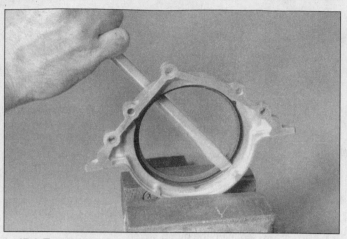

17.4 To remove the old seal from the rear main seal retainer, mount the retainer in bench vise and pry out the old seal with a screwdriver

17.5 To install the new seal into the seal retainer, lay the retainer flat on a clean work space and drive the new seal into place with a block of wood and hammer

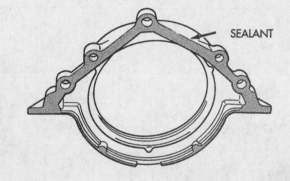
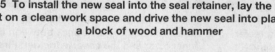

17.6 Before installing the rear main oil seal retainer onto the block, coat the mating surfaces of the retainer with RTV sealant

If any of the clearances are excessive, replace the entire oil pump assembly.

11 Pack the oil pump cavities with petroleum jelly to prime it. Assemble the oil pump and tighten the screws to the torque in this Chapter's Specifications. Install the oil pressure relief valve, spring, and washer, then tighten the oil pressure relief valve plug to the torque in this Chapter's Specifications.

Installation

12 Apply a thin film of RTV sealant to the new oil pump gasket.

13 Installation of the remaining components is the reverse of removal. Align the flats on the crankshaft with the flats in the inner rotor of the oil pump. Tighten all fasteners to the torque in this Chapter's Specifications.

16 Driveplate - removal and installation

This procedure is essentially the same for all engines. Refer to Chapter 2A, Sec-

tion 15, and follow the procedure outlined there, but use the bolt torque in this Chapter's Specifications.

17 Rear main oil seal - replacement

Refer to illustrations 17.3, 17.4, 17.5 and 17.6

Note: *It's possible to pry out the old seal and install a new one without removing the seal retainer, but we don't recommend it, because it's easy to nick or scratch the crankshaft or the seal bore. If you're not extremely careful, you can damage the new seal lip during installation. However, if circumstances prevent removing the oil pan and the retainer, use the procedure outlined in Chapter 2A, Section 16 (but be advised that the following method is the recommended way to change the rear main seal).*

1   Remove the transaxle (see Chapter 7).
2   Remove the oil pan (See Section 14).
3   Remove the rear main oil seal retainer bolts and the retainer **(see illustration)**.

4   Put the retainer in a bench vise and pry out the old seal **(see illustration)**.
5   To install the new seal, lay the retainer on a clean, flat surface and carefully drive in the seal with a block of wood and a hammer **(see illustration)**.
6   Coat the mating surface of the retainer with RTV sealant **(see illustration)**, apply a light coating of clean oil to the seal lip, install the retainer, and tighten the retainer bolts to the torque in this Chapter's Specifications.
7   Installation of the remaining components is the reverse of removal.

18 Engine mounts - check and replacement

This procedure is essentially the same for all engines. See Chapter 2A , Section 17, and follow the procedure outlined there.

Chapter 2 Part C
3.3L and 3.8L V6 engines

Contents

	Section
Camshaft and bearings - removal, inspection and installation	See Chapter 2D
Check Engine light	See Chapter 6
Crankshaft front oil seal - replacement	9
Crankshaft pulley - removal and installation	6
Cylinder compression check	See Chapter 2D
Cylinder heads - removal and installation	13
Drivebelt check, adjustment and replacement	See Chapter 1
Driveplate - removal and installation	17
Engine mounts - check and replacement	19
Engine oil and filter change	See Chapter 1
Engine overhaul - general information	See Chapter 2D
Engine - removal and installation	See Chapter 2D
Exhaust manifolds - removal and installation	5
General information	1
Hydraulic roller lifters - removal, inspection and installation	11

	Section
Intake manifold - removal and installation	4
Oil cooler - removal and installation (2001 and later models)	16
Oil pan - removal and installation	14
Oil pump - removal, inspection and installation	15
Rear main oil seal - replacement	18
Repair operations possible with the engine in the vehicle	2
Rocker arms and pushrods - removal, inspection and installation	10
Spark plug replacement	See Chapter 1
Timing chain and sprockets - removal, inspection and installation	8
Timing chain cover - removal and installation	7
Top Dead Center (TDC) for number one piston - locating	See Chapter 2D
Vacuum gauge diagnostics checks	See Chapter 2D
Valve cover(s) - removal and installation	3
Valve springs, retainers and seals - replacement	12
Water pump - removal and installation	See Chapter 3

Specifications

General

Bore	
3.3L	3.66 inches
3.8L	3.779 inches
Stroke	
3.3L	3.188 inches
3.8L	3.425 inches
Compression ratio	
3.3L	8.9:1
3.8L	9.6:1
Displacement	
3.3L	201 cubic inches
3.8L	231 cubic inches
Cylinder numbers (drivebelt end-to-transmission end)	
Front bank (radiator side)	2-4-6
Rear bank	1-3-5
Firing order	1-2-3-4-5-6
Oil pressure	
At idle speed	5 psi (minimum)
At 3000 rpm	30 to 80 psi

30011-2C-SPECS HAYNES

Cylinder and coil terminal locations

Camshaft

Bearing journal diameter
    No. 1 .... 1.997 to 1.999 inches
    No. 2 .... 1.981 to 1.983 inches
    No. 3 .... 1.966 to 1.968 inches
    No. 4 .... 1.950 to 1.952 inches
Bearing bore diameter
    No. 1 .... 2.001 to 2.000 inches
    No. 2 .... 1.985 to 1.984 inches
    No. 3 .... 1.970 to 1.969 inches
    No. 4 .... 1.954 to 1.953 inches
Bearing clearance .... 0.001 to 0.003 inch
End play .... 0.005 to 0.012 inch
Lobe lift .... 0.400 inch

Oil pump

Cover warpage limit .... 0.001 inch
Outer rotor thickness (minimum) .... 0.301 inch
Inner rotor thickness (minimum) .... 0.301 inch
Rotor-to-pump cover clearance .... 0.004 inch
Outer rotor-to-housing clearance .... 0.015 inch
Inner rotor-to-outer rotor lobe clearance .... 0.008 inch

Torque specifications

	Ft-lbs (unless otherwise indicated)
Camshaft sprocket bolt	40
Camshaft thrust plate bolt	105 in-lbs
Crankshaft pulley bolt	40
Cylinder head bolts	
Step 1 (bolts 1 through 8)	45
Step 2 (bolts 1 through 8)	65
Step 3 (bolts 1 through 8)	65
Step 4 (bolts 1 through 8)	Tighten an additional 90-degrees (1/4 turn)
Step 5 (bolt 9)	25
Driveplate-to-crankshaft bolts	70
Engine mount plate bolts	40
Exhaust manifold-to-cylinder head bolts	17
Exhaust manifold-to-catalytic converter bolts (2001 and later)	27
Exhaust crossover bolts	
1996 through 2000	25
2001 and later	30
Hydraulic lifter retaining bolts	105 in-lbs
Intake manifold gasket retaining bolts	105 in-lbs
Intake manifold-to-cylinder head	200 in-lbs
Oil cooler fitting	20
Oil pan drain plug	20
Oil pan bolts/nuts	105 in-lbs
Oil pump pick-up tube mounting bolts	21
Oil pump cover (plate) bolts	105 in-lbs
Valve cover-to-cylinder head bolts	105 in-lbs
Rear main oil seal retainer bolts	105 in-lbs
Rocker arm shaft bolts	
1996 through 2000	21
2001 and later	17
Timing chain cover bolts	
M8	20
M10	40
Timing chain snubber (guide)	105 in-lbs
Timing chain sprocket-to-camshaft bolt	35
Water pump bolts	105 in-lbs

3.4 Remove the valve cover mounting bolts (arrows)

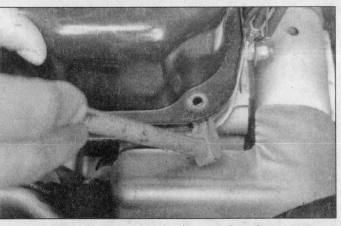

3.5 Be careful not to bend or damage the valve cover or cylinder head when prying

1 General information

Chapter 2C is devoted to in-vehicle repair procedures for the 3.3L and 3.8L V6 engines. These engines utilize a cast-iron engine block with six cylinders arranged in a "V" shape with a 60-degree angle between the two banks. The overhead valve aluminum cylinder heads are equipped with replaceable valve guides and seats. An in-block camshaft, chain driven from the crankshaft, and hydraulic roller lifters actuate the valves through tubular pushrods.

Information concerning engine removal and installation and engine block and cylinder head overhaul can be found in Chapter 2D. The following repair procedures are based on the assumption that the engine is installed in the vehicle. If the engine has been removed from the vehicle and mounted on a stand, many of the steps outlined in Chapter 2C do not apply.

The Specifications included in Chapter 2C apply only to the procedures contained in Chapter 2C. Chapter 2D contains the Specifications required for cylinder head and engine block building.

2 Repair operations possible with the engine in the vehicle

Many major repair operations can be done without removing the engine from the vehicle.

Clean the engine compartment and the exterior of the engine with degreaser before any work is done. It'll make the job easier and help keep dirt out of internal parts of the engine.

It may be helpful to remove the hood to improve engine access when repairs are performed (see Chapter 11). Cover the fenders to prevent damage to the paint. Special pads are available, but an old bedspread or blanket will also work.

If vacuum, exhaust, oil, or coolant leaks develop, indicating a need for gasket or seal replacement, the repairs can generally be done with the engine in the vehicle. The intake and exhaust manifold gaskets, timing chain cover gasket, oil pan gasket, crankshaft oil seals, and cylinder head gaskets are all accessible with the engine in the vehicle.

Exterior engine components, such as the intake and exhaust manifolds, the oil pan, the oil pump, the timing chain cover, the water pump, the starter motor, the alternator, and fuel system components can be removed for repair with the engine in the vehicle.

Cylinder heads can be removed without pulling the engine. Valve component servicing can also be done with the engine in the vehicle. Replacement of the timing chain and sprockets is also possible with the engine in the vehicle, but the camshaft <u>cannot</u> be removed with the engine in the vehicle.

Repair or replacement of piston rings, pistons, connecting rods, and rod bearings is possible with the engine in the vehicle, however, this practice is not recommended because of the cleaning and preparation work that must be done to the components.

3 Valve covers - removal and installation

Removal

Refer to illustrations 3.4 and 3.5

Front (radiator side) valve cover

1 Disconnect the negative battery cable.
2 Remove the ignition wires from the spark plugs (see Chapter 1). Label each wire before removal to ensure correct reinstallation.
3 Remove the crankcase vent hose from the valve cover.
4 Remove the valve cover bolts **(see illustration)**.
5 Remove the valve cover. **Note:** *If the valve cover sticks to the cylinder head, use a wood block and a hammer to dislodge it. If the valve cover still won't come loose, pry on it carefully, but don't distort the sealing flange* **(see illustration)**.

Rear (firewall side) valve cover

6 Disconnect the negative battery cable.
7 Remove the wiper unit (see Chapter 12).
8 Label and detach the vacuum lines from the throttle body.
9 Remove the serpentine drivebelt (see Chapter 1).
10 Remove the alternator (see Chapter 5).
11 Remove the ignition wires from the spark plugs (see Chapter 1). Label each wire before removal to ensure correct reinstallation.
12 Remove the ignition coil pack (see Chapter 5).
13 Remove the air intake plenum (see Chapter 4).
14 Remove the breather hose from the PCV valve.
15 Remove the valve cover bolts **(see illustration 3.4)**.
16 Detach the valve cover. **Note:** *If the valve cover sticks to the cylinder head, use a wood block and a hammer to dislodge it. If the valve cover still won't come loose, pry on it carefully, but don't distort the sealing flange* **(see illustration 3.5)**.

Installation

17 The mating surfaces of the cylinder heads and valve covers must be perfectly clean when the valve covers are installed. Use a gasket scraper to remove all traces of sealant or old gasket material, then clean the mating surfaces with lacquer thinner or acetone (if there's sealant or oil on the mating surfaces when the valve cover is installed, oil leaks may develop). Be extra careful not to nick or gouge the mating surfaces with the scraper.
18 Clean the mounting bolt threads with a die, if necessary, to remove corrosion and restore damaged threads. Use a tap to clean the threaded holes in the cylinder heads.
19 Place the valve cover and new gasket in position, then install the bolts. Tighten the bolts in several steps to the torque listed in this Chapter's Specifications.
20 Installation of the remaining components is the reverse of removal.
21 Start the engine and check carefully for oil leaks.

4.2 Disconnect the coolant bypass hose from the intake manifold near the thermostat housing

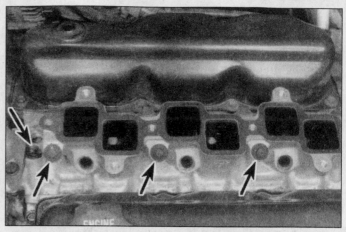

4.3a Remove the intake manifold bolts using a circular pattern, starting with the outer bolts first

4.3b Pry on the intake manifold only in the areas where the gasket mating surface will not get damaged

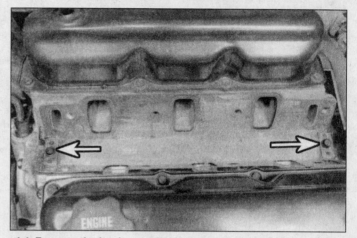

4.4 Remove the intake manifold gasket retainer screws (arrows)

4   Intake manifold - removal and installation

Removal (1996 through 2000 models)

Refer to illustrations 4.2, 4.3a, 4.3b and 4.4

1   Remove the intake manifold cover, the intake manifold plenum and the fuel rail and injectors (see Chapter 4).

2   Remove the upper radiator hose, bypass hose and rear intake manifold hose (see illustration).

3   Remove the intake manifold bolts, and the intake manifold (see illustration) and separate the intake manifold from the engine (see illustration). If the intake manifold is stuck, carefully pry on a casting protrusion - don't pry between the intake manifold and cylinder heads, as damage to the gasket sealing surfaces may result. If you're installing a new intake manifold, transfer all fittings and sensors to the new intake manifold.

4   Remove the intake manifold gasket retaining screws (see illustration) and clamps and lift the gasket from the engine block.

Installation (1996 through 2000 models)

Refer to illustration 4.7

Note: The mating surfaces of the cylinder heads, engine block, and intake manifold must be perfectly clean when the intake manifold is installed. Gasket removal solvents are available at most auto parts stores and may be helpful when removing old gasket material that's stuck to the cylinder heads and intake manifold (the intake manifold is made of aluminum - aggressive scraping can cause damage). Be sure to follow the directions printed on the solvent container.

5   Lift the old gasket off. Use a gasket scraper to remove all traces of sealant and old gasket material, then clean the mating surfaces with lacquer thinner or acetone. If there's old sealant or oil on the mating surfaces when the intake manifold is installed, oil or vacuum leaks may develop. Use a vacuum cleaner to remove gasket material that falls into the intake ports or the lifter valley.

6   Use a tap of the correct size to chase the threads in the bolt holes, then use compressed air (if available) to remove debris from the holes. Warning: Wear safety glasses or a face shield to protect your eyes when using compressed air!

7   Apply a 1/4-inch bead of RTV sealant or equivalent to the four cylinder head-to-engine block junctions (see illustration).

8   Install the intake manifold gasket and tighten the retainer screws.

9   Carefully lower the intake manifold into place and install the mounting bolts/nuts finger tight.

4.7 Apply RTV sealant to the corners of the cylinder head and engine block

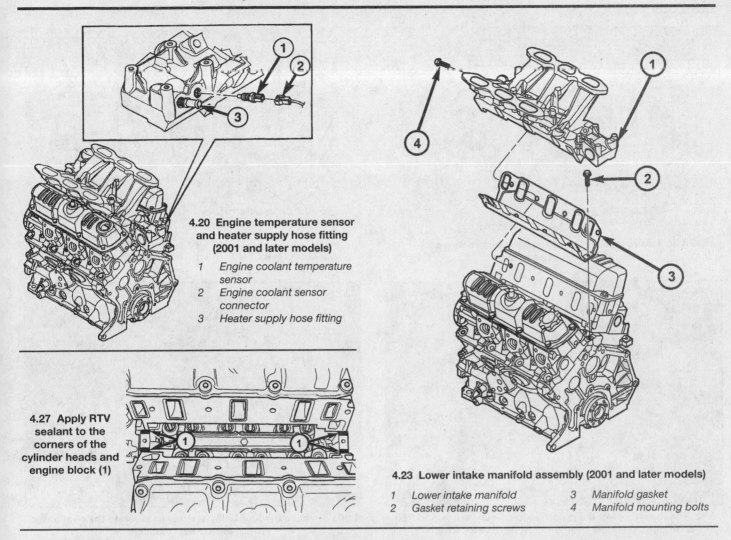

4.20 Engine temperature sensor and heater supply hose fitting (2001 and later models)

1 *Engine coolant temperature sensor*
2 *Engine coolant sensor connector*
3 *Heater supply hose fitting*

4.27 Apply RTV sealant to the corners of the cylinder heads and engine block (1)

4.23 Lower intake manifold assembly (2001 and later models)

1 *Lower intake manifold*
2 *Gasket retaining screws*
3 *Manifold gasket*
4 *Manifold mounting bolts*

10 Tighten the mounting bolts in three steps, working from the center out, in a criss-cross pattern, to the torque listed in this Chapter's Specifications.
11 Installation of the remaining components is the reverse of removal.
12 Change the oil and filter and refill the cooling system (see Chapter 1).
13 Start the engine and check for leaks.

Removal (2001 and later models)

Refer to illustrations 4.20 and 4.23
14 Relieve the system pressure (see Chapter 4).
15 Disconnect the cable from the negative terminal of the battery.
16 Drain the cooling system (see Chapter 3).
17 Remove the upper intake manifold (see Chapter 4).
18 Refer to Chapter 4 and disconnect the fuel hose quick disconnect fitting.
19 Remove the ignition coil pack and bracket (see Chapter 5).
20 Disconnect the heater supply hose and the engine temperature sensor **(see illustration)**.

21 Disconnect the fuel injector rail assembly (see Chapter 4).
22 Disconnect the upper radiator hose.
23 Remove the lower intake manifold bolts and the lower intake manifold and separate the lower intake manifold from the engine **(see illustration)**. If the lower intake manifold is stuck, carefully pry on the casting protrusion - don't pry between the lower intake manifold, and the cylinder heads, as damage to the gasket sealing surfaces may result. If you're installing a new lower intake manifold, transfer all fittings and sensors to the new lower intake manifold.
24 Remove the lower intake manifold gasket retaining screws and remove the gasket from the cylinder block **(see illustration 4.23)**.

Installation (2001 and later models)

Refer to illustration 4.27 and 4.30
Note: *The mating surfaces of the cylinder heads, cylinder block, and the intake manifold must be perfectly clean when the lower intake manifold is installed. Gasket removal solvents are available at most auto parts stores and may be helpful when removing old gasket*

material that's stuck to the cylinder heads, cylinder block and lower intake manifold (the lower intake manifold is made of aluminum - aggressive scrapping can cause damage). Be sure to follow the instructions printed on the solvent container.
25 Use a gasket scraper to remove all traces of sealant and old gasket material, then clean the mating surfaces with lacquer thinner or acetone. If there's old sealant or oil on the mating surfaces when the lower intake manifold is installed, oil or vacuum leaks may develop. Use a vacuum cleaner to remove gasket material that falls into the intake ports or the lifter valley.
26 Use a tap of the correct size to chase the threads in the bolt holes, then use compressed air (if available) to remove debris from the holes. **Warning:** *Wear safety glasses or a face shield to protect your eyes when using compressed air!*
27 Apply a 1/4-inch bead of RTV sealant or equivalent to the four cylinder heads-to-engine block junctions **(see illustration)**.
28 Install the lower intake gasket and tighten the retainer screws.
29 Carefully lower the lower intake manifold into place and install the mounting bolts finger-tight.

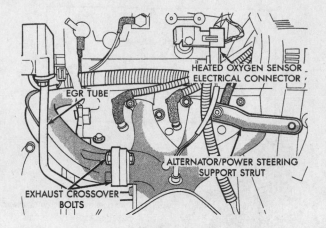

4.30 Lower intake manifold bolt tightening sequence (2001 and later models)

5.9 Disconnect the EGR tube from the exhaust manifold

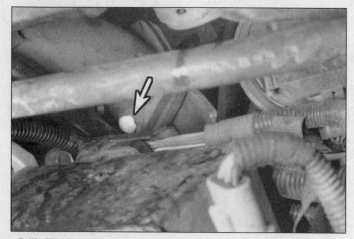

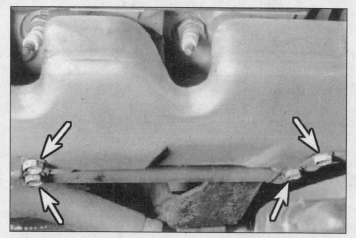

5.12 The lower bolt for the crossover pipe can be reached from under the engine compartment with an extension and swivel socket

5.15a Remove the four bolts (arrows) to separate the heat shield from the exhaust manifold

30   Tighten the mounting bolts in three steps, following the recommended tightening sequence **(see illustration)**, to the torque listed in this Chapter's Specifications.

5   Exhaust manifolds - removal and installation

Removal (1996 through 2000 models)

Refer to illustrations 5.9, 5.12 , 5.15a, 5.15b, 5.16 and 5.17

1   Disconnect the negative battery cable.
2   Remove the air cleaner assembly (see Chapter 4).
3   Let the engine cool completely, then drain the coolant (see Chapter 1) and disconnect the coolant bypass tube.
4   Remove the accessory drive belt (see Section 1).
5   Remove the alternator (see Chapter 5).
6   Raise the vehicle, support it securely on jackstands, and disconnect the exhaust pipe(s) from the exhaust manifold(s) at the flex-joint.

7   Disconnect the down stream oxygen sensor connector.
8   Lower the exhaust system to gain access to the rear exhaust manifold.
9   Disconnect the EGR tube from the exhaust manifold and the heated oxygen sensor lead wire **(see illustration)**.
10   Remove the heat shield from the rear engine mount.
11   Remove the alternator/power steering support strut **(see illustration 5.9)**.
12   Unbolt the exhaust crossover pipe **(see illustration 5.9)** where it joins the front exhaust manifold. **Note:** *The lower bolt is accessed from under the engine compartment* **(see illustration)**.
13   Disconnect the up stream oxygen sensor connector.
14   Remove the bolts attaching the rear exhaust manifold to the cylinder head, and remove the exhaust manifold.
15   Lower the vehicle and remove the screws attaching the front heat shield(s) to the exhaust manifold(s) **(see illustrations)**.
16   Remove the bolts fastening the crossover pipe to the front exhaust manifold **(see illustration)**.

17   Remove the mounting bolts and the exhaust manifold(s) from the cylinder head **(see illustration)**. Be sure to spray penetrating lubricant on the bolts and threads before attempting to remove them.

Installation (1996 through 2000 models)

18   Clean the mating surfaces to remove all traces of old gasket material, then inspect the exhaust manifold for distortion and cracks. Check for warpage with a precision straightedge held against the mating flange. If a feeler gauge thicker than 0.030-inch can be inserted between the straightedge and the flange surface, take the exhaust manifold to an automotive machine shop for resurfacing.
19   Place the exhaust manifold in position with a new gasket and install the bolts finger tight. **Note:** *Be sure to identify the exhaust manifold gaskets by the correct cylinder designation and the position of the exhaust ports on the gasket.*
20   Starting in the middle and working toward the ends, tighten the mounting bolts to the torque listed in this Chapter's Specifications.

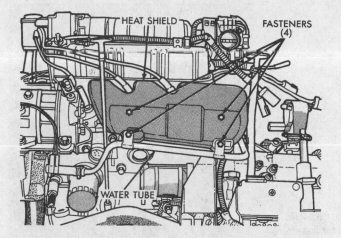

5.15b Remove the mounting bolts from the heat shield attached to the rear exhaust manifold

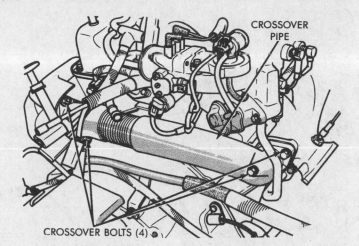

5.16 Remove the bolts from the crossover pipe

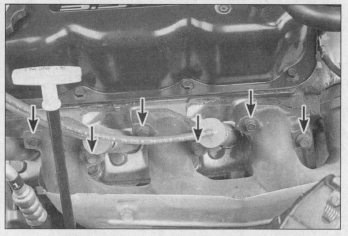

5.17 Remove the exhaust manifold bolts (arrows)

5.26 Remove the two crossover pipe mounting bolts

21   Installation of the remaining components is the reverse of removal.

22   Start the engine and check for exhaust leaks between the exhaust manifold and cylinder head and between the exhaust manifold and exhaust pipe.

Removal (2001 and later models)

Rear exhaust manifold

Refer to illustration 5.26, 5.27, 5.32 and 5.36

23   Disconnect the cable from the negative terminal of the battery.

24   Remove the windshield wiper motor assembly (see Chapter 12).

25   Disconnect the rear bank of spark plug wires.

26   Unbolt the crossover pipe where it joins the rear exhaust manifold **(see illustration)**.

27   Disconnect and remove the upstream oxygen sensor connector **(see illustration)**. Remove the upstream oxygen sensor (see Chapter 6).

28   Remove the bolts and the upper heat shield **(see illustration 5.27)**.

5.27 Rear exhaust manifold assembly

1	Heat shield screw	4	Lower heat shield
2	Upper heat shield	5	Rear exhaust manifold
3	Exhaust manifold bolt	6	Upstream oxygen sensor

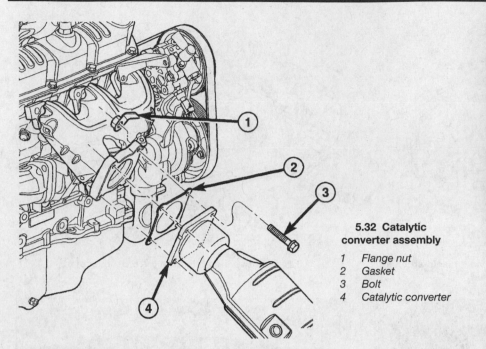

5.32 Catalytic converter assembly
1   *Flange nut*
2   *Gasket*
3   *Bolt*
4   *Catalytic converter*

5.36 Remove the two crossover pipe mounting bolts

29   Raise the vehicle, support it securely on jackstands, and remove the drive belt shield.
30   Loosen the power steering pump support strut lower bolt.
31   Disconnect the downstream oxygen sensor connector.
32   Remove the bolts and disconnect the catalytic converter from the exhaust manifold **(see illustration)**.
33   Lower the vehicle and remove the power steering pump support upper bolt.
34   Remove the bolts attaching the rear exhaust manifold to the cylinder head, and remove the rear exhaust manifold.

Front exhaust manifold

35   Disconnect the cable from the negative terminal of the battery.
36   Unbolt the crossover pipe where it joins the front exhaust manifold **(see illustration)**.

37   Disconnect the front bank of spark plug wires.
38   Remove the bolts and the upper heat shield.
39   Remove the bolts attaching the front exhaust manifold to the cylinder head, and remove the front exhaust manifold.

Installation (2001 and later models)

40   Clean the mating surfaces to remove all traces of old gasket material, then inspect the exhaust manifolds for distortion and cracks. Check for warpage with a precision straight edge held against the mating surface. If a feeler gauge thicker than 0.030-inch can be inserted between the straightedge and the mating surface, take the exhaust manifold(s) to an automotive machine shop for resurfacing.

41   Place the exhaust manifold in position with a new gasket and install the mounting bolts finger tight. **Note:** *Be sure to identify the exhaust manifold gasket by the correct cylinder designation and the position of the exhaust ports on the gasket.*
42   Starting in the middle and working out toward the ends, tighten the bolts to the torque listed in this Chapter's Specifications.
43   Installation of the remaining components is the reverse of removal.
44   Start the engine and check for exhaust leaks between the exhaust manifolds and the cylinder heads and between the exhaust manifolds, crossover pipe and catalytic converter.

6   Crankshaft pulley - removal and installation

Removal

Refer to illustrations 6.6a, 6.6b and 6.7
1   Disconnect the negative battery cable.
2   Loosen the lug nuts on the right front wheel, raise the vehicle, and support it securely on jackstands.
3   Remove the wheel.
4   Remove the right front inner fender splash shield (see Chapter 11).
5   Remove the serpentine drivebelt (see Chapter 1).
6   Remove the driveplate cover and position a large screwdriver in the ring gear teeth to keep the crankshaft from turning **(see illustration)** while a helper removes the crankshaft pulley-to-crankshaft bolt **(see illustration)**.
7   Pull the crankshaft pulley off the crankshaft with a two-jaw puller attached to the inner hub as shown **(see illustration)**.
Caution: *Do not attach the puller to the outer edge of the pulley or damage to the pulley may result.*

6.6a Use a large screwdriver or prybar wedged into the corner of the bellhousing to lock the driveplate in place

6.6b Remove the crankshaft pulley bolt (arrow) with a breaker bar and a socket

6.7 Remove the crankshaft pulley with a two-jaw puller attached to the inner hub - DO NOT pull on the outer edge of the pulley or damage may result!

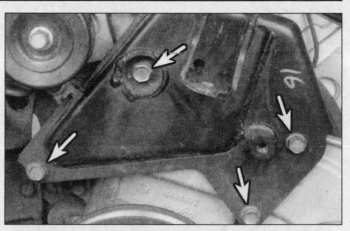

7.8 Remove the bolts (arrows) that retain the engine mounting plate to the engine

Installation

8   Install the crankshaft pulley with a special installation tool that threads to the crankshaft in place of the crankshaft pulley bolt (available at most automotive parts stores). Be sure to apply clean engine oil or multi-purpose grease to the seal contact surface of the damper hub (if it isn't lubricated, the seal lip could be damaged and oil leakage would result). If the tool isn't available, the crankshaft pulley bolt and several washers used as spacers, may be used as long as the crankshaft pulley bolt torque is not exceeded.

9   Remove the tool and install the crankshaft pulley bolt and tighten it to the torque listed in this Chapter's Specifications.

10   Installation of the remaining components is the reverse of removal.

7   Timing chain cover - removal and installation

Refer to illustrations 7.8 and 7.13

Removal (1996 through 2000 models)

1   Disconnect the negative battery cable.

2   Remove the serpentine drivebelt (see Chapter 1).

3   Drain the coolant and remove the water pump pulley (see Chapter 3).

4   Raise the vehicle and support it securely on jackstands. Drain the engine oil (see Chapter 1).

5   Support the transmission with a floor jack and a wood block and remove the engine mount closest to the timing chain (right side) of the engine (see Section 18).

6   Remove the oil pan (see Section 14) and the oil pump pick-up tube.

7   Remove the right wheel and inner splash shield (see Chapter 11). Remove the crankshaft pulley (see Section 6).

8   Unbolt the idler pulley and remove the

engine mounting plate **(see illustration)**.

9   Unbolt the air conditioning compressor from its bracket and set it off to the side. Use mechanics wire to tie the assembly to the fender to keep it away from the work area (see Chapter 3). **Warning:** *The refrigerant hoses are under pressure - don't disconnect them.*

10   Remove the drivebelt tensioner from the engine.

11   Remove the cam sensor from the timing chain cover (see Chapter 4).

12   Disconnect the canister purge hose from the fenderwell area.

13   Remove the timing chain cover-to-engine block bolts **(see illustration)**. **Note:** *Draw a diagram showing the locations and sizes of the timing cover bolts to aid in installation.*

Removal (2001 and later models)

Refer to illustrations 7.24 and 7.28

14   Disconnect the cable from the negative terminal of the battery.

15   Drain the coolant (see Chapter 1).

16   Raise the vehicle and support it securely on jackstands. Drain the engine oil (see Chapter 1).

17   Remove the right wheel and inner splash shield (see Chapter 1).

18   Remove the oil pan (see Section 14) and the oil pump pick-up tube.

19   Remove the serpentine drive belt (see Chapter 1).

20   Unbolt the air conditioning compressor from its bracket and set it off to one side. Use mechanics wire to tie the assembly to the fender to keep it away from the work area (see Chapter 3). **Warning:** *The refrigerant hoses are under pressure - don't disconnect them.*

21   Remove the crankshaft pulley (see Section 6).

22   Remove the radiator lower hose (see Chapter 3). Remove the heater hose from the timing chain cover housing, or water pump inlet (oil cooler equipped models).

23   Remove the right side engine mount (see Section 18).

24   Unbolt and remove the idler pulley from the engine bracket **(see illustration)**.

25   Remove the bolts and remove the engine mount bracket. Remove the camshaft sensor from the timing chain cover **(see illustration 7.24)**.

26   Remove the water pump (see Chapter 3).

7.13 Remove the timing chain cover bolts from the engine (be sure to mark the location of each bolt to aid in proper installation)

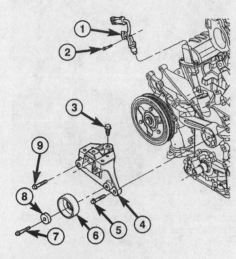

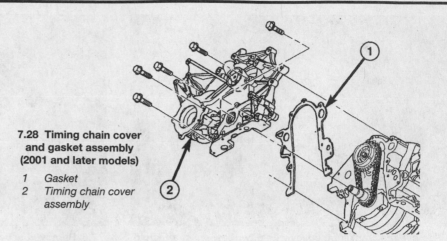

7.28 Timing chain cover and gasket assembly (2001 and later models)

1 *Gasket*
2 *Timing chain cover assembly*

7.24 Engine mounting bracket and camshaft sensor assembly (2001 and later models)

1 *Camshaft sensor*
2 *Camshaft sensor bolt*
3 *Mounting bracket vertical bolt*
4 *Engine mounting bracket*
5 *Mounting bracket horizontal bolt*
6 *Idler pulley*
7 *Idler pulley bolt*
8 *Idler pulley bolt spacer*
9 *Mounting bracket horizontal bolt*

27   Remove the bolt and remove the power steering pump support strut to the front cover.
28   Remove the timing chain cover-to engine block bolts **(see illustration)**. **Note:** *Draw a diagram showing the locations and sizes of the timing cover bolts to aid in installation.*

Installation (all models)

29   Use a gasket scraper to remove all traces of old gasket material and sealant from

8.2 Timing chain and sprocket alignment details

A   Crankshaft sprocket alignment mark
B   Camshaft sprocket alignment mark
C   Camshaft sprocket bolt

the cover and engine block. The cover is made of aluminum, so be careful not to nick or gouge it. Clean the gasket sealing surfaces with lacquer thinner or acetone.
30   Apply a thin film of RTV sealant to both sides of the new gasket, then position it on the engine block. Attach the cover to the engine block, making sure the flats of the oil pump gear are aligned with the flats on the crankshaft. Install the bolts and tighten them in a criss-cross pattern, in three steps, to the torque listed in this Chapter's Specifications.
31   Installation of the remaining components is the reverse of removal.
32   Add oil and coolant (see Chapter 1), start the engine and check for leaks.

8   Timing chain and sprockets - removal, inspection and installation

Removal

> **** CAUTION ****
>
> The timing system is complex. Severe engine damage will occur if you make any mistakes. Do not attempt this procedure unless you are highly experienced with this type of repair. If you are at all unsure of your abilities, consult an expert. Double-check all your work and be sure everything is correct before you attempt to start the engine.

Refer to illustration 8.2
1   Remove the timing chain cover (see Section 7).
2   Temporarily install the crankshaft pulley bolt and turn the crankshaft with the bolt to align the timing marks on the crankshaft and camshaft sprockets. The crankshaft arrow should be at the top (12 o'clock position) and the camshaft sprocket arrow should be in the 6 o'clock position **(see illustration)**.
3   Remove the camshaft sprocket bolt. Do not turn the camshaft in the process (if you do, realign the timing marks before the sprocket is removed).

4   Use two large screwdrivers to carefully pry the camshaft sprocket off the camshaft dowel pin.
5   Timing chains and sprockets should be replaced in sets. If you intend to install a new timing chain, remove the crankshaft sprocket with a puller and install a new one. Be sure to align the key in the crankshaft with the keyway in the sprocket during installation.

Inspection

6   Inspect the timing chain dampener (guide) for cracks and wear and replace it, if necessary.
7   Clean the timing chain and sprockets with solvent and dry them with compressed air (if available). **Warning:** *Wear eye protection when using compressed air.*
8   Inspect the components for wear and damage. Look for teeth that are deformed, chipped, pitted, and cracked.
9   The timing chain and sprockets should be replaced with a new one if the engine has high mileage, the chain has visible damage, or total freeplay midway between the sprockets exceeds one-inch. Failure to replace a worn timing chain and sprockets may result in erratic engine performance, loss of power, and decreased fuel mileage. Loose chains can "jump" timing. In the worst case, chain "jumping" or breakage will result in severe engine damage.

Installation

> **** CAUTION ****
>
> Before starting the engine, carefully rotate the crankshaft by hand through at least two full revolutions (use a socket and breaker bar on the crankshaft pulley center bolt). If you feel any resistance, STOP! There is something wrong - most likely, valves are contacting the pistons. You must find the problem before proceeding. Check your work and see if any updated repair information is available.

Refer to illustration 8.10
10   Turn the camshaft to position the dowel

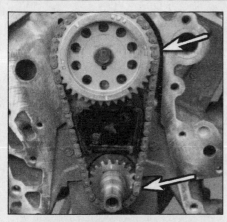

8.10 Be sure the timing chain colored reference links align with marks on the sprockets (arrows)

9.2 Be very careful not to damage the crankshaft surface when removing the front seal

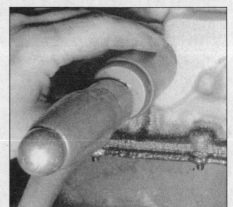

9.3 Use a large deep socket and gently tap the seal into place

pin at 6 o'clock (see illustration 8.2). Mesh the timing chain with the camshaft sprocket, then engage it with the crankshaft sprocket. The timing marks should be aligned (see illustration 8.2). **Note:** *If the crankshaft has moved, turn it until the arrow stamped on the crankshaft sprocket is exactly at the top. If the camshaft was turned, install the sprocket temporarily and turn the camshaft until the sprocket timing mark is at the bottom, opposite the mark on the crankshaft sprocket. The arrows should point to each other. The timing chain colored reference links should align with the camshaft and crankshaft timing marks that are in the 3 o'clock position (see illustration).* If you are using replacement parts, check this alignment.

11 Install the camshaft sprocket bolt and tighten it to the torque listed in this Chapter's Specifications.

12 Lubricate the chain and sprocket with clean engine oil. Install the timing chain cover (see Section 7).

13 Installation of the remaining components is the reverse of removal.

9 Crankshaft front oil seal - replacement

Refer to illustrations 9.2 and 9.3

1 Remove the crankshaft pulley (see Section 6).

2 Note how the seal is installed - the new one must be installed to the same depth and face the same way. Carefully pry the oil seal out of the cover with a seal puller or a large screwdriver (see illustration). Be very careful not to distort the cover or scratch the crankshaft! Wrap tape around the tip of the screwdriver to avoid damage to the crankshaft.

3 Apply clean engine oil or multi-purpose grease to the outer edge of the new seal, then install it in the cover with the lip (spring side) facing IN. Drive the seal into place (see illustration) with a large socket and a hammer (if a large socket isn't available, a piece of pipe of the proper diameter will also work). Make sure the seal enters the bore squarely. Stop when

the front face is at the proper depth.

4 Reinstall the crankshaft pulley.

10 Rocker arms and pushrods - removal, inspection and installation

Refer to illustrations 10.2 and 10.3

Removal (1996 through 2000 models)

1 Remove the valve covers (see Section 3).

2 On shaft-mounted rocker arms, loosen each rocker arm shaft bolt a little at a time until they are all loose enough to be removed by hand (see illustration). If the rocker arms are removed from the shaft, be sure to note how they are positioned. On pedestal-type rocker arms, remove each individual pedestal bolt and remove the rocker arm, along with the pedestal. Mark each rocker arm and pedestal so they can be reassembled the same way.

3 Remove the pushrods and store them in order to make sure they don't get mixed up during installation (see illustration).

Inspection (all years)

4 Inspect each rocker arm for wear, cracks, and other damage, especially where the pushrods and valve stems make contact.

5 Check each rocker arm pivot area and shaft or pedestal for wear, cracks, and galling. If the rocker arms or shafts/pedestals

are worn or damaged, replace them with new ones.

6 On shaft-mounted rocker arms, inspect the shafts for galling and excessive wear. Inspect the oil holes for plugging.

7 Inspect the pushrods for cracks and excessive wear at the ends. Roll each pushrod across a piece of plate glass to see if it's bent (if it wobbles, it's bent).

Installation (1996 through 2000 models)

8 Lubricate the lower end of each pushrod with clean engine oil or moly-base grease and install them in their original locations. Make sure each pushrod seats completely in the lifter socket.

10.2 Remove the rocker arm shaft bolts from the cylinder head - be sure to start with the outer ones first

10.3 Be sure to store the pushrods in an organized manner to make sure they're reinstalled in their original locations

9   Apply moly-base grease to the ends of the valve stems and the upper ends of the pushrods.

10   Apply moly-base grease to the rocker arm shaft or pedestal. Install the rocker arms on the shaft or pedestals and lower the assembly onto the cylinder head. Tighten the bolts. On shaft-mounted rocker arms, tighten a little at a time (working from the center out), to the torque listed in this Chapter's Specifications. As the bolts are tightened, make sure the pushrods engage properly in the rocker arms. **Caution:** *Allow the engine to set for 20 minutes before starting.*

11   Install the valve covers.

Removal (2001 and later models)

Refer to illustrations 10.13 and 10.14

12   Remove the valve covers (see Section 3).

13   Loosen each rocker arm shaft bolt a little at a time, until they are all loose enough to be removed by hand **(see illustration)**.

14   Remove the rocker arm and shaft assembly. If the rocker arms, washers and shaft retainer/spacers are going to be removed from the shaft, be sure to note how they are positioned **(see illustration)**. To remove the bolts and retainer/spacers, use adjustable pliers and grip the edges of the retainer/spacers and pull them straight up off the shaft.

15   Remove the pushrods and store them in order to make sure they don't get mixed up during installation **(see illustration 10.3)**.

Installation (2001 and later models)

16   Lubricate the lower end of each pushrod with clean engine oil or moly-base grease and install them in their original locations. Make sure each pushrod seats completely in the lifter socket.

17   Apply moly-base grease to the ends of the valve stems and the upper ends of the pushrods.

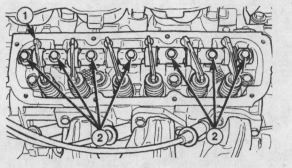

10.13 Rocker arms and shaft assembly

1   *Rocker arm*
2   *Rocker arm shaft bolts*

18   Apply moly-base grease to the rocker arm shaft. If removed, install the rocker arms, washers, shaft retainer/spacers and bolts in the correct order **(see illustration 10.14)**. Install the rocker arm assembly onto the cylinder head. Tighten the bolts, a little at a time (working from the center out), to the torque listed in this Chapter's Specifications. As the bolts are tightened, make sure the pushrods engage properly in the rocker arms. **Caution:** *Allow the engine to set for 20 minutes before staring.*

19   Install the valve covers.

11 Hydraulic roller lifters - removal, inspection and installation

Refer to illustrations 11.6, 11.7, 11.8 and 11.9

1   A noisy valve lifter can be isolated when the engine is idling. Hold a mechanic's stethoscope or a length of hose near each valve while listening at the other end. Another method is to remove the valve cover and, with the engine idling, touch each of the valve spring retainers, one at a time. If a valve lifter is defective, it'll be evident from the shock felt at the retainer each time the valve seats.

2   The most likely causes of noisy valve lifters are dirt trapped inside the lifter and lack of oil flow, viscosity, or pressure. Before condemning the lifters, check the oil for fuel contamination, correct level, cleanliness, and correct viscosity.

Removal

3   Remove the intake manifold (see Section 4) and valve covers (see Section 3).

4   Remove the rocker arms and pushrods (see Section 10).

5   Remove the cylinder heads from the engine block (see Section 13).

6   Remove the retaining plate bolts **(see illustration)** and lift the plate to gain access to the hydraulic roller lifters.

7   Each pair of lifters is retained with an alignment yoke. Lift the yoke from the lifters **(see illustration)**.

8   There are several ways to extract the lifters from the bores. A special tool designed to grip and remove lifters is manufactured by many tool companies and is available at most automotive parts stores, but it may not be required in every case. On newer engines without a lot of varnish buildup, the lifters can often be removed with a small magnet or even with your fingers **(see illustration)**. A machinist's scribe and bent end can be used to pull the lifters out by positioning the point under the retainer ring in the top of each lifter. **Caution:** *Don't use pliers to remove the lifters unless you intend to replace them with new ones. The pliers may damage the precision machined and hardened lifters, rendering them useless.*

9   Store the lifters in a box clearly labeled to ensure they're reinstalled in their original locations **(see illustration)**.

10.14 Rocker arms, washers, shaft retainer/spacer and shaft assembly

1   *Rocker arm shaft oil feed bolt (longer length)*
2   *Shaft retainer/spacer (0.84 inch)*
3   *Shaft retainer/spacer (1.47 inch)*
4   *Shaft retainer/spacer (1.61 inch)*
5   *Rocker arm - exhaust*
6   *Washer*
7   *Rocker arm - intake (larger offset)*
8   *Rocker arm lubrication feed hole (position upward and toward the valve spring)*

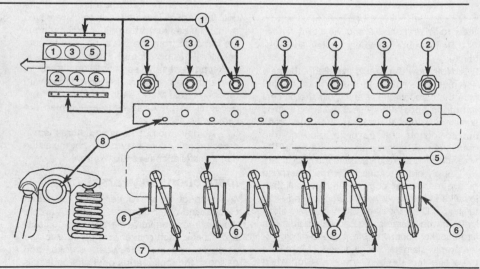

11.6 Remove the bolts (arrows) that attach the lifter retaining plate

11.7 Lift off the alignment yokes

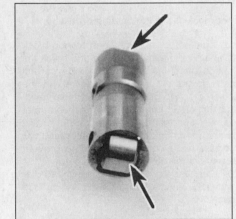

11.8 On engines with low mileage, the roller lifters can be removed by hand - if the lifters are coated with varnish, a special lifter removal tool may be required

11.9 Store the lifters in a box so each one will be reinstalled in its original bore

11.11 Check the roller for pitting or excessive looseness and the lifter surfaces for gouges, scoring, wear or damage (arrows)

Inspection

Refer to illustration 11.11

10   Clean the lifters with solvent and dry them thoroughly. Do not mix them up.

11   Check each lifter wall and pushrod seat for scuffing, score marks, and uneven wear. If the lifter walls are damaged or worn inspect the lifter bores in the engine block (**see illustration**).

12   Check the roller of each lifter for freedom of movement, excessive looseness, flat spots, or pitting. The camshaft must also be inspected for signs of abnormal wear. **Note:** *Used roller lifters can be reinstalled with a new camshaft or the original camshaft can be used if new roller lifters are installed, provided the used components are in good condition.*

Installation

13   When installing used lifters, make sure they're replaced in their original bores. On 2001 and later models, position the valve lifter with the lubrication hole facing upward toward the middle of the engine block. Soak the lifters in oil to remove trapped air. Coat the lifters with moly-based grease or engine assembly lube prior to installation.

14   Installation of the remaining compo-

nents is the reverse of removal.

15   Tighten the retaining plate bolts to the torque listed in this Chapter's Specifications.

16   Run the engine and check for oil leaks.

12   Valve springs, retainers and seals - replacement

This procedure is essentially the same as the one for the 2.4L four-cylinder engines. Refer to Chapter 2A, Section 11 and follow the procedure outlined there.

13   Cylinder heads - removal and installation

Refer to illustration 13.9

Caution: *Allow the engine to cool completely before loosening the cylinder head bolts.*

Removal

1   Disconnect the negative battery cable.

2   Remove the intake manifold (see Section 4).

3   Disconnect all wires and vacuum hoses from the cylinder heads. Label them to simplify reinstallation.

4   Disconnect the ignition wires and remove the spark plugs (see Chapter 1). Label the ignition wires to simplify reinstallation.

5   Remove the exhaust manifold (see Section 5).

6   Remove the valve covers (see Section 3).

7   Remove the rocker arms and pushrods (see Section 10).

8   Using the new cylinder head gasket, outline the cylinders and bolt pattern on a piece of cardboard (see Chapter 2A). Be sure to indicate the front (timing chain end) of the engine for reference. Punch holes at the bolt locations. Loosen each of the cylinder head mounting bolts, 1/4-turn at a time, until they can be removed by hand - work from bolt-to-bolt in a pattern that's the reverse of the tightening sequence (**see illustration 13.18**). Store the bolts in the cardboard holder as they're removed - this will ensure they are reinstalled in their original locations, which is absolutely essential.

9   Lift the cylinder heads from the engine. If resistance is felt, don't pry between the cylinder head and engine block, damage to the mating surfaces will result. Recheck for cylinder head bolts that may have been over-

13.9 Do not pry on the cylinder head near the gasket mating surface - use the corners under the casting protrusions

13.12 Use a putty knife or gasket scraper to remove the gasket from the cylinder head

13.15 Be sure the stamped designations are facing up and forward

looked, then use a hammer and wood block to tap up on the cylinder head and break the gasket seal **(see illustration)**. Be careful because there are locating dowels in the engine block to position each cylinder head. As a last resort, pry each cylinder head up at the rear corner only and be careful not to damage anything. After removal, place the cylinder head on wood blocks to prevent damage to the gasket surfaces.

10   See Chapter 2D, for cylinder head disassembly, inspection, and valve service procedures.

Installation

Refer to illustrations 13.12, 13.15, 13.17 and 13.18

11   The mating surfaces of each cylinder head and the engine block must be perfectly clean when the cylinder head is installed.

12   Use a gasket scraper to remove all traces of carbon and old gasket material **(see illustration)**, then clean the mating surfaces with lacquer thinner or acetone. If there's oil on the mating surfaces when the cylinder head is installed, the gasket may not seal correctly and leaks may develop. When working on the engine block, it's a good idea to cover the lifter valley with shop rags to keep debris out of the engine. Use a shop rag

or vacuum cleaner to remove any debris that falls into the cylinders.

13   Check the engine block and cylinder head mating surfaces for nicks, deep scratches, and other damage. If damage is slight, it can be removed with a file; if it's excessive, machining may be the only alternative.

14   Use a tap of the correct size to chase the threads in the cylinder head bolt holes. Dirt, corrosion, sealant, and damaged threads will affect torque readings.

15   Position the new gasket over the dowel pins in the engine block. Some gaskets are marked TOP or FRONT to ensure correct installation **(see illustration)**.

16   Carefully position the cylinder head on the engine block without disturbing the gasket.

17   Check the threads of the cylinder head bolts for stretching **(see illustration)**. Replace any bolts that have stretched.

18   Tighten bolt numbers 1 through 8 in the recommended sequence to the torque listed in this Chapter's Specifications (Step 1) **(see illustration)**. Next, tighten bolts 1 through 8 following the recommended sequence to the torque listed in this Chapter's Specifications (Step 2). Tighten the same bolts to the same torque again as a double check (Step 3). Tighten each bolt (except for number 9) an additional 90-degrees (1/4-turn) following the

recommended sequence (Step 4). Do not use a torque wrench for this step, apply a paint mark to the bolt head or use a torque-angle meter (available at most automotive parts stores) and a socket and breaker bar to tighten each bolt exactly 90-degrees further. After all the cylinder head bolts (numbers 1 through 8) have been sufficiently torqued, tighten cylinder head bolt number 9 to the torque listed in this Chapter's Specifications (Step 5).

19   Installation of the remaining components is the reverse of removal.

20   Change the oil and filter (see Chapter 1).

14   Oil pan - removal and installation

Removal

Refer to illustrations 14.7a and 14.7b

1   Disconnect the negative battery cable.

2   Raise the front of the vehicle and support it securely on jackstands. Apply the parking brake and block the rear wheels to keep it from rolling off the stands.

3   Remove the lower splash pan (see Section 11) and the bending brace to transmission bolt.

4   Drain the engine oil (see Chapter 1).

5   Remove the lower driveplate cover.

6   Remove the starter (see Chapter 5).

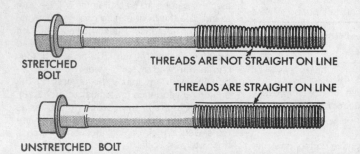

13.17 To check a cylinder head bolt for stretching, lay it against a straightedge - if any threads don't contact the straightedge, replace the bolt

13.18 Cylinder head bolt TIGHTENING sequence

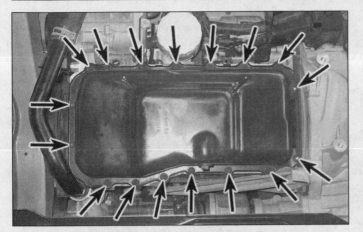

14.7a Remove the bolts from the oil pan

14.7b Use a soft faced hammer to loosen the oil pan - be careful not to dent the pan

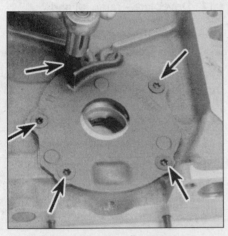

15.2 Remove the oil pump cover bolts (arrows)

15.4 Place a straightedge across the oil pump cover and check it for warpage with a feeler gauge

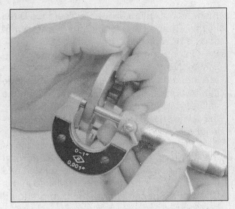

15.6 Use a micrometer to measure the thickness of the inner rotor

7   Remove the bolts and nuts, then carefully separate the oil pan from the engine block **(see illustration)**. Don't pry between the engine block and the pan or damage to the sealing surfaces could occur and oil leaks may develop. Tap the pan with a soft-face hammer to break the gasket seal **(see illustration)**.

Installation

8   Clean the pan with solvent and remove all old sealant and gasket material from the engine block and pan mating surfaces. Clean the mating surfaces with lacquer thinner or acetone and make sure the bolt holes in the engine block are clear. Check the oil pan flange for distortion, particularly around the bolt holes. If necessary, place the pan on a wood block and use a hammer to flatten and restore the gasket surface.

9   Apply a bead of RTV sealant to the bottom surface of the timing chain cover and to the bottom of the rear main oil seal retainer. Install a new gasket on the oil pan flange.

10   Place the oil pan in position on the engine block and install the nuts/bolts.

11   Tighten the bolts to the torque listed in this Chapter's Specifications. Starting at the center, follow a criss-cross pattern and work up to the final torque in three steps.

12   Installation of the remaining components is the reverse of removal.

13   Refill the engine with oil (see Chapter 1), run it until normal operating temperature is reached, and check for leaks.

15   Oil pump - removal, inspection and installation

Removal

Refer to illustration 15.2

1   Remove the oil pan (see Section 14).

2   Remove the timing chain cover (see Section 7). Remove the oil pump cover (plate) from the timing chain cover **(see illustration)**.

Inspection

Refer to illustrations 15.4, 15.6, 15.7, 15.8 and 15.9

3   Clean all parts thoroughly in solvent and carefully inspect the rotors, pump cover, and timing chain cover for nicks, scratches, or burrs. Replace the assembly if it is damaged.

4   Use a straightedge and a feeler gauge to measure the oil pump cover for warpage **(see illustration)**. If it's warped more than the limit listed in this Chapter's Specifications, the pump should be replaced.

5   Measure the thickness of the outer rotor. If the thickness is less than the value listed in this Chapter's Specifications, the pump should be replaced.

6   Measure the thickness of the inner rotor **(see illustration)**. If the diameter is less than the value listed in this Chapter's Specifications, the pump should be replaced.

7   Insert the outer rotor into the timing chain cover/oil pump housing and measure the clearance between the rotor and housing **(see illustration)**. If the measurement is more

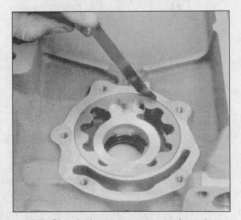

15.7 Check the outer rotor-to-housing clearance with a feeler gauge

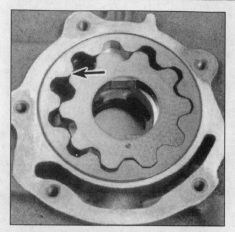

15.8 Check the clearance between the lobes of the inner and outer rotor (arrow)

15.9 Using a straightedge and feeler gauge, check the clearance between the surface of the oil pump cover and the rotors

than the maximum allowable clearance listed in this Chapter's Specifications, the pump should be replaced.

8   Install the inner rotor in the oil pump assembly and measure the clearance between the lobes on the inner and outer rotors **(see illustration)**. If the clearance is more than the value listed in this Chapter's Specifications, the pump should be replaced. **Note:** *Install the inner rotor with the mark facing up.*

9   Place a straightedge across the face of the oil pump assembly **(see illustration)**. If the clearance between the pump surface and the rotors is greater than the limit listed in this Chapter's Specifications, the pump should be replaced.

Installation

10   Install the pump cover and tighten the bolts to the torque listed in this Chapter's Specifications.

11   To install the pump, turn the flats in the rotor so they align with the flats on the crankshaft.

12   Install the timing chain cover (see Section 7) and tighten the bolts to the torque listed in this Chapter's Specifications.

13   Installation of the remaining components is the reverse of removal.

16   Oil cooler - removal and installation (2001 and later models)

Removal

Refer to illustrations 16.4 and 16.5

1   Disconnect the cable from the negative terminal of the battery.

2   Drain the coolant (see Chapter 1).

3   Raise the vehicle and support it securely on jackstands. Drain the engine oil and remove the oil filter (see Chapter 1).

4   Disconnect the coolant hoses from the inlet and outlet ports **(see illustration)**.

5   Unscrew and remove the oil cooler fitting and remove the oil cooler **(see illustration)**.

Installation

6   Lubricate the oil cooler connector on the oil filter adapter with clean engine oil.

7   Position the flat side of the oil cooler parallel to the oil pan and install the oil cooler onto the adapter. Install the fitting and tighten to the torque listed in this Chapter's Specifications.

8   Install the oil filter and refill the engine with oil (see Chapter 1).

9   Refill the cooling system (see Chapter 1). Run the engine until normal operating temperature is reached, and check for leaks.

17   Driveplate - removal and installation

This procedure is essentially the same for all engines. Refer to Chapter 2A , Section 15, and follow the procedure outlined there, but use the torque listed in this Chapter's Specifications.

18   Rear main oil seal - replacement

This procedure is essentially the same for all engines. Refer to Chapter 2A , Section 16, and follow the procedure outlined there.

19   Engine mounts - check and replacement

This procedure is essentially the same for all engines. Refer to Chapter 2A , Section 17, and follow the procedure outlined there.

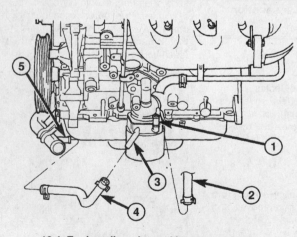

16.4 Engine oil cooler and hoses assembly

1	Oil cooler inlet tube	4	Outlet hose
2	Inlet hose	5	Water pump inlet tube
3	Oil cooler outlet tube		

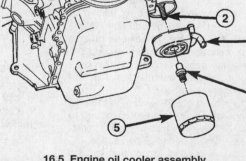

16.5 Engine oil cooler assembly

1	Oil filter adapter	4	Fitting
2	Connector	5	Oil filter
3	Oil cooler		

Chapter 2 Part D
General engine overhaul procedures

Contents

	Section
Balance shafts (four-cylinder engine only) - removal, inspection and installation	16
Camshaft and bearings (3.3L and 3.8L V6 engines only) - removal and inspection	14
Camshaft (3.3L and 3.8L V6 engines only) - installation	27
Crankshaft - inspection	22
Crankshaft installation and main bearing oil clearance check	26
Crankshaft - removal	17
Cylinder compression check	4
Cylinder head - cleaning and inspection	11
Cylinder head - disassembly	10
Cylinder head - reassembly	13
Cylinder honing	20
Engine block - cleaning	18
Engine block - inspection	19
Engine overhaul - disassembly sequence	9
Engine overhaul - general information	2

	Section
Engine overhaul - reassembly sequence	24
Engine rebuilding alternatives	8
Engine - removal and installation	7
Engine removal - methods and precautions	6
General information	1
Initial start-up and break-in after overhaul	30
Main and connecting rod bearings - inspection	23
Pistons and connecting rods - inspection	21
Pistons and connecting rods - installation and rod bearing oil clearance check	29
Pistons and connecting rods - removal	15
Piston rings - installation	25
Rear main oil seal - installation	28
Top Dead Center (TDC) for number one piston - locating	3
Vacuum gauge diagnostics checks	5
Valves - servicing	12

Specifications

Four-cylinder engines

General

Displacement	148 cubic inches
Cylinder compression pressure	170 to 225 psi
Maximum variation between cylinders	25%
Oil pressure	
At idle speed	4 psi minimum
At 3000 rpm	25 to 80 psi
Firing order	1-3-4-2
Engine block	
Cylinder bore diameter	3.445 inches
Cylinder taper limit	0.002 inch
Cylinder out-of-round limit	0.002 inch

Pistons and rings

Piston diameter	3.4434 to 3.4441 inches
Piston-to-bore clearance	0.0009 to 0.0022 inch
Piston ring side clearance	
Top compression ring	
Standard	0.0011 to 0.0031 inch
Service limit	0.004 inch
Second compression ring	
Standard	0.001 to 0.0026 inch
Service limit	0.004 inch
Top compression ring	0.0098 to 0.020 inch
Second compression ring	0.009 to 0.018 inch
Oil ring	0.0098 to 0.025 inch

Crankshaft and connecting rods

Endplay
    Standard.. 0.0035 to 0.0094 inch
    Service limit.. 0.015 inch
Main bearing journal
    Diameter... 2.361 to 2.3625 inches
    Out-of-round/taper limits.. 0.0001 inch
Connecting rod journal
    Diameter... 1.967 to 1.9685 inches
    Out-of-round/taper limits.. 0.0001 inch
Main bearing oil clearance
    Standard.. 0.0007 to 0.0023 inch
    Service limit.. 0.003 inch
Connecting rod bearing oil clearance
    Standard.. 0.0009 to 0.0027 inch
    Service limit.. 0.003 inch
Connecting rod endplay (side clearance).. 0.0051 to 0.0150 inch

Cylinder head and valves

Head warpage limit... 0.004 inch
Valve seat angle.. 45-degrees
Valve face angle.. 44-1/2 to 45-degrees
Valve margin width
    Intake
        Standard .... 0.050 to 0.063 inch
        Service limit... Not available
    Exhaust
        Standard .... 0.038 to 0.051 inch
        Service limit... Not available
Valve stem diameter
    Intake.. 0.234 inch
    Exhaust... 0.233 inch
Valve stem-to-guide clearance
    Intake .... 0.0018 to 0.0025 inch
    Exhaust... 0.0029 to 0.0037 inch
Valve spring free length .... 1.905 inches
Valve spring installed height .... 1.496 inches

Camshaft

Endplay
    Standard.. 0.0019 to 0.0066 inch
    Service limit.. Not available
Lobe lift
    Intake.. 0.324 inch
    Exhaust... 0.256 inch
Bearing clearance... 0.0027 to 0.003 inch
Bearing journal diameter... 1.021 to 1.022 inches

Torque specifications*

	Ft-lbs (unless otherwise indicated)
Camshaft sprocket bolt	75
Crankshaft main bearing cap/bedplate bolts	
Step 1 (bedplate bolts Nos. 11, 17 and 20 only)	Finger tight
Step 2 (bedplate bolts Nos. 11, 17 and 20 only	Tighten evenly until bedplate contacts block
Step 3 (bedplate bolts Nos. 11, 17 and 20 only)	20
Step 4 (bearing cap bolts Nos. 1 through 10)	30
Step 5 (bearing cap bolts Nos. 1 through 10)	Tighten an additional 90-degrees
Step 6 (remaining bedplate bolts)	20
Crankshaft damper bolt	100
Connecting rod bearing cap nuts	20 plus 1/4-turn
Counterbalance shafts	
Carrier to block bolts	40
Gear cover double-ended stud	105 in-lbs
Sprocket bolts	21
Chain tensioner bolts	105 in-lbs
Carrier cover	105 in-lbs

* **Note:** *Refer to Part A for additional torque specifications.*

3.0L V6 engine

General

Displacement	181 cubic inches
Cylinder compression pressure	170 at 250 rpm
Maximum variation between cylinders	25%
Oil pressure	
At idle speed	10 psi
At 3000 rpm	45 to 75 psi
Firing order	1-2-3-4-5-6

Engine block

Cylinder bore diameter	3.587 inches
Cylinder taper limit	0.001 inch
Cylinder out-of-round limit	0.0003 inch

Pistons and rings

Piston diameter	3.585 to 3.586 inches
Piston ring side clearance	
Top compression ring	
Standard	0.0020 to 0.0035 inch
Service limit	0.0039 inch
Second compression ring	
Standard	
1996-1998	0.0016 to 0.0033 inch
1999	0.0008 to 0.0024 inch
Piston ring end gap	
Top compression ring	
Standard	0.012 to 0.018 inch
Service limit	0.031 inch
Second compression ring	
Standard	0.018 to 0.024 inch
Service limit	0.031 inch
Oil ring	
Standard	0.008 to 0.024 inch
Service limit	0.039 inch

Crankshaft and connecting rods

Endplay	
Standard	0.002 to 0.010 inch
Service limit	0.012 inch
Main bearing journal	
Diameter	2.361 to 2.362 inches
Taper limit	0.0002 inch
Out-of-round limit	0.001 inch
Connecting rod journal	
Diameter	1.968 to 1.969 inches
Taper limit	0.0002 inch
Out-of-round limit	0.001 inch
Main bearing oil clearance	0.0007 to 0.0014 inch
Connecting rod bearing oil clearance	0.0007 to 0.0014 inch
Connecting rod endplay (side clearance)	
Standard	0.004 to 0.010 inch
Service limit	Not available

Cylinder head and valves

Head warpage limit	0.002 inch
Valve seat angle	44 to 44.5 degrees
Valve face angle	45 to 45.5 degrees
Valve margin width	
Intake	
Standard	0.047 inch
Service limit	0.027 inch
Exhaust	
Standard	0.079 inch
Service limit	0.059 inch
Valve stem-to-guide clearance	
Intake	
Standard	0.001 to 0.002 inch
Service limit	0.004 inch

Cylinder head and valves (continued)
Exhaust
    Standard .... 0.0019 to 0.003 inch
    Service limit... 0.006 inch
Valve spring free length
    Standard... 1.960 inches
    Service limit.. 1.9213 inches
Valve spring installed height
    Standard... 1.590 inches
    Service limit.. Not available
Valve stem diameter
    Intake.. 0.313 to 0.314 inch
    Exhaust... 0.312 to 0.3125 inch
Camshaft
    Lobe height
        Standard .... 1.624 inches
        Service limit... 1.604 inches
Journal diameter.. Not available

Torque specifications*
Ft-lbs (unless otherwise indicated)
Crankshaft Main bearing mono-block bolts 60
Connecting rod bearing cap bolts 38

Note: *Refer to Part B for additional torque specifications.*

3.3L and 3.8L V6 engines

General
Displacement
    3.3L .... 201 cubic inches
    3.8L .... 231 cubic inches
Cylinder compression pressure .... 170 at 250 rpm
Maximum variation between cylinders 25%
Oil pressure
    At idle .... 5 psi
    At 3000 rpm .... 30 to 80 psi
Firing order 1-2-3-4-5-6

Engine block
Cylinder bore diameter
    3.3L .... 3.661 inches
    3.8L .... 3.779 inches
Cylinder taper limit
    Standard... 0.002 inch
    Service limit.. Not available
Cylinder out-of-round limit
    Standard... 0.003 inch
    Service limit.. Not available

Piston and piston rings
Piston diameter
    3.3L .... 3.6594 to 3.6602 inches
    3.8L .... 3.7776 to 3.7783 inches
Piston-to-bore clearance... 0.001 to 0.0022 inch
Piston ring side clearance
    Top and second compression ring
        Standard .... 0.0012 to 0.0037 inch
        Service limit... 0.004 inch
    Oil ring (steel rails)
        Standard .... 0.005 to 0.0089 inch
        Service limit... 0.0090 inch
Piston ring end gap
    Top and second compression ring
        Standard .... 0.0118 to 0.0217 inch
        Service limit... 0.039 inch
    Oil ring (steel rails)
        Standard .... 0.098 to 0.0394 inch
        Service limit... 0.074 inch

Crankshaft and connecting rods

Endplay
    Standard... 0.0036 to 0.0095 inch
    Service limit.. 0.015 inch
Main bearing journal
    Diameter... 2.5202 to 2.5195 inches
    Out-of-round/taper limit .... 0.001 inch
Connecting rod journal
    Diameter... 2.2837 inches
    Out-of-round/taper limits .... 0.001 inch
Main bearing oil clearance
    Standard... 0.0005 to 0.0024 inch
    Service limit.. 0.003 inch
Connecting rod bearing oil clearance
    Standard... 0.0008 to 0.0029 inch
    Service limit.. 0.003 inch
Connecting rod endplay (side clearance)
    Standard... 0.005 to 0.013 inch
    Service limit.. 0.015 inch

Cylinder head and valves

Head warpage limit .... 0.002 inch
Valve seat angle.. 45 to 45.4 degrees
Valve face angle.. 44.5 degrees
Valve margin width
    Intake
        Standard .... 0.031 inch
        Service limit... Not available
    Exhaust
        Standard .... 0.0469 inch
        Service limit... Not available
Stem-to-guide clearance
    Intake
        1999-2000... 0.001 to 0.003 inch
        2001 and later.. 0.001 to 0.0025 inch
    Exhaust
        1999-2000... 0.002 to 0.006 inch
        2001 and later.. 0.002 to 0.0037 inch
Valve spring free length .... 1.909 inches
Valve spring installed height .... 1.662 to 1.681 inches
Valve stem diameter
    Intake... 0.312 to 0.313 inch
    Exhaust.. 0.3112 to 0.3119 inch

Camshaft

Endplay.. 0.005 to 0.012 inch
Lobe lift... 0.2678 inch
Camshaft bearing clearance
    Standard... 0.001 to 0.003 inch
    Service limit.. 0.005 inch
Camshaft journal diameter
    No. 1... 1.997 to 1.999 inches
    No. 2... 1.981 to 1.983 inches
    No. 3... 1.966 to 1.968 inches
    No. 4... 1.950 to 1.952 inches
Camshaft bearing diameter (inside)
    No. 1... 2.000 to 2.001 inches
    No. 2... 1.984 to 1.985 inches
    No. 3... 1.969 to 1.970 inches
    No. 4... 1.953 to 1.954 inches

Torque specifications*

Ft-lbs (unless otherwise indicated)
Main bearing cap bolts .... 30 plus 1/4-turn
Camshaft thrust plate bolts .... 105 in-lbs
Camshaft sprocket bolt 40
Connecting rod bearing cap nuts .... 40 plus 1/4 turn

* **Note:** *Refer to Part C for additional torque specifications.*

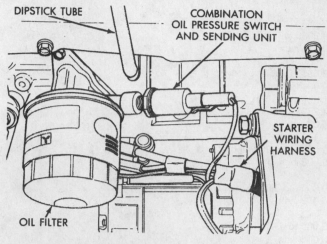

2.4a Location of the oil pressure sending unit on the 3.0L V6 engine

2.4b The oil pressure sending unit on 3.3L and 3.8L V6 engines is next to the oil filter

1   General information

This Chapter contains the general overhaul procedures for the cylinder head(s) and internal engine components.

The information ranges from advice concerning preparation for an overhaul and the purchase of replacement parts to detailed, step-by-step procedures covering removal and installation of internal engine components and parts inspection.

This Chapter was written based on the assumption the engine has been removed from the vehicle. For information concerning in-vehicle engine repair, as well as removal and installation of external components for engine overhaul, see Chapter 2A (four-cylinder engine), Chapter 2B (3.0L V6 engine), and Chapter 2C (3.3L and 3.8L V6 engines).

The Specifications included in Chapter 2D are only those necessary for the inspection and overhaul procedures which follow. Refer to Chapters 2A, 2B, and 2C for additional Specifications.

2   Engine overhaul - general information

Refer to illustrations 2.4a and 2.4b

It's not easy to determine when, or if, an engine should be completely overhauled. A number of factors must be considered.

High mileage isn't necessarily an indication an overhaul is needed, and low mileage doesn't preclude the need for an overhaul. Frequency of servicing is the most important consideration. An engine that's had regular and frequent oil and filter changes, as well as other required maintenance, will probably give many thousands of miles of reliable service. A neglected engine may require an overhaul very early in its life.

Excessive oil consumption is an indication that piston rings, valve seals and/or valve guides need repair. Before deciding that the

rings and/or guides are worn, make sure that oil leaks are not responsible for oil loss. Do a cylinder compression check (see Section 4) to determine the extent of work required.

Check the oil pressure with a gauge installed in place of the oil pressure sending unit **(see illustrations)** and compare it with this Chapter's Specifications. As a general rule, engines should have ten psi oil pressure for every 1,000 rpm. If the pressure is extremely low, the main and connecting rod bearings, and/or oil pump are probably worn out.

Loss of power, rough running, knocking or metallic engine noises, excessive valve train noise and high fuel consumption may also point to the need for an overhaul, especially if they're all present at the same time. If a complete tune-up doesn't remedy the situation, major mechanical work is the only solution.

Engine overhaul involves restoring internal engine parts to new specifications. During an overhaul, the piston rings are replaced and the cylinder walls are reconditioned (rebored and/or honed). If a rebore is done by an automotive machine shop, new oversize pistons will also be installed. New main bearings, connecting rod bearings and camshaft bearings are usually installed, and, if necessary, the crankshaft reground to restore the journals. The valves should be reground as well, they're usually worn by this time. When the engine is being overhauled, other components, such as the distributor, starter and alternator can be rebuilt as well. The final result should be a like-new engine that will give many trouble free miles. **Note:** *Critical cooling system components such as hoses, drivebelts, the thermostat and water pump MUST be replaced when an engine is overhauled. The radiator should be checked carefully to ensure it isn't clogged or leaking (see Chapter 3). It is a good idea to replace the oil pump whenever the engine is overhauled. We don't recommend overhauling the oil pump.*

Before beginning the engine overhaul, read the entire procedure to familiarize yourself with the size of the job. Overhauling an

engine isn't difficult, if you follow all the instructions, have the necessary tools and equipment, and pay close attention to all specifications. It can, however, be time consuming. Plan on the vehicle being tied up for a minimum of two weeks, especially if parts must be taken to an automotive machine shop for repair or rebuilding. Check on parts availability, and make sure that special tools and equipment are obtained in advance. Most work can be done with typical hand tools, although a number of precision measuring tools are required for parts inspection to determine if parts must be replaced. The automotive machine shop can inspect parts, and offer advice concerning rebuilding and/or replacement. **Note:** *Always wait until the engine has been completely disassembled and until all components (especially the engine block/crankcase and the crankshaft) have been inspected before deciding what service and repair operations must be done by an automotive machine shop. The condition of the block will be the major factor to consider when determining whether to overhaul the original engine or buy a rebuilt one. Do not purchase parts or have machine work done on other components until the block has been thoroughly inspected. As a general rule, time is the primary cost of an overhaul, so it doesn't pay to install worn or substandard parts.*

To ensure maximum life and minimum trouble from a rebuilt engine, everything must be assembled with care in a spotlessly clean environment.

3   Top Dead Center (TDC) for number one piston - locating

Note: *The following procedure is based on the assumption that the spark plug wires and distributor (if equipped) are correctly installed. If you are trying to locate TDC to install the distributor correctly, piston position must be determined by feeling for compression at the number one spark plug hole as the crankshaft*

3.13a Use a felt-tip marker or chalk to mark the distributor housing directly beneath the number 1 spark plug wire terminal, but note that . . .

3.13b . . . the terminals inside the distributor cap are offset from their respective spark plug wire terminals on top of the cap, so it's easy to become confused by the rotor's position relative to the apparent spark plug wire terminal when the number one piston is at TDC

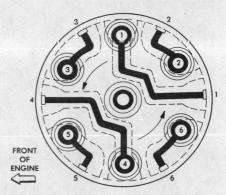

3.13c To avoid confusion, refer to this terminal guide for the distributor cap whenever you're trying to locate TDC for the number one piston (or doing any procedure that involves alignment of the rotor with the correct terminal) - this view is from the top of the cap

is slowly turned clockwise, then aligning the ignition timing marks.

1   Top Dead Center (TDC) is the highest point in the cylinder that each piston reaches as it travels up-and-down when the crankshaft rotates. Each piston reaches TDC on the compression stroke and again on the exhaust stroke, but TDC refers to the piston position on the compression stroke. The timing mark on the crankshaft timing belt sprocket on the front of the crankshaft refers to the number 1 piston.

2   Positioning the piston(s) at TDC is an essential part of many procedures such as camshaft and timing belt/sprocket removal and distributor removal.

3   Before beginning this procedure, be sure to place the transmission in Neutral and apply the parking brake or block the rear wheels. Disable the ignition system by disconnecting the spark plug wire from each spark plug and connecting each wire securely to a ground connection with a jumper wire (see Chapter 1).

4   Disconnect the negative battery cable.

5   In order to bring any piston to TDC, the crankshaft must be turned using one of the methods outlined below. When looking at the drivebelt end of the engine, normal crankshaft rotation is clockwise.

a) *The preferred method is to turn the crankshaft with a ratchet and socket on the bolt in the front of the crankshaft.*

b) *A remote starter switch can also be used. Follow the instructions included with the switch. Once the piston is near TDC, use a socket and ratchet as described in the previous paragraph.*

c) *If a helper is available to turn the ignition switch to the Start position in short bursts, you can get the piston close to TDC without a remote starter switch. Make sure your assistant is out of the vehicle, away from the ignition switch, then use a socket and ratchet as described in Step 5a to complete the procedure.*

6   On 3.0L V6 engines, note the position of

the terminal for the number one spark plug wire on the distributor cap. If the terminal isn't marked, follow the plug wire from the number one cylinder spark plug to the cap.

Four-cylinder engines

Note: *The crankshaft timing marks on these engines aren't visible until after the timing belt cover(s) have been removed.*

7   Remove the accessory drivebelt splash shield (see Chapter 11) to gain access to the crankshaft damper/pulley bolt.

8   Install a compression gauge (screw-in type with a hose) in the number 1 cylinder spark plug hole. Place the gauge dial where you can see it while turning the crankshaft damper/pulley bolt. **Note:** *The number 1 cylinder is located at the front (drivebelt end) of the engine.*

9   Rotate the crankshaft clockwise until you see compression building up on the gauge - indicating you are on the compression stroke.

10   Remove the timing belt upper cover (see Chapter 2A, Section 6). Rotate the crankshaft clockwise until the camshaft sprocket timing marks are aligned **(see illustration 6.11 in Chapter 2A).** The crankshaft is now located at number 1 piston TDC on the compression stroke. **Note:** *If you turn the crankshaft too far, rotate the crankshaft clockwise approximately 1-3/4 turns to approach the compression stroke again.*

11   After the number 1 piston has been positioned at TDC on the compression stroke, TDC for the remaining pistons can be located by turning the crankshaft exactly 180-degrees (1/2 turn) from that position, following the spark plug firing order (see Chapter 1 Specifications). The first 180-degree rotation from number 1 piston TDC will bring the number 3 cylinder piston to TDC on it's compression stroke, another 180-degree rotation will bring the number 4 cylinder piston to TDC on it's compression stroke, etc.

3.0L V6 engine

Refer to illustrations 3.13a, 3.13b, 3.13c and 3.15

12   Note the position of the terminal for the number one spark plug wire on the distributor cap. If the terminal isn't marked, follow the plug wire from the number one cylinder spark plug to the cap.

13   Use a felt-tip pen or chalk to make a mark on the distributor body directly under the terminal. To do this, it will be necessary to refer to the accompanying illustrations, as the distributor cap on these engines has offset terminals - the terminals inside the cap are offset from their respective spark plug wire terminals on the top of the cap **(see illustrations).**

14   Detach the cap from the distributor and set it aside (see Chapter 1, if necessary).

15   Turn the crankshaft (see Step 5 above) until the "0" notch in the crankshaft pulley is aligned with the timing indicator (located at the front of the engine **(see illustration).**

16   Look at the distributor rotor - it should be pointing directly at the mark you made on the distributor body. If it is, go to Step 12.

17   If the rotor is 180-degrees off, the number one piston is at TDC on the exhaust stroke - proceed to the next Step.

18   To get the piston to TDC on the compression stroke, turn the crankshaft one complete turn (360-degrees) clockwise. The rotor should now be pointing at the mark on the distributor. When the rotor is pointing at the number one spark plug wire terminal inside the distributor cap and the ignition timing marks are aligned, the number one piston is at TDC on the compression stroke.

19   After the number one piston has been positioned at TDC on the compression stroke, TDC for any of the remaining pistons can be located by turning the crankshaft and following the firing order. Mark the remaining spark plug wire terminal locations on the dis-

3.15 To bring the number one piston to TDC on a 3.0L V6 engine, watch the timing notch on the edge of the crankshaft pulley and align it with the 0-degree mark on the timing cover

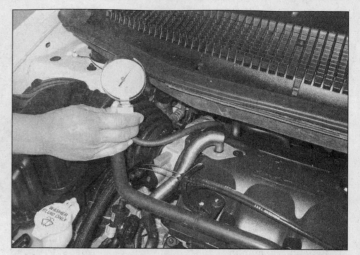

4.6 A compression gauge with a threaded fitting for the spark plug hole is preferred over the type that requires hand pressure to maintain the seal

tributor body just like you did for the number one terminal, then number the marks to correspond with the cylinder numbers. As you turn the crankshaft, the rotor will also turn. When it's pointing directly at one of the marks on the distributor, the piston for that particular cylinder is at TDC on the compression stroke.

3.3L and 3.8L V6 engines

20 Remove the valve cover closest to the radiator (see Chapter 2B).
21 Remove the spark plugs (see Chapter 1).
22 Use a socket and ratchet on the crankshaft pulley bolt to turn the crankshaft clockwise until the rocker arms for the number 2 cylinder (the cylinder closest to the right fender) can be rotated. With the engine at this position, approximate TDC for cylinder number 2 has been found. To bring the engine to TDC (approximate) for cylinder number 1, make a mark on the crankshaft pulley and a corresponding mark on the engine, and then turn the crankshaft 120-degrees counterclockwise.
23 This position will be adequate for most operations requiring the engine to be set at TDC, but if exact TDC must be found, a degree wheel and a dial indicator (with the proper spark plug hole adapter) must be used.
24 Install the degree wheel (available from many auto parts stores), on the crankshaft pulley.
25 Position the engine at TDC (approximate) for cylinder number 2 as described in Step 22. Use the proper adapter to install the dial indicator in the number 2 spark plug hole.
26 Slowly turn the crankshaft in a clockwise direction until the dial indicator shows the piston has reached its highest point.
27 Align the zero mark on the degree wheel with the mark made on the engine.
28 Rotate the crankshaft 120-degrees counterclockwise. The engine is now positioned at TDC for cylinder number 1.

29 TDC for any of the remaining cylinders can be located by turning the crankshaft clockwise 120-degrees at a time and re-aligning the timing marks. Follow the firing order in this Chapter's Specifications.

4   Cylinder compression check

Refer to illustration 4.6

1 A compression check will tell you the mechanical condition of the upper end (pistons, rings, valves, and head gaskets) of your engine. It can tell you if the compression is down due to leakage caused by worn piston rings, defective valves and seats, or a blown head gasket. **Note:** *The engine must be at normal operating temperature and the battery must be fully charged for this check. The choke must be all the way open to get an accurate compression reading (if the engine is warm, the choke should be open).*
2 Clean the area around the spark plugs before you remove them (use compressed air if available, a small brush, or a bicycle tire pump) to prevent dirt from getting into the cylinders while the compression check is being done.
3 Remove all of the spark plugs from the engine (see Chapter 1).
4 Block the throttle wide open.
5 Detach the coil wire from the center of the distributor cap and ground it on the engine block. Use a jumper wire with alligator clips on each end to ensure a good ground.
6 Install the compression gauge in the number one spark plug hole **(see illustration)**.
7 Crank the engine over at least seven compression strokes and watch the gauge. The compression should build up quickly in a healthy engine. Low compression on the first stroke, followed by gradually increasing pressure on successive strokes, indicates worn piston rings. A low compression reading on the first stroke, which doesn't build up during

successive strokes, indicates leaking valves or a blown head gasket (a cracked head may also be the cause). Deposits on the undersides of the valve heads can also cause low compression. Record the highest reading obtained.
8 Repeat the procedure for the remaining cylinders and compare the results with this Chapter's Specifications.
9 Add some engine oil (about three squirts from a plunger-type oil can) to each cylinder, through the spark plug hole, and repeat the test.
10 If the compression increases after the oil is added, the piston rings are definitely worn. If the compression doesn't increase significantly, the leakage is occurring in the valves or head gasket. Leakage past the valves may be caused by burned valve seats and/or faces or warped, cracked, or bent valves.
11 If two adjacent cylinders have equally low compression, the head gasket between them is probably blown. Coolant in the combustion chambers or the crankcase would verify this condition.
12 If a cylinder is 20 percent lower than the others, and the engine has a slightly rough idle, a worn exhaust lobe on the camshaft may be the cause.
13 If the compression is unusually high, the combustion chambers are probably coated with carbon deposits. The cylinder head should be removed and decarbonized.
14 It is a good idea to have a leak-down test done by an automotive repair shop if compression is way down or varies substantially between cylinders. This test will pinpoint where the leakage is occurring and its severity.

5   Vacuum gauge diagnostic checks

1 A vacuum gauge provides valuable, low cost information about an engine's condition. You can check for worn rings or cylinder

walls, leaking cylinder head or intake manifold gaskets, incorrect carburetor adjustments, restricted exhaust, stuck or burned valves, weak valve springs, improper ignition or valve timing, and ignition problems.

2   Vacuum gauge readings are easy to misinterpret, so they should be used in conjunction with other tests to confirm the diagnosis.

3   Both the absolute readings and the rate of needle movement are important for an accurate vacuum diagnosis. Most gauges measure vacuum in inches of mercury (in-Hg). As vacuum increases (or atmospheric pressures decreases), the reading will decrease. For every 1,000 foot increase in elevation above sea level; the gauge readings will decrease about one inch of mercury.

4   Connect the vacuum gauge directly to intake manifold vacuum, not to ported vacuum. Be sure no hoses are left disconnected during the test or false readings will result.

5   Warm up the engine completely before you begin the test. Block the wheels and set the parking brake. With the transmission in Park, start the engine and allow it to run at normal idle speed. **Warning:** *Carefully inspect the fan blades for cracks or damage before starting the engine. Keep your hands and the vacuum tester clear of the fan and do not stand in front of the vehicle or in line with the fan when the engine is running.*

6   Refer to the following vacuum gauge readings and what they indicate about the engine's condition:

a)   *A low steady reading usually indicates a leaking gasket between the intake manifold and carburetor or throttle body, a leaky vacuum hose, late ignition timing or incorrect camshaft timing. Check ignition timing with a timing light and eliminate all other possible causes. Use the tests in this Chapter before you remove the timing chain cover to check the timing marks.*

b)   *If the reading is three to eight inches vacuum below normal and it fluctuates at that low reading, an intake manifold gasket leak at an intake port or a faulty injector may be the problem.*

c)   *If the needle has regular drops of about two to four inches vacuum at a steady rate, the valves are probably leaking. Do a compression or leak-down test to confirm this.*

d)   *An irregular drop or down-flick of the needle can be caused by a sticking valve or an ignition misfire. Do a compression or leak-down test and examine the spark plugs.*

e)   *A rapid fluctuation of about four inches vacuum at idle combined with exhaust smoke indicates worn valve guides. Do a leak-down test to confirm this. If rapid fluctuation occurs with an increase in engine speed, check for a leaking intake manifold gasket or cylinder head gasket, weak valve springs, burned valves, or ignition misfire.*

f)   *A small fluctuation, of one inch up and down, may mean ignition problems. Check the usual tune-up items and, if necessary, run the engine on an ignition analyzer.*

g)   *If there is a large fluctuation, do a compression or leak-down test to look for a weak or dead cylinder or a blown cylinder head gasket.*

h)   *If the needle moves slowly through a wide range, check for a clogged PCV system, incorrect idle fuel mixture, or throttle body or intake manifold gasket leaks.*

i)   *Check for a slow return after revving the engine quickly to about 2,500 rpm and letting off the gas. The reading should drop to near zero, rise above normal idle reading (about 5 in-Hg over) and then return to the previous idle reading. If the vacuum returns slowly and doesn't peak when the throttle is released, the rings may be worn. If there is a long delay, look for a restricted exhaust system (often the muffler or catalytic converter). An easy way to check this is to temporarily disconnect the exhaust ahead of the suspected restriction and redo the test.*

6   Engine removal - methods and precautions

If you decide the engine must be removed for overhaul or major repair work, several steps should be taken.

Find a suitable place to work with adequate work and storage space. If a workshop or garage is not available, a flat, level, clean work surface (concrete or asphalt) is required.

Cleaning the engine compartment and engine/transmission before removing the engine/transmission will help keep tools clean and organized.

An engine hoist or A-frame will be necessary. Make sure the equipment is load-rated higher than the combined weight of the engine and transmission. Safety is of primary importance, considering the potential hazards in lifting the engine/transmission from the vehicle.

A helper should be available if this is the first time you remove an engine. Advice and help from someone more experienced would also be helpful. There are many cases when one person cannot do all of the required operations simultaneously when lifting the engine out of the vehicle.

Plan the operation ahead of time. Before starting work, rent or buy all of the tools and equipment you'll need. Some of the equipment required to do engine/transmission removal and installation safely and easily (in addition to an engine hoist) include: a heavy duty floor jack, a complete set of wrenches and sockets (described in the Introduction section of this manual), wooden blocks and

plenty of rags and cleaning solvent for mopping up spilled oil, coolant, and gasoline. If the hoist must be rented, make sure to reserve it in advance and do all of the operations possible without it beforehand. This will save you time and money.

Plan for the vehicle to be out of use for quite a while. An automotive machine shop will be required to do some of the work which the do-it-yourselfer can't accomplish without special equipment. These shops are usually busy, so talk with them before removing the engine, in order to accurately estimate the amount of time required to rebuild or repair components.

Be extremely careful when removing and installing the engine. Serious injury can result from carelessness. Plan ahead and take your time, a job of this nature, although major, can be accomplished successfully.

7   Engine - removal and installation

Warning: *Gasoline is extremely flammable, so take extra precautions when disconnecting any part of the fuel system. Don't smoke or allow open flames or bare light bulbs in or near the work area and don't work in a garage where a natural gas appliance (such as a clothes dryer or water heater) is installed. If you spill gasoline on your skin, rinse it off immediately. Have a Class B fire extinguisher handy and know how to use it! Also, the air conditioning system is under high pressure - have a dealer service department or service station discharge the system before disconnecting any of the hoses or fittings.*
Note: *Read through the following steps carefully and familiarize yourself with the procedure before beginning work. The engine, together with the transaxle, must be removed from under the vehicle, which requires a vehicle hoist and engine/transaxle cradle assembly.*

Removal
Refer to illustrations 7.15 and 7.19

1   If the vehicle is equipped with air conditioning, have the air conditioning system discharged by a dealer service department or service station.

2   Relieve the fuel system pressure (see Chapter 4).

3   Disconnect the negative battery cable.

4   Cover the fenders and cowl and remove the hood (see Chapter 11). Special pads are available to protect the fenders, but an old bedspread or blanket will also work.

5   Remove the battery cover, battery, and battery tray, with integral vacuum reservoir (see Chapter 1).

6   Block off the heater hoses to rear heater assembly, if equipped.

7   Drain the cooling system. Label and disconnect all coolant hoses from the engine (see Chapter 1).

8   Disconnect the heater hoses (see Chapter 3).

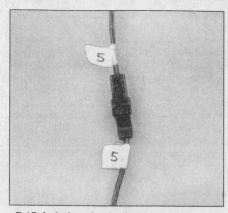

7.15 Label each wire before unplugging the connector

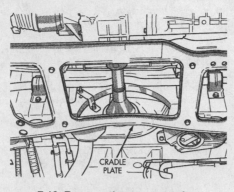

7.19 Remove the crossmember cradle plate

9   Remove the fan module (see Chapter 3), the radiator, and the coolant and windshield wiper reservoirs.

10   Disconnect the automatic transmission shift linkage (see Chapter 7).

11   Disconnect the throttle body linkage and vacuum hoses from the throttle body (see Chapter 4).

12   Remove the accessory drive belts (see Chapter 1)

13   Remove the air conditioning compressor from the engine (see Chapter 3).

14   Disconnect the alternator wiring harness and remove the alternator (see Chapter 5).

15   Label all remaining vacuum lines, emissions system hoses, wiring connectors, ground straps and fuel lines to ensure correct reinstallation, then detach them. Pieces of masking tape with numbers or letters written on them work well **(see illustration)**. If there's any possibility of confusion, make a sketch of the engine compartment and clearly label the lines, hoses and wires.

16   Disconnect the fuel lines running from the engine to the chassis (see Chapter 4). Plug or cap all open fittings/lines.

17   Raise the vehicle, being sure it's safely supported.

18   Remove the right and left inner splash shields (see Chapter 11).

19   Remove the crossmember cradle plate **(see illustration)**.

20   Drain the engine oil and remove the filter (see Chapter 1).

21   Remove the driveaxles (see Chapter 8).

22   Disconnect the exhaust pipe from the manifold (see Chapter 4).

23   Remove the front engine mount and bracket (see Chapter 2A).

24   Remove the rear transmission mount and bracket (see Chapter 2A).

25   Remove the power steering pump and bracket assembly (see Chapter 10).

26   Remove the wiring harness and connectors from the engine.

27   Remove the reinforcement strut and collar and transmission inspection cover (see Chapter 7).

28   Match/mark the driveplate and torque converter.

29   Remove the driveplate to torque con-

verter bolts (see Chapter 7).

30   Lower the vehicle to the ground and remove the vehicle ground straps (see Chapter 12).

31   Recheck to be sure nothing is still connecting the engine to the vehicle (or transmission, where applicable). Disconnect anything still remaining.

32   **Warning:** *When raising the vehicle this time, be sure it's supported solidly and has the rear two hoist lifting points as far to the rear as possible. When the engine and transaxle are detached from the vehicle, the vehicle center of gravity will change, and it's possible for the vehicle to fall off the lift if the hoist is not positioned properly. Raise the vehicle on a hoist enough to allow the engine/transaxle cradle assembly to be positioned under the engine/transaxle assembly. The Chrysler cradle assembly consists of special tool Numbers 6710, 6135, 6408 and 6848. The purpose of this cradle assembly is to safely support the engine/transaxle assembly while the vehicle is lifted off it with a hoist. Alternative cradle assemblies may be able to accomplish this. Consult equipment rental yards for suggestions.*

33   Lower the vehicle until the engine and transmission just touches the cradle. Recheck to make sure that the cradle is configured to handle both the engine and transmission.

34   Lower the vehicle so the weight of only the engine and transmission is on the floor jack.

35   Remove the right engine mount and left transmission mount through bolt (see Chapter 2A).

36   Raise the vehicle slowly. It may be necessary to move the engine/transmission assembly on the cradle for removal around body flanges.

37   Once the engine/transmission assembly is out of the vehicle, lower it slowly and carefully to the ground and support it on wood blocks. Remove the transmission-to-engine block bolts and carefully separate the engine from the transmission. Be sure the torque converter stays in place (clamp a pair of vise-grips to the housing to keep the converter from sliding out).

38   Remove the driveplate and mount the engine on an engine stand.

Installation

39   Check the engine and transmission mounts. If they're worn or damaged, replace them.

40   Rejoin the engine with the transmission. **Caution:** *DO NOT use the transmission-to-engine bolts to force the transmission and engine together. Be very careful when installing the torque converter (see Chapter 7).*

41   Carefully raise the engine/transmission into the engine compartment - make sure the mounts line up. Installation of the remaining components is the reverse of removal. Double-check to make sure everything is hooked up right.

42   Add coolant, oil, power steering and transmission fluid as needed. If the brake master cylinder was removed, bleed the brakes (see Chapter 9). Recheck the fluid level and test the brakes.

43   Run the engine and check for leaks and proper operation of all accessories, then install the hood and test drive the vehicle.

44   If the air conditioning system was discharged, have it evacuated, recharged and leak tested by the shop that discharged it.

8   Engine rebuilding alternatives

The do-it-yourselfer has a number of options when doing an engine overhaul. The decision to replace the engine block, piston/connecting rod assemblies, and crankshaft depends on a number of factors. The number one consideration is the condition of the block. Other considerations are cost, access to automotive machine shop facilities, parts availability, time required to complete the project, and the extent of prior mechanical experience on the part of the do-it-yourselfer.

Some rebuilding alternatives include:

Individual parts - If the inspection shows that the engine block and most engine components are reusable, purchasing individual parts may be the most economical alternative. The block, crankshaft and piston/connecting rod assemblies should all be inspected carefully. Even if the block shows little wear, the cylinders should be honed.

Short block - A short block consists of an engine block with a crankshaft and piston/connecting rod assemblies already installed. All new bearings are installed and all clearances correct. The existing camshaft, valve train components, cylinder head(s), and external parts can be bolted to the short block with little or no automotive machine shop work required.

Long block - A long block consists of a short block, oil pump, oil pan, cylinder head(s), rocker arm cover(s), camshaft and valve train components, timing sprockets, and chain or gears and timing cover. All components are installed with new bearings, seals, and gaskets. Installation of manifolds and external parts is all that's required.

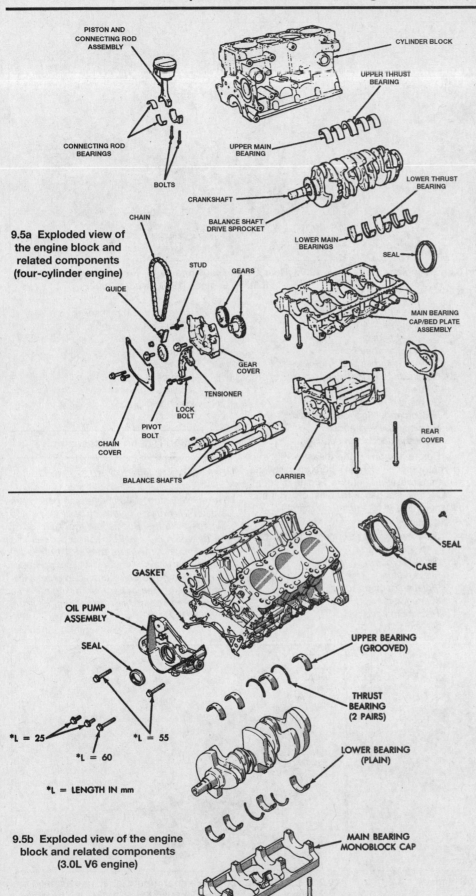

9.5a Exploded view of the engine block and related components (four-cylinder engine)

Labels: PISTON AND CONNECTING ROD ASSEMBLY, CYLINDER BLOCK, UPPER THRUST BEARING, CONNECTING ROD BEARINGS, UPPER MAIN BEARING, BOLTS, CRANKSHAFT, LOWER THRUST BEARING, CHAIN, BALANCE SHAFT DRIVE SPROCKET, LOWER MAIN BEARINGS, SEAL, STUD, GEARS, GUIDE, MAIN BEARING CAP/BED PLATE ASSEMBLY, GEAR COVER, TENSIONER, LOCK BOLT, PIVOT BOLT, CHAIN COVER, BALANCE SHAFTS, CARRIER, REAR COVER

9.5b Exploded view of the engine block and related components (3.0L V6 engine)

Labels: GASKET, SEAL, CASE, OIL PUMP ASSEMBLY, SEAL, UPPER BEARING (GROOVED), *L = 25, *L = 55, *L = 60, THRUST BEARING (2 PAIRS), CRANKSHAFT, LOWER BEARING (PLAIN), *L = LENGTH IN mm, MAIN BEARING MONOBLOCK CAP

Used Engine - While overhaul provides the best assurance of a like-new engine, used engines available from wrecking yards and importers are often a very simple and economical solution. Many used engines come with warranties, but always give any used engine a thorough diagnostic check-out before purchase. Check compression and also for signs of oil leakage. If possible, have the seller run the engine either in the vehicle or on a test stand so you can be sure it runs smoothly with no knocking or other noises.

Decide which alternative is best for you and discuss the situation with a local automotive machine shop, auto parts dealer, or experienced rebuilder before ordering or purchasing replacement parts.

9 Engine overhaul - disassembly sequence

Refer to illustrations 9.5a, 9.5b, 9.5c, 9.5d and 9.5e

1   It's much easier to disassemble and work on the engine if it's mounted on a portable engine stand. A stand can be rented quite cheaply from an equipment rental yard. The driveplate should be removed from the engine before it's mounted on a stand.

2   If a stand isn't available, it's possible to disassemble the engine with it blocked up on the floor. Be extra careful not to tip or drop the engine when working without a stand.

3   If you're going to obtain a rebuilt engine, all external components must come off first, and be transferred to the replacement engine, just as they will if you're doing a complete engine overhaul yourself. These components include:

> Alternator and sbrackets
> Emissions control components
> Ignition coil/module assembly, spark plug wires, and spark plugs
> Thermostat and housing cover
> Water pump
> EFI components
> Intake/exhaust manifolds
> Oil filter
> Engine mounts
> Driveplate

Note: *When removing external components from the engine, pay close attention to details that may be helpful or important during installation. Note the installed positions of gaskets, seals, spacers, pins, brackets, washers, bolts, and other small items.*

4   If you're obtaining a short block (see Section 8), the cylinder head(s), oil pan, and oil pump will have to be removed as well. For additional information, see Section 8.

5   If you're planning a complete overhaul, the engine must be disassembled and the internal components removed in the following general order **(see illustrations):**

9.5c End (timing chain) view of the 3.3L and 3.8L V6 engines
(1996 through 2000)

9.5d Rear side (exhaust manifold) view of the 3.3L and
3.8L V6 engines (1996 through 2000)

Four-cylinder engine

Intake and exhaust manifolds
Valve cover
Timing belt covers
Timing belt and sprockets
Camshafts
Cam followers (rocker arms) and
    hydraulic lash adjusters
Water pump
Cylinder heads
Oil pan and oil pickup tube
Oil pump
Balance shaft carrier
Piston/connecting rod assemblies
Crankshaft and main bearing cap/or
    mono-block

V6 engines

Valve covers
Exhaust manifolds
Rocker arm assemblies and camshafts
    (3.0L V6 engine)
Rocker arms and pushrods (3.3L and
    3.8L V6 engines)
Intake manifold(s)

Valve roller lifters (3.3L and 3.8L
    V6 engines)
Cylinder heads
Timing chain/belt cover
Timing chain/belt and sprockets
Camshaft (3.0L V6 engine)
Oil pan
Oil pump
Piston/connecting rod assemblies
Rear main oil seal housing
Crankshaft and main bearings

6   Before beginning the disassembly and
overhaul procedures, make sure the following
items are available. Refer to Engine overhaul
- reassembly sequence for a list of tools and
materials needed for engine reassembly.

Common hand tools
Small cardboard boxes or plastic bags
    for storing parts
Gasket scraper
Ridge reamer
Vibration damper puller
Micrometers
Telescoping gauges
Dial indicator set

Valve spring compressor
Cylinder surfacing hone
Piston ring groove cleaning tool
Electric drill motor
Tap and die set
Wire brushes
Oil gallery brushes
Cleaning solvent

10   Cylinder head - disassembly

*Refer to illustrations 10.2, 10.3, 10.4a, 10.4b
and 10.4c*

Note: *New and rebuilt cylinder heads are
available for most engines at dealerships and
auto parts stores. Specialized tools necessary
for disassembly and inspection procedures
and replacement parts may not be readily
available. It may be more practical and economical for the home mechanic to purchase a
replacement head rather than taking the time
to disassemble, inspect and recondition the
original.*

1   Cylinder head disassembly involves

9.5e Front view of the 3.3L and 3.8L V6 engines
(1996 through 2000)

10.2 A small plastic bag, with appropriate label, can be used to
store the valve train components so they can be kept together
and reinstalled in the original locations

10.3 Use a valve spring compressor to compress the spring, then remove the keepers from the valve stems

10.4a Remove the valve from the cylinder head (four-cylinder engine shown) . . .

removal of the intake and exhaust valves and related components. If they're still in place, remove the bearing caps, camshafts, cam followers (rocker arms) and lash adjusters. Label the parts or store them separately so they can be reinstalled in their original locations.

2 Before the valves are removed, label and store them, along with their related components, so they can be kept separate and reinstalled in the same valve guides they are removed from **(see illustration)**.

3 Compress the springs on the first valve with a spring compressor and remove the keepers **(see illustration)**. Carefully release the valve spring compressor and remove the retainer and the spring.

4 Pull the valve out of the head, remove the valve stem seal with pliers, and remove the spring seat from the guide **(see illustrations)**. Note: *On the four-cylinder engines the valve stem seal and spring seat are an assembly. If the valve binds in the guide (won't pull through), push it back into the head and deburr the area around the keeper groove and stem tip with a fine file or whetstone **(see illustration)**.*

5 Repeat the procedure for the remaining

valves. Remember to keep all the parts for each valve together so they can be reinstalled in their original locations.

6 Once the valves and related components have been removed and stored in an organized manner, the head should be thoroughly cleaned and inspected. If a complete engine overhaul is being performed, finish the engine disassembly procedures before beginning the cylinder head cleaning and inspection process.

11 Cylinder head - cleaning and inspection

1 Thorough cleaning of the cylinder head(s) and related valve train components, followed by a detailed inspection, will enable you to decide how much valve service work must be done during the engine overhaul. Note: *If the engine was severely overheated, the cylinder head is probably warped.*

Cleaning

2 Scrape all traces of old gasket material and sealant off the head gasket, intake manifold, and exhaust manifold mating surfaces.

Be very careful not to gouge the cylinder head. Special gasket removal solvents that soften gaskets and make removal much easier are available at auto parts stores.

3 Remove built up scale from the coolant passages.

4 Run a stiff wire brush through the various holes to remove corrosion and deposits.

5 Run an appropriate size tap into each of the threaded holes to remove corrosion and thread sealant. If compressed air is available, use it to clear the holes of debris. **Warning:** *Wear eye protection when using compressed air!*

6 Clean the rocker arm bolt threads with a wire brush.

7 Clean the cylinder head with solvent and dry it thoroughly. Compressed air will speed the drying process and ensure that holes and recessed areas are clean. **Note:** *Decarbonizing chemicals are available and may prove very useful when cleaning cylinder heads and valve train components. They're very caustic and should be used with caution. Be sure to follow the instructions on the container.*

8 Clean the rocker arms, shafts, and pushrods (3.3L and 3.8L V6 engines only) with solvent and dry them thoroughly (don't mix them up). Compressed air speeds the drying process and can be used to clean out oil passages.

9 Clean all the valve springs, spring seats, keepers, and retainers with solvent and dry them thoroughly. Do the components from one valve at a time to avoid mixing parts.

10 Scrape off heavy deposits that may have formed on the valves, then use a motorized wire brush to remove deposits from the valve heads and stems. Make sure the valves don't get mixed up.

Inspection

Refer to illustrations 11.12, 11.14, 11.15, 11.16, 11.17 and 11.18

Note: *Be sure to perform all of the following inspection procedures before deciding that machine shop work is required. Make a list of items that need attention.*

10.4b . . . then use pliers to remove the valve stem seal from the valve guide

10.4c If the valve won't pull through the guide, deburr the edge of the stem end and the area around the top of the keeper groove with a file or whetstone

11.12 Check the cylinder head gasket surface for warpage by trying to slip a feeler gauge under the straightedge (see this Chapter's Specifications for the maximum warpage allowed and use a feeler gauge of that thickness)

11.14 A dial indicator can be used to determine the valve stem-to-guide clearance (move the valve stem as indicated by the arrows)

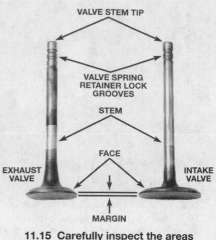

11.15 Carefully inspect the areas indicated for valve wear or damage

Cylinder head

11   Inspect the head very carefully for cracks, evidence of coolant leakage, and other damage. If cracks are found, check with an automotive machine shop about repair. If repair isn't possible, a new cylinder head is required.

12   Use a straightedge and feeler gauge to check the head gasket mating surface for warpage **(see illustration)**. If warpage exceeds the limit in this Chapter's Specifications, it can be resurfaced at an automotive machine shop. **Note:** *If the V6 engine heads are resurfaced, the intake manifold flanges also require machining.*

13   Examine the valve seats in each of the combustion chambers. If they're pitted, cracked or burned, the head will require valve service that's beyond the scope of the home mechanic.

14   Check the valve stem-to-guide clearance by measuring the lateral movement of the valve stem with a dial indicator attached to the head **(see illustration)**. The valve must be in the guide and approximately 1/16-inch off the seat. The total valve stem movement indicated by the gauge needle must be

divided by two to obtain the actual clearance. If there's still doubt about the condition of the valve guides, they should be checked by an automotive machine shop (the cost should be minimal).

Valves

15   Carefully inspect each valve face for uneven wear, deformation, cracks, pits, and burned areas. Check the valve stem for scuffing and galling and the neck for cracks. Rotate the valve and check for obvious indications that it's bent. Look for pits and excessive wear on the end of the stem. Any of these conditions **(see illustration)** indicates the need for valve service by an automotive machine shop.

16   Measure the margin width on each valve **(see illustration)**. Valves with a margin narrower than specified in this Chapter's Specifications have to be replaced.

Valve components

17   Check each valve spring for wear (on the ends) and pits. Measure the free length and compare it to this Chapter's Specifications **(see illustration)**. Any springs that are shorter than specified should be replaced. Spring tension should be checked with a

special fixture before deciding they're suitable for use in a rebuilt engine (take the springs to an automotive machine shop for this check).

18   On four-cylinder and 3.0L V6 engines, stand each spring on a flat surface and check it for squareness **(see illustration)**. If the springs are distorted or sag, replace all of them. **Note:** *The springs on the 3.3L and 3.8L V6 engines are not flat-sided. Springs that look damaged should be examined by a qualified machine shop.*

19   Check spring retainers and keepers for obvious wear and cracks. Questionable parts should be replaced with new ones, extensive damage will occur if they fail during engine operation.

Rocker arm components (3.3L and 3.8L V6 engines only)

20   Check the rocker arm faces (the areas that contact the pushrod ends and valve stems) for pits, wear, galling, score marks and rough spots. Check the rocker arm pivot contact areas as well. Look for cracks in each rocker arm and bolt.

21   Inspect the pushrod ends for scuffing and excessive wear. Roll each pushrod on a flat surface to determine if it's bent.

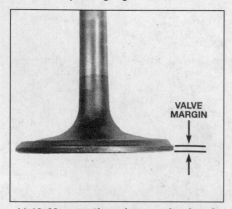

11.16 Measure the valve margin of each valve before and after machining (if necessary) to verify it is acceptable for reuse

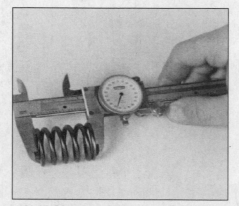

11.17 Measure the free length of each valve spring with a dial or vernier caliper

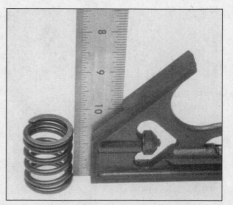

11.18 Check each valve spring for squareness

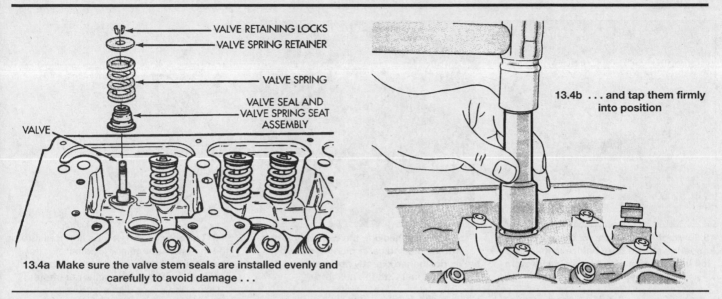

VALVE RETAINING LOCKS
VALVE SPRING RETAINER
VALVE SPRING
VALVE SEAL AND VALVE SPRING SEAT ASSEMBLY
VALVE

13.4a Make sure the valve stem seals are installed evenly and carefully to avoid damage . . .

13.4b . . . and tap them firmly into position

22 Check the rocker arm bolt mounts in the cylinder heads for damaged threads and secure installation.
23 Damaged or excessively worn parts must be replaced.

All components
24 If inspection indicates the valve components are in generally poor condition and worn beyond specified limits, usually the case in an engine that's being overhauled, reassemble the valves in the cylinder head and refer to Section 12 for valve servicing recommendations.

12 Valves - servicing

1 Because of the complex nature of the job and the special tools and equipment required, servicing the valves, the valve seats and the valve guides, commonly known as a valve job, should be done by a professional.
2 The home mechanic can remove and disassemble the head, do the initial cleaning and inspection, then reassemble and deliver it to an automotive machine shop for the actual valve job. The inspection will allow you

to see what condition the head and valve train components are in and ensure that you know what work and new parts are required.
3 The automotive machine shop, will remove the valves and springs, rebuild or replace the valves and valve seats, rebuild the valve guides, check and replace the valve springs, spring retainers and collets (as necessary), replace the valve seals, reassemble the valve components, and make sure the installed spring height is correct. The cylinder head gasket surface will be resurfaced if its warped.
4 After a professional valve job, the head will be in like-new condition. When the head is returned, be sure to clean it again before installation on the engine to remove metal particles and abrasive grit that may be present from the valve job or head resurfacing operations. Use compressed air, if available, to blow out all the oil holes and passages.

13 Cylinder head - reassembly

Refer to illustrations 13.4a, 13.4b, 13.6a, 13.6b and 13.6c
1 Make sure the cylinder head is clean

before beginning reassembly, even if it was sent to an automotive repair shop for valve servicing.
2 If the head was sent out for valve servicing, the valves and related components will already be in place. Begin the reassembly procedure with Step 8.
3 Install the spring seats or valve rotators (if equipped) before the valve seals.
4 Install new seals on each of the valve guides. Use a hammer and a deep socket or seal installation tool to gently tap each seal in place until it's completely seated on the guide **(see illustrations)**. Don't twist or cock the seals during installation or they won't seal properly on the valve stems.
5 Begin at one end of the head and lubricate and install the first valve. Apply moly-base grease or clean engine oil to the valve stem.
6 Position the valve springs (and shims, if used) over the valves. Compress the springs with a valve spring compressor and carefully install the keepers in the groove. Slowly release the compressor and make sure the keepers seat properly. Apply a small dab of grease to each keeper to hold it in place **(see illustrations)**.

13.6a Install the spring over the valve guide and onto the seat (3.0L V6 engine shown) . . .

13.6b . . . and place the retainer on the spring

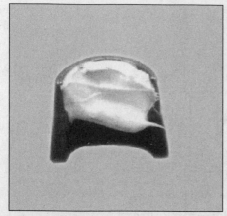

13.6c Apply a small dab of grease to each keeper as shown here before installation - it'll hold them in place on the valve stem as the spring is released

14.3 When checking the camshaft lobe lift, the dial indicator plunger must be positioned directly above and in line with the pushrod

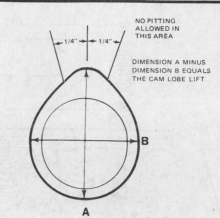

14.9 To verify camshaft lobe lift, measure the major (A) and minor (B) diameters of each lobe with a micrometer or vernier caliper - subtract each minor diameter from the major diameter to arrive at the lobe lift

7   Repeat the procedure for the remaining valves. Be sure to return components to their original locations - don't mix them up!

8   Check the installed valve spring height with a ruler graduated in 1/32-inch increments or a dial caliper. If the head was sent out for service, the installed height should be correct (but don't automatically assume it is). The measurement is taken from the top of each spring seat to the bottom of the retainer. If the height is greater than called for in this Chapter's Specifications, shims can be added under the springs to correct it. **Caution:** *Do not shim the springs to the point where the installed height is less than specified.*

9   Apply moly-base grease to the rocker arm faces and the shaft, then install the rocker arm assembly on the cylinder head.

10   If you're working on an overhead camshaft engine, refer to Chapter 2A, or 2B and install the camshafts, hydraulic lash adjusters and rocker arm assemblies on the head.

14   Camshaft and bearings (3.3L and 3.8L V6 engines only) - removal and inspection

Note: *This procedure applies to the 3.3 and 3.8 liter V6 engines only. Since there isn't enough room to remove the camshaft with the engine in the vehicle, the engine must be out of the vehicle and mounted on a stand to perform this procedure.*

Camshaft lobe lift check
With cylinder head installed
Refer to illustration 14.3

1   The lobe lift should be checked prior to camshaft removal In order to determine the extent of cam lobe wear. Refer to Chapter 2C and remove the valve covers.

2   Position the number one piston at TDC (see Section 3).

3   Begin with the number one cylinder

valves and mount a dial indicator on the engine. Position the plunger against the top surface of the first rocker arm, directly above and in line with the pushrod **(see illustration)**.

4   Zero the dial indicator. Very slowly turn the crankshaft in the normal direction of rotation (clockwise) until the indicator needle stops and begins to move in the opposite direction. The point at which it stops indicates maximum cam lobe lift.

5   Record this figure for future reference, then reposition the piston at TDC on the compression stroke.

6   Move the dial indicator to the other number one cylinder rocker arm and repeat the check. Be sure to record the results for each valve.

7   Repeat the check for the remaining valves. Each piston must be at TDC on the compression stroke for this procedure. Work from cylinder-to-cylinder following the firing order sequence.

8   After the check is complete, compare the results to this Chapter's Specifications. If camshaft lobe lift is less than specified, the cam lobes are worn and a new camshaft is required.

With cylinder head removed
Refer to illustration 14.9

9   If the cylinder head has been removed, an alternate method of lobe measurement can be used. Remove the camshaft as described in steps 11 through 14 below. Use a micrometer to measure the lobe at its highest point. Then measure the base circle perpendicular (90-degrees) to the lobe **(see illustration)**. Do this for each lobe and record the results.

10   Subtract the base circle measurement from the lobe height. The difference is the lobe lift. See Step 8 above.

Removal
Refer to illustration 14.12

11   Remove the timing chain and sprockets (see Chapter 2C, Section 8), lifters and

pushrods (see Chapter 2C, Section 10).

12   Remove the bolts and the camshaft thrust plate from the engine block **(see illustration)**.

13   Use a long bolt in the camshaft sprocket bolt hole as a handle when removing the camshaft from the block.

14   Carefully pull the camshaft out. Support the cam in the block so the lobes don't nick or gouge the bearings as the cam is pulled out.

Inspection
Refer to illustration 14.16

15   After the camshaft has been removed, cleaned with solvent, and dried, inspect the bearing journals for uneven wear, pitting, and evidence of seizure. If the journals are damaged, the bearing inserts in the block are probably damaged. Both the camshaft and bearings will have to be replaced.

16   Measure the bearing journals with a micrometer **(see illustration)** to determine if they're excessively worn or out-of-round. Refer to this Chapter's Specifications for the correct diameter.

17   Check the camshaft lobes for heat discoloration, score marks, chipped areas, pitting, and uneven wear. If the lobes and gears are in good condition and the lobe lift measurements are as specified, the cam can be reused.

18   Check the cam bearings for wear and damage. Look for galling, pitting, and discolored areas.

19   The inside diameter of each bearing can be determined with a small hole gauge and outside micrometer or an inside micrometer. Subtract the camshaft bearing journal diameters from the corresponding bearing inside diameters to determine the bearing oil clearance. If it's excessive, new bearings will be required regardless of the condition of the originals. Check this Chapter's Specifications.

20   Camshaft bearing replacement requires special tools and expertise that place it out-

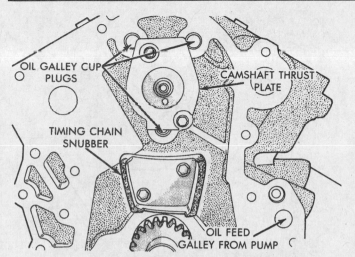

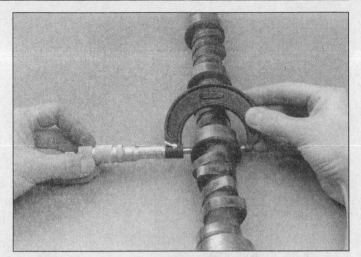

14.12 Remove the thrust plate from the front of the engine

14.16 Check the diameter of each camshaft bearing journal to pinpoint excessive wear and out-of-round conditions

side the scope of most home do-it-your-selfers. Take the block to an automotive machine shop to ensure the job is done correctly.

15 Pistons and connecting rods - removal

Refer to illustrations 15.1, 15.3, 15.4 and 15.6
Note: *Prior to removing the piston/connecting rod assemblies, remove the cylinder head(s), the oil pan and the oil pump by referring to the appropriate Sections in Chapters 2A, 2B and 2C.*

1   Use your fingernail to feel if a ridge has formed at the upper limit of ring travel (about 1/4-inch down from the top of each cylinder). If carbon deposits or cylinder wear have produced ridges, they must be removed with a special tool **(see illustration)**. Follow the manufacturer's instructions provided with the tool. Failure to remove the ridges before removing the piston/connecting rod assemblies may result in piston breakage.

2   After the cylinder ridges have been removed, turn the engine upside-down so the crankshaft is facing up.

3   Before the connecting rods are removed, check the endplay with feeler gauges. Slide them between the first connecting rod and the crankshaft throw until all the play is removed **(see illustration)**. The endplay is equal to the thickness of the feeler gauge(s). If the endplay exceeds the limit in this Chapter's Specifications, new connecting rods are required. If new rods (or a new crankshaft) are installed, the endplay may fall under the minimum in this Chapter's Specifications (if it does, the rods will have to be machined to restore it - consult an automotive machine shop for advice if necessary). Repeat the procedure for the remaining connecting rods.

4   Check the connecting rods and caps for identification marks. If they aren't plainly marked, use a small center punch to make

15.1 A ridge reamer is required to remove the ridge from the top of each cylinder - do this before removing the pistons!

the appropriate number of indentations on each rod and cap (1, 2, 3, etc., depending on the engine type and cylinder they're associated with) **(see illustration)**.

5   Loosen each of the connecting rod cap nuts 1/2-turn at a time until they can be removed by hand. Remove the number one

15.4 If the connecting rods and caps are not identified, use a center punch or numbered impression stamps to mark the caps to the rods by cylinder number (No. 4 connecting rod shown)

15.3 Check the connecting rod side clearance with a feeler gauge as shown

connecting rod cap and bearing insert. Don't drop the bearing insert out of the cap.

6   Slip a short length of plastic or rubber hose over each connecting rod cap bolt to protect the crankshaft journal and cylinder wall when the piston is removed **(see illustration)**.

15.6 To prevent damage to the crankshaft journals and cylinder walls, slip sections of rubber or plastic hose over the rod bolts before removing the pistons

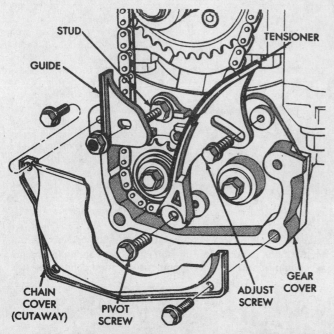

16.2 Balance shaft chain cover, guide and tensioner

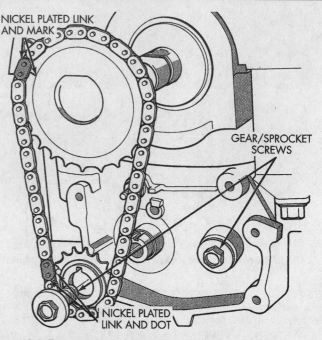

16.4 Remove the balance shaft chain sprocket, chain, and crankshaft bolts

7   Remove the bearing insert and push the connecting rod/piston assembly through the top of the engine. Use a wooden or plastic hammer handle to push on the upper bearing surface in the connecting rod. Double-check to make sure all of the ridge was removed from the cylinder if resistance is felt.

8   Repeat the procedure for the remaining cylinders.

9   After removal, reassemble the connecting rod caps and bearing inserts in their respective connecting rods and install the cap nuts finger tight. Leave the old bearing inserts in place until reassembly to prevent the connecting rod bearing surfaces from being accidentally nicked or gouged.

10   Don't separate the pistons from the connecting rods (see Section 21).

16   Balance shafts (four-cylinder engine only) - removal, inspection and installation

Note: *This procedure assumes that the engine has been removed from the vehicle and the driveplate, timing belt, oil pan and oil pump have also been removed (see Chapter 2A).* **Caution:** *With the timing belt removed, do not rotate the crankshaft unless the camshafts have first been removed (see Chapter 2A); valve damage may occur.*

Removal

Refer to illustrations 16.2, 16.4, 16.5 and 16.6

1   The balance shafts are installed in a carrier mounted to the main bearing cap/bed-plate on the lower part of the engine block. The shafts are connected through two gears which rotate them in opposite directions. These gears are driven by a chain from the crankshaft and are designed to rotate at a 2:1 ratio with the crankshaft (one turn of the crankshaft equals two turns of the balance shafts), which counterbalances reciprocating masses within the engine.

2   Remove the chain cover, guide and tensioner from the engine block **(see illustration)**.

3   Keep the crankshaft from rotating and remove the balance shaft bolts. **Note:** *A block of wood placed tightly between the engine block and the crankshaft counterbalance weight will prevent crankshaft rotation.*

4   Remove the balance shaft chain sprock-

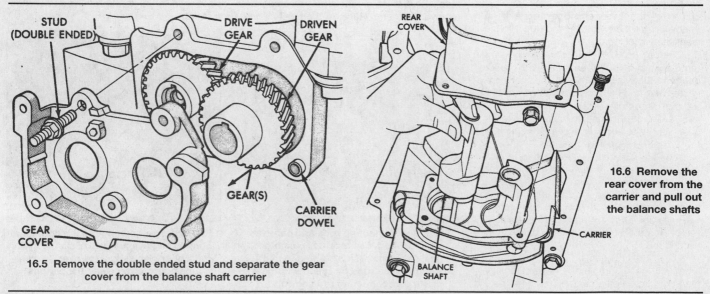

16.5 Remove the double ended stud and separate the gear cover from the balance shaft carrier

16.6 Remove the rear cover from the carrier and pull out the balance shafts

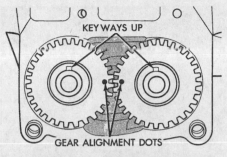

16.12 After gear installation, the balance shaft keyways should be parallel and facing the crankshaft, and the gear alignment dots should be together as shown

et, chain, and crankshaft chain sprocket **(see illustration)**. Use two prybars to work the sprocket back and forth until it is free from the crankshaft. **Note:** *The carrier assembly may be removed from the main bearing cap/bedplate at this time, if balance shaft removal is not required.*

5   Remove the special stud (double-ended) from the gear cover. Then remove the gear cover and balance shaft gears **(see illustration)**.
6   Remove the rear cover from the carrier and pull out the balance shafts **(see illustration)**.
7   Remove the bolts that hold the carrier to the main bearing cap/bedplate, and separate the carrier from the engine.

Cleaning and inspection

8   Clean all components with solvent and dry thoroughly. Inspect all components for damage and wear. Pay close attention to the chain, sprocket and gear teeth and the bearing surfaces of the carrier and balance shafts. Replace defective parts as necessary.

Installation

Refer to illustrations 16.12 and 16.15

9   Install the balance shaft carrier on the main bearing cap/bedplate and tighten the bolts to the torque in this Chapter's Specifications.
10   Lubricate the balance shafts with clean engine oil and insert them into the carrier.
11   Install the rear cover and tighten the bolts to the torque in this Chapter's Specifications.
12   Rotate the balance shafts until both shaft keyways are parallel and face the crankshaft. Install the short hub drive gear on the sprocket driven shaft and the long hub gear on the gear driven shaft. After installation, the timing marks (dots) should be together and the keyways positioned as shown **(see illustration)**.
13   Install the gear cover and tighten the double-ended stud to the torque in this Chapter's Specifications.
14   Install the sprocket on the crankshaft with the timing mark facing out, be careful not to cock the sprocket as its being installed.
15   Position the crankshaft so the timing mark on the chain sprocket is lined up with the parting line on the left side of the number 1 main bearing cap **(see illustration)**.
16   Place the chain on the crankshaft sprocket so that the nickel plated link of the chain is located at the timing mark on the crankshaft sprocket **(see illustration 16.15)**.
17   Install the balance shaft sprocket in the chain so that the timing mark on the sprocket (yellow dot) mates with the nickel plated link on the chain (8 links from the upper nickel plated link) **(see illustration 16.15)**.
18   Slide the balance shaft sprocket on the balance shaft. If the sprocket is difficult to install, it may be necessary to loosen the rear cover and push the balance shaft slightly out of the carrier to ease sprocket installation. **Note:** *The timing mark on the balance shaft sprocket and the nickel plated link should align with the notch on the side of the gear cover* **(see illustration 16.15)**.
19   Install the balance shaft bolts. Keep the crankshaft from rotating and tighten the balance shaft bolts to the torque in this Chapter's Specifications. **Note:** *A block of wood placed tightly between the engine block and the crankshaft counterbalance will prevent crankshaft rotation.*

Chain tensioning

Refer to illustration 16.20

20   Install the chain tensioner loosely. Place a 0.039 x 2.75 inch shim (a feeler gauge cut to the appropriate size can be used) between the tensioner and the chain **(see illustration)**. Push the tensioner against the chain. Apply pressure (approximately 5.5 to 6.5 lbs) directly behind the adjustment slot to remove the slack.
21   With pressure applied, tighten the top tensioner bolt first then the bottom pivot bolt. Tighten the bolts to the torque in this Chapter's Specifications. Remove the shim.
22   Place the chain guide on the double-ended stud making sure the tab on the guide fits into the slot on the gear cover. Tighten the nut to the torque in this Chapter's Specifications.
23   Install the chain cover and tighten the bolts securely.

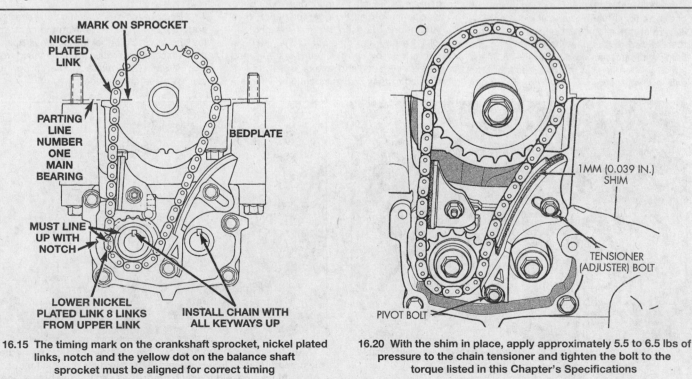

16.15 The timing mark on the crankshaft sprocket, nickel plated links, notch and the yellow dot on the balance shaft sprocket must be aligned for correct timing

16.20 With the shim in place, apply approximately 5.5 to 6.5 lbs of pressure to the chain tensioner and tighten the bolt to the torque listed in this Chapter's Specifications

17.1 Checking crankshaft endplay with a dial indicator

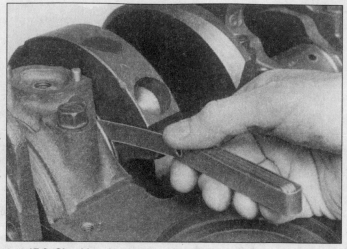

17.3 Checking the crankshaft endplay with a feeler gauge

17 Crankshaft - removal

Refer to illustrations 17.1, 17.3, 17.4a and 17.4b

Note: *The crankshaft can be removed only after the engine has been removed from the vehicle. Remove the driveplate, crankshaft balancer/vibration damper, timing chain or belt, oil pan, oil pump, counterbalance shafts (if equipped), and piston/connecting rod assemblies by referring to the appropriate Sections in Chapters 2A, 2B and 2C. The rear main oil seal housing must be unbolted and separated from the block before removing the crankshaft.*

1   Check the endplay before the crankshaft is removed. Mount a dial indicator with the stem in line with the crankshaft, touching one of the crankshaft throws **(see illustration)**.

2   Push the crankshaft all the way to the rear and zero the dial indicator. Pry the crankshaft as far as possible to the front and check the reading on the dial indicator. The distance it moves is the endplay. If it's greater than the endplay in this Chapter's Specifications, check the crankshaft thrust surfaces for wear. If no wear is evident, new main bearings should correct the endplay.

3   If a dial indicator isn't available, feeler gauges can be used. Gently pry or push the crankshaft all the way to the front of the engine. Slip feeler gauges between the crankshaft and the front face of the thrust main bearing to determine the clearance **(see illustration)**. **Note:** *The thrust main bearing is located at the Number Two main bearing cap on 3.3L and 3.8L V6 engines and at the Number Three main bearing cap on four-cylinder and 3.0L V6 engines.*

4   Check the main bearing caps to see if they're marked. They should be numbered consecutively from the front of the engine to the rear. If they aren't, mark them with number stamping dies or a center-punch **(see illustrations)**. Loosen the main bearing cap bolts 1/4-turn at a time each, until they can be removed by hand. Check to see if stud bolts are used and make sure they're returned to their original locations when the crankshaft is reinstalled.

5   Gently tap the caps with a soft-face hammer, then separate them from the engine block. If necessary, use the bolts as levers to remove the caps. Try not to drop the bearing inserts if they come out with the caps.

6   Carefully lift the crankshaft out of the engine. It may be a good idea to have a helper available, since the crankshaft is quite heavy. Leave the bearing inserts in the engine block and main bearing caps, and put the caps in their respective locations on the engine block. Tighten the bolts finger tight.

18 Engine block - cleaning

Refer to illustrations 18.4a, 18.4b, 18.8 and 18.10

1   Remove the main bearing caps and separate the bearing inserts from the caps and the engine block. Label the bearings to indicate which cylinder they were removed from and whether they were in the cap or the block, and set them aside.

17.4a The main bearing cap numerals (arrows) are easily visible on the 3.0L V6 engines

17.4b Use a centerpunch or number stamping dies to mark the main bearing caps to ensure installation in their original locations of the block (make the punch marks near one of the bolt heads)

18.4a Use a hammer and a large punch to knock the core plugs sideways in their bores . . .

18.4b . . . then pull the core plugs out with pliers

2   Use a gasket scraper to remove all traces of gasket material from the engine block. Be careful not to nick or gouge the gasket sealing surfaces.

3   Remove all of the covers and threaded oil gallery plugs from the block. The plugs are usually very tight - they may have to be drilled out and the holes retapped. Use new plugs when the engine is reassembled.

4   Remove the core plugs from the block **(see illustrations)**. **Caution:** *The core plugs (also known as freeze or soft plugs) may be difficult or impossible to retrieve if they're driven into the block coolant passages, so be very careful.*

5   If the engine is extremely dirty, it should be taken to an automotive machine shop to be steam cleaned or hot tanked.

6   After the block is returned, clean all oil holes and oil galleries again. Brushes specifically designed for this purpose are available at most auto parts stores. Flush the passages with warm water until the water runs clear, dry the block thoroughly and wipe all machined surfaces with a light, rust preventive oil. If you have compressed air, use it to speed the drying process and blow out all the oil holes and galleries. **Warning:** *Wear eye protection when using compressed air!*

7   If the block isn't extremely dirty or sludged up, you can do an adequate cleaning job with hot soapy water and a stiff brush. Take plenty of time and do a thorough job. Regardless of the cleaning method, be sure to clean all oil holes and galleries thoroughly. Dry the block completely and coat all machined surfaces with light oil.

8   The threaded holes in the block must be clean to ensure accurate torque readings during reassembly. Run the proper size tap into each of the holes to remove rust, corrosion, thread sealant or sludge, and restore damaged threads **(see illustration)**. If possible, use compressed air to clear the holes of debris. Clean the threads on the head bolts and the main bearing cap bolts as well.

9   Reinstall the main bearing caps and tighten the bolts finger tight.

10   After coating the sealing surfaces of the new core plugs with Permatex no. 2 sealant, install them in the engine block **(see illustration)**. Make sure they're driven in straight and seated properly or leakage could result. Special tools are available for this purpose, but a large socket, with an outside diameter that will just slip into the core plug, a 1/2-inch drive extension and a hammer will work just as well.

11   Apply non-hardening sealant (such as Permatex no. 2 or Teflon pipe sealant) to the new oil gallery plugs and thread them into the holes in the block. Make sure they're tightened securely.

12   If the engine isn't going to be reassembled right away, cover it with a large plastic trash bag to keep it clean.

18.8 All holes in the block - particularly the main bearing cap and head bolt holes - should be cleaned and restored with a tap (be sure to remove debris from the holes after this is done)

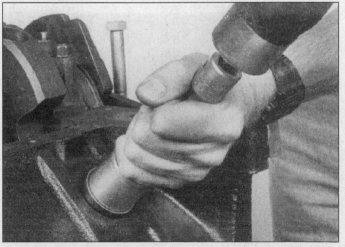

18.10 A large socket on an extension can be used to drive the new core plugs into the bores

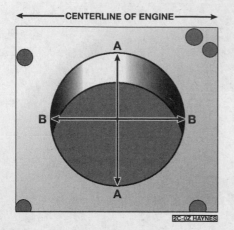

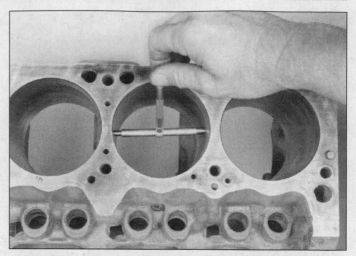

19.4a Measure the diameter of each cylinder at a right angle to the engine centerline (A) and parallel to the engine centerline (B) - the cylinder out-of-round is the difference between (A) and (B); the cylinder taper is the difference between (A) and (B) at the top of the cylinder and (A) and (B) at the bottom of the cylinder

19.4b The ability to "feel" when the telescoping gauge is at the correct point will be developed over time, so work slowly and repeat the check until you're satisfied the bore measurement is accurate

19   Engine block - inspection

Refer to illustrations 19.4a, 19.4b, 19.4c and 19.13

1   The block should be cleaned before it is inspected (see Section 18).

2   Check the block for cracks, rust and corrosion. Look for stripped threads. Its a good idea to have the block checked for hidden cracks by an automotive machine shop that has special equipment to do this type of work. If defects are found, have the block repaired, or replaced.

3   Check the cylinder walls for scuffing and scoring.

4   Measure the diameter of each cylinder at the top (just under the ridge area), center and bottom of the cylinder, parallel to the crankshaft axis **(see illustrations)**.

5   Measure each cylinder's diameter at the same three locations across the crankshaft axis. Compare the results to this Chapter's Specifications.

6   If precision measuring tools aren't available, the piston-to-cylinder clearances can be obtained using feeler gauge stock. Feeler gauge stock comes in 12-inch lengths and various thicknesses and is available in auto parts stores.

7   To check the clearance, select a feeler gauge and slip it into the cylinder along with the matching piston. The piston must be positioned exactly as it normally would be. The feeler gauge must be between the piston and cylinder on one of the thrust faces (90-degrees to the wrist pin).

8   The piston should slip through the cylinder (with the feeler gauge in place) with moderate pressure.

9   If it falls through or slides through easily, the clearance is excessive and a new piston is required. If the piston binds at the lower end of the cylinder and is loose toward the top, the cylinder is tapered. If tight spots are encountered as the piston/feeler gauge is rotated in the cylinder, the cylinder is out-of-round.

10   Repeat the procedure for the remaining pistons and cylinders.

11   If the cylinder walls are badly scuffed or scored, or if they're out-of-round or tapered beyond the limits in this Chapter's Specifications, have the engine block rebored and honed at an automotive machine shop. If the block is rebored, oversize pistons and rings will be required.

12   If the cylinders are in reasonably good condition and not worn beyond specified limits, and if the piston-to-cylinder clearances can be maintained, they don't have to be rebored. Honing is all that is required (see Section 20).

13   Use a precision straightedge and a feeler gauge to check the block deck (the surface that mates with the cylinder head) for distortion **(see illustration)**. If it's distorted

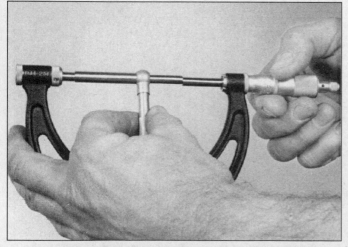

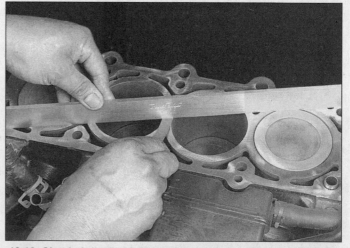

19.4c The gauge is then measured with a micrometer to determine the bore size

19.13 Check the cylinder block head gasket surface for warpage by placing a precision straightedge across the surface and trying to slip a feeler gauge between the block and the straightedge

20.2a A "bottle brush" hone will produce better results if you've never honed cylinders before

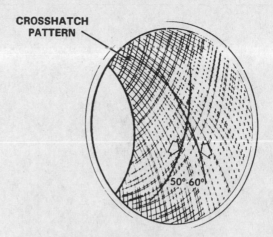

CROSSHATCH PATTERN

50°-60°

20.2b The cylinder hone should leave a smooth, crosshatch pattern with the lines intersecting at approximately a 60-degree angle

beyond the tolerance in this Chapter's Specifications, it can probably be resurfaced by an automotive machine shop.

20 Cylinder honing

Refer to illustrations 20.2a and 20.2b

1   Prior to engine reassembly, the cylinder bores must be honed so the new piston rings will seat correctly and provide the best possible combustion chamber seal. **Note:** *If you don't have the tools or don't want to tackle the honing operation, most automotive machine shops will do it for a reasonable fee.*

2   Two types of cylinder hones are commonly available - the flex hone or "bottle brush" type and the more traditional surfacing hone with spring-loaded stones. Both will do the job, but for the less experienced mechanic the "bottle brush" hone will probably be easier to use. You'll also need some honing oil (kerosene will work if honing oil isn't available), rags and an electric drill motor. Proceed as follows:

a) *Mount the hone in the drill motor, compress the stones and slip it into the first cylinder* **(see illustration)**. *Be sure to wear safety goggles or a face shield!*

b) *Lubricate the cylinder with plenty of honing oil, turn on the drill and move the hone up-and-down in the cylinder at a pace that will produce a fine crosshatch pattern on the cylinder walls. The crosshatch lines should intersect at approximately a 60-degree angle* **(see illustration)**. *Be sure to use plenty of lubricant and don't take off more material than is absolutely necessary to produce the desired finish.* **Note:** *Piston ring manufacturers may specify a smaller crosshatch angle than the traditional 60-degrees - read and follow any instructions included with the new rings.*

c) *Don't withdraw the hone from the cylinder while it's running. Shut the drill off and continue moving the hone up-and-down in the cylinder until it comes to a complete stop, then compress the stones and withdraw the hone. If you're using a "bottle brush" type hone, stop the drill motor, then turn the chuck in the normal direction of rotation while withdrawing the hone from the cylinder.*

d) *Wipe the oil out of the cylinder and repeat the procedure for the remaining cylinders.*

3   After the honing is complete, chamfer the top edges of the cylinder bores with a small file so the rings won't catch when the pistons are installed. Be very careful not to nick the cylinder walls with the end of the file.

4   The entire engine block must be washed again very thoroughly with warm, soapy water to remove all traces of the abrasive grit produced during the honing operation. **Note:** *The bores can be considered clean when a lint-free white cloth - dampened with clean engine oil doesn't pick up any more honing*

residue, which shows up as gray areas on the cloth. Be sure to run a brush through all oil holes and galleries and flush them with running water.

5   After rinsing, dry the block and apply a coat of light rust preventive oil to all machined surfaces. Wrap the block in a plastic trash bag to keep it clean and set it aside until reassembly.

21 Pistons and connecting rods - inspection

Refer to illustrations 21.2, 21.4a, 21.4b, 21.10 and 21.11

1   Before the inspection can be done, the piston/connecting rod assemblies must be cleaned and the original piston rings removed from the pistons. **Note:** *Always use new piston rings when the engine is reassembled.*

2   Use a piston ring installation tool and carefully remove the rings from the pistons **(see illustration)**. Do not to nick or gouge the pistons in the process.

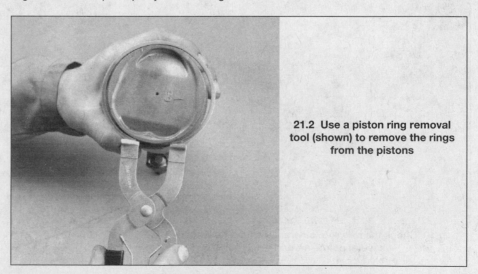

21.2 Use a piston ring removal tool (shown) to remove the rings from the pistons

21.4a The piston ring grooves can be cleaned with a special tool, as shown here . . .

21.4b . . . or a section of a broken ring

3   Scrape all traces of carbon from the top of the piston. A hand-held wire brush or a piece of fine emery cloth can be used when the majority of the deposits have been scraped away. Do not use a wire brush mounted in a drill motor to remove deposits from the pistons. The piston material is soft and may be worn away by the wire brush.

4   Use a piston ring groove cleaning tool to remove carbon deposits from the ring grooves. If a tool isn't available, a piece broken off the old ring will do the job. Be careful to remove only the carbon deposits - don't remove any metal and do not nick or scratch the sides of the ring grooves **(see illustrations)**.

5   When the deposits have been removed, clean the piston/rod assemblies with solvent and dry them with compressed air (if available). **Warning:** *Wear eye protection. Make sure the oil return holes in the back sides of the ring grooves are clear.*

6   If the pistons and cylinder walls aren't damaged or excessively worn, and the engine block isn't rebored, new pistons won't be necessary. Normal piston wear appears as even vertical wear on the piston thrust surfaces and slight looseness of the top ring in its groove. New piston rings should always be used when an engine is rebuilt.

7   Inspect each piston for cracks around the skirt, at the pin bosses, and at the ring lands.

8   Look for scoring and scuffing on the thrust faces of the skirt, holes in the piston crown, and burned areas at the edge of the crown. If the skirt is scored or scuffed, the engine may have overheated. The cooling and lubrication systems should be thoroughly checked. A hole in the piston crown indicates abnormal combustion (preignition) occurred. Burned areas at the edge of the piston crown indicates spark knock (detonation). If any of the above problems exist, the causes must be corrected or the damage will occur again. The causes may include intake air leaks, incorrect fuel/air mixture, low octane fuel, ignition timing, and EGR system malfunctions.

9   Corrosion of the piston, in the form of small pits, indicates coolant leaks into the combustion chamber and/or the crankcase. The cause must be corrected or the problem may persist in the rebuilt engine.

10   Measure the piston ring side clearance by laying a new piston ring in each ring groove and slipping a feeler gauge in beside it **(see illustration)**. Check the clearance at three or four locations around each groove. Be sure to use the correct ring for each groove - they are different. If the side clearance is greater than specified in this Chapter's Specifications, new pistons are required.

11   Check the piston-to-bore clearance by measuring the bore (see Section 19) and the piston diameter. Make sure the pistons and bores are correctly matched. Measure the piston across the skirt, at a 90-degree angle to the piston pin **(see illustration)**. The measurement must be taken at a specific point, depending on the engine type, to be accurate.

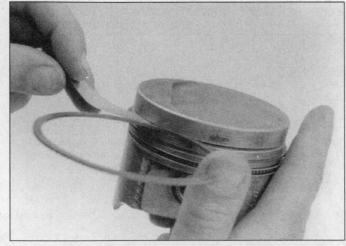

21.10 Check the ring side clearance with a feeler gauge at several points around the groove

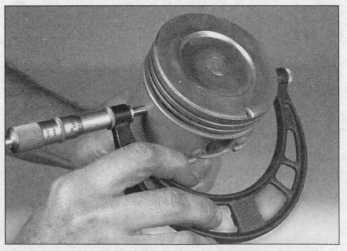

21.11 Measure the piston diameter 90-degrees from the piston pin

22.1 The oil holes should be chamfered so sharp edges don't gouge or scratch the new bearings

22.2 Use a wire or stiff plastic bristle brush to clean the oil passages in the crankshaft

a) *Four-cylinder engines are measured 0.563 inches above the bottom of the piston.*
b) *3.0L V6 engine pistons are measured 0.080 inches above the bottom of the piston skirt.*
c) *3.3L V6 engine pistons are measured 1.65 inches below the top of the piston.*
d) *3.8L V6 engine pistons are measured 1.42 inches below the top of the piston.*

12   Subtract the piston diameter from the bore diameter to obtain the clearance. If it's greater than specified in this Chapter's Specifications, the block will have to be rebored and new pistons and rings installed.

13   Check the piston-to-rod clearance by twisting the piston and rod in opposite directions. Any noticeable play indicates excessive wear, which must be corrected. The piston/connecting rod assemblies should be taken to an automotive machine shop to have the pistons and rods resized and new pins installed.

14   If the pistons must be removed from the connecting rods for any reason, they should be taken to an automotive machine shop. Also

have the machine shop check the connecting rods for bend and twist; automotive machine shops have special equipment for this purpose. **Note:** *Unless new pistons and/or connecting rods must be installed, do not disassemble the pistons and connecting rods.*

15   Check the connecting rods for cracks and other damage. Temporarily remove the rod caps, lift out the old bearing inserts, wipe the rod and cap bearing surfaces clean and inspect them for nicks, gouges and scratches. After checking the rods, replace the old bearings, slip the caps into place and tighten the nuts finger tight. **Note:** *If the engine is being rebuilt because of a connecting rod knock, be sure to install new rods.*

22   Crankshaft - inspection

Refer to illustrations 22.1, 22.2, 22.4, 22.6 and 22.8

1   Remove burrs from the crankshaft oil holes with a stone, file, or scraper **(see illustration)**.
2   Clean the crankshaft with solvent and

dry it with compressed air (if available). **Warning:** *Wear eye protection when using compressed air.* Be sure to clean the oil holes with a stiff brush **(see illustration)** and flush them with solvent.

3   Check the main and connecting rod bearing journals for uneven wear, scoring, pits, and cracks.

4   Rub a penny across each journal several times **(see illustration)**. If a journal picks up copper from the penny, it's too rough and must be reground.

5   Check the rest of the crankshaft for cracks and other damage. It should be magnafluxed to reveal hidden cracks - an automotive machine shop can handle the procedure.

6   Use a micrometer to measure the diameter of the main and connecting rod journals and compare the results to this Chapter's Specifications **(see illustration)**. Measure the diameter at a number of points around each journal's circumference to determine whether the journal is out-of-round. Take the measurement at each end of the journal, near the crank throws, to determine if the journal is tapered.

22.4 Rubbing a penny lengthwise on each journal will reveal its condition - if copper rubs off and is embedded in the crankshaft, the journals should be reground

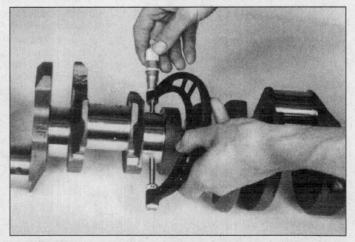

22.6 Measure the diameter of each crankshaft journal at several points to detect taper and out-of-round conditions

22.8 If the seals have worn grooves in the crankshaft journals, or if the seal contact surfaces are nicked or scratched, the new seals will leak

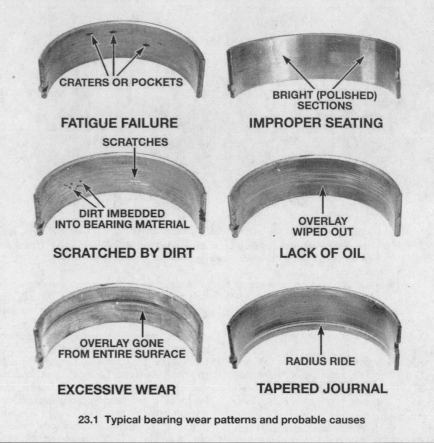

23.1 Typical bearing wear patterns and probable causes

7   If the crankshaft journals are damaged, tapered, out-of-round, or worn beyond the limits in this Chapter's Specifications, have the crankshaft reground by an automotive machine shop. Be sure to use the correct size bearing inserts if the crankshaft is reconditioned.

8   Check the oil seal journals at each end of the crankshaft for wear and damage. If the seal has worn a groove in the journal, or if it's nicked or scratched **(see illustration)**, the new seal may leak when the engine is reassembled. An automotive machine shop may be able to repair the journal by pressing on a thin sleeve. If repair isn't feasible, a new or different crankshaft should be installed.

9   Refer to Section 23 and examine the main and rod bearing inserts.

23 Main and connecting rod bearings - inspection

Refer to illustration 23.1

1   Main and connecting rod bearings should be replaced with new ones during engine overhaul. The old bearings should be retained. They may reveal valuable information about the condition of the engine **(see illustration)**.

2   Bearing failure occurs because of lack of lubrication, the presence of dirt or foreign particles, overloading the engine, and corrosion. Regardless of the cause of bearing failure, it must be corrected before the engine is reassembled to prevent it from happening again.

3   To examine the bearings, remove them from the engine block, the main bearing caps, the connecting rods, and the rod caps. Lay them on a clean surface in the same position as their location in the engine. This will enable you to match bearing problems with the corresponding crankshaft journal.

4   Dirt and foreign particles can get into the engine in a variety of ways. It may be left in the engine during assembly, or it may pass through filters or the PCV system. It may get into the oil, and from there into the bearings. Metal chips from machining operations and normal engine wear are often present. Abrasives are sometimes left in engine components after reconditioning, especially when parts aren't thoroughly cleaned. Whatever the source, these foreign objects often end up embedded in the soft bearing material. Large particles won't embed in the bearing and will score or gouge the bearing and journal. The best prevention for this cause of bearing failure is to clean all parts thoroughly and keep everything spotlessly clean during engine assembly. Frequent and regular engine oil and filter changes are also recommended.

5   Lack of lubrication (or lubrication breakdown) has a number of interrelated causes. Excessive heat (which thins the oil), overloading (which squeezes the oil from the bearing face) and oil leakage or throw off (from excessive bearing clearances, worn oil pump or high engine speeds) all contribute to lubrication breakdown. Blocked oil passages, usually the result of misaligned oil holes in a bearing shell, will oil starve a bearing and destroy it. When lack of lubrication is the cause of bearing failure, the bearing material is wiped or extruded from the steel backing of the bearing. Temperatures may increase to the point where the steel backing turns blue from overheating.

6   Driving habits can have a definite effect on bearing life. Full throttle, low speed operation (lugging the engine) puts very high loads on bearings, which tends to squeeze out the oil film. These loads cause the bearings to flex, producing fine cracks in the bearing face (fatigue failure). Eventually the bearing material will loosen in pieces and tear away from the steel backing. Short trip driving leads to corrosion of bearings because insufficient engine heat is produced to drive off the condensed water and corrosive gases. These products collect in the engine oil, forming acid and sludge. As the oil is carried to the engine bearings, the acid attacks and corrodes the bearing material.

7   Incorrect bearing installation during engine assembly will lead to bearing failure as well. Tight fitting bearings leave insufficient oil clearance and will result in oil starvation. Dirt or foreign particles trapped behind a bearing insert can result in high spots on the bearing, leading to failure.

24 Engine overhaul - reassembly sequence

1   Before beginning engine reassembly, make sure you have all the necessary new parts, gaskets and seals as well as the following items on hand:

Common hand tools
Torque wrench (1/2-inch drive)
Piston ring installation tool
Piston ring compressor
Vibration damper installation tool

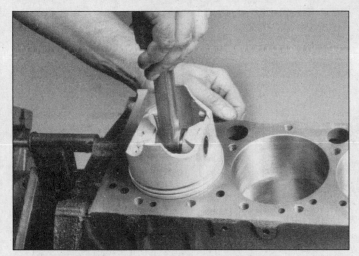

25.3 When checking piston ring end gap, the ring must be square in the cylinder bore (this is done by pushing the ring down with the top of a piston as shown)

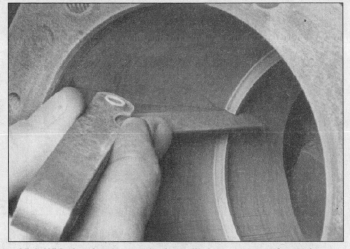

25.4 With the ring square in the cylinder, measure the end gap with a feeler gauge

Short lengths of rubber or plastic hose to fit over connecting rod bolts
Plastigage
Feeler gauges
Fine-tooth file
New engine oil
Engine assembly lube or moly-base grease
Gasket sealant
Thread locking compound

2   In order to save time and avoid problems, engine reassembly must be done in the following general order:

Four-cylinder engine

Piston rings installed on pistons
Crankshaft and main bearings
Piston/connecting rod assemblies
Rear main oil seal
Balance shaft carrier
Front case and oil pump assembly
Oil pan
Cylinder head(s) assembly
Water pump
Timing belt and sprockets
Timing belt cover(s)
Rocker arm cover(s)
Intake and exhaust manifolds
Driveplate

3.0 V6 engine

Crankshaft and main bearings
Rear main oil seal housing
Piston/connecting rod assemblies
Oil pump
Oil pan
Timing belt cover
Timing belt and sprockets
Cylinder heads and camshafts
Intake and exhaust manifolds
Valve covers
Driveplate

3.3L and 3.8L V6 engines

Crankshaft and main bearings
Rear main oil seal housing
Piston/connecting rod assemblies
Oil pump

Camshaft
Timing chain and sprockets
Timing chain cover
Oil pan
Cylinder heads
Valve lifters
Rocker arms and pushrods
Intake and exhaust manifolds
Valve covers
Driveplate

25 Piston rings - installation

Refer to illustrations 25.3, 25.4, 25.5, 25.9a, 25.9b, 25.11 and 25.12

1   Before installing the piston rings, the ring end gaps must be checked. It's assumed the piston ring side clearance has been checked and verified correct (see Section 21).
2   Lay out the piston/connecting rod assemblies and the new ring sets so the ring sets will be matched with the same piston and cylinder during the end gap measurement and engine assembly.
3   Insert the top (number one) ring into the first cylinder and square it up with the cylin-

der walls by pushing it in with the top of the piston (see illustration). The ring should be near the bottom of the cylinder, at the lower limit of ring travel. **Note:** *On 3.3L and 3.8L V6 engines, the measurement should be taken at least 0.500 inch from the bottom of the cylinder bore.*
4   To measure the end gap, slip feeler gauges between the ends of the ring until a gauge equal to the gap width is found (see illustration). The feeler gauge should slide between the ring ends with a slight amount of drag. Compare the measurement to this Chapter's Specifications. If the gap is larger or smaller than specified, double-check to make sure you have the correct rings before proceeding.
5   If the gap is too small, it must be enlarged or the ring ends may come in contact with each other during engine operation, which can cause serious engine damage. The end gap can be increased by filing the ring ends very carefully with a fine file. Mount the file in a vise equipped with soft jaws, slip the ring over the file with the ends contacting the file teeth and slowly move the ring to remove material from the ends. When performing this operation, file only from the outside in (see illustration).

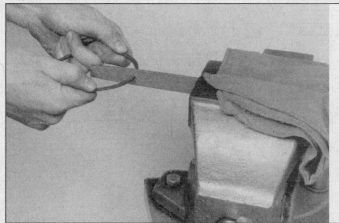

25.5 If the end gap is too small, clamp a file in a vise and file the ring ends (from the outside in only) to enlarge the gap slightly

25.9a Installing the spacer/expander in the oil control ring groove

25.9b DO NOT use a piston ring installation tool when installing the oil ring side rails

6   Excess end gap isn't critical unless it's greater than 0.040-inch. Double-check to make sure you have the correct rings for the engine.

7   Repeat the procedure for each ring to be installed in the first cylinder and for each ring in the remaining cylinders. Remember to keep rings, pistons and cylinders matched up.

8   When the ring end gaps have been checked/corrected, the rings can be installed on the pistons.

9   The oil control ring (lowest one on the piston) is usually installed first. It's composed of three separate components. Slip the spacer/expander into the groove (see illustration). If an anti-rotation tang is used, make sure it's inserted into the drilled hole in the ring groove. Next, install the lower side rail. Don't use a piston ring installation tool on the oil ring side rails; they may be damaged. Instead, place one end of the side rail into the groove between the spacer/expander and the ring land, hold it firmly in place and slide a fin-ger around the piston while pushing the rail into the groove (see illustration). Install the upper side rail in the same manner.

10   After the three oil ring components have been installed, check to make sure both the upper and lower side rails can be turned smoothly in the ring groove.

11   The number two (middle) ring is installed next. It's usually stamped with a mark, which must face up, toward the top of the piston (see illustration). Note: *Always follow the instructions printed on the ring package or box - different manufacturers may require different approaches. Don't mix the top and middle rings, as they have different cross sections.*

12   Use a piston ring installation tool and make sure the identification mark is facing the top of the piston (see illustration). Slip the ring into the middle groove on the piston. Don't expand the ring any more than necessary to slide it over the piston.

13   Install the number one (top) ring in the same manner. Make sure the mark is facing

up. Be careful not to confuse the number one and number two rings.

14   Repeat the procedure for the remaining pistons and rings.

26 Crankshaft - installation and main bearing oil clearance check

Refer to illustrations 26.3a, 26.3b, 26.3c, 26.5, 26.11, 26.13a, 26.13b and 26.15

1   Crankshaft installation is the first step in engine reassembly. It's assumed at this point that the engine block and crankshaft have been cleaned, inspected, and repaired or reconditioned.

2   Position the engine with the bottom facing up.

3   Remove the main bearing cap bolts and lift out the caps. Lay them out in the proper order to ensure correct installation (see illustrations).

4   If they're still in place, remove the original bearing inserts from the block and the main bearing caps. Wipe the bearing surfaces of the block and caps with a clean, lint-free cloth. They must be kept spotlessly clean.

Main bearing oil clearance check

Note: *Don't touch the faces of the new bearing inserts with your fingers. Oil and acids from your skin can etch the bearings.*

5   Clean the back sides of the new main bearing inserts and lay one in each main bearing saddle in the block (see illustration). If one of the bearing inserts from each set has a large groove in it, make sure the grooved insert is installed in the block. Lay the other bearing from each set in the corresponding main bearing cap. Make sure the tab on the bearing insert fits into the recess in the block or cap. **Caution:** *The oil holes in the block must line up with the oil holes in the bearing inserts. Do not hammer the bearing into place and don't nick or gouge the bearing faces. No lubrication should be used at this time.*

6   The flanged thrust bearing must be installed in the number two cap and saddle (counting from the front of the engine) on 3.3L and 3.8L V6 engines. On the four-cylinder and 3.0L V6 engines, the thrust bearing must be installed in the number three (center) cap and saddle. Note that the 3.0L V6 engine uses separate thrust washers.

7   Clean the faces of the bearings in the block and the crankshaft main bearing journals with a clean, lint-free cloth.

8   Clean the oil holes in the crankshaft, any dirt here can go only one way - straight through the new bearings.

9   When the crankshaft is clean, carefully lay it in position in the main bearings.

10   Before the crankshaft can be permanently installed, the main bearing oil clearance must be checked.

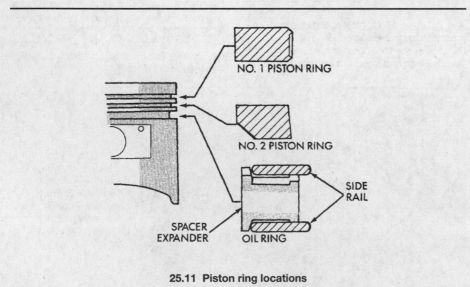

25.11 Piston ring locations

NO. 1 PISTON RING

NO. 2 PISTON RING

SIDE RAIL

SPACER EXPANDER

OIL RING

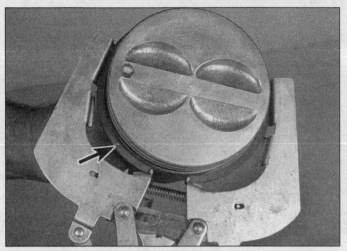

25.12 Installing the compression rings with a ring expander - the mark on the ring must face up

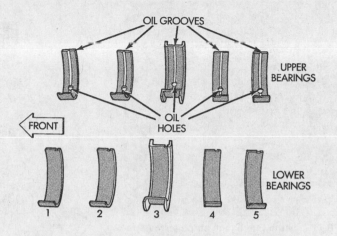

26.3a Four-cylinder main bearings - the No. 3 bearing is the thrust bearing

26.3b On the 3.0L V6 engine, separate thrust washers, located at the number three bearing, are used. Use thick engine assembly grease to hold them in place during assembly

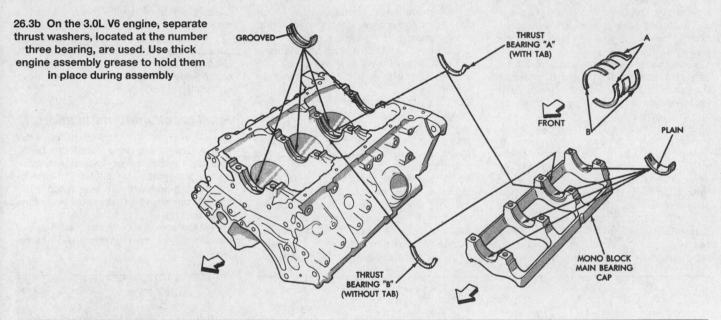

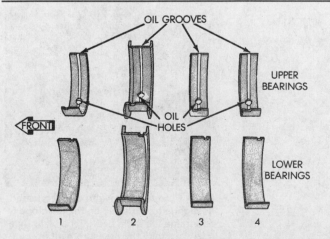

26.3c The thrust bearing is located on the number 2 journal on the 3.3L and 3.8L V6 engines

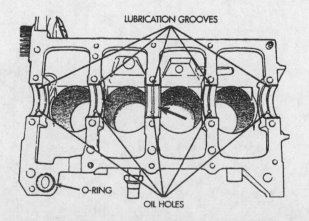

26.5 On four-cylinder engines, install the upper bearings (with grooves and holes) into the engine block. Be sure to align the oil holes and install the thrust bearing in the center bearing position (arrow)

26.11 Lay the Plastigage strips (arrow) on the main bearing journals, parallel to the crankshaft centerline

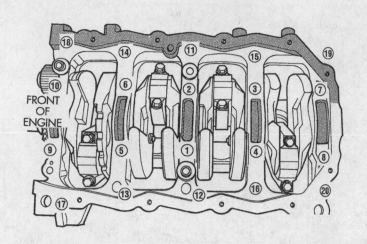

26.13a Four-cylinder engine main bearing cap/bedplate assembly bolt tightening sequence

11   Cut several pieces of the appropriate size Plastigage (they should be slightly shorter than the width of the main bearings) and place one piece on each crankshaft main bearing journal, parallel with the journal axis **(see illustration)**.

12   Clean the faces of the bearings in the caps and install the caps in their original locations (don't mix them) with the arrows pointing toward the front of the engine. Don't disturb the Plastigage.

13   Start with the center main bearing and work out toward the ends, tighten the main bearing cap bolts, in three steps, to the torque in this Chapter's Specifications. Don't rotate the crankshaft during this operation. **Note 1:** *On the four-cylinder engine cap/bedplate and the 3.0L V6 engine Mono-block, be sure to torque in the correct sequence* **(see illustrations)**. **Note 2:** *On four-cylinder engines, it is only necessary to torque the larger main bearing cap bolts for this check.*

14   Remove the bolts and carefully lift off the main bearing caps. Keep them in order. Don't disturb the Plastigage or rotate the crankshaft. If any of the main bearing caps are difficult to remove, tap them gently from side-to-side with a soft-face hammer to loosen them.

15   Compare the width of the crushed Plastigage on each journal to the scale printed on the Plastigage envelope to obtain the main bearing oil clearance **(see illustration)**. Check this Chapter's Specifications to make sure it's correct.

16   If the clearance is not correct, the bearing inserts may be the wrong size (which means different ones will be required). Before deciding different inserts are needed, make sure no dirt or oil was between the bearing inserts and the caps or block when the clearance was measured. If the Plastigage was wider at one end than the other, the journal may be tapered (see Section 22).

17   Carefully scrape all traces of the Plastigage material off the main bearing journals and/or the bearing faces. Use your fingernail or the edge of a credit card - don't nick or scratch the bearing faces.

Final crankshaft installation

18   Carefully lift the crankshaft out of the engine. Clean the bearing faces in the block, then apply a thin, uniform layer of moly-base grease or engine assembly lube to each of the bearing surfaces. Be sure to coat the thrust faces as well as the journal face of the thrust bearing.

19   Make sure the crankshaft journals are clean, then lay the crankshaft back in the block.

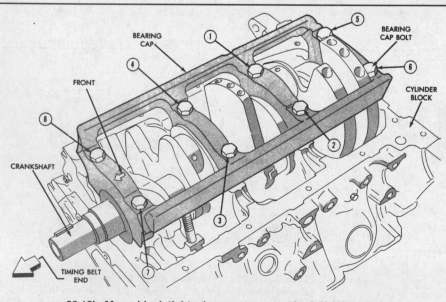

26.13b Mono-block tightening sequence on the 3.0L V6 engine

26.15 Compare the width of the crushed Plastigage to the scale on the envelope to determine the main bearing oil clearance (always take the measurement at the widest point of the Plastigage); be sure to use the correct scale - standard and metric ones are included

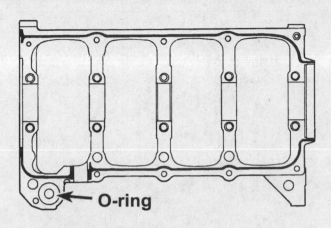

26.20 On four-cylinder engines, apply a 0.059- to 0.078-inch bead of the specified anaerobic sealant to the engine block as shown

27.1 Coat the lobes and journals with cam lube

Four-cylinder engines

Refer to illustration 26.20

20   Clean the bedplate-to-cylinder block mating surfaces. They must be free of oil residue. Apply a 0.059- to 0.078-inch bead of Mopar Torque Cure Gasket Maker (or equivalent) to the cylinder block as shown **(see illustration). Caution:** *You must use the correct anaerobic sealant on the bedplate or damage may occur to the engine.*

21   Install the the bedplate/main bearing cap assembly on the engine block and tighten the bolts in the stages listed in the Specifications in the recommended sequence **(see illustration 26.13a). Note:** *Replace any O-ring seals between the cap assembly and the engine block, if equipped.*

V6 engines

22   Install the caps or mono-block in the original locations with the arrows pointing toward the front of the engine.
23   Install the bolts.
24   Tighten all except the thrust bearing cap

bolts to the torque in this Chapter's Specifications (work from the center and finish the torque in three steps).
25   Tighten the thrust bearing cap bolts to 10-to-12 ft-lbs.
26   Tap the ends of the crankshaft forward and backward with a lead or brass hammer to line up the main bearing and crankshaft thrust surfaces.
27   Retighten all main bearing cap bolts to the torque in this Chapter's Specifications, starting with the center main and working out toward the ends.

All engines

28   Rotate the crankshaft a number of times by hand to check for binding.
29   The final step is to check the crankshaft endplay with feeler gauges or a dial indicator (see Section 17). The endplay should be correct if the crankshaft thrust faces aren't worn or damaged and new bearings have been installed.
30   Install the new rear main oil seal (see Section 28).

27   Camshaft (3.3L and 3.8L V6 engines only) - installation

Refer to illustration 27.1
Note: *This procedure applies to 3.3L and 3.8L V6 engines only.*
1   Lubricate the camshaft bearing journals and cam lobes with moly-base grease or engine assembly lube **(see illustration)**.
2   Slide the camshaft into the engine. Support the cam near the block and be careful not to scrape or nick the bearings.
3   Install the thrust plate and bolts. Tighten the bolts to the torque in this Chapter's Specifications.
4   See Chapter 2C for the timing chain installation procedure.

28   Rear main oil seal - installation

Refer to illustrations 28.1, 28.2 and 28.3
Note: *The crankshaft must be installed and the main bearing caps bolted in place before the new seal and housing assembly can be bolted to the block.*
1   Remove the old seal from the housing with a hammer and punch. Drive it out from the back side **(see illustration)**. Look to see how far it's recessed into the housing bore before removing it; the new seal will have to be recessed the same amount. Be careful not to scratch or damage the bore in the housing or oil leaks could develop.
2   Clean the housing, and apply a thin coat of engine oil to the outer edge of the new seal. The seal must be pressed squarely into the housing bore. Hammering it into place isn't recommended. If you don't have access to a press, sandwich the housing and seal between two smooth pieces of wood and press the seal into place with the jaws of a large vise. If you don't have a large enough vise, lay the housing on a workbench and drive the seal into place with a block of wood

28.1 To remove the old rear main oil seal from the housing, support the housing on a pair of wood blocks and drive out the seal with a punch or screwdriver and hammer - make sure you don't damage the seal bore

28.2 To install the new seal in the housing, simply lay the housing on a clean, flat workbench, lay a block of wood on the seal and carefully tap it into place with a hammer

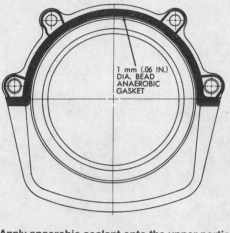

28.3 Apply anaerobic sealant onto the upper portion of the retainer

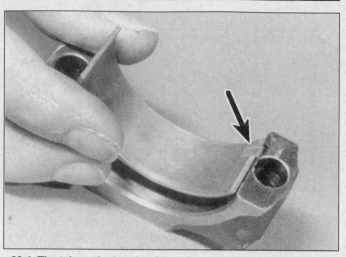

29.4 The tab on the bearing (arrow) must fit into the cap recess so the bearing will seat properly

and hammer **(see illustration)**. The wood must be thick enough to distribute the force evenly around the entire circumference of the seal. Work slowly making sure the seal enters the bore squarely.

3   Apply anaerobic sealant to the upper portion of the retainer **(see illustration)** before installing the housing. Lubricate the seal lips with clean engine oil or multi-purpose grease before you slip the seal/housing over the crankshaft and bolt it to the block.

4   Tighten the housing bolts a little at a time until they're all snug.

29   Pistons and connecting rods - installation and rod bearing oil clearance check

1   Before installing the piston/connecting rod assemblies, the cylinder walls must be perfectly clean, the top edge of each cylinder must be chamfered, and the crankshaft must be in place.

2   Remove the cap from the end of the number one connecting rod (check the marks made during removal). Remove the original bearing inserts and wipe the bearing surfaces of the connecting rod and cap with a clean, lint-free cloth. They must be kept spotlessly clean.

Connecting rod bearing oil clearance check

Refer to illustrations 29.4, 29.5, 29.9a, 29.9b, 29.11, 29.13, 29.14 and 29.17

Note: *Don't touch the faces of the new bearing inserts with your fingers. Oil and acids from your skin can etch the bearings.*

3   Clean the back side of the new upper bearing insert, then lay it in place in the connecting rod. Make sure the tab on the bearing fits into the recess in the rod. Don't hammer the bearing insert into place and be careful not to nick or gouge the bearing face. Do not lubricate the bearing at this time.

4   Clean the back side of the other bearing insert and install it in the rod cap. Make sure

the tab on the bearing fits into the recess in the cap **(see illustration)**. Do not apply lubricant. It's very important that the mating surfaces of the bearing and connecting rod are perfectly clean and oil free when they're assembled.

5   Position the piston ring gaps at 120-degree intervals around the piston **(see illustration)**.

6   Slip a section of plastic or rubber hose over each connecting rod cap bolt.

7   Lubricate the piston and rings with clean engine oil and put the piston ring compressor on the piston. Leave the skirt protruding about 1/4-inch to guide the piston into the cylinder. The rings must be compressed until they're flush with the piston.

8   Rotate the crankshaft until the number one connecting rod journal is at BDC (bottom dead center) and apply a coat of engine oil to the cylinder walls.

9   With the mark or notch on top of the piston **(see illustrations)** facing the front of the engine, gently insert the piston/connecting rod assembly into the number one cylinder bore and rest the bottom edge of the ring compressor on the engine block. If you're working on a four-cylinder engine, make sure the oil hole in the lower end of the connecting rod faces the front (timing belt) side of the engine.

10   Tap the top edge of the ring compressor to make sure it's contacting the block around its entire circumference.

11   Gently tap on the top of the piston with the end of a wooden or plastic hammer handle **(see illustration)** while guiding the end of the connecting rod into place on the crankshaft journal. The piston rings may try to pop out of the ring compressor just before entering the cylinder bore, keep downward pressure on the ring compressor. Work slowly, and if any resistance is felt as the piston enters the cylinder, stop immediately. Find out what's hanging up and fix it before proceeding. Do not force the piston into the cylinder - you might break a ring and/or the piston.

29.5 Position the ring gaps as shown here before installing the piston/connecting rod assemblies in the engine

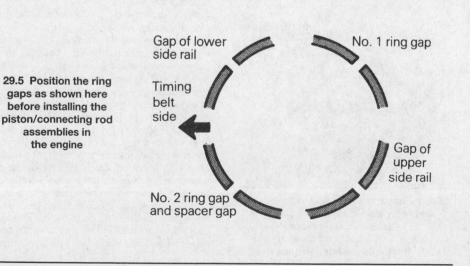

Gap of lower side rail

No. 1 ring gap

Timing belt side

Gap of upper side rail

No. 2 ring gap and spacer gap

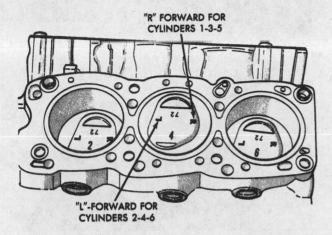

"R" FORWARD FOR CYLINDERS 1-3-5

"L"-FORWARD FOR CYLINDERS 2-4-6

29.9a Piston orientation after installation (3.0L V6 engine)

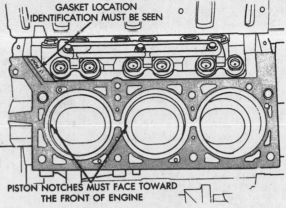

GASKET LOCATION IDENTIFICATION MUST BE SEEN

PISTON NOTCHES MUST FACE TOWARD THE FRONT OF ENGINE

29.9b Piston orientation after installation (1996 through 2000 3.3L and 3.8L V6 engines)

29.11 Gently drive the piston into the cylinder bore with the end of a wooden or plastic hammer handle

29.13 Lay the Plastigage strips on each rod bearing journal, parallel to the crankshaft centerline

12   When the piston/connecting rod assembly is installed, the connecting rod bearing oil clearance must be checked before the rod cap is permanently bolted into place.

13   Cut a piece of the appropriate size Plastigage slightly shorter than the width of the connecting rod bearing and lay it in place on the number one connecting rod journal, parallel with the journal axis **(see illustration)**.

14   Clean the connecting rod cap bearing face, remove the protective hoses from the connecting rod bolts and install the rod cap. Make sure the mating mark on the cap is on the same side as the mark on the connecting rod **(see illustration)**.

15   Install the nuts and tighten them to the torque in this Chapter's Specifications. Work up to it in three steps. **Note:** *Use a thin-wall socket to avoid erroneous torque readings that can result if the socket is wedged between the rod cap and nut. If the socket tends to wedge itself between the nut and the cap, lift up on it slightly until it no longer contacts the cap. Do not rotate the crankshaft at any time during this operation.*

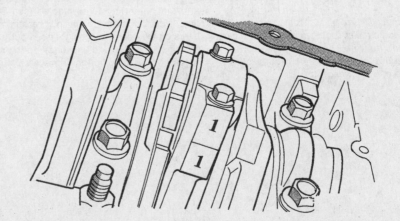

29.14 Install the connecting rod cap, making sure the cap and rod identification numbers match

16   Remove the nuts and detach the rod cap, be very careful not to disturb the Plastigage.

17   Compare the width of the crushed Plastigage to the scale printed on the Plastigage envelope to obtain the oil clearance **(see illustration)**. Compare it to this Chapter's Specifications to make sure the clearance is correct.

18   If the clearance is not as specified, the bearing inserts may be the wrong size (which means different ones will be required). Before deciding different inserts are needed, make sure no dirt or oil was between the bearing inserts and the connecting rod or cap when the clearance was measured. Recheck the journal diameter. If the Plastigage was wider at one end than the other, the journal may be tapered (refer to Section 22).

Final connecting rod installation

19   Carefully scrape all traces of the Plastigage material off the rod journal and/or bearing face. Be careful not to scratch the bearing - use your fingernail or the edge of a credit card.

20   Make sure the bearing faces are perfectly clean, then apply a uniform layer of clean moly-base grease or engine assembly lube to both of them. Push the piston into the cylinder to expose the face of the bearing insert in the connecting rod - be sure to slip the protective hoses over the rod bolts first.

21   Slide the connecting rod into place on the journal, remove the protective hoses from the rod cap bolts, install the rod cap, and tighten the nuts to the torque in this Chapter's Specifications. Work up to the torque in three steps.

22   Repeat the entire procedure for the remaining pistons/connecting rods.

23   The important points to remember are :

a) *Keep the back sides of the bearing inserts and the insides of the connecting rods and caps perfectly clean when assembling them.*

b) *Make sure you have the correct piston/rod assembly for each cylinder.*

c) *The arrow or mark on the piston must face the front (timing chain end) of the engine.*

d) *Lubricate the cylinder walls with clean oil.*

e) *Lubricate the bearing faces when installing the rod caps after the oil clearance has been checked.*

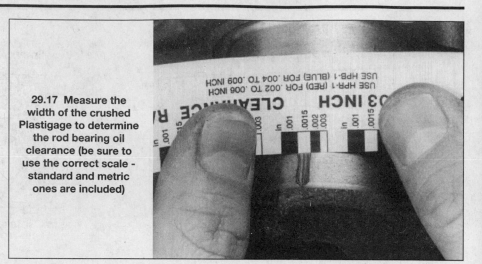

29.17 Measure the width of the crushed Plastigage to determine the rod bearing oil clearance (be sure to use the correct scale - standard and metric ones are included)

24   After all the piston/connecting rod assemblies have been installed, rotate the crankshaft a number of times by hand to check for binding.

25   Check the connecting rod endplay (see Section 15).

26   Compare the endplay to this Chapter's Specifications to make sure it's correct. If it was correct before disassembly and the original crankshaft and rods were reinstalled, it should still be right. If new rods or a new crankshaft were installed, the endplay may be inadequate. If so, the rods will have to be removed and taken to an automotive machine shop for resizing.

30   Initial start-up and break-in after overhaul

Warning: *Have a Class B fire extinguisher handy when starting the engine for the first time.*

1   Double-check the engine oil and coolant levels.

2   With the spark plugs out of the engine and the ignition system disabled (see Section 4), crank the engine until oil pressure registers on the gauge or the light goes out.

3   Install the spark plugs, hook up the plug wires and restore the ignition system functions (see Section 4).

4   Start the engine. It may take a few moments for the fuel system to build up pressure, but the engine should start without a great deal of effort. **Note:** *If backfiring occurs through the throttle body, recheck the valve and ignition timing.*

5   After the engine starts, it should be allowed to warm up to normal operating temperature. While the engine is warming up, make a thorough check for fuel, oil and coolant leaks.

6   Shut the engine off and recheck the engine oil and coolant levels.

7   Drive the vehicle to an area with minimum traffic. Accelerate at full throttle from 30 to 50 mph, then allow the vehicle to slow to 30 mph with the throttle closed. Repeat the procedure 10 or 12 times. This will load the piston rings and cause them to seat properly against the cylinder walls. Check again for oil and coolant leaks.

8   Drive the vehicle gently for the first 500 miles (no sustained high speeds) and keep a constant check on the oil level. It isn't unusual for an engine to use oil during the break-in period.

9   At approximately 500 to 600 miles, change the oil and filter.

10   For the next few hundred miles, drive the vehicle normally. Don't pamper it or abuse it.

11   After 2000 miles, change the oil and filter again and consider the engine broken in.

Chapter 3
Cooling, heating and air conditioning systems

Contents

	Section		Section
Air conditioning compressor - removal and installation	14	Drivebelt check, adjustment and replacement	See Chapter 1
Air conditioning condenser - removal and installation	16	Engine cooling fans and circuit - check and replacement	4
Air conditioning filter/drier - removal and installation	15	General information	1
Air conditioning and heating system - check and maintenance	13	Heater/air conditioner blower motor (front) - removal and installation	10
Antifreeze - general information	2	Heater core (front) - replacement	11
Auxiliary (rear) heating and air conditioning system - general information	17	Heater/air conditioner control assembly - removal and installation	12
Auxiliary (rear) heating and air conditioning components - removal and installation	18	Radiator/transmission oil cooler - removal and installation	5
Coolant reservoir - removal and installation	6	Thermostat - check and replacement	3
Coolant level check	See Chapter 1	Underhood hose check and replacement	See Chapter 1
Coolant temperature sending unit - check and replacement	9	Water pump - check	7
Cooling system check	See Chapter 1	Water pump - replacement	8
Cooling system servicing (draining, flushing and refilling)	See Chapter 1		

Specifications

General
Radiator cap pressure rating .... 10 to 18 psi
Thermostat rating (opening temperature) .... 192 degrees F
Cooling system capacity .... See Chapter 1
Refrigerant capacity
  Without rear air conditioning .... 34 ounces
  With rear air conditioning .... 48 ounces

Torque specifications
Ft-lbs (unless otherwise indicated)
Radiator upper mounting bracket nut .... 105 in-lbs
Thermostat housing bolts
  Four-cylinder and 3.3L/3.8L V6 21
  3.0L V6 .... 105 in-lbs
Transaxle Oil cooler Hose clamps .... 18 in-lbs
Water pump inlet tube bolts
  Four-cylinder 21
  3.0L V6 .... 94 in-lbs
Water pump pulley bolts (3.3L/3.8L V6) 21
Water pump mounting bolts
  Four-cylinder and 3.3L/3.8L V6 .... 105 in-lbs
  3.0L V6 20

1 General information

Engine cooling system

All vehicles covered by this manual employ a pressurized engine cooling system with thermostatically controlled coolant circulation. An impeller-type water pump mounted on the front of the engine pumps coolant through the engine. The pump mounts on the timing chain case on the 3.3L/3.8L V6 engine, and directly on the engine block on the four-cylinder and 3.0L V6 engines. The coolant flows around the combustion chambers and toward the rear of the engine. Cast-in coolant passages direct coolant near the intake ports, exhaust ports, and spark plug areas.

A wax pellet-type thermostat is located in a housing near the front of the engine. During warm-up, the closed thermostat prevents coolant from circulating through the radiator. As the engine nears normal operating temperature, the thermostat opens and allows hot coolant to travel through the radiator, where it's cooled before returning to the engine.

The cooling system is sealed by a pressure-type cap, which raises the boiling point of the coolant and increases the cooling efficiency of the system. If the system pressure exceeds the cap pressure relief value, the excess pressure in the system forces the spring-loaded valve inside the cap off its seat and allows the coolant to escape through the overflow tube into a coolant reservoir. When the system cools, the excess coolant is automatically drawn from the reservoir back into the radiator.

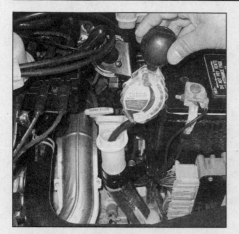

2.4 An inexpensive hydrometer can be used to test the level of anti-freeze protection in your coolant

3.10 Remove the thermostat housing cover mounting bolts (arrows) (later model shown)

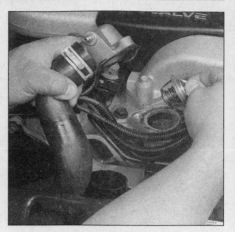

3.11 Remove the thermostat, noting the installed direction (spring end down) (early model shown)

The coolant reservoir does double duty as both the point at which fresh coolant is added to the cooling system to maintain the proper fluid level and as a holding tank for overheated coolant. This type of cooling system is known as a closed design because coolant that escapes past the pressure cap is saved and reused. The location of the tank compared to the radiator makes it the highest point in the system, and the best place to keep air out of the system.

An automatic transmission oil cooler is mounted in the radiator left tank on four-cylinder engine models to cool the transmission fluid. If the model is equipped with a trailer tow package an auxiliary transmission oil cooler is located in the right radiator tank.

Heating system

The heating system consists of blower fans and a heater core located in the heater box, with hoses connecting the heater core to the engine cooling system. Hot engine coolant is circulated through the heater core. When the heater mode on the heater/air conditioning control head on the dashboard is activated, a flap door opens to expose the heater box to the passenger compartment. A fan switch on the control head activates the blower motor, which forces air through the core, heating the air. Some models are equipped with an auxiliary heating/air conditioning system mounted in the right rear quarter panel. An optional accessory on all models is an engine block heater which is operated by ordinary house current through a power cord located behind the radiator grille.

Air conditioning system

The air conditioning system consists of a condenser mounted in front of the radiator, an evaporator mounted adjacent to the heater core, a compressor mounted on the engine, receiver/drier which contains a high pressure relief valve and the plumbing connecting all of the above components. Some models are equipped with an auxiliary heating/air conditioning system mounted in the

right rear quarter panel.

A blower fan forces the warmer air of the passenger compartment through the evaporator core, transferring the heat from the air to the refrigerant (sort of a "radiator in reverse"). The liquid refrigerant boils off into low pressure vapor, taking the heat with it when it leaves the evaporator.

2   Antifreeze - general information

Refer to illustration 2.4
Warning: *Do not allow antifreeze to come in contact with your skin or painted surfaces of the vehicle. Rinse off spills immediately with plenty of water. Antifreeze is highly toxic if ingested. Never leave antifreeze lying around in an open container or in puddles on the floor; children and pets are attracted by it's sweet smell and may drink it. Antifreeze is also flammable, so don't store or use it near open flames. Check with local authorities about disposing of used antifreeze. Many communities have collection centers which will see that antifreeze is disposed of safely. Never dump used anti-freeze on the ground or into drains.*
Note: *Non-Toxic coolant is available at local auto parts stores. Although the coolant is non-toxic when fresh, proper disposal is still required.*

The cooling system should be filled with a water/ethylene glycol based antifreeze solution, which will prevent freezing down to at least 20-degrees F, or lower if local climate requires it. It also provides protection against corrosion and increases the coolant boiling point.

The cooling system should be drained, flushed and refilled at the specified intervals (see Chapter 1). Old or contaminated antifreeze solutions are likely to cause damage and encourage the formation of rust and scale in the system. Use distilled water with the antifreeze.

Before adding antifreeze, check all hose connections, because antifreeze tends to leak through very minute openings. Engines don't

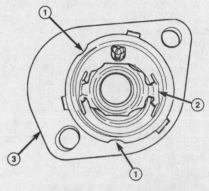

3.13a Thermostat position in the housing cover

1   Locating notch
2   Thermostat
3   Thermostat housing cover

normally consume coolant, so if the level goes down, find the cause and correct it.

The exact mixture of antifreeze-to-water which you should use depends on the relative weather conditions. The mixture should contain at least 50-percent antifreeze, but should never contain more than 70 percent antifreeze. The manufacturer recommends a mixture of 50/50 ethylene glycol and distilled water. Consult the mixture ratio chart on the antifreeze container before adding coolant. Hydrometers are available at most auto parts stores to test the coolant **(see illustration)**. Use antifreeze that meets the vehicle manufacturer's specifications.

3   Thermostat - check and replacement

Warning: *Do not remove the coolant tank cap, drain the coolant or replace the thermostat until the engine has cooled completely.*

Check

1   Before assuming the thermostat is to blame for a cooling system problem, check

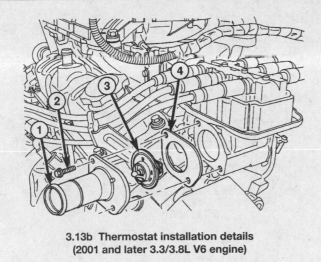

**3.13b Thermostat installation details
(2001 and later 3.3/3.8L V6 engine)**

1	Coolant outlet connector	3	Thermostat
2	Bolt	4	Gasket

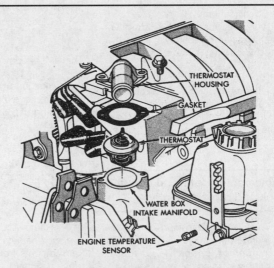

3.13c Thermostat installation details - four-cylinder engine

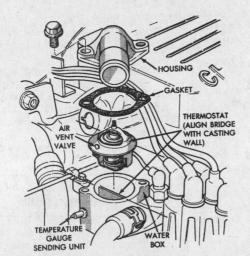

3.13d Thermostat installation details - 3.0L V6 engine

**3.13e Thermostat installation details - 3.3L/3.8L V6 engine
(1996 through 2000)**

the coolant level, drivebelt tension (see Chapter 1) and temperature gauge operation.

2   If the engine seems to be taking a long time to warm up (based on heater output or temperature gauge operation), the thermostat is probably stuck open. Replace the thermostat with a new one.

3   If the engine runs hot, use your hand to check the temperature of the upper radiator hose. If the hose isn't hot, but the engine is, the thermostat is probably stuck closed, preventing the coolant inside the engine from escaping to the radiator. Replace the thermostat. **Caution:** *Don't drive the vehicle without a thermostat. The computer may stay in open loop and emissions and fuel economy will suffer.*

4   If the upper radiator hose is hot, it means that the coolant is flowing and the thermostat is open. Consult the Troubleshooting Section at the front of this manual for cooling system diagnosis.

Replacement

Refer to illustrations 3.10, 3.11, 3.13a, 3.13b and 3.13c

5   Disconnect the cable from the negative terminal of the battery.

6   Drain the cooling system (see Chapter 1). If the coolant is relatively new or in good condition, save it and reuse it.

7   Follow the upper radiator hose to the engine to locate the thermostat housing.

8   Loosen the hose clamp, then detach the hose from the fitting. If it's stuck, grasp it near the end with a pair of adjustable pliers and twist it to break the seal, then pull it off. If the hose is old or deteriorated, cut it off and install a new one.

9   If the outer surface of the large fitting that mates with the hose is deteriorated (corroded, pitted, etc.) it may be damaged further by hose removal. If it is, the thermostat housing cover will have to be replaced.

10   Remove the fasteners and detach the housing cover **(see illustration)**. If the cover is stuck, tap it with a soft-face hammer to jar it loose. Be prepared for some coolant to spill as the gasket seal is broken.

11   Note how it's installed, then remove the thermostat **(see illustration)**.

12   Remove all traces of old gasket material and sealant from the housing and cover with a gasket scraper.

13   On 2001 and later 3.3/3.8L V6 engines, install the thermostat into the housing cover aligning the two notches on the thermostat with the cover **(see illustration)**. Position the new gasket over the thermostat and cover, lining up the bolt holes and install the assembly onto the intake manifold **(see illustration)**. On all other models, install the thermostat into the housing, or intake manifold, spring-end first **(see illustrations)**. Dip a new gasket in water and place it over the thermostat, lining up the bolt holes.

4.1 Disconnect the fan connector (arrow) and try operating the fan with a fused battery-voltage jumper wire and a ground wire

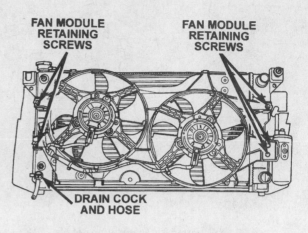

4.11 Location of fan module retaining screws

14   Install the cover and fasteners. Tighten the fasteners to the torque listed in this Chapter's Specifications.

15   Reattach the hose to the fitting and tighten the hose clamp securely.

16   Refill the cooling system (see Chapter 1).

17   Start the engine and allow it to reach normal operating temperature, then check for leaks and proper thermostat operation (as described in Steps 2 through 4). See Chapter 1 for the cooling system air-bleeding procedure.

4   Engine cooling fans and circuit - check and replacement

Warning: *To avoid possible injury or damage, DO NOT operate the engine with a damaged fan. Do not attempt to repair fan blades or shroud assembly - replace as an assembly.*

Note: *Always be sure to check for blown fuses before attempting to diagnose an electrical circuit problem.*

Check

Refer to illustrations 4.1

1   If the engine is overheating and the cooling fan is not operating, unplug the electrical connector at the motor and use fused jumper wires to connect the fan motor directly to the battery **(see illustration)**. If the fan still doesn't work, replace the motor. Test each motor separately.

2   If the motors are OK, but the cooling fan doesn't come on when the engine gets hot, the fault may be in the coolant temperature sensors, the fan relays, the Powertrain Control Module (PCM) or the wiring which connects the components.

3   Carefully check all wiring and connections (wiring diagrams are included at the end of Chapter 12). If no obvious problems are found, further diagnosis should be done by a dealer service department or repair shop with the proper diagnostic equipment.

Replacement

Refer to illustrations 4.11 and 4.15

4   Disconnect the cable from the negative terminal of the battery, then disconnect the fan module electrical connectors if you haven't already done so.

5   Raise the vehicle and support it securely on jackstands.

6   Remove the radiator outlet hose from its retaining clip and remove the clip from the shroud.

7   Remove the lower transmission cooler lines from their clips on the shroud.

8   Lower the vehicle and remove the air intake resonator from the throttle body and air cleaner assembly.

9   Remove the coolant reservoir attaching screw from the upper crossmember.

10   Remove the upper grill to crossmember valence panel and disconnect the upper radiator mounts from the crossmember. Remove the crossmember.

11   Remove the air cleaner assembly and remove the fan module retaining bolts **(see illustration).**

12   On vehicles equipped with transmission coolers remove the cooler lines from the retaining clips on the module.

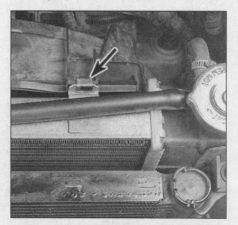

4.15 There are also two retaining clips at the top of the radiator

13   Disconnect and plug the transmission line from the radiator fitting on the lower left side.

14   Raise the vehicle, support it securely on jackstands and remove the fan module and radiator mounting bolts located on the lower left side. Detach the air conditioning filter/drier and position it aside.

15   Lower the vehicle and remove the retaining clips holding the fan module to the radiator **(see illustration)** then carefully lift the fan module out of the engine compartment.

16   Installation is the reverse of removal.

5   Radiator/transmission oil cooler - removal and installation

Warning: *Wait until the engine is completely cool before beginning this procedure. Do not remove the cylinder block plug or the radiator draincock with the system hot and under pressure because serious burns from coolant can occur.*

Radiator

Removal

Refer to illustrations 5.3, 5.5, 5.7, 5.9, 5.10 and 5.11

1   Disconnect the cable from the negative terminal of the battery.

2   Drain the cooling system (see Chapter 1). If the coolant is relatively new and in good condition, save it and reuse it.

3   Remove the air intake resonator and detach the coolant reservoir hose from the fitting **(see illustration)**.

4   Disconnect the fans from the connector located on the left side of the fan module and remove the coolant reservoir retaining screw from the panel crossmember.

5   Disconnect the upper radiator mounting screws from the crossmember **(see illustration)** and disconnect the engine block heater wire, if equipped.

6   Remove the upper radiator closure

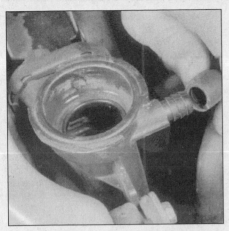

5.3 Detach the coolant reservoir hose from the fitting

5.5 Remove the screws from the upper radiator mounting bracket (arrow)

off and install new ones. Remove the lower clip from the fan module.

9 Remove the air conditioning condenser fasteners **(see illustration)** and separate the condenser from the radiator. Be sure that the condenser is supported in position.

10 Remove the air conditioning filter/drier mounting bracket, two bolts to the fan module, and the two nuts to the filter/drier **(see illustration)**.

11 Carefully lift out the radiator **(see illustration)**. Care should be taken not to damage radiator cooling fins or water tubes. Don't spill coolant on the vehicle or scratch the paint

12 Check the radiator for leaks and damage. If it needs repair, have a radiator shop or dealer service department perform the work, as special techniques are required.

13 Remove bugs and dirt from the radiator with compressed air and a soft brush (don't bend the cooling fins).

Installation

14 Inspect the radiator mounts for deterioration and make sure there's no dirt or gravel

panel crossmember and remove the air cleaner assembly.

7 Disconnect the transmission oil cooler lines **(see illustration)** at the radiator and plug them.

8 Loosen the hose clamps, then detach the upper and lower coolant hoses from the radiator. If they're stuck, grasp each hose near the end with a pair of adjustable pliers and twist it to break the seal, then pull it off - be careful not to distort the radiator fittings! If the hoses are old or deteriorated, cut them

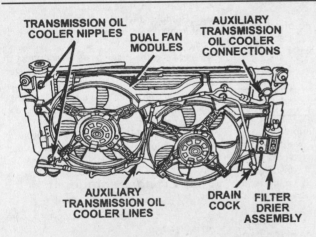

5.7 Transmission oil cooler connections including the optional tow package auxiliary cooler connection

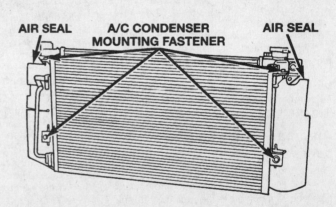

5.9 Location of the four air conditioning condenser-to-radiator mounting fasteners (arrows)

5.10 Remove two fasteners (arrows) attaching the air conditioning filter/drier

5.11 Carefully lift the radiator out of the engine compartment

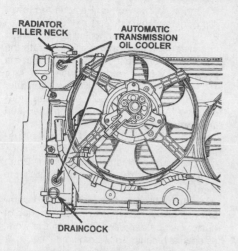

5.18 Location of the automatic transmission oil cooler

in them when the radiator is installed.

15   Installation is the reverse of the removal procedure. Make sure the air seals are in position and seat the radiator on the lower mounting isolators before fastening the top brackets.

16   After installation, fill the cooling system with the proper mixture of antifreeze and water (see Chapter 1).

17   Start the engine and check for leaks. Allow the engine to reach normal operating temperature, indicated by the upper radiator hose becoming hot. Recheck the coolant level and add more if required. Check the automatic transmission fluid level and add fluid as needed.

Automatic transmission oil coolers

Refer to illustration 5.18

18   The oil cooler is an internal oil to coolant type and is mounted in the radiator left tank **(see illustration)**. On models with the trailer tow package a second transmission oil cooler is located in the right radiator tank.

19   It is recommended that you use only approved transmission oil cooler hoses if replacement becomes necessary. These rubber oil hoses are molded to fit the available space. Straight hoses will kink when bent and restrict or stop the flow of transmission oil through the cooler. If the flow through the cooler is restricted or stopped the oil will not cool properly which may cause it to burn (turning the oil from a red color to a brown color). This may cause the transmission to fail prematurely.

6   Coolant reservoir - removal and installation

Refer to illustration 6.3

1   This system works with the radiator pressure cap to keep the coolant free of trapped air and provides a convenient method for checking coolant level and provide some reserve coolant. All vehicles have this system with various shapes and forms.

2   Detach the hoses at the reservoir and plug them to prevent leakage.

3   Remove the reservoir retaining bolts and lift the reservoir out of the engine compartment **(see illustration)**.

4   Installation is the reverse of removal. While the tank is off the vehicle, it should be cleaned with soapy water and a brush to remove any deposits inside.

7   Water pump - check

1   A failure in the water pump can cause serious engine damage due to overheating.

2   There are three ways to check the operation of the water pump while it's installed on the engine. If the pump is defective, it should be replaced with a new or rebuilt unit.

3   Water pumps are equipped with weep or vent holes. If a failure occurs in the pump seal, coolant will leak from the hole. In most cases you'll need a flashlight to find the hole on the water pump from underneath to check

for leaks. **Note:** *Some small black staining around the weep hole is normal. If the stain is heavy brown or actual coolant is evident, replace the pump.*

4   If the water pump shaft bearings fail there may be a howling sound at the front of the engine while it's running. With the engine off, shaft wear can be felt if the water pump pulley is rocked up and down. Don't mistake drivebelt slippage, which causes a squealing sound, for water pump bearing failure.

5   A quick water pump performance check is to put the heater on. If the pump is failing, it won't be able to efficiently circulate hot water all the way to the heater core like it used to.

8   Water pump - replacement

Warning: *Wait until the engine is completely cool before beginning this procedure.*

All engines

1   Disconnect the cable from the negative terminal of the battery.

2   Drain the cooling system (see Chapter 1). If the coolant is relatively new or in good condition, save and reuse it.

3   Remove the splash shield under the right front fender for easy access to the water pump bolts.

4   Loosen the clamps and disconnect the hoses from the water pump. If they're stuck grasp each hose near the end with a pair of adjustable pliers and twist it to break the seal, then pull it off. If the hoses are deteriorated, cut them off and install new ones.

5   If you are installing a new pump, compare the new pump to the old pump to make sure that they are identical.

Four-cylinder engine

Refer to illustrations 8.11 and 8.12

6   Raise the vehicle and support it securely on jackstands.

7   Remove the accessory drivebelts (see Chapter 1).

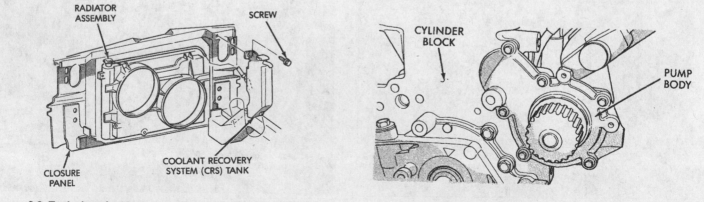

6.3 Typical coolant recovery reservoir installation details

8.11 Water pump location - four-cylinder engine

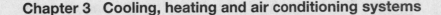

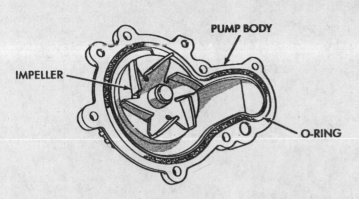

8.12 Seat the O-ring in the water pump body - four-cylinder engine

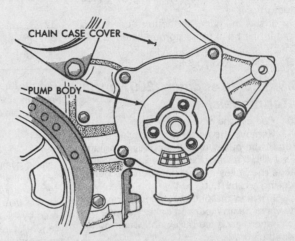

8.16 Water pump installation details - 3.0L V6 engine

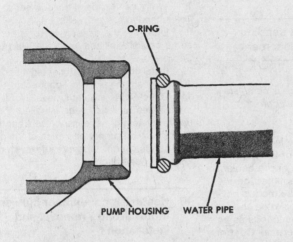

8.18 Install a new O-ring on the water pipe

8.24 Water pump location - 3.3L/3.8L V6 engines (1996 through 2000)

8   Support the engine from the underneath and remove the right engine mount, then remove the right engine mount bracket (see Chapter 2).

9   Remove the timing belt and timing belt idler pulley (see Chapter 2). **Caution:** *Do not turn the crankshaft or camshafts while the belt is disconnected, or camshaft timing will be disturbed.*

10   Clamp or otherwise hold the camshafts to prevent rotation with the belt removed and while removing the camshaft sprocket bolts. Remove both camshaft sprockets. **Note:** *If clamping is not sufficient, special tools are available at the dealer or automotive parts stores for holding the camshafts while removing the camshaft sprockets.*

11   Remove the rear timing belt cover and remove the bolts attaching the water pump to the engine **(see illustration)**.

12   Install the new pump with a new O-ring **(see illustration)** wetting it with water for easier installation in the groove. **Caution:** *Make sure the O-ring is properly seated in the water pump groove before tightening the*

bolts. *An improperly located O-ring may cause damage to the O-ring and cause a coolant leak.* Apply a thin coat of RTV sealant on the flange outside the O-ring and install the pump, tightening the bolts to the torque listed this Chapter's Specifications.

13   Proceed to Step 30.

3.0L V6 engine

Refer to illustrations 8.16 and 8.18

14   The 3.0L V6 engine uses metal piping beyond the lower radiator hose to route coolant to the water pump, which is located in the V of the cylinder banks.

15   Follow procedures (see Chapter 2) for removal of timing belt to gain access to the water pump.

16   Remove the water pump mounting bolts and separate the pump from the water inlet pipe **(see illustration)**.

17   Clean all gasket and O-ring surfaces on pump and water pipe inlet tube.

18   Install a new O-ring on the water inlet pipe **(see illustration)** wetting the O-ring with water to ease assembly. **Caution:** *Keep the*

O-ring free of oil or grease.

19   Install new gasket on water pump and install pump inlet opening over the water pipe, press the water pipe into the pump housing.

20   Install the water pump mounting bolts and tighten them to the torque listed in this Chapter's Specifications.

21   Proceed to Step 39.

3.3L and 3.8L V6 engines (1996 through 2000 models)

Refer to illustrations 8.24 and 8.27

22   Remove the drivebelt (see Chapter 1).

23   Remove the water pump pulley bolts and remove the pulley.

24   Remove the bolts and detach the water pump from the front cover **(see illustration)**.

25   Clean the bolt threads and the threaded holes in the front cover to remove any corrosion and sealant.

26   Remove and discard the old O-ring and clean the mating surfaces. Be careful not to gouge or scratch the mating surfaces.

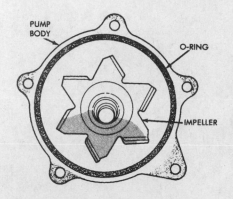

8.27 Seat a new O-ring in the water pump body - 3.3L/3.8L V6 engines

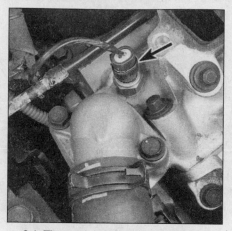

9.1 The coolant temperature sensor (arrow) is located at the front of the engine, next to the thermostat

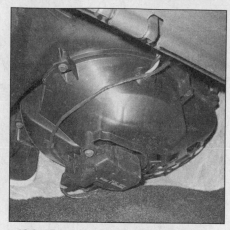

10.3a Remove the screws retaining the blower motor cover

27 Install a new O-ring into the groove (see illustration).
28 Install the pump to the front cover and tighten the bolts to the torque listed in this Chapter's Specifications.
29 Proceed to Step 39.

3.3/3.8L V6 engines (2001 and later models)

30 Remove the drive belt.
31 Remove the water pump pulley bolts. Rotate the pulley until the pulley openings align with the water pump drive hub spokes. Move the pulley inward between the pump housing and the hub.
32 Position the pulley to allow access to the water pump mounting bolts. Remove the bolts and detach the pulley and water pump from the front cover.
33 Clean the bolt threads and threaded holes in the front cover to remove any corrosion and sealant.
34 Remove and discard the old seal and clean the mating surfaces. Be sure not to gouge or scratch the mating surfaces.
35 Install a new seal into the groove.
36 **Note:** *The water pump pulley must be positioned loosely between the pump housing and the drive hub before installing the water pump.* Position the water pump pulley loosely between the pump housing and drive hub.
37 Install the water pump and pulley onto the front cover and tighten the bolts to the torque listed in this Chapter's Specifications.
38 Position the pulley onto the drive hub and tighten the bolts to the torque listed in this Chapter's Specifications.
39 Proceed to Step 39.

All engines

40 The remainder of installation is the reverse of removal.
41 Refer to Chapter 2 for procedures to reinstall the timing belt, timing belt tensioner, and accessory drivebelts as necessary.
42 Refill the cooling system and operate the engine to check for leaks. Lower the vehicle, if it had been raised and connect the battery.

9 Coolant temperature sending unit - check and replacement

Refer to illustration 9.1
Warning: *Wait until the engine is completely cool before beginning this procedure.*

Check

1 The coolant temperature indicator system is composed of a light or temperature gauge mounted in the dash and a coolant temperature sending unit mounted on the engine (see illustration). In the models covered by this manual, there is only one coolant temperature sensor, which functions as an indicator to both the Powertrain Control Module (PCM) and the instrument panel.
2 If an overheating indication occurs, check the coolant level in the system and then make sure the wiring between the light or gauge and the sending unit is secure and all fuses are intact.
3 When the ignition switch is turned on and the starter motor is turning, the indicator light (if equipped) should be on (overheated engine indication).
4 If the light is not on, the bulb may be burned out, the ignition switch may be faulty or the circuit may be open.
5 As soon as the engine starts, the light should go out and remain out unless the engine overheats. Failure of the light to go out may be due to a grounded wire between the light and the sending unit, a defective sending unit or a faulty ignition switch. See Chapter 6, Section 5 for a diagnostic check of the coolant temperature sensor. Check the coolant to make sure it's the proper type. **Note:** *Plain water may have too low a boiling point to activate the sending unit.*

Replacement

Warning: *Wait until the engine is completely cool before beginning this procedure.*
6 Disconnect the electrical connector from the sensor.

7 Wrap the threads of the new sensor with Teflon tape to prevent leaks.
8 Unscrew the sensor. Be prepared for some coolant spillage (read the **Warning** in Section 2).
9 Install the sensor and tighten it securely.
10 Connect the electrical connector.
11 Check the coolant level after the replacement unit has been installed and top up the system, if necessary (see Chapter 1). Check now for proper operation of the gauge and sending unit. Observe the system for leaks after operation.

10 Heater/air conditioner blower motor (front) - removal and installation

Refer to illustrations 10.3a, 10.3b, 10.4, 10.5a and 10.5b

1996 through 2000 models

Warning: *These models have airbags. Always disconnect the negative battery cable and wait two minutes before working in the vicinity of the impact sensors, steering column or instrument panel to avoid the possibility of accidental deployment of the airbag, which could cause personal injury (see Chapter 12).*
1 Disconnect the cable from the negative terminal of the battery.
2 Remove the glove box (see Chapter 11).
3 Remove the four hex screws retaining the blower motor cover (see illustration) and then remove the mounting screws for the blower motor (see illustration).
4 Holding the blower assembly, allow it to drop down and rest on the floor board (see illustration).
5 Disconnect the blower wiring connector (see illustration), remove the grommet and wiring harness through the blower housing (see illustration). Remove the blower motor from the vehicle.
6 The fan (wheel assembly) is balanced with the blower motor, and is available only

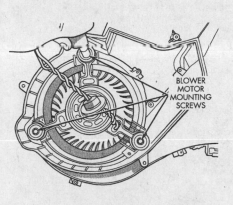

10.3b Remove the blower motor mounting screws

10.4 After removing mounting screws, lower the blower motor . . .

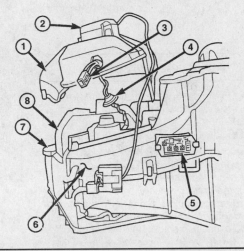

10.5a . . . disconnect the blower motor electrical connector . . .

10.5b . . . and pull the wiring harness and grommet (arrow) from the blower housing

10.10 Lower air intake assembly

1   *Lower air intake housing*
2   *Recirculation air door actuator*
3   *Blower motor pigtail wire connector*
4   *Rubber grommet*
5   *Blower motor resistor/power module*
6   *Lower evaporator housing*
7   *Upper air intake air housing*
8   *Recirculation air door*

as an assembly. If the fan is damaged, both fan and blower motor must be replaced.
7   Installation is the reverse of removal.

2001 and later models

Refer to illustrations 10.10 and 10.14
Warning: *These models have airbags. Always disconnect the negative battery cable and wait two minutes before working in the vicinity of the impact sensors, steering column or instrument panel to avoid the possibility of accidental deployment of the airbag, that could cause personal injury (see Chapter 12).*
8   Disconnect the cable from the negative terminal of the battery.
9   Partially remove the instrument panel to gain access to the heating and air conditioning unit (see Chapter 11).
10   Disconnect the blower motor pigtail wire harness connector from the receptacle of either the blower motor resistor or the power module **(see illustration)**.
11   Remove the two screws that secure the recirculation door actuator and disconnect the wire harness from its clips on the lower intake housing.
12   Remove the two screws retaining the air housing to the lower intake air housing.
13   Remove the three screws retaining the

lower air intake housing to the lower half of the evaporator housing.
14   Push the rubber grommet on the blower motor pigtail wires through the hole in the lower intake air housing **(see illustration)**.
15   Remove the lower intake air housing from the evaporator housing and upper intake air housing.
16   Carefully push the blower motor pigtail wires and harness connector out through the grommet hole in the lower intake air housing.

17   Carefully move the recirculation air door as necessary to gain access, then remove the three screws securing the blower motor to the blower housing in the lower half of the evaporator housing.
18   Gently flex the recirculation air door far enough to remove the blower motor and blower wheel from the blower housing in the lower half of the evaporator housing. Remove the blower motor and wheel.
19   Installation is the reverse of removal.

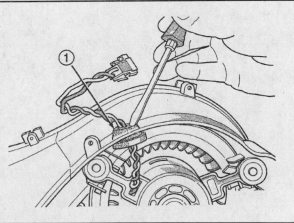

10.14 Use a screwdriver and push the rubber grommet wires through the hole in the lower intake air housing

11.2a Remove the safety pin, nut and pinch bolt to separate the steering column shaft coupler from the steering gear intermediate shaft

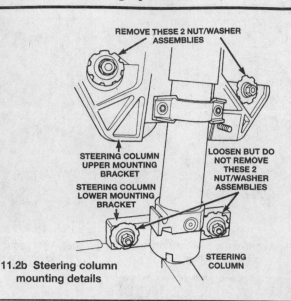

11.2b Steering column mounting details

11   Heater core - replacement

Refer to illustrations 11.2a, 11.2b, 11.3, 11.4, 11.5, 11.7, 11.8a and 11.8b

1996 through 2000 models

Warning: *These models have airbags. Always disconnect the negative battery cable and wait two minutes before working in the vicinity of the impact sensors, steering column or instrument panel to avoid the possibility of accidental deployment of the airbag, which could cause personal injury (see Chapter 12).*

1   Drain the cooling system (see Chapter 1). If the coolant is relatively new or in good condition, save it and reuse it.

2   Remove the lower steering column cover and knee blocker reinforcement (see Chapter 11). Place the steering wheel in the locked position and remove the key. Remove the steering column as follows **(see illustra-**

tions): Caution: *Do not allow the steering shaft to rotate with the steering column removed or damage to the airbag clockspring could occur.*

 a) *Remove the airbag module and steering wheel (see Chapter 10).*
 b) *Disconnect the wiring harness connectors from the steering column.*
 c) *Remove the safety pin, nut and pinch bolt from the steering column shaft coupler.*
 d) *Detach the steering column shaft coupler from the steering gear shaft.*
 e) *Loosen, but do not remove the two lower steering column mounting bracket nuts.*
 f) *Remove the two upper steering column mounting bracket nut/washer assemblies.*
 g) *Carefully remove the steering column from the vehicle.*

3   Disconnect the ABS module electrical connector and remove the module and

bracket **(see illustration).**

4   Disconnect the instrument panel-to-body harness connector and position the harness connector and bracket aside **(see illustration).**

5   Remove the lower column insulation boot at the base of steering shaft **(see illustration).**

6   Pinch off the heater hoses under the hood using locking pliers.

7   Remove the heater core cover and place some towels under the heater core tubes. Remove the screw securing the heater core tubes to the heater core and pull the tubes out of the heater core **(see illustration).**

8   Depress the heater core retaining clips with a flat bladed screwdriver **(see illustration).** Pull up on the accelerator pedal and slide the heater core past **(see illustration).** Depress the brake pedal and remove the heater core from the housing.

9   Installation is the reverse of removal.

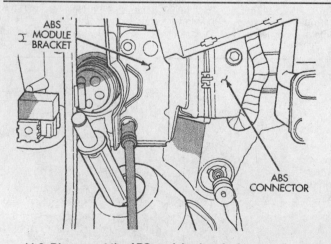

11.3 Disconnect the ABS module electrical connector and remove the module and bracket

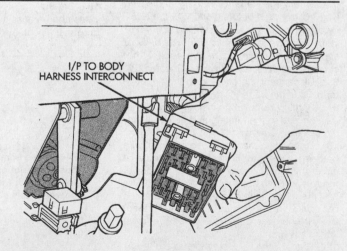

11.4 Disconnect the instrument panel-to-body harness connector

Chapter 3 Cooling, heating and air conditioning systems

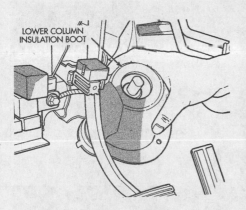

11.5 Remove the lower steering column insulation boot

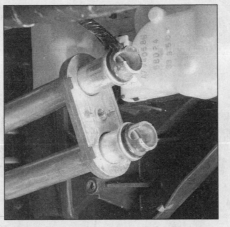

11.7 Separate the heater core tubes and retaining plate from the heater core

11.8a Detach the heater core retaining clips (arrows) . . .

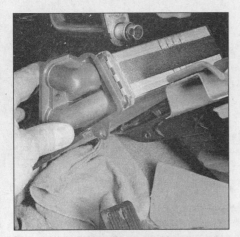

11.8b . . . and withdraw the heater core from the housing

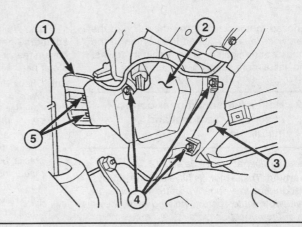

11.15 Heater core shield assembly

1 Heater/air conditioning housing
2 Heater core shield
3 Distribution housing
4 Screws
5 Location tabs

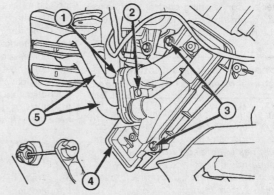

11.16 Heater core and tubes assembly

1 Sealing plate
2 Screw
3 Screws
4 Heater core
5 Heater core tubes

Install screws to retain the heater core in the housing and replace the heater core tube inlet O-rings. Securely tighten the heater core tube retaining plate. Tighten the steering column mounting bracket nuts to 105 in-lbs.

2001 and later models

Refer to illustrations 11.15 and 11.16
Warning: These models have air bags. Always disconnect the negative battery cable and wait two minutes before working in the vicinity of the impact sensors, steering column or instrument panel to avoid the possibility of accidental deployment of the airbag, that could cause personal injury (see Chapter 12).
10 Disconnect the cable from the negative terminal of the battery.
11 Drain the cooling system (see Chapter 1). If the coolant is relatively new or in good condition, save it and reuse it.
12 Remove the silencer boot fasteners at the base of the lower steering shaft and push the silencer aside.
13 Remove the brake lamp switch from the bracket and set it aside.
14 Remove the pin and disconnect the

power brake booster push rod from the brake pedal arm.
15 Remove the three screws securing the heater core shield to the left side of the heater/air conditioning distribution housing **(see illustration)**. Pull the heater core shield rearward and disengage the two locating tabs and remove the heater core shield.
16 Place some towels under the heater core tubes. Remove the screw securing the heater core tube sealing plate to the heater core supply and return ports **(see illustration)**.

17 Push both heater core tubes toward the instrument panel and disengage their fittings from the heater core supply and return ports. Plug the openings.
18 Remove the two screws securing the heater core mounting plate to the distribution housing **(see illustration 11.16)**.
19 Pull up on the accelerator pedal and push down on the brake pedal to allow clearance, then pull the heater core out of the distribution housing.
20 Installation is the reverse of removal. Each heater tube has a slot that must be

12.3a Remove the heater/air conditioning control module and bezel as an assembly (1996 through 2000)

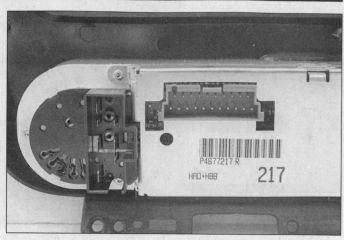

12.3b Disconnect the electrical connectors from the back of the heater/air conditioning control module

indexed to a location tab within each of the heater core ports. Adjust the portion of the tubes so the sealing plate fits flush against the heater core supply and return ports.

12 Heater/air conditioner control assembly - removal and installation

Refer to illustrations 12.3a and 12.3b
Warning: *These models have airbags. Always disconnect the negative battery cable and wait two minutes before working in the vicinity of the impact sensors, steering column or instrument panel to avoid the possibility of accidental deployment of the airbag, which could cause personal injury (see Chapter 12).*
1　Disconnect the cable from the negative terminal of the battery.
2　Remove the radio and heater/air conditioning control module and bezel assembly from the instrument panel (see Chapter 11).
3　Disconnect the electrical connectors from the back of the heater/air conditioning control module and from the rear blower switch **(see illustrations)**. On 2001 and later models equipped with the optional Automatic Temperature Control system, disconnect the infrared sensor jumper harness connector.
4　Installation is the reverse of removal. If the heater/air conditioning control module is replaced, calibration/diagnostic tests will need to be performed (see Section 13).

13 Air conditioning and heating system - check and maintenance

Warning: *The air conditioning system is under high pressure. Do not loosen any hose fittings or remove any components until after the system has been discharged by a dealer service department or service station. Always wear eye protection when disconnecting air conditioning system fittings.*

1　The following maintenance checks should be performed on a regular basis to ensure the air conditioner continues to operate at peak efficiency.
   a) *Check the compressor drivebelt. If it's worn or deteriorated, replace it (see Chapter 1).*
   b) *Check the drivebelt tension and, if necessary, adjust it (see Chapter 1).*
   c) *Check the system hoses. Look for cracks, bubbles, hard spots and deterioration. Inspect the hoses and all fittings for oil bubbles and seepage. If there's any evidence of wear, damage or leaks, replace the hose(s).*
   d) *Inspect the condenser fins for leaves, bugs and other debris. Use a "fin comb" or compressed air to clean the condenser.*
   e) *Make sure the system has the correct refrigerant charge.*
   f) *Check the evaporator housing drain tube for blockage.*
2　It's a good idea to operate the system for about 10 minutes at least once a month, particularly during the winter. Long term non-use can cause hardening, and subsequent failure, of the seals.
3　Because of the complexity of the air conditioning system and the special equipment necessary to service it, in-depth troubleshooting and repairs are not included in this manual (refer to the *Haynes Automotive Heating and Air Conditioning Repair Manual*). However, simple checks and component replacement procedures are provided in this Chapter.
4　The most common cause of poor cooling is simply a low system refrigerant charge. If a noticeable drop in cool air output occurs, the following quick check will help you determine if the refrigerant level is low.

Checking the refrigerant charge

5　Warm the engine up to normal operating temperature.

6　Place the air conditioning temperature selector at the coldest setting and the blower at the highest setting. Open the doors (to make sure the air conditioning system doesn't cycle off as soon as it cools the passenger compartment).
7　With the compressor engaged - the clutch will make an audible click and the center of the clutch will rotate. If the compressor discharge line feels warm and the compressor inlet pipe feels cool, the system is properly charged.
8　Place a thermometer in the dashboard vent nearest the evaporator and add refrigerant to the system until the indicated temperature is around 40 to 45 degrees F. If the ambient (outside) air temperature is very high, say 110 degrees F, the duct air temperature may be as high as 60 degrees F, but generally the air conditioning is 30 to 50 degrees F cooler than the ambient air. **Note:** *Humidity of the ambient air also affects the cooling capacity of the system. Higher ambient humidity lowers the effectiveness of the air conditioning system.*

Adding refrigerant

Refer to illustration 13.12
9　Buy an automotive charging kit at an auto parts store. A charging kit includes a 14-ounce can of refrigerant, a tap valve and a short section of hose that can be attached between the tap valve and the system low side service valve. Because one can of refrigerant may not be sufficient to bring the system charge up to the proper level, it's a good idea to buy a couple of additional cans. Make sure that one of the cans contains red refrigerant dye. If the system is leaking, the red dye will leak out with the refrigerant and help you pinpoint the location of the leak. **Caution:** *The models covered by this manual use the environmentally-friendly R-134a refrigerant. This refrigerant (and the appropriate refrigerant oil) are not compatible with R-12 refrigerant and must never be mixed or components will be damaged. Use only R-134a*

13.12 Cans of R-134A refrigerant are available in auto parts stores that can be added to your system with a simple recharging kit

14.5 Remove the nuts (arrows), detach and plug the refrigerant lines at the compressor

refrigerant in the models covered by this book. **Warning:** *Never add more than two cans of refrigerant to the system.*

10 Hook up the charging kit by following the manufacturer's instructions. **Warning:** *DO NOT hook the charging kit hose to the system high side!* The fittings on the charging kit are designed to fit **only** on the low side of the system.

11 Back off the valve handle on the charging kit and screw the kit onto the refrigerant can, making sure first that the O-ring or rubber seal inside the threaded portion of the kit is in place. **Warning:** *Wear protective eyewear when dealing with pressurized refrigerant cans.*

12 Remove the dust cap from the low-side charging connection and attach the quick-connect fitting on the kit hose **(see illustration)**.

13 Warm up the engine and turn on the air conditioner. Keep the charging kit hose away from the fan and other moving parts. **Note:** *The charging process requires the compressor to be running. Your compressor may cycle off if the pressure is low due to a low charge. If the clutch cycles off, you can pull the low-pressure cycling switch plug and attach a jumper wire. This will keep the compressor ON.*

14 Turn the valve handle on the kit until the

stem pierces the can, then back the handle out to release the refrigerant. You should be able to hear the rush of gas. Add refrigerant to the low side of the system until both the receiver-drier surface and the evaporator inlet pipe feel about the same temperature. Allow stabilization time between each addition.

15 If you have an accurate thermometer, you can place it in the center air conditioning duct inside the vehicle and keep track of the "conditioned" air temperature. A charged system that is working properly should put out air that is 40 degrees F. If the ambient (outside) air temperature is very high, say 110 degrees F, the duct air temperature may be as high as 60 degrees F, but generally the air conditioning is 30 to 50 degrees F cooler than the ambient air.

16 When the can is empty, turn the valve handle to the closed position and release the connection from the low-side port. Replace the dust cap.

17 Remove the charging kit from the can and store the kit for future use with the piercing valve in the UP position, to prevent inadvertently piercing the can on the next use.

Diagnosis and testing

18 The heater/air conditioning control module **(see illustration 12.3a)** is capable of trou-

bleshooting the system during dealer or repair shop servicing. If a problem is detected an error code is displayed by flashing lights on the dashboard pushbuttons. The error code cannot be erased until the condition is repaired and diagnostic tests performed. If the heater/air conditioning control module is replaced, calibration/diagnostic tests will need to be performed. Because of the detailed sequencing procedure and the complexity of display codes, these diagnosis and testing should be done by a dealer or qualified repair shop.

14 Air conditioning compressor - removal and installation

Refer to illustrations 14.5 and 14.6
Warning: *The air conditioning system is under high pressure. DO NOT disassemble any part of the system (hoses, compressor, line fittings, etc.) until after the system has been evacuated and the refrigerant recovered by a dealer service department or air conditioning service station.*
Note: *The filter/drier (see Section 15) should be replaced whenever the compressor is replaced.*

1 Have the system discharged (see Warning above).

2 Disconnect the cable from the negative terminal of the battery.

3 Drain the engine coolant and remove the upper radiator hose.

4 Remove the drivebelt (see Chapter 1).

5 On 2001 and later 3.3/3.8L V6 models, disengage the retainer on the engine wire harness compressor clutch coil and remove it from the bracket on top of the compressor. On all other models, disconnect the compressor clutch electrical connector. On all models, remove the refrigerant lines from the compressor **(see illustration)**. Plug the open fittings to prevent entry of dirt and moisture.

6 Unbolt the compressor from the mounting bracket and lift it out of the vehicle **(see illustration)**.

14.6 Remove the bolts (arrows) and compressor from its mounting bracket

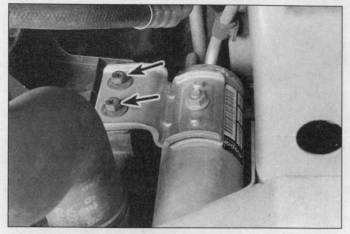

15.4 Remove the two bolts (arrows) retaining the filter/drier bracket

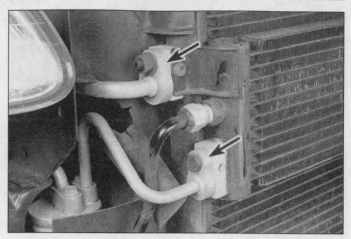

16.6 Remove the bolts and detach the refrigerant lines from the condenser (arrows)

7   If a new compressor is being installed, pour out the oil from the old compressor into a graduated container and add that amount of new refrigerant oil to the new compressor. Also follow any directions included with the new compressor.

8   The clutch may have to be transferred from the original to the new compressor.

9   Installation is the reverse of removal. Replace all O-rings with new ones specifically made for use with R-134a refrigerant and lubricate them with R-134a-compatible refrigerant oil.

10   Have the system evacuated, recharged and leak tested by the shop that discharged it.

15 Air conditioning filter/drier - removal and installation

Refer to illustration 15.4

Warning: *The air conditioning system is under high pressure. DO NOT disassemble any part of the system (hose, compressor, line fittings, etc.) until after the system has been evacuated and the refrigerant recovered by a dealer service department or service station.*

Caution: *Replacement filter/drier/receiver-drier units are so effective at absorbing moisture that they can quickly saturate upon exposure to the atmosphere. When installing a new unit, have all tools and supplies ready for quick reassembly to avoid having the system open any longer than necessary.*

1   The filter/drier acts as a reservoir for the system refrigerant. It's located on the right side of the engine compartment, next to the radiator and condenser.

2   Have the system discharged (see the **Warning** at the beginning of this Section).

3   Disconnect the cable from the negative terminal of the battery.

4   Remove the two bolts retaining the filter/drier bracket to the radiator fan module bracket **(see illustration)**.

5   Disconnect the refrigerant lines from the filter/drier.

6   Plug the open fittings to prevent entry of dirt and moisture.

7   Remove the upper radiator crossmember then pull up on the radiator and slide the filter/drier from the mounting location.

8   Installation is the reverse of removal, but before installation replace both refrigerant line O-rings.

9   Take the vehicle back to the shop that discharged it. Have the system evacuated, recharged and leak tested.

16 Air conditioning condenser - removal and installation

Refer to illustrations 16.6 and 16.7

Warning: *The air conditioning system is under high pressure. DO NOT disassemble any part of the system (hoses, compressor, line fittings, etc.) until after the system has been evacuated and the refrigerant recovered by a dealer service department or service station.*

Note: *Special effort must be used to keep all system components moisture-free. Moisture in the oil is very difficult to remove and will cause a reliability problem with the compressor. The receiver-drier should be replaced whenever the condenser is replaced (see Section 15).*

1   Have the system discharged (see **Warning** above).

2   Disconnect the cable from the negative terminal of the battery.

3   Refer to Chapter 11 and remove the front bumper cover and grill assembly.

4   Remove the upper radiator crossmember.

5   On 2001 and later models, perform the following:

   a) *Remove the five small screws attaching the front fascia grille inserts to the radiator shield.*

   b) *Remove the radiator sight shield from the radiator closure panel crossmember.*

   c) *Remove the two screws attaching the hood latch unit to the front of the radiator closure panel crossmember and move the latch out of the way over the top of the crossmember. Mark the latch location.*

6   Remove the refrigerant lines from the condenser **(see illustration)**. Plug the open fittings to prevent entry of dirt and moisture.

7   Remove the condenser mounting bolts **(see illustration)**.

8   Carefully pulling straight up remove the condenser from the vehicle.

9   Inspect the rubber insulator pads (on the lower crossmember) on which the radiator sits. Replace them if they're dried or cracked.

16.7 Remove the condenser mounting bolts (arrows)

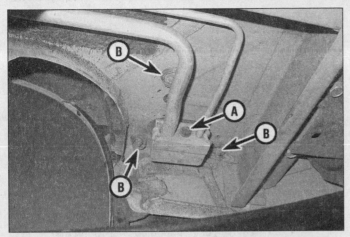

18.2 Location of the rear air conditioning refrigerant lines (A) and rear unit mounting bolts (B)

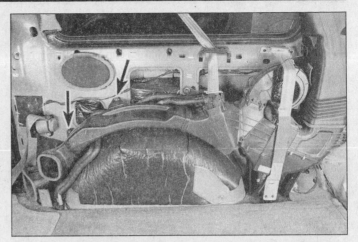

18.5 Remove the screws (arrows) holding the lower ducts

18.6a Pinch off the heater hoses using locking pliers

18.6b Release heater hose clamps (arrows) and carefully detach the hoses from the heater core

10   If the original condenser will be reinstalled, store it with the line fittings on top to prevent oil from draining out. If a new condenser is being installed, pour one ounce of R-134a-compatible refrigerant oil into it prior to installation.

11   Before installation, replace all O-rings and gaskets, coat all sealing surfaces with approved refrigerant oil. Reinstall the components in the reverse order of removal. Be sure the rubber pads are in place under the condenser.

12   Have the system evacuated, recharged and leak tested by the shop that discharged it.

17   Auxiliary (rear) heating and air conditioning system - general information

The auxiliary rear heating-air/conditioning unit is located in the right rear quarter panel. The rear heater air conditioning control operates in conjunction with the front heater air conditioning control. A four position two

speed blower (override) switch is located on the front heater air conditioning control panel. The system can be operated from the front blower switch on the dashboard, regardless of the settings of the rear controls.

Air is drawn into the air intake, then enters the blower housing and is pushed through the heater core or the air conditioning evaporator. The air direction, floor or overhead is determined by the position of the driver's temperature control lever on the front heater/air conditioning control panel.

18   Auxiliary (rear) heating and air conditioning components - removal and installation

Warning: *The air conditioning system is under high pressure. DO NOT disassemble any part of the system (hoses, compressor, line fittings, etc.) until after the system has been evacuated and the refrigerant recovered by a dealer service department or service station. The engine cooling system must also be relieved of all pressure.*

Heater/air conditioning unit

Refer to illustrations 18.2, 18.5, 18.6a, 18.6b, 18.8a and 18.8b

Warning: *Wait until the engine is completely cool before beginning this procedure.*

Note: *Special effort must be used to keep all system components moisture-free. Moisture in the oil is very difficult to remove and will cause a reliability problem with the compressor.*

1   Have the system discharged (see the Warning at the beginning of this Section). Raise the vehicle and support it securely on jackstands.

2   Remove the refrigerant lines at the lower pan flange, then remove the three air conditioning unit floor mounting nuts (**see illustration**).

3   Lower the vehicle.

4   Remove the right quarter trim panel and D-pillar trim (see Chapter 11).

5   Remove the screws holding the air distribution duct to the rear wheel housing (**see illustration**).

6   Pinch off the heater hoses at the rear heater core using locking pliers (**see illustration**), then remove the heater hoses at the heater core (**see illustration**).

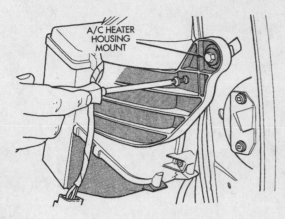

18.8a   Remove the screw to release the upper duct trim

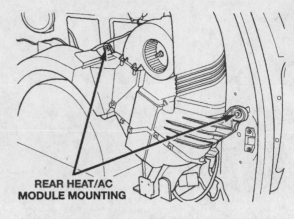

18.8b   Remove the mounting bolts securing the air conditioning module

7   Remove the quarter trim panel mounting bracket and disconnect the blower motor wiring connector.

8   Remove the rear upper duct trim screw and the two mounting bolts retaining the unit to the vehicle **(see illustrations)**.

9   Pull upon the upper air conditioning duct while tilting the unit outward. Lift the air conditioning unit high enough to clear the floor and remove it from the vehicle.

10   Installation is the reverse of removal, installing new O-rings at the refrigerant lines. Refill the cooling system. Have the system evacuated, recharged and leak tested. **Note:** *If the heater core was emptied and was not prefilled, it is necessary to thermal cycle the vehicle TWICE. The heater core is positioned higher than the radiator fill cap, and will not gravity fill to level. To thermal cycle the vehicle, it must be operated until the thermostat opens, then turned off and allowed to cool. In order to verify that the auxiliary unit is filled completely, the following procedure can be used:*

a)   *Vehicle must be at room temperature.*
b)   *Engine is brought up to operating temperature.*

c)   *Front unit is OFF, and temperature slides are at full HEAT position.*
d)   *Engine is at idle with rear motor set on HIGH.*
e)   *The discharge air temperature, measured at the dual register located on C-pillar base should be between 135-degrees and 145-degrees F.*

Rear heater core

Refer to illustration 18.13

11   Remove the right quarter trim panel (see Chapter 11).

12   Isolate and disconnect the lines from the heater core **(see illustration 18.6a)**.

13   Remove the heater core retaining screws and carefully pull the heater core and tubes up and straight out of the unit **(see illustration)**.

14   Installation is the reverse of removal. Prefill the heater core and test for leaks and overall performance. **Note:** *If the heater core was emptied and was not prefilled, it is necessary to thermal cycle the vehicle TWICE. The heater core is positioned higher than the radiator fill cap, and will not gravity fill to level. To thermal cycle the vehicle, it must be operated until the thermostat opens, then turned*

off and allowed to cool. In order to verify that the auxiliary unit is filled completely, the procedure of Step 10 can be used.

Rear blower motor

Refer to illustration 18.16

15   Remove the right quarter trim panel (see Chapter 11).

16   Remove the screws securing the blower motor housing to the heater/air conditioning unit (one screw is located on the evaporator cover) **(see illustration)**.

17   Twist the motor out of the housing and disconnect the wiring connector.

18   Installation is the reverse of removal.

Rear heater air conditioning auxiliary condenser

19   If the vehicle is equipped with a 3.3L or 3.8L V6 engine with rear heater and air conditioning, it will be equipped with an auxiliary condenser, the auxiliary condenser is mounted on the primary condenser in front of the radiator. Both condensers must be removed as an assembly and then separated. See Section 16 for removal and installation of the condenser.

18.13   Carefully pull the heater core straight out

18.16   Remove the blower motor mounting screws (not all screws visible)

Chapter 4
Fuel and exhaust systems

Contents

	Section
Accelerator cable - replacement	10
Air cleaner assembly - removal and installation	9
Air filter replacement	See Chapter 1
Air intake plenum or upper intake manifold (V6 models) - removal and installation	16
CHECK ENGINE light	See Chapter 6
Exhaust system check	See Chapter 1
Exhaust system servicing - general information	17
Fuel filter replacement	See Chapter 1
Fuel injection system - check	12
Fuel injection system - general information	11
Fuel rail and injectors - check, removal and installation	14
Fuel level sending unit - check and replacement	6

	Section
Fuel lines and fittings - replacement	4
Fuel pressure relief procedure	2
Fuel pump, fuel pressure regulator and inlet strainer - removal and installation	5
Fuel pump/fuel pressure - check	3
Fuel system check	See Chapter 1
Fuel tank - removal and installation	7
Fuel tank cleaning and repair - general information	8
General information	1
Idle Air Control (IAC) valve - check and replacement	15
Idle speed check and adjustment	See Chapter 1
Throttle body - check, removal and installation	13
Throttle linkage check	See Chapter 1

Specifications

General

Fuel pressure	49 psi
Fuel injector resistance	12 ohms @ 68-degrees F

Torque specifications
Ft-lbs (unless otherwise indicated)

Air intake plenum bolts	
3.0L V6	130 in-lbs
3.3L and 3.8L V6	105 in-lbs
Throttle body bolts	19
Fuel rail mounting bolts	
Four-cylinder	16
3.0L V6	115 in-lbs
3.3L and 3.8L V6	95 in-lbs

1 General information

The vehicles covered by this manual are equipped with a Multi-Port Fuel Injection (MPI) system. This system uses timed impulses to sequentially inject the fuel directly into the intake ports of each cylinder. The injectors are controlled by the Powertrain Control Module (PCM). The PCM monitors various engine parameters and delivers the exact amount of fuel, in the correct sequence, into the intake ports.

All models are equipped with an electric fuel pump, mounted in the fuel tank. It is necessary to remove the fuel tank for access to the fuel pump. The fuel level sending unit is an integral component of the fuel pump and it must be removed from the fuel tank in the same manner.

The exhaust system consists of exhaust manifolds, a catalytic converter, an exhaust pipe and a muffler. Each of these components is replaceable. For further information regarding the catalytic converter, refer to Chapter 6.

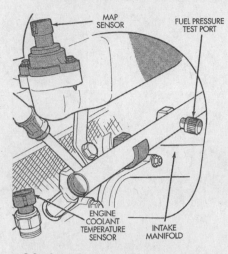

2.2a Location of the fuel pressure test port on the four-cylinder engine

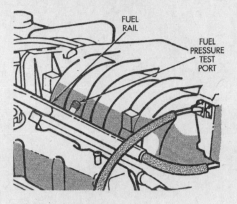

2.2b Location of the fuel pressure test port on the 3.3L and 3.8L V6 engines

3.5 Install a fuel pressure gauge at the fuel rail test port - check fuel pressure with the engine idling

2   Fuel pressure relief procedure

Warning: *Gasoline is extremely flammable, so take extra precautions when you work on any part of the fuel system. Don't smoke or allow open flames or bare light bulbs near the work area, and don't work in a garage where a natural gas-type appliance (such as a water heater or a clothes dryer) with a pilot light is present. Since gasoline is carcinogenic, wear latex gloves when there's a possibility of being exposed to fuel, and, if you spill any fuel on your skin, rinse it off immediately with soap and water. Mop up any spills immediately and do not store fuel-soaked rags where they could ignite. The fuel system is under constant pressure, so, if any fuel lines are to be disconnected, the fuel pressure in the system must be relieved first. When you perform any kind of work on the fuel system, wear safety glasses and have a Class B type fire extinguisher on hand.*

All except 3.0L V6 engine

Refer to illustrations 2.2a and 2.2b

1   Disconnect the cable from the negative terminal of the battery. Unscrew the fuel filler cap to relieve pressure built up in the fuel tank.
2   Carefully place several shop towels around the fuel pressure test port and the fuel rail. Remove the cap from the fuel pressure test port located on the fuel rail **(see illustrations)**.
3   Use one of the two following methods:
 a) *Attach a fuel pressure gauge to the Schrader valve on the fuel rail (see Section 3). Place the gauge bleeder hose in an approved fuel container. Open the valve on the gauge to relieve pressure, then disconnect the cable from the negative terminal of the battery.*
 b) *Using the tip of a screwdriver, depress the Schrader valve and let the fuel drain into the shop towels. Be careful to catch any fuel that might spray upward by using another shop towel.*

4   Unless this procedure is followed before servicing fuel lines or connections, fuel spray (and possible injury) may occur.
5   Install the cap onto the fuel pressure test port.

3.0L V6 engine

6   Remove the fuel pump relay from the Power Distribution Center (PDC). Refer to the underside of the PDC cover for relay location.
7   Start the engine and run until it stalls.
8   Attempt restarting the engine until it will no longer run.
9   Turn the ignition key OFF.
10   Disconnect the cable from the negative battery terminal.
11   Replace the fuel pump relay in the Power Distribution Center (PDC).
12   Any DTC (trouble code) that may have been stored in the PCM memory due to fuel pump relay removal must be cleared (erased) using a DRB scan tool. When work is completed, you may need to see a dealer or repair shop for this step.

3   Fuel pump/fuel pressure - check

Warning: *Gasoline is extremely flammable, so take extra precautions when you work on any part of the fuel system. Don't smoke or allow open flames or bare light bulbs near the work area, and don't work in a garage where a natural gas-type appliance (such as a water heater or a clothes dryer) with a pilot light is present. Since gasoline is carcinogenic, wear latex gloves when there's a possibility of being exposed to fuel, and, if you spill any fuel on your skin, rinse it off immediately with soap and water. Mop up any spills immediately and do not store fuel-soaked rags where they could ignite. The fuel system is under constant pressure, so, if any fuel lines are to be disconnected, the fuel pressure in the system must be relieved first (see Section 2 for more information). When you perform any kind of work on the fuel system, wear safety glasses and have a Class B type fire extinguisher on hand.*

Preliminary check

Note: *On all models, the fuel pump is located inside the fuel tank (see Section 5).*
1   If you suspect insufficient fuel delivery, first inspect all fuel lines to ensure that the problem is not simply a leak in a line.
2   Set the parking brake and have an assistant turn the ignition switch to the ON position while you listen to the fuel pump (inside the fuel tank). You should hear a "whirring" sound, lasting for a couple of seconds. Start the engine. The whirring sound should now be continuous (although harder to hear with the engine running). If there is no sound, either the fuel pump fuse, fuel pump, fuel pump relay, ASD relay or related circuits (see Chapter 12) are defective (proceed to Step 16).

Pressure check

Refer to illustration 3.5
Note: *A special fuel gauge (capable of reading high pressure) and the appropriate fittings and adapters are needed to properly test the fuel pump on all models.*
3   Relieve the fuel pressure (see Section 2).
4   On all except 3.0L V6 models, attach a fuel pressure gauge to the fuel pressure test port located on the fuel rail **(see illustrations 2.2a and 2.2b)**. On 3.0L V6 models, disconnect the quick-connect fuel line fitting at the fuel rail (see Section 4) and install the fuel gauge into the fuel line using the appropriate T-fitting and adapters.
5   Start the engine and check the pressure on the gauge **(see illustration)**, comparing your reading with the pressure listed in this Chapter's Specifications. With the engine idling, measure the fuel pressure. It should be as specified.
6   If the fuel pressure is not as specified, check the following:
 a) *If the pressure is higher than specified, check for a pinched or clogged fuel return hose or pipe. If the return line is not obstructed, see below for fuel pressure regulator.*

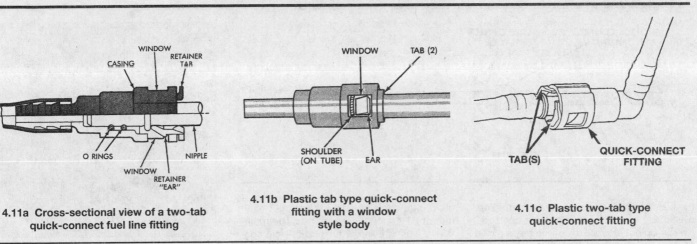

4.11a Cross-sectional view of a two-tab quick-connect fuel line fitting

4.11b Plastic tab type quick-connect fitting with a window style body

4.11c Plastic two-tab type quick-connect fitting

b) *If the pressure is lower than specified:*
1) *Inspect the fuel filter - make sure it's not clogged (see Chapter 1).*
2) *Look for a pinched or clogged fuel hose between the fuel tank and the fuel rail.*
3) *Check the pressure regulator for a malfunction (see below).*
4) *Look for leaks in the fuel line.*

7   If there are no problems with any of the above-listed components, check the fuel pump (see below).

Component checks

Fuel pressure regulator

8   The fuel pressure regulator is a mechanical regulator device located in the fuel tank as part of the fuel pump module. the pressure regulator is not controlled by the PCM or engine vacuum. Check as described above in *Pressure Check.* Compare your readings with the values listed in this Chapter's Specifications.

9   If the fuel pressure is not correct, the fuel pump or regulator may be defective or there is a kink or other restriction in the fuel line. Check the fuel return line (from filter to pump module) and blow through it to check for blockage. Replace the fuel regulator by removal of the fuel pump module from the fuel tank (see Section 5).

Fuel pump

10   If you suspect a problem with the fuel pump, verify the pump actually runs. Have an assistant turn the ignition switch to ON - you should hear a brief "whirring" noise as the pump comes on and pressurizes the system. Have the assistant start the engine. This time you should hear a constant whirring sound from the pump (but it's more difficult to hear with the engine running).

11   If the pump does not come on (makes no sound), proceed to the next step.

12   Remove the trunk liner and access the fuel pump module on top of the tank (see Section 5). Disconnect the electrical connector from the fuel pump.

13   Working on the harness side of the fuel pump electrical connector, check for battery voltage to the fuel pump with the ignition key ON (engine not running). Battery voltage should be present. Also check for continuity to ground on the fuel pump ground circuit. If voltage is available, the ground is good and the fuel pump doesn't run when connected, replace the fuel pump (see Section 5). If no voltage is available, check the main relays (see below).

Fuel pump and ASD relays

Note: *The Automatic Shutdown (ASD) relay and the fuel pump relay must both be tested to insure proper fuel pump operation. Testing procedures for the ASD relay and the fuel pump relay are identical (see Chapter 6).*

4   Fuel lines and fittings - replacement

Warning: *Gasoline is extremely flammable, so take extra precautions when you work on any part of the fuel system. Don't smoke or allow open flames or bare light bulbs near the work area, and don't work in a garage where a natural gas-type appliance (such as a water heater or a clothes dryer) with a pilot light is present. Since gasoline is carcinogenic, wear latex gloves when there's a possibility of being exposed to fuel, and, if you spill any fuel on your skin, rinse it off immediately with soap and water. Mop up any spills immediately and do not store fuel-soaked rags where they could ignite. The fuel system is under constant pressure, so, if any fuel lines are to be disconnected, the fuel pressure in the system must be relieved first (see Section 2 for more information). When you perform any kind of work on the fuel system, wear safety glasses and have a Class B type fire extinguisher on hand.*

1   Always relieve the fuel pressure before servicing fuel lines or fittings (see Section 2).

2   The fuel feed, return and vapor lines extend from the fuel tank to the engine compartment. The lines are secured to the underbody with clip and screw assemblies. These lines must be occasionally inspected for leaks, kinks and dents.

3   If evidence of dirt is found in the system or fuel filter during disassembly, the line should be disconnected and blown out. Check the fuel strainer on the fuel gauge sending unit (see Section 6) for damage and deterioration.

4   In the event of any fuel line damage (metal or flexible lines) it is necessary to replace the damaged lines with factory replacement parts. Others may fail from the high pressures of this system.

Steel tubing

5   If replacement of a fuel line or emission line is called for, use tubes/hoses meeting the manufacturers specification or its equivalent.

6   Don't use copper or aluminum tubing to replace steel tubing. These materials cannot withstand normal vehicle vibration.

7   Because fuel lines used on fuel-injected vehicles are under high pressure, they require special consideration.

8   Some fuel lines have threaded fittings with O-rings. Any time the fittings are loosened to service or replace components:
a) *Use a backup wrench while loosening and tightening the fittings.*
b) *Check all O-rings for cuts, cracks and deterioration. Replace any that appear hardened, worn or damaged.*
c) *If the lines are replaced, always use original equipment parts, or parts that meet the original equipment standards specified in this Section.*

Flexible hose

Refer to illustrations 4.11a, 4.11b, 4.11c, 4.11d and 4.11e

Warning: *Use only original equipment replacement hoses or their equivalent. Others may fail from the high pressures of this system.*

9   Relieve the fuel pressure.

10   Remove all fasteners attaching the lines to the vehicle body.

11   There are various methods depending upon the type of quick-connect fitting on the fuel line **(see illustrations).** Carefully remove

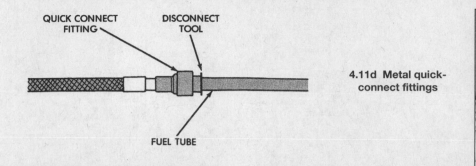

4.11d Metal quick-connect fittings

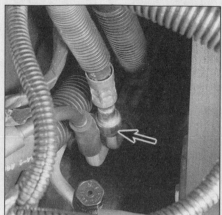

4.11e Disconnect the engine compartment fuel feed line by pushing up on the plastic clip (arrow) using an open end wrench. Gently pull the fitting open

the fuel lines from the chassis. **Caution:** *The plastic ring type fittings are not serviced separately. Do not attempt to service these types of fuel lines in the event the clip or line becomes damaged. Replace the entire fuel line as an assembly.*

12   Installation is the reverse of removal. Be sure to use new O-rings at the threaded fittings (if equipped).

13   Don't route fuel hose within four inches of any part of the exhaust system or within ten inches of the catalytic converter. Metal lines and rubber hoses must never be allowed to chafe against the frame. A minimum of 1/4-inch clearance must be maintained around a line or hose to prevent contact with the frame.

5   Fuel pump, fuel pressure regulator, and inlet strainer - removal and installation

Warning: *Gasoline is extremely flammable, so take extra precautions when you work on any part of the fuel system. Don't smoke or allow open flames or bare light bulbs near the work area, and don't work in a garage where a natural gas-type appliance (such as a water heater or a clothes dryer) with a pilot light is present. Since gasoline is carcinogenic, wear latex gloves when there's a possibility of being exposed to fuel, and, if you spill any fuel on your skin, rinse it off immediately with soap and water. Mop up any spills immediately and do not store fuel-soaked rags where they could ignite. The fuel system is under constant pressure, so, if any fuel lines are to be disconnected, the fuel pressure in the system must be relieved first (see Section 2 for more information). When you perform any kind of work on the fuel system, wear safety glasses and have a Class B type fire extinguisher on hand.*

Removal

Refer to illustrations 5.5, 5.6, 5.7 and 5.9

1   Relieve the fuel system pressure (see Section 2).

2   Disconnect the cable from the negative terminal of the battery.

3   Unbolt the fuel tank and lower the tank slightly (see Section 7).

4   Clean the area around the fuel tank pump module to keep dirt and other material out of the tank.

5   Disconnect the fuel pump module electrical connector **(see illustration)**.

6   Disconnect the fuel lines from the pump module inlet and return pipe connectors **(see illustration)**.

7   Using a strap wrench (or a fabricated tool), turn the plastic lock nut counterclockwise to release the pump module **(see illustration)**.

8   Carefully remove the fuel pump module and O-ring from the tank. Discard the old O-ring.

5.5 Remove the plastic locking pin and disconnect the fuel pump module electrical connector

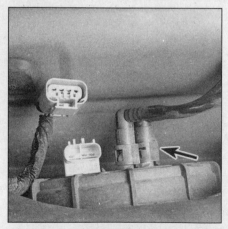

5.6 Disconnect the fuel lines from the tank by depressing the quick-connect retainer tabs

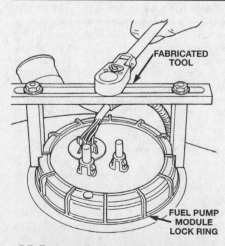

5.7 Remove the fuel pump module lock ring with a strap wrench or a tool similar to that shown

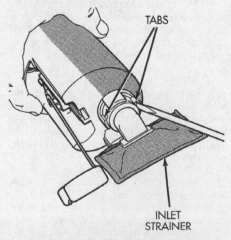

5.9 Pry the locking tabs upward to release the inlet strainer from the fuel pump module

5.13a Spread the tangs on the fuel pump module pressure regulator retainer away from the tabs

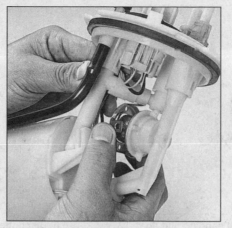

5.13b Remove the retainer and carefully pry the pressure regulator out of the fuel pump module

5.13c Remove the O-rings from the pressure regulator

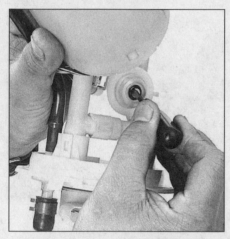

5.13d Apply clean engine oil to the O-rings and install them into the fuel pump module, making sure they are properly seated

9   The fuel pump inlet strainer is removed by using a thin screwdriver to pry back the locking tabs on the fuel pump reservoir and removing the strainer **(see illustration)**.
10   Remove the strainer O-ring from the fuel pump reservoir body.

Installation

Refer to illustrations 5.13a, 5.13b, 5.13c and 5.13d

11   If necessary, clean out the fuel tank.
12   When installing the inlet strainer, lubricate the strainer O-ring with clean engine oil. Insert the strainer O-ring into the outlet of the strainer so that it sits evenly on the step inside of the outlet. Push the strainer onto the inlet of the fuel pump reservoir body, until the locking tabs engage securely.
13   Remove the fuel pressure regulator from the fuel pump module by spreading the tangs on the pressure regulator retainer, removing the retainer, and prying the pressure regulator out **(see illustrations)**. Replace the pressure regulator O-rings.
14   Fuel pump module installation is the reverse of removal.

---

6   Fuel level sending unit - check and replacement

Warning: *Gasoline is extremely flammable, so take extra precautions when you work on any part of the fuel system. Don't smoke or allow open flames or bare light bulbs near the work area, and don't work in a garage where*

a natural gas-type appliance (such as a water heater or a clothes dryer) with a pilot light is present. Since gasoline is carcinogenic, wear latex gloves when there's a possibility of being exposed to fuel, and, if you spill any fuel on your skin, rinse it off immediately with soap and water. Mop up any spills immediately and do not store fuel-soaked rags where they could ignite. The fuel system is under constant pressure, so, if any fuel lines are to be disconnected, the fuel pressure in the system must be relieved first (see Section 2 for more information). When you perform any kind of work on the fuel system, wear safety glasses and have a Class B type fire extinguisher on hand.

Check

Refer to illustrations 6.2, 6.3 and 6.4

1   Follow Steps 1 to 8 of Section 5 to remove the fuel pump module from the fuel tank to allow testing of the fuel level sending unit.
2   Position the probes of an ohmmeter onto the fuel level sending unit electrical connector terminals and check for resistance **(see illustration)**.
3   Carefully lifting the fuel tank float arm, check the resistance of the sending unit to simulate a full fuel tank **(see illustration)**. The resistance (ohms) of the sending unit should

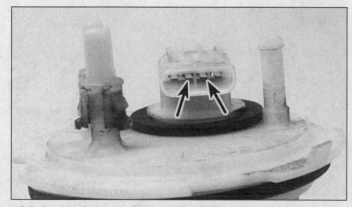

6.2 Attach ohmmeter leads to check the fuel level sending unit resistance between these two terminals (arrows)

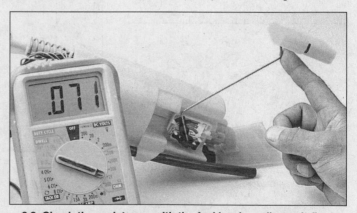

6.3 Check the resistance with the fuel level sending unit float lifted to simulate a full fuel tank - it should be low

6.4 Check the resistance with the fuel level sending unit float lowered to simulate an empty fuel tank - it should be high

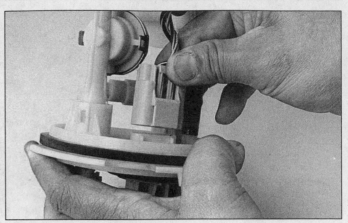

6.6 Disconnect the internal electrical connector from the fuel pump module

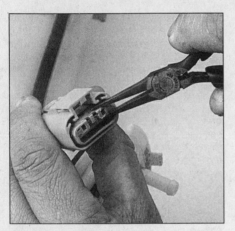

6.7 Use a needlenose pliers and carefully pull out and remove the blue locking wedge

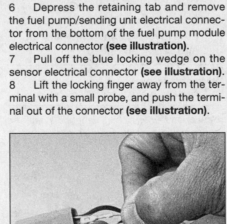

6.8 Lift the locking terminal away from the wire terminal

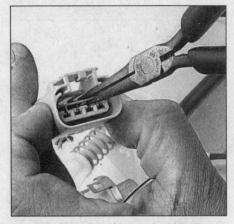

6.9a With the wire terminal loose, carefully push the terminal out of the connector

be low (approximately 8 ohms).

4   Then carefully release the fuel tank float arm to simulate an empty tank of fuel and check the resistance of the sending unit again **(see illustration)**. The resistance should be high (approximately 100 ohms).

5   If the readings are incorrect or there is very little change in resistance as the float travels from full to empty, replace the fuel level sending unit sensor assembly.

Replacement

Refer to illustrations 6.6, 6.7, 6.8, 6.9a, 6.9b, 6.9c, 6.10, 6.11 and 6.13

6   Depress the retaining tab and remove the fuel pump/sending unit electrical connector from the bottom of the fuel pump module electrical connector **(see illustration)**.

7   Pull off the blue locking wedge on the sensor electrical connector **(see illustration)**.

8   Lift the locking finger away from the terminal with a small probe, and push the terminal out of the connector **(see illustration)**.

9   Push the sending unit signal and ground terminals out of the connector **(see illustrations)**.

10   Insert a screwdriver between the fuel pump module and the top of the sending unit housing **(see illustration)**. Push the sending unit down slightly to separate it from the module.

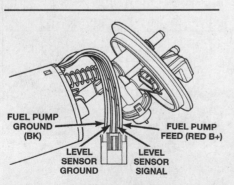

6.9b Fuel sending unit level sensor connector wiring identification

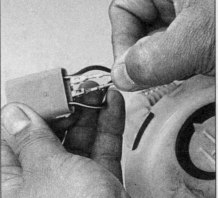

6.9c Pull the sending unit wires out of the connector

6.10 Insert a screwdriver between the fuel pump module and the top of the fuel level sensor and push the sensor down slightly

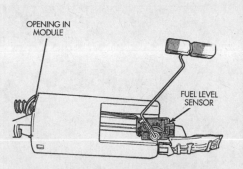

6.11 Slide the sending unit wires through the fuel pump module opening and then slide the sending unit out of the channel

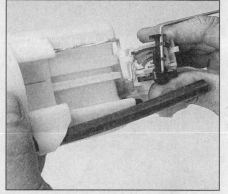

6.13 To reinstall the sending unit level sensor, feed the wires into the guide grooves, then slide the sending unit up the channel until it snaps in place solidly

7.7 Support the fuel tank and remove both tank strap bolts (arrows)

11 Slide the fuel level sensor wires through the fuel pump module assembly **(see illustration)**. Then slide the sending unit out of the module.
12 Lift the fuel level sending unit from the assembly.
13 Installation is the reverse of removal. Feed the wires into the guide grooves and slide the fuel level sensor up into the channel until it snaps into place **(see illustration)**. Ensure that the tab at the bottom of the sensor locks into place.

7   Fuel tank - removal and installation

Refer to illustration 7.7
Warning: *Gasoline is extremely flammable, so take extra precautions when you work on any part of the fuel system. Don't smoke or allow open flames or bare light bulbs near the work area, and don't work in a garage where a natural gas-type appliance (such as a water heater or a clothes dryer) with a pilot light is present. Since gasoline is carcinogenic, wear latex gloves when there's a possibility of being exposed to fuel, and, if you spill any fuel on your skin, rinse it off immediately with*

soap and water. Mop up any spills immediately and do not store fuel-soaked rags where they could ignite. The fuel system is under constant pressure, so, if any fuel lines are to be disconnected, the fuel pressure in the system must be relieved first (see Section 2 for more information). When you perform any kind of work on the fuel system, wear safety glasses and have a Class B type fire extinguisher on hand.
Note: *The following procedure is much easier to perform if the fuel tank is empty. Some tanks have a drain plug for this purpose. If the tank does not have a drain plug, the fuel can be siphoned from the tank using a siphoning kit, available at most auto parts stores. NEVER start the siphoning action with your mouth!*
1 Remove the fuel tank filler cap to relieve fuel tank pressure.
2 Relieve the fuel system pressure (see Section 2).
3 Disconnect the cable from the negative terminal of the battery.
4 Insert fuel siphon hose into fuel filler neck and push it down into the fuel tank, using a siphoning kit (available at most auto

parts stores). Siphon the fuel until the fuel tank is dry, into an approved and properly labeled GASOLINE container.
5 Working on a flat, level surface, raise the vehicle and support it securely on jackstands.
6 Using a transmission jack or equivalent, position a piece of wood between the jack head and the fuel tank to protect the tank, support the fuel tank.
7 Remove the bolts from the fuel tank straps **(see illustration)** and lower the tank slightly.
8 Disconnect fuel lines, hoses and electrical connectors (see Section 5) and remove the tank from the vehicle.
9 If necessary, remove the fuel pump module from the fuel tank (see Section 5).
10 Fuel tank installation is the reverse of removal.

8   Fuel tank cleaning and repair - general information

1 The fuel tanks installed in the vehicles covered by this manual are made of plastic and are not repairable.
2 If the fuel tank is removed from the vehicle, it should not be placed in an area where sparks or open flames could ignite the fumes coming out of the tank. Be especially careful inside a garage where a natural gas-type appliance is located, because the pilot light could cause an explosion.

9   Air cleaner assembly - removal and installation

1996 through 2000 models
Refer to illustrations 9.2, 9.4 and 9.5
1 Disconnect the cable from the negative terminal of the battery.
2 Remove the air resonator **(see illustration)**.
3 Loosen the 3 clamps holding the air cleaner housing halves together.
4 Remove the left side of the air cleaner housing **(see illustration)**.
5 Lift out the air cleaner element **(see**

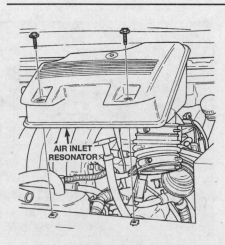

9.2 Remove the air inlet resonator bolts and lift off the unit

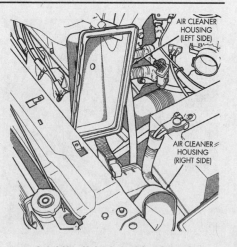

9.4 Lift off the left side of the air cleaner housing

9.5 Pull out the air cleaner element

9.9 Unsnap the two clips (arrows) and lift off the air cleaner cover

9.10 Lift up and remove the air cleaner element from the air box

illustration). Clean any dirt or other foreign material out of the air cleaner housing.

6   Unbolt the air cleaner housing bottom from the vehicle.

7   Installation is the reverse of removal.

2001 and later models

Refer to illustrations 9.9 and 9.10

8   Disconnect the cable from the negative terminal of the battery.

9   Unsnap the two clips holding the air cleaner housing halves together **(see illustration)**.

10   Lift up the cover and remove the air cleaner element **(see illustration)**.

11   Lift the cover, pull toward the engine, disengage the tabs and remove the cover.

12   Disconnect the inlet air temperature sensor.

13   Disconnect the inlet hose from the air box.

14   Detach the bolt securing the air cleaner air box to the upper radiator crossmember.

15   Pull the air cleaner air box up and off the single locating pin and remove the air box.

16   Installation is the reverse of removal.

10 Accelerator cable - replacement

Refer to illustrations 10.2a, 10.2b, 10.2c, 10.4a, 10.4b, 10.4c, 10.7a and 10.7b

1   Disconnect the cable from the negative terminal of the battery.

2   Working inside the engine compartment, hold the throttle lever at the throttle body in the wide open position. Remove the throttle cable from the throttle body cam **(see illustrations)**.

3   From inside the vehicle, hold up the pedal and remove the cable retainer and throttle cable from the pedal.

4   Remove the retainer clip **(see illustrations)** from the throttle cable.

5   Remove the grommet at the firewall throttle cable opening.

6   From the engine compartment, pull the cable through the firewall.

7   Remove the throttle cable from the throttle bracket by carefully compressing both retaining ears and pulling the throttle cable from the bracket **(see illustrations)**.

8   Installation is the reverse of removal.

11 Fuel injection system - general information

The Multi-Port Fuel Injection (MPI) system consists of three sub-systems: air intake, electronic control and fuel delivery. The system uses a Powertrain Control Module (PCM) along with the sensors (Engine Coolant Temperature sensor (ECT), Throttle Position Sensor (TPS), Manifold Absolute Pressure (MAP) sensor, oxygen sensor, etc.) to determine the proper air/fuel ratio under all operating conditions.

The fuel injection system and the emissions and engine control system are linked electronically to function together for operating efficiency and powertrain control. For additional information, refer to Chapter 6.

Air intake system

The air intake system consists of the air cleaner, the air intake ducts, the throttle body, the idle control system, the air intake plenum and the intake manifold.

A throttle position sensor is attached to

10.2a On four-cylinder models, remove the throttle cable cover . . .

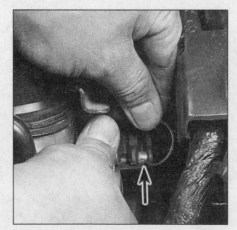

10.2b . . . and with the accelerator pedal held down, disconnect the throttle cable from the slot in the throttle body cam

10.2c On V6 engines, hold the accelerator pedal down and disconnect the throttle cable from the throttle body cam

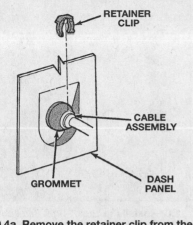

10.4a Remove the retainer clip from the accelerator cable at the firewall grommet area

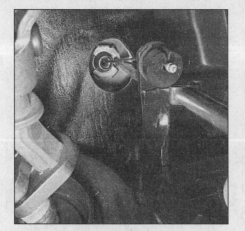

10.4b Pull the accelerator cable to create slack in the cable

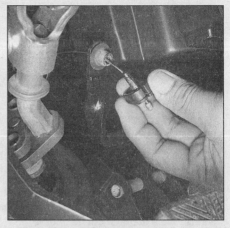

10.4c Remove the grommet, sliding the cable through the slot

the throttle shaft to monitor changes in the throttle opening.

When the engine is idling, the air/fuel ratio is controlled by the idle air control system, which consists of the Powertrain Control Module (PCM) and the Idle Air Control (IAC) valve. The IAC valve is controlled by the PCM and is opened and closed depending upon the running conditions of the engine (air conditioning system, power steering, cold and warm running etc.). This valve regulates the amount of airflow past the throttle plate and into the intake manifold, thus increasing or decreasing the engine idle speed. The PCM receives information from the sensors (throttle opening, vehicle speed, engine coolant temperature, air pressure and temperature, air conditioning, power steering mode, etc.) and adjusts the idle according to the demands of the engine and driver.

Electronic emissions and engine control system

The electronic emissions and engine control system is explained in detail in Chapter 6.

Fuel delivery system

The fuel delivery system consists of these components: The fuel pump, the pressure regulator, the fuel injectors, the fuel rail, the Automatic Shutdown (ASD) Relay and the fuel pump relay (main relays).

The fuel pump is an in-line, direct drive type. Fuel is drawn through a filter into the pump, flows past the armature through the one-way valve, passes through another filter and is delivered to the injectors. A relief valve prevents excessive pressure build-up by opening in the event of a blockage in the discharge side and allowing fuel to flow from the high to the low pressure side. The pressure regulator maintains a constant fuel pressure to the injectors.

The injectors are solenoid-actuated, constant stroke, pintle types consisting of a solenoid, plunger, needle valve and housing.

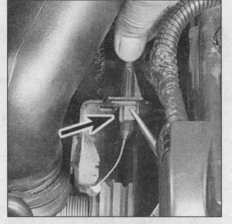

10.7a Use needlenose pliers to depress the tabs, disconnect the cable retainer and release the accelerator cable from the bracket

When current is applied to the solenoid coil, the needle valve raises and pressurized fuel fills the injector housing and squirts out the nozzle. The injection quantity is determined by the length of time the valve is open (the length of time during which current is supplied to the solenoid coils).

Because it determines opening and closing intervals, which in turn, determines the air-fuel mixture ratio - injector timing must be quite accurate. To attain the best possible injector response, the current rise time, when voltage is being applied to each injector coil, must be as short as possible.

The Automatic Shutdown (ASD) relay and the fuel pump relay are contained within the Power Distribution Center, which is located in the left side of the engine compartment. The ASD relay connects battery voltage to the fuel injectors and the ignition coil while the fuel pump relay connects battery voltage only to the fuel pump. If the PCM senses there is NO signal from the camshaft or crankshaft sensors while the ignition key is turned to the RUN or START positions, the PCM will de-energize both relays.

10.7b Typical accelerator cable retainer (arrow)

12 Fuel injection system - check

Refer to illustrations 12.7, 12.8a and 12.8b
Note: The following procedure is based on the assumption that the fuel pressure is adequate (see Section 3).
1 Check all wiring harness connectors that are related to the system. Check the ground wire connections on the intake manifold for tightness. Loose connectors and poor grounds can cause many problems that resemble more serious malfunctions.
2 Check to see that the battery is fully charged, as the control unit and sensors depend on an accurate supply voltage in order to properly meter the fuel.
3 Check the air-filter element - a dirty or partially blocked filter will severely impede performance and economy (see Chapter 1).
4 If a blown fuse is found, replace it and see if it blows again. If it does, search for a grounded wire in the harness to the fuel pump.
5 Check the air intake duct to the intake manifold for leaks, which will result in an excessively lean mixture. Also check the condition of all vacuum hoses connected to the intake manifold.

12.7 Use a stethoscope to check if the injectors are working properly - they should make a steady clicking sound that rises and falls with engine speed changes

12.8a Remove the fuel injector electrical connectors (arrows) for injector testing (later model shown, early model similar)

12.8b Install the "noid" light (available at most auto parts stores) into each injector electrical connector and confirm that it blinks when the engine is cranking or running

6   Remove the air intake duct from the throttle body and check for dirt, carbon or other residue build-up. If it's dirty, see Section 13 for the cleaning procedure.

7   With the engine running, place an automotive stethoscope against each injector, one at a time, and listen for a clicking sound, indicating operation **(see illustration)**. If you don't have a stethoscope, place the tip of a long screwdriver against the injector and listen with your ear at the screwdriver handle.

8   Disconnect the electrical connector from each injector and using an ohmmeter, measure the resistance across the terminals **(see illustration)**. Compare your measurement with the fuel injector resistance listed in this Chapter's Specifications. Replace any injector with abnormally high or low resistance. Install an injector test light ("noid" light) into each injector electrical connector, one at a time **(see illustration)**. Crank the engine over. Observe that the light flashes evenly on each connector. This will test for voltage to the injector. If the light doesn't flash, check the wiring harness (see Chap-

ter 12). If the wiring harness is not damaged or shorted, check the wiring between the PCM and the injector(s) for a short circuit, or a break in the wire or bad connection.

9   The remainder of the system checks can be found in the following Sections.

13   Throttle body - check, removal and installation

Check

Refer to illustration 13.6

1   On the throttle body, locate the vacuum hose and detach it from the throttle body. Connect a vacuum gauge to this port on the throttle body.

2   Start the engine and warm it to its normal operating temperature (wait until after the cooling fan turns on). Verify the gauge indicates no vacuum.

3   Open the throttle slightly from idle and verify that the gauge indicates vacuum. If the gauge indicates no vacuum, check the port to make sure it is not clogged. Clean it with aerosol carburetor cleaner if necessary.

4   Stop the engine and verify the accelerator cable and throttle valve operate smoothly without binding or sticking.

5   If the accelerator cable or throttle valve binds or sticks, check for a build-up of sludge on the cable or throttle shaft.

6   If a build-up of sludge is evident, try cleaning with aerosol carburetor cleaner (engine must be off) or a similar solvent **(see illustration)**. Make sure the inside of the throttle body is clean (see Step 7).

7   With the engine off, hold the throttle wide open and check the backside of the throttle plate. If cleaning fails to remedy the problem, replace the throttle body.

Removal and installation

Refer to illustration 13.11

Warning: *Wait until the engine is completely cool before beginning this procedure.*

13.6 Clean the throttle body bore and throttle plate with an aerosol-type cleaner

8   Disconnect the cable from the negative terminal of the battery.

9   Remove the air inlet resonator. Disconnect the accelerator and cruise control cables (if equipped) from the throttle lever (see Section 10).

10   Disconnect the throttle position sensor and the idle air control motor electrical connectors from the throttle body. Label and detach any vacuum hoses from the throttle body.

11   Remove the throttle body mounting bolts/nuts. Remove the throttle body and gasket **(see illustration)**. Remove all traces of old gasket material from the throttle body and intake manifold.

12   Installation is the reverse of removal. Be sure to use a new gasket. Adjust the accelerator cable (see Section 10).

14   Fuel rail and injectors - check, removal and installation

Warning: *Gasoline is extremely flammable, so take extra precautions when you work on any part of the fuel system. Don't smoke or allow open flames or bare light bulbs near the*

13.11 Remove the throttle body bolts (arrows) and the accelerator cable bracket - separate the throttle body from the intake manifold

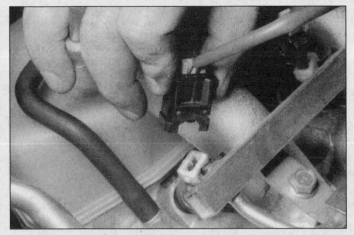

14.10 Release the security locks and disconnect the connector from the fuel injector

14.11 Remove the fuel rail mounting bolts (arrows) - be sure to cover the intake manifold ports first

14.13 Carefully lift the fuel rail assembly with fuel injectors attached from the intake manifold - while removing, wiggle the fuel rail to loosen the injectors

14.14a Release the retaining clip and separate the fuel injector from the fuel rail

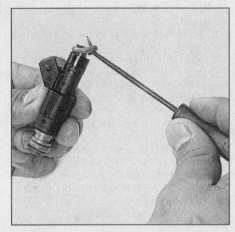

14.14b Remove and discard the O-rings - always install new O-rings when the fuel injectors are removed

work area, and don't work in a garage where a natural gas-type appliance (such as a water heater or a clothes dryer) with a pilot light is present. Since gasoline is carcinogenic, wear latex gloves when there's a possibility of being exposed to fuel, and, if you spill any fuel on your skin, rinse it off immediately with soap and water. Mop up any spills immediately and do not store fuel-soaked rags where they could ignite. The fuel system is under constant pressure, so, if any fuel lines are to be disconnected, the fuel pressure in the system must be relieved first (see Section 2 for more information). When you perform any kind of work on the fuel system, wear safety glasses and have a Class B type fire extinguisher on hand.

Check

1   Connect a tachometer to the engine according to the tool manufacturers instructions. Start the engine and warm it to its normal operating temperature.
2   With the engine idling, unplug each fuel injector one at a time, note the change in idle speed, then reconnect the injector. If the idle speed drop is approximately the same for each cylinder, the injectors are operating correctly.
3   If unplugging a particular injector fails to change the idle speed, turn the engine off and perform the injector resistance and electrical checks as described in Section 12.

Removal

Refer to illustrations 14.10, 14.11, 14.13, 14.14a, 14.14b and 14.15

4   Relieve the fuel pressure (see Section 2).
5   Disconnect the cable from the negative terminal of the battery.
6   On four-cylinder models, remove the intake manifold (see Chapter 2A).
7   On 2001 and later V6 models, remove the upper intake manifold (see Section 16). On all other V6 models, remove the air intake plenum (see Section 16).
8   Cover the open ports on the cylinder head or intake manifold while working on the engine.
9   Disconnect the fuel line quick-connect fitting from the fuel rail (see Section 4) (wrap a shop towel around the hose/tube line to catch any gasoline spillage).
10   Label each fuel injector electrical connector with the corresponding cylinder number and disconnect the connector **(see illustration).**
11   Remove the fuel rail attachment bolts **(see illustration).** On 1996 through 2000 3.3/3.8 V6 engines, spread the retainer bracket to allow fuel rail clearance later.
12   As necessary, disconnect the camshaft position sensor and engine coolant sensor.
13   Remove the fuel rail and fuel injectors as an assembly, being careful not to damage the injector O-rings **(see illustration).**
14   Remove the injectors from the fuel rail and discard the O-rings **(see illustrations).**
Note: *Whether you're replacing an injector or a leaking O-ring, it's a good idea to remove all the injectors from the fuel rail and replace all the O-rings.*

Installation

Refer to illustration 14.15
15   Coat the new O-rings with clean engine

14.15 Coat the new O-rings with clean engine oil and insert each injector into the fuel rail - make sure it is seated fully

15.1a Throttle Position Sensor (TPS) (upper arrow) and Idle Air Control (IAC) valve (lower arrow) locations - 1996 through 2000 V6 engines

15.1b Throttle Position Sensor (top arrow) Idle Air Control (IAC) (lower arrow) locations - 2001 and later V6 engines

oil and slide them onto the injectors **(see illustration)**.

16   Insert each injector into its corresponding bore in the fuel rail.

17   Install the injector and fuel rail assembly. Tighten the fuel rail mounting nuts to the torque listed in this Chapter's Specifications.

18   The remainder of installation is the reverse of removal.

19   After the injector/fuel rail assembly installation is complete, turn the ignition switch to ON, but don't operate the starter (this activates the fuel pump for about two seconds, which builds up fuel pressure in the fuel lines and the fuel rail). Repeat this about two or three times, then check the fuel lines, rail and injectors for fuel leakage.

15   Idle Air Control (IAC) valve - check and replacement

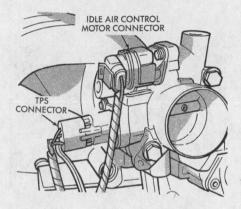

15.1c Throttle Position Sensor (TPS) and Idle Air Control (IAC) valve locations - four-cylinder engine

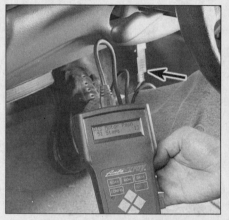

15.4 Connect the SCAN tool into the diagnostic test connector (arrow) under the driver's dash and switch to the IAC mode for accurate testing of the IAC valve

Refer to illustrations 15.1a, 15.1b, 15.1c, 15.4 and 15.6

1   The idle speed is controlled by the IAC valve located on the throttle body **(see illustrations)**. The IAC valve controls idle speed by changing the amount of air that will bypass the throttle plate and flow into the intake manifold. The IAC valve has a pintle valve that protrudes into the air bypass passage and regulates air flow, as controlled by the PCM. The IAC valve is opened and closed depending upon the running conditions of the engine (TPS, crankshaft position, camshaft position, engine coolant temperature, air conditioning system, power steering, cold and warm running etc.). Sudden release of the accelerator pedal by the driver can cause an engine to stall, so the IAC system is also designed to slow the engine deceleration by increasing bypass airflow when the throttle is closed quickly after driving at speed.

Check

2   The IAC valve can accumulate deposits that affect its operation. Idle speed and IAC circuits will set a DTC (trouble code) in the

PCM if a problem occurs.

3   Disconnect the electrical connector from the IAC valve and listen carefully for a change in the idle. Connect the IAC valve electrical connector and turn the air conditioning on and listen for a change in idle rpm. When the engine is cold, the IAC valve should vary the idle as the engine begins to warm-up and also when the air conditioning compressor is turned ON. If there are no obvious signs that the IAC valve is working, have the IAC valve and electrical circuit diagnosed by a dealer service department or other qualified repair shop.

4   There is an alternate method for testing the IAC valve. A SCAN tool is available from some automotive parts stores and specialty tool companies that can be connected into the diagnostic connector for the purpose of monitoring the computer and the sensors (see Chapter 6). Install the SCAN tool **(see illustration)** and switch to the IAC position mode and monitor the steps (valve winding position). The SCAN tool should indicate steps depending upon the rpm range. Allow the engine to idle for several minutes and

while observing the count reading, snap the throttle to achieve high rpm (under 3,500 rpm). Repeat the procedure several times and observe the SCAN tool steps when the engine returns to idle. The readings should be within 5 to 10 steps each time. If the readings fluctuate greatly, replace the IAC valve. **Note:** *When the IAC valve electrical connector is disconnected for testing, the PCM will have to "relearn" its idle mode. In other words, it will take a certain amount of time before the idle valve resets for the correct idle speed. Make sure the idle is smooth before connecting the SCAN tool.*

Replacement

5   Disconnect the electrical connector from the IAC valve.

6   Remove the two mounting screws from the IAC valve and withdraw it from the throttle body **(see illustration)**. Make sure the O-ring is removed with the IAC valve.

7   Before installing the IAC valve, check that the pintle is not extended more than 1 inch. If the pintle is extended more than 1

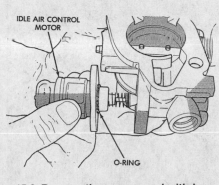

15.6 Remove the screws and withdraw the IAC valve from the throttle body

inch, it must be retracted using the DRB scan tool Idle Air Control Motor Open/Close Test. Take the vehicle to a dealer or repair shop for pintle resetting. Be sure to install a new O-ring.

16 Air intake plenum or upper intake manifold (V6 models) removal and installation

3.0L V6 engine

Refer to illustrations 16.11a, 16.11b and 16.12

1   Relieve the fuel system pressure (see Section 2).
2   Disconnect the cable from the negative terminal of the battery.
3   Drain the cooling system (see Chapter 3).
4   Remove the air inlet resonator.
5   Disconnect the accelerator cable and cruise control cable from the throttle lever and bracket (see Section 10).
6   Disconnect the IAC and TPS wiring connectors from the throttle body.
7   Remove the vacuum hose harness from the throttle body. Remove the throttle body

(see Section 13). **Note:** *If you are replacing the air intake plenum, remove the throttle body. If you are simply removing the air intake plenum to service the lower intake manifold, cylinder heads, etc., you do not need to remove the throttle body from the air intake plenum.*

8   Remove the PCV, brake booster vacuum hoses, and the remaining vacuum connections from the air intake plenum.
9   Remove the electrical connector from the engine coolant temperature sensor, located near the distributor and radiator hose thermostat housing on the top of the engine.

10   Remove the ignition coil from the air intake plenum (see Chapter 5).
11   Remove the air intake plenum fasteners **(see illustrations)** and remove the air intake plenum from the engine. Cover the intake manifold while working in the engine compartment.
12   Installation is the reverse of removal. Carefully clean the gasket surfaces. Use new air intake plenum gaskets; install the gaskets with the beaded sealant side up. Tighten the air intake plenum bolts/nuts in the recommended sequence **(see illustration)** to the torque listed in this Chapter's Specifications.

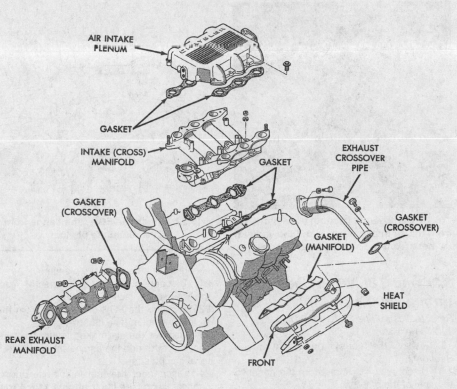

16.11a 3.0L V6 engine intake and exhaust system components

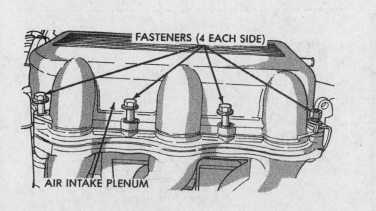

16.11b Remove the air intake plenum bolts/nuts - 3.0L V6 engine

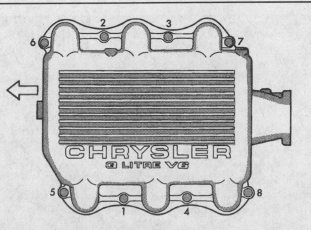

16.12 Air intake plenum tightening sequence - 3.0L V6 engine

16.18 Remove the vacuum hose harness from the air intake plenum and the vacuum hose from the throttle body (arrows)

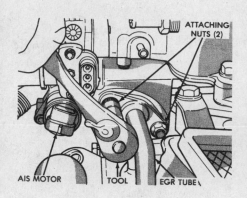

16.22 Detach the EGR tube flange from the air intake plenum

16.26 Remove alternator bracket mounting bolts (arrows)

3.3L and 3.8L V6 engines (1996 through 2000)

Refer to illustrations 16.18, 16.22, 16.26, 16.27 and 16.28

13　Relieve the fuel system pressure (see Section 2).

14　Disconnect the cable from the negative terminal of the battery.

15　Remove the intake manifold cover and air inlet resonator.

16　Disconnect the accelerator cable and cruise control cable from the throttle lever and bracket (see Section 10).

17　Disconnect the IAC and TPS wiring connectors from the throttle body.

18　Remove the vacuum hose harness from the throttle body and intake manifold **(see illustration)**.

19　Remove the throttle body (see Section 13). **Note:** *If you are replacing the air intake plenum, remove the throttle body. If your are simply removing the air intake plenum to service the lower intake manifold, cylinder heads, etc., you do not need to remove the throttle body from the air intake plenum.*

20　Remove the PCV, brake booster vacuum hoses, and the remaining vacuum con-

nections from the air intake plenum.

21　Disconnect electrical connector from the MAP sensor (see Chapter 6).

22　Remove the EGR tube flange from the air intake plenum **(see illustration)**.

23　Remove the air intake plenum to cylinder head strut and the engine-mounted electrical ground strap.

24　Disconnect the fuel inlet hose quick-connect fitting **(see illustration 4.11d)**. Wrap a shop rag around the fitting to absorb spilled fuel.

25　Remove the Direct Ignition System (DIS) coil assembly (see Chapter 5).

26　Remove the alternator bracket to intake manifold bolt. Loosen the top alternator bolts and move the bracket up so the intake manifold plenum can clear the mounting studs **(see illustration)**.

27　Remove the air intake plenum bolts/nuts **(see illustration)** and remove the air intake plenum from the lower intake manifold, rotating the plenum over the rear valve cover. Cover the ports in the lower intake manifold while working in the engine compartment.

28　Installation is the reverse of removal. Use new gaskets and carefully clean the gasket surface. Tighten the air intake plenum bolts/nuts in several steps, in the recom-

mended sequence **(see illustration)**, to the torque listed in this Chapter's Specifications.

3.3L and 3.8L V6 engines (2001 and later)

Refer to illustrations 16.36, 16.37a, 16.37b, 16.42 and 16.43

29　Relieve the fuel pressure (see Section 2).

30　Disconnect the cable from the negative terminal of the battery.

31　Disconnect the air inlet sensor electrical connector.

32　Remove the air inlet resonator to throttle body hose assembly.

33　Disconnect the accelerator cable and cruise control cable from the throttle lever bracket (see Section 10).

34　Disconnect the make-up air hose support clip from the throttle cable bracket.

35　Disconnect the ASI and TPS wiring connectors from the throttle body.

36　Disconnect the MAP sensor electrical connector **(see illustration)**.

37　Disconnect the EGR transducer vacuum hose from the bottom of the upper intake manifold **(see illustration)**. On 3.3L V6 engines, remove the EGR fitting from the top of the upper intake manifold **(see illustration)**. Remove the EGR tube assembly.

16.27 Remove the air intake plenum bolts/nuts (arrows)

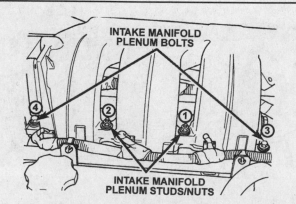

16.28 Air intake plenum tightening sequence - 3.3L and 3.8L V6 engines

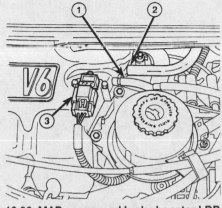

16.36 MAP sensor and brake booster LDP vacuum hoses locations

1   *LDP and speed control vacuum hose*
2   *Brake booster vacuum hose*
3   *MAP sensor*

16.37b Remove the mounting bolts (arrows) securing the EGR fitting

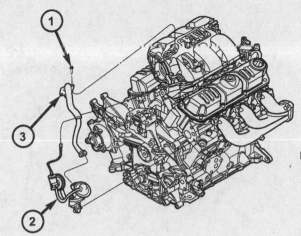

16.37a EGR component locations (3.3L V6 shown)

1   *Bolt*
2   *EGR valve assembly*
3   *EGR tube*

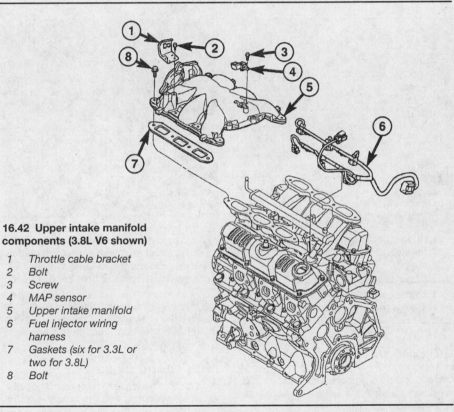

16.42 Upper intake manifold components (3.8L V6 shown)

1   *Throttle cable bracket*
2   *Bolt*
3   *Screw*
4   *MAP sensor*
5   *Upper intake manifold*
6   *Fuel injector wiring harness*
7   *Gaskets (six for 3.3L or two for 3.8L)*
8   *Bolt*

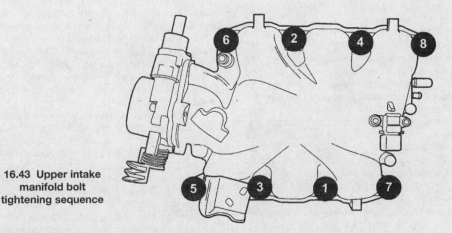

16.43 Upper intake manifold bolt tightening sequence

38   Disconnect the vapor vacuum hose from the throttle body.

39   Disconnect the PCV hose from the valve cover and upper intake manifold. Remove the hose.

40   Disconnect the brake booster and leak detector pump (LDP) hoses from the intake manifold **(see illustration 4.36)**.

41   Remove the bolts attaching the power steering reservoir. Loosen, do not remove, the single nut. Lift the reservoir up and disengage the lower mount from the stud. Move the reservoir aside, do not disconnect the hose.

42   Remove the upper intake manifold bolts **(see illustration)** and remove the upper intake manifold from the lower intake manifold. Cover the ports in the lower intake manifold while working in the engine compartment.

43   Installation is the reverse of removal. Gaskets in good condition can be reused, but new gaskets are recommended. Carefully clean the gaskets and recesses before installation. Do not scrape or use chemical gasket removers on the composite manifold assembly. Tighten the upper intake manifold bolts in the recommended sequence **(see illustration)** to the torque listed in this Chapter's Specifications.

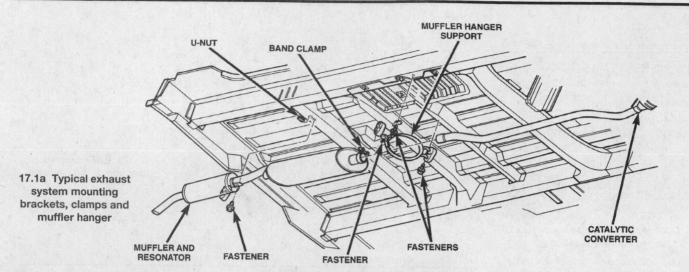

17.1a Typical exhaust system mounting brackets, clamps and muffler hanger

17.1b Inspect the muffler hanger for damage or deteriorated rubber

17.1c The catalytic converter is connected to the exhaust pipe with a flex joint - when working around the exhaust system, be careful not to bend or dent the flex joint

17   Exhaust system servicing - general information

Refer to illustration 17.1a, 17.1b and 17.1c

Warning: *Inspection and repair of exhaust system components should be done only after enough time has elapsed after driving the vehicle to allow the system components to cool completely. Also, when working under the vehicle, make sure it is securely supported on jackstands.*

1   The exhaust system consists of the exhaust manifold(s), the catalytic converter, the muffler, the tailpipe and all connecting pipes, brackets, hangers and clamps. The exhaust system is attached to the body with mounting brackets and hangers **(see illustrations)**. If any of the parts are improperly installed, excessive noise and vibration will be transmitted to the body. Heat shields are needed to protect the vehicle and the floor pan from high temperatures, and are located at the toe board for the catalytic converter and the underbody for the muffler. A flex joint is welded into the catalytic converter **(see illustration)** to secure the catalytic converter to the engine manifold; this joint moves as

the engine moves, preventing breakage that could otherwise occur from the rocking motion of the front mounted transverse engine arrangement.

Muffler and pipes

2   Conduct regular inspections of the exhaust system to keep it safe and quiet. Look for any damaged or bent parts, open seams, holes, loose connections, excessive corrosion or other defects which could allow exhaust fumes to enter the vehicle. Also check the catalytic converter when you inspect the exhaust system (see below). Deteriorated exhaust system components should not be repaired; they should be replaced with new parts.

3   If the exhaust system components are extremely corroded or rusted together, exhaust repair shop cutting equipment will probably be required to remove them. The convenient way to accomplish this is to have a muffler repair shop remove the corroded sections with a cutting torch. If, however, you want to save money by doing it yourself (and you don't have a welding outfit with a cutting torch), simply cut off the old components

with a hacksaw. If you have compressed air, special pneumatic cutting chisels can also be used. If you do decide to tackle the job at home, be sure to wear safety goggles to protect your eyes from metal chips and work gloves to protect your hands.

4   Here are some simple guidelines to follow when repairing the exhaust system:

a) *Work from the back to the front when removing exhaust system components.*

b) *Apply penetrating oil to the exhaust system component fasteners to make them easier to remove.*

c) *Use new gaskets, hangers and clamps when installing exhaust systems components.*

d) *Apply anti-seize compound to the threads of all exhaust system fasteners during reassembly.*

e) *Be sure to allow sufficient clearance between newly installed parts and all points on the underbody to avoid overheating the floor pan and possibly damaging the interior carpet and insulation. Pay particularly close attention to the catalytic converter and heat shield.*

Catalytic converter

Warning: *The converter gets very hot during operation. Make sure it has cooled down before you touch it.*

Note: *See Chapter 6 for more information on the catalytic converter.*

5   Periodically inspect the heat shield for cracks, dents and loose or missing fasteners.

6   Remove the heat shield and inspect the converter for cracks or other damage.

7   If the converter must be replaced, remove the mounting nuts from the flanges at each end, detach the rubber mounts and separate the converter from the exhaust system (you should be able to push the exhaust pipes at each end out of the way to clear the converter studs.

8   Installation is the reverse of removal. Be sure to use new gaskets and make sure the heat shield is in place.

Chapter 5
Engine electrical systems

Contents

	Section		Section
Alternator - removal and installation	11	General information	1
Battery cables - check and replacement	3	Ignition coil - check and replacement	7
Battery check, maintenance and charging	See Chapter 1	Ignition system - check	6
Battery - emergency jump starting	2	Ignition system - general information	5
Battery - removal and installation	4	Spark plug replacement	See Chapter 1
Charging system - check	10	Spark plug wire, distributor cap and rotor check	
Charging system - general information and		and replacement	See Chapter 1
precautions	9	Starter motor - in-vehicle check	14
CHECK ENGINE light	See Chapter 6	Starter motor - removal and installation	15
Distributor (3.0L V6 engine only) - removal, inspection		Starting system - general information and	
and installation	8	precautions	13
Drivebelt check, adjustment and		Voltage regulator - general information	12
replacement	See Chapter 1		

Specifications

Ignition system

Ignition coil
  Four cylinder engine
    Primary resistance

1996 through 1998	0.45 to 0.65 ohms @ 70 to 80-degrees F
1999	
Weastec (steel towers)	0.45 to 0.65 ohms @ 70 to 80-degrees F
Diamond (brass towers)	0.53 to 0.65 ohms @ 70 to 80-degrees F

    Secondary resistance

1996 through 1998	7,000 to 15,800 ohms @ 70 to 80-degrees F
1999	
Weastec (steel towers)	11,500 to 13,500 ohms @ 70 to 80-degrees F
Diamond (brass towers)	10,900 to 14,700 ohms @ 70 to 80-degrees F

  3.3L and 3.8L V6 engines (1996 through 2000) (2001 and later - not available)

Primary resistance	0.45 to 0.65 ohms @ 70 to 80-degrees F
Secondary resistance	7,000 to 15,800 ohms @ 70 to 80-degrees F
3.0L V6 engine	Not available

Spark plug wire resistance (maximum)
  Four cylinder engine

No. 1 and 4	4.2 K-ohms
No. 2 and 3	3.2 K-ohms

  3.0L V6 engine

No. 1	14.0 K-ohms
No. 2	10.4 K-ohms
No. 3	14.9 K-ohms
No. 4	11.5 K-ohms
No. 5	17.5 K-ohms
No. 6	10.3 K-ohms
Coil Lead	11.1 K-ohms

  3.3L and 3.8L V6 engines (1996 through 2000)

No. 1	18.5 K-ohms
No. 2	15.5 K-ohms
No. 3	20.4 K-ohms
No. 4	21.2 K-ohms
No. 5	27.7 K-ohms
No. 6	26.7 K-ohms

Ignition system (continued)

3.3/3.8L V6 engines (2001 and later)

No. 1	22.5 K ohms
No. 2	22.8 K ohms
No. 3	19.3 K ohms
No. 4	19.3 K ohms
No. 5	13.6 K ohms
No. 6	16.4 K ohms

1   General information

Engine electrical systems include all ignition, charging and starting components. Because of their engine-related functions, these components are discussed separately from chassis electrical devices such as the lights, the instruments, etc. (see Chapter 12).

Always observe the following precautions when working on the electrical systems:

a) *Be extremely careful, when servicing engine electrical components. They are easily damaged if checked, connected or handled improperly.*

b) *Never leave the ignition switch on for long periods of time with the engine off.*

c) *Don't disconnect the battery cables while the engine is running.*

d) *Maintain correct polarity when connecting a battery cable from another vehicle during jump starting.*

e) *Always disconnect the negative cable first and hook it up last or the battery may be shorted by the tool being used to loosen the cable clamps.*

It's also a good idea to review the safety-related information regarding the engine electrical systems located in the *Safety first!* Section near the front of this manual before beginning any operation in this Chapter.

2   Battery - emergency jump starting

Refer to the *Booster battery (jump) starting* procedure at the front of this manual.

3   Battery cables - check and replacement

1   Periodically inspect the entire length of each battery cable for damage, cracked or burned insulation and corrosion. Poor battery cable connections can cause starting problems and decreased engine performance.

2   Check the cable-to-terminal connections at the ends of the cables for cracks, loose wire strands, and corrosion. The presence of white, fluffy deposits under the insulation at the cable terminal connection is a sign that the cable is corroded and should be replaced. Check the terminals for distortion, missing mounting bolts, and corrosion.

3   When removing the cables, always disconnect the negative cable first and hook it up last or the battery may be shorted by the tool used to loosen the cable clamps. Even if only the positive cable is being replaced, disconnect the negative cable from the battery first.

4   Disconnect the old cables from the battery, then trace each of them to their opposite ends and detach them from the starter solenoid and ground terminals. Note the routing of each cable to ensure correct installation.

5   If you replace either or both of the old cables, take them with you when buying new cables. It is vitally important that you replace the cables with identical parts. Cables have characteristics that make them easy to identify: positive cables are usually red and larger in cross-section; ground cables are usually black and smaller in cross section.

6   Clean the threads of the solenoid or ground connection with a wire brush to remove rust and corrosion. Apply a light coat of battery terminal corrosion inhibitor, or petroleum jelly, to the threads to prevent future corrosion.

7   Attach the cable to the solenoid or ground connection and tighten the mounting nut/bolt securely.

8   Before connecting a new cable to the battery, make sure that it reaches the battery post without having to be stretched.

9   Connect the positive cable first, followed by the negative cable.

4   Battery - removal and installation

Refer to illustrations 4.2, 4.4 and 4.6

1   Verify that the ignition switch and all accessories are OFF.

2   Disconnect both cables from the battery terminals **(see illustration). Caution:** *Always disconnect the negative cable (the black one) first and hook it up last or the battery may be shorted by the tool being used to loosen the cable clamps.*

3   Remove the battery heat shield.

4   Remove the battery hold down **(see Illustration).**

5   Lift out the battery. Be careful - it's heavy. **Note:** *Battery straps and handlers are available at most auto parts stores for a reasonable price. They make it easier to remove and carry the battery.*

6   Remove the carrier tray bolts and the carrier tray, if necessary and inspect for corrosion **(see illustration). Note:** *Remove the speed control servo attachment bolt from the battery tray and disconnect the vacuum lines.*

7   If there is corrosion below the tray, use baking soda to clean it and prevent further oxidation.

8   If you are replacing the battery, make sure you get one that's identical, with the same dimensions, amperage rating, cold cranking rating, etc.

9   Installation is the reverse of removal.

5   Ignition system - general information

The ignition system is regulated by the Powertrain Control Module (PCM) which supplies battery voltage to the ignition coil(s) through the Automatic Shutdown (ASD) Relay. The PCM also controls the ground circuit for the ignition coil and ignition timing.

During the crank-start period the PCM advances the ignition timing a set amount. During engine operation, the amount of spark advance provided by the PCM is determined by the following input:

a) *Manifold vacuum*

b) *Barometric pressure*

c) *Engine coolant temperature*

d) *Engine RPM*

e) *Intake air temperature (four cylinder engine only)*

f) *Throttle position*

The PCM also regulates the fuel injection system. **Note:** *All engines use a fixed ignition timing system. Basic ignition timing is not adjust-able. All spark advance is determined by the PCM.*

The four cylinder, 3.3L V6 and 3.8L V6 engines are equipped with a distributorless ignition system (DIS). The entire ignition system consists of the ignition switch, the battery, the coil packs, the primary (low voltage) and secondary (high voltage) wiring circuits, the ignition wires and spark plugs, the camshaft position sensor, the crankshaft position sensor, and the PCM. The crankshaft and camshaft sensors are both Hall Effect timing devices. Refer to Chapter 6 for testing and replacement procedures for the crankshaft sensor and camshaft sensor.

The crankshaft sensor and camshaft sensor generate pulses that are input to the PCM. The PCM determines crankshaft position from these two sensors and then calcu-

4.2 Disconnect the cables (arrows) from the battery terminals (negative first, then positive)

4.4 Remove the nut (arrow) and detach the hold-down clamp from the battery tray

lates injector sequence and ignition timing.

The computerized ignition system provides complete control of the ignition timing by determining the optimum timing using a micro computer in response to engine speed, coolant temperature, throttle position and vacuum pressure in the intake manifold. These parameters are relayed to the PCM by the camshaft position sensor, crankshaft position sensor, the Throttle Position Sensor (TPS), coolant temperature sensor and Manifold Absolute Pressure (MAP) sensor. Ignition timing is altered during warm-up, idling and warm running conditions by the PCM.

The 3.0L V6 engine uses a conventional distributor, distributor pickup, camshaft sensor, crankshaft sensor and ignition coil.

Refer to a dealer parts department or auto parts store for questions concerning the availability of the ignition parts and assemblies. Testing of the camshaft position sensor and the crankshaft position sensor is covered in Chapter 6.

6   Ignition system - check

Refer to illustrations 6.3 and 6.14
Warning: *Because of the very high voltage generated by the ignition system (40,000 volts in the direct ignition system), extreme care should be taken whenever an operation is performed involving ignition components. This includes the coil, camshaft position sensor and spark plug wires, as well as related items connected to the system such as the plug connections, tachometer and any test equipment.*

1   With the ignition switch turned to the "ON" position, a glowing instrument panel "Battery" light or "Oil Pressure" light is a basic check for battery supply to the ignition system and PCM.

2   Check all ignition wiring connections for tightness, cuts, corrosion or any other signs of a bad connection.

3   If the engine turns over but won't start, disconnect the spark plug wires (one at a time) and attach it to a calibrated ignition

tester (available at most auto parts stores or specialty tool companies) to verify adequate secondary voltage (25,000 volts) at each spark plug **(see illustration).** Make sure you use an ignition tester calibrated for electronic ignition systems. A faulty or poor connection at that plug could also result in a misfire. Also, check for carbon deposits inside the spark plug boot.

4   If a tester is not available, use an insulated tool and hold the end of the spark plug wire about 1/4-inch from a good ground. **Caution:** *Spark plug cables may be damaged if this test is performed with more than 1/4-inch clearance between the cable and engine ground.*

5   Crank the engine and watch the end of the tester or spark plug wire to see if bright blue, well-defined sparks occur. If you're not using a calibrated tester, have a helper crank the engine for you. **Warning:** *Keep clear of drivebelts and other moving engine components that could injure you.*

6   If sparks occur, sufficient voltage is reaching the plug to fire it (repeat the check at the remaining plug wires to verify the wires and coils) (four cylinder, 3.3L V6 and 3.8L V6 engines) or wires, distributor cap and rotor (3.0L V6 engine) are OK. However, the plugs themselves may be fouled, so remove and

4.6 Remove the bolts (arrows) retaining the battery carrier tray

check them (see Chapter 1).

7   If NO spark or INTERMITTENT sparks occur on a DIS-type system, check the coil pack (see Section 7). On a conventional system, if no sparks or intermittent sparks occur, remove the distributor cap and check the cap and rotor (see Chapter 1). If moisture is present, dry out the cap and rotor, then reinstall the cap.

6.3 To use a calibrated ignition tester, simply disconnect a spark plug wire, connect it to the tester, clip the tester to a convenient ground and crank the engine over - if there's enough power to fire the plug, sparks will be visible between the electrode tip and the tester body

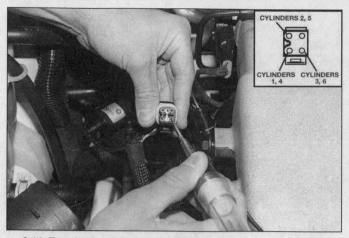

6.14 Touch the probe of an LED test light to each coil driver circuit and observe that the test light flashes while the engine is cranked over

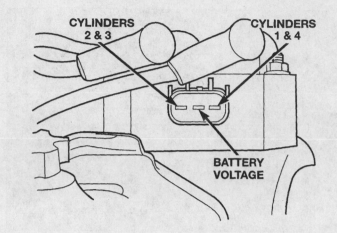

7.7a Check the primary resistance of each coil across the center terminal and each outside terminal - four-cylinder engine

8   If there is still no spark you may have to cycle the ignition key on and off several times to make this check because the computer shuts off the ignition feed if it senses the engine is not cranking. Refer to the ignition wiring schematic at the end of Chapter 12 for additional wiring harness information.

9   Use an ohmmeter, to check the resistance between the coil terminals (see Section 7). If an open is found (verified by an infinite reading), replace the coil.

10   Use an ohmmeter to check the resistance of the spark plug wires (see spark plug cable resistance in this Chapter's Specifications).

11   Check the operation of the Automatic Shutdown (ASD) relay (see Chapter 4).

12   Check the operation of the crankshaft position sensor (see Chapter 6).

13   Check the operation of the camshaft position sensor (see Chapter 6).

14   If all the checks are correct, check the coil driver circuits from the computer (DIS system). Using a test light (an LED-type test light works best for this check) connected to the positive battery terminal, disconnect the coil pack electrical connector and probe the dark blue/tan, gray/red and red/yellow connector terminals while an assistant cranks the engine **(see illustration). Caution:** *Do not touch the dark green/orange wire terminal with the test light connected to the positive battery terminal or damage to the PCM may result.* If the circuits are functioning properly, the light will rapidly blink on and off as the

PCM grounds the circuit. If there is no flashing from the test light, most likely the computer is defective. Have the PCM diagnosed by a dealer service department.

15   Additional checks should be performed by a dealer service department or an automotive repair shop.

7   Ignition coil - check and replacement

Check

1   Disconnect the cable from the negative terminal of the battery.

3.0L V6 engine

Note: *Although coil primary and secondary resistance values are not available from the manufacturer, the resistance values given are general in nature and should help to determine if the ignition coil is defective.*

2   Disconnect the electrical connector and coil-wire (high-tension lead) from the ignition coil.

3   Using an ohmmeter, measure the primary resistance across the two terminals. Primary resistance is generally less than 1-ohm.

4   Measure the secondary resistance across the positive primary terminal (terminal corresponding to the dark green/orange wire) and the high-tension terminal. The resistance should be considerably higher (approxi-

mately 10 to 15 K-ohms). Replace the coil if either circuit is open or the resistance is abnormally high.

Four cylinder, 3.3L V6 and 3.8L V6 engines

Refer to illustrations 7.7a, 7.7b, 7.7c, 7.8a and 7.8b

Note: *On the four cylinder engine, coil one fires cylinders 1 and 4 and coil two fires cylinders 2 and 3. On the 3.3L V6 and 3.8L V6 engines, coil one fires cylinders 1 and 4, coil two fires cylinders 2 and 5, and coil three fires cylinders 3 and 6. Each coil tower is labeled with the number of the corresponding cylinder.*

5   Clearly label the spark plug wires, then detach them from the coil pack.

6   Disconnect the electrical connector from the coil pack.

7   Measure the resistance on the primary side of each coil with a digital ohmmeter **(see illustrations)**. At the coil, connect an ohmmeter between the B+ pin and the pin corresponding to the particular cylinder. Compare your readings with the resistance values listed

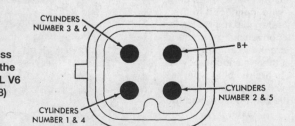

7.7b Check the primary resistance of each coil across the B+ terminal and each of the other terminals - 3.3L and 3.8L V6 engines (1996 through 1998)

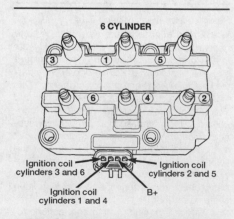

7.7c Check the primary resistance of each coil across the B+ relay output terminal and each of the other terminals - 3.3L and 3.8L engines (1999)

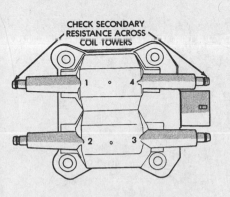

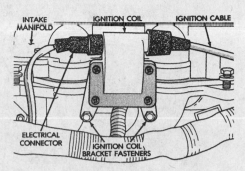

7.8a Check the secondary resistance across the paired coil towers (1-4 and 2-3) - four cylinder engine

7.8b Check the secondary resistance across the paired coil towers (3-6, 1-4 and 5-2) - 3.3L and 3.8L V6 engine (through 1998)

7.9 The ignition coil is located at the back of the intake manifold

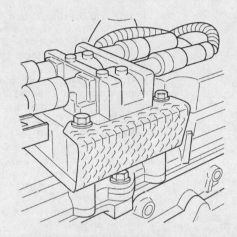

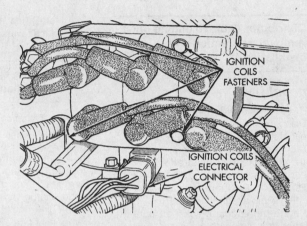

7.16a Remove the ignition coil pack mounting bracket bolts

7.16b Disconnect the electrical connector and remove the coil pack mounting bolts (1996 through 2000 3.3L and 3.8L V6 engines)

in this Chapter's Specifications. Replace the coil if resistance is not within specifications.

8 Measure the secondary resistance of the coil between the paired high tension towers of each group of cylinders **(see illustrations)**. Compare your readings with the resistance values listed in this Chapter's Specifications. Replace the coil if resistance is not within specifications.

Replacement

3.0L V6 engine

Refer to illustration 7.9

9 The ignition coil is located at the back of the intake manifold **(see illustration)**.

10 Remove the air cleaner assembly.

11 Disconnect the ignition cable from the coil. Disconnect the wiring harness connector from the coil.

12 Remove the coil mounting screws.

Four cylinder, 3.3L V6 and 3.8L V6 engines

Refer to illustrations 7.16a, 7.16b and 7.16c

13 On 2001 and later 3.3L and 3.8L V6

engines, perform the following:
a) *Remove the accelerator and cruise control cable from the cable clip.*
b) *Remove the bolts attaching the power steering reservoir. Loosen, do not remove, the single nut. Lift the reservoir up and disengage the lower mount from the stud. Move the reservoir aside, do not disconnect the hose.*

14 Clearly label the spark plug wires, then disconnect them from the coil pack.

15 Unplug the primary electrical connectors from the coil pack.

16 Remove the coil pack mounting bolts and nuts **(see illustrations)** and lift the coil pack from the engine compartment.

17 Installation of these components is the reverse of removal.

7.16c Remove the bolts and nuts securing the ignition coil pack

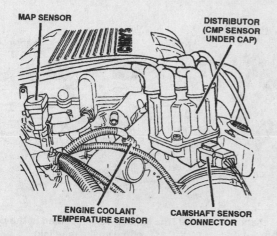

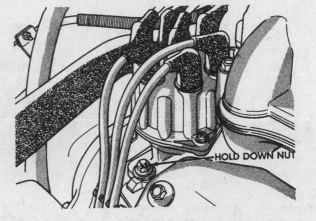

8.2 Disconnect the electrical connector from the distributor

8.5 Remove the distributor hold-down nut

8   Distributor (3.0L V6 engine only) - removal, inspection and installation

Removal

Refer to illustrations 8.2 and 8.5

1   Disconnect the cable from the negative terminal of the battery.

2   Disconnect the electrical connector from the distributor **(see illustration)**.

3   Loosen the screws and lift the cap off the distributor. Position the cap, with the spark plug wires attached, aside.

4   Rotate the engine crankshaft until the distributor rotor points to the intake manifold plenum. Scribe a mark on the plenum in line with the rotor. The scribe line indicates where to position the rotor when reinstalling the distributor.

5   Remove the distributor hold down nut **(see illustration)**.

6   Carefully lift the distributor from the engine. **Note:** *Do NOT turn the crankshaft while the distributor is out of the engine, or the alignment marks will be useless.*

Installation

7   Position the distributor in the engine. Make sure that the O-ring is properly seated on the distributor. If the O-ring is cracked or nicked, replace it with a new one.

8   Carefully engage the distributor drive with the gear on the camshaft. When the distributor is installed properly, the rotor will be in line with the scribe mark on the air intake plenum. **Note:** *If the engine was rotated while the distributor was removed, position the number one piston at TDC (see Chapter 2D) and install the distributor with the rotor pointing at the number one spark plug wire terminal inside the distributor cap (be aware that when the rotor is pointing to the number one spark plug wire terminal inside the cap it is NOT pointing to the number one spark plug wire tower outside the cap).*

9   Installation of the remaining components is the reverse of removal.

9   Charging system - general information and precautions

Refer to illustration 9.1

The charging system includes the alternator, a charge indicator light, the battery, the battery temperature sensor, the Electronic Voltage Regulator (EVR) circuitry within the Powertrain Control Module (PCM), the Automatic Shutdown Relay (ASD), a voltmeter, a fusible link and the wiring between all the components **(see illustration)**. The charging system supplies electrical power to maintain the battery at its full charge capacity.

The alternator control system within the PCM varies the voltage generated at the alternator in accordance with driving conditions. Depending on electric load, vehicle speed, engine coolant temperature, accessories (air conditioning system, radio, cruise control etc.) and the intake air temperature, the system will adjust the amount of voltage generated, creating less load on the engine.

The purpose of the EVR is to limit the alternator's voltage to a preset value. This prevents power surges, circuit overloads, etc., during peak voltage output. The voltage regulator is contained within the PCM and in the event of failure, the PCM must be replaced as a single unit.

These models are equipped with a Nippondenso 90 or 120 amp alternator. The alternator must be replaced as a single unit in the event of failure.

The charging system doesn't ordinarily require periodic maintenance. However, the drivebelt, battery, harness wires and connections should be inspected at the intervals outlined in Chapter 1.

The dashboard warning light should come ON when the ignition key is turned to ON, but it should go off immediately after the engine is started. If it remains on, there is a malfunction in the charging system (see Section 11). Some vehicles are also equipped with a voltmeter. If the voltmeter indicates abnormally high or low voltage, check the charging system.

Be very careful when making electrical circuit connections to a vehicle equipped with an alternator and note the following:

a)   *When reconnecting wires to the alternator from the battery, be sure to note the polarity.*

b)   *Before using arc welding equipment to repair any part of the vehicle, disconnect the wires from the alternator and the battery terminals.*

c)   *Never start the engine with a battery charger connected.*

d)   *Always disconnect both battery cables before using a battery charger.*

e)   *The alternator is turned by an engine drivebelt which could cause serious injury if your hands, hair or clothes become entangled in it with the engine running.*

f)   *Because the alternator is connected directly to the battery, it could arc or cause a fire if overloaded or shorted out.*

g)   *Wrap a plastic bag over the alternator and secure it with rubber bands before steam cleaning the engine.*

10   Charging system - check

Refer to illustration 10.3
Note: *These vehicles are equipped with an On Board Diagnostic (OBD) system that is useful for detecting charging system problems. Refer to Chapter 6 for the trouble code extracting procedures.*

1   If a malfunction occurs in the charging circuit, do not immediately assume that the alternator is causing the problem. First check the following items:

a)   *The battery cables where they connect to the battery. Make sure the connections are clean and tight.*

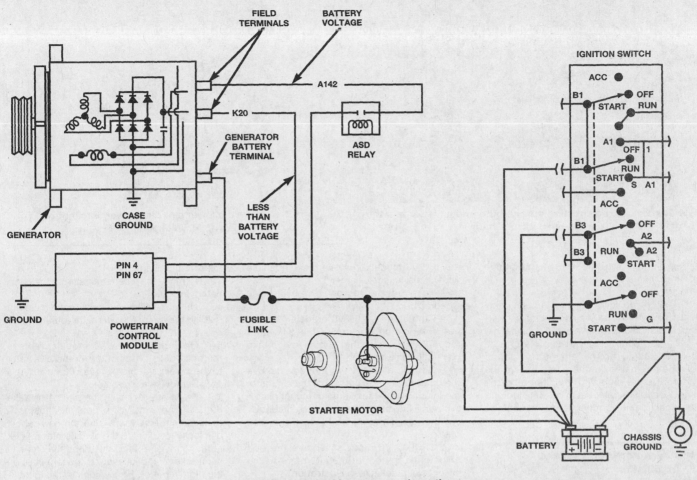

9.1 Typical charging system schematic

b) *The battery electrolyte specific gravity. If it is low, charge the battery.*

c) *Check the external alternator wiring and connections.*

d) *Check the drivebelt condition and tension* (see Chapter 1).

e) *Check the alternator mounting bolts for tightness.*

f) *Run the engine and check the alternator for abnormal noise.*

2 Using a voltmeter, check the battery voltage with the engine off. It should be approximately 12-volts.

3 Start the engine and check the battery voltage again. It should now be approximately 13 to 15-volts **(see illustration)**.

4 If the indicated voltage reading is more or less than the specified charging voltage, have the PCM checked at a dealer service department. The voltage regulator on these models is contained within the PCM and it cannot be adjusted, removed or tampered with in any way.

5 Due to the special equipment necessary to test or service the alternator, it is recommended that if a fault is suspected, the vehi-cle be taken to a dealer or a shop with the proper equipment. Because of this, the home mechanic should limit maintenance to checking connections and the inspection and replacement of the alternator.

6 Some models are equipped with an ammeter on the instrument panel that indicates charge or discharge - current passing in or out of the battery. With the electrical equipment switched ON, and the engine idling, the gauge needle may show a discharge condition. At fast idle or normal driving speeds the needle should stay on the charge side of the gauge, with the charged state of the battery determining just how far over (the lower the battery state of charge, the farther the needle should swing toward the charge side).

7 Some models are equipped with a voltmeter on the instrument panel that indicates

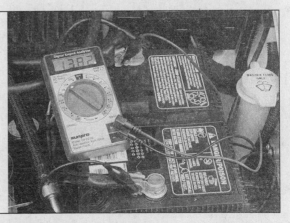

10.3 To check the charging system, attach the voltmeter leads to the battery terminals (engine OFF) and note the voltage; start the engine - the voltage should increase

11.4 Remove the bolt holding the alternator mount bracket to the engine air intake plenum

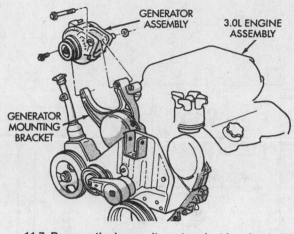

11.7 Remove the lower alternator pivot bracket bolt (3.0L V6 engine)

battery voltage with the key on and engine off, and alternator output when the engine is running.

8   The charge light on the instrument panel illuminates with the key on and engine not running, and should go out when the engine runs.

9   If the gauge does not show a charge when it should or the alternator light (if equipped) remains on, there is a fault in the system. Before replacing the alternator, the battery condition, alternator belt tension and electrical cable connections should be checked.

11   Alternator - removal and installation

Removal (All Four cylinder and 1996 through 2000 V6 engines)

Refer to illustrations 11.4, 11.7 and 11.14

1   Disconnect the cable from the negative terminal of the battery.

2   On V6 models, remove the windshield wiper housing (see Chapter 12).

3   Remove the accessory drive belt(s) (see Chapter 1).

4   On 3.3L and 3.8L V6 models, remove the bolt holding the top of the alternator mount bracket to the engine air intake plenum **(see illustration)**.

5   On 3.3L and 3.8L V6 models, remove the bolts holding the outside of the alternator mount bracket to the alternator mount plate.

6   On all V6 models, remove the bolt holding the top of the alternator to the mount bracket.

7   On 3.0L V6 models, remove the bolt holding the bottom of the alternator to the lower pivot bracket **(see illustration)**.

8   On 3.3L and 3.8L V6 models, remove the alternator mount bracket from the vehicle.

9   On 3.3L and 3.8L V6 models, rotate the alternator toward the rear of the vehicle.

10   Disconnect the push-in field wire connector from the back of the alternator.

11   Remove the nut holding the B+ wire terminal to the alternator.

12   Remove the wire/terminal from the alternator.

13   On four cylinder models, remove the nut holding the top of the alternator to the adjustable T-bolt.

14   On 3.3L and 3.8L V6 models, remove the bolt holding the bottom of the alternator to the lower pivot bracket **(see illustration)**.

15   Remove the alternator.

16   If you are replacing the alternator, take the old one with you when purchasing a replacement unit. Make sure the new/rebuilt unit looks identical to the old alternator. Look at the terminals - they should be the same in number, size and location as the terminals on the old alternator. Finally, look at the identification numbers - they will be stamped into the housing or printed on a tag attached to the housing. Make sure the numbers are the same on both alternators.

17   Many new/rebuilt alternators do not have a pulley installed, so you may have to switch the pulley from the old unit to the new/rebuilt

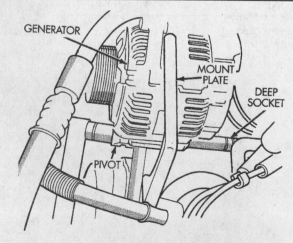

11.14 Remove the lower alternator pivot bracket bolt (3.3L and 3.8L V6 engines)

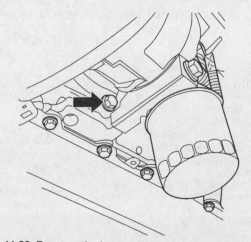

11.23 Remove the lower mounting bolt securing the oil dipstick tube

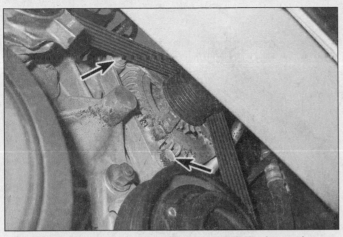

11.25a Remove the two lower mounting bolts (arrows)...

11.25b ...then the upper bolt

one. When buying an alternator, find out the shop's policy regarding pulleys; some shops will perform this service free of charge.

Removal (2001 and later V6 engines)

Refer to illustrations 11.23, 11.25a and 11.25b
Note: *The alternator is equipped with a de-coupler type driven pulley. This pulley is designed to reduce drive belt tension and is non-serviceable.*
18   Disconnect the cable from the negative terminal of the battery.
19   Disconnect the push-in field wire connector from the back of the alternator.
20   Remove the nut holding the B+ wire terminal to the alternator. Separate the B+ terminal from the alternator.
21   Remove the accessory drive belt (see Chapter 1).
22   Raise the vehicle, support it securely on jackstands.
23   Remove the oil dipstick tube lower mounting bolt **(see illustration)**.
24   Remove the wiring harness from the oil dipstick tube.
25   Remove the three bolts securing the alternator to the engine **(see illustrations)**.
26   Lower the vehicle to the ground.
27   Remove the dipstick tube from the engine.
28   Remove the alternator.

Installation (all models)

29   Installation is the reverse of removal.
30   After the alternator is installed, adjust the drivebelt tension (see Chapter 1).
31   Check the charging voltage to verify proper operation of the alternator (see Section 10).

12   Voltage regulator - general information

The Electronic Voltage Regulator (EVR) is not a separate component. It is actually a voltage regulating circuit located within the Powertrain Control Module (PCM). The EVR is not serviced separately. If replacement is necessary, the PCM must be replaced as a unit.

The amount of DC current produced by the alternator is controlled by the EVR circuitry contained within the PCM. The circuitry is connected in series with the alternators second rotor field terminal and its ground.

Voltage is regulated by cycling the ground path to control the strength of the rotor magnetic field. The EVR circuitry monitors system line voltage and battery temperature (voltage will be higher at colder temperatures and reduced at warmer temperatures) . It then compensates and regulates the alternator accordingly.

13   Starting system - general information and precautions

The starting system consists of the battery, the starter motor, the starter solenoid, the starter relay, the Powertrain Control Module (PCM), the Neutral starting and back up switch, and the wires connecting them.

The starter motor on all models is a Nippondenso conventional gear train design. The starter motor is an integral assembly with the solenoid and the unit is sold strictly as a complete assembly. Check with your local dealer parts department before disassembly.

The solenoid/starter motor assembly is installed on the lower part of the engine, next to the transmission bellhousing.

When the ignition key is turned to the Start position, the starter solenoid is actuated through the starter control circuit which includes a starter relay located in the Power Distribution Center. The starter solenoid then connects the battery to the starter. The battery supplies the electrical energy to the starter motor, which does the actual work of cranking the engine.

Always observe the following precautions when working on the starting system:

a) *Excessive cranking of the starter motor can overheat it and cause serious damage. Never operate the starter motor for more than 15 seconds at a time without pausing to allow it to cool for at least two minutes.*
b) *The starter is connected directly to the battery and could arc or cause a fire if mishandled, overloaded, or shorted out.*
c) *Always detach the cable from the negative terminal of the battery before working on the starting system.*

14   Starter motor - in-vehicle check

Refer to illustration 14.6
Caution: *Before performing any starter tests, the ignition and fuel systems must be disabled.*
Note: *Before diagnosing starter problems, make sure the battery is fully charged.*
1   If the starter motor does not turn at all when the switch is operated, make sure the shift lever is in Neutral or Park.
2   Make sure the battery is charged and all cables, both at the battery and starter solenoid terminals, are clean and secure.
3   If the starter motor spins but the engine is not cranking, the overrunning clutch in the starter motor is slipping and the starter motor must be replaced. Also, the ring gear on the flywheel or driveplate may be worn.
4   If, when the switch is actuated, the starter motor does not operate at all but the solenoid clicks, the problem is either the battery, the main solenoid contacts or the starter motor itself (or the engine is seized).
5   If the solenoid plunger cannot be heard when the switch is actuated, the battery is bad, the fusible link is burned (the circuit is open) or the solenoid itself is defective.
6   To check the solenoid, locate and remove the starter relay from the PDC. Connect a remote starter switch between the battery and terminal 87 of the starter relay con-

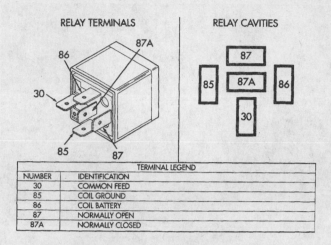

14.6 Connect a remote starter switch between the battery and terminal 87 of the starter relay connector

TERMINAL LEGEND	
NUMBER	IDENTIFICATION
30	COMMON FEED
85	COIL GROUND
86	COIL BATTERY
87	NORMALLY OPEN
87A	NORMALLY CLOSED

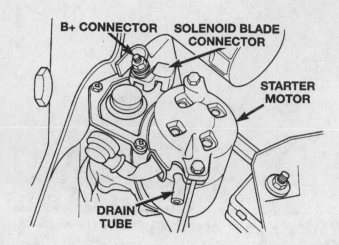

15.4 Remove the nut holding the B+ wire to the starter terminal

nector **(see illustration)**. If the starter motor operates when the remote switch is activated, the solenoid is OK and the problem is in the ignition switch, neutral start switch, starter relay or the wiring.

7   To check the starter relay, remove the starter relay from the PDC. The de-energized starter relay should have continuity between terminals 87A and 30, and no continuity between terminals 87 and 30. If this checks out OK, go to step 8. If not OK, replace the faulty relay.

8   The resistance between terminals 85 and 86 should be 70 to 80 ohms. If OK go to step 9. If not OK, replace the faulty relay.

9   Connect a positive battery lead to terminal 86 and a ground lead to terminal 85 to energize the relay. The relay should click. Also test for continuity between terminals 30 and 87, and no continuity between terminals 87A and 30 with the relay energized. If OK, the ignition switch, the relay circuit, or the wiring is bad. If not OK, replace the faulty relay.

10   If the starter motor still does not operate, remove the starter/solenoid assembly for

testing and repair. **Note:** *The starter/solenoid assembly must be exchanged as a complete unit.*

11   If the starter motor cranks the engine at an abnormally slow speed, first make sure that the battery is charged and that all terminal connections are clean and tight. If the engine is partially seized, or has the wrong viscosity oil in it, it will crank slowly.

12   Run the engine until normal operating temperature is reached, then remove the fuel pump relay from the power distribution center to keep the engine from starting.

13   Connect a voltmeter positive lead to the positive battery post and connect the negative lead to the negative post.

14   Crank the engine and take the voltmeter readings as soon as a steady figure is indicated. Do not allow the starter motor to turn for more than I5 seconds at a time. A reading of nine volts or more, with the starter motor turning at normal cranking speed, is normal. If the reading is nine volts or more but the cranking speed is slow, the motor, solenoid contacts or circuit connections are faulty. If

the reading is less than nine volts and the cranking speed is slow, the starter motor is probably bad.

15   Starter motor - removal and installation

Refer to illustration 15.4

1   Disconnect the cable from the negative terminal of the battery.

2   Raise the vehicle and support it securely on jackstands.

3   Disconnect the solenoid wire connector from the terminal.

4   Remove the nut holding the B+ wire to the terminal **(see illustration)**.

5   Disconnect the solenoid and B+ wires from the starter terminals.

6   Remove the bolts holding the starter to the transmission bellhousing.

7   Remove the starter.

8   Installation is the reverse of removal.

Chapter 6
Emissions and engine control systems

Contents

	Section
Catalytic converter	9
CHECK ENGINE or MIL light	4
Evaporative Emissions Control (EVAP) system	8
Evaporative Emissions Control (EVAP) system check	See Chapter 1
Exhaust Gas Recirculation (EGR) system	7
Exhaust Gas Recirculation (EGR) system check	See Chapter 1
General information	1
Information sensors - general description, check and replacement	5

	Section
Multi-Port Fuel Injection (MPI) system and information sensors	2
Positive Crankcase Ventilation (PCV) system	6
Positive Crankcase Ventilation (PCV) valve check and replacement	See Chapter 1
Powertrain Control Module (PCM) - removal and installation	3
On Board Diagnostic (OBD) system and trouble codes	4

Specifications

Torque specifications

	Ft-lbs (unless otherwise indicated)
Crankshaft sensor retaining bolt	105 in-lbs
Camshaft sensor retaining bolt	105 in-lbs
EGR valve bolts	16
EGR tube nuts/bolts	105 to 200 in-lbs
Knock sensor	84 in-lbs

Idle Specifications

Four-cylinder engine	550 to 875 rpm
3.0L V6 engine	610 to 910 rpm
3.3L and 3.8L V6 engines	575 to 875 rpm

1   General information

Refer to illustrations 1.3a, 1.3b, 1.3c, 1.7a and 1.7b

To prevent pollution of the atmosphere from incompletely burned and evaporating gases, and to maintain good driveability and fuel economy, a number of emission control systems are incorporated. The principal systems are:

Positive Crankcase Ventilation (PCV) system
Evaporative Emission Control (EVAP) system
Exhaust Gas Recirculation (EGR) system
Oxygen sensor (O_2) system
Catalytic converter (Three-Way Catalyst - TWC)
Powertrain Control Module (PCM) and information sensors

The Sections in this Chapter include general descriptions, checking procedures within the scope of the home mechanic and component replacement procedures (when possible) for each of the systems listed above.

Before assuming an emissions control system is malfunctioning, check the fuel and ignition systems carefully. The diagnosis of some emission control devices requires specialized tools, equipment and training. If checking and servicing become too difficult or if a procedure is beyond your ability, consult a dealer service department. Remember,

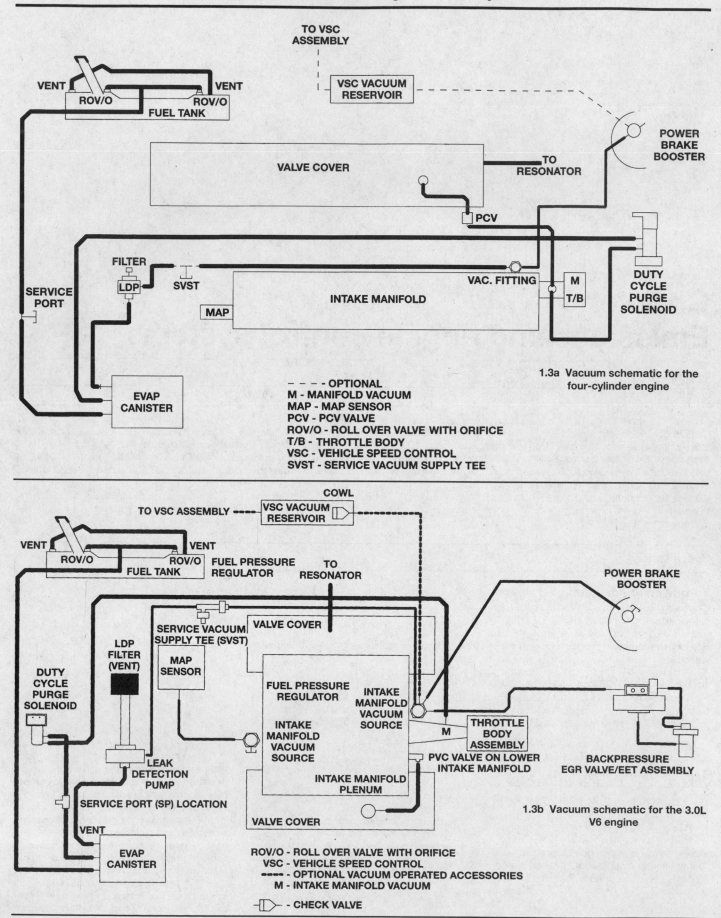

1.3a Vacuum schematic for the
four-cylinder engine

– – – – - OPTIONAL
M - MANIFOLD VACUUM
MAP - MAP SENSOR
PCV - PCV VALVE
ROV/O - ROLL OVER VALVE WITH ORIFICE
T/B - THROTTLE BODY
VSC - VEHICLE SPEED CONTROL
SVST - SERVICE VACUUM SUPPLY TEE

1.3b Vacuum schematic for the 3.0L
V6 engine

ROV/O - ROLL OVER VALVE WITH ORIFICE
VSC - VEHICLE SPEED CONTROL
– – – - OPTIONAL VACUUM OPERATED ACCESSORIES
M - INTAKE MANIFOLD VACUUM

– ⊳ - CHECK VALVE

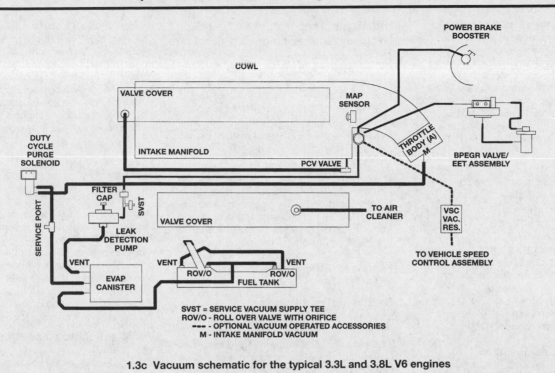

1.3c Vacuum schematic for the typical 3.3L and 3.8L V6 engines

the most frequent cause of emissions problems is simply a loose or broken vacuum hose or wire, so always check the hose and electrical connections first **(see illustrations)**.

This doesn't mean, however, that emission control systems are particularly difficult to maintain and repair. You can quickly and easily perform many checks and do most of the regular maintenance at home with common tune-up and hand tools. **Note:** *Because of a Federally mandated extended warranty which covers the emission control system components, check with your dealer about warranty coverage before working on any emissions-related systems. Once the warranty has expired, you may wish to perform some of the component checks and/or replacement procedures in this Chapter to save money.*

Pay close attention to any special precautions outlined in this Chapter. It should be noted that the illustration of the various systems may not exactly match the system installed on your vehicle because of changes made by the manufacturer during production or from year-to-year.

A Vehicle Emission Control Information (VECI) label is located in the engine compartment **(see illustrations)**. This label contains important emission specifications and adjustment information on the idle speed adjustment, ignition timing, the location of the emission control devices on your vehicle, vacuum line routing, etc. When servicing the engine or emission systems, the VECI label in your particular vehicle should always be checked for up-to-date information.

2 Multi-Port Electronic Fuel Injection (MPI) system and information sensors

1   The engines are equipped with electrically operated fuel injectors. A fuel injector is located in each intake port. The system fires each injector in sequence, timed with the opening of each intake valve. The Multi-Port Electronic Fuel Injection (MPI) system provides the correct air-fuel ratio under all driving conditions.

2   The "brain" of all MPI systems is the Powertrain Control Module (PCM). The PCM is located at the front corner of the engine compartment.

3   The PCM receives variable voltage inputs from a variety of sensors, switches and relays. All inputs are converted into digital signals which are "read" by the PCM, which constantly fine-tunes such variables as ignition timing, spark advance, ignition coil dwell, fuel injector pulse width and idle speed to minimize exhaust emissions and enhance driveability. It also controls the operation of the radiator cooling fan, the alternator charging rate and such emissions-related components as the EGR solenoids and the purge solenoid for the EVAP canister. The PCM even updates and revises its own programming in response to changing operating conditions.

4   The PCM also constantly monitors many of its own input and output circuits. If a fault is found in the MPI system, the information is stored in the PCM memory. The diagnosis process begins with reading any stored fault codes to identify the general location of a problem, followed by a thorough visual inspection of the system components to

1.7a On 1999 through 2000 models, the Vehicle Emission Control Information (VECI) label is located under the hood on the suspension strut tower . . .

1.7b . . . or on the radiator cross member on 2001 and later models

ensure that everything is properly connected. The most common cause of a problem in any MPI system is a loose or corroded electrical connector or a loose vacuum line. If no obvious problems are found, proceed to check the relevant sensors as described in Section 5. To learn how to output this information and display it on the CHECK ENGINE light (also called the MIL or Malfunction Indicator Light) on the dash, refer to Section 4.

Information sensors

5   Various components provide basic information to the PCM; they include:

Air conditioning clutch relay
Auto shutdown (ASD) relay
Brake switch
Camshaft position sensor
Intake air temperature sensor
Engine coolant temperature sensor
Crankshaft position sensor
Manifold Absolute Pressure (MAP) sensor
Heated oxygen sensor (O2)
Throttle Position Sensor (TPS)
Knock sensor
Vehicle speed sensor (VSS)

Air conditioning clutch relay

6   The air conditioning clutch relay is controlled by the PCM. The air conditioning compressor clutch is operated by switching the ground circuit for the air conditioning clutch relay on and off. When the PCM receives a request from the air conditioning (climate control system) it will adjust the idle air control motor position. The air conditioning clutch control relay is located in the Power Distribution Center next to the battery. For checks of the clutch and clutch coil, see Chapter 3.

Automatic shutdown (ASD) relay

7   If there is no ignition (distributor) signal or camshaft or crankshaft reference sensor signal present when the ignition key is turned to the RUN position, the auto shutdown relay interrupts power to the electric fuel pump, the fuel injectors, the ignition coil and the heated oxygen sensor. The cut-out relay is located in the Power Distribution Center next to the battery. For ASD relay and fuel pump relay locations and testing procedures, refer to Chapter 4.

Camshaft position sensor

8   The camshaft position sensor provides cylinder identification to the PCM to synchronize the fuel system with the ignition system. The synchronizing signal is generated from a rotating pulse ring located on the camshaft sprocket. The sensor generates pulses as groups of notches on the camshaft sprocket pass underneath it. When metal aligns with the sensor the voltage pulses low (approximately 0.3 volts) and when the notch aligns with the sensor, voltage increases suddenly to about 5.0 volts. These voltage pulses are in turn processed by the PCM which in turn determines ignition timing.

Intake Air Temperature (IAT) sensor - four-cylinder engine

9   The air temperature sensor, mounted in the intake manifold, measures the temperature of the incoming air and sends this information to the PCM. This data is used by the PCM to modify the air/fuel mixture.

Engine Coolant Temperature (ECT) sensor

10   The coolant temperature sensor, which is threaded into the intake manifold near the thermostat housing, monitors coolant temperature and sends this information to the PCM. This data, along with the information from the air temperature sensor, is used by the PCM to determine the correct air/fuel mixture and idle speed while the engine is warming up. The sensor is also used to turn on the radiator fan.

Crankshaft position sensor

11   The crankshaft position sensor is mounted on the transmission bellhousing. This sensor sends information to the PCM regarding engine crankshaft position. The sensor "reads" the slots on the torque converter driveplate.

Manifold Absolute Pressure (MAP) sensor

12   The MAP sensor is located on the intake manifold plenum. It monitors intake manifold vacuum. The MAP sensor transmits this data, along with data on barometric pressure, in the form of a variable voltage output to the PCM. When combined with data from other sensors, this information helps the PCM determine the correct air-fuel mixture ratio.

Miscellaneous switches

13   Various switches (such as the air conditioning clutch switch, the speed control switch and the brake light switch) provide information to the PCM, which adjusts engine operation in accordance with switch states present at these inputs. The state of these switch inputs (high/low) is determined using the DRB II diagnostic SCAN tool at the dealer.

Heated oxygen sensor

14   The oxygen sensors, which are mounted in the exhaust manifold and downstream of the catalytic converter, produce a voltage signal when exposed to the oxygen present in the exhaust gases. The sensor is electrically heated internally for faster switching when the engine is running. When there is extra oxygen present (lean mixture), the sensor produces a low voltage signal; when there is little oxygen present (rich mixture), it produces a signal of higher voltage. By monitoring the oxygen content and converting it to electrical voltage, the sensor acts as a lean-rich switch. The voltage signal to the PCM alters the pulse width of the injectors.

Throttle Position Sensor (TPS)

15   The TPS, which is located on the throttle body, monitors the angle of the throttle plate. The voltage produced increases or decreases in accordance with the opening angle of the throttle plate. This data, when relayed to the PCM, along with data from several other sensors, enables the PCM to adjust the air/fuel ratio in accordance with the operating conditions, such as acceleration, deceleration, idle and wide open throttle.

Knock sensor

Note: *A knock sensor is not used on the 3.0L V6 engine.*
16   The knock sensor is mounted in the side of the engine block and detects a knock in any cylinder during the combustion process. The electrical signal generated is sent to the PCM. The PCM, in turn, retards the ignition timing by a certain amount to reduce the uncontrolled detonation. The knock sensor consists of a small crystal that vibrates with engine vibration. If the engine detonation exceeds the normal limit, the vibration causes an increase in the voltage signal from the knock sensor.

Vehicle distance (speed) sensor

17   The vehicle distance (speed) sensor, which is located in the transmission housing, senses vehicle motion. The sensor generates pulses for every revolution of the driveaxle and transmits them as voltage signals to the PCM. These signals are compared by the PCM with the throttle signal from the throttle position sensor so it can distinguish between a closed throttle deceleration and normal idle (vehicle stopped) condition. Under deceleration conditions, the PCM controls the idle air control (IAC) valve to maintain the desired MAP value; under idle conditions, the PCM adjusts the IAC valve to maintain the desired engine speed.

3   Powertrain Control Module (PCM) - removal and installation

1996 through 2000 models

Refer to illustrations 3.3 and 3.5
Note: *Avoid static electricity damage to the PCM by grounding yourself to the body of the vehicle before touching the PCM and using a special anti-static pad to store the PCM on once it is removed.*
1   Disconnect the cable from the negative terminal of the battery.
2   Remove the battery from the engine compartment (see Chapter 5).
3   Remove the screws retaining the Power Distribution Center (PDC) to the bracket and position the PDC aside to access the PCM **(see illustration)**.
4   Disconnect the PCM electrical connector.
5   Remove the screws that retain the PCM to the body and remove the PCM **(see illustration)**.
6   Installation is the reverse of removal.

2001 and later models

Refer to illustrations 3.11a and 3.11b
Note: *Avoid static electricity damage to the*

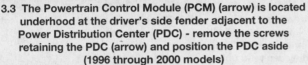

3.3 The Powertrain Control Module (PCM) (arrow) is located underhood at the driver's side fender adjacent to the Power Distribution Center (PDC) - remove the screws retaining the PDC (arrow) and position the PDC aside (1996 through 2000 models)

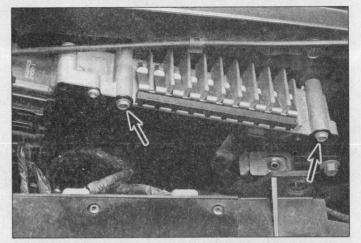

3.5 Remove the Powertrain Control Module (PCM) mounting screws (arrows) (1996 through 2000 models)

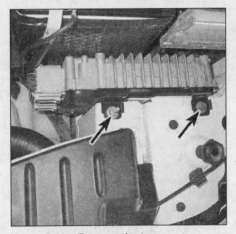

3.11a Remove the two upper mounting screws...

3.11b ... and the lower screw in the headlight area and remove the PCM

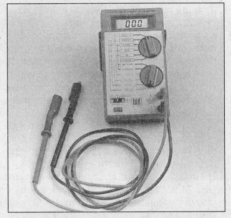

4.4 Digital multimeters can be used for testing all types of circuits; their high impedance makes them more accurate than analog meters for measuring voltage in low-voltage computer or sensor circuits

PCM by grounding yourself to the body of the vehicle before touching the PCM and using a special anti-static pad to store the PCM on once it is removed.

7   Disconnect the cable from the negative terminal of the battery.

8   Remove the battery heat shield (see Chapter 5).

9   Disconnect the two PCM electrical connectors.

10   Remove the left side headlight housing (see Chapter 12).

11   Remove the two upper screws and the lower screw that retain the PCM **(see illustrations)** and remove the PCM.

12   Installation is the reverse of removal.

4   On Board Diagnosis (OBD) system and trouble codes

General description

1   The On Board Diagnosis-II (OBD-II) is a second-generation self diagnosis system specified by the CARB and EPA regulations.

This system incorporates a series of diagnostic monitors that detect and identify emissions systems faults and store the information in the PCM memory. This updated system also tests sensors and output actuators, diagnoses drive cycles, freezes data and clears codes. This powerful diagnostic computer must be accessed using an OBD-II SCAN tool and the 16 pin Data Link Connector (DLC) located under the driver's dash area. All engines and powertrain combinations described in this manual are equipped with the On Board Diagnosis II (OBD-II) system. This system consists of an onboard computer, known as the Powertrain Control Module (PCM), and information sensors, which monitor various functions of the engine and send data to the PCM. Based on the data and the information programmed into the PCM's memory, the PCM generates output signals to control various engine functions via control relays, solenoids and other output actuators.

2   The PCM is the "brain" of the system. It receives data from a number of sensors and other electronic components (switches,

relays, etc.). Based on the information it receives, the PCM generates output signals to control various relays, solenoids and other actuators. The PCM is specifically calibrated to optimize the emissions, fuel economy and driveability of the vehicle.

3   Because of a Federally-mandated extended warranty and because any owner-induced damage to the PCM, the sensors and/or the control devices may void the warranty. It is recommended that you take the vehicle to a dealer service department if the PCM or a system component malfunctions while the vehicle is under warranty.

Diagnostic tool information

Refer to illustrations 4.4, 4.5 and 4.7

4   A digital multimeter is necessary for checking fuel injection and emissions-related components **(see illustration)**. A digital volt-ohmmeter is preferred over the older style analog multimeter for several reasons. The analog multimeter cannot display the volts-ohms or amps measurement in hundredths

and thousandths increments. When working with electronic circuits which are often very low voltage, this accurate reading is most important. Another good reason for the digital multimeter is the high impedance circuit. The digital multimeter is equipped with a high resistance internal circuitry (10 million ohms). Because a voltmeter is hooked up in parallel with the circuit when testing, it is vital that none of the voltage being measured should be allowed to travel the parallel path set up by the meter itself. This dilemma does not show itself when measuring larger amounts of voltage (9 to 12 volt circuits), but if you are measuring a low voltage circuit such as the oxygen sensor signal voltage, a fraction of a volt may be a significant amount when diagnosing a problem. Obtaining the diagnostic trouble codes is one exception where using an analog voltmeter is necessary.

5   Hand-held scanners are the most powerful and versatile tools for analyzing engine management systems used on later model vehicles **(see illustration)**. Early model scanners handle codes and some diagnostics for many OBD I systems. Each brand scan tool must be examined carefully to match the year, make and model of the vehicle you are working on. Often interchangeable cartridges are available to access the particular manufacturer (Ford, GM, Chrysler, etc.). Some manufacturers will specify by continent (Asia, Europe, USA, etc.).

6   With the arrival of the Federally mandated emission control system (OBD-II), a specially designed scanner must be used. OBD-II scan tools for the home mechanic may be available through local auto parts stores.

Obtaining trouble codes

7   The self-diagnosis information contained in the Powertrain Control Module (PCM) can be accessed either by the ignition key or by using a special tool called the Diagnostic Readout Box (DRB II). This tool is attached to the diagnostic connector (Data Link Connector) **(see illustration)** and reads the codes and parameters on the digital display screen. The tool is expensive and most home mechanics prefer to use the alternate ignition key method. The drawback with the ignition key method is that it does not access all the available codes for display. Most problems can be solved or diagnosed quite easily and if the information cannot be obtained readily, have the vehicle's self-diagnosis system analyzed by a dealer service department or other qualified repair shop. The PCM monitors circuits in the fuel injection, ignition, emission, and engine systems.

8   To obtain the codes using the ignition key method, first set the parking brake and put the shift lever in Park. Raise the engine speed to approximately 2,500 rpm and slowly let the speed down to idle. Also cycle the air conditioning system (on briefly, then off). Next, with your foot on the brake, select each position on the transmission (Reverse, Drive, Low, etc.), finally bring the shifter back to

4.5 Scanners like the Actron Scantool and the AutoXray are powerful diagnostic aids - programmed with comprehensive diagnostic information, they can read out most of the stored PCM information

Park and turn off the engine. This will allow the PCM to obtain any fault codes that might be linked to any of the sensors controlled by the transmission, engine speed or air conditioning system.

9   To display the codes on the dashboard CHECK ENGINE light or Malfunction Indicator Light (MIL), with the engine NOT running, turn the ignition key ON, OFF, ON, OFF and finally ON. The codes will begin to flash. The light will blink the number of the first digit then pause and blink the number of the second digit. For example: Code 23, intake air temperature sensor circuit, would be indicated by two flashes, then a pause followed by three flashes.

10   Certain criteria must be met for a DTC to be stored in the PCM memory. The criteria might be a specific range of engine rpm, engine temperature or input voltage to the engine controller. It's possible that a DTC for a particular monitored circuit may not be entered into the PCM memory despite a malfunction. This may happen because one of the DTC criteria has not been met. For example, the engine must be operating between 750 and 2,000 rpm in order to monitor the MAP sensor circuit correctly. If the engine speed is raised above 2,400 rpm, the MAP sensor output circuit shorts to ground and will not allow a DTC to be entered into the memory. Then again, the exact opposite could occur: A DTC is entered into the memory that suggests a malfunction within another component that is not monitored by the PCM. For example, a fuel pressure problem cannot register a fault directly but instead, it will cause a rich or lean fuel mixture problem. Consequently, this will cause an oxygen sensor malfunction resulting in a stored code in the PCM for the oxygen sensor. Or pulling a spark plug wire to perform a spark test may set the misfire DTC. Be aware of the interrelationship of the sensors and circuits and the overall relationship of the emissions control and fuel injection systems. If a problem in a non-emissions system com-

4.7 The diagnostic Data Link Connector is located under the dash

ponent or system is repaired or ceases to be a problem, the PCM will cancel the DTC after 40 warm-up cycles.

Clearing codes

11   To clear the codes from the PCM memory, install the OBD-II SCAN tool, scroll the menu for the function that describes "CLEARING CODES' and follow the prescribed method for that particular SCAN tool. If necessary, have the codes cleared by a dealer service department or other qualified repair facility. **Caution:** *Do not disconnect the battery from the vehicle to clear the codes. This will erase stored operating parameters from the memory and cause the engine to run rough for a period of time while the PCM relearns the information.*

Trouble code identification

Refer to illustration 4.12

Note 1: *On the models covered by this manual, the CHECK ENGINE light or MIL light, located in the instrument panel, flashes on for three seconds as a bulb test when the engine is started. The light comes on and stays on when there's a problem in the emissions system.*

Note 2: *These models are equipped with the OBD-II system. The engine codes can be accessed using the ignition key but it will be necessary to use a special factory SCAN tool (DRB-II) to interpret the diagnostic information. The codes indicated in the text are designed and mandated by the EPA for all OBD-II vehicles produced by automobile manufacturers, and some listed are manufacturer's specific trouble codes. Consult a dealer service department for additional information. General information on the system sensors and actuators for all models is described in the following text. See the Troubleshooting Section at the beginning of this manual for some basic diagnostic aids. Because the OBD-II system requires a special SCAN tool to access the trouble codes, have the vehicle diagnosed by a dealer service department or other qualified automotive repair facility if the proper SCAN tool is not available.*

MIL CODE	GENERIC SCAN TOOL CODE	DRB SCAN TOOL DISPLAY	DESCRIPTION OF DIAGNOSTIC TROUBLE CODE
12*		Battery Disconnect	Direct battery input to PCM was disconnected within the last 50 Key-on cycles.
55*			Completion of fault code display on Check Engine lamp.
54**	P0340	No Cam Signal at PCM	No camshaft signal detected during engine cranking.
53**	P0601	Internal Controller Failure	PCM Internal fault condition detected.
47***		Charging System Voltage Too Low	Battery voltage sense input below target charging during engine operation. Also, no significant change detected in battery voltage during active test of generator output circuit.
46***		Charging System Voltage Too High	Battery voltage sense input above target charging voltage during engine operation.
42*		Auto Shutdown Relay Control Circuit	An open or shorted condition detected in the auto shutdown relay circuit.
41***		Alternator Field Not Switching Properly	An open or shorted condition detected in the alternator field control circuit.
37**	P0743	Torque Converter Clutch Soleniod/Trans Relay Circuits	An open or shorted condition detected in the torque converter part throttle unlock solenoid control circuit (3 speed auto RH trans. only).
35**	P1491	Rad Fan Control Relay Circuit	An open or shorted condition detected in the low speed radiator fan relay control circuit.
34*		Speed Control Solenoid Circuits	An open or shorted condition detected in the Speed Control vacuum or vent solenoid circuits.
33*		A/C Clutch Relay Circuit	An open or shorted condition detected in the A/C clutch relay circuit.
32**	P0403	EGR Solenoid Circuit	An open or shorted condition detected in the EGR transducer solenoid circuit.
31**	P0443	EVAP Purge Solenoid Circuit	An open or shorted condition detected in the duty cycle purge solenoid circuit.
27**	P0203	Injector #3 Control Circuit	Injector #3 output driver does not respond properly to the control signal.
	or P0202	Injector #2 Control Circuit	Injector #2 output driver does not respond properly to the control signal.

4.12 Diagnostic Trouble Code (DTC) descriptions

Note 3: *Before outputting the trouble codes, thoroughly inspect ALL electrical connectors and hoses. Make sure all electrical connections are tight, clean and free of corrosion; make sure all hoses are properly connected, fit tightly and are in good condition (no cracks or tears).*
Note 4: ** indicates that the MIL (Malfunction Indicator Light/check engine lamp) will not*

illuminate if a Diagnostic Trouble Code (DTC) was recorded. Cycle the ignition key as described to observe the code flashed by the MIL.
** indicates that the MIL will illuminate if the DTC was recorded - this would be an emissions-related problem.
*** indicates that the generator lamp is illuminated.

12   The accompanying listing gives DTC's which may be encountered while diagnosing the systems (**see illustration**). Also included are simplified troubleshooting procedures. If the problem persists after these checks have been made, more detailed service procedures will have to be performed by a dealer service department or other qualified repair shop.

MIL CODE	GENERIC SCAN TOOL CODE	DRB SCAN TOOL DISPLAY	DESCRIPTION OF DIAGNOSTIC TROUBLE CODE
	or P0201	Injector #1 Control Circuit	Injector #1 output driver does not respond properly to the control signal.
25**	P0505	Idle Air Control Motor Circuits	A shorted or open condition detected in one or more of the idle air control motor circuits.
24**	P0122	Throttle Position Sensor Voltage Low	Throttle position sensor input below the minimum acceptable voltage
	or P0123	Throttle Position Sensor Voltage High	Throttle position sensor input above the maximum acceptable voltage.
22**	P0117	ECT Sensor Voltage Too Low	Engine coolant temperature sensor input below minimum acceptable voltage.
	or P0118	ECT Sensor Voltage Too High	Engine coolant temperature sensor input above maximum acceptable voltage.
21**	P0134	Right Rear (or just) Upstream O2S Stays at Center	Neither rich or lean condition detected from the oxygen sensor.
17*		Engine Is Cold Too Long	Engine did not reach operating temperature within acceptable limits.
15**	P0500	No Vehicle Speed Sensor Signal	No vehicle speed sensor signal detected during road load conditions.
14**	P0107	MAP Sensor Voltage Too Low	MAP sensor input below minimum acceptable voltage.
	or P0108	MAP Sensor Voltage Too High	MAP sensor input above maximum acceptable voltage.
13**	P1297	No Change in MAP From Start to Run	No difference recognized between the engine MAP reading and the barometric (atmospheric) pressure reading from start-up.
11*		No Crank Reference Signal at PCM	No crank reference signal detected during engine cranking.
43**	P0353	Ignition Coil #3 Primary Circuit	Peak primary circuit current not achieved with maximum dwell time.
	or P0352	Ignition Coil #2 Primary Circuit	Peak primary circuit current not achieved with maximum dwell time.
	or P0351	Ignition Coil #1 Primary Circuit	Peak primary circuit current not achieved with maximum dwell time.
42*		No ASD Relay Output Voltage at PCM	An Open condition Detected In The ASD Relay Output Circuit.
32**	P0401	EGR System Failure	Required change in air/fuel ratio not detected during diagnostic test.

Diagnostic Trouble Code (DTC) descriptions (continued)

MIL CODE	GENERIC SCAN TOOL CODE	DRB SCAN TOOL DISPLAY	DESCRIPTION OF DIAGNOSTIC TROUBLE CODE
62*	P1697	PCM Failure SRI Miles Not Stored	Unsuccessful attempt to update EMR mileage in the PCM EEPROM.
63**	P1696	PCM Failure EEPROM Write Denied	Unsuccessful attempt to write to an EEPROM location by the PCM.
23**	P0112	Intake Air Temp Sensor Voltage Low	Intake air temperature sensor input below the minimum acceptable voltage.
	or		
	P0113	Intake Air Temp Sensor Voltage High	Intake air temperature sensor input above the maximum acceptable voltage.
61**	P0106	Barometric Pressure Out Of Range	MAP sensor has a baro reading below an acceptable value.
27**	P0204	Injector #4 Control Circuit	Injector #4 output driver does not respond properly to the control signal.
21**	P0132	Right Rear (or just) Upstream O2S Shorted to Voltage	Oxygen sensor input voltage maintained above the normal operating range.
53**	P0600	PCM Failure SPI Communications	PCM Internal fault condition detected.
27**	P0205	Injector #5 Control Circuit	Injector #5 output driver does not respond properly to the control signal.
	or		
	P0206	Injector #6 Control Circuit	Injector #6 output driver does not respond properly to the control signal.
77*		SPD CTRL PWR RLY; or S/C 12v Driver CKT	Malfunction detected with power feed to speed control servo solenoids.
33		A/C Pressure Sensor Volts Too High	Sensor input voltage is above 4.9 volts.
	or		
		A/C Pressure Sensor Volts Too Low	Sensor input voltage is below .098 volts.
66	P1698	No CCD Messages From TCM	No messages received from Transmission Control Module.
	or		
	P1695	No CCD Message From Body Control Module	No messages received from Body Control Module.
42*		Fuel Pump Relay Control Circuit	An open or shorted condition detected in the fuel pump relay control circuit.
21**	P0133	Right Bank Upstream O2S Slow Response	Oxygen sensor response slower than minimum required switching frequency.
	or		
	P0135	Right Rear (or just) Upstream O2S Heater Failure	Upstream oxygen sensor heating element circuit malfunction.

Diagnostic Trouble Code (DTC) descriptions (continued)

MIL CODE	GENERIC SCAN TOOL CODE	DRB SCAN TOOL DISPLAY	DESCRIPTION OF DIAGNOSTIC TROUBLE CODE
	P0141	Right Rear (or just) Downstream O2S Heater Failure	Oxygen sensor heating element circuit malfunction.
43**	P0300	Multiple Cylinder Mis-fire	Misfire detected in multiple cylinders.
	or		
	P0301	Cylinder #1 Mis-fire	Misfire detected in cylinder #1.
	or		
	P0302	Cylinder #2 Mis-fire	Misfire detected in cylinder #2.
	or		
	P0303	Cylinder #3 Mis-fire	Misfire detected in cylinder #3.
	or		
	P0304	Cylinder #4 Mis-fire	Misfire detected in cylinder #4.
72**	P0420	Right Rear (or just) Catalyst Efficency Failure	Catalyst efficiency below required level.
31*	P0441	Evap Purge Flow Monitor Failure	Insufficient or excessive vapor flow detected during evaporative emission system operation.
37**	P1899	P/N Switch Stuck in Park or in Gear	Incorrect input state detected for the Park/Neutral switch, auto. trans. only.
52**	P0172	Right Rear (or just) Fuel System Rich	A rich air/fuel mixture has been indicated by an abnormally lean correction factor.
51**	P0171	Right Rear (or just) Fuel System Lean	A lean air/fuel mixture has been indicated by an abnormally rich correction factor.
21**	P0138	Right Rear (or just) Downstream O2S Shorted to Voltage	Oxygen sensor input voltage maintained above the normal operating range.
17**	P0125	Closed Loop Temp Not Reached	Engine does not reach 20°F within 5 minutes with a vehicle speed signal.
21**	P0140	Right Rear (or just) Downstream O2S Stays at Center	Neither reich or lean condition detected from the downstream oxygen sensor.
24**	P0121	TPS Voltage Does Not Agree With MAP	TPS signal does not correlate to MAP sensor.
45**	P0700	EATX Controller DTC Present	An automatic transmission input DTC has been set in the transmission controller.
25**	P1294	Target Idle Not Reached	Actual idle speed does not equal target idle speed.
71**	P1496	5 Volt Supply Output Too Low	5 volt output from regulator does not meet minimum requirement.
37*	P0740	Torq Conv Clu, No RPM Drop At Lockup	Relationship between engine speed and vehicle speed indicates no torque converter clutch engagement (auto. trans. only).

Diagnostic Trouble Code (DTC) descriptions (continued)

MIL CODE	GENERIC SCAN TOOL CODE	DRB SCAN TOOL DISPLAY	DESCRIPTION OF DIAGNOSTIC TROUBLE CODE
42*	or	Fuel Level Sending Unit Volts Too Low	Open circuit between PCM and fuel gauge sending unit.
	or	Fuel Level Sending Unit Volts Too High	Circuit shorted to voltage between PCM and fuel gauge sending unit.
		Fuel Level Unit No Change Over Miles	No movement of fuel level sender detected.
65**	P0703	Brake Switch Stuck Pressed or Released	No release of brake switch seen after too many accelerations.
44**	P1493	Ambient/Batt Temp Sen VoltsToo Low	Battery temperature sensor input voltage below an acceptable range.
	or		
	P1492	Ambient/Batt Temp Sensor VoltsToo High	Battery temperature sensor input voltage above an acceptable range.
21**	P0131	Right Rear (or just) Upstream O2S Shorted to Ground	O2 sensor voltage too low, tested after cold start.
	or		
	P0137	Right Rear (or just) Downstream O2S Shorted to Ground	O2 sensor voltage too low, tested after cold start.
	or		
11**	P1391	Intermittent Loss of CMP or CKP	Intermittent loss of either camshaft or crankshaft position sensor.
31**	P0442	Evap Leak Monitor Small Leak Detected	A small leak has been detected by the leak detection monitor.
	or		
	P0455	Evap Leak Monitor Large Leak Detected	The leak detection monitor is unable to pressurize Evap system, indicating a large leak.
43**	P0305	Cylinder #5 Mis-fire	Misfire detected in cylinder #5.
	or		
	P0306	Cylinder #6 Mis-fire	Misfire detected in cylinder #6.
31**	P1495	Leak Detect ion Pump Solenoid Circuit	Leak detection pump solenoid circuit fault (open or short).
	or		
	P1494	Leak Detect Pump Sw or Mechanical Fault	Leak detection pump switch does not respond to input.
11**	P1398	Mis-fire Adaptive Numerator at Limit	CKP sensor target windows have too much variation.
31**	P1486	Evap Leak Monitor Pinched Hose Found	Plug or pinch detected between purge solenoid and fuel tank.
64**	P1290	CNG System Pressure Too High	Compressed natural gas pressure sensor reading above acceptable voltage.
21	P0153	Cat Mon Slow O2 Upstream	Oxygen sensor response slower than minimum required switching frequency during catalyst monitor.

Diagnostic Trouble Code (DTC) descriptions (continued)

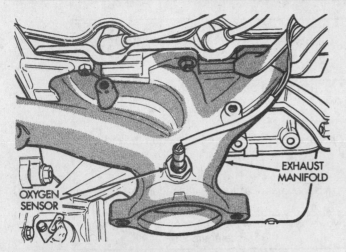

5.1a The upstream oxygen sensor is threaded into the exhaust manifold

5.1b The downstream oxygen sensor is located at the catalytic converter in the exhaust pipe directly behind the catalytic converter

5   Information sensors - general description, check and replacement

Note: *These models are equipped with the OBD-II system. The engine codes can be accessed using the ignition key as described in Section 4, but it will be necessary to use a special factory SCAN tool (DRB-II) to interpret the diagnostic information. Have the vehicle diagnosed by a dealer service department if following the sensor checking procedures fails to turn up a problem.*

Oxygen sensor

General description

Refer to illustrations 5.1a, 5.1b, 5.12a and 5.12b

1   The oxygen sensors, one upstream which is located in the exhaust manifold, and one downstream at the catalytic converter, monitor the oxygen content of the exhaust gas stream **(see illustrations)**. The oxygen content in the exhaust reacts with the oxygen sensor to produce a voltage output which varies from 0.1-volt (high oxygen, lean mixture) to 0.9-volts (low oxygen, rich mixture). The PCM constantly monitors this variable voltage output to determine the ratio of oxygen to fuel in the mixture. The PCM alters the air/fuel mixture ratio by controlling the pulse width (open time) of the fuel injectors. A mixture ratio of 14.7 parts air to 1 part fuel is the ideal mixture ratio for minimizing exhaust emissions, thus allowing the catalytic converter to operate at maximum efficiency. It is this ratio of 14.7 to 1 which the PCM and the oxygen sensor attempt to maintain at all times.

2   The oxygen sensor produces no voltage when it is below its normal operating temperature of about 600 degrees F. During this initial period before warm-up, the PCM operates in OPEN LOOP mode.

3   If the engine reaches normal operating temperature, the PCM will set a DTC if it detects any problem with the oxygen sensor circuit.

4   When there is a problem with the oxygen sensor or its circuit, the PCM operates in the open loop mode - that is, it controls fuel delivery in accordance with a programmed default value instead of feedback information from the oxygen sensor.

5   The proper operation of the oxygen sensor depends on four conditions:

a) *Electrical - The low voltages generated by the sensor depend upon good, clean connections which should be checked whenever a malfunction of the sensor is suspected or indicated.*

b) *Outside air supply - The sensor is designed to allow air circulation to the internal portion of the sensor. Whenever the sensor is removed and installed or replaced, make sure the air passages are not restricted.*

c) *Proper operating temperature - The PCM will not react to the sensor signal until the sensor reaches approximately 600-degrees F. This factor must be taken into consideration when evaluating the performance of the sensor.*

d) *Unleaded fuel - The use of unleaded fuel is essential for proper operation of the sensor. Make sure the fuel you are using is of this type.*

6   In addition to observing the above conditions, special care must be taken whenever the sensor is serviced.

a) *The oxygen sensor has a permanently attached pigtail and electrical connector which should not be removed from the sensor. Damage or removal of the pigtail or electrical connector can adversely affect operation of the sensor.*

b) *Grease, dirt and other contaminants should be kept away from the electrical connector and the louvered end of the sensor.*

c) *Do not use cleaning solvents of any kind on the oxygen sensor.*

d) *Do not drop or roughly handle the sensor.*

e) *The silicone boot must be installed in the correct position to prevent the boot from being melted and to allow the sensor to operate properly.*

Check

Note: *An OBD II SCAN tool is needed to check the working parameters of the oxygen sensor, but the heating element can be checked as described below.*

7   Locate the oxygen sensor electrical connector and disconnect the oxygen sensor. The white wires in the connector are the heater power and ground circuits. **Note:** *Consult the wiring diagrams at the end of Chapter 12 for oxygen sensor electrical connector wire color designations.*

8   Connect an ohmmeter to the terminals of the white wires in the sensor connector. The resistance should be between 4 and 7 ohms.

9   Replace the heated oxygen sensor if the resistance is not correct.

Replacement

Note: *Because it is installed in the exhaust manifold or pipe, which contracts when cool, the oxygen sensor may be very difficult to loosen when the engine is cold. Rather than risk damage to the sensor (assuming you are planning to re-use it in another manifold or pipe), start and run the engine for a minute or two, then shut it off. Be careful not to burn yourself during the following procedure.*

10   Disconnect the cable from the negative battery terminal.

11   Raise the vehicle and support it securely on jackstands.

12   Carefully disconnect the electrical connector from the sensor and unscrew the sensor from the exhaust system **(see illustrations)**.

13   Anti-seize compound must be used on the threads of the sensor to facilitate future removal. The threads of new sensors will already be coated with this compound, but if an old sensor is removed and reinstalled,

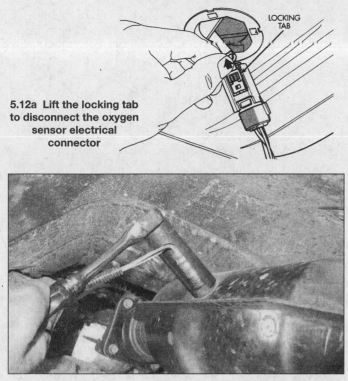

5.12a Lift the locking tab to disconnect the oxygen sensor electrical connector

5.12b Use a box wrench or a special slotted socket to remove the oxygen sensor

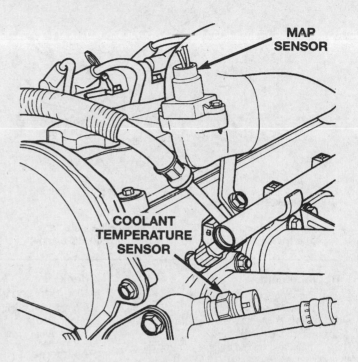

5.17a MAP sensor location - four-cylinder engine

recoat the threads.

14   Install the sensor and tighten it securely.

15   Reconnect the electrical connector of the pigtail lead to the main engine wiring harness.

16   Lower the vehicle, take it on a test drive and check to see that no trouble codes set.

Manifold Absolute Pressure (MAP) sensor

General description

Refer to illustrations 5.17a and 5.17b

17   The Manifold Absolute Pressure (MAP) sensor monitors intake manifold pressure changes resulting from changes in engine load and speed and converts the information into a voltage output. The MAP sensor is located on the side of the intake manifold plenum **(see illustrations)**. The PCM uses the MAP sensor to control fuel delivery and ignition timing. The PCM will receive information as a voltage signal that will vary from 4 to 5 volts with the ignition switch ON and the engine not running, and then drop to between 1.5 and 2.1 volts at idle (closed throttle, high vacuum).

18   A failure in the MAP sensor circuit should set a DTC.

Check

Refer to illustration 5.20

19   Check the electrical connector at the sensor for a snug fit. Check the terminals in the connector and the wires leading to it for looseness and breaks. Repair as required.

20   Disconnect the MAP sensor connector, and connect a voltmeter to terminals 1 and 2 of the harness connector **(see illustration)**. Turn the ignition key ON (engine not running), there should be approximately 4 to 5 volts. Using an ohmmeter, check for continuity to ground on terminal 1. If the supply voltage is not available or the ground circuit is open, check the wiring harness from the sensor to the PCM.

21   Connect the electrical connector to the MAP sensor and using suitable probes (such as straight pins), backprobe terminals 2 and 3. Connect a voltmeter to the probes. Turn the ignition key On - voltage should be approximately 4 to 5 volts; now start the engine - the voltage should drop to 1.5 to 2.0 volts. If the MAP sensor does not operate as described, replace the sensor.

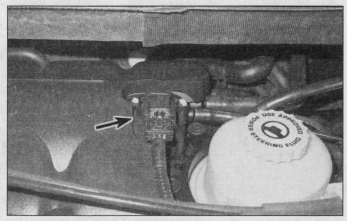

5.17b Map sensor location (arrow) - V6 engines (2001 and later models shown)

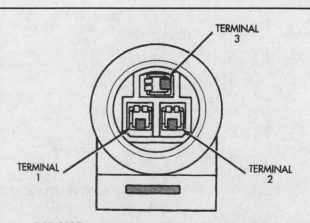

5.20 MAP sensor connector terminal identification

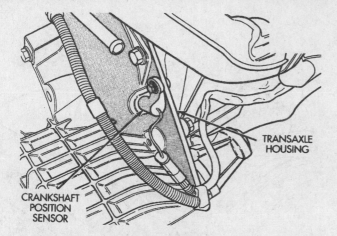

5.25 The crankshaft position sensor is located at the transaxle bellhousing (1996 through 2000 V6 engine)

5.31a Engine Coolant Temperature (ECT) sensor - four-cylinder engine

Replacement

22   Disconnect the electrical connector from the MAP sensor.

23   Remove the screws and the MAP sensor from the intake plenum.

24   Installation is the reverse of removal.

Crankshaft position sensor

General description

Refer to illustration 5.25

25   On these models, the crankshaft position sensor determines the timing for the fuel injection and ignition on each cylinder. It also detects engine RPM.

26   The crankshaft position sensor is a Hall-Effect device that is mounted either on the rear of the engine near the accessory drive belt on four-cylinder engines, or on the bell housing on 1996 through 2000 V6 engines or near the rear portion of the transmission housing on 2001 and later V6 engines. The sensor output voltage will fluctuate from 0.3 volts (metal under the sensor) to 5.0 volts (slots under the sensor). The engine will not operate if the PCM does not receive a crankshaft position sensor output.

Check

27   An OBD II SCAN tool is required to check the crankshaft position sensor, have the system checked at a dealership service department or other properly equipped repair facility.

Replacement

28   Disconnect the crankshaft sensor wiring harness connector.

29   Remove the crankshaft sensor mounting bolts. Use only the original bolts to mount the sensor, they are machined to correctly space the sensor to the flywheel.

30   Installation is the reverse of removal. Tighten the bolt(s) to the torque listed in this Chapter's Specifications.

Engine Coolant Temperature (ECT) sensor

General description

Refer to illustrations 5.31a, 5.31b and 5.31c

31   The engine coolant temperature sensor is a thermistor (a variable resistor which changes resistance in accordance with temperature changes). The change in the resistance values will directly affect the voltage signal from the coolant temperature sensor. The ECT sensor **(see illustrations)** provides an input voltage to the PCM, which varies with coolant temperature. The ECT is also used for cooling fan on/off control by the PCM. A failure in the coolant sensor circuit should set either a DTC, indicating a failure in the coolant temperature circuit, so the appropriate solution to the problem will be either repair of a wire or replacement of the sensor. The sensor can also be checked with an ohmmeter, by measuring its resistance when cold, then warming up the engine and taking another measurement.

Check

Refer to illustration 5.32

32   To check the sensor, check the resistance values of the coolant temperature sensor with an ohmmeter connected to terminals A and B of the sensor connector **(see illustration)**. With the engine cold (approximately 70 degrees F), the resistance should be approximately 7,000 to 13,000 ohms. Next, start the engine and warm it up until it reaches operating temperature (approximately 200 degrees F). The resistance should

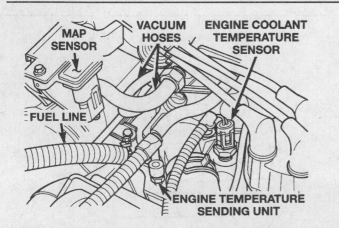

5.31b Engine Coolant Temperature (ECT) sensor - 3.0L V6 engine

5.31c Engine Coolant Temperature (ECT) sensor - 3.3L and 3.8L V6 engines (typical)

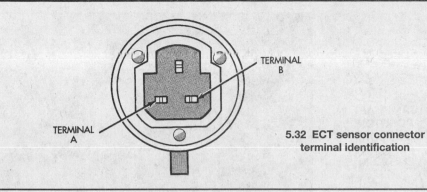

5.32 ECT sensor connector terminal identification

be 700 to 1,000 ohms.

33   If there is not a definite change in temperature, remove the coolant temperature sensor and check the resistance in a pan of heated water to simulate operating conditions. If the sensor tests are good, check the wiring harness from the sensor to the PCM.

Replacement

Warning: *Wait until the engine is completely cool before beginning this procedure.*

34   To remove the sensor, release the locking tab, disconnect the electrical connector, then carefully unscrew the sensor. **Caution:** *Handle the coolant sensor with care. Damage to this sensor will affect the operation of the entire fuel injection system.*

35   Before installing the new sensor, wrap the threads with Teflon sealing tape to prevent leakage and thread corrosion.

36   Installation is the reverse of removal.

Throttle Position Sensor (TPS)

General description

37   The Throttle Position Sensor (TPS) is located on the end of the throttle shaft on the throttle body (see Chapter 4). The PCM determines fuel delivery based on throttle valve angle (driver demand). A broken or loose TPS can cause intermittent bursts of fuel from the injector and an unstable idle because the PCM senses that the throttle is moving.

Check

38   Locate the Throttle Position Sensor (TPS) on the throttle body.

39   Disconnect the TPS electrical connector and using a digital voltmeter, check the 5 volt reference voltage and ground circuits from the PCM by connecting the voltmeter positive probe to the connector violet/white wire terminal and the negative probe to the black/light blue wire terminal. With the ignition switch ON approximately 5 volts should be present. If it isn't, check the wiring harness from the sensor to the PCM.

40   Next, reconnect the connector the sensor and check the sensor output voltage by backprobing the TPS connector center terminal (orange/dark blue wire) and the ground terminal (black/light blue) wire with a voltmeter (use suitable probes, such as straight pins to backprobe the connector and connect the meter to the probes). Turn the ignition switch ON (engine not running). At closed throttle the voltage should be approximately 0.38 volts to 1.2 volts. At wide-open throttle, voltage should be approximately 3.1 volts to 4.4 volts. The output voltage should gradually increase as the throttle moves slowly from closed to wide-open throttle.

41   If the TPS sensor voltage readings are incorrect, replace the TPS sensor.

42   A problem in any of the TPS circuits will set a DTC. Once a DTC is set, the PCM will use an artificial default value for throttle position and some vehicle performance will return. Complete testing of the TPS and related circuitry, the use of the dealer DRB II scan tool is recommended.

Replacement

Refer to illustrations 5.44 and 5.45

43   Disconnect the electrical connector from the TPS.

44   Remove the mounting screws from the TPS and remove the TPS from the throttle body **(see illustration)**.

45   When installing the TPS, be sure to align the socket locating tangs on the TPS with the throttle shaft in the throttle body **(see illustration)**.

46   Installation is the reverse of removal. Be sure the throttle valve is fully closed once the TPS is mounted. If it isn't, rotate the TPS to allow complete closure (idle) before tightening the mounting screws.

47   If idle condition is not satisfactory, shut off the engine and remove and clean the throttle body with an aerosol cleaner, cleaning the inside of the throttle body bore and both sides and the edges of the throttle plate until free of deposits (see Chapter 4).

Intake Air Temperature sensor (four-cylinder engine only)

General information

48   The intake air temperature sensor (IAT) is located in the intake manifold. This sensor operates as a negative temperature coefficient (NTC) device, which means that as the sensor temperature DECREASES, the resistance values will INCREASE. As the sensor temperature INCREASES, the resistance values will DECREASE. In most cases, the solution to a problem with the IAT will be either repair of a wire or replacement of the sensor.

Check

49   To check the sensor, with the ignition switch OFF, disconnect the electrical connector from the air temperature sensor,

5.44 Remove the Throttle Position Sensor (TPS) mounting screws (arrows) and separate the TPS from the throttle body

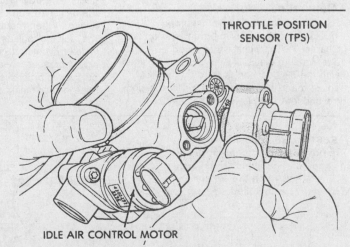

5.45 When installing the Throttle Position Sensor (TPS), align the socket locating tangs on the TPS with the throttle shaft

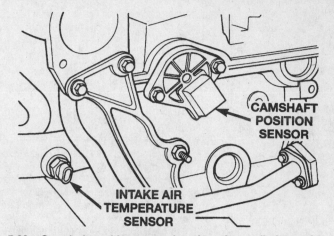

5.60a Camshaft position sensor location - four-cylinder engine

5.60b Camshaft position sensor location (arrow) -
3.3L and 3.8L V6 engines

which is located on the intake manifold. Using an ohmmeter, measure the resistance between the two terminals on the sensor while it is completely cold, then start the engine and warm it up until it reaches operating temperature. The resistance should be higher when the engine is cold and lower when the engine is hot.

50   If the sensor resistance test results are incorrect, replace the air temperature sensor.

51   If the sensor checks out okay but there is still a problem, have the vehicle checked at a dealer service department or other qualified repair shop, as the PCM may be malfunctioning.

Replacement

52   Disconnect the electrical connector from the air temperature sensor.

53   Unscrew the sensor from the intake manifold and remove the air temperature sensor.

54   Installation is the reverse of removal.

Vehicle Speed Sensor

Note: *3.3L and 3.8L V6 engines with the 41TE transaxle are NOT equipped with a vehicle speed sensor.*

General description

55   The Vehicle Speed Sensor (VSS) is located on the side of the transmission (see Chapter 7). This sensor that produces a voltage signal to the PCM. This signal, combined with the TPS sensor, is used by the PCM to adjust the idle air control motor for fuel control and for transmission shift control.

Check

56   An OBD II SCAN tool is required to check the VSS, have the system checked at a dealership service department or other properly equipped repair facility.

Replacement

57   To replace the VSS, disconnect the electrical connector from the VSS.

58   Remove the retaining bolt and lift the VSS from the transmission.

59   Installation is the reverse of removal.

Camshaft position sensor

General description

Refer to illustrations 5.60a and 5.60b

Note: *The general description and replacement procedures below do not apply to the 3.0L V6 engine, which has the camshaft position sensor located in the distributor.*

60   The camshaft position sensor **(see illustrations)** provides cylinder identification to the PCM to synchronize the fuel and spark systems.

61   The signal is generated from a rotating pulse ring located on the camshaft sprocket, generating pulses as groups of notches on the camshaft sprocket pass underneath the sensor. When metal aligns with the sensor the voltage pulses low (under 0.5 volts). When the notch aligns with the sensor, voltage increases to about 5.0 volts. These pulses are processed by the PCM to determine ignition timing.

Check

62   An OBD II SCAN tool is required to check the camshaft position sensor, have the system checked at a dealership service department or other properly equipped repair facility.

Replacement

Refer to illustration 5.66

Note: *The 3.0L V6 engine camshaft position sensor, located in the distributor, requires distributor removal and replacement (see Chapter 5).*

63   Disconnect the negative terminal from the battery.

64   Disconnect the electrical connector from the camshaft position sensor.

65   Remove the bolt from the camshaft position sensor and lift the sensor from the timing cover.

66   Installation is the reverse of removal. Be sure to install the paper spacer **(see illustration)** onto the camshaft sensor and tighten the camshaft sensor bolt to the torque listed in this Chapter's Specifications. The paper spacer sets a proper clearance and will absorb in engine oil after running the engine.

Automatic Shutdown (ASD) and fuel pump relays

General description

67   The ASD relay provides battery voltage to the fuel injectors, electronic ignition coil, and the heating elements in the oxygen sensors. The ASD and fuel pump relays are located in the Power Distribution Center (PDC) in the engine compartment, adjacent to the battery (see Chapter 12) and are fused in the PDC. The PDC supplies voltage to the solenoid side and contact side of the relays. The PCM controls the ASD relay by switching the ground path on and off. The ground path is off when the ignition switch is OFF. When the ignition switch is in the ON or CRANK position, the PCM determines if it is sensing crankshaft position sensor and camshaft position sensor signals; if none are sensed, the ASD relay will be de-energized, cutting voltage to the fuel injectors electronic ignition coil, and the heating elements in the

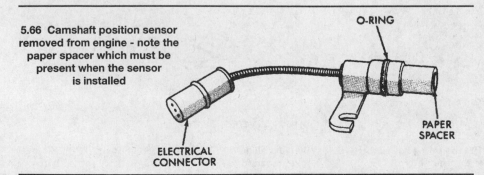

5.66 Camshaft position sensor removed from engine - note the paper spacer which must be present when the sensor is installed

O-RING

PAPER SPACER

ELECTRICAL CONNECTOR

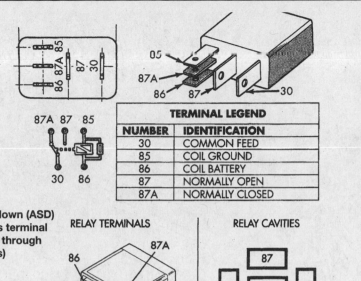

TERMINAL LEGEND	
NUMBER	IDENTIFICATION
30	COMMON FEED
85	COIL GROUND
86	COIL BATTERY
87	NORMALLY OPEN
87A	NORMALLY CLOSED

5.68 Automatic Shutdown (ASD) and fuel pump relays terminal identification (1996 through 1998 models)

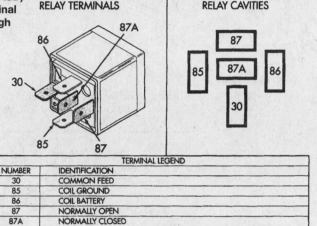

RELAY TERMINALS   RELAY CAVITIES

NUMBER	IDENTIFICATION
30	COMMON FEED
85	COIL GROUND
86	COIL BATTERY
87	NORMALLY OPEN
87A	NORMALLY CLOSED

oxygen sensors. As for the fuel pump relay, the PCM will de-energize the relay if it does not detect engine rotation.

Check

Refer to illustration 5.68

68   To check the ASD or Fuel Pump relays, remove the relay to be checked **(see illustration)**. Use an ohmmeter to check resistance between terminals 85 and 86. The resistance should be between 70 and 80 ohms.

69   Check for continuity between terminals 30 and 87A. The meter should indicate continuity.

70   Check for continuity between terminals 30 and 87. The meter should <u>not</u> indicate continuity.

71   Connect a jumper wire to terminal 85 and a good chassis ground, then connect another jumper from terminal 86 to a 12 volt source (such as the positive terminal of the vehicle battery). This actuates the relay. Recheck using the ohmmeter between terminals 30 and 87; the meter should now indicate continuity. Disconnect the jumper wires.

72   Replace the relay if it did not pass continuity or resistance checks.

Knock sensor

General description

Rofor to illuotration 5.73

Note: *A knock sensor is not used on the 3.0L and 3.3L V6 engines.*

73   The knock sensor **(see illustration)** is mounted into the side of the engine block. If the knock sensor detects a knock in the cylinder during the combustion process it sends an electrical signal to the PCM. The PCM, in turn, retards the ignition timing by a certain amount to reduce the uncontrolled detonation. The knock sensor consists of a small crystal that oscillates with engine vibration, and as the intensity of the engine knock vibration increases, the voltage signal from the knock sensor to the PCM also increases.

Check

74   Connect a digital voltmeter to the knock sensor terminals and set the voltmeter to AC. With the engine running, check the output is approximately 20 mV at about 700 RPM and then approximately 600 mV (0.6 volts) at 5,000 RPM.

75   In the event of knock sensor failure, have the system checked at a dealer service department.

Replacement

76   Disconnect the electrical connector(s) and unscrew the knock sensor(s) from the engine block.

77   Installation is the reverse of removal.

Park Neutral position switch

78   Refer to Chapter 7 for all the checks and replacement procedures for the Park/Neutral position switch.

6   Positive Crankcase Ventilation (PCV) system

Refer to illustrations 6.1a, 6.1b, 6.1c and 6.3

1   The Positive Crankcase Ventilation (PCV) system **(see illustrations)** reduces hydrocarbon emissions by scavenging

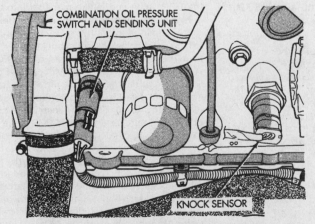

5.73 Typical knock sensor location - 3.3L and 3.8L V6 engines shown

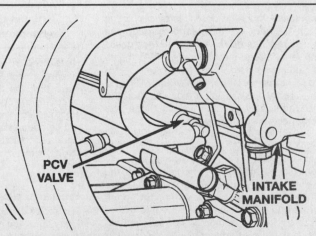

6.1a Positive Crankcase Ventilation (PCV) valve - four-cylinder engine

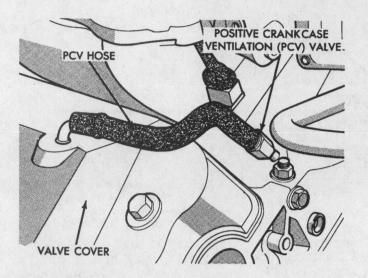

6.1b Positive Crankcase Ventilation (PCV) valve - 3.0L V6 engine

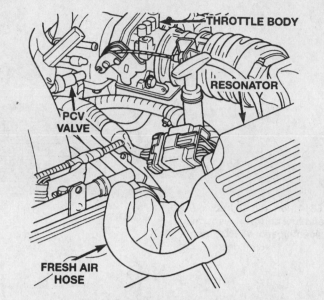

6.1c Positive Crankcase Ventilation (PCV) valve and fresh air hose - 3.3L and 3.8L V6 engines (typical)

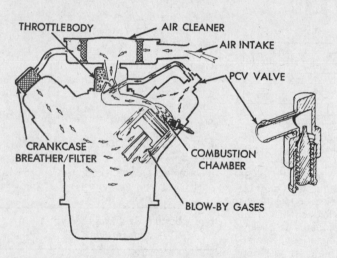

6.3 Typical PCV system flow for burning of crankcase blow-by gases

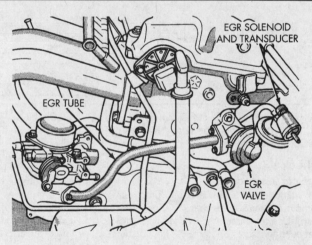

7.2a EGR valve mounted on the 2.4L engine (1999 and 2000 models)

crankcase vapors. It does this by circulating fresh air from the air cleaner through the crankcase, where it mixes with blow-by gases and is then rerouted through a PCV valve to the intake manifold.

2   The main components of the PCV system are the PCV valve, a blow-by filter and the vacuum hoses connecting these two components with the engine.

3   To maintain idle quality, the PCV valve restricts the flow when the intake manifold vacuum is high. If abnormal operating conditions (such as piston ring problems) arise, the system is designed to allow excessive amounts of blow-by gases to flow back through the crankcase vent tube into the air cleaner to be consumed by normal combustion **(see illustration)**.

4   Checking and replacement of the PCV valve is covered in Chapter 1.

7   Exhaust Gas Recirculation (EGR) system

Note 1: *1996 through 1998 four-cylinder engines are not equipped with an EGR system*
Note 2: *If the EGR valve control solenoid becomes disconnected or damaged, the electrical signal will be lost and the EGR valve will be open at all times during warm-up and driving conditions. The symptoms will be poor performance, rough idle and driveability problems.*

General description
Refer to illustrations 7.2a, 7.2b, 7.2c, 7.2d, 7.2e, 7.6, 7.18a and 7.18b

1   The EGR system reduces oxides of nitrogen by recirculating exhaust gas through the EGR valve and intake manifold into the combustion chambers. This system helps reduce oxides of nitrogen in the engine exhaust and helps prevent spark knock.

2   The EGR system consists of the EGR valve, EGR backpressure transducer and the EGR control solenoid valve, the Powertrain Control Module (PCM) and various sensors **(see illustrations)**. The PCM memory is programmed to produce the ideal EGR valve lift for each operating condition. The PCM operates the EGR control solenoid and the exhaust system back pressure controls the EGR transducer. Engine vacuum is ported to the transducer when the PCM de-energizes the solenoid. When exhaust system back pressure is high, if fully closes a bleed valve in the transducer; when the PCM de-energizes the solenoid and back pressure closes the transducer bleed valve, vacuum is ported

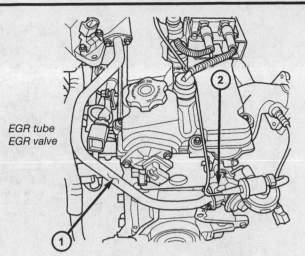

1 EGR tube
2 EGR valve

7.2b EGR valve mounted on the 2.4L engine (2001 and later models)

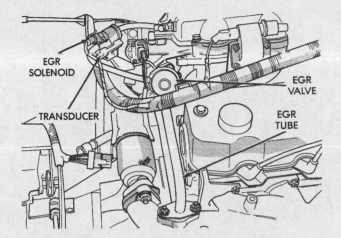

7.2c Exhaust Gas Recirculation (EGR) component locations - 3.0L V6 engine

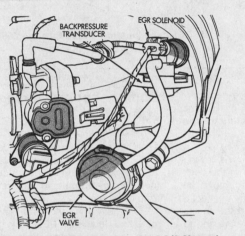

7.2d EGR valve mounted on the 3.3/3.8L engine (2000 and earlier models)

7.2e EGR valve (lower arrow) and tube connection (upper arrow) on 2001 and later models

to the transducer to operate the EGR valve. Varying the strength of the vacuum applied to the EGR valve changes the amount of EGR supplied to the engine intake, which is exhaust gas recirculation. There is no EGR at idle, and operates at all coolant temperatures above 60 degrees F.

Check

Refer to illustration 7.6

3   Start the engine and warm it to its normal operating temperature.

4   Check the condition of all the EGR system hoses and tubes for leaks, cracks, kinks or hardening of the rubber hoses. Make sure all the hoses are intact before proceeding with the EGR check.

5   Check the underhood vacuum schematic for the correct EGR system hose routing. Reroute the hoses if necessary.

6   Detach the vacuum hose from the EGR valve diaphragm (top vacuum hose) and attach a hand-held vacuum pump to the valve **(see illustration)**.

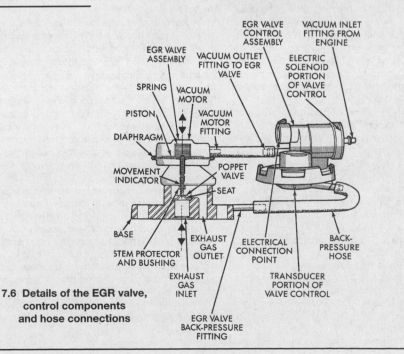

7.6 Details of the EGR valve, control components and hose connections

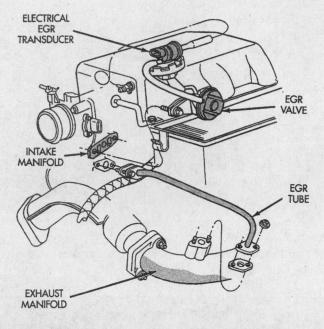

7.18a EGR tube installation details - 3.0L V6 engine

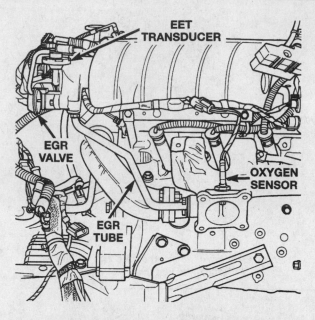

7.18b EGR tube location - 1996 through 2000
3.3L and 3.8L V6 engines

7   Start the engine and apply 5 in-Hg vacuum to the EGR valve. With the engine at idle speed, the idle speed should drop considerably or even stall as vacuum is applied. This indicates that the EGR system is operating properly.

8   If the engine speed does not change, this indicates a possible faulty EGR valve, blocked or plugged EGR tube or passages in the intake and exhaust manifolds that may be plugged with carbon.

9   Apply vacuum to the EGR valve and observe the stem on the EGR valve for movement. If the valve opens and closes correctly and the engine does not stall, check the passages.

10   Install a vacuum gauge into the EGR Transducer vacuum line **(see illustration 7.6)**, apply 15 in-Hg vacuum and observe the pump gauge reading. If the gauge reading drops, the diaphragm in the EGR valve is defective.

11   With the EGR valve operating properly or replaced if found defective above, disconnect the small rubber hose on the back pressure fitting at the base of the EGR valve **(see illustration 7.6)**. Remove the air cleaner housing from the engine (see Chapter 4).

12   Using compressed air and a nozzle with a rubber tip, apply approximately 50 psi of regulated air to the metal back pressure fitting on the EGR valve.

13   By hand, open the throttle to wide open. Air should not be heard coming from the intake manifold. If air is heard, the poppet valve at the base of the EGR valve is leaking. Replace the EGR valve. **Note:** *If the EGR valve is severely plugged with carbon deposits, do not attempt to scrape them out. Replace the unit.*

14   Check that the EGR valve diaphragm is not leaking by connecting a hand-held vacuum pump at the back pressure fitting at the bottom of the EGR valve **(see illustration 7.6)**. Apply 10 in-Hg vacuum; if the vacuum leaks, replace the EGR valve.

15   Check that the engine vacuum is flowing from the inlet to the outlet side of the back pressure transducer valve. First, remove the vacuum hose from the engine and connect a vacuum gauge to this hose. Start the engine and bring it to operating temperature and to approximately 1500 rpm. Check for steady engine vacuum; if no vacuum is present, repair the vacuum line. Reconnect the hose to the solenoid valve.

16   Next, disconnect the back pressure solenoid outlet hose which connects to the EGR diaphragm. Connect a vacuum gauge to the outlet fitting on the back pressure solenoid **(see illustration 7.6)**. Disconnect the back pressure solenoid electrical connector. Start the engine and bring it to operating temperature. Hold at 2,000 rpm and check for full engine manifold vacuum. It may be necessary to build exhaust system back pressure for this test; do this by wearing thick leather gloves and partially covering the tailpipe while observing the vacuum gauge. Do not cover the tailpipe for more than one or two second's time. Full engine (manifold) vacuum should be observed. **Note:** *At idle speed, it is normal for the vacuum gauge reading to be erratic.* Replace the back pressure transducer assembly if full manifold vacuum is not measured at the back pressure solenoid valve outlet fitting (the fitting connecting the to the EGR diaphragm) and if vacuum was present at the vacuum inlet fitting (the fitting connecting to the engine vacuum).

Component replacement

EGR valve

Refer to illustrations 7.18a and 7.18b

17   Disconnect the electrical connector for the EGR valve back pressure solenoid.

18   Remove the EGR tube mounting bolts **(see illustrations)** and separate the tube from the engine.

19   Remove the nuts that secure the EGR valve and detach the EGR valve. Lift the EGR valve and the back pressure solenoid valve out as a single unit.

20   Clean the mating surfaces of the EGR valve and adapter.

21   Install the EGR valve, using a new gasket. Tighten the nuts securely.

22   Connect the electrical connector to the EGR back pressure solenoid.

EET control solenoid

23   Disconnect the electrical connector to the back pressure solenoid.

24   Disconnect the vacuum hoses from the back pressure solenoid to the EGR valve.

25   Lift the back pressure solenoid from the engine compartment.

26   Installation is the reverse of removal.

---

8   Evaporative Emissions Control (EVAP) system

General description

Refer to illustrations 8.5a through 8.5e and 8.6

1   The fuel evaporative emissions control system absorbs fuel vapors and, during engine operation, releases them into the engine intake where they mix with the incoming air-fuel mixture.

8.5a Location of the EVAP canister under the vehicle body (1996 through 2000 models)

8.5b Location of the front EVAP canister . . .

2   The evaporative system employs a canister filled with activated charcoal to absorb fuel vapors. When fuel evaporates in the fuel tank, vapors pass through vent hoses or tubes to the evaporative canister.

3   The fuel filler cap is fitted with a relief valve as a safety device. The valve vents fuel vapors to the atmosphere if the evaporative control system fails.

4   Another fuel cut-off valve (fuel tank rollover valve), mounted on the fuel tank, regulates fuel vapor flow from the fuel tank to the charcoal canister, based on the pressure or vacuum caused by temperature changes.

5   Fuel vapor is carried by vent hoses to the charcoal canister under the passenger compartment **(see illustrations)**. The activated charcoal in the canister absorbs and stores these vapors The canister temporarily holds the vapors, and during engine operation, the PCM ports intake manifold vacuum to draw vapors into the intake throttle body to burn the vapors as fuel. The system controls vapor flow with a purge solenoid which regulates the flow rate of vapor to the engine. When the engine is running and warmed to a preset temperature, a duty cycle EVAP purge

8.5c . . . and the rear EVAP canister under the driver's seat (2001 and later models)

solenoid or proportional surge solenoid **(see illustrations)**, allows a purge control diaphragm valve in the charcoal canister to be opened by intake manifold vacuum. Fuel vapors from the canister are then drawn through the purge control diaphragm valve by intake manifold vacuum. During cold running conditions and hot start time delay, the

PCM does not energize the solenoid (NO PURGING VAPORS). After the engine has warmed up to the correct operating temperatures the PCM purges the vapors into the throttle body according to the running conditions of the engine. The PCM will cycle (ON then OFF) the purge control solenoid about 5 to 10 times per second. The flow rate will be

8.5d The canister duty cycle purge control valve - located in the engine compartment

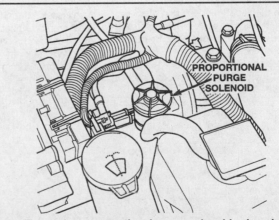

8.5e The canister proportional purge solenoid valve - located in the engine compartment

controlled by the pulse width or length of time the solenoid is allowed to be energized

6   A leak detection pump, located under the engine cradle near the steering gear **(see illustration)**, automatically detects EVAP system leaks. When the engine is started and is cold, the pump pressurizes the EVAP system temporarily and if there is a leak, the pump will flow at a flowrate determined by the size of the leak, which the PCM pump monitor compares to the required detection limit. If there is a leak, the PCM will set a DTC trouble code.

Check

Note: *The evaporative control system, like all emission control systems, is protected by a Federally-mandated extended warranty. The EVAP system probably won't fail during the service life of the vehicle; however, if it does, the hoses or charcoal canister are usually to blame.*

7   Always check the hoses first. A disconnected, damaged or missing hose is the most likely cause of a malfunctioning EVAP system. Refer to the Vacuum Hose Routing Diagram (attached to the radiator support) to determine whether the hoses are correctly routed and attached. Repair any damaged hoses or replace any missing hoses as necessary.

8   Disconnect the vacuum hose from the purge control diaphragm valve (located on the intake manifold) and connect a vacuum gauge to the hose. Start the engine and allow it to idle. There should be NO vacuum present with the engine cold. If vacuum is present, have the fuel tank rollover valve tested by a dealer or repair shop.

9   Warm the engine up to normal operating temperature. There should be vacuum present with the engine hot.

10   An OBD II SCAN tool will be required for a complete diagnosis of the EVAP system, have the system checked at a dealership service department or other properly equipped repair facility.

Component replacement

EVAP Purge Solenoid

11   Detach the vacuum hoses and electrical connectors from the purge solenoid and remove the purge solenoid and its rubber boot from the bracket.

12   Install the new purge solenoid with the word TOP upwards. The solenoid will not operate properly unless it is installed correctly. Reconnect the electrical connectors, vacuum hoses, and rubber boot.

8.6 The EVAP system leak detection pump is located under the engine cradle

Fuel tank rollover valve

13   Two rollover valves are located on the fuel tank. On these vehicles, the rollover valves are not serviceable. The fuel tank must be removed and replaced with a new tank in the event that the rollover valves require servicing. Remove and replace the fuel tank (see Chapter 4).

9   Catalytic converter

Note: *Because of a Federally mandated extended warranty which covers emissions-related components such as the catalytic converter, check with a dealer service department before replacing the converter at your own expense.*

General description

1   The catalytic converter (see Chapter 4) is an emission control device added to the exhaust system to reduce pollutants from the exhaust gas stream. The three-way catalyst lowers the levels of oxides of nitrogen (NOx) as well as hydrocarbons (HC) and carbon monoxide (CO).

Check

2   The test equipment for a catalytic converter is expensive and highly sophisticated. If you suspect that the converter on your vehicle is malfunctioning, take it to a dealer or authorized emissions inspection facility for diagnosis and repair.

3   Whenever the vehicle is raised for servicing of underbody components, check the converter for leaks, corrosion, dents and other damage. Check the welds/flange bolts that attach the front and rear ends of the converter to the exhaust system. If damage is discov-

ered, the converter should be replaced.

4   Although catalytic converters don't fail often, they can become plugged. The easiest way to check for a restricted converter is to use a vacuum gauge to diagnose the effect of a blocked exhaust on intake vacuum.

a) *Open the throttle until the engine speed is about 2000 rpm.*

b) *Release the throttle quickly.*

c) *If there is no restriction, the gauge will quickly drop to not more than 2 in-Hg or more above its normal reading.*

d) *If the gauge does not show 5 in-Hg or more above its normal reading, or seems to momentarily hover around its highest reading for a moment before it returns, the exhaust system, or the converter, is plugged (or an exhaust pipe is bent or dented, or the core inside the muffler has shifted).*

5   The dual oxygen sensor system monitors the efficiency of the catalytic converter by continuously monitoring the oxygen storage capacity of the catalyst and then calculating its efficiency. The upstream oxygen sensor detects the amount of oxygen in the exhaust gas ahead of the catalytic converter, while the downstream oxygen sensor is affected as the catalytic converter chemical reaction changes as oxygen content from a lean or rich engine condition occurs. The system is monitored so that when catalyst efficiency deteriorates and exhaust emissions increase to the limit, the MIL (Check Engine light) will be illuminated. Take the vehicle to the dealer or repair shop for repair, or replace the catalytic converter.

Replacement

6   Refer to the exhaust system removal and installation in Chapter 4.

Chapter 7
Automatic transaxle

Contents

	Section
Automatic transaxle - removal and installation	8
Automatic transaxle band adjustment (3-speed 31TH transaxle)	9
Diagnosis - general	2
Fluid and filter change	See Chapter 1
Fluid level check	See Chapter 1
General information	1
Neutral start/back-up light switch - check and replacement	7
Oil seal - replacement	3
Shift cable - check and adjustment	5
Transaxle throttle cable (3-speed 31TH transaxle) - check and adjustment	6
Transaxle mount - check and replacement	4

Specifications

Fluid type and capacity	See Chapter 1
Band adjustment (3-speed 31TH transaxle)	
Kickdown (backed off from 72 in-lbs)	2-1/4 turns
Low-reverse (backed off from 41 in-lbs)	3-1/2 turns

Torque specifications

Ft-lbs (unless otherwise indicated)

Driveplate-to-torque converter bolts	
31TH 3-speed	50
41TE 4-speed	55
Driveplate-to-crankshaft bolts	
31TH 3-speed	55
41TE 4-speed	70
Neutral start switch	24
Throttle cable-to-transaxle case bolt (31TH)	105 in-lbs
Manual cable-to-transaxle case bolt (31TH)	21
Manual control lever screw (31TH)	105 inch-lbs
Throttle cable adjustment swivel lock screw (31TH)	100 inch-lbs
Transaxle to engine block bolt (31TH)	70
Output speed sensor (41TE)	20
Solenoid assembly to case (41TE)	105 inch-lbs
Gearshift cable adjustment screw	70 inch-lbs
Kickdown band adjusting screw locknut	35
Low-reverse band adjusting screw locknut	10

1   General information

All vehicles covered in this manual come equipped with a 3-speed or 4-speed automatic transaxles. The compact front-wheel-drive system transaxle consists of a torque converter attached to the crankshaft through a driveplate, an automatic transmission, and a differential in one unit.

The 3-speed 31TH automatic transaxle includes the torque converter, transaxle area, and differential in an aluminum housing. The differential sump is common with the transaxle sump and separate filling of the differential is not possible; automatic transmission fluid only is used (see Chapter 1). The torque converter is attached to the crankshaft by a flexible driveplate. The torque converter is cooled by circulating transaxle fluid through a remote cooler located in the radiator side tank and/or an oil-to-air heat exchanger. The transaxle fluid is filtered by an internal filter on the valve body. The transaxle is conventional in that it uses hydraulic clutches to shift a planetary geartrain. A torque converter clutch is standard, activated in drive gear by an electric solenoid actuated by the Powertrain Control Module (PCM)

The 4-speed 41TE is a fully-adaptive controlled automatic transaxle and is similar to the above in construction except for the controls, bands, the number and types of clutches and accumulators. The 41TE adaptive controls are based on real-time feedback sensor information from various sensors and signals from the PCM and the Transmission Control Module (TCM). The TCM is located underhood on the passenger side of the engine compartment. Three pressure switches indicate solenoid application, two speed sensors read input (torque converter) speed and output (parking sprag) speed. There is also a manual shift lever position switch, and engine speed, throttle position, temperature, and other conditions are also read from the engine sensors and from the PCM. The 41TE is identified by an identification code on the transaxle case near the solenoid assembly, which control the shift clutches. The adaptive controls electronically read and store ("learn") information for clutching element release and engagement to be more precise and smooth as driving speed changes, compensating for changes in engine or transmission torque (below 16 miles per hour), and relearns these as the unit wears. Onboard diagnostics (OBD II) is a feature of the 41TE transaxle, and faults or problems can be read out as described in Chapter 6 (Diagnostic Trouble Code 45).

Due to the complexity of the automatic transaxles and the need for special equipment and expertise to perform most service operations, this Chapter contains only general diagnosis, seal replacement, adjustments and removal and installation procedures.

If the transaxle requires major work or a trouble code is detected for the transaxle (see Chapter 6), it should be left to a dealer service department or an automatic transmission repair shop.

2   Diagnosis - general

Note: *Automatic transaxle malfunctions may be caused by five general conditions: Poor engine performance, improper adjustments, hydraulic-mechanical, or electronic malfunctions. Diagnosis of these problems should always begin with a check of the easily repaired items: fluid level and condition (see Chapter 1), shift linkage adjustment and throttle cable adjustment (see Sections 5 and 6). Next, perform a road test to determine if the problem has been corrected or if more diagnosis is necessary. If the problem persists after the preliminary tests and corrections are completed, additional diagnosis should be done by a dealer service department or transmission repair shop. Refer to the Troubleshooting Section at the front of this manual for transaxle problem diagnosis or Chapter 6 if a trouble code is readout from the MIL (Malfunction Indicator Light) on the dashboard.*

Preliminary checks

1   Drive the vehicle to warm the transaxle to normal operating temperature. For vehicles with the 4-speed 41TE transaxle, see a dealer or transmission repair shop if a MIL light is ON and a trouble code 45 is detected (see Chapter 6).
2   Check the fluid level as described in Chapter 1:

a) *If the fluid level is unusually low, add enough to bring the level within the designated area on the dipstick, then check for external leaks.*
b) *If the fluid level is abnormally high, drain off the excess, then check the drained fluid for contamination by coolant. The presence of engine coolant in the automatic transmission fluid indicates that a failure has occurred in the internal radiator walls that separate the coolant from the transmission fluid (see Chapter 3).*
c) *If the fluid is foaming, drain it and refill the transaxle, then check for coolant in the fluid or a high fluid level.*

3   Check the engine idle speed. **Note:** *If the engine is malfunctioning, don't proceed with the preliminary checks until it has been repaired and runs normally.*
4   Check the throttle valve cable on 3-speed 31TH model transaxles for freedom of movement. Adjust it if necessary (see Section 6). **Note:** *The throttle valve cable may function properly when the engine is off and cold, but may malfunction once the engine is hot. Check it cold and at normal engine operating temperature.*
5   Inspect the shift linkage (see Section 5). Make sure it is properly adjusted and operates smoothly.

Fluid leak diagnosis

6   Most fluid leaks are easy to locate visually. Repair usually consist of replacing a seal or gasket. If a leak is difficult to find, the following procedure may help.
7   Identify the fluid. Make sure it's transmission fluid and not engine oil or brake fluid (automatic transmission fluid is a deep red color).
8   Try to pinpoint the source of the leak. Drive the vehicle several miles, then park it over a large sheet of cardboard. After a minute or two you should be able to locate the leak by determining the source of the fluid dripping onto the cardboard.
9   Make a careful visual inspection of the suspected component and the areas immediately around it. Pay particular attention to gasket mating surfaces. A mirror is often helpful for finding leaks in areas that are hard to see.
10   If the leak still can't be found, clean the suspected area thoroughly with a degreaser or solvent, then dry it.
11   Drive the vehicle for several miles at normal operating temperature and varying speeds. After driving the vehicle, visually inspect the suspected component again.
12   Once the leak has been located, the cause must be determined before it can be properly repaired. If a gasket is replaced but the sealing flange is bent, the new gasket won't stop the leak. The bent flange must be straightened.
13   Before attempting to repair a leak, check to make sure the following conditions are corrected or they may cause another leak. **Note:** *Some of the following conditions cannot be fixed without highly specialized tools and expertise. Such problems must be referred to a transmission shop or a dealer service department.*

Gasket leaks

14   Check the pan periodically. Make sure the bolts are all in place (and none are missing) and tight, the gasket is good condition and the pan is flat (dents in the pan may indicate damage to the valve body inside).
15   If the pan gasket is leaking, the fluid level or the fluid pressure may be too high, the vent may be plugged, the pan bolts may be too tight, the pan sealing flange may be warped, the sealing surface of the transaxle housing may be damaged, the gasket may be damaged or the transaxle casting may be cracked or porous. If sealant is used in place of a gasket, it may be the wrong sealant.

Seal leaks

16   If a transaxle seal is leaking, the fluid level or pressure may be too high, the vent may be plugged (these models are vented through the hollow dipstick), the seal bore may be damaged, the seal itself may be damaged or improperly installed, the surface of the shaft protruding through the seal may be damaged or a loose bearing may be causing excessive shaft movement. Check for a leak

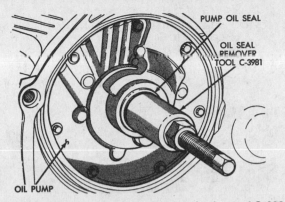

3.3 Transaxle housing oil pump seal removal using tool C-3981-B

3.4 Transaxle oil pump seal installation using tools C-4171 and C-4193

at the oil pump seal by removing the torque converter inspection plate and looking for trails of fluid or a puddle of fluid in the torque converter housing.

17 Make sure the dipstick tube seal is in good condition and the tube is properly seated. Periodically check the area around the speedometer gear or sensor for leakage. If transmission fluid is evident, check the O-ring for damage. Also inspect the side gear shaft oil seals for leakage.

Case leaks

18 If the case itself appears to be leaking, the casting is porous and will have to be repaired or replaced.

19 Make sure the oil cooler hose fittings are tight and in good condition.

Fluid comes out of the filler opening

20 If this condition occurs, the transaxle is overfilled, there is coolant in the fluid, the case is porous, the dipstick is incorrect, the vent is plugged or the drain back holes are plugged.

3 Oil seal - replacement

Refer to illustrations 3.3, 3.4, 3.8 and 3.9

1 **Note:** *If your vehicle has been sitting for* *any length of time (six months or longer), the transaxle oil pump seal may leak. The leaking seal(s) will have to be replaced, as the manufacturer does not recommend the use of any fluid additives or sealers.*

Oil pump seal

Note: *The transaxle oil pump (front) seal can be replaced without removing the oil pump.*

2 To replace the transaxle oil pump seal, the transaxle and torque converter will have to be removed. Refer to Section 8 for transaxle removal.

3 If available, use the factory seal removal tool (number C-3981-B). Screw the seal remover into the seal, then tighten the screw to draw the seal out **(see illustration)**. If the factory tool is not available, use a hook-type seal removal tool (available from automotive tool suppliers). If a hook-type tool is not available, try using a screwdriver or other prying tool to pry the seal up, moving around the seal. Be careful not to scratch the input shaft or the seal bore.

4 If available, use the factory tools (numbers C-4193 [the installer] and C-4171 [the handle]) to install the new seal. Place the seal in the opening (lip side facing in), then drive the seal in until it bottoms in the seal bore **(see illustration)**. If the factory tools are not available, use a small block of wood and a hammer to carefully tap the seal into place,

tapping all the way around the seal until it bottoms in the seal bore.

Extension housing (right side driveaxle) seal

Note: *Replacing the left side driveaxle oil seal requires removing the differential bearing retainer (a special tool is needed) and pressing the new seal into the retainer with an arbor press. This procedure is beyond the scope of the home mechanic.*

5 The extension housing seal is located in the extension housing, which is bolted to the right side of the transaxle.

6 Raise the vehicle and support it securely on jackstands.

7 Remove the right driveaxle (see Chapter 8).

8 Using a screwdriver or other prying tool, pry the seal out of the extension housing **(see illustration)**.

9 Coat the lip and outside diameter of the new seal with transmission fluid. Place the new seal over the opening (lip side facing in). Use a socket the same size as the outside diameter of the seal or a wood block and carefully tap the socket or wood with a hammer, driving the seal into place. If available, you should use the factory tool (numbers L-4520 and C-4171 handle). With these tools drive the new seal into the extension housing **(see illustration)**.

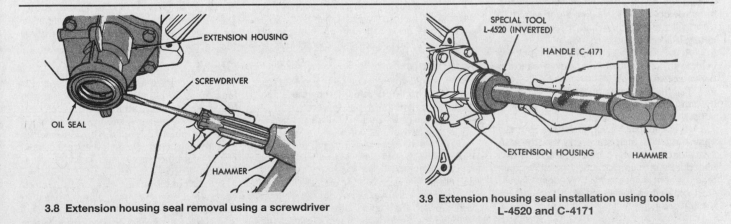

3.8 Extension housing seal removal using a screwdriver

3.9 Extension housing seal installation using tools L-4520 and C-4171

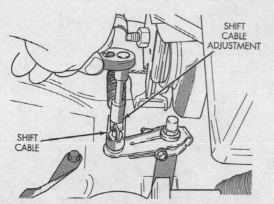

5.3 Shift linkage adjustment - 3-speed and 4-speed automatic transaxles

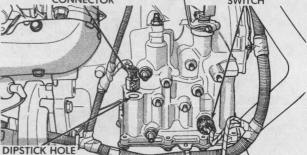

7.1a Neutral start/back-up light switch location - 3-speed automatic transaxle

4   Transaxle mount - check and replacement

This procedure is covered with the *Engine mounts - check and replacement procedures in Chapter 2.*

5   Shift cable - check and adjustment

Check

1   Check the operation of the transaxle in each shift lever position (try to start the engine in each position - the starter should operate in the Park and Neutral positions only). Also, place the shift lever in Park position and remove the ignition key to confirm that the shift lever is in the gated Park (P) position. If operation is not as described, try adjusting the shift cable, as described below. If operation still is not correct, check the neutral start switch (see Section 7).

Adjustment

Refer to illustration 5.3

2   With the vehicle level, set the parking brake. Place the shift lever in Park position and remove the ignition key.

3   Working in the engine compartment, loosen the cable adjustment screw on the transaxle operating lever **(see illustration)**.

4   Pull the shift lever all the way to the detent (Park position) by hand.

5   Release the parking brake, then rock the vehicle to assure it is Park lock. Reset the parking brake.

6   Tighten the cable adjustment screw to the torque listed in this Chapter's Specifications.

7   Check the shift lever and try to start the engine in all the shift stops and that the shift indicator displays the proper gears. If the display does not read correctly, gearshift cable readjustment is necessary. The engine should start only when the lever is in the Park or Neutral position.

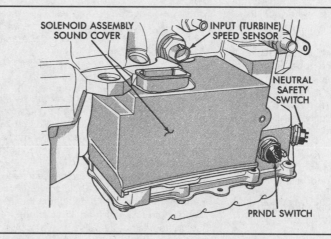

7.1b Neutral start/ back-up light switch location - 4-speed automatic transaxle

6   Transaxle throttle cable (3-speed 31TH transaxle) - check and adjustment

Note: *The 4-speed 41TE transaxle does not have a transaxle throttle cable.*

Check

1   The transaxle throttle pressure cable adjustment is important to the proper operation of the transaxle. If the adjustment is long, the transaxle will shift early. If the adjustment is too short, the transaxle will shift late.

2   The transaxle throttle cable controls a valve in the transaxle which governs the shift quality and speed. If shifting is harsh or erratic, the throttle cable should be adjusted.

Adjustment

3   The adjustment must be made with the engine at normal operating temperature and the idle speed of the engine correct.

4   Loosen the transaxle throttle cable adjustment swivel lock screw.

5   To ensure proper adjustment, the swivel must be free to slide back-and-forth on the flat end of the throttle rod. If necessary, remove it and clean the slot and sliding surfaces.

6   Hold the transaxle throttle cable lever firmly toward the engine, against its internal stop, to the limit of its travel. Tighten the

swivel lock screw to the torque listed in this Chapter's Specifications.

7   The adjustment is finished and the linkage backlash was automatically removed by the preload spring.

8   Lubricate the sliding parts if required.

7   Neutral start/back-up light switch - check and replacement

Refer to illustrations 7.1a, 7.1b and 7.7
Note: *On vehicles equipped with the 4-speed 41TE transaxle, no switch is installed. A Transaxle Range Sensor (TRS) is used instead. The TRS requires factory service equipment for service. We recommend professional assistance regarding this component.*

Check

1   The neutral start/back-up light switch is located at the lower front edge of the transaxle **(see illustrations)**. The switch controls the back-up lights and the starting of the engine in Park and Neutral. The center terminal of the switch grounds the starter solenoid circuit when the transaxle is in Park or Neutral, allowing the engine to start.

2   Prior to checking the neutral start/back-up light switch, make sure the gearshift linkage is properly adjusted (see Section 5).

3   Unplug the switch connector and use an

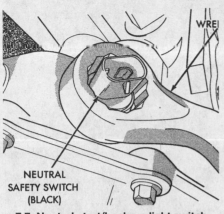

7.7 Neutral start/back-up light switch removal - 4-speed automatic transaxle

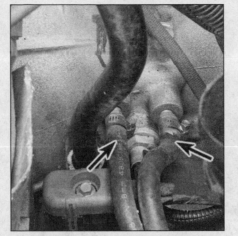

8.2 Transmission cooler line connections at the transaxle - typical

8.4 Removal of the transaxle shift cable from the transaxle manual valve lever

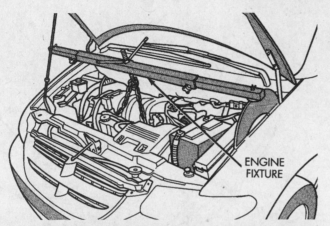

8.5 The weight of the engine must be supported with the special fixture as the transaxle is removed - an alternate support method is to use a floor jack to support the engine

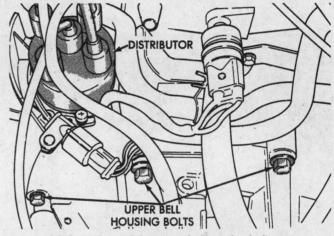

8.6 Locations of the upper bellhousing bolts

ohmmeter to check for continuity between the center terminal and the case. Continuity should exist only when the transaxle is in Park or Neutral.

4   Check for continuity between the two outer terminals. Continuity should exist only when the transaxle is in Reverse. No continuity should exist between either outer terminal and the case.

5   If the neutral switch fails any of the tests, replace it with a new one.

Replacement

6   Position a drain pan under the neutral switch to catch the fluid released when the neutral switch is removed. If not already done, unplug the electrical connector from the neutral switch.

7   Unscrew the neutral start safety switch from the transaxle, using a box-end wrench to avoid damage to the switch housing (see illustration)

8   Move the shift lever from Park to Neutral while checking that the neutral switch operating fingers are centered in the opening.

9   Install the new neutral switch with a new

seal, tighten it to the torque listed in this Chapter's Specifications. Repeat the checks on the new neutral switch and plug in the electrical connector.

10   Check the fluid level and add fluid as required (see Chapter 1).

---

8   Automatic transaxle - removal and installation

Refer to illustrations 8.2, 8.4, 8.5, 8.6, 8.7, 8.10, 8.13, 8.16, 8.17a, 8.17b and 8.18
Warning: *Wait until the engine is completely cool before beginning this procedure.*

Removal

Note: *Transaxle removal does not require engine removal. The transaxle and torque converter must be removed as an assembly; otherwise, the torque converter driveplate, pump bushing or soil seal may be damaged. The driveplate will not support the transaxle weight, so be sure to support the transaxle during removal.*

1   Disconnect the cable from the negative terminal of the battery. If you're working on a model with a 3.0L V6 engine, drain the engine coolant.

2   Remove the oil cooler lines (see illustration). Plug the lines to prevent the entry of dirt or foreign material. If equipped with the 3.0L V6 engine, remove the coolant return extension from above the bell housing.

3   Remove the air cleaner and air cleaner hoses/duct. On the 4-speed model 41TE, remove the heater tube mounting bolt from the transaxle.

4   Remove the transaxle shift cable (see illustration). Move the cables out of the way. Remove the transaxle dipstick and dipstick tube. On 3-speed model 31TH, disconnect the transaxle throttle cable.

5   Support the engine from above with the special fixture (see illustration), or from below with a jack (place a block of wood between the jack and the engine oil pan to prevent damage).

6   Remove the upper bellhousing bolts (see illustration).

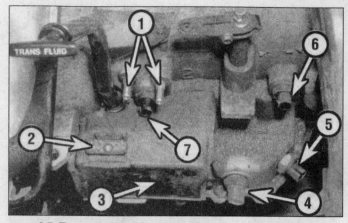

8.7 Transaxle left side - 4-speed transaxle model 41TE

1   *Transaxle cooler lines*
2   *Electrical connector*
3   *Solenoid assembly cover*
4   *PRNDL switch*

5   *Neutral start/back-up light switch*
6   *Output speed sensor*
7   *Input turbine speed sensor*

8.10 Front engine mount insulator and bracket

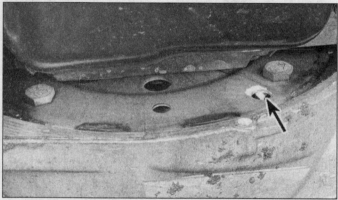

8.13 Be sure to mark the torque converter and driveplate so they can be reattached in the same position

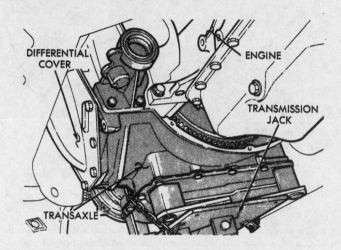

8.16 Transaxle jack positioning (note the safety chain)

7   Unplug all electrical connectors (**see illustration**) (see Section 7).

8   Raise the vehicle and support it securely on jackstands. **Note:** *If the engine is supported from below as described in Step 5 above, and you are not using the top-mounted support fixture shown in illustration 8.5, then make sure that the engine is always supported as you raise the vehicle.*

9   Drain the transaxle fluid (see Chapter 1).

10 On the 3-speed model 31TH, remove rear engine mount bracket and the rear engine mount shield and the left engine mount through-bolt and left engine mount (see Chapter 2). On 4-speed model 41TE, remove the front engine mount insulator and bracket (**see illustration**), remove the rear engine mount bolt from the top, and remove the rear engine mount shield screw (see Chapter 2).

11 Remove bolts securing the exhaust flex joint to the exhaust manifold.

12 Remove the torque converter cover.

13 Mark the torque converter and drive-plate so they can be reinstalled in the same position (**see illustration**). Rotate the engine clockwise by turning the crankshaft with a large wrench on the crankshaft pulley bolt and remove the torque converter-to-drive-plate bolts.

14 Remove the starter motor (see Chapter 5). **Note:** *Do not allow the starter to hang from the battery cable.*

15 Remove the tires, remove the front wheel hub nuts, and remove both driveaxles (see Chapter 8).

16 Support the transaxle with a jack - preferably a special jack made for this purpose. Safety chains will help steady the transaxle on the jack (**see illustration**).

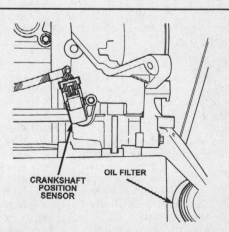

8.17a Four-cylinder engine crankshaft position sensor location - remove the sensor before transaxle removal

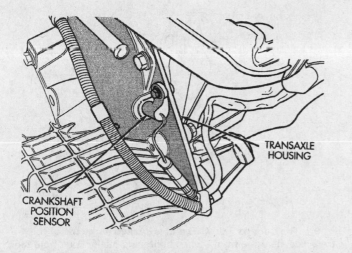

8.17b V6 engine crankshaft position sensor location - remove the sensor before transaxle removal

8.18 Use a large screwdriver to pry the transaxle away from the engine

17   Remove the lower bell housing bolts securing the transaxle to the engine. On 4-speed model 41TE, remove the crankshaft position sensor from the bell housing before transmission removal **(see illustrations)**.

18   Move the transaxle back to disengage it from the engine block dowel pins. You may have to use a prybar or a large screwdriver to pry the transaxle from the engine **(see illustration)**. On the 3-speed model 31TH, disengage the torque converter hub from the end of the crankshaft and attach a small C-clamp to the edge of the bell housing to hold the torque converter in place during transaxle removal. **Note:** *Secure the torque converter to the transaxle with wire from two bolt holes 180-degrees apart so it won't fall out during removal.*

19   Lower the transaxle from the vehicle. Remove the torque converter from the transaxle.

Installation

20   Prior to installation, be sure to align the transmission pump inner gear pilot flats with the torque converter impeller hub flats; this will ensure that the torque converter hub is securely engaged in the transmission pump.

21   With the transaxle secured to the jack and the torque converter secured to the transaxle, raise it into position.

22   Turn the torque converter to line up with the holes in the driveplate. Line up the marks you made on the torque converter and driveplate.

23   Move the transaxle forward carefully until the dowel pins and transaxle housing are engaged.

24   Install the transaxle housing-to-engine bolts. Tighten them securely.

25   Install the torque converter-to-driveplate bolts. Tighten the bolts to the torque listed in this Chapter's Specifications.

26   Install the engine mounts and bracket.

Tighten the engine mount bolts and nuts to the torque listed in Chapter 2 Specifications.

27   Remove the jack supporting the transaxle.

28   Install the starter motor (see Chapter 5).

29   Attach the transaxle shift and throttle cables.

30   Connect all the electrical connectors.

31   Install the torque converter cover.

32   Install the driveaxles (see Chapter 8).

33   Connect the exhaust flex connector.

34   Lower the vehicle. Check the wheel lug nut torque (see Chapter 1).

35   Adjust the shift cable (see Section 5).

36   Fill the transaxle with transmission fluid (see Chapter 1), run the vehicle and check for leaks.

Torque converter break-in - 4-speed model 41TE

Refer to illustrations 8.39 and 8.40

Note: *On 4-speed model 41TE, if the torque converter was replaced with a new unit, per-*

form the following torque converter clutch break-in procedure below to properly program and reset the Transmission Control Module (TCM). Failure to perform this step may cause transaxle shudder when driving.

37   The current trouble code (DTC) will have to be reset to the start of break-in by a dealer or transmission service shop using a DRB scan tool and scan tool cartridge to read or reset the status.

38   If a new TCM is installed in the vehicle, no modification of the break-in DTC is needed. However, if a new TCM is installed, the dealer or transmission repair shop will be required to reset the Pinion Factor for proper speedometer operation.

39   On 1996 through 2000 models to remove the TCM, disconnect the cable from the negative terminal of the battery, remove the TCM connector by unbolting the connector **(see illustration, lower arrow)**, and unscrewing the TCM mounting screws **(see illustration, upper arrow)**. Installation is the reverse of removal.

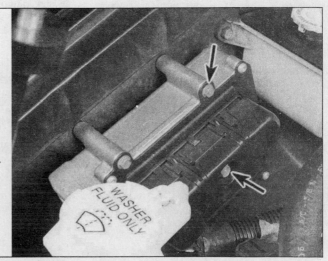

8.39 Transmission Control Module (TCM) located underhood at the right front fender - remove the electrical connector bolt (lower arrow) and the TCM mounting screws (upper arrow) (1996 through 2000 models)

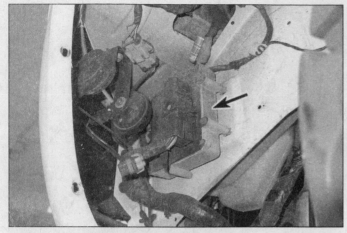

8.40 On 2001 and later models, the Transmission Control Module (TCM) is located behind the inner splash shield in the front left side wheel well - disconnect the electrical cable and remove the three screws

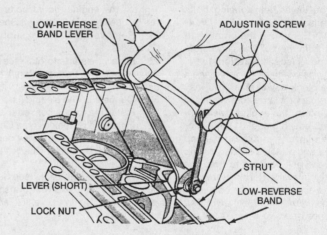

9.1 The front (kickdown) band is located at the top of the transaxle, near the front - when tightening the locknut, hold the adjustment screw so it can't move, then tighten the nut

40   On 2001 and later models to remove the TCM, disconnect the cable from the negative terminal of the battery, remove the left side front wheel and pull back the inner splash shield. Disconnect the connector and remove the three TCM mounting screws, then remove the TCM **(see illustration)**. Installation is the reverse of removal.

Transaxle Quick Learn - 4-speed automatic transaxle model 41TE

41   The quick learn procedure recalibrates the electronic transaxle system to provide the best transaxle operation. Quick Learn must be done by the dealer or transmission repair shop using the DRB scan tool and scan tool cartridge will be required to if the following procedures are performed:

a) *Transaxle replacement*
b) *TCM replacement*
c) *Solenoid replacement*
d) *Clutch plate and or seal replacement*
e) *Valve body replacement or repair*

9.6 The rear (low-reverse) band is located under the transaxle fluid pan, next to the valve body

9   Automatic transaxle band adjustment (3-speed 31TH transaxle)

Kickdown band (front)

Refer to illustration 9.1

1   To adjust the kickdown band, loosen the lock nut approximately 5 turns **(see illustration)**.

2   With the lock nut loose the adjusting screw should turn freely in the case.
3   Tighten the adjusting screw to 72 in-lbs then loosen it exactly 2-1/4 turns.
4   Hold the adjusting screw from turning while tightening the lock nut to 35 ft-lbs.

Low-reverse band (rear)

Refer to illustration 9.6

5   Remove the transaxle oil pan (see Chapter 1).

6   To adjust the low-reverse band, loosen the lock nut approximately 5 turns **(see illustration)**.
7   With the lock nut loose the adjusting screw should turn freely in the lever.
8   Tighten the adjusting screw to 41 in-lbs then loosen it exactly 3-1/2 turns.
9   Hold the adjusting screw from turning while tightening the lock nut to 10 ft-lbs.

Chapter 8   Driveaxles

Contents

	Section		Section
Driveaxle boot check	See Chapter 1	Driveaxle - removal and installation	2
Driveaxle boot replacement and CV joint inspection	3	Driveaxles - general information and inspection	1

Specifications

Torque specifications   Ft-lbs

Driveaxle hub nut	180
Wheel lug nuts	See Chapter 1

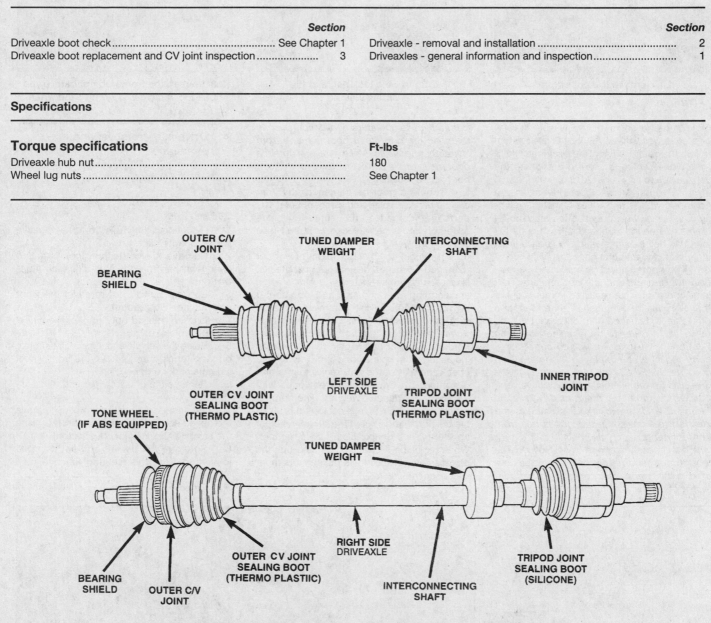

1.1 **The left driveaxle (above) and right driveaxle (below) assemblies**

1   Driveaxles - general information and inspection

Refer to illustration 1.1

1   Power is transmitted from the transaxle to the wheels through a pair of driveaxles **(see illustration)**. The inner end of each driveaxle is splined into its corresponding differential side gear inside the transaxle; the outer end of each driveaxle has a stub shaft that is splined to the front hub and bearing assembly and locked in place with a large nut and cotter pin combination.

2   The inner ends of the driveaxles are equipped with sliding tripod-type Constant Velocity (CV) joints, which are capable of both angular and axial motion. Each inner tripod CV joint assembly consists of a tripod-type bearing and a housing in which the joint is free to slide in-and-out as the driveaxle

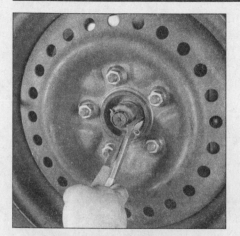

2.2a Remove the cotter pin . . .

2.2b . . . the lock nut, and the spring washer

2.3 Loosen the front hub nut before you raise the vehicle and remove the wheel

moves up-and-down with the wheel. On vehicles equipped with an Antilock Brake System (ABS), the outer CV joints are equipped with a tone wheel which is used to determine the vehicle speed for proper ABS operation.

3   The outer ends of the driveaxles are equipped with Rzeppo-type Constant Velocity (CV) joints, which permits the high movements of steering maneuvers. Each outer CV joint has ball bearings which run between an inner race and an outer cage.

4   The boots should be inspected periodically for damage and leaking lubricant. Torn joint boots must be replaced immediately or the joints will be damaged. If either boot of a driveaxle is damaged, that driveaxle must be removed in order to replace the boot (see Section 2). **Note 1:** *Some auto parts stores carry "split" type replacement boots, which can be installed without removing the driveaxle from the vehicle. This is convenient, but we recommend that the driveaxle be removed and the joint disassembled and cleaned to ensure that the joint is free from contaminants, such as moisture and dirt, which will accelerate joint wear.* **Note 2:** *The inner tripod joint boots on the vehicles covered in this manual are constructed from different materials: The left inner boot is made*

from a high-temperature application silicone material; the right inner boot is made from Hytrel thermoplastic. Make sure you obtain a boot made of the correct material for the joint boot you're replacing.

5   Should a boot be damaged, the joint can be disassembled and cleaned, but if any parts are damaged, the entire driveaxle assembly must be replaced as a unit (see Section 3).

6   The most common symptom of worn or damaged CV joints, besides lubricant leaks, is a clicking noise in turns, a clunk when accelerating after coasting and vibration at highway speeds. To check for wear in the CV joints and axleshafts, grasp each axle (one at a time) and rotate it in both directions while holding the joint housings, feeling for play indicating worn splines or sloppy joints. Also check the axleshafts for cracks, dents and distortion. The driveaxles are equipped with tuned rubber damper weights. The damper weight on the right side (if equipped) is a single clamp style damper. The damper weight on the left is a double clamp style damper. When replacing a driveaxle, be sure that the replacement driveaxle has the same damper weight as the original.

2   Driveaxle - removal and installation

Removal

Refer to illustrations 2.2a, 2.2b, 2.3, 2.7, 2.9, 2.10 and 2.11

1   Disconnect the cable from the negative terminal of the battery.

2   Remove the cotter pin, lock nut, and spring washer from the stub axle **(see illustrations)**.

3   Loosen (but do not remove) the front hub nut **(see illustration)**.

4   Loosen, but do not remove, the wheel lug nuts.

5   Raise the vehicle and support it securely on jackstands, then remove the front wheel lug nuts and the wheel.

6   Remove the brake caliper and disc (see Chapter 9).

7   If equipped with antilock brakes, remove the speed sensor cable routing bracket from the steering knuckle **(see illustration)**.

8   Separate the tie rod end and the ball joint stud from the steering knuckle (see Chapter 10).

9   Remove the hub nut and pull the steer-

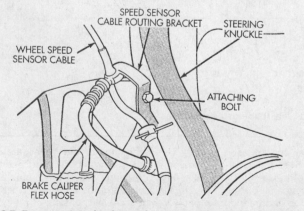

2.7 Remove the wheel speed sensor cable routing bracket

2.9 Pull the steering knuckle away from the outer CV joint

2.10 Using a large pry bar, pry the inner tripod CV joint out sharply to disengage the snap-ring from the differential gears inside the transaxle

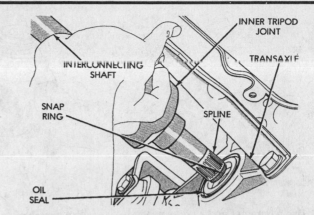

2.11 When withdrawing the inner tripod CV joint from the transaxle, be careful not to damage the oil seal with the splines

ing knuckle out and away from the outer CV joint of the driveaxle **(see illustration)**. Strike the end of the stub shaft with a soft-faced hammer to separate the splines from the hub and bearing assembly, if necessary.

10   Support the outer end of the driveaxle and insert a pry bar between the inner tripod CV joint and the transaxle case **(see illustration)**. Pry out sharply to disengage the inner tripod CV joint from the transaxle. Make sure you have a drain pan under the transaxle, as some oil will leak out.

11   Carefully withdraw the inner tripod CV joint from the transaxle **(see illustration)**. Do not let the spline or the snap-ring drag across the sealing lip of the driveaxle-to-transaxle oil seal. **Caution:** *The driveaxle acts as a bolt, when installed, that secures the front hub/bearing assembly. If the vehicle must be supported or moved with the driveaxle removed, a proper sized bolt and nut must be secured through the front hub. Tighten the bolt and nut to the torque listed in this Chapter's Specifications.*

Installation

11   Installation is the reverse of the removal procedure, noting the following additional points:

a) *Thoroughly clean the splines and bearing shield on the outer CV joint. This is very important, as the bearing shield protects the wheel bearings from water and contamination. Also clean the wheel bearing area of the steering knuckle.*

b) *Thoroughly clean the splines and oil seal sealing surface on the inner tripod CV joint. Apply an even bead of multi-purpose grease around the oil seal sealing surface of the tripod CV joint.*

c) *When installing the driveaxle, push it sharply in to seat the snap-ring on the tripod CV joint stub shaft into its groove in the differential gears inside the transaxle. Pull out sharply to ensure it's seated.*

d) *Tighten the driveaxle/hub nut to the torque listed in this Chapter's Specifications.*

e) *Install the wheel and lug nuts, lower the vehicle and tighten the lug nuts to the*

torque listed in the Chapter 1 Specifications.

f) *The steering knuckle-to-ball joint stud clamping bolt and nut should not be reused. A new clamping bolt and nut should always be used.*

---

3 Driveaxle boot replacement and CV joint inspection

Note 1: *If the CV joints or boots must be replaced, explore all options before beginning the job. Complete, rebuilt driveaxles may be available on an exchange basis, eliminating much time and work. Whichever route you choose to take, check on the cost and availability of parts before disassembling the vehicle.*
Note 2: *On 1997 and later models, the outer CV joint can not be removed from the axleshaft. These driveaxles must be serviced as a complete unit if the CV joint or boot fails.*
Note 3: *The inner tripod CV joint boots are constructed from different materials: The left boot is a high-temperature application silicone; the right boot is Hytrel thermoplastic. Make sure you obtain a boot of the correct material for the tripod CV joint boot you're replacing.*

1   Remove the driveaxle (see Section 2).
2   Mount the driveaxle in a vise with wood-

lined jaws (to prevent damage to the axleshaft). Check the CV joints for excessive play in the radial direction, which indicates worn parts. Check for smooth operation throughout the full range of motion for each CV joint. If a boot is torn, the recommended procedure is to disassemble the joint, clean the components and inspect for damage due to loss of lubrication and possible contamination by foreign matter. If the CV joint is in good condition, lubricate it with CV joint grease and install a new boot.

Inner CV joint

Disassembly

Refer to illustrations 3.4, 3.5, and 3.7
3   Cut the boot clamps with side-cutters, remove and discard them.
4   Using a screwdriver, carefully pry up on the edge of the CV boot, pull it off the CV joint housing and slide it down the axleshaft, exposing the tripod spider assembly. To separate the axleshaft and spider assembly from the inner CV joint housing, simply pull them straight out **(see illustration)**. **Note:** *When removing the spider assembly, hold the rollers in place on the spider trunion to protect the rollers and the needle bearings from falling free.*
5   Remove the spider assembly snap-ring with a pair of snap-ring pliers **(see illustration)**.

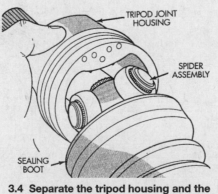

3.4 Separate the tripod housing and the spider assembly

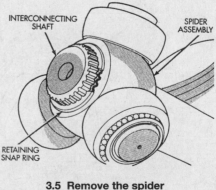

3.5 Remove the spider assembly snap-ring

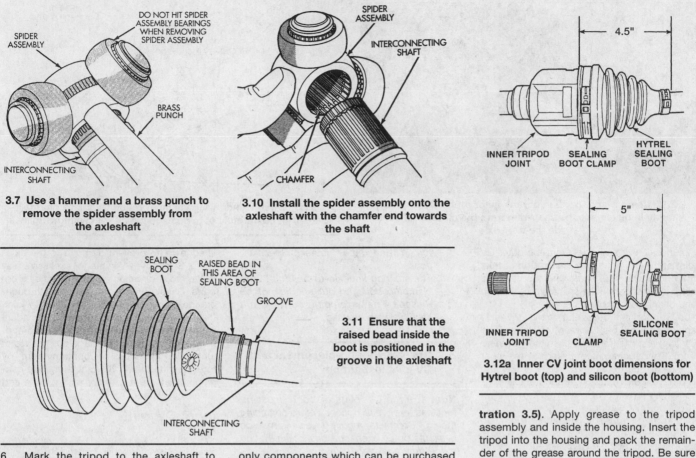

3.7 Use a hammer and a brass punch to remove the spider assembly from the axleshaft

3.10 Install the spider assembly onto the axleshaft with the chamfer end towards the shaft

3.11 Ensure that the raised bead inside the boot is positioned in the groove in the axleshaft

3.12a Inner CV joint boot dimensions for Hytrel boot (top) and silicon boot (bottom)

6   Mark the tripod to the axleshaft to ensure that they are reassembled properly.

7   Use a hammer and a brass drift to drive the spider assembly from the axleshaft **(see illustration)**.

8   Slide the boot off the shaft.

Inspection

9   Thoroughly clean all components with solvent until the old CV joint grease is completely removed. Inspect the bearing surfaces of the inner tripods and housings for cracks, pitting, scoring and other signs of wear. If any part of the inner CV joint is worn, you must replace the entire driveaxle assembly (inner CV joint, axleshaft and outer CV joint). The

only components which can be purchased separately are the boots themselves and the boot clamps.

Reassembly

Refer to illustrations 3.10, 3.11, 3.12a, 3.12b, 3.13a, 3.13b, 3.13c and 3.13d

10   Wrap the splines on the inner end of the axleshaft with electrical or duct tape to protect the boots from the sharp edges of the splines. Slide the clamps and boot onto the axleshaft. Remove the tape and place the tripod spider on the axleshaft with the chamfer toward the shaft **(see illustration)**. Tap the spider onto the shaft with a brass drift until it's seated and install the snap ring **(see illus-**

tration 3.5)**. Apply grease to the tripod assembly and inside the housing. Insert the tripod into the housing and pack the remainder of the grease around the tripod. Be sure to work the entire tube of CV joint grease (included with the boot kit) into the bearing assembly. **Caution:** *Do not use any other type of grease.*

11   Slide the boot onto the tripod housing, making sure the raised bead inside the small end of the boot seats in the groove on the axleshaft **(see illustration)**.

12   Slide the axleshaft in or out of the inner CV joint so that the dimensions of the boot and joint are as shown **(see illustration)**. Once this dimension is set, equalize the pressure inside the boot by inserting a small, dull, flat screwdriver tip between the boot and the CV joint housing **(see illustration)**. Then

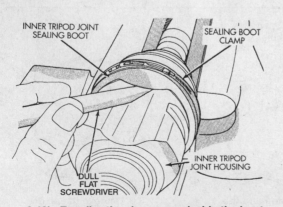

3.12b Equalize the air pressure inside the boot

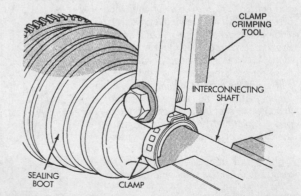

3.13a Place the crimping tool over the bridge of the boot clamp . . .

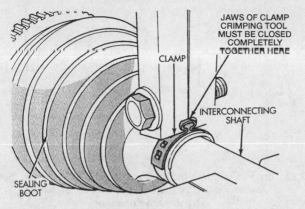

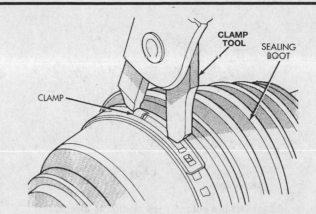

3.13b . . . then tighten the nut on the crimping tool until the jaws close

3.13c For the low profile latching type boot clamp, place the prongs of the clamping tool in the holes of the clamp . . .

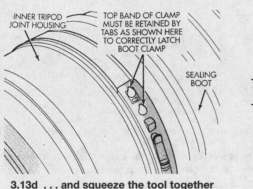

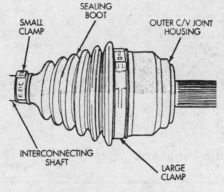

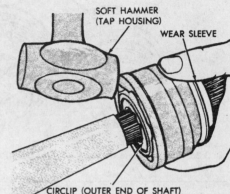

3.13d . . . and squeeze the tool together until the top band latches behind the tabs of the lower band

3.15 Remove the boot clamps

3.17 Strike the edge of the CV joint housing sharply with a soft-faced hammer to dislodge the CV joint from the shaft

remove the screwdriver tip.

13   Two types of clamps are used on the inner CV joint. If a crimp-type clamp is used, clamp the new boot clamps onto the boot with a special crimping tool (available at automotive parts stores). Place the crimping tool over the bridge of each new boot clamp, then tighten the nut on the crimping tool until the jaws are closed **(see illustrations)**. If a low profile latching-type clamp is used, clamp the sealing boot onto the axleshaft with the special clamping tool (available at automotive parts stores). Place the prongs of the clamp locking tool in the holes of the clamp and squeeze the tool together until the top band of the clamp is latched behind the two tabs on the lower band of the clamp **(see illustrations)**.

14   The driveaxle is now ready for installation (see Section 2).

Outer CV joint (1996 models only)

Note: *The outer CV joints and boots on 1997 and later models are not serviceable and must be replaced as a unit.*

Disassembly

Refer to illustrations 3.15 and 3.17

15   Cut the boot clamps with side-cutters,

remove and discard them **(see illustration)**.

16   Slide the boot away from the outer CV joint, and clean the CV joint and the interconnecting parts.

17   Strike the edge of the CV joint housing sharply with a soft-faced hammer to dislodge the outer CV joint housing from the axleshaft **(see illustration)**.

18   Slide the outer CV joint and the sealing boot off the axleshaft.

Inspection

Refer to illustration 3.19

19   Thoroughly clean all components with solvent until the old CV grease is completely removed. Inspect the bearing surfaces of the inner tripods and housings for cracks, pitting, scoring, and other signs of wear **(see illustration)**. If any part of the outer CV joint is worn, you must replace the entire driveaxle assembly (inner CV joint, axleshaft and outer CV joint). The only components which can be purchased separately are the boots themselves and the boot clamps.

Reassembly

Refer to illustrations 3.21, 3.22, 3.26, 3.27a, 3.27b, 3.28a and 3.28b

20   Slide a new sealing boot clamp and sealing boot onto the axleshaft **(see illustration 3.11)**. **Note:** *The sealing boot must be*

3.19 After the CV joint has been thoroughly cleaned and dried, rotate the outer joint housing through its full range of motion and inspect the bearing surfaces for wear or damage - if any of the balls, the race or cage look damaged, replace the driveaxle assembly

positioned on the shaft so the raised bead on the inside of the boot is in the groove on the shaft.

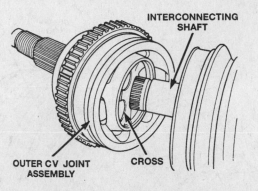

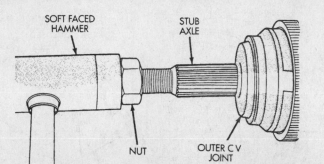

3.21 Start the outer CV joint onto the axleshaft

3.22 Thread a nut onto the stub axle to protect the shaft threads and drive the CV joint onto the axleshaft with a soft-faced hammer

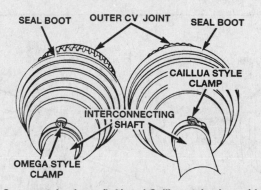

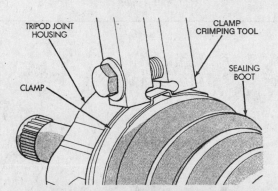

3.26 Omega style clamp (left) and Caillua style clamp (right)

3.27a For the Omega style boot clamp, place the crimping tool over the bridge of the boot clamp . . .

21   Align the splines on the axleshaft with the splines on the outer CV joint assembly and start the outer CV joint onto the axleshaft **(see illustration)**.
22   Thread a nut loosely onto the stub axle and use a soft-faced hammer to strike the nut (the nut is installed to protect the threads) **(see illustration)**.
23   Drive the CV joint onto the axleshaft until the CV joint is seated to the axleshaft. **Note:** *The outer CV joint is not completely installed until the small snap-ring on the end of the shaft locks into the groove in the cross of the outer CV joint.*
24   Place half the grease provided in the

sealing boot kit into the outer CV joint assembly housing. Put the remaining grease into the sealing boot. **Note:** *Lubricant requirements and quantities are different between the inner joint and the outer joint.* **Caution:** *Do not use any other type of grease.*
25   Install the outer CV joint sealing boot to the axleshaft.
26   Two different types of clamps are used to clamp the CV joint sealing boot to the axleshaft. Determine which type of clamp is present, and perform the appropriate steps as described below **(see illustration)**.
27   If the driveaxle uses the Omega style boot clamp, clamp the sealing boot onto the

axleshaft with the special crimping tool (available at automotive parts stores). Place the crimping tool over the bridge of the clamp. Tighten the nut on the crimping tool until the jaws on the tool are closed completely **(see illustrations)**.
28   If the driveaxle uses the Caillua style boot clamp, clamp the sealing boot onto the axleshaft with the special crimping tool (available at automotive parts stores). Place the crimping tool on the boot clamp with the sealing clamp tabs between the jaws of the tool. Squeeze the jaws of the special tool together until the locking tabs of the clamp are latched together **(see illustrations)**.

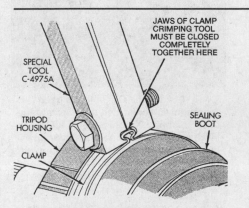

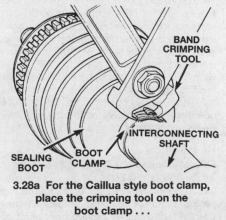

3.27b . . . then tighten the nut on the crimping tool until the jaws close

3.28a For the Caillua style boot clamp, place the crimping tool on the boot clamp . . .

3.28b . . . and squeeze the jaws until the locking tabs are latched together

Chapter 9 Brakes

Contents

	Section
Anti-lock Brake System (ABS) - general information	2
Brake check	See Chapter 1
Brake disc - inspection, removal and installation	5
Brake fluid level check	See Chapter 1
Brake hoses and lines - inspection and replacement	10
Brake system - bleeding	11
Brake light switch - check, replacement and adjustment	16
Disc brake caliper - removal and installation	4
Disc brake pads - replacement	3
Drum brake shoes - replacement	6
General information	1

	Section
Master cylinder - removal, installation and vacuum seal replacement	8
Parking brake cables - replacement	14
Parking brake pedal assembly - removal, installation and adjustment	13
Parking brake shoes (models with rear disc brakes) - replacement	15
Power brake booster - check, removal and installation	12
Proportioning valves - check and replacement	9
Wheel cylinder - removal and installation	7

Specifications

General
Brake fluid type	DOT 3

Disc brakes
Brake pad minimum thickness (metal backing plus lining)	5/16 inch
Disc lateral runout limit	0.005 inch
Disc minimum thickness	Cast into disc
Thickness variation	0.0005 inch

Drum brakes
Minimum brake lining thickness	1/8 inch
Maximum drum diameter	Cast into drum

Torque specifications   Ft-lbs (unless otherwise indicated)

Note: *One foot-pound of torque is equivalent to 12 inch-pounds of torque. Torque values below approximately 15-ft-lbs. are expressed in inch-pounds, since most foot pound torque wrenches are not accurate at these smaller values.*

Brake booster mounting nuts	250 in-lbs
Brake hose banjo bolt-to-caliper	35
Caliper bracket bolts (2001 and later)	125
Caliper guide pin bolts	
1996 through 1998	30
1999 and 2000	195 inch-lbs
2001 and later	26
Master cylinder-to-brake booster mounting nuts	225 in-lbs
Parking brake mechanism mounting bolts	250 in-lbs
Wheel cylinder-to-backing plate mounting nuts	75 in-lbs
Wheel speed sensor bolt	60 in-lbs
Wheel lug nuts	See Chapter 1

1 General information

General

All models covered by this manual are equipped with a hydraulically operated brake system. The front brakes are disc type and the rear brakes are either drum or disc type. Both brake types are self-adjusting. Disc brakes automatically compensate for pad wear, while drum brakes incorporate an adjustment mechanism which is activated as the brakes are applied.

The hydraulic system is split diagonally - the left front and right rear brakes are on one circuit; the right front and left rear on the other. If one circuit fails, the other circuit will remain functional and a warning indicator will illuminate on the dashboard when a substantial amount of brake fluid is lost, showing that a failure has occurred.

Before disconnecting any electrical connector from a vehicle equipped with an anti-lock brake system (ABS), make sure the ignition is in the OFF position and the battery has been disconnected at the negative terminal. If any weld repair is going to be performed on a vehicle equipped with an ABS system, disconnect the CAB or ICU electrical connector (see Section 2) or damage to the electronics may occur.

Calipers

All disc brakes used by the vehicles covered in this manual are equipped with a double-pin floating caliper, a single-piston design that "floats" on two steel guide pins. When the brake pedal is depressed, hydraulic pressure pushing on the piston is transmitted to the inner brake pad and against the inner surface of the brake disc. As the force against the disc from the inner pad is increased, the caliper assembly moves in, sliding on the guide pins and pulling the outer pad against the disc, providing a pinching force on the disc.

Master cylinder

The master cylinder is located in the engine compartment on the driver's side near the firewall, and can be identified by the large fluid reservoir on top. The master cylinder has two separate circuits to accommodate the diagonally split system.

Power brake booster

The power brake booster uses engine manifold vacuum to provide assistance to the brakes. It is mounted on the firewall in the engine compartment, directly behind the master cylinder.

Parking brake system

The parking brake actuates the rear brakes via two cables. On drum brake models, the parking brake cables pull on a lever attached to the brake shoe assembly, causing the shoes to expand against the drum. On models with rear disc brakes, the cables pull on actuators that expand the parking brake shoes, which are like small drum brake shoes in the center portion of the rear brake disc.

Precautions

There are some general precautions and warnings related to the hydraulic brake system:

a) *Use only brake fluid conforming to DOT 3 specifications.*
b) *The brake pads and linings may contain asbestos fibers which are hazardous to your health if inhaled. Whenever you work on brake system components, DO NOT blow it out with compressed air and DO NOT inhale it. DO NOT use gasoline or petroleum-based solvents to clean components. Brake system cleaner should be used to flush the dust into a drain pan. After the brake components are wiped clean with a rag, dispose of the contaminated rags and cleaner in a labeled, covered container. Do not allow the fine dust to become airborne.*
c) *Safety should be paramount whenever any servicing of the brake components is performed. Do not use parts or fasteners which are not in perfect condition, and be sure all clearances and torque specifications are adhered to. If you are at all unsure about a certain procedure, seek professional advice. Upon completion of any brake system work, test the brakes carefully in a controlled area before driving the vehicle in traffic.*
d) *If a problem is suspected in the brake system, don't drive the vehicle until it's been corrected.*

2　Anti-lock Brake System (ABS) - general information

Description

1　The Anti-lock Brake System (ABS) prevents wheel lock-up under heavy braking conditions on virtually any road surface. Preventing the wheels from locking up maintains vehicle maneuverability, preserves directional stability, and allows optimal deceleration on all surfaces. How does ABS work? Basically, by monitoring the rotational speed of the wheels and controlling the brake line pressure to the calipers/wheel cylinders at each wheel during extreme braking.

Components

Controller Anti-lock Brake (CAB)

Refer to illustration 2.2

2　The CAB consists of a pair of microprocessors which monitor wheel speeds and control the anti-lock and traction control functions. The CAB receives two identical signals and processes the information independently of one another. The results are compared to make sure that they agree. If they don't, the CAB turns off the ABS and traction control functions, and turns on the warning lights. The CAB is mounted on the bottom of the HCU **(see illustration)**.

Hydraulic Control Unit (HCU)

3　The Hydraulic Control Unit (HCU) is mounted near the front suspension cradle **(see illustration 2.2)**. The HCU contains the valve block assembly, fluid accumulators, the pump/motor assembly and relay box.

Integrated Control Unit (ICU) - 1998 and later models only

4　On 1998 and later models a new ABS brake system was introduced which functions very much like the previous ABS system except it combines the HCU and CAB into one unit. The ICU is located in the same location as the HCU on previous models (see above).

Valve block assembly

5　The valve block assembly contains eight valve/solenoids: four inlet valves and four outlet valves. The inlet valves are spring-loaded in the open position and the outlet valves are

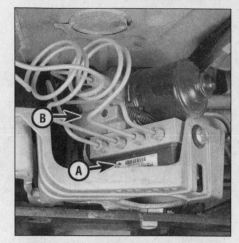

2.2 The Controller Anti-lock Brake (A) is the brain of the ABS system; it's mounted to the bottom of the Hydraulic Control Unit (B)

spring-loaded in the closed position. During ABS operation, these valves are cycled to maintain the proper slip ratio for each channel. If a wheel locks, the inlet valve is closed to prevent a further increase in pressure. Simultaneously, the outlet valve is opened to release the pressure back to the accumulators until the wheel is no longer slipping. Once the wheel no longer slips, the outlet valve closes and the inlet valve opens to allow pressure to the wheel caliper or wheel cylinder.

Pump/motor assembly

6　The pump/motor assembly consists of an electric motor and a dual-piston pump. The pump provides high-pressure brake fluid to the hydraulic control unit when the ABS system is activated.

Fluid accumulators

7　The two fluid accumulators located inside the HCU are for the primary and secondary hydraulic circuits, respectively. The accumulators temporarily store brake fluid that is blocked during ABS operation. This fluid is re-routed to the pump.

Proportioning valves

8　Refer to Section 9.

Wheel Speed Sensors (WSS)

Refer to illustrations 2.9a and 2.9b

9　A speed sensor is mounted at each wheel **(see illustrations)**. The speed sensors send variable voltage signals to the HCU. These analog voltage outputs are proportional to the speed of rotation of each wheel.

Diagnosis and repair

10　The ABS system has self-diagnostic capabilities. Each time the ignition key is turned to ON, the system runs a self-test. If it finds a problem, the ABS and traction control warning lights come on and remain on. If there's no problem with the system, the lights go out after a second or two.

2.9a Location of the front wheel speed sensor (arrow)

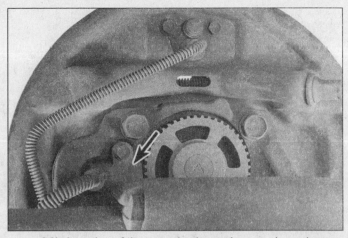
2.9b Location of the rear wheel speed sensor (arrow)

11 If the ABS and traction control warning lights come on and stay on during vehicle operation, there is a problem in the ABS system. Two things now happen: The controller stores a diagnostic trouble code (which can be displayed with a DRB II scanner at the dealer) and the ABS system is shut down. Once the ABS system is disabled, it will remain disabled until the problem is corrected and the trouble code is erased. However, the regular brake system will continue to function normally.

12 Although a DRB II (a special electronic tester) is necessary to properly diagnose the system, you can make a few preliminary checks before taking the vehicle to a dealer for service:

a) Make sure the brake calipers and linings are in good condition.
b) Check the electrical connector at the CAB, HCU or ICU as applicable.
c) Check the fuses.
d) Follow the wiring harness to the wheel speed sensors and brake light switch and make sure all connections are clean, secure and the wiring isn't damaged.

If the above preliminary checks don't rectify the problem, the vehicle should be diagnosed by a dealer service department.

3 Disc brake pads - replacement

Refer to illustrations 3.2, 3.3, 3.4a through 3.4z

Warning: *Disc brake pads must be replaced on both front or rear wheels at the same time - never replace the pads on only one wheel. Also, the dust created by the brake system may contain asbestos, which is harmful to your health. Never blow it out with compressed air and don't inhale any of it. An approved filtering mask should be worn when working on the brakes. Do not, under any circumstances, use petroleum-based solvents to clean brake parts. Use brake system cleaner only!*

Note: *On 2001 and later models, there are two different brake caliper assemblies used on the various models. Models equipped with*

front disc and rear drum brake combination are equipped with a caliper manufactured by TRW. Models equipped with front disc and rear disc brake combination are equipped with a caliper manufactured by Continental Teves. These are two completely different caliper assemblies and none of the parts are interchangeable.

1 Loosen the front or rear wheel lug nuts 1/4 turn, raise the vehicle and support it securely on jackstands. Apply the parking brake. Remove the wheels.

2 Using a syringe or equivalent, remove approximately two-thirds of the fluid from the master cylinder reservoir and discard it. Position a drain pan under the brake assembly and clean the caliper and surrounding area with brake system cleaner **(see illustration)**.

3 Push the piston back into its bore using a C-clamp **(see illustration)**. As the piston is depressed to the bottom of the caliper bore, the fluid in the master cylinder will rise as the brake fluid is displaced. Make sure it doesn't overflow. If necessary, remove more of the fluid.

3.2 Spray the disc and brake pads with brake cleaner to remove brake dust; DO NOT blow brake dust off with compressed air - collect the contaminated fluid in a suitable container and dispose of it properly!

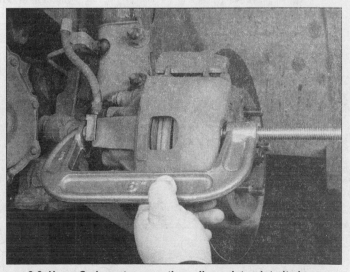
3.3 Use a C-clamp to press the caliper piston into its bore

2000 and earlier models

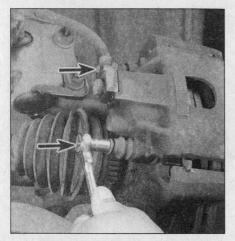

3.4a To remove the brake caliper, remove the two guide pin bolts (arrows)

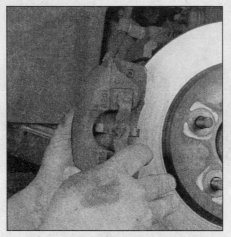

3.4b Lift the caliper off the steering knuckle

3.4c Remove the pads from the caliper

3.4d Hang the caliper from the spring with a piece of wire - don't let it hang by the brake hose

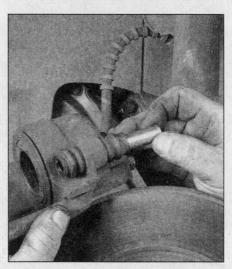

3.4e Remove the guide pin bushings and the bushing boots. Inspect them for damage and replace if necessary

4　To replace the front brake pads on 1996 through 2000 models, follow **illustrations 3.4a through 3.4j**. To replace the front brake pads on 2001 and later models, start with **illustration 3.4k**. On rear disc brake models, to replace the rear brake pads on 2001 and later models, follow **illustrations 3.4k through 3.4x**.

5　On rear disc brake models, continue with the following steps:

a) *Hang the caliper from the spring with a piece of wire - don't let it hang by the brake hose.*

b) *Push the outer brake pad in toward the piston and disengage the two metal protrusions on the pad, then slide the brake pad off the caliper.*

c) *Pull the inner brake pad from the caliper.*

d) *Remove the guide pin bushings and the bushing boots. Inspect them for damage and replace if necessary.*

e) *Lubricate the guide pin bushings with multi-purpose grease before installing them.*

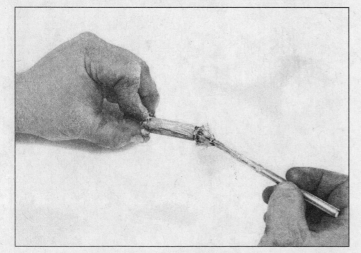

3.4f Lubricate the guide pin bushings with multi-purpose grease before installing them

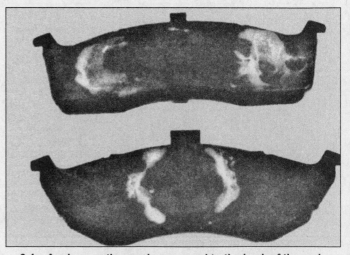

3.4g Apply an anti-squeal compound to the back of the pads where they mate with the caliper and piston

3.4h Install the inner brake pad - make sure the retaining spring is fully seated into the piston bore

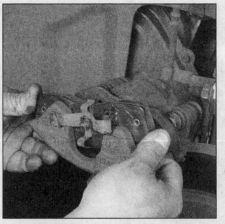

3.4i Install the outer brake pad, making sure the retaining spring is properly engaged with the caliper body

3.4j Place the caliper/brake pad assembly onto the steering knuckle, install the guide pin bolts and tighten them to the torque listed in this Chapter's Specifications

2001 and later models

3.4k Use a screwdriver and remove the anti-rattle spring

3.4l On the Teves caliper, to remove the brake caliper, remove the guide pin bolts

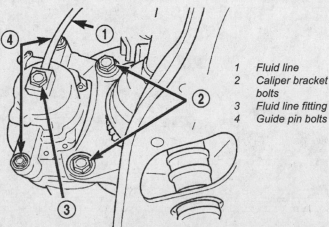

1　Fluid line
2　Caliper bracket bolts
3　Fluid line fitting
4　Guide pin bolts

3.4m On the TRW caliper, to remove the brake caliper, remove the guide pin bolts

3.4n Lift the caliper off the steering knuckle

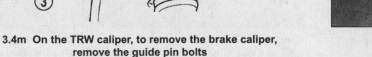

3.4o On the Teves caliper, remove the outer brake pad from the caliper bracket

3.4p On the Teves caliper, remove the inner brake pad from the caliper. On the TRW caliper, remove the inner and outer pad from the caliper bracket

3.4q Hang the caliper from the spring with a piece of wire - don't let it hang by the brake hose

3.4r Remove the guide pin bushings and the bushing boots. Inspect them for damage and replace if necessary

3.4s Lubricate the guide pin bushings with multi-purpose grease before installing them

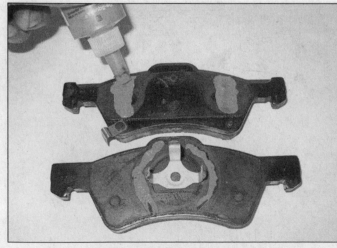

3.4t Apply an anti-squeal compound to the back of the pads where they mate with the caliper and piston

3.4u On the Teves caliper, install the inner brake pad - make sure the retaining spring is fully seated into the piston bore

3.4v On the Teves caliper, install the outer brake pad into the caliper bracket. On the TRW caliper, install both brake pads onto the caliper bracket and onto the anti-rattle clips

3.4w Place the caliper/brake pad assembly onto the steering knuckle, install the guide pin bolts and tighten them to the torque listed in this Chapter's Specifications

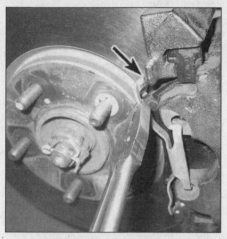

3.4x Install the anti-rattle spring and hook the end over the caliper bracket tab

3.4y Rear caliper guide pin golt locations

3.4z To remove the rear brake caliper, first rotate the caliper up from the caliper bracket, then pull the rear of the caliper and outboard brake shoe anti-rattle spring from under the rear abutment on the caliper bracket (arrow). Lift the rear caliper off the caliper bracket

f) Apply an anti-squeal compound to the back of the pads where they mate with the caliper and piston.

g) Install the inner brake pad - make sure the retaining spring is fully seated into the piston bore.

h) Install the outer brake pad into the caliper bracket. Make sure it is seated squarely against the caliper outer fingers.

i) Place the caliper/brake pad assembly onto the caliper bracket, install the guide pin bolts and tighten them to the torque listed in this Chapter's Specifications.

j) Install the anti-rattle spring and hook the end over the caliper bracket tab.

6   While the pads are removed, inspect the caliper for brake fluid leaks and ruptures of the piston dust boot. Replace the caliper if necessary (see Section 4). Also inspect the brake disc carefully (see Section 5). If machining is necessary, follow the information in that Section to remove the disc. Inspect the brake

hoses for damage and replace if necessary (see Section 10).

7   Before installing the caliper guide pin bolts, clean and check them for corrosion and damage. If they're significantly corroded or damaged, replace them. Be sure to tighten the caliper guide pin bolts to the torque listed in this Chapter's Specifications.

8   Repeat the procedure for the opposite wheel, then install the wheels, lug nuts and lower the vehicle. Tighten the lug nuts to the torque listed in the Chapter 1 Specifications. Add the appropriate brake fluid to the reservoir until it's full (see Chapter 1 if necessary).

9   Pump the brakes several times to seat the pads against the disc, then check the brake fluid level in the reservoir again. Top it up as necessary.

10   Carefully test the operation of the brakes before resuming normal operation. Try to avoid heavy brake applications until the brakes have been applied lightly several times to seat the pads.

4   Disc brake caliper - removal and installation

Refer to illustration 4.2

Warning: *Dust created by the brake system may contain asbestos, which is harmful to your health. Never blow it out with compressed air and don't inhale any of it. An approved filtering mask should be worn when working on the brakes. Do not, under any circumstances, use petroleum-based solvents to clean brake parts. Use brake system cleaner only.*

Note: *If replacement is indicated (usually because of fluid leaks, a stuck piston or broken bleed screw), replace the calipers with new or factory rebuilt calipers which are available on an exchange basis. Always replace the calipers in pairs - never replace just one of them.*

4.2 The brake hose is connected to the caliper with a banjo fitting bolt (be sure to replace the sealing washers upon installation)

5.2 The brake pads on this vehicle were obviously neglected, as they wore down to the rivets, then cut deep grooves into the disc, which must now be replaced

5.3 Use a dial indicator to check disc runout - if the reading exceeds the specified runout limit, the disc will have to be machined or replaced

Removal

1   Loosen the front or rear wheel lug nuts 1/4 turn, raise the vehicle and support it securely on jackstands. Remove the wheels.

2   Unscrew the banjo bolt from the caliper and detach the hose **(see illustration)**. **Note:** *If you're just removing the caliper for access to other components, don't disconnect the hose.* Discard the sealing washers on each side of the fitting and use new ones during installation. Plug the hose to prevent fluid loss and contamination.

3   Refer to the first few steps in Section 3 (caliper removal is the first part of the brake pad replacement procedure). Clean the caliper assembly with brake system cleaner. **Warning:** *DO NOT, under any circumstances, use kerosene, gasoline or petroleum-based solvents to clean brake parts!* Be sure to check the pads as well and replace them if necessary (see Section 3).

Installation

4   Install the brake pads and caliper (see Section 3). Tighten the caliper guide pin bolts to the torque listed in this Chapter's Specifications.

5   Connect the brake hose to the caliper using new sealing washers. Tighten the banjo

bolt to the torque listed in this Chapter's Specifications.

6   Firmly depress the brake pedal a few times to bring the pads into contact with the disc. Check the fluid level in the master cylinder reservoir and add more if necessary.

7   Bleed the brakes (see Section 11).

8   Install the wheels and lug nuts. Lower the vehicle and tighten the lug nuts to the torque listed in the Chapter 1 Specifications.

9   Carefully check for fluid leaks and test the operation of the brakes before resuming normal operation.

---

5   Brake disc - inspection, removal and installation

Note: *On 2001 and later models, there are two different brake caliper assemblies and brake discs used on the various models. Models equipped with front disc and rear drum brake combination are equipped with a caliper manufactured by TRW. Models equipped with front disc and rear disc brake combination are equipped with a caliper manufactured by Continental Teves. These are two completely different caliper and disc assemblies and none of the parts are inter-changeable. If the brake*

discs are interchanged, noise and wear problems can result.

Inspection

Refer to illustrations 5.2, 5.3, 5.4a and 5.4b

1   Loosen the wheel lug nuts 1/4 turn, raise the vehicle and support it securely on jackstands. Apply the parking brake if working on the front brakes. Remove the wheels. Reinstall the lug nuts, to hold the disc firmly against the hub. **Note:** *Washers may be required.*

2   Remove the brake caliper (see Section 4), but don't disconnect the brake hose. Visually inspect the disc surface for score marks and other damage **(see illustration)**. Light scratches and shallow grooves are normal after use and won't affect brake operation. Deep grooves - over 0.015-inch deep - require disc removal and refinishing by an automotive machine shop, or may require replacement if they are deep enough. Be sure to check both sides of the disc.

3   To check the disc runout, place a dial indicator at a point about 1/2-inch from the outer edge of the disc **(see illustration)**. Rotate the disc until you find the lowest point on the disc. Set the dial indicator to zero and turn the disc again. The indicator reading should not exceed the runout limit listed in this Chapter's Specification Section. Check the runout on both sides of the disc. If the runout exceeds specification, the disc must be refinished by an automotive machine shop, or replaced. **Note:** *Professionals recommend resurfacing the brake discs regardless of the dial indicator reading (to produce a smooth, flat surface that will eliminate brake pedal pulsations and other undesirable symptoms related to questionable discs). At the very least, if you elect not to have the discs resurfaced, deglaze them with sandpaper or emery cloth.*

4   The disc must not be machined to a thickness less than the specified minimum thickness. The minimum (or discard) thickness is cast into the disc **(see illustration)**. The disc thickness should be checked with a micrometer **(see illustration)**.

5.4a The minimum thickness is cast into the inside of the disc

5.4b Use a micrometer to measure the thickness of the disc at several points

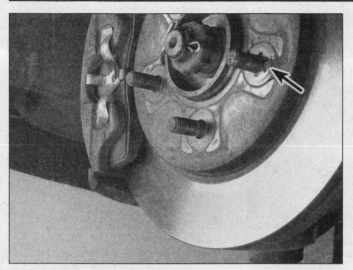

5.7 Remove and discard the retaining clips, if present (it isn't necessary to reinstall them)

6.3 Before disassembling the brake shoe assembly, spray it with brake cleaner to remove brake dust; DO NOT blow brake dust off with compressed air - collect the contaminated fluid in a suitable container and dispose of it properly!

Removal

Refer to illustration 5.7

5   Loosen the wheel lug nuts 1/4 turn, raise the vehicle and place it securely on jackstands. Remove the wheel. **Note:** *If you're removing a rear disc, release the parking brake.*

6   Remove the caliper, but don't disconnect the brake hose (see Section 4).

7   Remove the retaining clips, if present, from the wheel studs **(see illustration)**.

8   Pull the disc off the hub.

Installation

9   Installation is the reverse of removal. Make sure you tighten the caliper guide pin bolts to the torque listed in this Chapter's Specifications.

***

6   Drum brake shoes - replacement

Refer to illustrations 6.3, 6.4a through 6.4x and 6.5

Warning: *Drum brake shoes must be replaced on both wheels at the same time - never replace the shoes on only one wheel. Also, the dust created by the brake system may contain asbestos, which is harmful to your health. Never blow it out with compressed air and don't inhale any of it. An approved filtering mask should be worn when working on the brakes. Do not, under any circumstances, use petroleum-based solvents to clean brake parts. Use brake system cleaner only!*

Caution: *Whenever the brake shoes are replaced, the hold-down springs should also be replaced. Due to the continuous heating/cooling cycle that the springs are subjected to, they lose their tension over a period of time and may allow the shoes to drag on the drum and wear at a much faster rate than normal.*

1   Loosen the wheel lug nuts 1/4 turn, raise the rear of the vehicle and support it securely on jackstands. Block the front wheels to keep

6.4a Remove the hold-down spring and pin from the leading brake shoe by depressing the retainer and turning it 90-degrees - the tool shown here is available at most auto parts stores and greatly simplifies this task

the vehicle from rolling. Release the parking brake. Remove the wheel. **Note:** *To avoid mixing up parts, work on one brake assembly at a time.*

2   Remove the brake drum. If the drum won't come off, create some slack in the parking brake cables by pulling the exposed section of the cable down and to the rear, to the point where it passes through the body brackets. Clamp a pair of locking pliers to the rear of the rearmost bracket.

3   Wash the brake assembly with brake system cleaner **(see illustration)**.

4   Follow **illustrations 6.4a through 6.4x** for inspection and replacement of the brake shoes. Be sure to stay in order and read the caption under each illustration.

5   Before reinstalling the drum, carefully examine it for cracks, score marks, deep scratches and hard spots, which will appear as small discolored areas. If the hard spots cannot be removed with fine emery cloth or if

6.4b Disconnect the upper return spring from the brake shoe

any of the other conditions listed above exist, the drum must be taken to an automotive machine shop to have it turned. **Note:** *Professionals recommend resurfacing the drums whenever a brake job is performed. Resurfac-*

6.4c Disconnect the adjustment lever spring from the brake shoe

6.4d Remove the upper return spring (A), the tension clip (B), and the automatic adjuster (C)

6.4e Remove the adjustment lever and the spring

6.4f Disconnect the two return springs from the leading brake shoe and remove the shoe

6.4g Remove the parking brake actuating strut

6.4h Remove the hold-down spring and pin from the trailing brake shoe

6.4i Remove the trailing brake shoe and the parking brake actuating lever

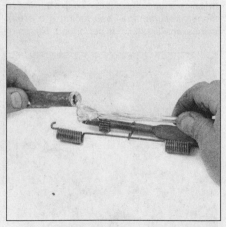

6.4j Lubricate the automatic adjuster screw threads

6.4k Lubricate the contact surfaces of the backing plate with high-temperature grease

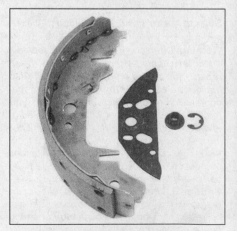

6.4l Remove the parking brake actuator from the old leading brake shoe and install it on the new leading shoe. Be sure the retaining clip seats properly

6.4m Connect the parking brake actuating lever to the parking brake cable

6.4n Install the trailing brake shoe

6.4o Install the hold-down pin and spring

6.4p Install the parking brake actuating strut

6.4q Install the automatic adjuster, the tension clip and the upper return spring

6.4r Install the leading brake shoe

6.4s Install the hold-down pin and spring

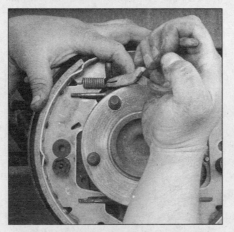

6.4t Connect the upper return spring to the leading brake shoe

6.4u Attach the automatic adjustment lever

6.4v Attach the actuating spring

6.4w Connect the top lower return spring

6.4x Connect the bottom lower return spring

ing will eliminate the possibility of out-of-round drums. If the drums are worn so much that they can't be resurfaced without exceeding the maximum allowable diameter (stamped into the drum) **(see illustration)**, then new ones will be required. At the very least, if you elect not to have the drums resurfaced, remove the glazing from the surface with emery cloth or sandpaper using a swirling motion.

6   Install the brake drum, mount the wheel and install the lug nuts.

7   Repeat the procedure for the opposite wheel, then remove the locking pliers from the parking brake cable (if it was necessary to slacken the cables).

8   To set the initial adjustment of the brake shoes, disconnect the parking brake cable from the equalizer (this will give you access to the adjuster screw star wheel. Remove the plug from the brake backing plate, directly below the brake line.

9   Check to make sure the parking brake is fully released. Insert a narrow screwdriver or brake adjusting tool through the hole in the backing plate and turn the star wheel until the brake shoes drag on the drum as the rear wheel is rotated. Now, insert another thin screwdriver or a straightened-out coathanger

into the hole and push the adjuster lever off the star wheel. As the lever is held in this position, back-off the star wheel until the shoes don't drag on the drum as the rear wheel is turned.

10   Repeat this procedure to the opposite brake, then install the plugs in the backing plates and reconnect the parking brake cables.

11   Lower the vehicle and tighten the lug nuts to the torque listed in the Chapter 1 Specifications.

12   Fully depress the parking brake pedal then release it. This will adjust the parking brake cables automatically.

13   Carefully test brake operation before resuming normal operation.

---

7   Wheel cylinder - removal and installation

Note: *If replacement is warranted (usually because of fluid leakage or sticky operation) explore all options before beginning the job. New wheel cylinders are available, which makes this job quite easy. Never replace only one wheel cylinder. Always replace both of them at the same time.*

Removal

Refer to illustration 7.2

1   Remove the rear brake shoes (see Section 6).

2   Using a flare-nut wrench (if available) disconnect the brake line fitting from the rear of the wheel cylinder **(see illustration)**. Don't pull the line away from the cylinder, as this could bend the line and make threading the fitting into the wheel cylinder difficult.

3   Remove the two bolts securing the wheel cylinder to the backing plate and remove the wheel cylinder. Plug the line to prevent excess fluid loss and contamination.

Installation

4   Apply a film of RTV sealant to the wheel cylinder mounting area on the brake backing plate. Installation is otherwise the reverse of removal. Tighten the wheel cylinder mounting bolts to the torque listed in this Chapter's Specification Section. Tighten the line fitting securely.

5   Install the brake shoes and the brake drum (see Section 6).

6   Bleed the brakes (see Section 11). Carefully test brake operation before resuming normal operation.

---

8   Master cylinder - removal, installation and vacuum seal replacement

---

Note: *The master cylinder used on these vehicles is not serviceable and must be replaced as a unit. However, you can replace the fluid reservoir and/or reservoir sealing grommets.*

Warning: *If your vehicle is equipped with an Anti-lock Brake System (ABS), the vehicle must be towed to a dealer service department or other repair shop equipped with a DRB II scan tool to have the hydraulic system properly bled after master cylinder replacement.*

6.5 The maximum allowable diameter is stamped into the drum

7.2 Disconnect the brake line fitting (arrow) from the wheel cylinder

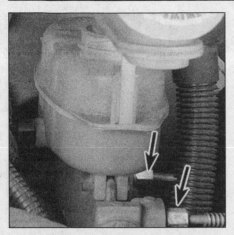

8.5 Disconnect the brake line fittings (arrows) with a flare-nut wrench

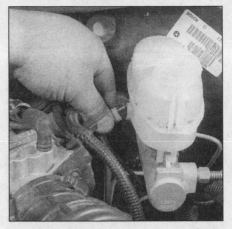

8.6 Unplug the electrical connector from the brake fluid level sensor

8.8 To detach the master cylinder from the power brake booster, remove the mounting nuts (arrows), then pull the master cylinder assembly straight off the mounting studs

Removal

Refer to illustrations 8.5, 8.6 and 8.8

1   **Caution:** *The vacuum in the power brake booster must be pumped down prior to removing the master cylinder, otherwise foreign matter may be sucked into the booster. With the ignition switch in the OFF position, pump the brake pedal until a firm pedal is obtained.*

2   If equipped, disconnect the cruise control electrical connector and detach the cruise control servo from its mounting on the battery tray and position it out of the way.

3   Using a syringe or equivalent, siphon the brake fluid from the master cylinder reservoir and dispose of it properly. **Caution:** *Brake fluid will damage paint. Cover all painted surfaces and avoid spilling fluid during this procedure.*

4   Place rags under the brake line fittings and prepare caps or plastic bags to cover the ends of the lines once they're disconnected.

5   Loosen the tube nuts at the ends of the brake lines where they enter the master cylinder. **Note:** *Non-ABS vehicles have four hydraulic lines attached to the master cylinder. To prevent rounding off the wrenching flats on these nuts, a flare-nut wrench, which wraps around the nut, should be used* (**see illustration**). Pull the brake lines away from the master cylinder slightly and plug the ends to prevent leakage and contamination. Also plug the openings in the master cylinder to prevent fluid spillage.

6   Unplug the electrical connector from the brake fluid level sensor (**see illustration**).

7   On ABS equipped models, clean the area where the master cylinder attaches to the vacuum booster using brake system cleaner.

8   Remove the two master cylinder mounting nuts (**see illustration**) and any brackets that may be attached. Slide the master cylinder off the studs and remove it from the vehicle.

9   On ABS equipped models, replace the front vacuum seal located in the vacuum booster (see below).

Installation

Note: *Read this entire procedure before beginning this operation.*

10   Install the master cylinder onto the power brake booster, making sure to engage the operating rod. Install any brackets as necessary and tighten the mounting nuts securely.

11   Before installing the brake lines to the master cylinder, it should be bled. Since you'll have to apply pressure to the master cylinder piston and at the same time, control flow from the brake line outlets, the aid of an assistant will be required.

12   Fill the reservoir with the recommended brake fluid (see Chapter 1).

13   Place rags or newspapers under the master cylinder to catch the fluid that will be expelled.

14   Have your assistant SLOWLY depress the brake pedal to expel the air from the master cylinder. Use a rag to catch any brake fluid that squirts out. A clear plastic bag placed over the master cylinder will help you guide the expelled fluid for collection and prevent it from squirting in unwanted areas.

15   To prevent air from being drawn back into the master cylinder, place your finger tightly over the ports before releasing the brake pedal. Wait several seconds for brake fluid to be drawn from the reservoir into the bore, then have your assistant depress the brake pedal again, removing your fingers as brake fluid is expelled.

16   Repeat the procedure until only brake fluid is expelled from the ports. Be sure to keep the master cylinder reservoir filled with brake fluid to prevent the introduction of air into the system.

17   Loosen the master cylinder mounting nuts and connect the brake lines to the master cylinder. Since the master cylinder is a bit loose, it can be moved slightly so the fittings can thread in easily.

18   Tighten the master cylinder mounting nuts to the torque given in this Chapter's Specifications. Now repeat the bleeding procedure by loosening each brake line, one at a time, until the fluid emerging from the fittings is free of air (this will bleed out the air that

may have entered when the lines were connected. Start with the port closest to the brake booster.

19   If equipped, install the cruise control servo onto the shock tower and plug in the electrical connector.

20   Fill the master cylinder reservoir with the recommended fluid (see Chapter 1), then bleed the entire brake hydraulic system (see Section 11).

Vacuum Seal Replacement

Refer to illustration 8.21

Caution: *The master cylinder is used to create a seal for holding vacuum in the vacuum booster. The vacuum seal on the master cylinder must be replaced whenever the master cylinder is removed from the vacuum booster.*

21   Using a non-metallic tool such as a toothpick or a pencil, pry the vacuum seal off the master cylinder (**see illustration**).

22   Carefully install a new seal on the master cylinder, making sure it is completely seated up against the mounting flange.

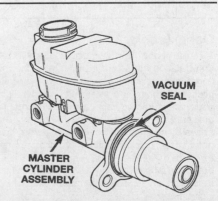

VACUUM SEAL

MASTER CYLINDER ASSEMBLY

8.21 The vacuum seal on the master cylinder must be replaced whenever the master cylinder is removed

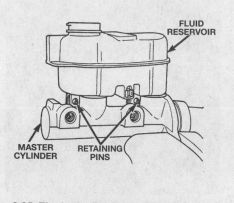

8.25 The brake fluid reservoir is secured to the master cylinder by the retaining pins

9.5 The proportioning valves are located on the bottom of the left rear frame rail

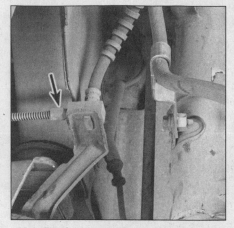

10.3 The front brake hose connection to the metal brake line

Fluid reservoir replacement

Refer to illustration 8.25

23   Using a syringe or equivalent, siphon the brake fluid from the master cylinder reservoir and dispose of it properly.

24   Disconnect the brake fluid level sensor electrical connector from the reservoir (**see illustration 8.6**).

25   Remove the fluid reservoir retaining pins with a hammer and a pin punch (**see illustration**).

26   To remove the reservoir, carefully rock it back-and-forth while gently pulling upward.

27   After removing the reservoir, remove the grommets from the master cylinder. **Note:** *New grommets should be installed anytime the reservoir is detached from the master cylinder.*

28   Remove the brake fluid level sensor from the reservoir, if necessary.

29   Installation is the reverse of removal. Coat the new grommets with clean brake fluid prior to installation.

9   Proportioning valves - check and replacement

Description

1   All models have two proportioning valves that balance front-to-rear braking by controlling the increase in rear system hydraulic pressure above a preset level. Under light pedal pressure, the valve allows full hydraulic pressure to the front and rear brakes. But above a certain pressure - known as the "split point" - the proportioning valve reduces the amount of pressure increase to the rear brakes in accordance with a predetermined ratio. This lessens the chance of rear wheel lock-up and skidding.

Check

2   If either rear wheel skids prematurely under hard braking, it could indicate a defective proportioning valve. If this occurs, have the system checked out by your local dealer service department or other qualified repair shop. A pair of special pressure gauges and fittings are required for proper diagnosis of the proportioning valves. While diagnosis is beyond the scope of the home mechanic, you may still save money by replacing the valves yourself.

Replacement

Refer to illustration 9.5

3   Raise the rear of the vehicle and support it securely on jackstands.

4   Block the front wheels to prevent the vehicle from rolling.

5   Loosen the brake lines from the proportioning valve with a flare-nut wrench to prevent rounding off the corners of the fittings (**see illustration**). Plug the ends of the lines to prevent loss of brake fluid and the entry of dirt.

6   Remove the mounting bolts (**see illustration 9.5**) and detach the valve and bracket.

7   Installation is the reverse of removal.

8   Bleed the brakes (see Section 11). Carefully test brake operation before resuming normal operation.

10   Brake hoses and lines - inspection and replacement

Brake hose inspection

1   Whenever the vehicle is raised and supported securely on jackstands, the rubber hoses which connect the steel brake lines with the front and rear brake assemblies should be inspected for cracks, chafing of the outer cover, leaks, blisters and other damage. These are important and vulnerable parts of the brake system and inspection should be thorough. A light and mirror will be helpful for a complete check. If a hose exhibits any of the above conditions, renew it immediately.

Flexible hose replacement

Refer to illustration 10.3

2   Clean all dirt away from the hose fittings.

3   Using a flare-nut wrench, disconnect the metal brake line from the hose fitting (**see illustration**). Be careful not to bend the frame bracket or line. If the threaded fitting is corroded, spray it with a penetrating oil and allow it to soak in for about 10 minutes, then try again. If you try to break loose a brake tube nut that's stuck, you will kink the metal line, which will then have to be replaced.

4   Remove the brake hose from the bracket (some are secured to a bracket with a retaining clip, others have an integral bracket/fitting). Detach the brake hose from the bracket or bracket from the vehicle as applicable.

5   Immediately plug the metal line to prevent excessive leakage and contamination.

6   On the front brake hose(s), unscrew the banjo bolt at the caliper and remove the hose, discarding the sealing washers on either side of the fitting.

7   Attach the new brake hose to the caliper. **Note:** *When replacing the front brake hoses, always use new sealing washers.* Tighten the banjo bolt or tube nut to the torque listed this Chapter's Specification Section.

8   Insert the other end of the new hose through the bracket or loosely attach the fitting/bracket to the vehicle as applicable, making sure the hose isn't kinked or twisted. Then connect the metal line to the hose (or hose fitting), tighten the hose bracket (if applicable) and tighten the brake fitting securely.

9   Carefully check to make sure the suspension or steering components don't make contact with the hose. Have an assistant push down on the vehicle while you watch to see whether the hose interferes with suspension operation. If you're replacing a front hose, have your assistant turn the steering wheel lock-to-lock while you make sure the hose doesn't interfere with the steering linkage or the steering knuckle.

10   After installation, check the master cylinder fluid level and add fluid as necessary. Bleed the brakes (see Section 11). Carefully test brake operation before resuming normal operation.

Metal brake line replacement

11 When replacing brake lines, be sure to use the correct parts. Do not use copper tubing for any brake system components. Purchase steel brake lines from a dealer parts department or auto parts store.

12 Prefabricated brake lines, with the tube ends already flared and fittings installed, are available at auto parts stores and dealer parts departments. These lines are also sometimes bent to the proper shapes. If it is necessary to bend a line, use a tubing bender tool to avoid kinking the line.

13 When installing the new line make sure it's well supported in the brackets and has plenty of clearance between moving or hot components. Make sure you tighten the fittings securely.

14 After installation, check the master cylinder fluid level and add fluid as necessary. Bleed the brakes (see Section 11). Carefully test brake operation before resuming normal operation.

11 Brake system - bleeding

Refer to illustration 11.9

Warning: *Wear eye protection when bleeding the brake system. If the fluid comes in contact with your eyes, immediately rinse them with water and seek medical attention.*

Note: *Bleeding the brake system is necessary to remove any air that's trapped in the system when it's opened during removal and installation of a hose, line, caliper, wheel cylinder or master cylinder.*

1 If a brake line was disconnected only at a wheel, then only that caliper or wheel cylinder must be bled.

2 On conventional (non-ABS) brake systems, if air has entered the system due to low fluid level or master cylinder replacement, all four brakes must be bled. **Warning:** *If this has occurred on a model with an Anti-lock Brake System (ABS), or if the lines to the Hydraulic Control Unit or Integrated Control Unit (1998 models) have been disconnected, the vehicle must be towed to a dealer service department or other repair shop equipped with a DRB II scan tool to have the system properly bled.*

3 If a brake line is disconnected at a fitting located between the master cylinder and any of the brakes, that part of the system served by the disconnected line must be bled.

4 Remove any residual vacuum from the brake power booster by applying the brake several times with the engine OFF.

5 Raise the vehicle and support it securely on jackstands. **Note:** *The wheels do not have to be removed for this process.*

6 Remove the master cylinder reservoir cover and fill the reservoir with brake fluid. Reinstall the cover. **Note:** *Check the fluid level often during the bleeding operation and add fluid as necessary to prevent the fluid level from falling low enough to allow air bubbles into the master cylinder.*

7 Have an assistant on hand, as well as a supply of new brake fluid, a clear container partially filled with clean brake fluid, a length of clear plastic or vinyl tubing to fit over the bleed screw and a box-end wrench to open and close the bleed screw.

8 Beginning at the left rear wheel, remove the bleed screw dust cap. Loosen the bleed screw slightly, then tighten it to a point where it's snug but can still be loosened quickly and easily. Use the box-end wrench to avoid rounding off the bleed screw corners.

9 With the wrench in place on the bleed screw, attach one end of the tubing over the bleed screw fitting and submerge the other end in a clear container filled with about 1 inch of new brake fluid **(see illustration).**

10 Have the assistant slowly push the brake pedal to the floor, then hold the pedal firmly depressed.

11 While the pedal is held depressed, open the bleed screw just enough to allow a flow of fluid to leave the valve. Watch for air bubbles to exit the submerged end of the tube. When the fluid flow slows after a couple of seconds, tighten the screw and have your assistant slowly release the pedal.

12 Repeat Steps 10 and 11 until no more air is seen leaving the tube, then tighten the bleed screw securely and proceed to the right front wheel, the right rear wheel and the left front wheel, in that order, and perform the same procedure. Be sure to check the fluid in the master cylinder reservoir frequently.

13 NEVER use old brake fluid. Brake fluid absorbs moisture from the atmosphere. When moisture is present in the hydraulic system, it can lower the boiling point of the fluid, which can render the brakes inoperative.

14 After bleeding the system, top up the brake fluid reservoir and reinstall the bleed screw dust caps.

15 Check the operation of the brakes. The pedal should feel solid when depressed, with no sponginess. If necessary, repeat the bleeding process. Check for leakage. **Warning:** *Do not operate the vehicle if the pedal feels low or spongy, if the ABS light on the dash won't go off, or if you are in doubt about the effectiveness of the brake system.*

12 Power brake booster - check, removal and installation

Operating check

1 Depress the pedal and start the engine. If the pedal goes down slightly, operation is normal.

2 Depress the brake pedal several times with the engine running and make sure that there is no change in the pedal reserve distance.

Airtightness check

3 Start the engine and turn it off after one or two minutes. Depress the brake pedal several

11.9 When bleeding the brakes, a hose is connected to the bleed screw at the caliper or wheel cylinder and then submerged in clean brake fluid - air will be seen as bubbles exiting the tube (all air must be expelled before moving to the next wheel)

times slowly. If the pedal goes down farther the first time but gradually rises after the second or third depression, the booster is airtight.

4 Depress the brake pedal while the engine is running, then stop the engine with the pedal depressed. If there is no change in the pedal reserve travel after holding the pedal for 30 seconds, the booster is airtight.

Removal

Refer to illustration 12.17 and 12.18

5 The power brake booster unit requires no special maintenance apart from periodic inspection of the vacuum hoses and the case. the booster should never be disassembled. If a problem develops, it must be replaced with a new one.

6 Remove any vacuum from the booster by pumping the pedal several times with the engine off, until the pedal feels hard to push.

7 Remove the air inlet resonator and the related ducting between the throttle body and the air cleaner (see Chapter 4).

8 Remove the battery thermal guard and the battery. If equipped, remove the cruise control servo electrical connector. Detach the unit from the battery tray and position it out of the way.

9 Remove the two nuts holding the battery tray, and remove the battery tray.

10 On models with 2.4L four-cylinder and 3.0L V6 engines, remove the electrical connector from the brake fluid level sensor on the master cylinder reservoir.

11 On models with 3.3L and 3.8L V6 engines, detach the wiring harness connectors from the EGR transducer, the throttle positioning sensor, and the AIS motor on the throttle body. Remove the throttle body and the throttle cable bracket from the intake manifold as a unit.

12 Clean the area where the master cylinder attaches to the power brake booster.

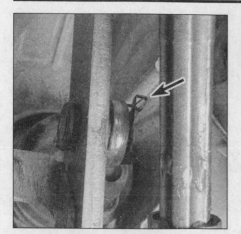

12.17 Power brake pedal-to-booster pushrod retaining clip (DO NOT reuse)

12.18 Power brake booster mounting nuts

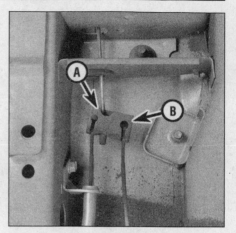

13.5 Disconnect the brake cable (a) from the brake equalizer (b)

13   Remove the clip that attaches the wiper module drain hose to the brake tube at the master cylinder and remove the drain hose from the wiper module.

14   Remove the nuts attaching the master cylinder to the vacuum booster **(see illustration 8.8)** and carefully position the master cylinder out of the way. **Note:** *It is not necessary to remove the brake tubes from the master cylinder when removing the master cylinder from the vacuum booster, but be careful not to kink the brake lines.* Lay the master cylinder on top of the left engine mount.

15   On 3.3L and 3.8L V6 engines, remove the EGR valve and the vacuum transducer as a unit (see Chapter 6).

16   Disconnect the vacuum hose from the vacuum booster check valve. **Warning:** *Don't remove the check valve from the booster.*

17   Working inside the vehicle under the dash, disconnect the brake pedal pushrod from the top of the brake pedal by prying off the retaining clip **(see illustration)**. For safety reasons, discard the old pushrod retaining clip and buy a new clip for reassembly.

18   Remove the nuts attaching the booster to the firewall **(see illustration)**.

19   Working back inside the engine compartment, carefully withdraw the power brake booster unit from the firewall and out of the engine compartment.

Installation

20   To install the booster, place it into position on the firewall and tighten the retaining nuts to the torque listed in this Chapter's Specification Section. Connect the brake pedal. **Warning:** *Use a new retainer clip. DO NOT reuse the old clip.*

21   The remaining installation steps are the reverse of removal. Be sure to install a new vacuum seal on the master cylinder **(see illustration 8.21)**.

22   Carefully test the operation of the brakes before placing the vehicle in normal operation.

13   Parking brake pedal assembly - removal, installation and adjustment

Removal

Refer to illustration 13.5

1   Disconnect the cable from the negative terminal of the battery. Remove the left door sill plate and the left side kick panel (see Chapter 11).

2   Remove the steering column cover and the reinforcement from the lower instrument panel (see Chapter 11).

3   Raise the vehicle and support it securely on jackstands.

4   Disconnect the parking brake cable equalizer by grabbing the exposed parking brake cable and pulling rearward on it. While holding the cable, install a pair of locking pliers on the cable, just rearward of the second body outrigger bracket.

5   Disconnect the brake cable from the brake cable equalizer **(see illustration)**.

6   Release the locking pliers from the brake cable.

7   Remove the three bolts attaching the wiring junction block to the instrument panel and position the junction block to the side.

8   Remove the lower bolt, the forward bolt, then the upper bolt from the parking brake pedal assembly. **Note:** *Push the brake pedal down five clicks to reach the lower mounting bolt.*

9   Disconnect the electrical connector from the switch on the pedal mechanism.

10   Pull down on the upper parking brake cable while rotating the pedal mechanism out from behind the junction block.

11   Once the pedal mechanism is clear of the instrument panel, unhook the parking brake cable end from the pedal mechanism.

12   Remove the ground switch for the brake warning light on the pedal mechanism.

13   Detach the cable casing from the parking brake mechanism.

Installation

14   Installation is the reverse of removal. Tighten the pedal mounting bolts to the torque listed in this Chapter's Specifications.

Adjustment

15   Cycle the parking brake pedal one time. This will seat the brake cables and it will allow the automatic adjuster to properly seat the cables.

14   Parking brake cables - replacement

Front cable

Removal

Refer to illustration 14.3

1   Raise the vehicle and support it securely on jackstands.

2   Disconnect the parking brake cable equalizer (see Step 4 in Section 13).

3   Remove the brake cable housing retainer from the body outrigger bracket by sliding a 1/2-inch box-end wrench over the end of the cable retainer to compress the retainer fingers **(see illustration)**.

4   Lower the vehicle.

5   Remove the left front door sill molding and the left kick panel (see Chapter 11).

6   Lift the floor mat for access to the parking brake cable and the floor pan.

7   Pull the seal and the parking brake cable out of the floor pan.

8   Disconnect the cable and the cable retainer from the pedal assembly.

9   Pull the cable out of the vehicle through the hole in the floor pan.

Installation

10   Installation is the reverse of removal. **Note:** *Be sure the foam collars are properly positioned on the cable to prevent the cable from rattling against the floor panels. Lower*

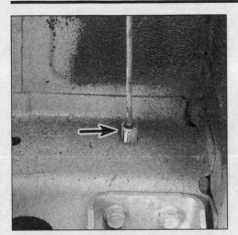

14.3 Sliding a 1/2-inch box-end wrench over the parking brake cable retainer will compress the retaining clip tabs so you can remove the cable from the bracket

the vehicle and apply the parking brake one time. This will automatically adjust the brake cables.

Intermediate cable

Removal
Note: *The removal and installation procedures for both the left and right intermediate cables are identical.*

11   Raise the vehicle and support it securely on jackstands.
12   Disconnect the parking brake cable equalizer (see Step 4 in Section 13).
13   Disconnect the intermediate parking brake cable from the rear parking brake cable.
14   Remove the cable from the cable guides on the frame rails.

Installation
15   Installation of the intermediate parking brake cable is the reverse of removal. **Note:** *Be sure the foam collars on the parking brake cable are properly positioned to prevent rattling against the floor panels. Lower the vehicle and apply the parking brake one time. This will automatically adjust the brake cables.*

Rear cables
Refer to illustration 14.25

Removal
Note: *The removal and installation procedures for both the left and right rear cables are identical.*

16   Loosen the lug nuts on the rear wheel.
17   Raise the vehicle and place it securely on jackstands.
18   Remove the rear wheel.
19   Remove the rear brake drum.
20   Disconnect the parking brake cable equalizer (see Step 4 in Section 13).
21   Disconnect the rear brake cable from the

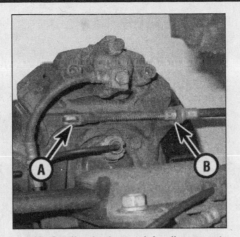

14.25 On disc-brake models, disconnect the parking brake cable from the actuator (A), then use a box-end wrench or hose clamp to compress the locking tabs on the retainer (B)

intermediate brake cable.
22   Remove the rear brake cable from the body bracket by sliding a 1/2-inch box end wrench over the end of the cable retainer to compress the retainer fingers **(see illustration 14.3)**.
23   Remove the brake shoes (see Section 6).
24   Disconnect the parking brake cable from the parking brake actuator lever.
25   On drum brake models, disconnect the parking brake cable from the brake backing plate. On disc brake models, disconnect the parking brake cable from the actuator **(see illustration)**. Use a box-end wrench and compress the locking tabs on the retainer and remove the parking brake cable.

Installation
26   Insert the rear of the cable through the hole in the brake backing plate. Make sure the cable casing is pushed through the hole far enough to allow the retaining tabs to expand all the way, locking the cable to the backing plate.

27   Connect the cable end to the parking brake lever on the trailing brake shoe and reassemble the rear brake assembly (see Section 6).
28   Connect the rear brake cable to the intermediate brake cable. Ensure the intermediate cable is connected to the forward cable, and the forward cable is properly configured.
29   Install the wheel and lug nuts, then lower the vehicle. Tighten the lug nuts to the torque listed in the Chapter 1 Specifications.
30   Pump the brake pedal once to automatically adjust the parking brake cables.

15 Parking brake shoes (models with rear disc brakes) - replacement

Refer to illustrations 15.5a through 15.5s
Warning: *Parking brake shoes must be replaced on both wheels at the same time - never replace the shoes on only one wheel. Also, the dust created by the brake system is harmful to your health. Never blow it out with compressed air and don't inhale any of it. An approved filtering mask should be worn when working on the brakes. Do not, under any circumstances, use petroleum-based solvents to clean brake parts. Use brake system cleaner only!*

1   Loosen the rear wheel lug nuts, raise the rear of the vehicle and support it securely on jackstands. Block the front wheels and remove the rear wheels. Release the parking brake.
2   Remove the rear calipers (see Section 4). Support the caliper assemblies with a coat hanger or heavy wire and don't disconnect the brake line from the caliper.
3   Remove the rear discs (see Section 5). Remove the rear hub and bearing assemblies (see Chapter 10).
4   Clean the parking brake assembly with brake system cleaner.
5   Follow the accompanying sequence of photos to replace the parking brake shoes **(see illustrations)**. Be sure to stay in order and read the caption under each illustration.

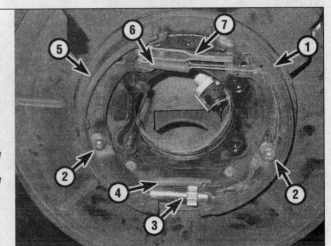

15.5a Parking brake details (right side)

1   Leading shoe
2   Hold-down spring and pin
3   Adjuster screw assembly
4   Lower return spring
5   Trailing shoe
6   Upper return spring
7   Parking brake actuator lever

15.5b Use a cable tie (or equivalent) to hold the brake backing plate in place

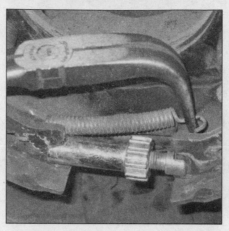

15.5c Remove the lower return spring

15.5d Remove the hold-down spring and pin from the leading shoe

15.5e Pull the leading shoe back and remove the adjuster screw assembly (note how it's installed; it must be reinstalled the same way)

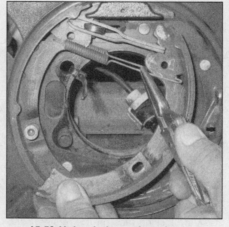

15.5f Unhook the outboard upper return spring . . .

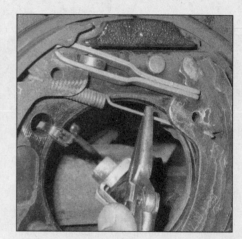

15.5g . . . then unhook the inboard upper return spring and remove the leading shoe

15.5h Remove the hold-down spring and pin from the trailing shoe . . .

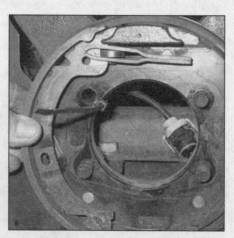

15.5i . . . and remove the trailing shoe

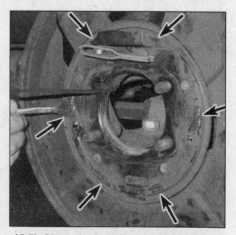

15.5j Clean the backing plate, then apply a thin coat of high-temperature grease to the shoe contact points on the backing plate

15.5k Clean and lubricate the threads of the adjuster screw assembly

15.5l Mount the trailing shoe on the backing plate, making sure the notch in the shoe engages with the actuator lever . . .

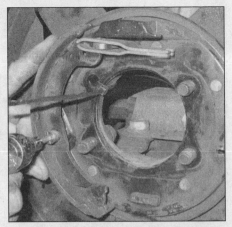

15.5m . . . and secure the shoe with the hold-down spring and pin

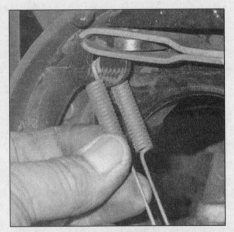

15.5n Connect the upper return springs to the top of the trailing shoe . . .

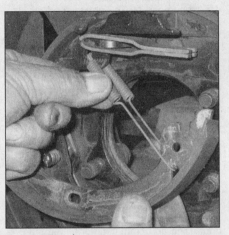

15.5o . . . and to the top of the leading shoe

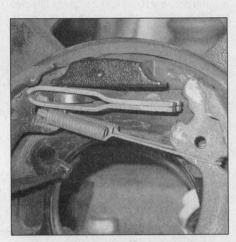

15.5p Place the leading shoe in position . . .

15.5q . . . and secure the shoe with the hold-down spring and pin

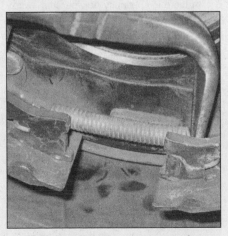

15.5r Install the lower return spring

15.5s Spread the shoes apart and install the adjuster screw assembly

16.7 The brake light switch (arrow) is located under the dash and mounted on a bracket near the brake pedal arm

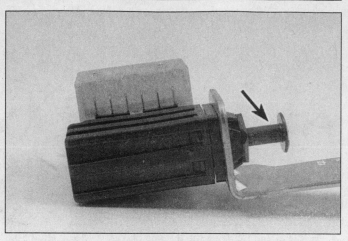

16.9 Pull the brake light switch plunger (arrow) out until it is fully extended

6   Inspect the drum surface inside the disc for score marks, deep grooves, hard spots (which appear as small, discolored areas) and cracks. If the disc/drum is worn, scored or out of round, it will have to be resurfaced by an automotive machine shop, or replaced.

7   Install the hub and bearing assemblies (see Chapter 10).

8   Install the disc/drum over the shoes. Using a screwdriver, turn the star wheel on the parking brake shoe adjuster until the shoes slightly drag as the disc is turned, then back-off the adjuster until the shoes don't drag. **Note:** *Access to the star wheel is through a plugged port on the brake backing plate. Remove the rubber plug near the bottom and backside of the backing plate.*

9   Install the caliper (see Section 4).

10   Repeat this sequence on the parking brake shoes for the other rear wheel.

---

16 Brake light switch - check, replacement and adjustment

---

1   The brake light switch is located near the top of the brake pedal and is attached to a bracket. When the brake pedal is applied, the pedal arm moves away from the switch and a spring-loaded plunger closes the circuit to the brake lights.

2   Models equipped with cruise control use a dual-purpose brake light switch that also deactivates the cruise control system when the brake pedal is depressed.

Check

3   Check the brake light fuse (see Chapter 12). If the fuse has blown, replace it. If it blows again, look for a short in the brake light circuit.

4   If the fuse is okay, use a test light or voltmeter to verify that there's voltage to the switch. If there's no voltage to the switch, look for an open or short in the power wire to the switch. Repair as necessary.

5   If the brake lights still don't come on when the brake pedal is applied, unplug the electrical connector from the brake light switch and, using an ohmmeter, verify that there is continuity between the switch terminals when the brake pedal is applied, i.e. when the switch is closed. If continuity is not detected, replace the switch.

6   If there is continuity between the switch terminals when the brake is applied (it closes the circuit), but the brake lights don't come on when the brake pedal is applied, check for power to the brake light bulb sockets when the pedal is depressed. If voltage is present, replace the bulbs (it isn't very likely that all of them would fail simultaneously, but it is possible that they could be burned out). If voltage

is not available, check the wiring between the switch and the brake lights for an open circuit and repair as necessary.

Replacement and adjustment
Refer to illustration 16.7 and 16.9

7   Depress and hold the brake pedal, then rotate the brake light switch about 30-degrees in a counterclockwise direction and remove it from the mounting bracket **(see illustration)**.

8   Unplug the electrical connector from the switch and remove the switch from the vehicle.

9   Grasp the switch plunger and pull it outward until it has ratcheted to its fully ex-tended position **(see illustration)**.

10   Depress the brake pedal as far as it will go, then install the switch in the bracket by aligning the index key on the switch with the slot at the top of the square hole in the mounting bracket. When the switch is fully installed in the bracket, rotate the switch clockwise about 30-degrees to lock the switch into the bracket.

11   Gently pull back on the brake pedal until the pedal stops moving. The switch plunger will ratchet backward to the correct position. **Caution:** *Don't use excessive force when pulling back on the brake pedal to adjust the switch. If you use too much force, you will damage the switch or the striker.*

12   Plug the electrical connector into the switch.

Chapter 10
Suspension and steering systems

Contents

	Section
Axle assembly (rear) - removal and installation	14
Balljoints - check and replacement	6
Control arm - removal, inspection and installation	5
General information	1
Hub and bearing assembly (front) - removal and installation	7
Hub and bearing assembly (rear) - removal and installation	15
Leaf springs - removal and installation	12
Leaf spring mounts - removal and installation	11
Power steering fluid level check	See Chapter 1
Power steering fluid cooler - removal and installation	21
Power steering pump - removal and installation	20
Power steering system - bleeding	22
Shock absorbers (rear) - removal and installation	13
Stabilizer bar and bushings (front) - removal, inspection and installation	2

	Section
Stabilizer bar (rear) - removal, inspection, and installation	9
Steering and suspension check	See Chapter 1
Steering gear - removal and installation	19
Steering knuckle - removal and installation	8
Steering system - general information	16
Steering wheel - removal and installation	17
Strut/coil spring - disassembly, inspection, and reassembly	4
Struts (front) - removal, inspection and installation	3
Tie-rod ends - removal and installation	18
Tire and tire pressure checks	See Chapter 1
Tire rotation	See Chapter 1
Track bar and mount - removal and installation	10
Wheel alignment - general information	24
Wheels and tires - general information	23

Specifications

Torque specifications

Ft-lbs (unless otherwise indicated)

Front suspension

Balljoint stud-to-steering knuckle pinch bolt nut	
1999 through 2000	123
2001 and later	80
Cradle plate bolts	
M14 bolts	
1999 through 2000	123
2001 and later	120
M12 bolts	80
Control arm pivot bolt	135
Control arm bushing retainer bolts	50
Front suspension cradle-to-body bolts	120
Hub and bearing-to-steering knuckle bolts	45
Stabilizer bar link-to-stabilizer bar nut	65
Stabilizer bar bushing/retainer bolts	50
Stabilizer bar link-to-strut nut	65
Steering knuckle-to-balljoint stud nut	100
Strut upper mounting nuts	21
Strut shaft nut	75
Strut-to-steering knuckle nuts	
Step 1	65
Step 2	Tighten an additional 90-degrees
Driveaxle/hub nut	180
Wheel stop bolts	70

Torque specifications

Ft-lbs (unless otherwise indicated)

Rear suspension

Hub and bearing-to-axle mounting bolts	95
Jounce bumper-to-frame rail..	25
Leaf spring rear mount bolts	45
Leaf spring front mount (hanger) bolts	45
Leaf spring front throughbolt...	115
Leaf spring axle plate bolts...	80
Shackle nuts	45
Shock absorber bolts	75
Stabilizer bar-to-link arm	45
Stabilizer bar bushing-to-axle bracket bolts	45
Stabilizer link arm-to-frame rail bracket	45
Stub axle nut..	180
Track bar bolts...	70
Track bar mount bolts	45

Steering system

Airbag module retaining screws	100 in-lbs
Intermediate coupler pinch bolt...	21
Power steering pump mounting bolts	40
Steering gear-to-cradle mounting bolts	
1996	100
1997 on	135
Steering wheel nut..	45
Tie-rod end-to-steering knuckle nut	40
Wheel lug nuts	See Chapter 1

1.1a Front suspension and steering components

1	*Steering gear*	*3*	*Outer CV joint*	*5*	*Cradle plate*	*7*	*Brake caliper*
2	*Stabilizer bar*	*4*	*Inner CV joint*	*6*	*Tie-rod ends*	*8*	*Balljoint*

1   General information

Refer to illustrations 1.1a, 1.1b, 1.2a and 1.2b

The front suspension **(see illustrations)** on these vehicles is by independent Mac-Pherson struts. The upper end of each strut/coil spring assembly bolts to the strut tower through a rubber isolated mount. The lower end of each strut bolts to the upper end of the steering knuckle. The lower end of the steering knuckle attaches to a balljoint mounted in the outer end of the control arm. The control arm is held longitudinally by the front suspension cradle. A stabilizer bar bolted to the frame and connected to the strut/coil assemblies reduces body roll while cornering.

The rear suspension **(see illustration)** on these vehicles is composed of leaf springs and a tube axle housing mounted in isolator bushings on axle mount brackets. The leaf springs are a mono-leaf design. Side-to-side axle movement is controlled by the rear track bar attached to the top of the axle housing and the frame. Further stability is provided by the rear stabilizer bar attached to the rear axle tube, and the rear frame rails through rubber-isolated bushings. Normal shock absorbers control vehicle "bounce", but self-leveling shock absorbers are available as an option.

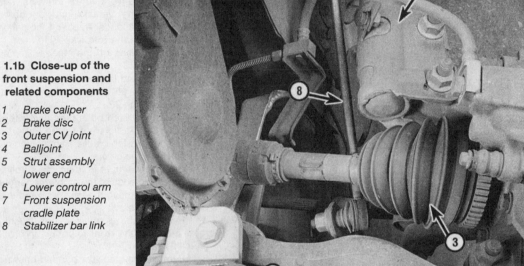

1.1b Close-up of the front suspension and related components

1   *Brake caliper*
2   *Brake disc*
3   *Outer CV joint*
4   *Balljoint*
5   *Strut assembly lower end*
6   *Lower control arm*
7   *Front suspension cradle plate*
8   *Stabilizer bar link*

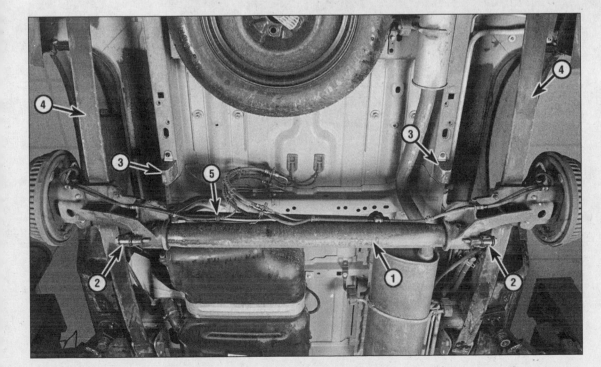

1.2a Rear suspension components (1996 through 2000 models)

1   *Axle assembly*
2   *Shock absorber*
3   *Jounce bumper*
4   *Leaf springs*
5   *Track bar*

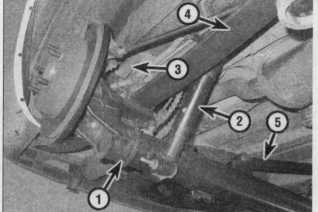

1.2b Rear suspension components (2001 and later models)

1. Axle assembly
2. Shock absorber
3. Jounce bumper
4. Leaf spring
5. Track bar

The power steering system consists of a rack-and-pinion steering gear, a power steering pump, the pressure hose, and the return line. The steering gear drives the tie-rods, which attach to the steering knuckles.

You may find fasteners which seem impossible to loosen when working on suspension or steering system components. Fasteners on the underside of the vehicle are subjected to water, road grime, mud, etc., and can become rusted or "frozen." To remove these fasteners without damaging them (or other components), soak them in penetrating oil. Use a wire brush to clean exposed threads, to ease nut or bolt removal, and to prevent thread damage. A sharp blow with a hammer and punch may break the bond between a nut and bolt threads, but be careful to keep the punch from slipping off the fastener and ruining the threads. Heating

fasteners with a torch may help, but isn't recommended because of the danger of fire. Long breaker bars and extension, or "cheater," pipes will increase leverage, but never use them on a ratchet - the ratcheting mechanism may be damaged. Tightening the nut or bolt first will sometimes help break it loose. Fasteners requiring drastic measures to remove should be replaced.

Most of the procedures in this Chapter involve jacking up the vehicle and working underneath it. A good pair of jackstands will be needed. A hydraulic floor jack is preferred to lift vehicles, and it can be used to support components during some repairs. **Warning:** *Never rely on a jack to support the vehicle while working on it. When suspension or steering fasteners are loosened or removed they must be inspected and, if necessary, replaced with new ones equivalent to original*

equipment quality and design. Torque specifications must be followed closely during reassembly. Do not heat or straighten any suspension or steering components. Replace bent or damaged parts with new ones.

2 Stabilizer bar and bushings (front) - removal, inspection and installation

Removal

Refer to illustrations 2.3, 2.4 and 2.5

1   Loosen the front wheel lug nuts, raise the front of the vehicle and support it securely on jackstands. Apply on the parking brake and block the rear wheels to keep the vehicle from rolling off the stands. Remove the front wheels.

2   On 2001 and later models, remove the power steering oil cooler from the cradle plate (see Section 23).

3   Remove the ten bolts **(see illustration)** attaching the cradle plate to the bottom of the front suspension cradle. Remove the cradle plate from the cradle.

4   Remove the nuts holding the stabilizer bar links to the ends of the stabilizer bar **(see illustration)**. Remove the links from the ends of the stabilizer bar.

5   Remove the stabilizer bar bushing retainers from the front suspension cradle **(see illustration)**.

6   Remove the stabilizer bar and bushings as an assembly from the front suspension cradle.

2.2 Remove the bolts attaching the cradle plate to the front suspension cradle

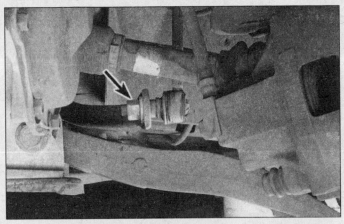

2.3 Remove the nuts holding the stabilizer bar links to the stabilizer bar

2.5 Stabilizer bar bushing locations (arrows) on the front suspension cradle

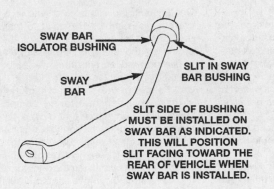

SWAY BAR ISOLATOR BUSHING

SLIT IN SWAY BAR BUSHING

SWAY BAR

SLIT SIDE OF BUSHING MUST BE INSTALLED ON SWAY BAR AS INDICATED. THIS WILL POSITION SLIT FACING TOWARD THE REAR OF VEHICLE WHEN SWAY BAR IS INSTALLED.

2.7 When installing the stabilizer bar bushings, make sure that the slit on each bushing faces forward and the square corner is towards the ground

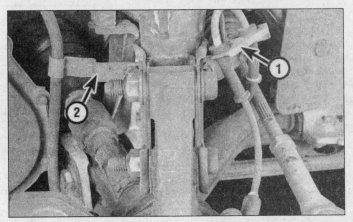

3.3 Remove the brake hose bracket (1) and the speed sensor cable routing bracket (2) from the strut bracket

Inspection

Refer to illustration 2.7

7　Inspect the bushings for cracks and tears. If either bushing is broken, damaged, distorted, or worn, replace both of them. **Note:** *Bushings must be installed on the stabilizer with the bushing slits facing the rear of the vehicle and the square corner towards the ground* **(see illustration).** Clean the stabilizer bar where the bushings are located. Lubricate the inside and outside of the new bushings with vegetable oil (used in cooking) to simplify reassembly. **Caution:** *Don't use petroleum or mineral-based lubricants or brake fluid - they will cause deterioration of the bushings.*

Installation

8　Align the stabilizer bar bushings with the depressions in the cradle, and install the stabilizer bar bushing retainers onto the crossmember, aligning the retainer with cutouts in the bushings. **Warning:** *Do not tighten the stabilizer bar bushings yet.*

9　Center the stabilizer bar on the cradle. Install the stabilizer bar links and nuts, and tighten the nuts to the torque listed in this Chapter's Specifications.

10　Install the stabilizer bar bushing retainer bolts to the torque listed in this Chapter's Specifications.

11　Install the front suspension cradle plate. Tighten the cradle plate bolts to the torque listed in this Chapter's Specifications.

12　On 2001 and later models, install the power steering oil cooler onto the cradle plate (see Section 23).

13　Install the wheels and snug the wheel lug nuts. Remove the jackstands and lower the vehicle. Tighten the wheel lug nuts to the torque listed in the Chapter 1 Specifications.

3　Struts (front) - removal, inspection and installation

Removal

Refer to illustrations 3.3, 3.4, and 3.6

1　Loosen the front wheel lug nuts, raise the vehicle and support it securely on jackstands. Remove the wheel.

2　Mark the strut assemblies, left and right, if both are to be removed. **Note:** *If the strut assembly is attached to the steering knuckle using a cam bolt in the lower slotted hole, mark the relationship of the cam bolt to the*

strut to preserve the wheel alignment setting on reassembly.

3　Remove the brake hose bracket and the speed sensor cable bracket from the strut bracket **(see illustration).**

4　Disconnect the stabilizer bar link from the strut assembly **(see illustration). Note:** *Hold the link stud to prevent it from turning.*

5　Remove the strut assembly-to-steering knuckle bolts. **Caution:** *The steering knuckle*

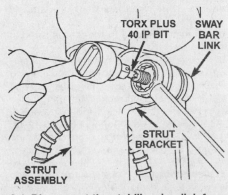

TORX PLUS 40 IP BIT　　SWAY BAR LINK

STRUT ASSEMBLY

STRUT BRACKET

3.4 Disconnect the stabilizer bar link from the strut assembly

3.6 Remove the strut assembly upper mount nuts

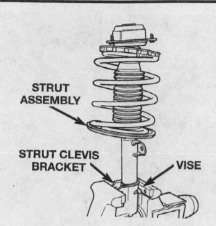

4.2a Mount the strut assembly in a vise, clamping the vise on the strut bracket

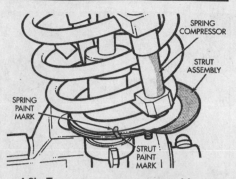

4.2b To ensure proper reassembly, use paint to mark the relationship of the upper end of the coil spring to the seat/bearing assembly and upper strut mount (not shown), and the lower end of the spring to the strut

to strut assembly bolts are serrated and must not turn during removal. Remove the nuts while holding the bolts stationary in the steering knuckles.

6   Remove the three nuts attaching the strut assembly upper mount to the strut tower **(see illustration). Warning:** *Do not loosen or remove the center strut shaft nut.*

7   Lower the strut assembly from the strut tower.

Inspection

8   Check the strut body for leakage, dents, cracks, and other damage that requires repair or replacement.

9   Check the coil spring for chips or cracks in the spring coating (this can cause corrosion and premature spring failure). Inspect the spring seat for cuts, hardness and deterioration.

10   If necessary, disassemble the strut (see Section 4).

Installation

11   Push the strut assembly into the strut tower and insert the three upper mounting studs through the holes in the shock tower. When the three studs protrude from the shock tower, install the nuts so the strut can't fall back through. This is done most easily with the help of an assistant, the strut is heavy and awkward.

12   Tighten the nuts to the torque listed in this Chapter's Specifications.

13   Align the strut assembly with the steering knuckle. Position the arm of the steering knuckle into the strut assembly bracket. Align the strut assembly bracket mounting holes with the steering knuckle mounting holes. Install the strut-to-steering knuckle bolts. **Note:** *If the strut assembly is attached to the steering knuckle using a cam bolt, the cam bolt must be installed in the lower slotted hole on the strut bracket. Bolts should be installed with the nuts facing the front of the vehicle. Align the cam bolt with the marks made in Step 2.* Tighten the strut assembly to steering knuckle bolts to the torque listed in this

Chapter's Specifications.

14   Install the stabilizer bar link on the bracket of the strut assembly. Install the stabilizer bar attaching link-to-strut bracket nut.

15   Tighten the stabilizer bar link nut to the torque listed in this Chapter's Specifications. **Note:** *When tightening the nut on the stud of the stabilizer bar attaching link, do not allow the stud to rotate.*

16   Install the brake hose and speed sensor cable brackets on the strut assembly brackets.

17   Install the wheel and lug nuts, lower the vehicle, and tighten the lug nuts to the torque listed in the Chapter 1 Specifications.

18   Drive the vehicle to an alignment shop to have the front end alignment checked and, if necessary, adjusted.

---

4   Strut/coil spring - disassembly, inspection, and reassembly

---

1   If the struts or coil springs show signs of wear (leaking fluid, loss of damping capability, chipped, sagging, or cracked coil springs) they may require replacement. Strut/shock absorber assemblies are not serviceable and must be replaced if a problem develops. Strut assemblies, complete with springs, may be available on an exchange basis, saving time and work. Whatever you do, check on the cost and availability of parts before disassembling your vehicle. **Warning:** *Disassembling a strut is potentially dangerous, and utmost attention must be directed to the job, or serious injury may result. Use only a high-quality spring compressor and follow the manufacturer's instructions furnished with the tool. After removing the coil spring from the strut assembly, set it in a safe, isolated area.*

Disassembly

Refer to illustrations 4.2a, 4.2b, 4.4, 4.5, 4.6, and 4.8

2   Remove the strut and spring assembly following the procedures in Section 3. Mount the strut assembly in a vise **(see illustration)**.

Don't tighten the vise excessively. To ensure correct reassembly, use paint to mark the relationship of the upper end of the coil spring to the seat/bearing assembly and upper strut mount, and the lower end of the spring to the strut **(see illustration)**.

3   Following the tool manufacturer's instructions, install the spring compressor (which can be purchased at most auto parts stores or rented) on the spring. Compress the spring enough to relieve pressure from the upper spring seat **(see illustration 4.2b)**. This can be verified by moving the spring.

4   Loosen and remove the strut shaft nut **(see illustration)** while holding the shaft with a wrench or socket. Use an offset box-end wrench to break the nut loose.

5   Remove the upper strut mount **(see illustration)**.

6   Remove the seat/bearing, dust shield and jounce bumper **(see illustration)**.

7   Carefully lift the compressed spring from the strut and set it in a safe place. **Warning:** *Never place your head or body near the end of a compressed spring!*

8   Remove the lower spring isolator from the strut **(see illustration)**.

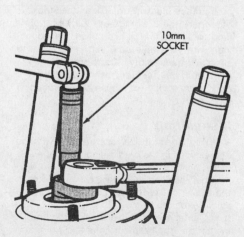

4.4 Remove the strut shaft nut

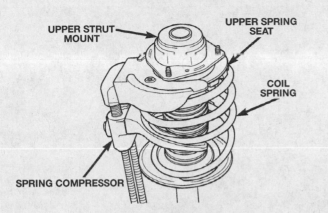

4.5 Remove the upper strut mount

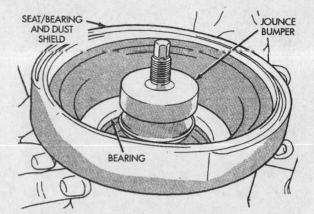

4.6 Remove the seat/bearing, dust shield and jounce bumper

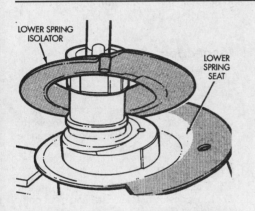

4.8 Remove the lower spring isolator from the strut assembly

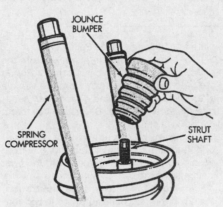

4.11 Extend the damper rod and install the jounce bumper

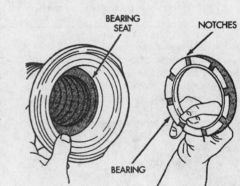

4.13 Install the strut bearing in the bearing seat with the notches facing down (1996 through 2000 models)

Inspection

9   Inspect all disassembled parts for signs of wear or failure and replace all broken, damaged, or worn parts. Replace the strut if it is leaking fluid. Check the strut for loss of gas charge. Push the strut shaft into the body and release it. If the strut shaft does not fully extend, it should be replaced.

Reassembly

Refer to illustrations 4.11, 4.13 and 4.14

10   Install the lower spring isolator.
11   Fully extend the strut shaft and install the jounce bumper **(see illustration)**.
12   Place the coil spring on the lower insulator. The marked end of the spring should align with the mark on the strut.
13   On 1996 through 2000 models, install the strut bearing in the bearing seat with the notches on the bearing facing down **(see illustration)**. On 2001 and later models, install the pivot bearing on the spring seat with the smaller diameter side toward the bearing seat. Make sure the pivot bearing is sitting flat on the bearing seat.
14   Lower the seat/bearing assembly and dust shield onto the strut/coil spring assembly. Align the paint mark on the seat/bearing assembly with the mark on the upper end of the coil spring **(see illustration)**.

15   Install the upper strut mount. Make sure the paint mark on the upper strut mount is aligned with the mark on the spring.
16   Using the same technique as in Step 4, tighten the strut damper shaft nut to the torque listed in this Chapter's Specifications. Use an offset box-end wrench to tighten the nut while holding the shaft with a wrench or socket.
17   Loosen the spring compressor. Back off each nut a turn at a time, alternating between the two nuts, until all tension is removed from the coil spring.
18   Install the strut in the vehicle (see Section 3).
19   Repeat this procedure for the other strut.
20   Drive the vehicle to an alignment shop and have the front end alignment checked and if necessary, adjusted.

5   Control arm - removal, inspection, and installation

Removal

Refer to illustrations 5.2, 5.3, 5.6, 5.7 and 5.8

1   Loosen the wheel lug nuts, raise the front of the vehicle and support it securely on jackstands. Remove the wheel.
2   Remove the wheel stop from the steer-

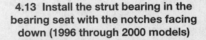

4.14 Lower the seat/bearing assembly and dust shield onto the strut/coil spring assembly; be sure to align the paint mark you made on the seat/bearing assembly with the mark on the upper end of the spring

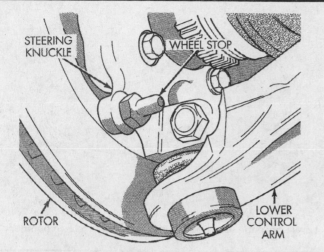

5.2 Remove the wheel stop from the steering knuckle

5.3 Remove the nut and bolt holding the steering knuckle to the balljoint stud

ing knuckle **(see illustration)**.

3   Remove the nut and bolt clamping the steering knuckle to the balljoint stud **(see illustration)**.

4   Remove the front suspension cradle

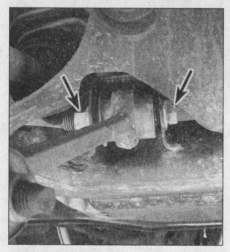

5.6 Loosen the pivot bolt and nut (arrows) that attach the control arm to the cradle

plate from the cradle (see Section 2).

5   Separate the steering knuckle from the balljoint stud with a prybar. **Caution:** *Pulling the steering knuckle away from the vehicle after releasing it from the balljoint can separate the inner CV joint.* Be careful not to cut the balljoint seal.

6   Loosen, but do not remove, the pivot bolt **(see illustration)** attaching the front bushing of the lower control arm to the front suspension cradle.

7   Remove the retainer **(see illustration)** attaching the rear bushing of the lower control arm to the front suspension cradle.

8   If you're removing the left control arm, support the left side of the cradle with a floor jack. Lower the front suspension cradle by loosening, but not fully removing, the left side suspension cradle-to-frame rail bolts **(see illustration)**. **Note:** *The front suspension cradle needs to be lowered for the pivot bolt to clear the transmission when the left lower control arm is removed.* Lower the left front corner of the suspension cradle until the pivot bolt clears the end of the transmission.

9   Remove the pivot bolt and lower the control arm.

Inspection

10   Make sure the control arm is straight. If it is bent, replace it. Do not attempt to straighten a bent control arm.

11   Inspect all bushings for cracks, distortion, and tears. If a bushing is torn or worn, take the assembly to an automotive machine shop and have it replaced.

Installation

12   Position the lower control arm in the front suspension cradle. Install the pivot bolt.

13   Install the pivot bolt in the front suspension cradle and lower control arm. **Note:** *Do not tighten the pivot bolt yet.*

14   Install the retainer attaching the rear bushing of the lower control arm to the suspension cradle. **Note:** *Be sure the raised rib on the rear bushing is positioned in the groove on the retainer. Do not fully tighten the bolts at this time.*

15   Insert the lower control arm balljoint stud into the steering knuckle. Install the bolt and nut clamping the steering knuckle to the balljoint stud. Tighten the clamping bolt/nut to the torque listed in this Chapter's Specifications.

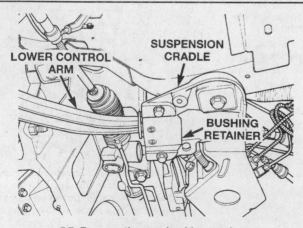

5.7 Remove the rear bushing retainer

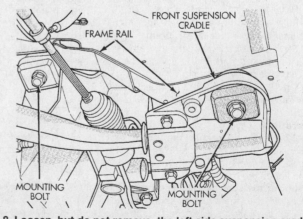

5.8 Loosen, but do not remove, the left side suspension cradle bolts to allow the cradle to lower

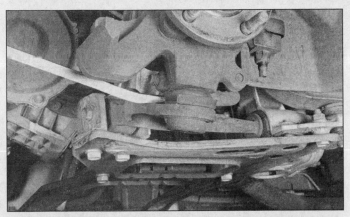

6.3 Use a prybar between the control arm and the steering knuckle to pry the knuckle up-and-down and side-to-side

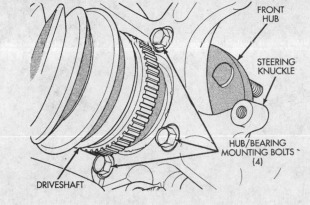

7.10 Remove the hub/bearing mounting bolts

16   Install the wheel stop, tightening it to the torque listed in this Chapter's Specifications.
17   Place a floor jack under the lower control arm (as close to the balljoints as possible). Raise the control arm to simulate normal ride height.
18   Tighten the control arm pivot bolt and the control arm bushing retainer bolts to the torque listed in this Chapter's Specifications.
19   Install the wheel and lug nuts, lower the vehicle and tighten the lug nuts to the torque listed in the Chapter 1 Specifications.
20   Have the front wheel alignment checked and, if necessary, adjusted after this job has been performed.

6   Balljoints - check and replacement

Refer to illustration 6.3
1   Reach under the vehicle and try to turn the balljoint grease fitting with your fingers. If you can move the grease fitting, the balljoint is worn out.
2   Raise the vehicle and support it securely on jackstands. Make sure the tires do not touch the ground.
3   Grab the tire at the top and bottom and try to rock it in and out. Balljoints on these vehicles are not designed to have freeplay. If there is any movement, the balljoint must be replaced.
4   Place a prybar or large screwdriver between the control arm and the underside of the steering knuckle and try to pry the knuckle up-and-down and side-to-side **(see illustration)**. If there is any movement, the balljoint must be replaced.
5   Balljoints on these vehicles are not serviceable. Remove the control arm (see Section 5) and take it to a dealer service department or automotive machine shop to have the old balljoint pressed out and a new one pressed in. **Note:** *The balljoint seal should be examined and replaced (if necessary) at the same time.*
6   Raise the vehicle, remove the jackstands, and lower the vehicle.

7   Hub and bearing assembly (front) - removal and installation

Warning: *Brake system dust may contain asbestos, which is harmful to your health. Never blow it out with compressed air and don't inhale it. Do not use petroleum-based solvents to clean brake parts. Use brake system cleaner only.*

Removal

Refer to illustrations 7.10 and 7.11
Note: *Replacement of the front hub/bearing assembly is usually done without removing the steering knuckle from the vehicle. If the hub/bearing is frozen in the steering knuckle and cannot be removed, it will have to be pressed out of the steering knuckle. If this is the case, remove the steering knuckle from the vehicle (see Section 8) and take the steering knuckle to an automotive machine shop to have the old hub and bearing assembly pressed out.*
1   Remove the cotter pin and the nut lock from the driveaxle.
2   Remove the spring wave washer from the end of the driveaxle.
3   Loosen (but do not remove) the driveaxle/hub nut.
4   Loosen the wheel lug nuts, raise the vehicle and support it securely on jackstands.
5   Remove the lug nuts and the front wheel.
6   Remove the brake caliper (see Chapter 9).
7   Support the caliper using a wire hook. Do not let the caliper assembly hang by a hydraulic hose.
8   Remove the brake disc from the front hub/bearing assembly.
9   Remove the hub nut and the washer from the end of the driveaxle.
10   Remove the four hub and bearing assembly mounting bolts from the rear of the steering knuckle **(see illustration)**.
11   Remove the hub and bearing assembly from the steering knuckle **(see illustration)**.
Note: *If the driveaxle splines stick in the hub, push the driveaxle out with a two-jaw puller.*

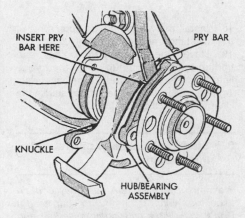

7.11 If the hub and bearing assembly is stuck in the steering knuckle, use a prybar to gently work it out

Installation

12   Make sure that the mounting surface inside the steering knuckle and on the driveaxle splines is smooth and free of burrs and nicks prior to installing the hub and bearing assembly.
13   Lubricate the driveaxle splines with multi-purpose grease. Install the hub/bearing assembly onto the driveaxle and into the steering knuckle until it is seated on the steering knuckle.
14   Install the hub/bearing assembly-to-steering knuckle bolts. Tighten the bolts equally in a criss-cross pattern until the hub/bearing assembly is seated securely against the steering knuckle. Tighten the bolts to the torque listed in this Chapter's Specifications.
15   Install the washer and the driveaxle/hub nut. Do not tighten the nut yet.
16   Install the brake disc on the hub and bearing assembly.
17   Install the brake caliper over the brake disc. Install the mounting bolts and tighten them to the torque listed in the Chapter 9 Specifications.

8.6 To remove the speed sensor from the steering knuckle, remove the sensor retaining bolt (arrow), then pull out the sensor

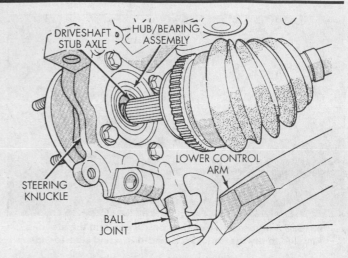

8.10 Separate the steering knuckle assembly from the outer CV joint/driveaxle assembly

18   Install the wheel and lug nuts, remove the jackstands, and lower the vehicle.

19   Have a helper apply the brakes, and tighten the driveaxle/hub nut to the torque listed in this Chapter's Specifications. Tighten the lug nuts to the torque listed in the Chapter 1 Specifications.

8   Steering knuckle - removal and installation

Warning: *Brake system dust may contain asbestos, which is harmful to your health. Don't blow it out with compressed air and don't inhale it. Do not use petroleum-based solvents to clean brake parts. Use brake system cleaner only.*
Note: *The steering knuckle is not a repairable component. It must be replaced if it is bent, broken, or damaged in any way.*

Removal

Refer to illustration 8.6, 8.10, and 8.11

1   Loosen the wheel lug nuts, raise the vehicle and support it securely on jackstands.
2   Remove the lug nuts and the wheel.
3   Remove the brake caliper and support it with a piece of wire. Remove the brake disc from the hub and bearing assembly (see Chapter 9).
4   Remove the driveaxle/hub nut.
5   Detach the tie-rod end from the steering knuckle (see Section 18).
6   Remove the front wheel speed sensor **(see illustration)** from the steering knuckle.
7   Remove the wheel stop **(see illustration 5.2)** from the steering knuckle.
8   Remove the steering knuckle-to-balljoint stud clamping nut and bolt **(see illustration 5.3)**.
9   Use a prybar to separate the steering knuckle from the balljoint stud. **Caution:** *Do not cut the balljoint seal when separating the balljoint stud from the steering knuckle.*
10   Pull the steering knuckle assembly off

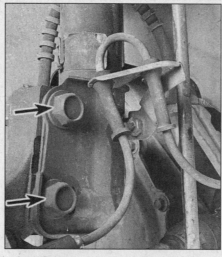

8.11 Remove the steering knuckle-to-strut bracket nuts and bolts (arrows)

the outer CV joint **(see illustration)**. **Caution:** *Do not separate the inner CV joint during this operation. Do not allow the driveshaft to hang by the inner CV joint. If the driveaxle splines stick in the hub, push the driveaxle out with a two-jaw puller.*
11   Remove the two steering knuckle-to-strut bracket bolts **(see illustration)**. **Caution:** *The steering knuckle to strut assembly bolts are serrated and must not be turned during removal.* **Note:** *If the strut assembly is attached to the steering knuckle using a cam bolt in the lower slotted hole, mark the relationship of the cam bolt to the strut to preserve the wheel alignment setting on reassembly.*
12   Remove the steering knuckle from the strut.

Installation

13   Installation is the reverse of removal. Be sure to tighten all suspension fasteners to the torque listed in this Chapter's Specifications.

Note: *If the strut assembly is attached to the steering knuckle using a cam bolt, the cam bolt must be installed in the lower slotted hole on the strut bracket. Bolts should be installed with the nuts facing the front of the vehicle. Align the cam bolt with the marks made in Step 11.*
14   Install the wheel, lower the vehicle and tighten the lug nuts to the torque listed in the Chapter 1 Specifications.
15   Drive the vehicle to an alignment shop and have the front end alignment checked and if necessary, adjusted.

9   Stabilizer bar (rear) - removal, inspection, and installation

Removal

1   Raise the vehicle and support it securely on jackstands. Block the front tires to keep the vehicle from moving.
2   Remove the two stabilizer bar-to-link arm bolts on each side of the vehicle.
3   Remove the stabilizer bar bracket bolts.
4   Remove the stabilizer bar from the vehicle.
5   If the link arms need to be replaced, remove the link arm-to-bracket bolt - then remove the link arm from the frame rail bracket.

Inspection

6   Inspect for broken or distorted clamps and bushings. Replace parts as necessary.

Installation

7   Connect the link arms to the frame rail brackets. Do not tighten them yet.
8   Place the stabilizer bar bushing on the stabilizer bar with the slit facing up.
9   Place the bar on the rear axle and install the brackets and bolts. Do not tighten them yet.
10   Install the link arm bolts on the stabilizer

10.2 Remove the lower track bar nut and bolt

10.4 To remove the track bar mount, remove these bolts (arrows)

bar. Do not tighten them yet.

11   Lower the vehicle so the weight of the vehicle is on the tires. Tighten all bolts to the torque listed in this Chapter's Specifications.

10   Track bar and mount - removal and installation

Removal

Refer to illustrations 10.2 and 10.4

1   Raise the vehicle and support it securely on jackstands. Block the front wheels to keep the vehicle from moving.

2   Remove the lower track bar bolt and nut at the axle (**see illustration**).

3   Remove the upper track bar bolt and nut. Remove the track bar.

4   To remove the mount, remove bolts retaining the mount to the body (**see illustration**).

Installation

5   Install the track bar mount, if removed.

Tighten the bolts to the torque listed in this Chapter's Specifications.

6   Install the track bar.

7   Install the track bar bolts with the bolt heads facing rearward. Do not tighten the bolts yet.

8   Lower the vehicle to the ground, with full vehicle weight on the wheels. Tighten the track bar bolts to the torque listed in this Chapter's Specifications.

11   Leaf spring mounts - removal and installation

Removal

Refer to illustrations 11.2 and 11.7

1   Raise the vehicle and support it securely on jackstands. Block the front tires to keep the vehicle from moving.

Rear mount

2   Remove the shackle bracket nuts (**see illustration**).

3   Place a floor jack under the axle and raise it until the weight is off the leaf spring.

4   Remove the lower shock absorber mounting bolt.

5   Remove the rear spring mount bolts (**see illustration 11.2**).

6   Lower the floor jack and the rear of the leaf spring. Remove the shackle from the leaf spring bushing.

Front mount

7   Loosen the leaf spring front pivot bolt (**see illustration**).

8   Place a floor jack under the axle and raise it until the weight is off the leaf spring.

9   Remove the lower shock absorber mounting bolt.

10   Remove the leaf spring front pivot bolt.

11   Lower the leaf spring, remove the front mount-to-body bolts and remove the mount.

Installation

12   Installation is the reverse of removal. Tighten the front mount-to-body bolts to the torque listed in this Chapter's Specifications.

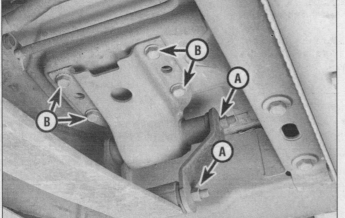

11.2 Remove the leaf spring shackle nuts (A) and the mount bolts (B)

11.7 Leaf spring front pivot bolt (lower arrow) and front mount-to-body bolts (upper arrows)

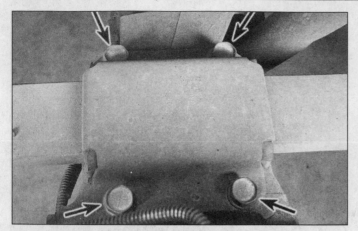

12.5   Remove the axle plate bolts (arrows)

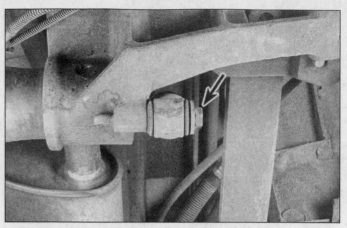

13.3   Remove the lower shock absorber bolt

13   Do not tighten the rear spring shackle nuts and the front pivot bolt until the vehicle is lowered and the full weight of the vehicle is on the rear wheels.

14   Tighten the nuts and bolts to the torque listed in this Chapter's Specifications.

12   Leaf spring - removal and installation

Removal

Refer to illustration 12.5

1   Raise the vehicle and support it securely on jackstands.
2   Support the axle with a floor jack.
3   Remove the lower shock absorber bolt **(see illustration 13.3)**.
4   Raise the axle assembly just enough to relieve the weight on the rear springs.
5   Loosen and remove the axle plate bolts on the leaf springs **(see illustration)**.
6   Lower the rear axle assembly, letting the springs hang free.
7   Loosen and remove four bolts from the front spring hanger **(see illustration 11.7)**.
8   Loosen and remove the rear spring shackle nuts and plate, remove the spring from the shackle **(see illustration 11.2)**.
9   Remove the leaf spring from the vehicle.
10   Loosen and remove the pivot bolt from the front spring mount.

Installation

11   Assemble the front spring mount to the front of the spring eye and install the pivot bolt and nut. Do not tighten the nut.
12   Raise the front of the spring and install the four hanger bolts. Tighten the bolts to the torque listed in this Chapter's Specifications.
13   Install the rear of the spring onto the rear spring shackle. Install the shackle plate, but do not tighten the nuts yet.
14   Position the lower leaf spring isolator.
15   Raise the axle assembly into position with the axle centered under the spring locator post.
16   Install the axle plate bolts and tighten them to the torque listed in this Chap-

ter's Specifications.
17   Install the shock absorber bolts. Do not tighten them yet.
18   Lower the vehicle to the floor with the full weight of the vehicle on the wheels. Tighten all components to the torque values listed in this Chapter's Specifications.

13   Shock absorbers (rear) - removal and installation

Removal

Refer to illustrations 13.3 and 13.4

1   Raise the vehicle and support it securely on jackstands. Block the front wheels to keep the vehicle from moving.
2   Support the axle with a floor jack. Raise the jack just enough to support the weight of the axle.
3   Remove the lower shock absorber bolt **(see illustration)**.
4   Remove the upper mounting bolt **(see illustration)**.

Installation

5   Install the upper shock absorber bolt finger tight.
6   Swing the shock absorber into position, and tighten the lower shock absorber bolt finger-tight.
7   Lower the vehicle to the ground and tighten the bolts to the torque listed in this Chapter's Specifications.

14   Axle assembly (rear) - removal and installation

Removal

1   Loosen the rear wheel lug nuts, raise the vehicle and support it securely on jackstands. Block the front wheels to keep the vehicle from moving.
2   Remove the rear wheels, brake drums, parking brake cables, ABS sensors and rear brake lines (see Chapter 9). Cap the open brake lines to prevent the loss of brake fluid.

13.4   Remove the upper shock absorber bolt

3   Support the axle with a floor jack.
4   Remove the shock absorber lower bolts.
5   Remove the track bar-to-axle bolt and nut.
6   Remove the axle plate **(see illustration 12.5)** bolts.
7   Lower the axle assembly.

Installation

8   Place the lower leaf spring isolator in the correct position.
9   Raise the axle assembly and align the mounting pad on the locator post on the leaf springs.
10   Install the axle plate and bolts. Tighten the bolts to the torque listed in this Chapter's Specifications.
11   Install the track bar bolt and nut. Do not tighten them yet.
12   Install the lower shock absorber bolts.
13   Install the rear wheels, drums, parking brake cables, ABS sensors and rear brake lines.
14   Lower the vehicle and tighten the track bar bolt and nut, and the shock absorber bolts to the torque values listed in this Chapter's Specifications.
15   Bleed the rear brakes before placing the vehicle back in service.

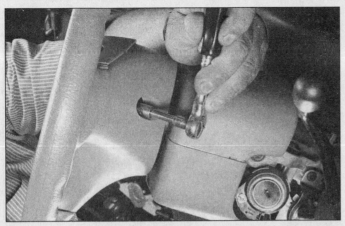

17.4 Remove the three bolts retaining the airbag module to the steering wheel

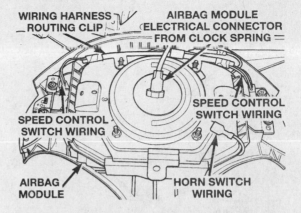

17.5 Remove the wiring harness connectors from the airbag, the horn switch wire, and the speed control switches

15 Hub and bearing assembly (rear) - removal and installation

The removal and installation procedure for the rear hub and bearing assembly is similar to the procedure for the front hub and bearing assembly (see Section 7), with the following exceptions:

a) *Refer to Chapter 9 and remove the brake drum.*

b) *Remove the rear wheel speed sensor (see Chapter 9).*

c) *Remove the four bolts retaining the hub and bearing assembly to the rear axle. If the hub/bearing assembly sticks in the axle, remove it with a slide hammer.*

d) *Tighten the hub/bearing mounting bolts to the torque listed in this Chapter's Specifications.*

16 Steering system - general information

All models covered in this manual are equipped with power-assisted rack-and-pinion steering. The power assist system con-

sists of a belt-driven pump and associated lines and hoses. The fluid level in the power steering pump reservoir should be checked periodically (see Chapter 1).

The steering wheel operates the steering shaft, which actuates the steering gear through a short steering column and a universal joint (referred to by Chrysler as the intermediate coupler). Looseness in the steering can be caused by wear in the universal joint, the steering gear, the tie-rod ends, and loose retaining bolts.

17 Steering wheel - removal and installation

Warning: *These models have airbags. Always disconnect the negative battery cable and wait two minutes before working in the vicinity of the impact sensors, steering column, or instrument panel to avoid accidental deployment of the airbag, which could cause personal injury (see Chapter 12).*

Removal

Refer to illustrations 17.4, 17.5, 17.6 and 17.8

1   Make sure the front wheels of the vehi-

cle are pointing straight ahead.

2   Disconnect the negative cable from the battery.

3   Turn the key to the locked position and remove the key. Turn the steering wheel a half turn to the left until the steering column lock engages.

4   Remove the three bolts (one in each spoke of the steering wheel) attaching the airbag module to the steering wheel **(see illustration)**. Remove the airbag module from the steering wheel and detach the electrical connector. **Warning:** *When handling an airbag, always carry the airbag module with the trim side facing away from your body and store the airbag module in a safe location with the trim side facing up.*

5   Remove the wiring harness connectors from the horn switch wire and the speed control switches **(see illustration)**. Remove the wiring harness routing clip from the airbag module studs.

6   Remove the steering wheel retaining nut from the steering column shaft **(see illustration)**.

7   Remove the steering wheel damper from the steering wheel.

8   Remove the steering wheel from the steering column shaft using a wheel puller

17.6 Remove the steering wheel retaining nut and the damper

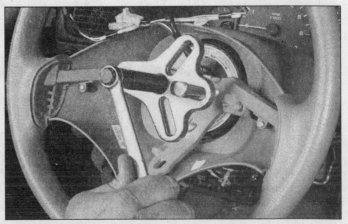

17.8 Use a steering wheel puller to remove the steering wheel from the steering shaft

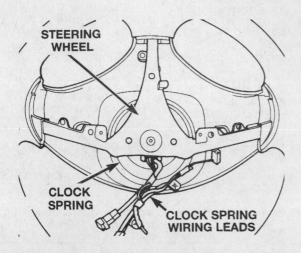

17.9 All wiring leads from the clock spring must be routed as shown

18.2a Loosen the tie-rod end jam nut . . .

18.2b . . . then mark the position of the tie-rod end

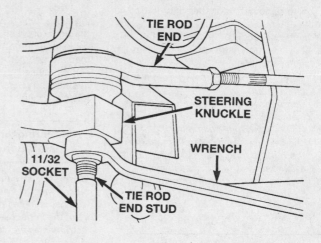

18.3 Remove the tie-rod end-to-steering knuckle nut

(see illustration). **Caution:** *Do not hammer on the steering wheel or steering column shaft when removing the steering wheel from the steering column shaft. When installing the steering wheel puller bolts in the steering wheel, do not thread the bolt into the steering wheel more than a half inch. If they are inserted more than half an inch, they will contact and damage the clock spring.*

Installation

Refer to illustration 17.9

9   Install the steering wheel with the master splines on the steering wheel aligned with the steering shaft and flats on the steering wheel with formations on the clock spring. Make sure the wiring is routed correctly **(see illustration)**.
10   Install the steering wheel damper on the steering wheel.
11   Install the steering wheel nut and tighten

it to the torque listed this Chapter's Specifications.
12   Connect the wiring leads from the clock spring on the airbag, horn switch wire, and speed control switches. Attach the wire routing clip to the studs on the airbag module.
13   Install the airbag module on the steering wheel.
14   Install the three bolts attaching the airbag module to the steering wheel and tighten them to the torque listed in this Chapter's Specifications.
15   Connect the cable to the negative battery terminal.
16 Turn the ignition key On and verify the airbag system is operating properly by watching the airbag warning light in the instrument cluster (see Chapter 12). **Warning:** *If the airbag system is not operating DO NOT drive the vehicle, have the airbag system repaired at a dealership service department or other qualified repair shop.*

18   Tie-rod ends - removal and installation

Removal

Refer to illustrations 18.2a, 18.2b, 18.3 and 18.4

1   Loosen the wheel lug nuts, raise the front of the vehicle and support it securely on jackstands. Block the rear wheels, set the parking brake, and remove the front wheel.
2   Loosen the tie-rod end jam nut then mark the position of the tie-rod end **(see illustrations)**.
3   Remove the nut attaching the tie-rod end to the steering knuckle **(see illustration)**. The nut is removed from the tie-rod end by holding the tie-rod end stud with a socket while the nut is removed with a wrench.
4   Remove the tie-rod end stud from the steering knuckle arm, using a balljoint separa-

18.4 Separate the tie-rod end from the steering knuckle with a balljoint separator

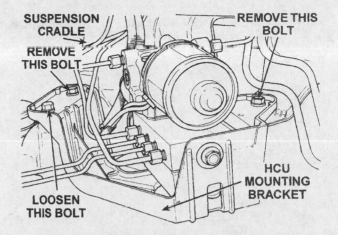

19.6 Loosen/remove the HCU-to-front suspension bolts

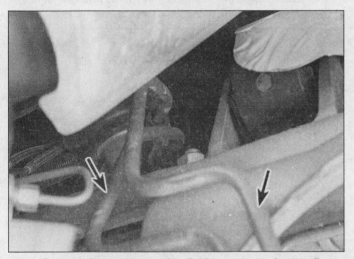

19.9 Remove the power steering fluid pressure and return lines

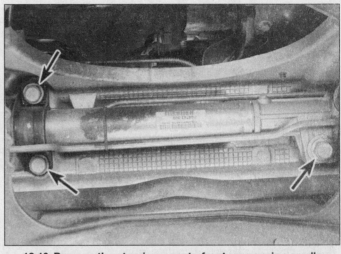

19.10 Remove the steering gear to front suspension cradle mounting nuts and bolts

tor tool or a two-jaw puller (see illustration).
5   Unscrew the tie-rod end.

Installation

6   Install the tie-rod end on the tie-rod, threading it on to the mark made during disassembly. Do not tighten the nut yet.
7   Connect the tie-rod end to the steering knuckle. Install and tighten the tie-rod end nut to the torque listed in this Chapter's Specifications.
8   Tighten the tie-rod jam nut securely.
9   Install the wheel and lug nuts. Lower the vehicle to the ground and tighten the lug nuts to the torque listed in the Chapter 1 Specifications.
10   Have the front end alignment checked and if necessary, adjusted by a properly equipped alignment shop.

19   Steering gear - removal and installation

Warning: Place the steering column in the locked position to prevent the clockspring from being over-extended when the steering column is disconnected from the intermediate coupler. If the clockspring is damaged, the airbag will not deploy in the event of a collision. Disable the airbag system before beginning this procedure (see Chapter 12).
Note: The power steering gear should not be serviced or adjusted. If a malfunction or oil leak occurs, the complete steering gear assembly must be replaced.

Removal

Refer to illustrations 19.6, 19.9, 19.10, and 19.11
1   Turn the ignition key to the locked position and turn the steering wheel to the left until the steering wheel is locked. Remove the key.
2   While the vehicle is still on the ground, disconnect the steering column shaft coupler from the steering gear intermediate coupler. Remove the cotter key, the nut, and the pinch bolt.
3   Loosen the wheel lug, raise the vehicle, support it securely on jackstands, and

remove the wheels.
4   Raise the insulating wrap on the power steering return hose to expose the hose clamp. Remove the hose clamp and detach the hose. Drain the power steering fluid from the system through the hose.
5   Remove both tie-rod ends from the steering knuckles (see Section 18).
6   Remove the two bolts and loosen the third (see illustration) attaching the antilock brakes Hydraulic Control Unit (HCU) to the front suspension cradle. Then, rotate the HCU rearward to allow access to the cradle plate nut and bolt just forward of the HCU.
7   Remove the nuts and bolts (see illustration 2.2) attaching the cradle plate to the bottom of the front suspension cradle. Then remove the cradle plate from the cradle.
8   Remove the bracket attaching the power steering fluid lines to the front suspension cradle.
9   Detach the power steering fluid pressure and return lines (see illustration) from the power steering gear.
10   Remove the three bolts and nuts (see illustration) mounting the steering gear to

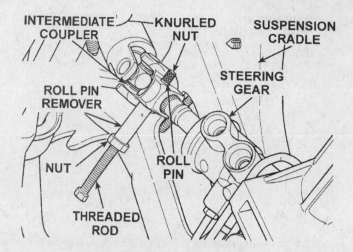

19.11 Install a roll pin remover/installer tool through the intermediate coupler roll pin and remove the roll pin

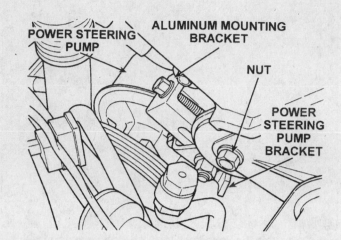

20.3 Loosen the power steering pump bracket nut

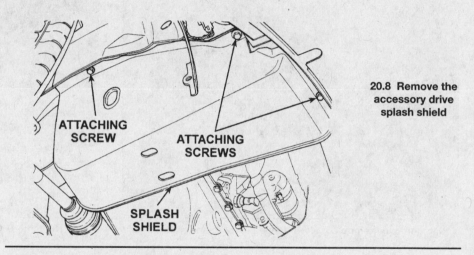

20.8 Remove the accessory drive splash shield

the front suspension cradle.

11   Lower the steering gear from the suspension cradle enough to allow access to the intermediate coupler roll pin. Install a roll pin remover/installer tool (or equivalent setup) **(see illustration)**. Pull the roll pin out of the intermediate coupler.

12   Separate the intermediate coupler from the shaft of the steering gear.

13   Remove the steering gear assembly from the front suspension cradle.

Installation

14   Install the steering gear in the front suspension cradle. Leave room to install the intermediate coupler.

15   Connect the immediate coupler to the steering gear shaft and install the roll pins, using the tool described in Step 11.

16   Insert the mounting bolts and nuts and tighten them to the torque listed in this Chapter's Specifications.

17   Attach the power steering fluid lines to the steering gear. Tighten the fittings securely.

18   Connect the tie-rods ends to the steering knuckles (see Section 18).

19   Install the cradle plate on the front suspension cradle and tighten the cradle plate bolts to the torque listed in this Chapter's Specifications.

20   Install the bracket attaching the power steering fluid tubes to the front suspension cradle.

21   Connect the return hose to the metal tube portion of the power steering fluid return line, securing it with a hose clamp. **Caution:** *Make sure the heat shield sleeves cover the entire hose and connection portion of the power steering pressure and return hoses.*

22   Install the wheels and lug nuts and lower the vehicle to a convenient working level. The tires should be just off the ground.

23   Use the intermediate coupler to turn the front wheels of the vehicle to the left until the intermediate coupler shaft is aligned with the steering column coupler. Connect the steer-

ing column shaft coupler to the steering gear intermediate coupler. Install the steering column coupler-to-intermediate shaft pinch bolt and tighten the bolt to the torque listed in this Chapter's Specifications.

24   Fill the power steering fluid reservoir with the recommended fluid (see Chapter 1), bleed the power steering system (see Section 22) and recheck the fluid level. Check for leaks.

25   Lower the vehicle to the ground and tighten the lug nuts to the torque listed in the Chapter 1 Specifications. Have the front end alignment checked and adjusted, if necessary by a properly equipped alignment shop.

20   Power steering pump - removal and installation

Warning: *Wait until the engine is completely cool before beginning this procedure.*
Note: *Remove the cap from the power steering reservoir and siphon as much power steering fluid as possible from the reservoir before beginning this procedure.*

Removal

Refer to illustrations 20.3, 20.8, 20.9, 20.10, 20.12, 20.13 and 20.16

1   Detach the negative battery cable.

2   Remove the accessory drive belts (see Chapter 1).

3   On four-cylinder models, loosen, but do not remove, the nut attaching the power steering pump front bracket to the mounting bracket **(see illustration)**.

4   Raise the vehicle and support it securely on jackstands.

5   Disconnect the oxygen sensor wiring harness from the vehicle wiring harness. Access to the connection is through the wiring harness grommet in the floor pan of the vehicle.

6   On all except 3.0L models, remove the catalytic converter from the exhaust manifold. Remove the exhaust system hangers/isolators from the brackets on the exhaust system.

7   Move the exhaust system as far to the rear and to the left side of the vehicle as possible.

8   Remove the accessory drive splash

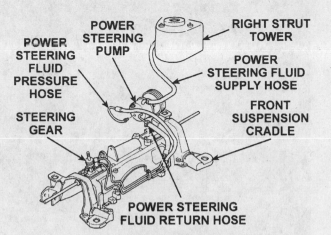

20.9 Remove the power steering fluid supply hose from the remote fluid reservoir

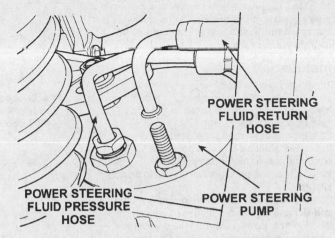

20.10 Remove the power steering fluid pressure line.

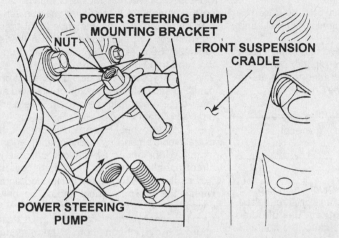

20.12 Remove the nut attaching the power steering pump to the mount bracket

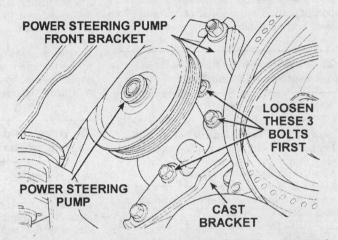

20.13 Remove the bolts attaching the power steering pump to the front mount bracket

shield (see illustration).

9   Detach the power steering supply hose coming from the fluid reservoir, from the fitting on the power steering pump (see illustration). Plug the hose to prevent excess fluid loss.

10   Remove the power steering fluid pressure line (see illustration) from the power steering pump. Plug the line.

11   Remove the power steering fluid return hose (see illustration 20.10) from the power steering pump. Plug the hose.

12   On all except 3.0L models, remove the nut attaching the rear of the power steering pump to the mounting bracket (see illustration).

13   On all except 3.0L models, loosen the three bolts attaching the power steering pump to the front mounting bracket (see illustration).

14   On all except 3.0L models, remove the power steering pump and the front bracket as an assembly.

15   On all except 3.0L models, remove the three bolts from Step 14 and separate the power steering pump from the front bracket.

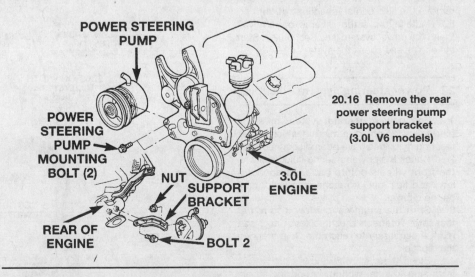

20.16 Remove the rear power steering pump support bracket (3.0L V6 models)

16   On 3.0L models, remove the support bracket at the rear of the power steering pump which attaches the pump to the rear of the engine (see illustration).

17   On 3.0L models, remove the power steering pump from the mounting bracket.

18 On 3.0L models, remove the power steering pump from the vehicle by pulling it out through the exhaust tunnel area in the floor pan of the vehicle.

Installation

19 Installation is the reverse of removal.
20 Tighten all power steering mounting hardware to the torque listed in this Chapter's Specifications.
21 Before connecting the pressure line to the power steering pump, inspect the O-ring on the pressure line for damage.
22 Tighten the pressure line-to-pump fitting securely.
23 Make sure the hoses are properly routed and all hose clamps are tightened securely.
24 Fill the power steering fluid reservoir with the recommended fluid (see Chapter 1).
25 Connect the negative battery cable to the battery.
26 Bleed the power system (see Section 22). Stop the engine, check the fluid level, and inspect the system for leaks.

21 Power steering fluid cooler - removal and installation

Refer to illustration 21.4

The power steering fluid cooler is designed to keep the power steering fluid temperature within a specific temperature level to maintain the maximum performance from the power steering system.
1 Use a shop syringe and remove as much of the power steering fluid from the fluid reservoir as possible.
2 Raise the vehicle, support it securely on jackstands.
3 Place a drip pan under the fluid cooler. Remove the hose clamps and disconnect both hoses from the fluid cooler.
4 Remove the two mounting bolts and remove the fluid cooler **(see illustration)**.
5 Installation is the reverse of removal. Bleed the power system (see Section 22). Start the engine and check the system for leaks.

22 Power steering system - bleeding

1 The power steering system must be bled following any operation in which power steering fluid lines have been disconnected.
2 Check the power steering fluid level with the front wheels pointed straight ahead. If low, add fluid until it reaches the Cold mark on the dipstick.
3 Start the engine and allow it to run at fast idle. Recheck the fluid level and add more if necessary to reach the Cold mark on the dipstick.
4 Bleed the system by turning the wheels from side to side, without hitting the stops. This will work the air out of the system. Keep the reservoir full of fluid while this is done.
5 When the air has been worked out of the system, turn the wheels straight ahead and

21.4 Location of power steering fluid cooler

leave the vehicle running for several more minutes before shutting it off.
6 Road test the vehicle to be sure the steering system is functioning normally and noise free.
7 Recheck the fluid level to be sure it is up to the Hot mark on the dipstick while the engine is at normal operating temperature. Add fluid if necessary (see Chapter 1).

23 Wheels and tires - general information

Refer to illustration 23.1

1 Vehicles in this manual are equipped with metric-sized fiberglass or steel belted radial tires **(see illustration)**. Use of other size or type of tires may affect the ride and

handling of the vehicle. Don't mix different types of tires, such as radials or bias belted, on the same vehicle. Handling may be seriously affected. It's recommended that tires be replaced in pairs, but if only one tire is replaced, be sure it's the same size, structure, and tread design as the other.
2 Tire pressure has a substantial effect on handling and wear, and should be checked at least once a month or before any extended trips (see Chapter 1).
3 Tire and wheel balance is important in overall vehicle handling, braking, and performance. Unbalanced wheels can adversely affect handling and ride characteristics as well as tire life. When a tire is installed on a wheel, the tire and wheel should be balanced.
4 Tire wear patterns can tell a great deal about the overall condition of the steering

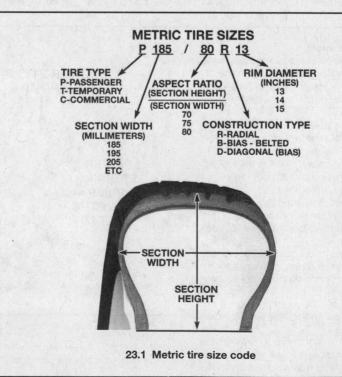

23.1 Metric tire size code

and suspension of a vehicle (see Chapter 1).
5   The spare tire is designed for emergency use only. The original tire should be repaired and reinstalled at the first opportunity, or a new tire purchased. Do not exceed speeds of 50 MPH.
6   Wheels must be replaced if they are bent, dented, leak air, have elongated bolt holes, are heavily rusted, are out of vertical symmetry, or if the lug nuts won't stay tight. Wheel repairs that use welding or peening are not recommended.

24   Wheel alignment - general information

Refer to illustration 24.1

Wheel alignment refers to the adjustments made to the front wheels to keep the proper angular relationship with the suspension and the ground. Wheels that are out of alignment affect vehicle control, and increase tire wear. Alignment angles normally measured are camber, caster and toe-in **(see illustration)**. Only toe-in is adjustable on these vehicles. The other angles should only be measured to check for bent or worn suspension parts. **Caution:** *Don't attempt to modify suspension or steering components to meet vehicle alignment specifications by heating or bending them.*

Proper wheel alignment is an exacting process, which requires complicated and expensive machines to perform the job properly. A technician with the proper equipment should perform these tasks. We will give you a basic idea of wheel alignment procedures so you can better understand the process and deal intelligently with the shop that does the work. **Note:** *Rear wheel alignment is not adjustable.*

Toe-in is the turning in of the front wheels. The purpose of toe-in is to ensure parallel rolling of the front wheels. In a vehicle with zero toe-in, the distance between the front edges of the wheels will be the same as

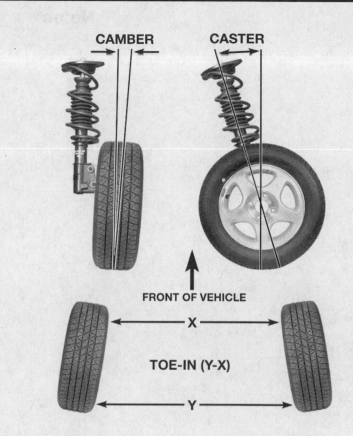

24.1 Front end alignment details

the distance between the rear edges of the wheels. Toe-in is normally only a fraction of an inch and is controlled by the tie-rod end position on the tie-rod. Incorrect toe-in will cause the tires to scrub against the road and wear improperly.

Camber is the vertical tilt of the wheels when viewed from one end of the vehicle. When the wheels tilt out at the top, the camber is said to be positive (+). When the wheels tilt in at the top, the camber is negative (-). Tilt is measured in degrees from vertical and is called the camber angle, which affects the amount of tire tread contacting the road. Camber angle also compensates for suspension geometry changes when the vehicle is cornering or traveling over an undulating surface.

Notes

Chapter 11 Body

Contents

	Section		Section
Body - maintenance	2	Hood latch and cable - removal and installation	10
Body repair - major damage	6	Instrument cluster bezel - removal and installation	25
Body repair - minor damage	5	Interior quarter trim panels - removal and installation	27
Bumpers - removal and installation	13	Liftgate - removal, installation and adjustment	18
Cowl cover - removal and installation	30	Liftgate strut - replacement	19
Dashboard panels - removal and installation	26	Lower console - removal and installation	23
Door latch, lock cylinder and outside handle - removal and installation	15	Mirrors - removal and installation	28
Door trim panels - removal and installation	14	Overhead console - removal and installation	24
Door window regulator - removal and installation	22	Seat belt check	32
Front door - removal and installation	16	Seats - removal and installation	31
Front door window glass - removal and installation	20	Sliding door - removal and installation	17
Front fender - removal and installation	12	Upholstery and carpets - maintenance	4
General information	1	Vinyl trim - maintenance	3
Grille - removal and installation	11	Wheelhouse splash shield - removal and installation	29
Hinges and locks - maintenance	7	Windshield and fixed glass - replacement	8
Hood - removal, installation and adjustment	9	Quarter window glass - removal and installation	21

1 General information

These models feature a "unibody" layout, using a floorpan with front and rear frame side rails which support the body components, front and rear suspension systems and other mechanical components. Certain components are particularly vulnerable to accident damage and can be unbolted and repaired or replaced. Among these parts are the body moldings, bumpers, front fenders, doors, the hood and liftgate and all glass. Only general body maintenance practices and body panel repair procedures within the scope of the do-it-yourselfer are included in this Chapter.

2 Body - maintenance

1   The condition of your vehicle's body is very important, because the resale value depends a great deal on it. It's much more difficult to repair a neglected or damaged body than it is to repair mechanical components. The hidden areas of the body, such as the wheel wells, the frame and the engine compartment, are equally important, although they don't require as frequent attention as the rest of the body.

2   Once a year, or every 12,000 miles, it's a good idea to have the underside of the body steam cleaned. All traces of dirt and oil will be removed and the area can then be inspected carefully for rust, damaged brake lines, frayed electrical wires, damaged cables and other problems. The front suspension components should be greased after completion of this job.

3   At the same time, clean the engine and the engine compartment with a steam cleaner or water-soluble degreaser.

4   The wheel wells should be given close attention, since undercoating can peel away and stones and dirt thrown up by the tires can cause the paint to chip and flake, allowing rust to set in. If rust is found, clean down to the bare metal and apply an anti-rust paint.

5   The body should be washed about once a week. Wet the vehicle thoroughly to soften the dirt, then wash it down with a soft sponge and plenty of clean soapy water. If the surplus dirt is not washed off very carefully, it

can wear down the paint.

6   Spots of tar or asphalt thrown up from the road should be removed with a cloth soaked in solvent.

7   Once every six months, wax the body and chrome trim. If a chrome cleaner is used to remove rust from any of the vehicle's plated parts, remember that the cleaner also removes part of the chrome, so use it sparingly.

3   Vinyl trim - maintenance

Don't clean vinyl trim with detergents, caustic soap or petroleum-based cleaners. Plain soap and water works just fine, with a soft brush to clean dirt that may be ingrained. Wash the vinyl as frequently as the rest of the vehicle. After cleaning, application of a high-quality rubber and vinyl protectant will help prevent oxidation and cracks. The protectant can also be applied to weatherstripping, vacuum lines and rubber hoses, which often fail as a result of chemical degradation, and to the tires.

4   Upholstery and carpets - maintenance

1   Every three months remove the floormats and clean the interior of the vehicle (more frequently if necessary). Use a stiff whisk broom to brush the carpeting and loosen dirt and dust, then vacuum the upholstery and carpets thoroughly, especially along seams and crevices.

2   Dirt and stains can be removed from carpeting with basic household or automotive carpet shampoos available in spray cans. Follow the directions and vacuum again, then use a stiff brush to bring back the "nap" of the carpet.

3   Most interiors have cloth or vinyl upholstery, either of which can be cleaned and maintained with a number of material-specific cleaners or shampoos available in auto supply stores. Follow the directions on the product for usage, and always spot-test any upholstery cleaner on an inconspicuous area (bottom edge of a backseat cushion) to ensure that it doesn't cause a color shift in the material.

4   After cleaning, vinyl upholstery should be treated with a protectant. **Note:** *Make sure the protectant container indicates the product can be used on seats - some products may make a seat too slippery.* **Caution:** *Do not use protectant on vinyl-covered steering wheels.*

5   Leather upholstery requires special care. It should be cleaned regularly with saddlesoap or leather cleaner. Never use alcohol, gasoline, nail polish remover or thinner to clean leather upholstery.

6   After cleaning, regularly treat leather upholstery with a leather conditioner, rubbed in with a soft cotton cloth. Never use car wax on leather upholstery.

7   In areas where the interior of the vehicle is subject to bright sunlight, cover leather seating areas of the seats with a sheet if the vehicle is to be left out for any length of time.

5   Body repair - minor damage

See photo sequence

Repair of scratches

1   If the scratch is superficial and does not penetrate to the metal of the body, repair is very simple. Lightly rub the scratched area with a fine rubbing compound to remove loose paint and built-up wax. Rinse the area with clean water.

2   Apply touch-up paint to the scratch, using a small brush. Continue to apply thin layers of paint until the surface of the paint in the scratch is level with the surrounding paint. Allow the new paint at least two weeks to harden, then blend it into the surrounding paint by rubbing with a very fine rubbing compound. Finally, apply a coat of wax to the scratch area.

3   If the scratch has penetrated the paint and exposed the metal of the body, causing the metal to rust, a different repair technique is required. Remove all loose rust from the bottom of the scratch with a pocket knife, then apply rust inhibiting paint to prevent the formation of rust in the future. Using a rubber or nylon applicator, coat the scratched area with glaze-type filler. If required, the filler can be mixed with thinner to provide a very thin paste, which is ideal for filling narrow scratches. Before the glaze filler in the scratch hardens, wrap a piece of smooth cotton cloth around the tip of a finger. Dip the cloth in thinner and then quickly wipe it along the surface of the scratch. This will ensure that the surface of the filler is slightly hollow. The scratch can now be painted over as described earlier in this section.

Repair of dents

4   When repairing dents, the first job is to pull the dent out until the affected area is as close as possible to its original shape. There is no point in trying to restore the original shape completely as the metal in the damaged area will have stretched on impact and cannot be restored to its original contours. It is better to bring the level of the dent up to a point which is about 1/8-inch below the level of the surrounding metal. In cases where the dent is very shallow, it is not worth trying to pull it out at all.

5   If the back side of the dent is accessible, it can be hammered out gently from behind using a soft-face hammer. While doing this, hold a block of wood firmly against the opposite side of the metal to absorb the hammer blows and prevent the metal from being stretched.

6   If the dent is in a section of the body which has double layers, or some other factor makes it inaccessible from behind, a different technique is required. Drill several small holes through the metal inside the damaged area,

particularly in the deeper sections. Screw long, self tapping screws into the holes just enough for them to get a good grip in the metal. Now the dent can be pulled out by pulling on the protruding heads of the screws with locking pliers.

7   The next stage of repair is the removal of paint from the damaged area and from an inch or so of the surrounding metal. This is easily done with a wire brush or sanding disk in a drill motor, although it can be done just as effectively by hand with sandpaper. To complete the preparation for filling, score the surface of the bare metal with a screwdriver or the tang of a file or drill small holes in the affected area. This will provide a good grip for the filler material. To complete the repair, see the subsection on *filling and painting*.

Repair of rust holes or gashes

8   Remove all paint from the affected area and from an inch or so of the surrounding metal using a sanding disk or wire brush mounted in a drill motor. If these are not available, a few sheets of sandpaper will do the job just as effectively.

9   With the paint removed, you will be able to determine the severity of the corrosion and decide whether to replace the whole panel, if possible, or repair the affected area. New body panels are not as expensive as most people think and it is often quicker to install a new panel than to repair large areas of rust.

10   Remove all trim pieces from the affected area except those which will act as a guide to the original shape of the damaged body, such as headlight shells, etc. Using metal snips or a hacksaw blade, remove all loose metal and any other metal that is badly affected by rust. Hammer the edges of the hole on the inside to create a slight depression for the filler material.

11   Wire brush the affected area to remove the powdery rust from the surface of the metal. If the back of the rusted area is accessible, treat it with rust inhibiting paint.

12   Before filling is done, block the hole in some way. This can be done with sheet metal riveted or screwed into place, or by stuffing the hole with wire mesh.

13   Once the hole is blocked off, the affected area can be filled and painted. See the following subsection on *filling and painting*.

Filling and painting

14   Many types of body fillers are available, but generally speaking, body repair kits which contain filler paste and a tube of resin hardener are best for this type of repair work. A wide, flexible plastic or nylon applicator will be necessary for imparting a smooth and contoured finish to the surface of the filler material. Mix up a small amount of filler on a clean piece of wood or cardboard (use the hardener sparingly). Follow the manufacturer's instructions on the package, otherwise the filler will set incorrectly.

15   Using the applicator, apply the filler paste to the prepared area. Draw the applicator across the surface of the filler to achieve

the desired contour and to level the filler surface. As soon as a contour that approximates the original one is achieved, stop working the paste. If you continue, the paste will begin to stick to the applicator. Continue to add thin layers of paste at 20-minute intervals until the level of the filler is just above the surrounding metal.

16   Once the filler has hardened, the excess can be removed with a body file. From then on, progressively finer grades of sandpaper should be used, starting with a 180-grit paper and finishing with 600-grit wet-or-dry paper. Always wrap the sandpaper around a flat rubber or wooden block, otherwise the surface of the filler will not be completely flat. During the sanding of the filler surface, the wet-or-dry paper should be periodically rinsed in water. This will ensure that a very smooth finish is produced in the final stage.

17   At this point, the repair area should be surrounded by a ring of bare metal, which in turn should be encircled by the finely feathered edge of good paint. Rinse the repair area with clean water until all of the dust produced by the sanding operation is gone.

18   Spray the entire area with a light coat of primer. This will reveal any imperfections in the surface of the filler. Repair the imperfections with fresh filler paste or glaze filler and once more smooth the surface with sandpaper. Repeat this spray-and-repair procedure until you are satisfied that the surface of the filler and the feathered edge of the paint are perfect. Rinse the area with clean water and allow it to dry completely.

19   The repair area is now ready for painting. Spray painting must be carried out in a warm, dry, windless and dust free atmosphere. These conditions can be created if you have access to a large indoor work area, but if you are forced to work in the open, you will have to pick the day very carefully. If you are working indoors, dousing the floor in the work area with water will help settle the dust which would otherwise be in the air. If the repair area is confined to one body panel, mask off the surrounding panels. This will help minimize the effects of a slight mismatch in paint color. Trim pieces such as chrome strips, door handles, etc., will also need to be masked off or removed. Use masking tape and several thickness of newspaper for the masking operations.

20   Before spraying, shake the paint can thoroughly, then spray a test area until the spray painting technique is mastered. Cover the repair area with a thick coat of primer. The thickness should be built up using several thin layers of primer rather than one thick one. Using 600-grit wet-or-dry sandpaper, rub down the surface of the primer until it is very smooth. While doing this, the work area should be thoroughly rinsed with water and the wet-or-dry sandpaper periodically rinsed as well. Allow the primer to dry before spraying additional coats.

21   Spray on the top coat, again building up the thickness by using several thin layers of paint. Begin spraying in the center of the

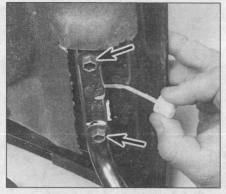

9.2 Mark the hinge plate and bolt head locations and loosen the bolts (arrows) for latch adjustment or removal

repair area and then, using a circular motion, work out until the whole repair area and about two inches of the surrounding original paint is covered. Remove all masking material 10 to 15 minutes after spraying on the final coat of paint. Allow the new paint at least two weeks to harden, then use a very fine rubbing compound to blend the edges of the new paint into the existing paint. Finally, apply a coat of wax.

6   Body repair - major damage

1   Major damage must be repaired by an auto body shop specifically equipped to perform unibody repairs. These shops have the specialized equipment required to do the job properly.

2   If the damage is extensive, the body must be checked for proper alignment or the vehicle's handling characteristics may be adversely affected and other components may wear at an accelerated rate.

3   Due to the fact that all of the major body components (hood, fenders, etc.) are separate and replaceable units, any seriously damaged components should be replaced rather than repaired. Sometimes the components can be found in a wrecking yard that specializes in used vehicle components, often at considerable savings over the cost of new parts.

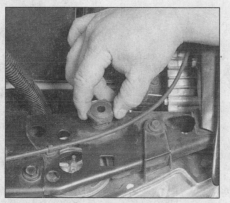

9.9 Adjust the hood height by screwing the hood bumpers in or out

7   Hinges and locks - maintenance

Once every 3000 miles, or every three months, the hinges and latch assemblies on the doors, hood and trunk should be given a few drops of light oil or lock lubricant. The door latch strikers should also be lubricated with a thin coat of grease to reduce wear and ensure free movement. Lubricate the door and trunk locks with spray-on graphite lubricant.

8   Windshield and fixed glass - replacement

Replacement of the windshield and fixed glass requires the use of special fast-setting adhesive/caulk materials and some specialized tools and techniques. These operations should be left to a dealer service department or a shop specializing in glass work.

9   Hood - removal, installation and adjustment

Note: *The hood is heavy and somewhat awkward to remove and install - at least two people should perform this procedure.*

Removal and installation
Refer to illustration 9.2

1   Use blankets or pads to cover the cowl area of the body and the fenders. This will protect the body and paint as the hood is lifted off.

2   Scribe alignment marks around the bolt heads and hinge attachment locations to insure proper alignment during installation - a permanent-type felt-tip marker also will work for this **(see illustration)**.

3   Remove the top bolts holding the hood to the hinge and loosen the bottom bolts until they can be removed by hand.

4   Have an assistant on the opposite side of the vehicle support the weight of the hood. Remove the bottom bolts holding the hood to the hinge and lift off the hood.

5   Installation is the reverse of removal.

Adjustment
Refer to illustrations 9.9 and 9.10

6   Front-and-back and side-to-side adjustment of the hood is done by moving the hood in relation to the hinge plate after loosening the bolts.

7   Scribe or trace a line around the entire hinge plate so you can judge the amount of movement.

8   Loosen the bolts or nuts and move the hood into correct alignment. Move it only a little at a time. Tighten the hinge bolts or nuts and carefully lower the hood to check the alignment.

9   Adjust the hood bumpers on the radiator support so the hood is flush with the fenders when closed **(see illustration)**.

These photos illustrate a method of repairing simple dents. They are intended to supplement *Body repair - minor damage* in this Chapter and should not be used as the sole instructions for body repair on these vehicles.

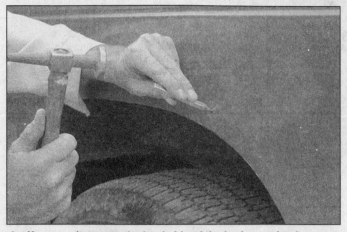

1   If you can't access the backside of the body panel to hammer out the dent, pull it out with a slide-hammer-type dent puller. In the deepest portion of the dent or along the crease line, drill or punch hole(s) at least one inch apart . . .

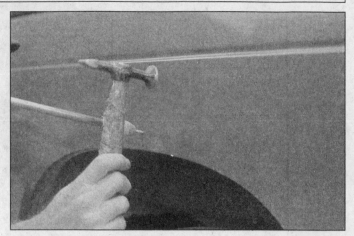

2   . . . then screw the slide-hammer into the hole and operate it. Tap with a hammer near the edge of the dent to help 'pop' the metal back to its original shape. When you're finished, the dent area should be close to its original contour and about 1/8-inch below the surface of the surrounding metal

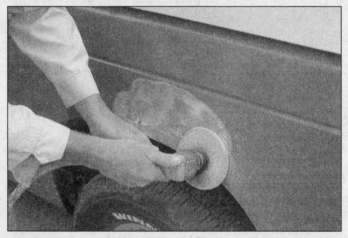

3   Using coarse-grit sandpaper, remove the paint down to the bare metal. Hand sanding works fine, but the disc sander shown here makes the job faster. Use finer (about 320-grit) sandpaper to feather-edge the paint at least one inch around the dent area

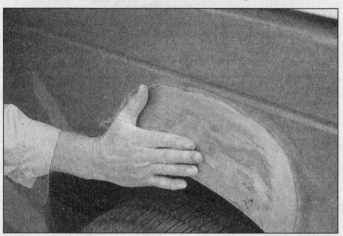

4   When the paint is removed, touch will probably be more helpful than sight for telling if the metal is straight. Hammer down the high spots or raise the low spots as necessary. Clean the repair area with wax/silicone remover

5   Following label instructions, mix up a batch of plastic filler and hardener. The ratio of filler to hardener is critical, and, if you mix it incorrectly, it will either not cure properly or cure too quickly (you won't have time to file and sand it into shape)

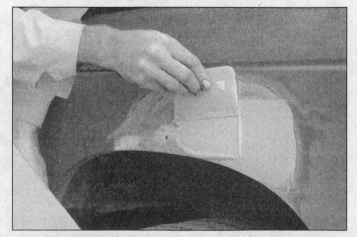

6   Working quickly so the filler doesn't harden, use a plastic applicator to press the body filler firmly into the metal, assuring it bonds completely. Work the filler until it matches the original contour and is slightly above the surrounding metal

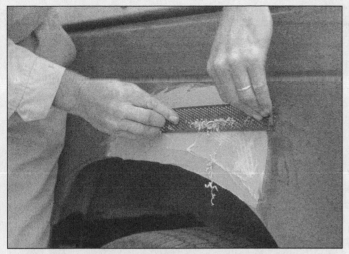

7   Let the filler harden until you can just dent it with your fingernail. Use a body file or Surform tool (shown here) to rough-shape the filler

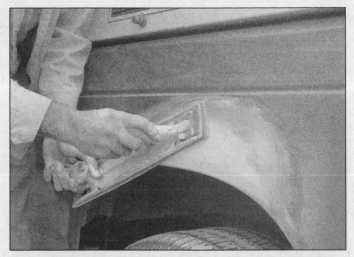

8   Use coarse-grit sandpaper and a sanding board or block to work the filler down until it's smooth and even. Work down to finer grits of sandpaper - always using a board or block - ending up with 360 or 400 grit

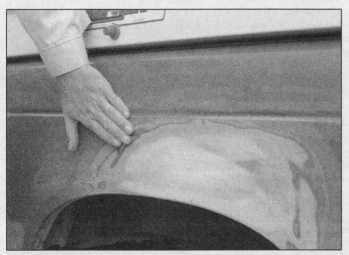

9   You shouldn't be able to feel any ridge at the transition from the filler to the bare metal or from the bare metal to the old paint. As soon as the repair is flat and uniform, remove the dust and mask off the adjacent panels or trim pieces

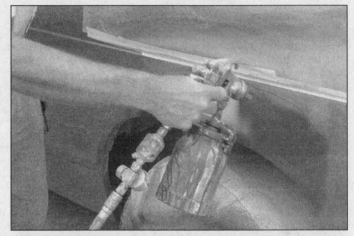

10   Apply several layers of primer to the area. Don't spray the primer on too heavy, so it sags or runs, and make sure each coat is dry before you spray on the next one. A professional-type spray gun is being used here, but aerosol spray primer is available inexpensively from auto parts stores

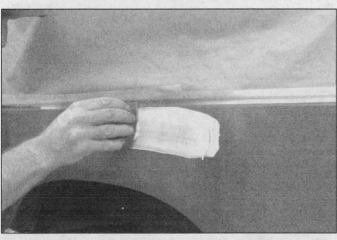

11   The primer will help reveal imperfections or scratches. Fill these with glazing compound. Follow the label instructions and sand it with 360 or 400-grit sandpaper until it's smooth. Repeat the glazing, sanding and respraying until the primer reveals a perfectly smooth surface

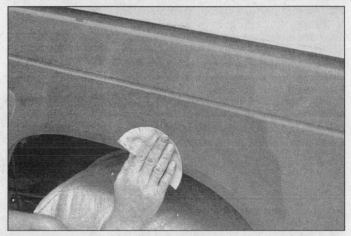

12   Finish sand the primer with very fine sandpaper (400 or 600-grit) to remove the primer overspray. Clean the area with water and allow it to dry. Use a tack rag to remove any dust, then apply the finish coat. Don't attempt to rub out or wax the repair area until the paint has dried completely (at least two weeks)

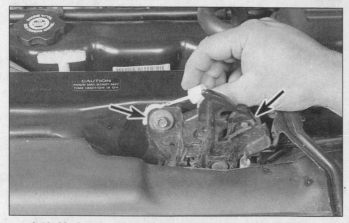

9.10 Mark the position of the hood latch, loosen the bolts (arrows) and move the latch to adjust the hood in the closed position

10.1 Hood latch assembly details

10   Mark the hood latch as a guide for adjustment (or removal and replacement). The hood latch assembly can also be adjusted up-and-down and side-to-side after loosening the bolts **(see illustration)**.

11   The hood latch assembly, as well as the hinges, should be periodically lubricated with white lithium-base grease to prevent sticking and wear.

10   Hood latch and cable - removal and installation

Warning: *These models have airbags. Always disconnect the negative battery cable and wait two minutes before working in the vicinity of the impact sensors, steering column or instrument panel to avoid the possibility of accidental deployment of the airbag, which could cause personal injury* (see Chapter 12).

Latch

Refer to illustration 10.1

1   Remove the bolts holding the hood latch to the radiator closure panel crossmember and detach the latch assembly **(see illustration)**.

2   Referring to Step 4, detach the hood release cable, then remove the latch from the cross member.

3   Installation is the reverse of removal.

Cable

Refer to illustrations 10.4 and 10.7

4   Release the cable end, then slide cable case end sideways in the keyhole slot of the hood latch while pinching the barb on the cable case closed **(see illustration)**.

5   Remove the cable from the latch.

6   In the passenger compartment, remove the lower steering column cover and knee blocker reinforcement (see Section 26).

7   Remove the screws and detach the hood release cable and handle assembly **(see illustration)**.

8   Under the dash remove the rubber cable insulator from the hole in the dash panel.

9   Connect a string or piece of wire to the engine compartment end of the cable, then detach the cable and pull it through the firewall into the passenger compartment.

10   Connect the string or wire to the new cable and pull it through the firewall into the engine compartment.

11   Installation is the reverse of Steps 1-8 above.

11   Grille - removal and installation

Warning: *These models have airbags. Always disconnect the negative battery cable and wait two minutes before working in the vicinity of the impact sensors, steering column or instrument panel to avoid the possibility of accidental deployment of the airbag, which could cause personal injury* (see Chapter 12).
Note: *The body-colored bumper cover has large openings that appear as a grille, but this procedure applies to the black plastic grille section attached to the bumper cover.*

1   Referring to Section 13, remove the front bumper cover.

2   Remove the clips securing the grille to the front bumper cover.

3   Using a 1/4-inch drill bit, drill out the

rivets holding the bottom of the grille to the bumper cover.

4   Carefully lift the grille away from the bumper cover.

5   Installation is the reverse of removal.

12   Front fender - removal and installation

Refer to illustrations 12.4 and 12.5
Warning: *These models have airbags. Always disconnect the negative battery cable and wait two minutes before working in the vicinity of the impact sensors, steering column or instrument panel to avoid the possibility of accidental deployment of the airbag, which could cause personal injury* (see Chapter 12).

1   Remove the bumper (see Section 13).

2   Loosen the front wheel lug nuts, raise the vehicle, support it securely on jackstands and remove the front wheel.

3   Remove the fender splash shield (see Section 29)

4   Remove the molding strip from the side-view mirror (see Section 28) and remove the fender bolt behind the mirror **(see illustration)**.

5   Remove the bolts at the front and rear edges of the fender and, working in the engine

10.4 Detach the cable end from the latch lever

10.7 Hood release handle mounting bolts (arrows)

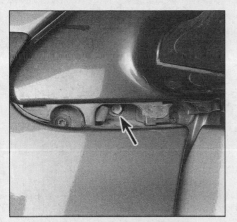

12.4 Remove the mirror molding to access the fender bolt (arrow) recessed behind the mirror

compartment, remove the upper bolts. There is also one nut at the lower rear of the fender **(see illustration)**. Detach the fender.

6   Installation is the reverse of removal.

7   Tighten all nuts, bolts and screws securely.

13 Bumpers - removal and installation

Warning: *These models have airbags. Always disconnect the negative battery cable and wait two minutes before working in the vicinity of the impact sensors, steering column or instrument panel to avoid the possibility of accidental deployment of the airbag, which could cause personal injury (see Chapter 12).*

Front bumper cover

Refer to illustrations 13.1 and 13.2

1   Release the hood latch and open the hood. Remove the screws attaching the grille to the radiator support panel **(see illustration)**.

2   Remove the bolts holding the bumper cover to the headlight mounting panel at each side of grille **(see illustration)**.

3   Raise the vehicle and support it securely on jackstands.

4   Remove the front wheels.

5   Remove the front wheelhouse splash shield fasteners as necessary to gain access

to the bolts holding the front cover to the fender (see Section 29).

6   Remove the bolts holding the bottom of the cover/air dam to the radiator closure panel.

7   Disconnect the fog light/parking and turn signal light electrical connector, if necessary.

8   Remove the bumper cover from the vehicle.

9   Installation is the reverse of removal.

Front bumper reinforcement bar

Refer to illustration 13.12

10   Remove the front bumper cover, as above.

11   Support the front bumper reinforcement bar on a suitable lifting device. Make a mark on the reinforcement bar to indicate the top.

12   Remove the nuts retaining the front bumper reinforcement bar to the frame rail **(see illustration)**.

13   Remove the front bumper reinforcement bar from the vehicle.

14   Installation is the reverse of removal.

12.5 Remove the lower fender attaching bolts

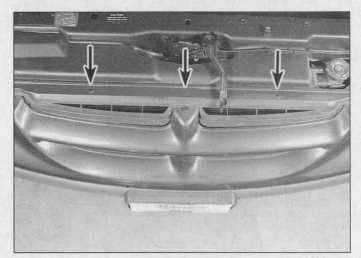

13.1 Remove the screws (arrows) attaching the grille to the radiator support panel

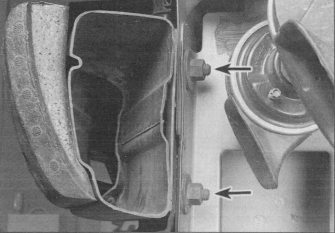

13.12 Front bumper reinforcement bar mounting bolts (arrows)

HEADLAMP MOUNTING PANEL

FRONT BUMPER REINFORCEMENT

FRONT BUMPER FASCIA

13.2 Typical front bumper cover assembly details

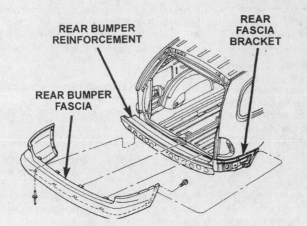

13.17 Typical rear bumper cover assembly details

13.24 Typical rear bumper reinforcement bar assembly details

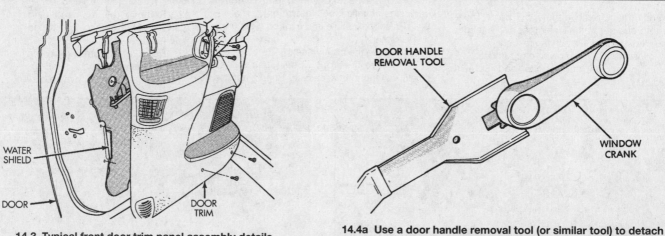

14.3 Typical front door trim panel assembly details

14.4a Use a door handle removal tool (or similar tool) to detach the retaining clip behind the window crank

Rear bumper cover

Refer to illustration 13.17

15   Release the liftgate latch and open the liftgate

16   Raise the vehicle and support it securely on jackstands.

17   Remove the screws holding the rear bumper cover to the rear cover brackets **(see illustration)**.

18   Release the hooks on the sides of the bumper cover from the tabs in the rear cover brackets.

19   Remove the rear bumper cover from the vehicle.

20   Installation is the reverse of removal.

Rear bumper reinforcement bar

Refer to illustration 13.24

21   Remove the rear bumper cover, as above.

22   Support the rear bumper reinforcement bar on a suitable lifting device.

23   Mark the position of the nuts on the frame rail extensions to aid installation.

24   Remove the nuts holding the rear bumper reinforcement bar to the frame rail

extensions **(see illustration)**.

25   Remove the rear bumper reinforcement bar from the vehicle.

26   Installation is the reverse of removal.

14   Door trim panels - removal and installation

Front door trim panel

Refer to illustrations 14.3, 14.4a, 14.4b, 14.4c, 14.4d, 14.5, 14.6a and 14.6b

1   Disconnect the cable from negative terminal of the battery.

2   Pry the courtesy light from the door trim and disconnect the wire connector.

3   Remove all door trim panel retaining screws and door pull/armrest assemblies **(see illustration)**.

4   On manual window models, remove the window crank **(see illustration)**. On power window models, remove the door switch panel and the control switch assembly **(see illustrations)**.

5   On models with memory seats/mirrors, use a small flat-bladed pry tool to remove the memory seat/mirror switch and disconnect

the wire connector **(see illustration)**.

6   Grasp the trim panel, lift up and pull out to detach it from the door **(see illustration)**. Disconnect the inner door handle lock rod from the handle **(see illustration)**. Unplug any electrical connectors remaining and remove the door panel.

7   To install, connect the wire harness connectors and place the panel in position in the

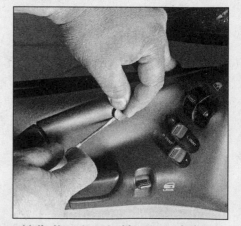

14.4b If equipped with power windows, pry off the trim panel screw covers . . .

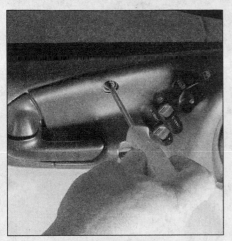

14.4c . . . remove the screws and lift the door switch panel off

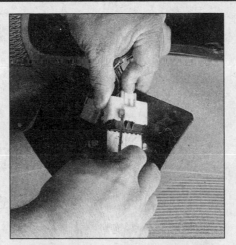

14.4d Disconnect the accessory switch electrical connector

door. Press the trim panel down into place until the hooks are seated.

8   Install the armrest/door pulls, the courtesy light and the window switch or crank. Reconnect the negative battery cable.

Sliding door trim panel

Refer to illustration 14.11

9   Close the door and remove the upper frame molding.
10   Remove the screws holding the trim panel to the inner door panel. If removing the left sliding door trim panel, remove the screw from inside the ash receiver bezel.
11   Remove the push-in fasteners and remove the trim panel from the vehicle (see illustration).
12   Installation is the reverse of removal.

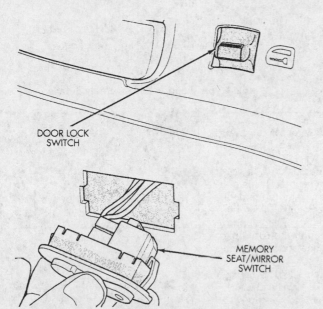

14.5 If equipped with a memory seat/mirror switch, detach the switch assembly from the door panel and disconnect the connector

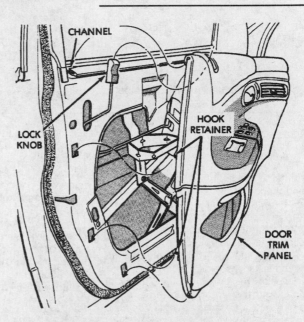

14.6a Lift the trim panel up and pull out to unhook the trim panel from the door frame

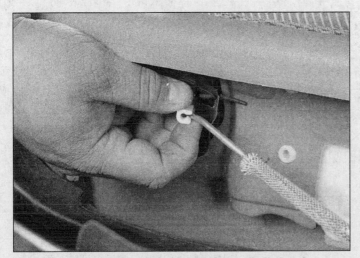

14.6b Disconnect the inner door handle lock rod

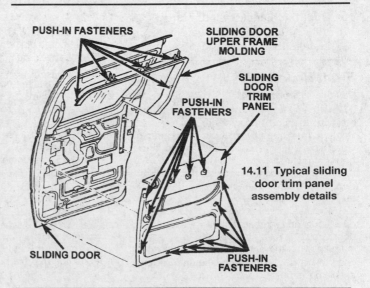

14.11 Typical sliding door trim panel assembly details

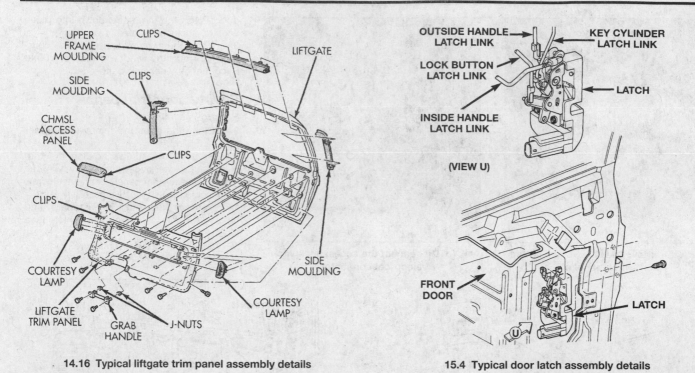

14.16 Typical liftgate trim panel assembly details

15.4 Typical door latch assembly details

Liftgate trim panel

Refer to illustration 14.16

13   Remove the liftgate upper frame molding and the side moldings. Remove the screws holding the assist handle and the fasteners around the perimeter of the lower trim panel.

14   If equipped with courtesy lamps, pry them from the trim and disconnect the wire connector from the lamp.

15   Remove the high-mount brake light cover and fasteners holding the trim panel.

16   Release the hidden clips holding the trim panel to the liftgate from around the edge of liftgate **(see illustration)** and remove trim panel.

17   Installation is the reverse of removal.

15   Door latch, lock cylinder and outside handle - removal and installation

Front door latch

Refer to illustration 15.4

1   Close the window completely and remove the front door trim panel (see Section 14). Carefully peel back the plastic water shield as needed to access the inner door components.

2   If equipped with power door locks, remove the wire connector from the power door lock motor.

3   Release the clips holding the linkage to door latch, and remove the linkages from the door latch.

4   Remove the screws holding the door latch to the door end frame **(see illustration)** and remove the latch from the door.

5   Installation is the reverse of removal. **Note:** *New screws must be used if the latch has been removed.*

6   After installing the door latch with new screws, insert the linkage into the latch, engage clips to hold the linkage to the door latch and connect the electrical connector to the power door lock motor, if equipped. Insert a hex wrench through the oval hole located in the door shut face above the latch and loosen the Allen head screw.

7   Pull outward on the outside door handle and release, then tighten the Allen head screw.

8   Check that the door latch and power door lock operate, then install the plastic shield and front door trim panel.

Front door outside handle

Refer to illustration 15.11

9   Close the window completely and remove the front door trim panel (see Section 14). Carefully peel back the plastic water shield as needed to access the inner door components. If equipped with the Vehicle Theft Security System (VTSS), use the access hole at the rear of the inner door panel and disconnect the switch connector from the door harness. Release the push-in fasteners holding the VTSS switch harness to the inner door reinforcement.

10   Release the clip holding the door latch linkage to the door latch and remove the latch linkage from the latch.

11   Release the clip holding the lock linkage to the door latch and remove the lock linkage from the latch **(see illustration)**.

12   Remove the nuts holding the outside door handle to the door outer panel and remove the handle from the vehicle.

15.11 Detach the outside door lock linkage from the latch (arrow)

Front door lock cylinder

Refer to illustrations 15.13 and 15.14

13   Proceed as above to remove the front door outside handle. Release the clip holding the lock cylinder into the outside handle **(see illustration)** and pull the lock from the door handle.

14   Install the lock cylinder retaining clip into the door handle. Position the link arm toward the rear of vehicle, push the lock cylinder into the door handle until the lock cylinder snaps into place **(see illustration)**. The remainder of installation is the reverse of removal.

Sliding door latch/lock control

Refer to illustrations 15.16, 15.17 and 15.18

15   Remove the sliding door trim panel (see Section 14), the door stop bumper, and the sound pad if equipped.

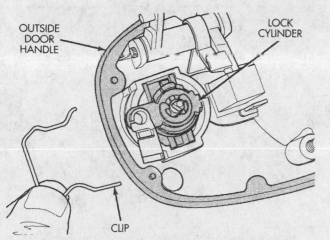

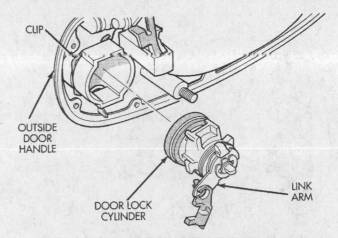

15.13 Remove the clip retaining the front door lock cylinder to the outside door handle

15.14 Install the clip into the door handle and press the lock cylinder in until it snaps into place

15.16 Remove the cover from the latch/lock

15.17 Detach the link rods (arrows) from the latch/lock control

16   Pull off the latch/lock control cover which is held in place by clips (see illustration).
17   With the sliding door slightly open, release the clip holding the rear latch link to the latch/lock control (see illustration).
18   Place a flat-head screwdriver between the metal clip ears and the bottom of the link (see illustration). Rotate the screwdriver to detach the link from the clip. Caution: Be very careful not to damage the metal clips, the entire latch/lock control assembly must

be replaced if any of the metal clips on the latch/lock control are bent or broken. Do not attempt to repair the clips to retain the links.
19   Remove the rear latch link from the latch/lock control.
20   Release the clip holding the outside door handle link to the latch/lock control as in Step 18 above, then remove the outside door handle link.
21   Release the clip holding the inside door handle bellcrank link to the control as in Step 18 above and separate the inside door

handle bellcrank link from the latch/lock control.
22   Remove the lock cylinder link from the control.
23   Release the clip holding the inside lock link to the control and remove the inside lock link from the control.
24   Release the lock tabs holding the open latch cable case to the latch/lock control and remove and hold open the latch cable ball end from the control.
25   Loosen the bolts holding the latch/lock control to the sliding door (If equipped with power door locks, disconnect the wire connector from the power door lock motor).
26   Remove the latch lock from the vehicle.
27   Installation is the reverse of removal.

Sliding door outside handle
Refer to illustration 15.31
28   Refer to Section 14 and remove the trim panel, the sliding door stop bumper and plastic shield as necessary to access the outside release fasteners.
29   Remove the latch/lock control cover and release the clip holding the outside door handle linkage to the door handle.

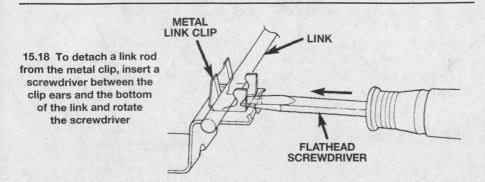

15.18 To detach a link rod from the metal clip, insert a screwdriver between the clip ears and the bottom of the link and rotate the screwdriver

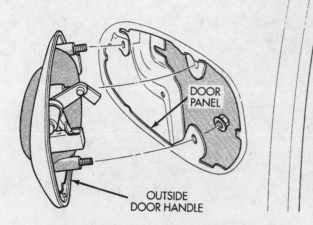

15.31 Sliding door outside latch assembly details

15.35 Disconnect the liftgate ajar switch electrical connector (arrow)

30   Separate the linkage from the outside door handle, then separate the linkage from the latch/lock control.

31   Remove the nuts holding the outside door handle to the outer door panel **(see illustration)** and remove the door handle from the vehicle.

32   Installation is the reverse of removal.

Liftgate latch

Refer to illustration 15.35

33   Remove the trim panel and watershield from the inside of liftgate (see Section 14).

34   Remove the outside handle link from the clip on the latch.

35   Disconnect the wire connector from the liftgate ajar switch **(see illustration)**.

36   Remove the screws holding the latch to the liftgate and remove it from the vehicle.

37   Installation is the reverse of removal.

Liftgate outside handle

Refer to illustration 15.41

38   Remove the liftgate trim panel (see Section 14) and power lock motor.

39   Release the outside handle link from the clip on the liftgate latch.

40   If equipped with a security system disconnect the VTSS switch from the back of the lock cylinder and disengage the lock nut.

41   Remove the nut attaching the outside liftgate handle to the liftgate **(see illustration)**.

42   Release the retaining groove holding the handle to the liftgate and remove the handle and links from the vehicle.

43   Installation is the reverse of removal.

Liftgate lock cylinder

Refer to illustrations 15.44 and 15.46

44   Remove the outside liftgate handle, as above and remove the lock cylinder clip from

the handle **(see illustration)**.

45   Remove the lock cylinder and arm from the handle.

46   To install, place the lock cylinder retaining clip into the liftgate handle and push the lock cylinder in until it snaps into place **(see illustration)**.

47   Install the outside liftgate handle and check to see that the lock works.

16   Front door - removal and installation

Refer to illustrations 16.2, 16.4 and 16.5
Caution: *If the hinge pin must be removed from the hinge, do not reuse the original pin. If you plan to remove the pin be sure you have a new one before starting the job. The retaining clips used on the door hinge pins should also be replaced with new ones.*

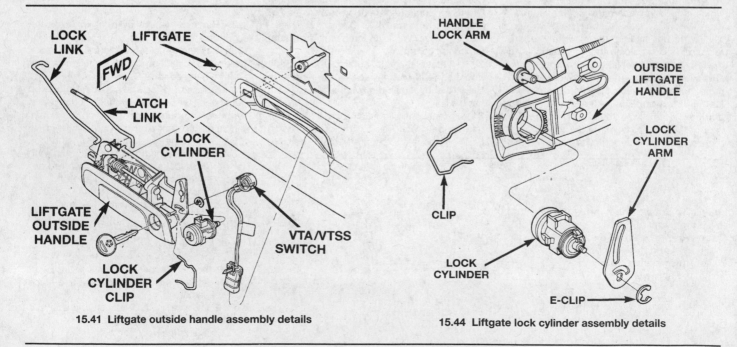

15.41 Liftgate outside handle assembly details

15.44 Liftgate lock cylinder assembly details

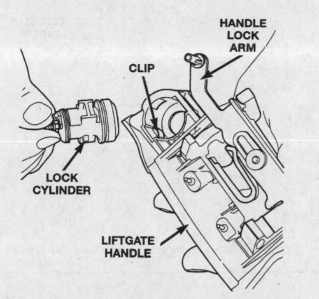

15.46 To install the lock cylinder, place the clip into the liftgate handle and press the cylinder in until it snaps into place

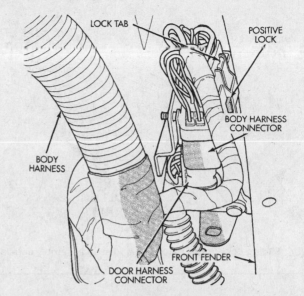

16.2 Release the positive lock slide on the side of the connector and disconnect the door harness wire connector

1   Remove the front wheelhouse splash shield (see Section 29).

2   Disconnect the door harness connector from the body harness **(see illustration)**.

3   Depress the lock tab holding the wire connector halves together and disconnect the door harness from the body wiring harness.

4   Scribe around the mounting bolt heads with a marking pen. Remove the bolts holding the door check strap to the A-pillar **(see illustration)**. Place a jack under the door or have an assistant on hand to support it when the hinge bolts are removed. **Note:** *If a jack is*

used, place a rag between it and the door to protect the door's painted surfaces.

5   Remove the bolts holding the lower hinge to the door end frame **(see illustration)**. Keeping door steady, remove the bolts holding the upper hinge to the door end frame and carefully lift off the door.

6   Installation is the reverse of removal, making sure to align the hinge with the marks made during removal before tightening the bolts.

7   Following installation of the door, check the alignment and adjust It if necessary as follows:

a) *Up-and-down and in-and-out adjustments are made by loosening the hinge-to-door bolts and moving the door as necessary.*

b) *Forward-and-backward adjustments are made by loosening the hinge-to-body bolts and moving the door as necessary.*

c) *The door lock striker can also be adjusted both up-and-down and sideways to provide positive engagement with the lock mechanism. This is done by loosening the mounting screws and moving the striker as necessary.*

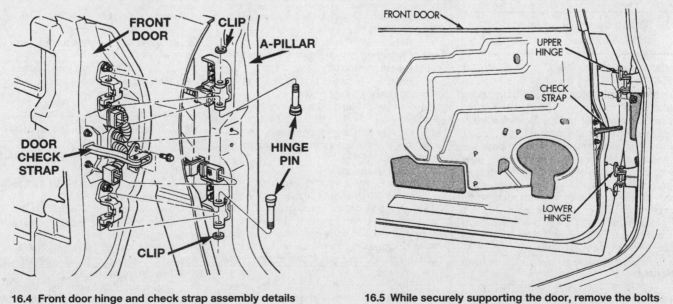

16.4 Front door hinge and check strap assembly details

16.5 While securely supporting the door, remove the bolts retaining the hinges to the door

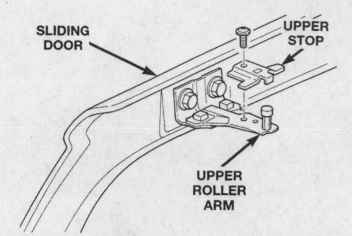

17.4 Sliding door upper roller arm and stop assembly details

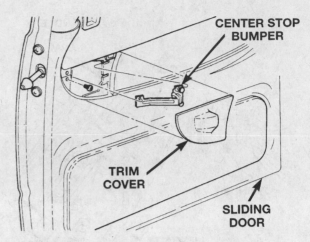

17.5 Sliding door center stop bumper assembly details

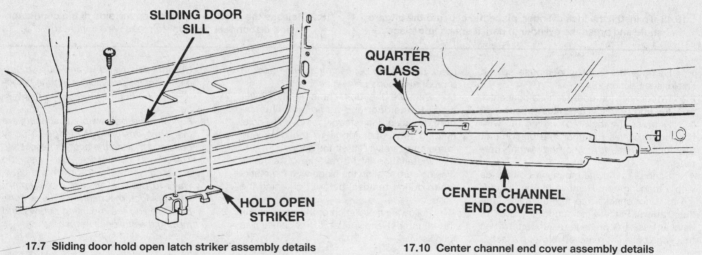

17.7 Sliding door hold open latch striker assembly details

17.10 Center channel end cover assembly details

17 Sliding door - removal and installation

Refer to illustrations 17.4, 17.5, 17.7, 17.10, 17.12a and 17.12b

Caution: *Apply several layers of masking tape to the body around the rear end of the upper roller channel and the forward edge of the quarter glass to avoid damaging the paint.*

Note: *This procedure applies to both the manual and electrically operated sliding door removal and installation and applies to both right and left side sliding doors. It does not apply to the electrically operated mechanism for the door.*

1   Apply masking tape to the outside surface of the quarter panel below the center roller channel, rearward of the door opening.
2   Release the sliding door latch and open the door.
3   Apply masking tape to the door jamb area, rearward of the upper roller channel.
4   Remove the screw holding the upper

roller arm stop bumper to the upper roller arm **(see illustration).**
5   Remove the stop bumper from the upper roller arm and the trim cover from the door **(see illustration).**
6   Remove the center and sliding door sill plate by removing the screws.
7   Remove the hold open striker **(see illustration).**
8   On power sliding door models, disconnect the electrical connector for the motor mechanism.
9   Open quarter glass.
10   Remove the center roller channel end cover **(see illustration).** Support the sliding door on a suitable lifting device that has a padded upper surface. The door must be moveable while on the lifting device. **Caution:** *Do not allow the center hinge roller to contact the quarter glass. This could break the glass.*
11   Roll the door rearward until the lower rollers disengage from the lower channel.
12   Roll the door rearward until the upper

and center hinge rollers exit the upper and center channels **(see illustrations).**
13   Remove the sliding door from the vehicle.
14   Installation is the reverse of removal. Be aware of cautions above about the hinge roller and quarter glass.

18 Liftgate - removal, installation and adjustment

Refer to illustration 18.5
1   Have an assistant support the liftgate in its fully open position.
2   Disconnect all cables and wire harness connectors that would interfere with removal of the liftgate.
3   Remove the liftgate upper frame molding and disconnect the rear window washer hose from the spray nozzle.
4   On power liftgate models, disconnect the lift mechanism actuator rod from the liftgate.

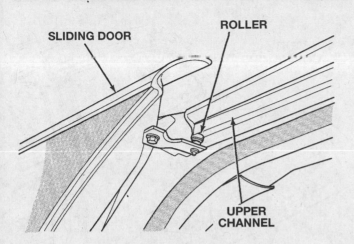

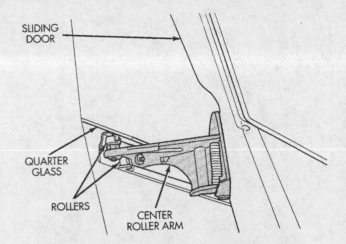

17.12a Sliding door upper roller assembly details

17.12b Sliding door center roller assembly details

18.5 Apply alignment marks around the liftgate hinges

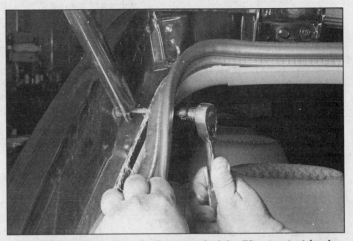

19.3 Remove the bolt at the lower end of the liftgate strut (make sure the liftgate is securely supported before removing these bolts)

5   Mark or scribe around the hinges **(see illustration)**.
6   While an assistant supports the liftgate, detach the support struts (see Section 19).
7   Remove the hinge bolts and detach the liftgate from the vehicle.
8   Installation is the reverse of removal.
9   After installation, close the liftgate and make sure it is in proper alignment with the surrounding body panels. Adjustments are made by changing the position of the hinge bolts in the slots. To adjust it, loosen the hinge bolts and reposition the hinges either side-to-side or front and back the desired amount and retighten the bolts.
10   The engagement of the liftgate can be adjusted by loosening the lock striker bolts, repositioning the striker and retightening the bolts.

19 Liftgate strut - replacement

Refer to illustration 19.3
1   Have an assistant support the liftgate in its fully open position.
2   Pull away the weatherstrip from the D-pillar flange next to the strut assembly end pivot.
3   Remove the mounting bolt where the strut attaches to the body **(see illustration)**.
4   Remove the bolt holding the strut to the liftgate, and remove the strut from the vehicle.
5   Installation is the reverse of removal.

20 Front door window glass - removal and installation

Refer to illustrations 20.3 and 20.5
1   Remove the door trim panel and plastic shield (see Section 14). Remove both inner and outer belt moldings and the radio speaker if installed.
2   Lower the glass so that you can get to the front and rear regulator lift plates through the front and rear access holes in the door panel.
3   Remove the clips that hold the door glass to the regulator lift plates **(see illustration)**, and remove the glass from the lift plates.

4   Remove the weatherstrip from the glass and then insert the front of the glass between the glass run channel and the outer door panel.

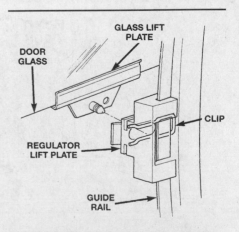

20.3 Front door glass regulator lift plate assembly details

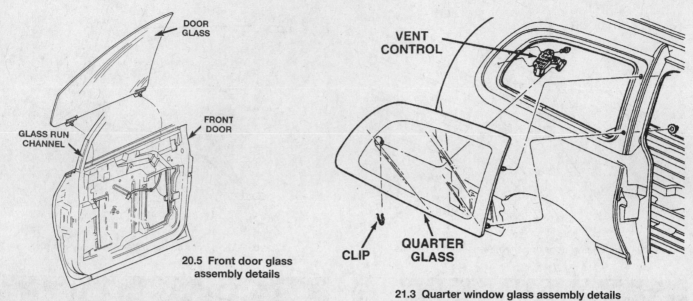

20.5 Front door glass assembly details

21.3 Quarter window glass assembly details

5   Carefully lift the glass upward and out of the exterior opening at the top of the door **(see illustration)**.
6   Installation is the reverse of removal.

21 Quarter window glass - removal and installation

Refer to illustration 21.3
1   Remove the interior trim that is around the window to be removed, then open the window to the vent position.
2   Remove the screw holding the window retainer to the vent motor arm and release the retainer from the motor arm.
3   Remove the nuts that hold the glass to the pillar **(see illustration)** and remove the glass from the vehicle.
4   Installation is the reverse of removal.

22 Door window regulator - removal and installation

Refer to illustrations 22.4 and 22.5
1   Remove the door trim panel and water-shield (see Section 14).
2   Remove the door glass retaining glass and allow the window glass to rest on the bottom of the door.
3   On power window models, unplug the electrical connector.
4   Loosen the screws holding the front and rear guide rails to the door panel **(see illustration)**.
5   Remove the screw heads on the guide rails from the key hole slots in the door panel, lift up to detach the regulator, then slide it rearward and remove it through the access hole in the door. Remove the front guide rail

through the front access hole and the rear guide rail through the rear access hole **(see illustration)**.
6   Installation is the reverse of removal.

23 Lower console - removal and installation

Refer to illustration 23.1a and 23.1b
Warning: *These models have airbags. Always disconnect the negative battery cable and wait two minutes before working in the vicinity of the impact sensors, steering column or instrument panel to avoid the possibility of accidental deployment of the airbag, which could cause personal injury (see Chapter 12).*
1   On 1999-2000 models, remove the two front screws holding the lower console to the

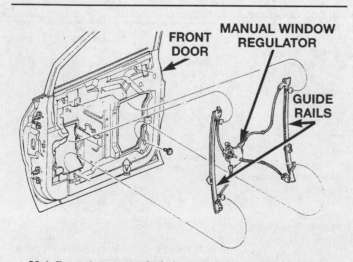

22.4 Front door manual window regulator assembly details

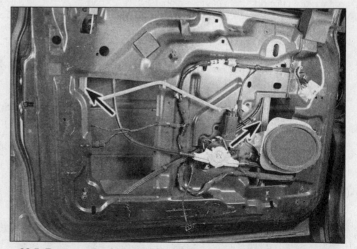

22.5 Remove the front guide rail through the front access hole (right arrow) and the rear guide rail through the rear access hole (left arrow)

23.1a Remove the screws retaining the lower console to the floor bracket

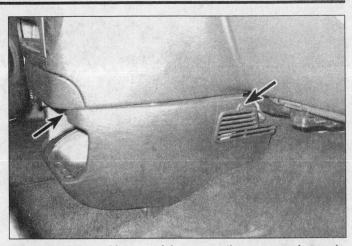

23.1b On 2001 and later models, remove these screws (arrows)

floor bracket and instrument panel **(see illustration)**. On 2001 and later models, remove the two front upper screws, two front lower screws and two rear screws holding the lower console to the floor bracket and instrument panel **(see illustration)**.
2   On models so equipped, disconnect the auxiliary power outlet wire connector.
3   Slide the console rearward from around the instrument panel supports, and remove the lower console.
4   Installation is the reverse of removal.

24   Overhead console - removal and installation

Refer to illustration 24.1

1996 through 2000 models

1   Open the transmitter bin door **(see illustration)** and remove the screw holding the console to the headliner.

2   Open the eyeglass bin door and press the retaining tab which is directly above the latch door. Lower the rear of the console away from the headliner.
3   Pull the console to the rear and release the clips that hold the front of the console to the roof armature and lower the console.
4   By fully depressing the lock tabs, disconnect all wire connectors and remove the overhead console.
5   Installation is the reverse of removal.

2001 and later models

Refer to illustration 24.8

6   Disconnect the cable from the negative terminal of the battery.
7   Remove the retaining screws at the front of the overhead console.
8   Grasp the sides of the overhead console **(see illustration)**, pull straight down evenly, and disengage the two snap clips at the rear.
9   Lower the overhead console sufficiently to gain access to the electrical connectors.

Disconnect the electrical connectors and remove the overhead console.
10   Installation is the reverse of removal.

25   Instrument cluster bezel - removal and installation

Refer to illustrations 25.2 and 25.4

1996 through 2000 models

Warning: *These models have airbags. Always disconnect the negative battery cable and wait two minutes before working in the vicinity of the impact sensors, steering column or instrument panel to avoid the possibility of accidental deployment of the airbag, which could cause personal injury* (see Chapter 12).
1   Remove the left instrument panel end cover and the upper and lower steering column covers (see Section 26).
2   Remove the two screws at the left end of the cluster bezel and one from each side of

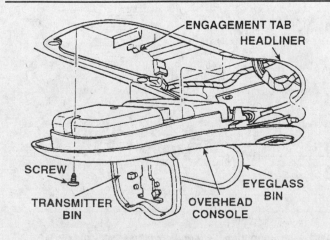

24.1 Overhead console assembly details

24.8 Grasp the sides of the overhead console and pull down evenly, then disengage the two snaps at the rear

25.2 Remove the two screws at the left end of the cluster bezel and one from each side of the steering column (screw on the right side of steering column not visible)

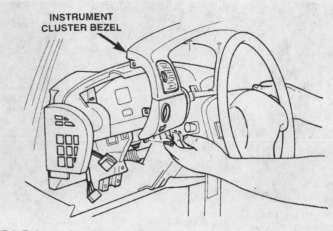

25.4 Release the clip above the right vent and pull the instrument cluster bezel to the rear

the steering column **(see illustration)**.

3 Disconnect the clip that holds the cluster bezel to the instrument panel from above the right vent louver.

4 Withdraw the cluster bezel from the instrument panel and disconnect the electrical connectors from the backside **(see illustration)**.

5 Installation is the reverse of removal.

2001 and later models

Refer to illustration 25.7

6 Firmly grasp the front edge of the steering column upper cover, pull upward quickly and disengage the cover from the instrument panel. Remove the upper cover.

7 Remove the four screws securing the instrument cluster. Withdraw the cluster from the bezel and disconnect the electrical connectors from the backside **(see illustration)**.

8 Remove the four screws securing the cluster bezel.

9 Move the steering column to the full down position.

10 Pull the cluster bezel out of the instrument panel and remove it.

11 Installation is the reverse of removal.

26 Dashboard panels - removal and installation

Warning: *These models have airbags. Always disconnect the negative battery cable and wait two minutes before working in the vicinity of the impact sensors, steering column or instrument panel to avoid the possibility of accidental deployment of the airbag, which could cause personal injury* (see Chapter 12).

Instrument panel end covers

Refer to illustration 26.1

1 On 1996 through 2000 models, for the left end cover, remove the lower steering column cover as necessary for clearance, then remove the attaching screw **(see illustration)**. The right end cap cover is only attached by clips and does not have a retaining screw.

2 On all models, grasp the cover securely (by the fuse box on the left cap or the heater vane on the right cap) and pull sharply to remove it. If necessary, gently pry with a screwdriver.

3 Installation is the reverse of removal.

Headlight switch bezel

4 Remove the instrument cluster bezel (see Section 25).

5 Separate the headlight switch bezel

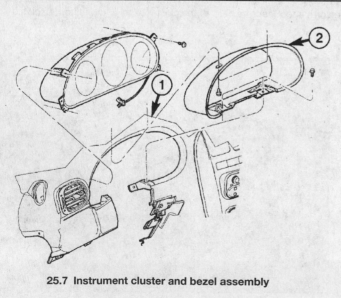

25.7 Instrument cluster and bezel assembly

1 Instrument cluster   2 Cluster bezel

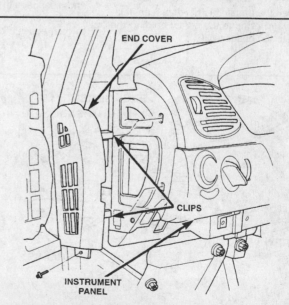

26.1 Instrument panel left end cover assembly details (1996 through 2000 models)

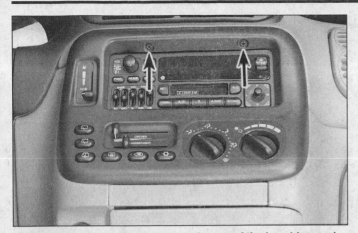

26.10 Remove the two screws at the top of the bezel (arrows)

26.11 On 2001 and later models, the bezel (arrow) comes off as one piece after removing the screws

26.15 Open the glove box door, remove the clip retaining the door-stop strap and unsnap the hinges

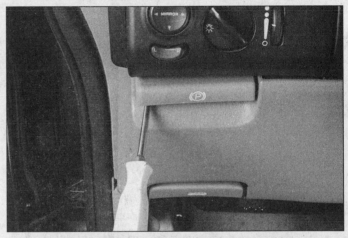

26.17 Remove the screws retaining the parking brake release handle

from the instrument cluster bezel.

6   Installation is the reverse of removal.

Radio and heater/air conditioning control panel bezel

Refer to illustrations 26.10 and 26.11

7   On 1996 through 2000 models, remove the cup holder (see Step 29).

8   Carefully insert a tape-covered screwdriver above the screw access panel cover below the heater/air conditioning control panel and pry the cover from the instrument panel (see Step 30).

9   Remove the bezel retaining screws behind the cover.

10   On 1996 through 2000 models, remove the screws retaining the top of the bezel to the instrument panel (**see illustration**).

11   On 1996 through 2000 models, remove the screws that hold the top of the bezel to the instrument panel. On 2001 and later models, remove the remaining side screws, disconnect the accessory switch electrical connectors and remove the bezel from the instrument panel (**see illustration**).

12   On 1996 through 2000 models, remove

the electrical connectors from the heater/air conditioning control panel and blower switch.

13   Installation is the reverse of removal.

Glove box

Refer to illustration 26.15

14   Open the glove box door, remove the contents and remove the clip retaining the door-stop strap.

15   Pivot the glove box downward, unsnap the hinges from the instrument panel and

remove the glove box (**see illustration**).

16   Installation is the reverse of removal.

Lower steering column cover

1996 through 2000 models

Refer to illustrations 26.17, 26.18 and 26.19

17   Remove the screws holding the parking brake release handle to the instrument panel (**see illustration**).

18   Remove the screws holding the cover to the instrument panel (**see illustration**).

26.18 Remove the screws retaining the lower steering column cover to the instrument panel (not all screws visible)

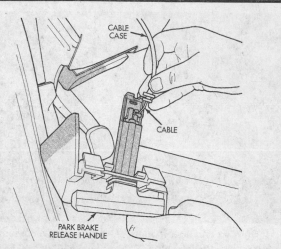

26.19 Detach the parking brake cable from the release handle

26.24a Remove the three screws retaining the upper steering column cover halves together and separate the halves

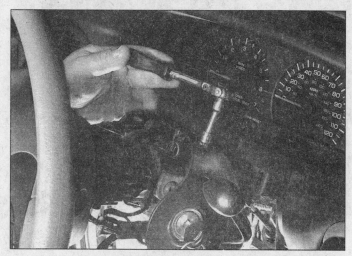

26.24b Remove the two screws (one on each side) and detach the bezel

26.27 Knee blocker reinforcement bolts (arrows)

19 Pull the cover back and detach the parking brake cable housing from the groove on the end of the release handle and disengage the cable end pivot from the slot on the handle **(see illustration)**.
20 Installation is the reverse of removal.

2001 and later models

21 Remove the side and lower screws holding the lower steering column cover to the instrument panel and remove the cover.
22 Installation is the reverse of removal.

Upper steering column covers

Refer to illustrations 26.24a and 26.24b
23 Remove the lower steering column cover.
24 Remove the screws retaining the upper steering column covers and separate the halves **(see illustration)**. To remove the steering column-to-instrument panel bezel, remove the instrument cluster bezel. Remove the screws and remove the bezel **(see illustration)**.
25 Installation is the reverse of removal.

Knee blocker reinforcement

Refer to illustration 26.27
26 Remove the lower steering column cover (see above).
27 Remove the bolts that hold the knee blocker reinforcement to the instrument panel, and remove the knee blocker reinforcement **(see illustration)**.
28 Installation is the reverse of removal.

Cup holder

1996 through 2000 models

Refer to illustrations 26.29, 26.30 and 26.31
29 Pull the cup holder out, press the tab at the rear and remove the holder **(see illustration)**.
30 Carefully insert a tape-covered screwdriver above the screw access cover below the heater/air conditioning control panel and pry the cover from the instrument panel **(see illustration)**. Remove the center bezel.
31 Remove the screws in the track and pull the track out to release the rear guide studs from the instrument panel **(see illustration)**.

32 Release the clip that holds the lamp to the track and pull out the cup holder track.

2001 and later models

33 Carefully insert a tape-covered screwdriver above the screw access panel cover

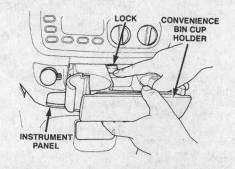

26.29 Pull the cup holder out and press the lock down

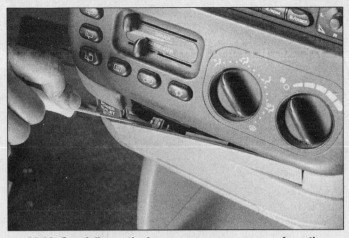

26.30 Carefully pry the lower screw access cover from the instrument panel and remove the screws behind the cover

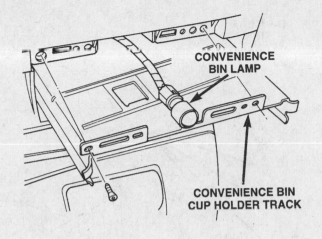

CONVENIENCE BIN LAMP

CONVENIENCE BIN CUP HOLDER TRACK

26.31 Remove the cup holder track

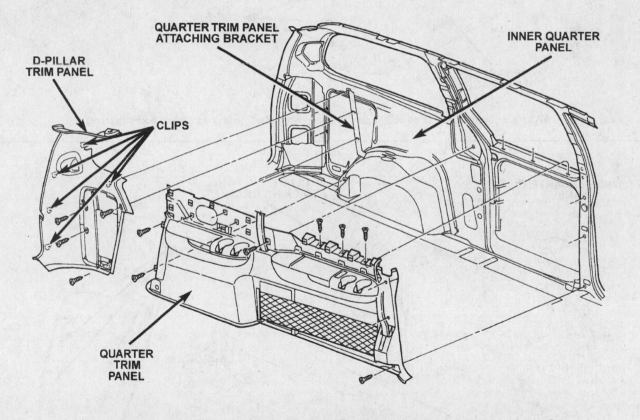

QUARTER TRIM PANEL ATTACHING BRACKET

INNER QUARTER PANEL

D-PILLAR TRIM PANEL

CLIPS

QUARTER TRIM PANEL

27.3a Left quarter and D-pillar trim panels - long wheel base with single sliding door (typical)

below the heater/air conditioning control panel and pry the cover from the instrument panel (see Step 30).

34 Remove the heater/air conditioning control panel.

35 Pull the cup holder assembly out from the lower instrument panel, disengage the rear guide studs and remove the cup holder.

36 Installation is the reverse of removal.

27 Interior quarter trim panels - removal and installation

Refer to illustrations 27.3a, 27.3b and 27.3c

1 Remove the first and, if equipped, the second rear seat.

2 Remove the plastic plugs from the trim panel that is being removed. Use a flat bladed screwdriver.

3 Remove all mounting screws with a screwdriver and release the mounting clips **(see illustrations)**. Disconnect any wire connectors from accessory power outlets, if so equipped.

4 Separate the trim panels from the body.

5 Installation is the reverse of removal.

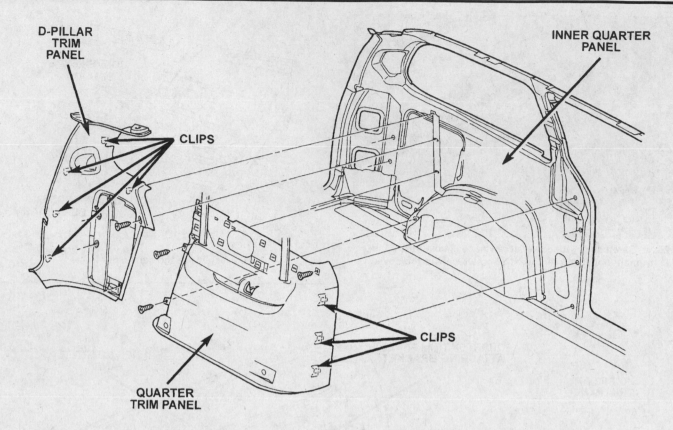

27.3b Left quarter and D-pillar trim panels - long wheel base with two sliding doors (typical)

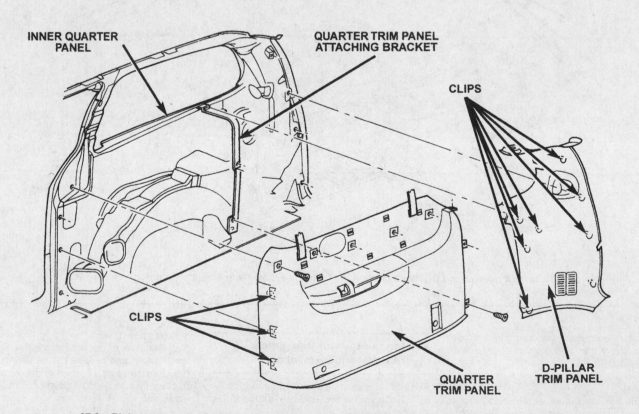

27.3c Right quarter and D-pillar trim panels - long wheel base with rear air conditioning (typical)

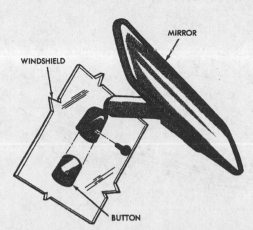

MIRROR

WINDSHIELD

BUTTON

28.1 Interior rear view mirror assembly details

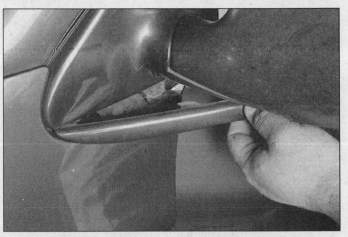

28.3 Remove the molding at the base of the side view mirror

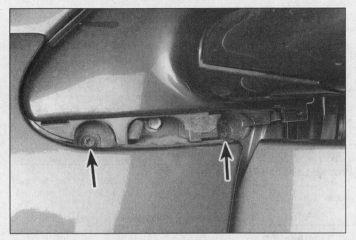

28.4a Side view mirror attaching screws (arrows)

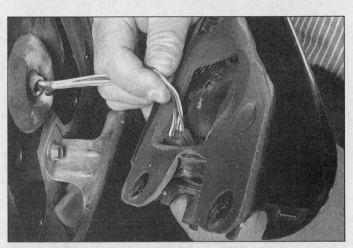

28.4b Disconnect the power mirror electrical connector

28 Mirrors - removal and installation

Refer to illustrations 28.1, 28.3, 28.4a and 28.4b

Interior

1 Use a Phillips head screwdriver to remove the set screw, then slide the mirror up off the button on the windshield **(see illustration)**.
2 Installation is the reverse of removal.

Exterior

3 Remove the screw holding the molding to the base of the mirror and remove the molding **(see illustration)**.
4 Remove the screws and detach the mirror **(see illustration)**. On power mirrors, unplug the electrical connector.
5 Installation is the reverse of removal.

29 Wheelhouse splash shield - removal and installation

Refer to illustration 29.2

1 Loosen the wheel lug nuts, raise the front of the vehicle and support it securely on jackstands. Remove the wheel(s).
2 Remove the push-in fasteners that hold the splash shield to the frame rails **(see illustration)**.

3 Remove the screws that hold the wheelhouse splash shield to the front fender and remove the splash shield from the vehicle.
4 Installation is the reverse of removal.

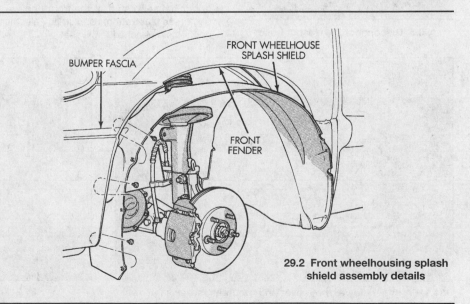

BUMPER FASCIA

FRONT WHEELHOUSE SPLASH SHIELD

FRONT FENDER

29.2 Front wheelhousing splash shield assembly details

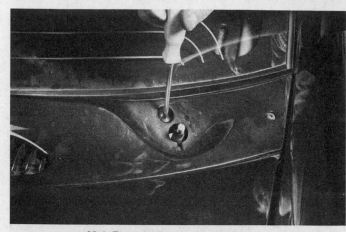

30.1 Remove the cowl cover screws

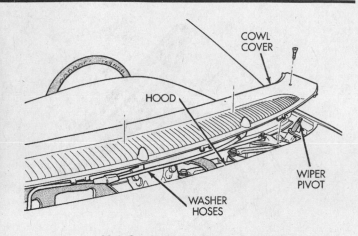

30.4 Cowl cover assembly details

30   Cowl cover - removal and installation

Refer to illustrations 30.1, 30.4 and 30.5

1   Remove the wiper arms, then remove the screws that hold the lower area of the cowl cover to the wiper module (see illustration).

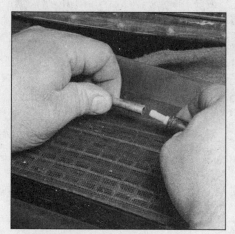

30.5 Disconnect the washer hose

2   Disengage the quarter-turn fasteners that hold the outer ends of the cowl cover to the wiper module.
3   Open the hood and release the wing nuts that hold the front of the cowl cover to the wiper module.
4   Close the hood but do not latch it. Now remove the outboard screws (see illustration) and lift the cowl cover up enough to get to the washer hose.
5   Disconnect the washer hose from the right washer nozzle (see illustration). Lift the cowl cover toward the windshield and off the vehicle.
6   Installation is the reverse of removal.

31   Seats - removal and installation

Refer to illustrations 31.1 and 31.2

Front

1   Move the seat forward and remove the seat trim screws (see illustration).
2   Remove the nuts from the seat track under the seat, start at the front and work back (see illustration). Unplug any electrical connectors attached to the seat.

3   Lift the seat from the vehicle.
4   Installation is the reverse of removal.

Rear

5   Lift the release latch handles on the lower sides of the seat and slide the seat toward the rear of the vehicle.
6   Installation is the reverse of removal.

32   Seat belt check

1   Check the seat belts, buckles, latch plates and guide loops for obvious damage and signs of wear.
2   See if the seat belt reminder light comes on when the key is turned to the Run or Start positions. A chime should also sound.
3   The seat belts are designed to lock up during a sudden stop or impact, yet allow free movement during normal driving. Make sure the retractors return the belt against your chest while driving and rewind the belt fully when the buckle is unlatched.
4   If any of the above checks reveal problems with the seat belt system, replace parts as needed.

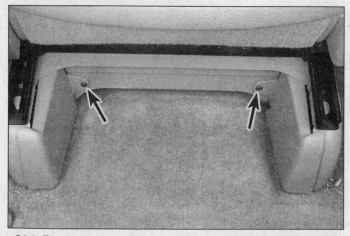

31.1 Front seat lower trim cover and mounting screws (arrows)

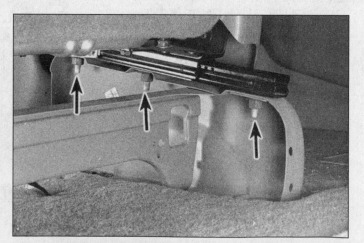

31.2 Front seat track retaining nuts (arrows)

Chapter 12
Chassis electrical system

Contents

	Section
Airbag system - general information	27
Antenna - removal and installation	16
Bulb replacement	13
Circuit breakers - general information	5
Cruise control system - description and check	23
Electric rear view mirrors - description and check	22
Electrical troubleshooting - general information	2
Fuses - general information	3
Fusible links - general information	4
General information	1
Headlight bulb - replacement	10
Headlight housing removal and installation	12
Headlight switch - check and replacement	14
Headlights - adjustment	11
Horn - check and replacement	21
Ignition switch and lock cylinder - removal and installation	8
Instrument cluster - removal and installation	20
Multifunction switch - check and replacement	9
Power door lock system - description and check	24
Power seats - description and check	26
Power window system - description and check	25
Radio and speakers - removal and installation	15
Rear window defogger - check and repair	19
Rear window defogger switch - removal and installation	18
Relays - general information	6
Turn signal/hazard flasher - check and replacement	7
Windshield wiper motor - check and replacement	17
Wiring diagrams - general information	28

Specifications

Light bulb types

Front
Headlight bulb
1996	9004
1997 through 2000 (except Town and Country)	9007

1998 through 2000 Town and Country
High beam	9005

Low beam
1998	905SLL
1999 through 2000	9005ZLSS
2001 and later	9007

Parking/Turn signal/Front side marker
1996 through 1998	3157NA
1999 through 2000	3157NAK
2001 and later	3157A
Parking/Turn signal Town & Country	4157NAK
Front side marker Town & Country	194NA

Fog light bulb
Except Town & Country	H3
Town & Country	9040

Interior

ABS/airbag indicator
   1996 through 2000 .... PC194
   2001 and later .... LED
Alarm set (security)
   1996 through 2000 .... PC194
   2001 and later PC74
Brake warning
   1996 through 2000 .... PC194
   2001 and later .... LED
Center rear dome lights 579
Center rear reading lights 578
Door ajar indicator lights
   1996 through 2000 .... PC194
   2001 and later .... LED
Door courtesy light
   1996 through 2000 567
   2001 and later 578
Engine compartment 579
Front door courtesy
   1996 through 2000 567
   2001 and later 578
Front header reading/center/rear dome lights
   1996 through 2000 579
   2001 and later 578
Glove compartment light 194
High beam indicator
   1996 through 2000 .... PC194
   2001 and later PC74
Liftgate flood lights
   1996 through 2000 567
   2001 and later 578
Liftgate ajar indicator lights
   1996 through 2000 .... PC74
   2001 and later .... LED
Low fuel indicator
   1996 through 2000 .... PC194
   2001 and later PC74
Low washer fluid, low voltage
   1996 through 2000 .... P74
   2001 and later .... LED
Low voltage indicator
   1996 through 2000 .... PC74
   2001 and later .... LED
Malfunction indicator
Indicator PC74
Base cluster .... LED
Oil pressure indicator
   1996 through 2000 .... PC194
   2001 and later PC74
Overhead console reading lights
   1996 through 2000 579
   2001 and later PC579
Seat belt indicator
   1996 through 2000 .... PC74
   2001 and later .... LED
Temperature indicator
   1996 through 2000 .... PC194
   2001 and later .... LED
Speedometer and instrument cluster light
   1996 through 2000 .... PC194
   2001 and later PC74
Visor vanity 6501966

Rear

Tail, stop, turn signal and side marker light
   1996 models 3157
   1997 and later models 3057

Back-up light bulb
   1996 models.. 921
   1997 and later models.. 3057
Center High Mounted Stop Light (CHMSL) bulb
   1996 models.. 922
   1997 and later models.. 921
License plate light.. 168

Note: *Do not use bulbs having a higher candle power than the bulbs listed. Do not touch halogen bulbs with fingers or any oily substance - clean with rubbing alcohol.*

1   General information

The electrical system is a 12-volt, negative ground type. Power for the lights and all electrical accessories is supplied by a lead/acid-type battery which is charged by the alternator.

This Chapter covers repair and service procedures for the various electrical components not associated with the engine. Information on the battery, alternator, distributor and starter motor can be found in Chapter 5. **Warning:** *When working on the electrical system, disconnect the cable from the negative terminal of the battery to prevent electrical shorts and/or fires.*

2   Electrical troubleshooting - general information

A typical electrical circuit consists of an electrical component, any switches, relays, motors, fuses, fusible links or circuit breakers related to the component and the wiring and connectors that link the component to both the battery and the chassis. To help pinpoint an electrical circuit problem, wiring diagrams are included at the end of this Chapter.

Before tackling any troublesome electrical circuit, first study the appropriate wiring diagrams to get a complete understanding of what makes up that individual circuit. Trouble spots, for instance, can often be narrowed down by noting if other components related to the circuit are operating properly. If several components or circuits fail at one time, chances are the problem is in a fuse or ground connection, because several circuits are often routed through the same fuse and ground connections.

Electrical problems usually stem from simple causes, such as loose or corroded connections, a blown fuse, a melted fusible link or a bad relay. Visually inspect the condition of all fuses, wires and connections in a problem circuit before troubleshooting it.

If testing instruments are going to be utilized, use the diagrams to plan ahead of time where to make the necessary connections to accurately pinpoint the trouble spot.

The basic tools needed for electrical troubleshooting include a circuit tester or voltmeter (a 12-volt bulb with a set of test leads can also be used), a continuity tester (which includes a bulb, battery and set of test leads) and a jumper wire, preferably with a circuit breaker incorporated, which can be used to bypass electrical components. Before attempting to locate a problem with test instruments, use the wiring diagram(s) to decide where to make the connections.

Voltage checks

Voltage checks should be performed if a circuit isn't functioning properly. Connect one lead of a circuit tester to either the negative battery terminal or a known good ground. Connect the other lead to a connector in the circuit being tested, preferably nearest to the battery or fuse. If the bulb of the tester lights, voltage is present, which means the part of the circuit between the connector and the battery is problem free. Continue checking the rest of the circuit in the same fashion. When you reach a point where no voltage is present, the problem lies between that point and the last test point with voltage. Most of the time the problem can be traced to a loose connection. **Note:** *Keep in mind that some circuits receive voltage only when the ignition key is in the Accessory or Run position.*

Finding a short

One method of finding a short in a circuit is to remove the fuse and connect a test light or voltmeter in its place to the fuse terminals. There should be no voltage present in the circuit. Move the wiring harness from side-to-side while watching the test light. If the bulb lights, there's a short to ground somewhere in that area, probably where the insulation has rubbed through. The same test can be performed on each component in the circuit, even a switch.

"Short finders" are also commonly available. These reasonably priced tools connect in place of a fuse and pulse voltage through the circuit. An inductive meter (included with the kit) is then run along the wiring for the circuit. When the needle on the meter stops moving, you've found the point of the short.

Ground check

Perform a ground test to check whether a component is properly grounded. Disconnect the battery and connect one lead of a self-powered test light, known as a continuity tester, to a known good ground. Connect the other lead to the wire or ground connection being tested. If the bulb lights, the ground is good. If the bulb doesn't light, the ground is no good.

Continuity check

A continuity check is done to determine if there are breaks in a circuit - if it's capable of passing electricity properly. With the circuit off (no power in the circuit), a self-powered continuity tester can be used to check it. Connect the test leads to both ends of the circuit (or to the "power" end and a good ground) - if the test light comes on the circuit is passing current properly. If the light doesn't come on, there's a break (open) somewhere in the circuit. The same procedure can be used to test a switch by connecting the continuity tester to the switch terminals. With the switch on, the test light should come on.

Finding an open circuit

When diagnosing for possible open circuits, it's often difficult to locate them by sight because oxidation or terminal misalignment are hidden by the connectors. Merely wiggling a connector on a sensor or in the wiring harness may correct the open circuit condition. Remember this when an open is indicated when troubleshooting a circuit. Intermittent problems may also be caused by oxidized or loose connections. Electrical troubleshooting is simple if you keep in mind that all electrical circuits are basically electricity running from the battery, through the wires, switches, relays, fuses and fusible links to each electrical component (light bulb, motor, etc.) and to ground, where it's passed back to the battery. Any electrical problem is an interruption in the flow of electricity to and from the battery.

3.1a Fuses, circuit breakers, and relays are located under the instrument panel on the Junction Block

3.1b The Power Distribution Center (PDC) is located in the engine compartment and contains both fuses and relays (1996 through 2000 models)

3   Fuses - general information

Refer to illustrations 3.1a, 3.1b, 3.1c and 3.3

The electrical circuits of the vehicle are protected by a combination of fuses, circuit breakers and fusible links. Interior fuses are mounted on the Junction Block located under the left side of the dashboard **(see illustration)**. On 1999 through 2000 models, additional fuses and the relay block, called the Power Distribution Center (PDC) are located on the left side of the engine compartment **(see illustration)**. On 2001 and later models, additional fuses and the relay block are located in the Integrated Power Module (IPM). The IPM is a combination of the Power Distribution Center (PDC) and the Front Control Module (FCM). The PDC mates with the FCM to form the IPM Fuse and Relay Center and it is located on the left side of the engine compartment **(see illustration)**. The under-dash Junction Block is accessed by first removing the lower steering column cover and kneepad (see Chapter 11).

Each of the fuses is designed to protect a specific circuit, and the various circuits are identified on the fuse panel itself.

Miniaturized fuses are employed in the fuse block. These compact fuses, with blade terminal design, allow fingertip removal and replacement. If an electrical component fails, always check the fuse first. A blown fuse is easily identified through the clear plastic body. Visually inspect the element for evidence of damage **(see illustration)**. If a continuity check is called for, the blade terminal tips are exposed in the fuse body.

Be sure to replace blown fuses with the correct type. Fuses of different ratings are physically interchangeable, but only fuses of the proper rating should be used. Replacing a fuse with one of a higher or lower value than specified is not recommended. Each electrical circuit needs a specific amount of protection. The amperage value of each fuse is molded into the fuse body.

If the replacement fuse immediately fails, don't replace it again until the cause of the problem is isolated and corrected. In most cases, the cause will be a short circuit in the wiring caused by a broken or deteriorated wire.

4   Fusible links - general information

Refer to illustrations 4.2a and 4.2b

Some circuits are protected by fusible links. The links are used in circuits which are not ordinarily fused, such as the ignition circuit.

Although the fusible links appear to be a heavier gauge than the wires they're protecting **(see illustration)**, the appearance is due to the thick insulation. All fusible links are four wire gauges smaller than the wire they're designed to protect. fusible links can't be repaired, but a new link of the same size wire can be installed. The procedure is as follows:

a) *Disconnect the cable from the negative terminal of the battery.*
b) *Disconnect the fusible link from the wiring harness.*

3.1c On 2001 and later models, the IPM Fuse and Relay Center is located in the engine compartment and contains both the PDC (A) and FCM (B)

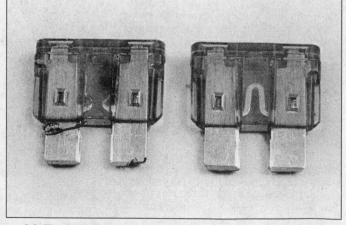

3.3 The fuses used on these models can be easily checked visually to determine if they are blown (good fuse on right, blown fuse on left)

4.2a **Typical fusible link (arrow) - this one is located at the Power Distribution Center (PDC)**

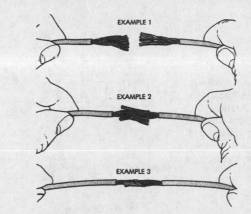

4.2b **To install a fusible link, cut out the damaged section, then join a new section by stripping the wire and twisting it together, as shown here. When securely joined, solder the connections and wrap them with electrical tape**

c) *Cut the damaged fusible link out of the wire just behind the connector.*
d) *Strip the insulation back approximately 1-inch.*
e) *Spread the strands of the exposed wire apart, push them together and twist them in place* **(see illustration).**
f) *Use rosin core solder for soldering the wires together to obtain a good connection.*
g) *Use plenty of electrical tape around the soldered joint. No wires should be exposed.*
h) *Connect the negative battery cable. Test the circuit for proper operation.*

5   Circuit breakers - general information

Refer to illustration 5.1a and 5.1b

Circuit breakers protect components such as power windows, power door locks, wipers, fuel pump, stop lights, Anti-Lock Brakes (ABS), airbags, the Powertrain Control Module (PCM) **(see illustrations)**, and the air conditioning compressor. Some circuit breakers are located in the fuse box. On some models the circuit breaker resets itself automatically, so an electrical overload in the circuit will cause it to fail momentarily, then come back on. If the circuit doesn't come back on, check it immediately. Once the condition is corrected, the circuit breaker will resume its normal function. Some circuit breakers must be reset manually.

6   Relays - general information

Several electrical accessories in the vehicle utilize relays to transmit current to the component. If the relay is defective, the component won't operate properly. The Junction Block, located under the dash (see Section 3) and the PDC, or the IPM, located in the engine compartment contain several relays **(see illustrations 3.1a, 3.1b and 3.1c).**

If a faulty relay is suspected, it can be removed and tested by a dealer service department or a repair shop. Defective relays must be replaced as a unit.

7   Turn signal/hazard flasher - check and replacement

Refer to illustration 7.1
Warning: *These models have airbags. Always disconnect the cable from the negative terminal of the battery and wait two minutes before working in the vicinity of the impact sensors, steering column or instrument panel to avoid the possibility of accidental deployment of the airbag, which could cause personal injury (see Section 27).*
1   The turn signal/hazard flasher/Daytime Running Light (DRL) module is located on the Junction Block, adjacent to and left of the

5.1a **The Powertrain Control Module (arrow) is directly adjacent to the Power Distribution Center (PDC) (1996 through 2000 models)**

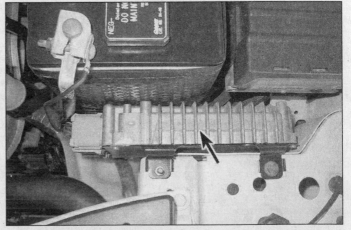

5.1b **The Power Control Module (arrow) is located directly in front of the battery and the IPM Fuse and Relay Center (2001 and later models)**

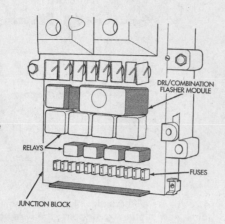

7.1 The combination turn signal/hazard flasher/Daytime Running Light (DRL) module is mounted under the dash on the Junction Block

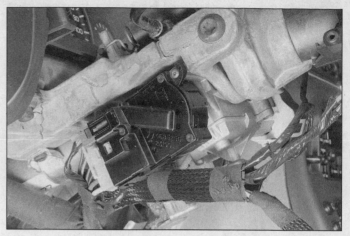

8.1 The ignition switch is located on the left side of the steering column

steering column **(see illustration)**. To access the Junction Block, first remove the lower steering column cover and knee pad panel (see Chapter 11).

2   When the flasher module is functioning properly, a click can be heard during its operation. If the turn signals fail on one side or the other and the flasher module doesn't make its characteristic clicking sound, a faulty turn signal bulb is indicated. If a rapidly flashing turn signal is observed, a light is burned out or there is a loose or open connection to a light. When the ignition is ON, the front turn signals are ON steadily (not flashing) for the Daytime Running Lights (DRL), and flash only when the turn signals or hazard flasher are operated.

3   If both turn signals or hazard lights fail to blink, the problem may be due to a blown fuse, a faulty combination flasher module, a broken switch or a loose or open connection. If a quick check of the fuse box indicates the turn signal fuse has blown, check the wiring for a short before installing a new fuse.

4   To replace the flasher module, simply detach it from its electrical connector and plug in the new one.

5   Make sure the replacement is identical to the original. Compare the new module to the old one before installing it.

6   Installation is the reverse of removal.

8   Ignition switch and lock cylinder - removal and installation

Warning: *These models have airbags. Always disconnect the cable from the negative terminal of the battery and wait two minutes before working in the vicinity of the impact sensors, steering column or instrument panel to avoid the possibility of accidental deployment of the airbag, which could cause personal injury (see Section 27).*

Ignition switch

Refer to illustration 8.1

1   The ignition switch is located on the left

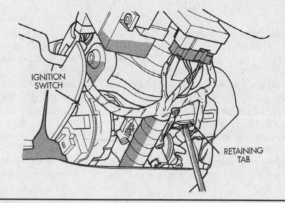

8.10 With the key in the Run position, depress the retaining tab and pull the lock cylinder out

side of the steering column and is actuated by the key lock cylinder **(see illustration)**.

2   Disconnect the cable from the negative terminal of the battery.

3   Remove the steering column cover screws under the steering column and near the parking brake handle. Lower the cover to access the parking brake handle.

4   Place the ignition key in the RUN position. Depress the lock cylinder retaining tab at the bottom of the lock cylinder, using a screwdriver.

5   Disconnect the electrical connectors from the ignition switch, remove the ignition switch mounting screws, depress the retaining tab behind the ignition switch, then detach the switch and lower it from the steering column. Note the position of the actuator shaft which connects to the lock cylinder.

6   To reinstall, insert the ignition switch and index the tab on the switch with the notch in the lock cylinder and install the screws securely.

Lock cylinder

Refer to illustration 8.10

7   Disconnect the cable from the negative terminal of the battery.

8   Remove the lower steering column shroud three screws under the steering column and remove the shroud.

9   Insert the key and turn it to the

Run position.

10   Depress the lock cylinder retaining tab (a small screwdriver may be required) to unseat the lock cylinder, then remove the lock cylinder **(see illustration)**.

11   Insert the lock cylinder in the LOCK position and, while pushing the lock cylinder in, insert the key and turn it clockwise to the Run position.

9   Multi-function switch - check and replacement

Warning: *These models have airbags. Always disconnect the cable from the negative terminal of the battery and wait two minutes before working in the vicinity of the impact sensors, steering column or instrument panel to avoid the possibility of accidental deployment of the airbag, which could cause personal injury (see Section 27).*

1   The multi-function switch is located on the left side of the steering column. It incorporates the turn signal, headlight dimmer and windshield wiper/washer functions into one switch.

2   Remove the lower steering column cover screws under the steering column. Lower the cover to access the multifunction switch.

3   Disconnect the electrical connector(s).

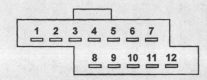

TURN SIGNAL MULTI-FUNCTION SWITCH TEST	
SWITCH POSITION	CONTINUITY BETWEEN
LEFT	4 AND 8
RIGHT	3 AND 8
HAZARD	1 AND 8
LO BEAM	9 AND 10
HI BEAM	9 AND 12

9.4a Turn signal, hazard flasher and dimmer switch terminal guide and continuity table (1996 through 2000 models)

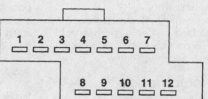

SWITCH POSITION	PIN NUMBER	RESISTANCE
LEFT	2 AND 3	1.7 Ω ± 5%
RIGHT	2 AND 3	1K Ω ± 5%
OPTICAL HORN	1 AND 3	4.87K Ω ± 5%
HI BEAM	1 AND 3	2.32K Ω ± 5%

9.4b Turn signal, optical horn and high beam switch terminal guide and resistance table (2001 and later models)

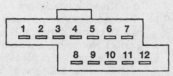

SWITCH POSITION	RESISTANCE VALUE BETWEEN
OFF	6 AND 7 MAX. 1.0 Ω
DELAY POSITION	
1ST	6 AND 7 1.91 K Ω ± 5 Ω
2ND	6 AND 7 1.00 K Ω ± 5 Ω
3RD	6 AND 7 617 Ω ± 5 Ω
4TH	6 AND 7 389 Ω ± 2 Ω
5TH	6 AND 7 256 Ω ± 2 Ω
6TH	6 AND 7 156 Ω ± 1 Ω
LOW	6 AND 7 65.4 Ω ± 0.5 Ω
HIGH	5 AND 8 MAX. 1.0 Ω
WASH	8 AND 11 CONTINUITY

9.4c Wiper/washer switch terminal guide and resistance table (1996 through 2000 models)

SWITCH POSITION	RESISTANCE VALUE BETWEEN
OFF	6 AND 7 = OPEN CIRCUIT
DELAY POSITION	
1ST	6 AND 7 = 8 K Ω ± 80 Ω
2ND	6 AND 7 = 6 K Ω ± 60 Ω
3RD	6 AND 7 = 4.5 K Ω ± 45 Ω
4TH	6 AND 7 = 3.5 K Ω ± 35 Ω
5TH	6 AND 7 = 2.5 K Ω ± 25 Ω
6TH	6 AND 7 = 1.5 K Ω ± 15 Ω
LOW	6 AND 7 = 1 K Ω ± 10 Ω
HIGH	6 AND 7 = 1 K Ω ± 10 Ω
WASH	6 AND 11 = CONTINUITY

9.4d Wiper/washer switch terminal guide and resistance table (2001 and later models)

Check

Refer to illustrations 9.4a, 9.4b, 9.4c and 9.4d

4   Use an ohmmeter or self-powered test light and the accompanying diagrams to check for continuity between the switch terminals with the switch in each position **(see illustrations)**.

Replacement

5   Remove the bolts, then detach the switch from the steering column.
6   Installation is the reverse of removal.

10 Headlight bulb - replacement

1996 through 2000 models

Refer to illustrations 10.4 and 10.5
Warning: *Halogen bulbs are gas-filled and*

under pressure and may shatter if the surface is scratched or the bulb is dropped. Wear eye protection and handle the bulbs carefully, grasping only the base whenever possible. Don't touch the surface of the bulb with your fingers because the oil from your skin could cause it to overheat and fail prematurely. If you do touch the bulb surface, clean it with rubbing alcohol.

1   Open the hood. On some models it will be necessary to remove the radiator closure panel sight shield for access (see Chapter 11).
2   Disconnect the cable from the negative terminal of the battery.
3   Remove the headlight housing (see Section 12)
4   Rotate the bulb retaining ring counterclockwise **(see illustration)**.
5   Pull the holder assembly out for access, grasp the bulb base and remove it from the

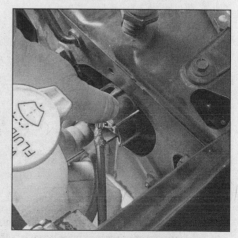

10.4 Rotate the bulb retaining ring counterclockwise to detach the bulb holder

10.5 Pull the holder assembly out for access, grasp the bulb base and unplug it from the holder

10.10 Turn the retaining ring counterclockwise to remove the bulb holder, then . . .

10.11 . . . remove the bulb from the holder

holder **(see illustration)**.

6   Insert the new bulb into the holder.

7   Install the bulb holder in the headlight assembly and connect the electrical connector.

8   Install the headlight assembly.

2001 and later models

Refer to illustrations 10.10 and 10.11

Warning: *Refer to previous warning relating to the handling of a Halogen bulb.*

9   Remove the headlamp housing module (see Section 12).

10   Rotate the bulb retaining ring counterclockwise and remove the bulb holder **(see illustration)**.

11   Remove the bulb from the holder and insert a new bulb **(see illustration)**.

12   Install the bulb holder, turn it clockwise and reconnect the electrical connector.

13   Install the headlamp housing module.

---

11   Headlights - adjustment

Refer to illustrations 11.1 and 11.3

Warning: *The headlights must be aimed correctly. If adjusted incorrectly, they could tem-*

porarily blind the driver of an oncoming vehicle and cause an accident or seriously reduce your ability to see the road. The headlights should be checked for proper aim every 12 months and any time a new headlight housing is installed or front end body work is performed.

1   The headlights on these models feature integral vertical and horizontal adjustment indicators with adjusting screws that allow the owner to check and adjust headlight alignment **(see illustration)**.

2   Adjustment should be made with the vehicle sitting level, the gas tank full and a normal load in the vehicle.

3   Open the hood and check the vertical bubble indicator **(see illustration)** to make sure the bubble is centered over the "0" area of the indicator.

4   If necessary, center the bubble by turning the up-and-down (vertical) adjusting screw - the adjusting screw near the top of the headlight module **(see illustration 11.1)**. **Note:** *Do not turn the calibration screw on the indicator itself.*

5   Check the arrow on the horizontal indicator decal to make sure the arrow is pointing at the "0". Turn the right-and-left (horizon-

tal) adjusting screw (the lower adjusting screw) to adjust if necessary **(see illustration 11.1)**.

6   This one adjustment of the low beams is the only adjustment necessary. The high beam will be correct if the low beam adjustment is correct. **Note:** *Fog lamps are optional and are separate from the headlight/turn signal modules. Fog lamp adjustment is correct when the light pattern is 4 inches below the fog lamp center height from the ground, with the vehicle 25 feet from the light screen or wall.*

7   If you have any problems achieving proper adjustment, take the vehicle to have the headlights checked by a dealer service department or service station as soon as possible.

---

12   Headlight housing - removal and installation

Refer to illustrations 12.3a, 12.3b, 12.5 and 12.6

1996 through 2000 models

Warning: *These models have airbags. Always disconnect the cable from the negative terminal of the battery and wait two minutes before*

11.1 Headlight module adjuster screws - the left arrow is the left and right (horizontal) adjuster and the right arrow is the up and down (vertical) adjuster

11.3 Headlight module bubble indicator - headlight removed for clarity

12.3a Remove the nuts at the back of the housing and the retaining bolt at the top of the headlight . . .

12.3b . . . then pull the housing out and unplug the bulb connector

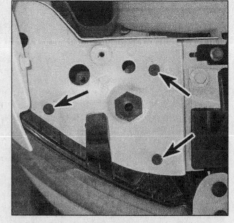

12.5 Remove the three screws and pull the headlight module out . . .

working in the vicinity of the impact sensors, steering column or instrument panel to avoid the possibility of accidental deployment of the airbag, which could cause personal injury (see Section 27).
1   Open the hood.
2   Inside the engine compartment, remove the nuts holding the headlight module to the radiator support panel.
3   Remove the retaining bolt on the top of the headlight module, pull the headlight module out and disconnect the electrical connector (see illustrations).
4   Installation is the reverse of removal. After you're done, check the headlight adjustment (see Section 11).

2001 and later models
Refer to illustrations 12.5 and 12.6
Warning: *These models have airbags. Always disconnect the negative battery cable and wait two minutes before working in the vicinity of the impact sensors, steering column or instrument panel to avoid the possibility of accidental deployment of the airbag, that could cause personal injury (see Chapter 12).*
5   Open the hood. Inside the engine com-

partment remove the three screws (see illustration) holding the headlight module to the radiator support panel.
6   Pull the headlight module out and disconnect the electrical connectors (see illustration).
7   Installation is the reverse of removal. After you're done, check the headlight adjustment (see Section 11).

13 Bulb replacement

Front parking/side marker/turn signal light

1996 through 2000 models
Refer to illustrations 13.1 and 13.3
1   From under the front wheel housing, remove the access cover behind the parking/turn signal light (see illustration).
2   Turn the bulb holder counterclockwise one quarter turn and pull it out of the housing.
3   Pull the socket out of the holder and pull the bulb from the socket (see illustration).
4   Installation is the reverse of removal.

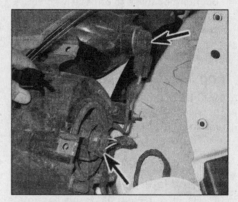

12.6 . . . then disconnect the electrical connectors

2001 and later models
Refer to illustration 13.6
5   Remove the headlamp housing module (see Section 12).
6   Rotate the bulb holder counterclockwise and remove the bulb holder (see illustration).
7   Remove the bulb from the holder and insert a new bulb.

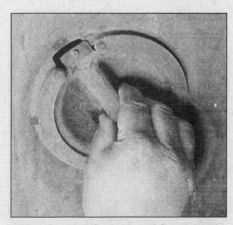

13.1 Remove the front park/turn signal access cover under the fenderwell

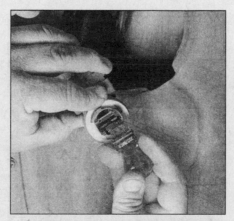

13.3 Pull the front park/turn signal bulb from its bulb holder and replace it

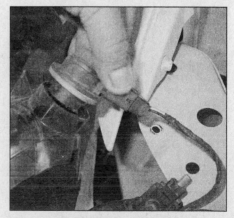

13.6 Rotate the bulb holder counterclockwise and remove it

13.19 After swinging the rear stop/turn signal assembly away from the vehicle body, rotate the bulb holder counterclockwise to remove it - pull the bulb straight out of the bulb holder

8   Install the bulb holder, turn it clockwise.
9   Install the headlamp housing module.

Fog light

1996 through 1998 models

10   Remove the fog light housing assembly retaining screws or nuts.
11   Remove the fog light housing assembly.
12   Remove the lens and replace the bulb.
13   Installation is the reverse of removal.

1999 and later models

14   Reach in behind the fascia and rotate the bulb and holder and remove it from the assembly.
15   Disconnect the wire connector from the bulb base.
16   Refer to the Warning relating to Halogen bulbs in Section 10 and replace the bulb.
17   Installation is the reverse of removal.

Tail light bulb and light assembly

Refer to illustration 13.19
18   Open the liftgate, remove the screws

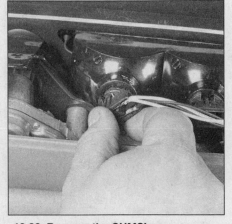

13.22 Remove the CHMSL access cover and rotate the bulb socket counterclockwise

holding the tail, stop, turn signal and back-up light assembly to the rear door opening. Separate the light assembly from the vehicle body, disengaging the hook holding the outer end of the light assembly to the body. Swing the housing out for access to the bulb holders.
19   Rotate the bulb holder and remove it from the light assembly **(see illustration)**. Pull the bulb straight out to remove it.
20   To completely separate the light assembly from the vehicle, depress the lock tab on the harness connector, then remove the connector from the light assembly.
21   Installation is the reverse of removal.

Center high-mounted brake light (CHMSL)

Refer to illustrations 13.22, 13.23 and 13.24
22   Open the liftgate. Disengage the clips holding the CHMSL access cover and remove the cover. Rotate the bulb socket counterclockwise on quarter turn **(see illustration)**.
23   Pull the bulb straight out of the socket and install the new one **(see illustration)**.

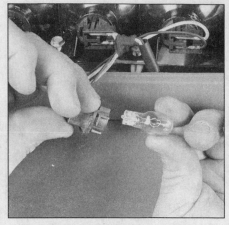

13.23 Pull the bulb straight out of the socket

24   To remove the CHMSL assembly, remove the retaining screws and separate the CHMSL assembly from the vehicle **(see illustration)**.
25   Installation is the reverse of removal.

Liftgate interior lights

Refer to illustrations 13.27 and 13.29
26   Open the liftgate.
27   Using a screwdriver, carefully pry off the liftgate interior light assembly **(see illustration)**.
28   Lift out the light assembly.
29   Separate the lens from the light base for access to the bulb **(see illustration)**.
30   Pull the bulb straight out of the holder.
31   Installation is the reverse of removal.

Instrument panel lights

Refer to illustration 13.33
32   To gain access to the instrument panel lights, the instrument cluster, back panel, wire connector, and printed circuit board must be removed (see Section 20).
33   Rotate the bulb holder counterclockwise one-quarter turn and remove it from the

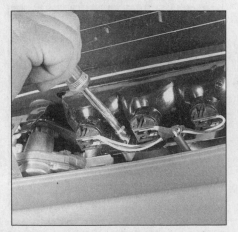

13.24 To remove the CHMSL assembly, remove the retaining screws

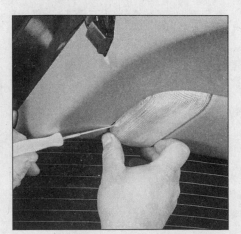

13.27 Carefully pry the lens off the liftgate interior light assembly

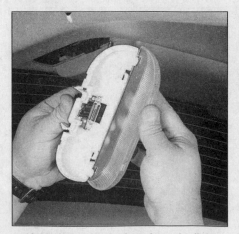

13.29 Separate the lens from the light base for access to the bulb

13.33 Instrument panel lights are mounted in grey plastic bulb holders. Rotate the bulb holder counterclockwise 1/4-turn to remove it. After the bulb holder is removed, the bulb can be pulled straight out

instrument cluster **(see illustration)**.
34 Pull the bulb straight out of the holder.
35 Installation is the reverse of removal.

License plate lights

Refer to illustrations 13.36 and 13.38
36 Remove the two screws and pull out the lamp assembly **(see illustration)**.
37 Remove the bulb holder.
38 Pull the bulb out of the holder **(see illustration)**.
39 Installation is the reverse of removal.

Interior lights - glovebox, vanity mirror, and others

Refer to illustrations 13.40, 13.41a, 13.41b and 13.41c
40 For replacement of the glovebox light, open the glovebox, and slide out the glovebox pin switch from its mounting. Pull out the bulb from the bulb holder **(see illustration)**

13.36 Remove the two license plate light screws and pull out the light assembly

and replace the bulb.
41 For overhead and other interior lights including the vanity mirror light, carefully pry off the lens and either unclip the bulb or rotate the bulbholder one-quarter turn to remove the bulb **(see illustrations)**. Replace the bulb.
42 Installation is the reverse of removal.

14 Headlight switch - check and replacement

Warning: *These models have airbags. Always disconnect the cable from the negative terminal of the battery and wait two minutes before working in the vicinity of the impact sensors, steering column or instrument panel to avoid the possibility of accidental deployment of the airbag, which could cause personal injury* (see Section 27).
1 Disconnect the cable from the negative terminal of the battery.
2 Remove the headlight switch (see Steps 4 through 6 below).

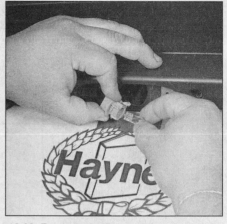

13.38 Remove the license plate light bulb holder and slide the bulb out of the holder

13.40 Open the glovebox and slide the glovebox door switch from its mounting - pull out the bulb to replace it

Check

Refer to illustrations 14.3a and 14.3b
3 Use an ohmmeter or self-powered test light and the accompanying diagram to check for continuity between the switch ter-

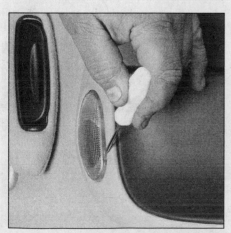

13.41a Carefully pry off the interior light lens

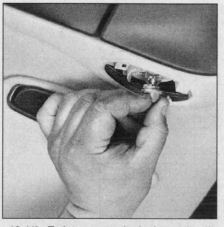

13.41b Twist counterclockwise and pull out the overhead light bulbholder. Pull the bulb straight out to replace it

13.41c After prying off the vanity mirror light lens, unclip the bulb and replace it - there is one bulb on each side of the light assembly

HEADLAMP SWITCH POSITION	8-WAY CONNECTOR TERMINALS	RESISTANCE VALUE
OFF	2 to 1	5.2 OHMS (avg.)
	2 to 5	OPEN
	2 to 6	OPEN
	2 to 7	OPEN
	2 to 8	OPEN
PARKING LAMPS ON	2 to 3	OPEN
	2 to 5	OPEN
	2 to 6	OPEN
	2 to 7	OPEN
	2 to 8	CONTINUITY
HEADLAMPS ON	2 to 3	CONTINUITY
	2 to 5	OPEN
	2 to 6	OPEN
	2 to 7	OPEN
	2 to 8	CONTINUITY
FRONT FOG LAMPS ON (WITH PARKING LAMPS OR HEADLAMPS)	2 to 3	CONTINUITY
	2 to 6	CONTINUITY
	2 to 8	CONTINUITY
	5 to 2	DIODE CONTINUITY
	7 to 2	DIODE CONTINUITY

THUMBWHEEL	12-WAY CONNECTOR TERMINALS	RESISTANCE VALUE
DOME LAMPS ON	6 to 4	CONTINUITY
	6 to 5	OPEN
	6 to 12	8k to 12k OHMS
	3 to 9	CONTINUITY
	10 to 11	OPEN
DAYTIME RUNNING MODE	6 to 4	OPEN
	6 to 5	CONTINUITY
	6 to 12	8k to 12k OHMS
	3 to 9	CONTINUITY
	10 to 11	CONTINUITY
I/P LAMPS IN BRIGHT POSITION	6 to 4	OPEN
	6 to 5	OPEN
	6 to 12	8k to 12k OHMS
	3 to 9	CONTINUITY
	10 to 11	CONTINUITY
I/P LAMPS IN DIM POSITION	6 to 4	OPEN
	6 to 5	OPEN
	6 to 12	0 to 500 OHMS
	3 to 9	CONTINUITY
	10 to 11	CONTINUITY
COURTESY LAMPS DEFEAT	6 to 4	OPEN
	6 to 5	OPEN
	6 to 12	0 to 500 OHMS
	3 to 9	OPEN
	10 to 11	CONTINUITY

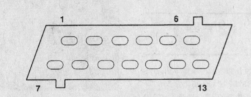

8-WAY CONNECTOR

14.3a Headlight switch terminal guide and continuity table (1996 through 2000 models)

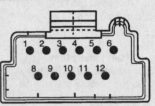

12-WAY CONNECTOR

HEADLAMP SWITCH POSITION	13 - WAY CONNECTOR TERMINAL	RESISTANCE
OFF	11 TO 6	3651 - 3729 Ω
PARKING LAMPS ON	11 TO 6	1697 - 2517 Ω
PARKING LAMPS WITH FRONT FOG LAMPS ON	11 TO 6	5765 - 5886 Ω
HEADLAMPS ON	11 TO 6	788 - 809 Ω
AUTO ON	11 TO 6	10056 - 10264 Ω
HEADLAMPS ON WITH FRONT FOG LAMPS	11 TO 6	1171 - 1200 Ω
AUTO ON WITH FRONT FOG LAMPS ON	11 TO 6	24278 - 24773 Ω

DIMMER POSITION	13 - WAY CONNECTOR TERMINAL	RESISTANCE
DOME	12 TO 6	15568 - 23357 Ω
PARADE	12 TO 6	5168 - 7757 Ω
DIM HIGH	12 TO 6	2288 - 3437 Ω
DIM LOW	12 TO 6	688 - 1037 Ω
OFF	12 TO 6	240 - 365 Ω

14.3b Headlight switch terminal guide and continuity table (2001 and later models)

minals with the switch in each position (see illustration). Note: On the headlight switch 8-way connector, terminals 5 to 2 and 7 to 2 are labeled diode continuity (listed in illustration 14.3) - to test these terminals, use a meter which has a diode test setting, and follow the meter instructions for diode testing. Remember that a diode can only pass current in one direction, so you must connect your meter red and black leads and check for continuity, then reverse your test lead polarity and check again for no continuity.

Replacement

Refer to illustration 14.5

4   Remove the instrument panel bezel from the dashboard (see Chapter 11).

5   Remove the headlamp switch mounting screws (see illustration).

14.5 Remove these two screws (arrows) and separate the headlight switch from the bezel

15.4 With the glovebox removed, disconnect the radio antenna lead (arrow)

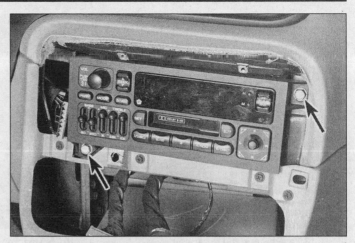

15.5a Remove the two screws (arrows) securing the radio

15.5b Pull the radio out and disconnect the electrical connectors

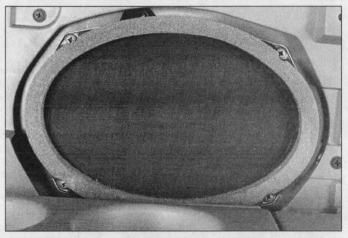

15.10 With the instrument panel top cover lifted, remove the four screws around the perimeter of the speaker and pull it out

6   Pull the switch assembly out of the bezel.

7   The headlamp switch light bulb may be replaced at this time, if necessary.

8   Installation is the reverse of removal.

15   Radio and speakers - removal and installation

Refer to illustrations 15.4, 15.5a and 15.5b
Warning: *These models have airbags. Always disconnect the cable from the negative terminal of the battery and wait two minutes before working in the vicinity of the impact sensors, steering column or instrument panel to avoid the possibility of accidental deployment of the airbag, which could cause personal injury (see Section 27).*

Radio

1   Disconnect the cable from the negative terminal of the battery.

2   Remove the ashtray. The ashtray light may be replaced with the ashtray removed.

Remove the dashboard radio/heater and A/C bezel screw access cover (Chapter 11). Then remove the attaching screws holding the bottom and top of the bezel. Pull the bezel out part way.

3   Disconnect the wire connector to the rear blower switch if equipped, and from the heater and A/C control.

4   Remove the glovebox (see Chapter 11). Disconnect the antenna lead **(see illustration)**.

5   Remove the mounting screws, pull the radio out of the instrument panel, disconnect the electrical connectors, then remove it from the vehicle **(see illustrations)**.

6   Installation is the reverse of removal.

Speakers

Door, pillar or quarter panel

7   Remove the front door trim panel (Chapter 11) for the door speakers; for the quarter panel and pillar speakers, remove the trim panel or speaker grille, as equipped.

8   Remove the speaker mounting screws. On the front door speaker, also detach the snap-in nut. Then pull the speaker out while disconnecting the electrical connector.

Instrument panel

Refer to illustration 15.10

9   Remove the instrument panel top cover by prying and detaching the clips at each end. Next, lift the rear edge and disengage the clips along the front edge.

10   Remove the screws **(see illustration)**, lift the speaker out while disconnecting the electrical connector. Remove the speaker from the vehicle.

Rear speakers

11   Installation is the reverse of removal, making sure that the wire connectors face forward.

16   Antenna - removal and installation

Refer to illustrations 16.7a, 16.7b and 16.7c

1   Disconnect the cable from the negative terminal of the battery.

2   Disconnect the antenna cable lead (see Section 15).

16.7a Remove the antenna cover

16.7b Unscrew the cap nut at the antenna base

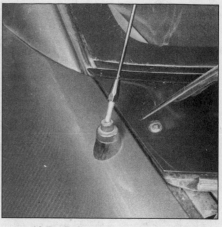

16.7c Pull out the antenna and antenna lead

17.3 Disconnect the wiper connector (arrow) to test for supply voltage

3   Remove the right kick trim panel (Chapter 11).
4   Loosen the rubber grommet insulator from the door hinge pillar. Pull the antenna cable through the hinge pillar to between the door hinges.

5   Jack up the front of the vehicle and securely place jackstands. Remove the right front wheel.
6   Remove the front wheel housing splash shield, and slide the plastic sleeve up on the antenna mast. Use a small wrench to unscrew the antenna mast, and remove the antenna mast from its base.
7   Remove the plastic cap from the cap nut, remove the cap nut from the antenna base, then pull out the antenna base from under the front fender (**see illustrations**).
8   Installation is the reverse of removal.

---

17   Windshield wiper motor - check and replacement

Front wipers
Refer to illustrations 17.3 and 17.13

Check
1   If the wiper motor does not run at all, first check the fuse block for a blown fuse and the power distribution center for a blown fuse or faulty relay (see Section 3).

2   Check the wiper switch (see Section 9).
3   Turn the ignition switch and wiper switch ON. Using a voltmeter, check for voltage at the motor connector (**see illustration**). If voltage is not measured, the problem is in the switch or wiring connection.
4   Check the wiper motor electrical ground by installing a temporary jumper wire between the wiper motor body and a body ground point, then again try to run the wipers. If the motor works now, repair the wiper motor ground connection.
5   Check for binding linkage.
6   If the wipers still don't work, have the system checked by a dealer service department or other qualified shop.
7   Replace the motor if found defective.

Replacement
8   Disconnect the cable from the negative terminal of the battery.
9   Detach the washer hoses, lift the wiper arm covers and mark the wiper arm locations on the pivot shaft for later reinstallation. Remove the wiper pivot nuts and remove the wiper arms.
10   Remove the cowl cover (see Chapter 11).
11   Open the hood. Disconnect the wiper motor electrical connector
12   Disconnect the windshield washer hose from the coupling inside the unit. Disconnect the drain tubes from the bottom of the wiper unit.
13   The wiper unit must be removed as a complete assembly to access the wiper motor. Remove the nuts holding the wiper unit to the lower windshield trim shield and the dash panel (**see illustration**).
14   Lift the wiper unit from the cowl area and place it on the work bench.
15   Working on the backside of the wiper unit, remove the wiper motor mounting bolts and separate the wiper motor from the wiper unit.
16   Installation is the reverse of removal. Wiper blade and wiper arm adjustment is

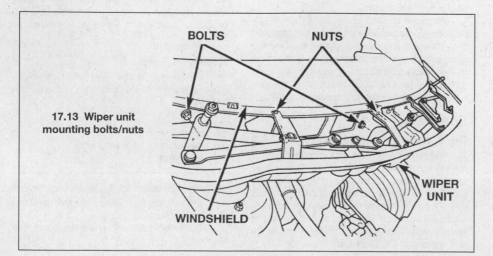

17.13 Wiper unit mounting bolts/nuts

BOLTS   NUTS

WINDSHIELD   WIPER UNIT

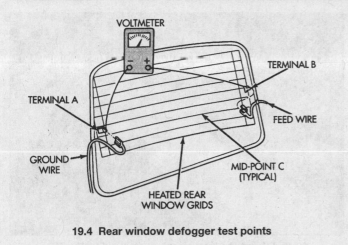

19.4 Rear window defogger test points

19.14 When repairing a broken grid, first apply a strip of tape to either side of the grid to mask off the area

measured with the wipers parked; correct adjustment is the lower wiper arm approximately 1-1/2 inches distance from the cowl cover and the upper wiper arm approximately 2-1/2 inches from the lower arm. Operate the wiper motor and check that the wiper motor parks when the wiper switch is OFF.

Rear wiper
Check
17   If the wiper motor does not run at all, first check the fuse block for a blown fuse and the power distribution center for a blown fuse or faulty relay (see Section 3).
18   Check the rear wiper switch.
19   Turn the ignition switch and wiper switch ON. Using a voltmeter, check for voltage at the motor connector. If voltage is not measured, the problem is in the switch or wiring connection.
20   Check the wiper motor electrical ground by installing a temporary jumper wire between the wiper motor body and a body ground point, then again try to run the wipers. If the motor works now, repair the wiper motor ground connection.
21   If the wipers still don't work, have the system checked by a dealer service department or other qualified shop.
22   Replace the motor if found defective.

Replacement
23   Disconnect the cable from the negative terminal of the battery.
24   Open the liftgate. Remove the liftgate trim panel (Chapter 11).
25   Disconnect the wiper motor electrical connector
26   Remove the wiper motor mounting screws. Remove the motor.
27   Installation is the reverse of removal.

18   Rear window defogger switch - removal and installation

Warning: *These models have airbags. Always disconnect the cable from the negative termi-*

nal of the battery and wait two minutes before working in the vicinity of the impact sensors, steering column or instrument panel to avoid the possibility of accidental deployment of the airbag, which could cause personal injury (see Section 27).
1   The defogger switch is part of the heater and air conditioning system control switch.
2   Remove the radio/heater and air conditioning bezel (see Chapter 11).
3   Detach the switch assembly, disconnect the electrical connector and remove the switch from the bezel.
4   Installation is the reverse of removal.

19   Rear window defogger - check and repair

Refer to illustrations 19.4 and 19.14
1   The rear window defogger consists of a number of horizontal elements baked onto the glass surface.
2   Small breaks in the element can be repaired without removing the rear window.

Check
3   Turn the ignition switch and defogger system switches ON. **Note:** *The rear window defogger is also activated when the Defrost Mode of the heater is selected.*
4   Ground the negative lead of a voltmeter to terminal B and the positive lead to terminal A of the heater grid **(see illustration)**.
5   The voltmeter should read between 10 and 12 volts. If the reading is lower, there is a poor ground connection.
6   Contact the negative lead to a good body ground. The reading should stay the same.
7   Connect the negative lead to terminal B, then touch each grid line at the mid-point with the positive lead.
8   The reading should be approximately six volts. If the reading is "0", there is a break between mid-point "C" and terminal "A".
9   A 10 to 12 volt reading is an indication of a break between mid-point "C". Move the lead toward the break; the voltage will change

when the break is crossed.
10   If the defogger grid does not receive voltage when the defogger switch is ON, either the heater and A/C switch, the defogger relay or the electrical connections are loose.

Repair
11   Repair the break in the line using a repair kit recommended specifically for this purpose, such as Mopar Repair Kit No. 4267922 (or equivalent). Included in this kit is plastic conductive epoxy.
12   Prior to repairing a break, turn off the system and allow it to de-energize for a few minutes.
13   Lightly buff the element area with fine steel wool, then clean it thoroughly with rubbing alcohol.
14   Use masking tape to mask off the area of repair **(see illustration)**.
15   Mix the epoxy thoroughly, according to the instructions on the package.
16   Apply the epoxy material to the slit in the masking tape, overlapping the undamaged area about 3/4-inch on either end.
17   Allow the repair to cure for 24 hours before removing the tape and using the defogger.

20   Instrument cluster - removal and installation

Refer to illustrations 20.4a, 20.4b, 20.5a and 20.5b
Warning: *These models have airbags. Always disconnect the cable from the negative terminal of the battery and wait two minutes before working in the vicinity of the impact sensors, steering column or instrument panel to avoid the possibility of accidental deployment of the airbag, which could cause personal injury* (see Section 27).
1   Disconnect the cable from the negative terminal of the battery.
2   Remove the upper steering column covers (Chapter 11).
3   Remove the instrument cluster bezel (see Chapter 11).

20.4a Remove the screws (arrows) securing the
instrument cluster

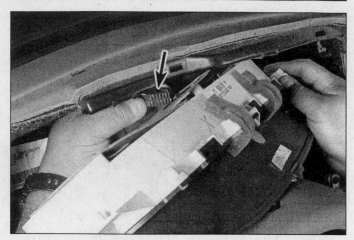

20.4b Lift out the instrument cluster and unplug the
electrical connectors

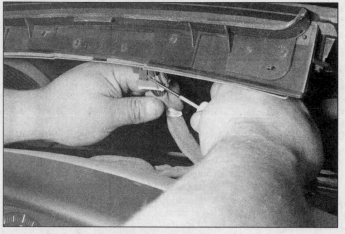

20.5a Unclip the upper dash cover to access the
electronic display

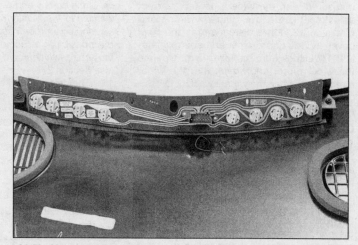

20.5b Upper dash panel electronic display - to remove the bulbs
(in the gray plastic holders), twist them counterclockwise 1/4-turn

4   Remove the screws retaining the instrument cluster to the instrument panel, pull the cluster back and disconnect the electrical connectors **(see illustrations)**.
5   Unclip the upper dash cover to access the top dash cover electronic instrument display **(see illustrations)**.
6   Disconnect the electrical wiring harness connectors.
7   Installation is the reverse of removal.

21 Horn - check and replacement

Refer to illustrations 21.2, 21.3a and 21.3b
Warning: *These models have airbags. Always disconnect the cable from the negative terminal of the battery and wait two minutes before working in the vicinity of the impact sensors, steering column or instrument panel to avoid the possibility of accidental deployment of the airbag, which could cause personal injury* (see Section 27).

Check

1   If the horns do not sound, check the horn fuse 6 in the Power Distribution Center

(underhood) and fuse 7 in the underdash Junction Block **(see illustrations 3.1a and 7.1)**. If the fuse is blown, replace it and retest. If it blows again, there is a short circuit in the horn or wiring between the horn and fuse block.
2   To test the horn, disconnect the electrical connector **(see illustration)**. Connect fused jumper wires from the positive and negative battery terminals to the positive and negative terminals of the horn. If the horn now sounds, the problem is a bad ground connection, faulty horn relay, faulty horn switch or problem in the wiring. If the horn does not sound, replace it.
3   Remove and check the horn relay **(see illustrations)**, located on the Junction Block as follows. Connect terminals 85 and 86 to the battery using fused jumper wires. The relay should click. With the jumper wires still connected, check that there's continuity between terminals 30 and 87. If there is continuity, the relay is OK. If the relay does not operate as described, replace it.

Replacement

4   The horns are located forward of the left

front wheel behind the bumper cover. To remove the horns, disconnect the electrical connector and remove the bracket bolt.
5   Installation is the reverse of removal.

22 Electric rear view mirrors - description and check

Refer to illustration 22.7
1   Electric rear view mirrors use two motors to move the glass; one for up-and-down adjustments and one for left-to-right adjustments. Heated mirrors may be equipped on models having a Rear Window Defogger. Memory mirrors may be equipped with models having the memory power seats.
2   The power mirror control switch on the headlamp switch bezel has a rocker switch which sends voltage to the left or right side mirror and a button for mirror Up, Down, Right, or Left. With the ignition ON but the engine OFF, roll down the windows and operate the mirror control switch through all functions (left-right and up-down) for both the left and right side mirrors.

21.2 To test a horn, disconnect its electrical connector (arrow)

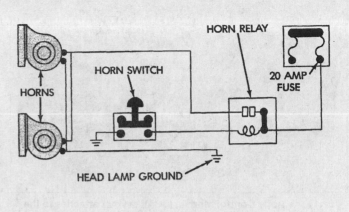

21.3a Horn circuit diagram

3   Listen carefully for the sound of the electric motors running in the mirrors.

4   If the motors can be heard but the mirror glass doesn't move, there is most likely a problem with the drive mechanism inside the mirror. Remove and disassemble the mirror to locate the problem.

5   If the mirrors don't operate and no sound comes from the mirrors, check the fuse (see Section 3).

6   If the fuse is OK, remove the mirror control switch from its mounting without disconnecting the wires attached to it. Turn the ignition ON and check for voltage at the switch. There should be voltage at one terminal. If there's no voltage at the switch, check for an open or short in the wiring between the fuse panel and the switch.

7   If there's voltage at the switch, disconnect it. Check the switch for continuity in all its operating positions **(see illustration)**. If the switch does not have continuity, replace it.

8   Reconnect the switch. Locate the wire going from the switch to ground. Leaving the switch connected, connect a jumper wire between this wire and ground. If the mirror works normally with this wire in place, repair the faulty ground connection.

9   If the mirror still doesn't work, remove the cover and check the wires at the mirror for voltage with a test light. Check with the ignition ON and the mirror selector switch on the appropriate side. Operate the mirror switch in all its positions. There should be voltage at one of the switch-to-mirror wires in each switch position (except the neutral "off" position).

10   If there is no voltage in each switch position, check the wiring between the mirror and control switch for opens and shorts.

11   If there is voltage, remove the mirror and test it off the vehicle with jumper wires.

12   Replace the mirror if it fails this test (see Chapter 11).

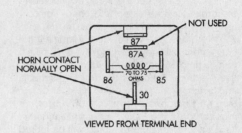

21.3b Horn relay terminal details

23   Cruise control system - description and check

1   The cruise control system maintains vehicle speed with a vacuum-actuated servo motor located in the engine compartment, which is connected to the throttle linkage by a cable. The system consists of the electronic Powertrain Control Module (PCM), brake switch, control switches, a relay, the vehicle speed sensor, steering wheel-mounted controls, and associated wiring. Listed below are some general procedures that may be used to locate common cruise control problems.

2   Locate and check the fuse (see Section 3). Also check the vacuum hose to the cruise control servo to make sure it's not plugged, cracked or soft (which will cause it to collapse in operation. With the engine off, check the servo by applying vacuum (with a hand vacuum pump) to the vacuum fitting on the servo - the servo should move the throttle linkage if it's working properly.

3   Have an assistant operate the brake lights while you check their operation (voltage from the brake light switch deactivates the cruise control).

4   If the brake lights do not come ON or OFF, correct the problem and retest the cruise control.

5   Inspect the cable linkage between the cruise control servo and the throttle linkage. it should operate freely without binding.

MIRROR SWITCH CONTINUITY			
MIRROR SELECT KNOB IN "LEFT" POSITION			
Move Lever	Continuity Between		
UP	PIN 9 - PIN 12,	PIN 6 - PIN 11,	PIN 9 - PIN 13
LEFT	PIN 9 - PIN 7,	PIN 6 - PIN 11,	PIN 9 - PIN 8
DOWN	PIN 9 - PIN 6,	PIN 12 - PIN 11,	PIN 13 - PIN 11
RIGHT	PIN 9 - PIN 6,	PIN 7 - PIN 11,	PIN 8 - PIN 11
MIRROR SELECT KNOB IN "RIGHT" POSITION			
Move Lever	Continuity Between		
UP	PIN 9 - PIN 13,	PIN 1 - PIN 11,	PIN 9 - PIN 12
LEFT	PIN 9 - PIN 8,	PIN 1 - PIN 11,	PIN 9 - PIN 7
DOWN	PIN 9 - PIN 1,	PIN 13 - PIN 11,	PIN 12 - PIN 11
RIGHT	PIN 9 - PIN 1,	PIN 8 - PIN 11,	PIN 7 - PIN 11
LAMP	PIN 5 - PIN 11		

22.7 Power rear view mirror switch terminal guide and continuity table

24.1 The Body Control Module (BCM) (arrow) attaches to the underdash Junction Block fuse and relay unit

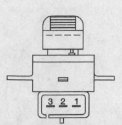

DOOR LOCK SWITCH TEST		
SWITCH POSITION	CONTINUITY BETWEEN	RESISTANCE VALUE
LOCK	2 and 3	1.5K Ohm ± 1%
UNLOCK	2 and 3	249 Ohm ± 1%

24.5 Door lock switch terminal guide and continuity table

6   Visually inspect the wires connected to the cruise control servo and check for corroded, damaged, or broken wires.

7   Test drive the vehicle to determine if the cruise control is now working. If it isn't, take it to a dealer service department or an automotive electrical specialist for further diagnosis and repair.

8   All functions of the speed control are monitored by the PCM Onboard Diagnostic (OBD) and any failure detected will be stored as a trouble code (see Chapter 6 for more information).

24 Power door lock system - description and check

Refer to illustrations 24.1, 24.5, 24.8 and 24.11

1   Power door lock systems are operated by door lock motors located in the front doors, the sliding door(s), the liftgate, and Lock/Unlock relays on the Junction Block, which receive a signal from the Body Control Module (BCM). The BCM is located under the dash to the left of the steering column, attached to the back of the Junction Block **(see illustration)**. The BCM automatically locks the doors and liftgate when the vehicle speed is greater than 16 mph. The automatic door lock feature can be disabled by the vehicle driver if desired (Disable/Enable feature). Actuation of the door locks is by the switches or the keyless remote, if equipped. The lock switches have two operating positions: Lock and Unlock.

2   Always check the circuit protection first. A 40 amp fuse is located in the Power Distribution Center (underhood). These vehicles use a combination of circuit breakers and fuses.

3   Operate the door lock switches in both directions (Lock and Unlock) with the engine off. Listen for the faint click of the relay operating.

4   If there's no click, check for voltage at the switches. If no voltage is present, check the wiring between the fuse panel and the switches for shorts and opens.

5   If voltage is present but no click is heard, test the switch for continuity **(see**

illustration). Replace it if there's not continuity in both switch positions.

6   If the switch has continuity but the relay doesn't click, check the wiring between the switch and relay for continuity. Repair the wiring if there is no continuity.

7   If the relay is receiving voltage from the switch but is not sending voltage to the lock motor, check for a bad ground at the relay case. If the relay case is grounding properly, replace the relay.

8   If all but one lock motor operates, remove the trim panel from the affected door (see Chapter 11) and check for voltage at the solenoid while the lock switch is operated **(see illustration)**. One of the wires should have voltage in the Lock position; the other should have voltage in the unlock position.

9   If the inoperative lock motor is receiving voltage, replace the solenoid.

10   If the inoperative lock motor isn't receiving voltage, check for an open or short in the wire between the lock motor and the relay. **Note:** *It's common for wires to break in the portion of the harness between the body and door (opening and closing the door fatigues*

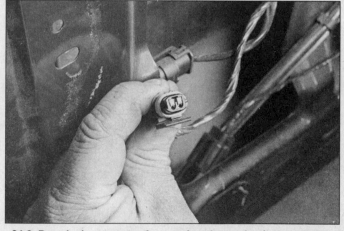

24.8 Door lock connector for supply voltage check - accessible with door panel removed

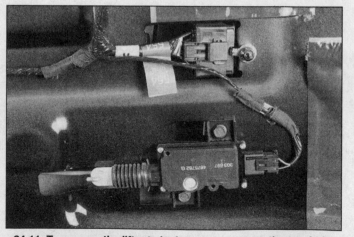

24.11 To remove the liftgate lock motor, unscrew the two bolts and disconnect the electrical connector, then rotate the motor to disengage the rod

and eventually breaks the wires).

11   To remove the liftgate lock motor, remove the liftgate trim panel (Chapter 11). Unbolt the lock motor **(see illustration)**, disconnect the electrical connector and disconnect the outside handle lock link from the lock motor shaft. Remove the lock motor from the vehicle.

12   To remove the sliding door lock motor, remove the sliding door trim panel (Chapter 11). Remove the latch/lock control cover and the control. Remove the screws holding the lock motor. If the sliding door lock contact is to be removed, remove the mounting screws and disconnect the electrical connector.

13   Installation is the reverse of removal.

25 Power window system - description and check

Refer to illustration 25.8a, 25.8b, 25.16a and 25.16b

1   The power window system consists of the separate driver's window and passenger's window control switches, separate right and left rear vent window switches (if equipped with power rear vent windows), the motors, window drive mechanisms (regulators), and associated wiring.

2   Power windows are wired so they can be lowered and raised from the master control switch by the driver or by remote switches located at the individual windows. Each window has a separate motor which is reversible. The position of the control switch determines the polarity and therefore the direction of motor operation. The driver's window has an automatic down switch position, using a power window switch that has two detent positions for either normal operation (first detent position) and automatic down (second detent position).

3   These procedures are general in nature, so if you cannot find the problem using them, take the vehicle to a dealer service department or other qualified repair shop.

4   The power window system operates when the ignition switch is ON. If none of the power windows work, check the fuse or circuit breaker.

5   If only the rear windows are inoperative, or if the windows only operate from the master control switch, check the rear window lockout switch for continuity in the unlocked position. Replace it if it doesn't have continuity.

6   Check the wiring between the switches and fuse panel for continuity. Repair the wiring, if necessary.

7   If only one window is inoperative from the master control switch, try the other control switch at the window. **Note:** *This doesn't apply to the driver's door window.*

8   If the same window works from one switch, but not the other, check the switch for continuity **(see illustrations)**.

9   If the switch tests OK, check for a short or open in the wiring between the affected

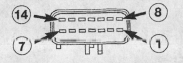

| DRIVER DOOR POWER WINDOW SWITCH TEST ||
SWITCH POSITION	CONTINUITY BETWEEN
OFF	13 and 1
	13 and 2
	13 and 3
	13 and 4
	13 and 5
	13 and 6
	13 and 7
	13 and 8
UP DRIVER	11 and 8
*DOWN DRIVER	11 and 6
*X DOWN DRIVER	11and 6
UP PASSENGER	9 and 4
DOWN PASSENGER	9 and 2
LEFT VENT OPEN	11 and 7
LEFT VENT CLOSE	9 and 3
RIGHT VENT OPEN	9 and 1
RIGHT VENT CLOSE	11 and 5

* MUST TEST WITH B+ ON PIN 9 AND GROUND ON PIN 13 FOR CONTINUITY BETWEEN PINS 11 AND 6

25.8a Terminal guide and continuity table for the driver's side power window control switch

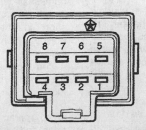

SWITCH POSITION	CONTINUITY BETWEEN
OFF	3 AND 8
OFF	2 AND 5
UP	4 AND 8
DOWN	4 AND 5

25.8b Terminal guide and continuity table for the passenger's side power window control switch

25.15a Two bolts secure the power rear vent window motor

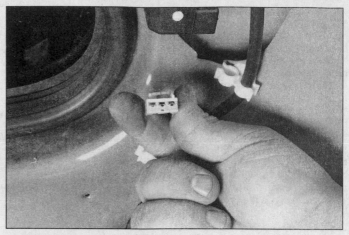

25.15b Power rear vent window electrical connector - check for supply voltage at the connector

switch and the window motor.

10   If one window is inoperative from both switches, remove the trim panel from the affected door (see Chapter 11) and check for voltage at the motor while the switch is operated.

11   If voltage is reaching the motor, disconnect the window glass from the regulator (see Chapter 11). Move the window up and down by hand while checking for binding and damage. Also check for binding and damage to the regulator. If the regulator is not damaged and the window moves up and down smoothly, replace the motor (see Chapter 11). If there's binding or damage, lubricate, repair or replace parts, as necessary.

12   If voltage isn't reaching the motor, check the wiring in the circuit for continuity between the switches and motors. Check that the relay is grounded properly and receiving voltage from the switches. Also check that the relay sends voltage to the motor when the switch is turned on. If it doesn't, replace the relay.

13   Test the windows after you are done to confirm proper repairs.

14   To remove the front door power window motor, remove the trim panel (Chapter 11), tape the window in position to support the weight of the window, cut the tie wrap on the window motor, disconnect the motor electrical connector, and remove the motor retaining screws and nuts, installing the new motor first without removing the old motor from the cables. **Note:** *Do not allow the cable drum to separate from the cable guide.* Then separate the original motor from the cable drum and cable guide. Insert the drum onto the new motor shaft; if necessary, have an assistant remove the tape holding the glass and lower the glass slightly to align the drum with the motor shaft.

15   To remove the vent window motor, remove the pillar trim panel, disconnect the electrical connector, remove the nut holding the crank to the vent glass, remove the power vent motor mounting bolts, and remove the vent window motor. Pull the vent window

crank arm from the motor. Cycle the replacement motor to the open position and install the vent window crank arm. Check the electrical circuit as described above in Steps 4, 9 and 12 **(see illustrations)** using two of the connector terminals.

16   For installation, cycle the motor to the window open position and the crank to its extended position.

17   Installation is the reverse of removal.

26   Power seats - description and check

Refer to illustrations 26.8a, 26.8b and 26.8c

1   Power seats, when equipped, allow you to adjust the position of the seat in eight directions: Up, down forward, back, tilt forward, and tilt rearward.

2   The power seat system consists of four reversing motors, a switch on the seat and a 40 amp fuse in the Power Distribution Center (PDC) located in the engine compartment, and a circuit breaker located in the wiring harness under the driver's seat.

3   If the seat does not move fully or stops short of full travel, look under the seat for any objects which may block the seat from moving.

4   If the seat does not work at all, check the condition of the battery and check the fuse.

5   With the engine off to reduce the noise level, operate the seat controls in all directions and listen for sound coming from the seat motor(s).

6   If the motor runs or clicks but the seat doesn't move, the integral seat drive mechanism is damaged and the motor assembly must be replaced.

7   If the motor doesn't work or makes noise, check for voltage at the motor circuit breaker under the seat, while an assistant operates the switch. If it still doesn't work, replace it.

8   If the motor isn't getting voltage, check for voltage at the switch. If there's no voltage

at the switch, check the wiring between the fuse panel and the switch. If there's voltage at the switch, check the switch for continuity in all its operating positions **(see illustration)**. Replace the switch if there's no continuity.

9   If the switch is OK, check for a short or open in the wiring between the switch and motor. If there's a relay between the switch and motor, check that it's grounded properly and there's voltage to the relay. Also check that there's voltage going from the relay to the motor when the switch is operated. If there's not, and the relay is grounded properly, replace the relay.

10   Test the completed repairs.

27   Airbag system - general information

Refer to illustration 27.3

Warning: *Always disconnect the cable from the negative terminal of the battery before beginning any service operation, especially involving the steering wheel servicing or Airbag System. Failure to disconnect the battery could result in accidental airbag deployment and possible injury. Allow the airbag system capacitor to discharge for two minutes before removing any airbag system component.*

These models are equipped with an Airbag restraint system. This system is designed to protect the driver and front seat passenger from serious injury in the event of head-on or frontal collision, if the driver and front seat passenger are wearing seat belts. It consists of airbag modules in the center of the steering wheel and the right side of the dashboard and one crash sensor.

The 2001 and later models are equipped with side impact airbags as well. This system is designed to protect the driver and front seat passenger from serious injury in the event of a side impact collision, if the driver and front seat passenger are wearing seat belts.

SWITCH POSITION	CONTINUITY BETWEEN PINS	
	DRIVER	PASSENGER
OFF	PIN 1 to 2 PIN 1 to 3 PIN 1 to 4 PIN 1 to 6 PIN 1 to 7 PIN 1 to 8 PIN 1 to 9 PIN 1 to 10	PIN 1 to 2 PIN 1 to 3 PIN 1 to 4 PIN 1 to 6 PIN 1 to 7 PIN 1 to 8 PIN 1 to 9 PIN 1 to 10
FRONT RISER UP	PIN 1 to 10 PIN 5 to 7	PIN 1 to 7 PIN 5 to 10
FRONT RISER DOWN	PIN 1 to 7 PIN 5 to 10	PIN 1 to 10 PIN 5 to 7
CENTER SWITCH FORWARD	PIN 1 to 3 PIN 5 to 6	PIN 1 to 3 PIN 5 to 6
CENTER SWITCH REARWARD	PIN 1 to 6 PIN 3 to 5	PIN 1 to 6 PIN 3 to 5
REAR RISER UP	PIN 1 to 9 PIN 5 to 8	PIN 1 to 8 PIN 5 to 9
REAR RISER DOWN	PIN 1 to 8 PIN 5 to 9	PIN 1 to 9 PIN 5 to 8
RECLINER UP	PIN 1 to 4 PIN 2 to 5	PIN 1 to 4 PIN 2 to 5
RECLINER DOWN	PIN 1 to 2 PIN 4 to 5	PIN 1 to 2 PIN 4 to 5

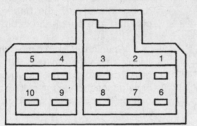

26.8a Power seat switch terminal guide and continuity table (1996 through 2000 models)

SWITCH POSITION	CONTINUITY BETWEEN PINS
	DRIVER
OFF	PIN 5 & 4 PIN 5 & 3 PIN 5 & 2 PIN 5 & 10 PIN 5 & 9 PIN 5 & 8 PIN 5 & 7 PIN 5 & 6
FRONT RISER UP	PIN 5 & 6 PIN 1 & 9
FRONT RISER DOWN	PIN 5 & 9 PIN 1 & 6
CENTER SWITCH FORWARD	PIN 5 & 3 PIN 1 & 10
CENTER SWITCH REARWARD	PIN 5 & 10 PIN 3 & 1
REAR RISER UP	PIN 5 & 7 PIN 1 & 8
REAR RISER DOWN	PIN 5 & 8 PIN 1 & 7
RECLINER UP	PIN 5 & 2 PIN 4 & 1
RECLINER DOWN	PIN 5 & 4 PIN 2 & 1

26.8b Driver side power seat switch terminal guide and continuity table (2001 and later models)

SWITCH POSITION	CONTINUITY BETWEEN PINS
	PASSENGER
OFF	PIN 5 & 4 PIN 5 & 3 PIN 5 & 2 PIN 5 & 10 PIN 5 & 9 PIN 5 & 8 PIN 5 & 7 PIN 5 & 6
FRONT RISER UP	PIN 5 & 9 PIN 1 & 6
FRONT RISER DOWN	PIN 5 & 6 PIN 1 & 9
CENTER SWITCH FORWARD	PIN 5 & 3 PIN 1 & 10
CENTER SWITCH REARWARD	PIN 5 & 10 PIN 3 & 1
REAR RISER UP	PIN 5 & 8 PIN 1 & 7
REAR RISER DOWN	PIN 5 & 7 PIN 1 & 8
RECLINER UP	PIN 5 & 2 PIN 4 & 1
RECLINER DOWN	PIN 5 & 4 PIN 2 & 1

26.8c Passenger side power seat switch terminal guide and continuity table (2001 and later models)

Airbag module

Each airbag module contains a housing incorporating the cushion (airbag) and inflator unit. The inflator assembly is mounted on the back of the housing over a hole through which gas is expelled, inflating the bag almost instantaneously when an electrical signal is sent from the system. The specially wound wire that carries this signal to the module is called a clockspring. The clockspring is a flat, ribbon-like electrically conductive tape which is wound so it can transmit an electrical signal regardless of steering wheel position.

Sensors

The system crash sensor is mounted in the Airbag Control Module (ACM) mounted just forward of the center console in the passenger compartment **(see illustration)**.

The crash sensor is a pressure sensitive switch that completes an electrical circuit during an impact of sufficient G force. The electrical signal from the crash sensor is sent to the ACM, which then completes the circuit and inflates the airbags.

Airbag Control Module (ACM)

The ACM checks the system every time the vehicle is started, causing the AIRBAG light to go on, then off, if the system is operating properly. If there is a fault in the system,

27.3 The Airbag Control Module (ACM) is located under the dash, forward of the center console

the light will go on and stay on and the ACM will store trouble codes indicating the nature of the fault. If the AIRBAG light does go on and stay on, the vehicle should be taken to your dealer immediately for service.

28   Wiring diagrams - general information

Since it isn't possible to include all wiring diagrams for every year covered by this manual, the following diagrams are those that are typical and most commonly needed.

Prior to troubleshooting any circuits, check the fuse and circuit breakers (if equipped) to make sure they're in good condition. Make sure the battery is properly charged and check the cable connections (see Chapter 1).

When checking a circuit, make sure that all connectors are clean, with no corroded, broken, or loose terminals. When disconnecting a connector, do not pull on the wires. Pull only on the connector housings themselves.

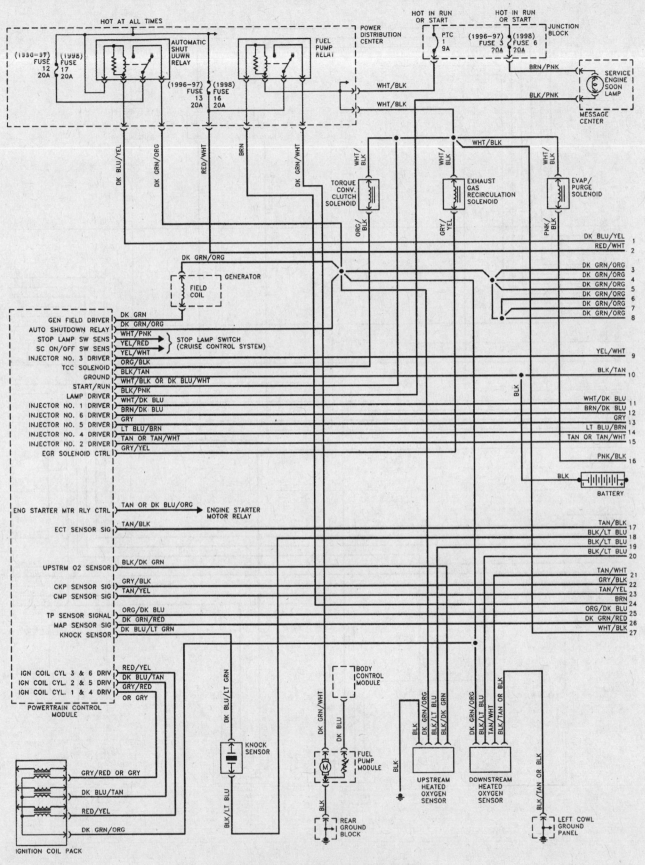

Typical engine control system (part 1 of 3)

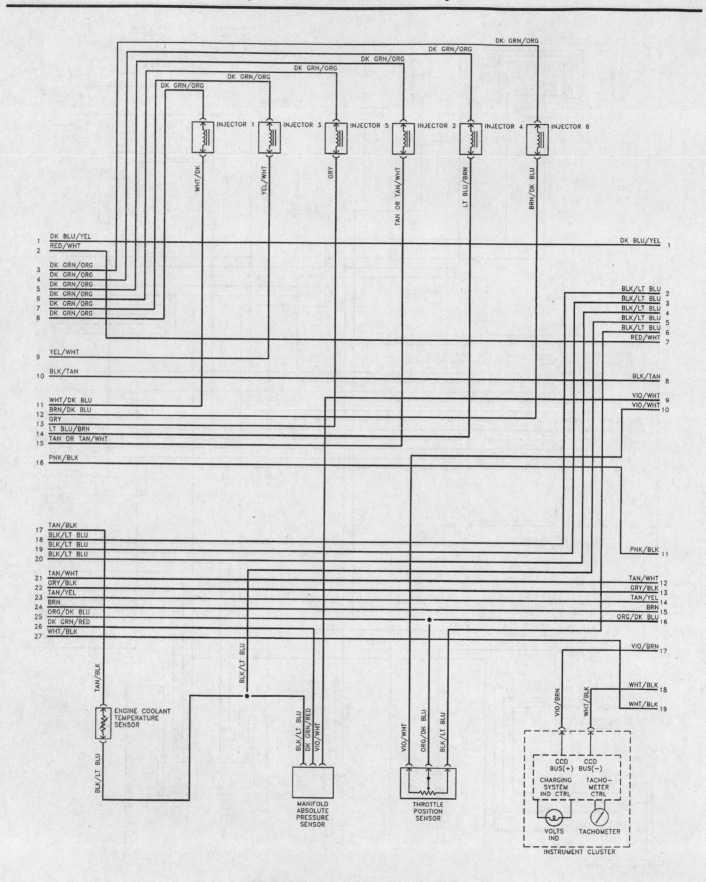

Typical engine control system (part 2 of 3)

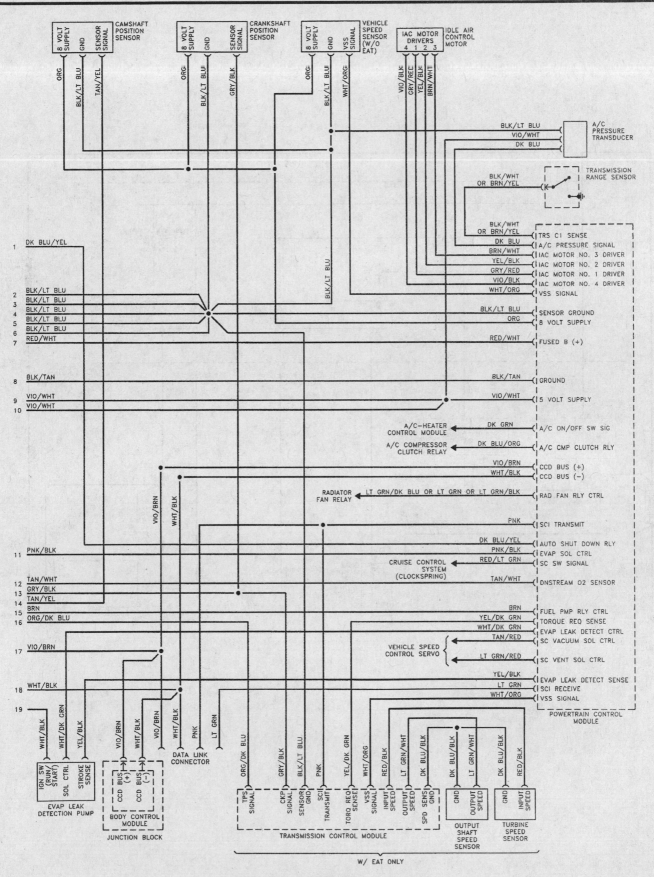

Typical engine control system (part 3 of 3)

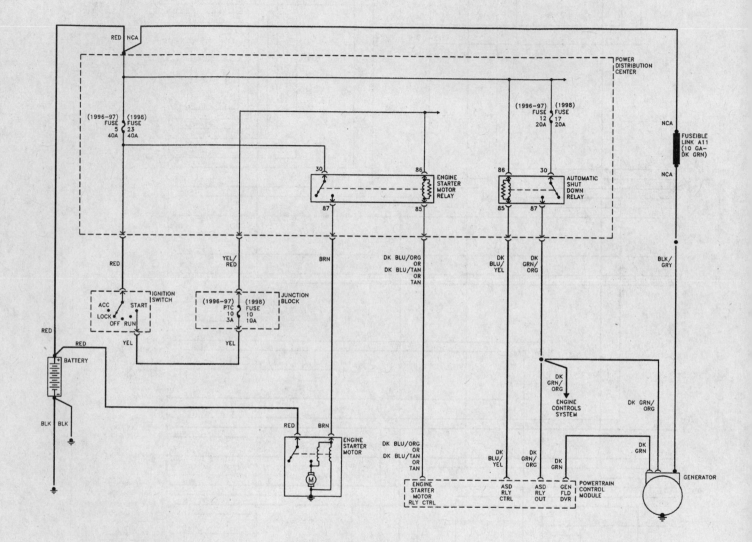

Typical starting and charging system

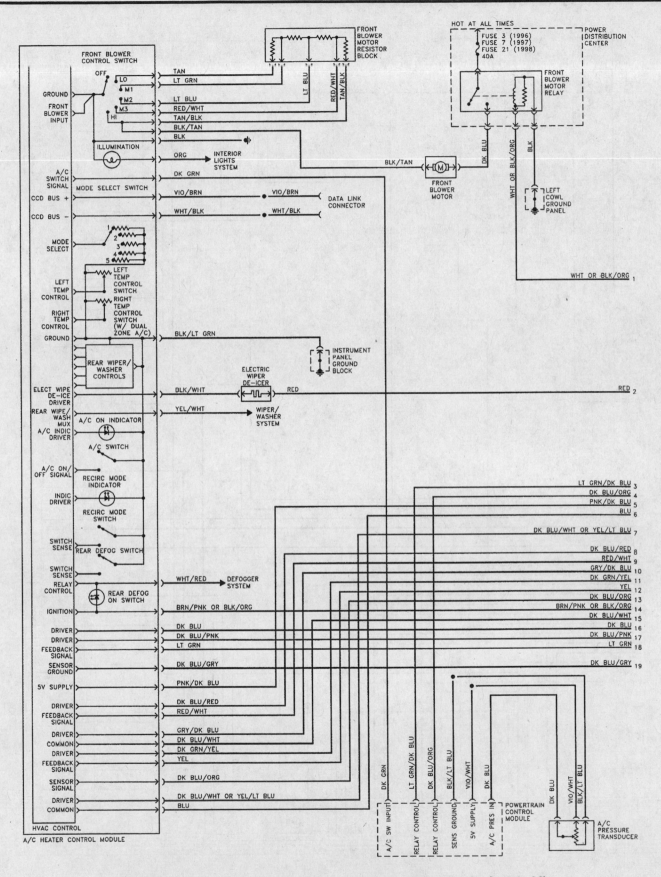

Typical heating and air conditioning system - includes engine cooling fan (part 1 of 2)

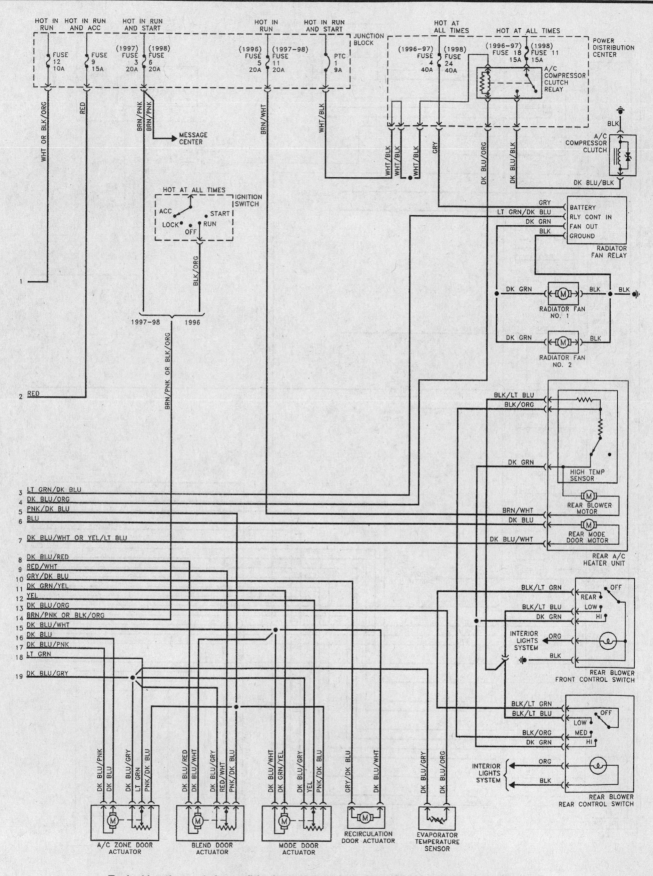

Typical heating and air conditioning system - includes engine cooling fan (part 2 of 2)

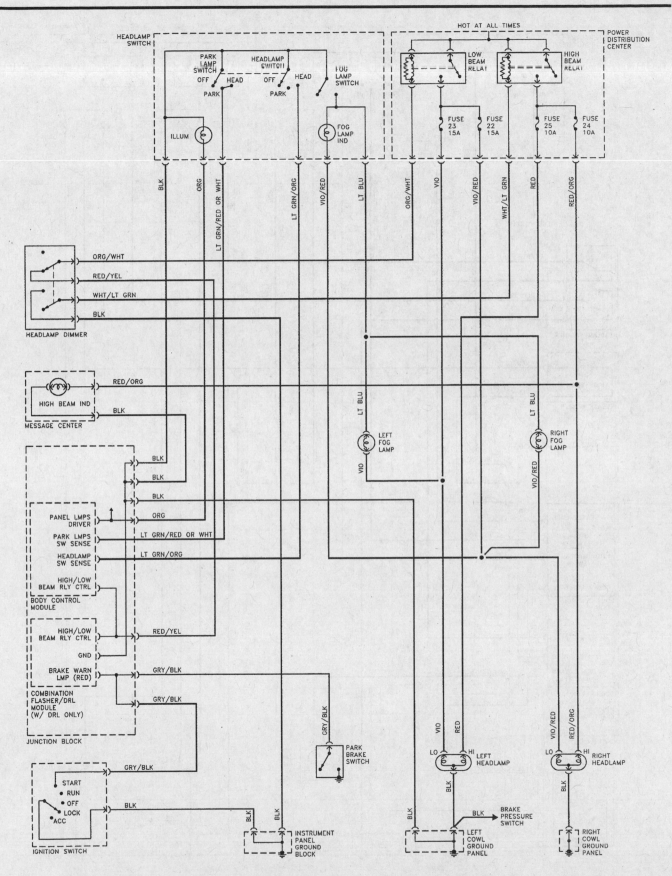

Typical headlight and fog light system - 1996 and 1997 models

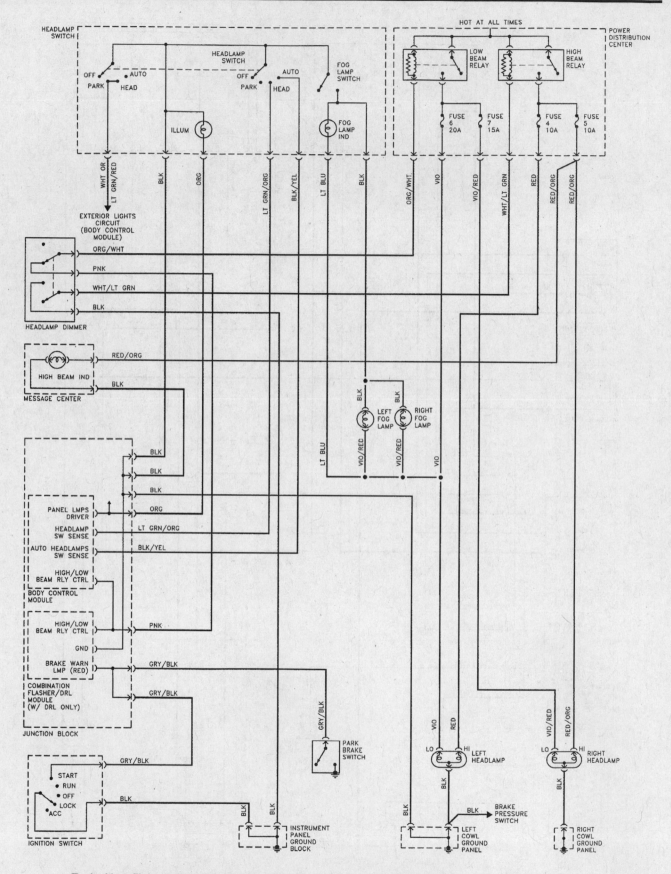

Typical headlight and fog light system - Plymouth Voyager and 1998 and later Caravan models

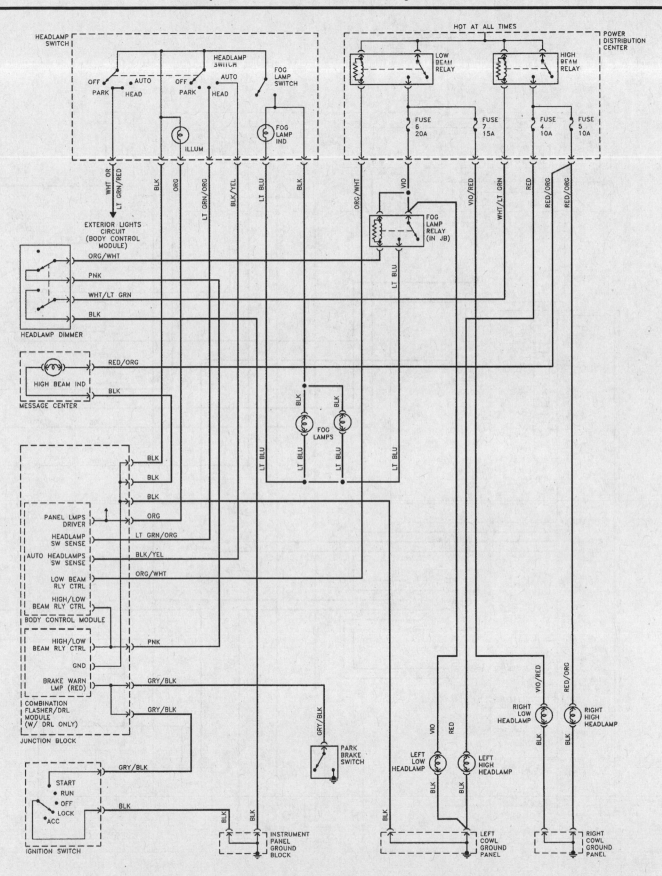

Typical headlight and fog light system - 1998 and later Chrysler Town & Country models

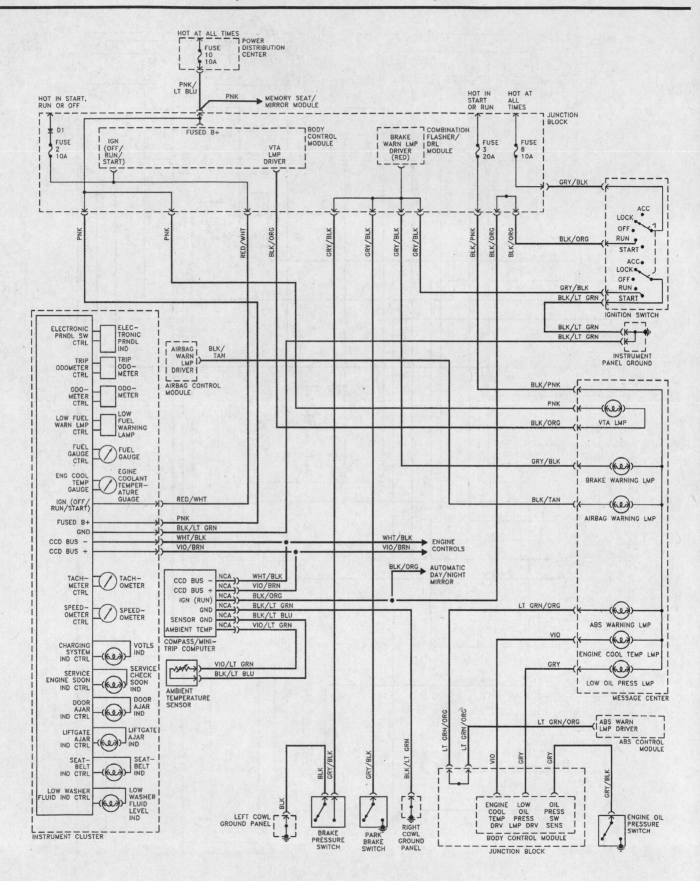

Typical engine warning system - 1996 models

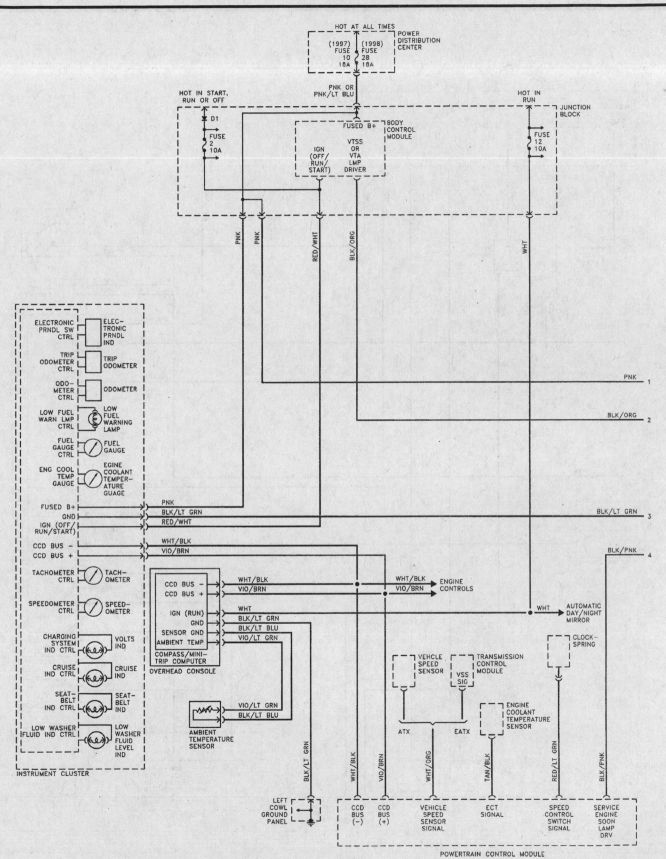

Typical engine warning system - 1997 and later models (part 1 of 2)

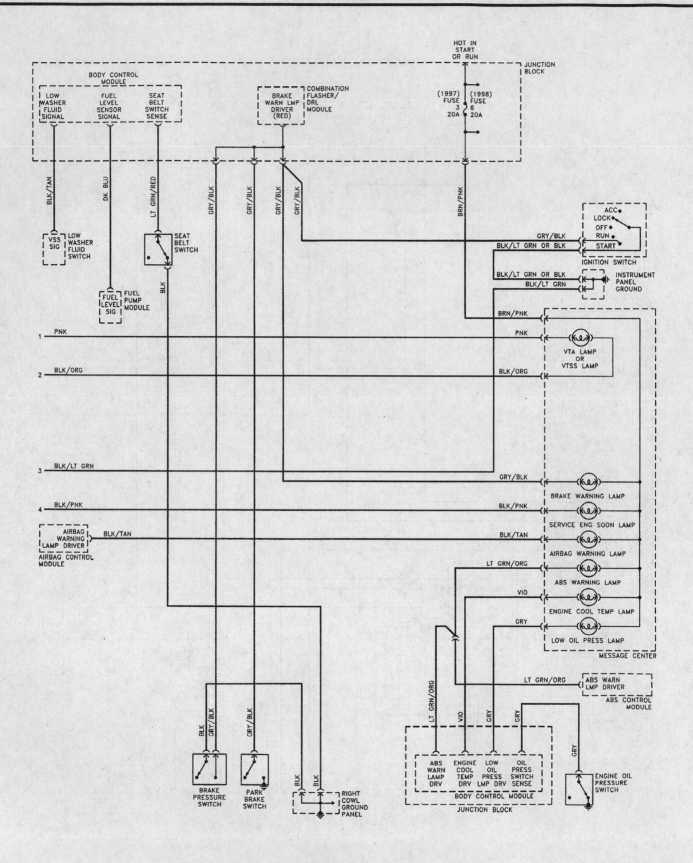

Typical engine warning system - 1997 and later models (part 2 of 2)

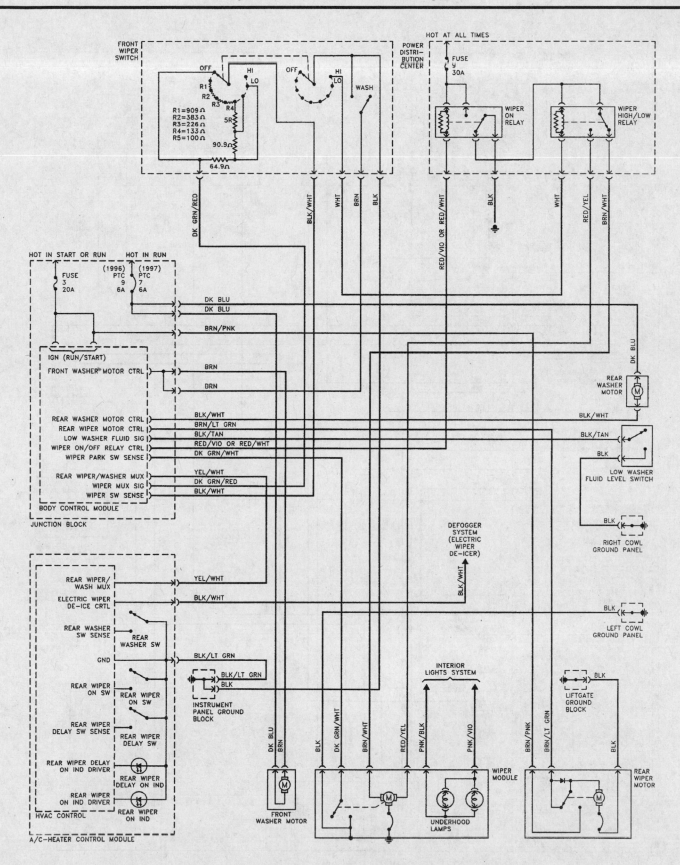

Typical windshield wiper system - 1996 and 1997 models

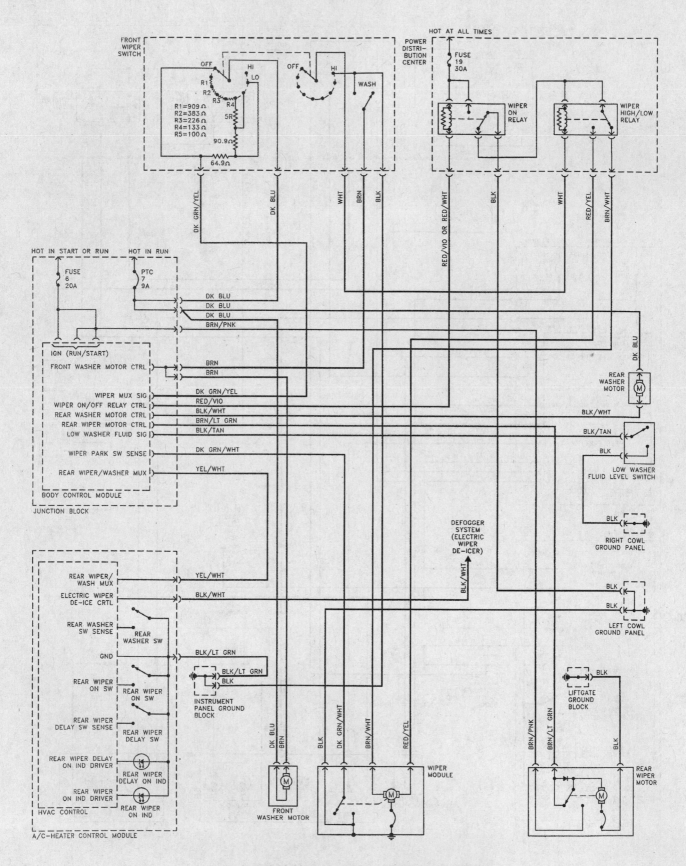

Typical windshield wiper system - 1998 and later models

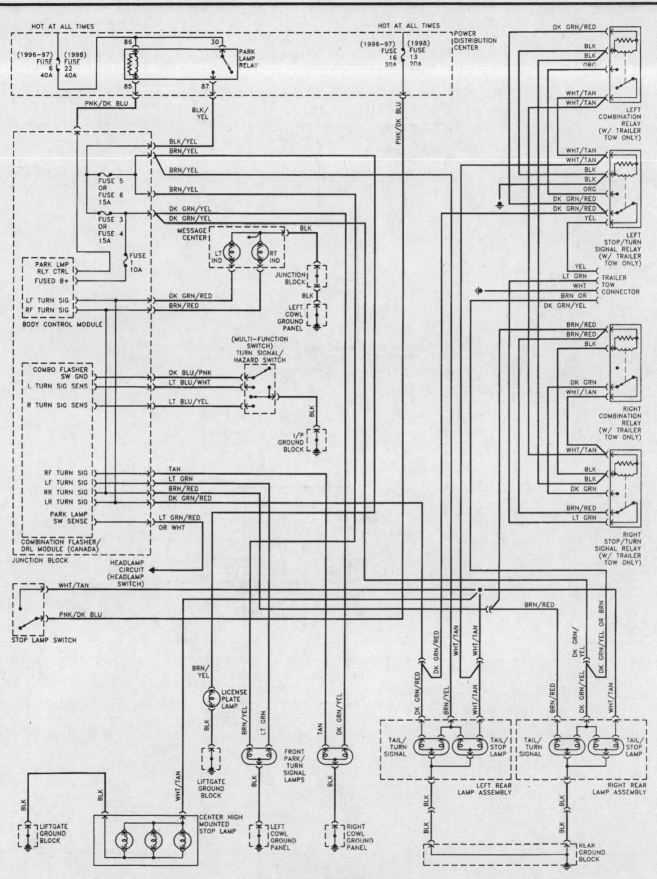

Typical exterior lighting system

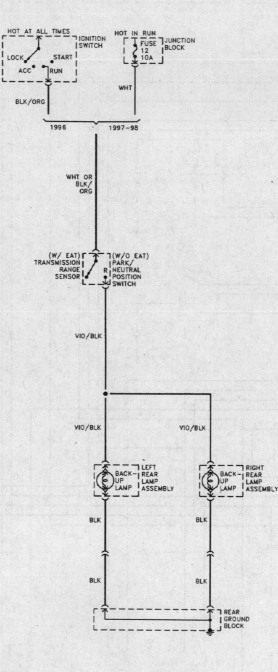

Typical back-up light system

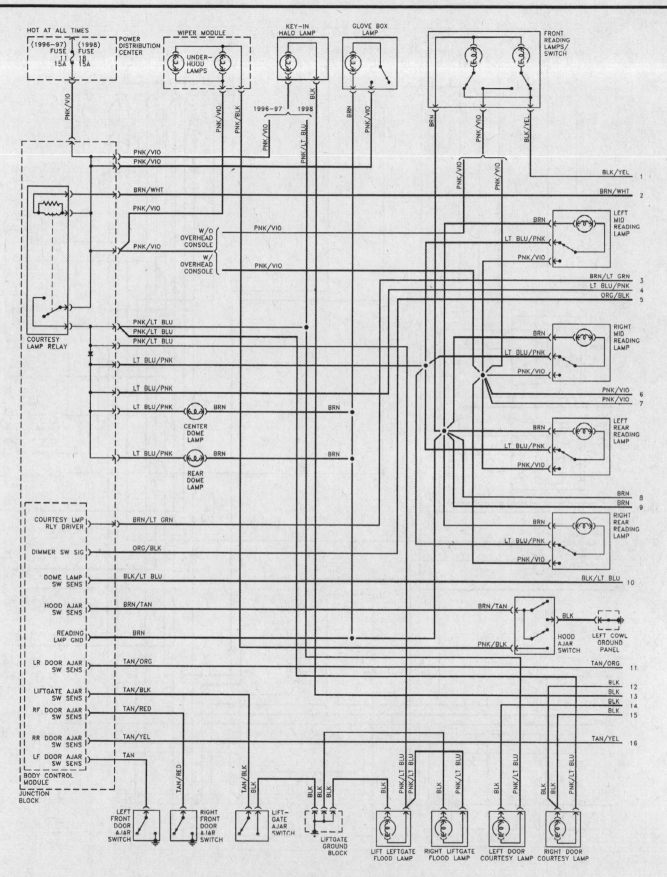

Typical interior lighting system (part 1 of 2)

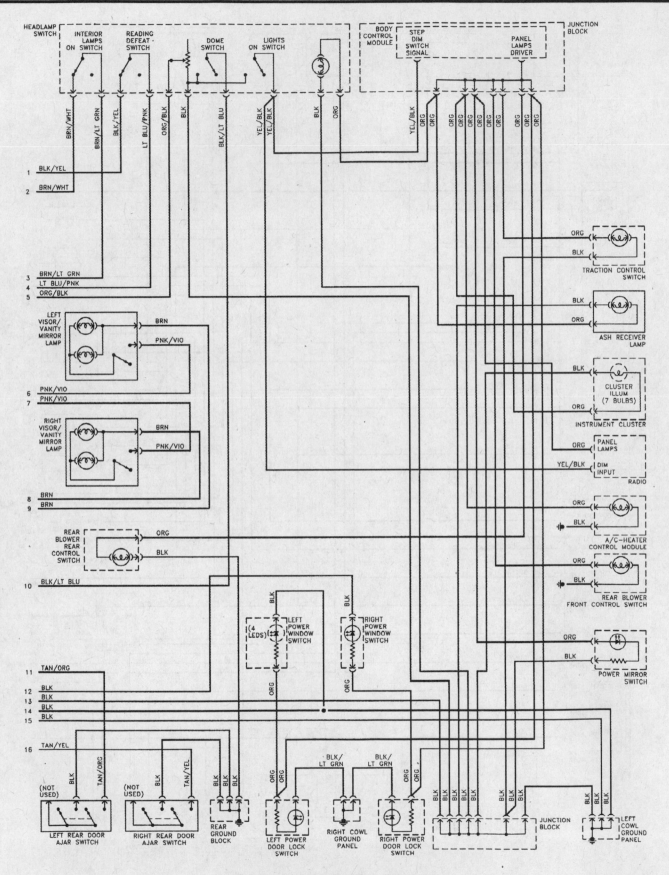

Typical interior lighting system (part 2 of 2)

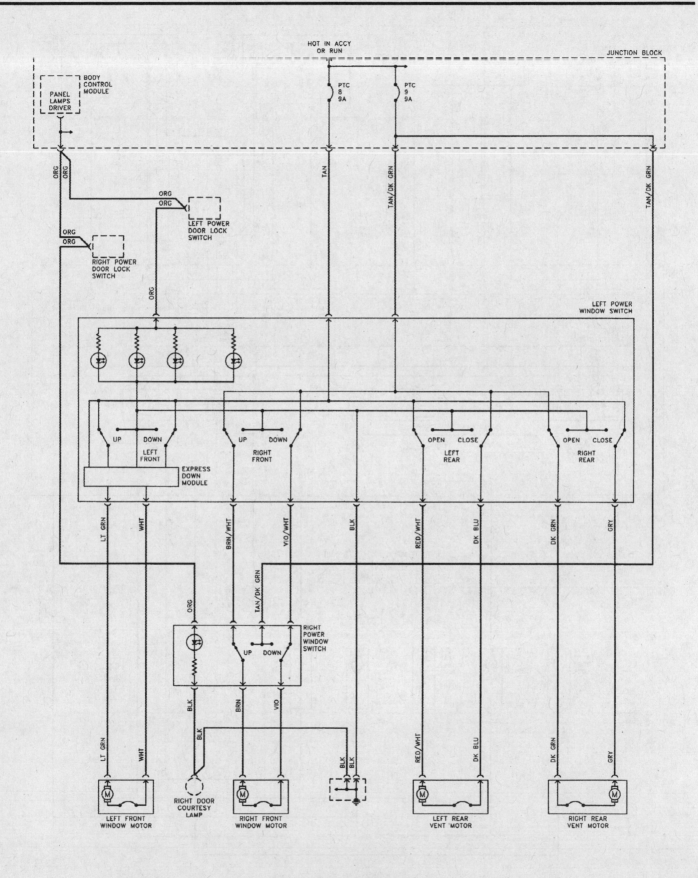

Typical power window system

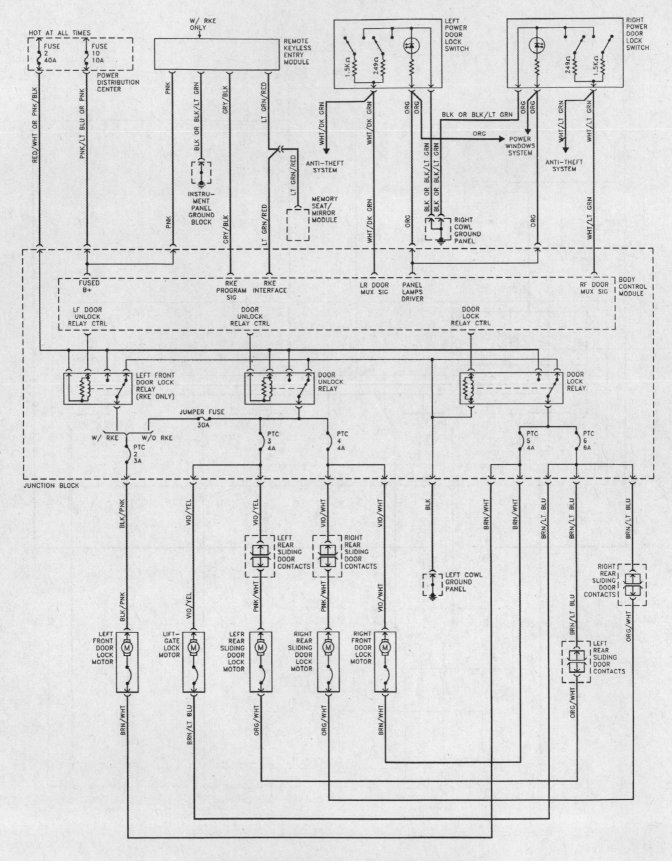

Typical power door lock system - 1996 and 1997 models

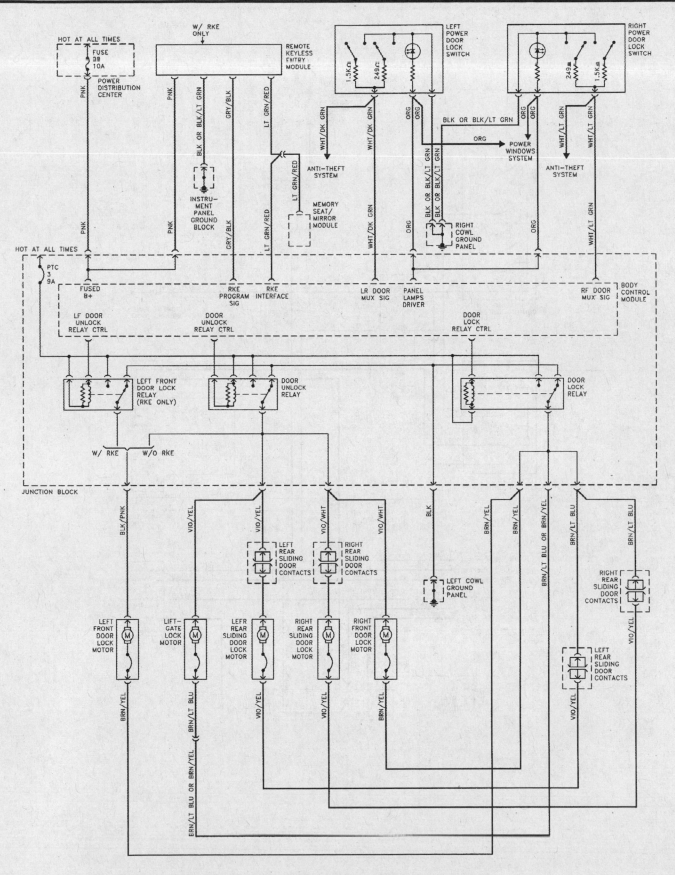

Typical power door lock system - 1998 and later models

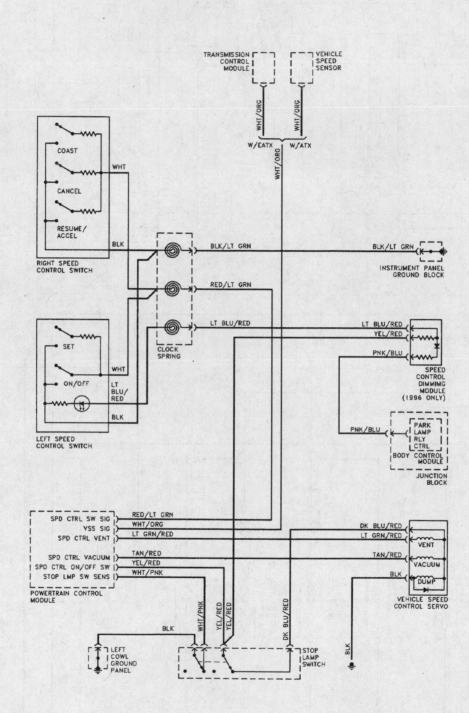

Typical cruise control system

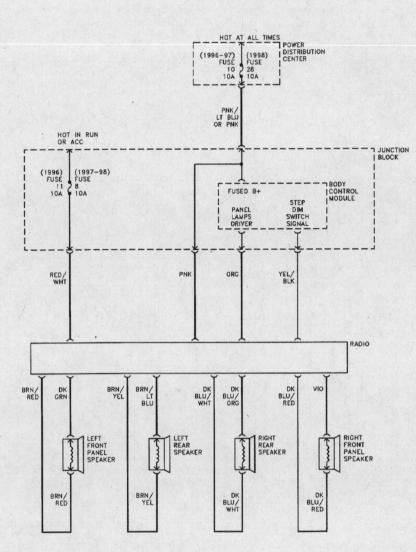

Typical audio system

Notes

Notes

Index

A

About this manual, 0-5
Accelerator cable, replacement, 4-8
Air cleaner assembly, removal and installation, 4-7
Air conditioning
    compressor, removal and installation, 3-13
    condenser, removal and installation, 3-14
    filter/drier, removal and installation, 3-14
Air conditioning and heating system, check and
    maintenance, 3-12
Air filter replacement, 1-21
Air intake plenum (V6 models), removal and installation, 4-13
Airbag system, general information, 12-20
Alternator, removal and installation, 5-8
Antenna, removal and installation, 12-13
Antifreeze, general information, 3-2
Anti-lock Brake System (ABS), general information, 9-2
Automatic transaxle, 7-1 through 7-8
    band adjustment (3-speed 31TH transaxle), 7-8
    diagnosis, general, 7-2
    fluid
        and filter change, 1-21
        level check, 1-11
    general information, 7-2
    neutral start/back-up light switch, check
        and replacement, 7-4
    oil seal, replacement, 7-3
    removal and installation, 7-5
    shift cable, check and adjustment, 7-4
    throttle cable, check and adjustment, 7-4
Automotive chemicals and lubricants, 0-17
Auxiliary (rear) heating and air conditioning
    components, removal and installation, 3-15
    system, general information, 3-15
Axle assembly (rear), removal and installation, 10-12

B

Balance shafts (four-cylinder engine only), removal,
    inspection and installation, 2D-18
Balljoints, check and replacement, 10-9
Battery
    cables, check and replacement, 5-2
    check, maintenance and charging, 1-13
    emergency jump starting, 5-2
    removal and installation, 5-2
Body, 11-1 through 11-24
    bumpers, removal and installation, 11-7
    cowl cover, removal and installation, 11-24
    dashboard panels, removal and installation, 11-18
    door
        latch, lock cylinder and outside handle, removal and
            installation, 11-10
        trim panels, removal and installation, 11-8
        window regulator, removal and installation, 11-16

front door
    removal and installation, 11-12
    window glass, removal and installation, 11-15
front fender, removal and installation, 11-6
grille, removal and installation, 11-6
hinges and locks, maintenance, 11-3
hood
    latch and cable, removal and installation, 11-6
    removal, installation and adjustment, 11-3
instrument cluster bezel, removal and installation, 11-17
interior quarter trim panels, removal and installation, 11-21
liftgate
    removal, installation and adjustment, 11-14
    strut, replacement, 11-15
lower console, removal and installation, 11-16
maintenance, 11-1
mirrors, removal and installation, 11-23
overhead console, removal and installation, 11-17
quarter window glass, removal and installation, 11-16
repair
    major damage, 11-3
    minor damage, 11-2
seat belt check, 11-24
seats, removal and installation, 11-24
sliding door, removal and installation, 11-14
upholstery and carpets, maintenance, 11-2
vinyl trim, maintenance, 11-2
wheelhouse splash shield, removal and installation, 11-23
windshield and fixed glass, replacement, 11-3
Booster battery (jump) starting, 0-16
Brakes, 9-1 through 9-20
    Anti-lock Brake System (ABS), general information, 9-2
    caliper, disc, removal and installation, 9-7
    disc, inspection, removal and installation, 9-8
    fluid, 1-10
    general information, 9-2
    hoses and lines, inspection and replacement, 9-14
    light switch, check, replacement and adjustment, 9-20
    master cylinder, removal, installation and vacuum seal
        replacement, 9-12
    pads, disc, replacement, 9-3
    parking brake
        cables, replacement, 9-16
        pedal assembly, removal, installation and adjustment, 9-16
        shoes (models with rear disc brakes), replacement, 9-17
    power brake booster, check, removal and installation, 9-15
    proportioning valves, check and replacement, 9-14
    shoes, drum, replacement, 9-9
    switch, 6-4
    system
        check, 1-17
        bleeding, 9-15
    wheel cylinder, removal and installation, 9-12
Bulb replacement, 12-9
Bumpers, removal and installation, 11-7
Buying parts, 0-8

C

Camshaft
  oil seal, replacement
    four-cylinder engine, 2A-9
    3.0L V6 engine, 2B-10
  removal, inspection and installation,
    four-cylinder engine, 2A-11
    3.0L V6 engine, 2B-14
    3.3L and 3.8L V6 engines
      removal and inspection, 2D-16
      installation, 2D-31
Catalytic converter, 6-22
Charging system
  check, 5-6
  general information and precautions, 5-6
Chassis electrical system
  airbag system, general information, 12-20
  antenna, removal and installation, 12-13
  bulb replacement, 12-9
  circuit breakers, general information, 12-5
  cruise control system, description and check, 12-17
  electric rear view mirrors, description and check, 12-16
  electrical troubleshooting, general information, 12-3
  fuses, general information, 12-4
  fusible links, general information, 12-4
  headlight(s)
    adjustment, 12-8
    bulb, replacement, 12-7
    housing, removal and installation, 12-8
    switch, check and replacement, 12-11
  horn, check and replacement, 12-16
  ignition switch and lock cylinder, removal
    and installation, 12-6
  instrument cluster, removal and installation, 12-15
  multi-function switch, check and replacement, 12-6
  power door lock system, description and check, 12-18
  power seats, description and check, 12-20
  power window system, description and check, 12-19
  radio and speakers, removal and installation, 12-13
  rear window defogger
    check and repair, 12-15
    switch, removal and installation, 12-15
  relays, general information, 12-5
  turn signal/hazard flasher, check and replacement, 12-5
  windshield wiper motor, check and replacement, 12-14
  wiring diagrams, 12-23
Chassis lubrication, 1-17
Circuit breakers, general information, 12-5
Control arm, removal, inspection, and installation, 10-7
Conversion factors, 0-18
Coolant reservoir, removal and installation, 3-6
**Coolant temperature sending unit, check and
replacement, 3-8**
Cooling system
  check, 1-15
  servicing, draining, flushing, and refilling, 1-21
**Cooling, heating and air conditioning systems,
3-1 through 3-16**
  air conditioning
    and heating system, check and maintenance, 3-12

    compressor, removal and installation, 3-13
    condenser, removal and installation, 3-14
    filter/drier, removal and installation, 3-14
  antifreeze, general information, 3-2
  auxiliary (rear) heating and air conditioning system
    general information, 3-15
    removal and installation, 3-15
  coolant
    reservoir, removal and installation, 3-6
    temperature sending unit, check and replacement, 3-8
  engine cooling fans and circuit, check and replacement, 3-4
  heater core, replacement, 3-10
  heater/air conditioner
    blower motor (front), removal and installation, 3-8
    control assembly, removal and installation, 3-12
  radiator/transmission oil cooler, removal and installation, 3-4
  thermostat, check and replacement, 3-2
  water pump
    check, 3-6
    replacement, 3-6
Cowl cover, removal and installation, 11-24
Crankshaft
  front oil seal, replacement
    four-cylinder engine, 2A-9
    3.0L V6 engine, 2B-10
    3.3L and 3.8L V6 engines, 2C-11
  position sensor, 6-4
  pulley, removal and installation, 2C-8
  pulley/vibration damper, removal and installation, 2B-6
  inspection, 2D-25
  installation and main bearing oil clearance
    check, 2D-28
    removal, 2D-20
Cruise control system, description and check, 12-17
CV joint inspection and driveaxle boot replacement, 8-3
Cylinder compression check, 2D-8
Cylinder head
  cleaning and inspection, 2D-13
  disassembly, 2D-12
  reassembly, 2D-15
  removal and installation
    four-cylinder engine, 2A-13
    3.0L V6 engine, 2B-15
    3.3L and 3.8L V6 engines, 2C-13
Cylinder honing, 2D-23

D

Dashboard panels, removal and installation, 11-18
Disc brake
  caliper, removal and installation, 9-7
  inspection, removal and installation, 9-8
  pads, replacement, 9-3
**Distributor (3.0L V6 engine only), removal, inspection
and installation, 5-6**
Door
  latch, lock cylinder and outside handle, removal and
    installation, 11-10
  trim panel, removal and installation, 11-8
  window regulator, removal and installation, 11-16

Driveaxles, 8-1 through 8-6
  boot
    check, 1-21
    replacement and CV joint inspection, 8-3
  general information and inspection, 8-1
  removal and installation, 8-2
Drivebelt check, adjustment and replacement, 1-18
Driveplate, removal and installation, 2A-17, 2B-18
Drum brake shoes, replacement, 9-9

E

**Electric rear view mirrors, description
and check, 12-16**
Electrical troubleshooting, general information, 12-3
Emissions and engine control systems, 6-1 through 6-22
  catalytic converter, 6-22
  Evaporative Emissions Control (EVAP) system, 6-20
  Exhaust Gas Recirculation (EGR) system, 6-18
  information sensors, 6-4
  information sensors, general description, check and
    replacement, 6-12
  Multi-Port Electronic Fuel Injection (MPI) system and
    information sensors, 6-3
  On Board Diagnosis (OBD) system and trouble codes, 6-5
  Positive Crankcase Ventilation (PCV) system, 6-17
  Powertrain Control Module (PCM), removal
    and installation, 6-4
Engine
  3.0L V6 engine, 2B-1 through 2B-18
    camshaft, removal, inspection and
      installation, 2B-14
    camshaft oil seal, replacement, 2B-10
    crankshaft
      front oil seal, replacement, 2B-10
      pulley/vibration damper, removal and
        installation, 2B-6
    cylinder head, removal and installation, 2B-15
    driveplate, removal and installation, 2B-18
    exhaust manifolds, removal, inspection
      and installation, 2B-4
    general information, 2B-2
    intake manifold, removal, inspection and installation, 2B-3
    mounts, check and replacement, 2B-18
    oil
      seal, replacement, 2B-10
      pan, removal and installation, 2B-15
      pump, removal, inspection and installation, 2B-16
    rear main oil seals, replacement, 2B-18
    repair operations possible with the engine
      in the vehicle, 2B-22
    rocker arm and hydraulic valve lash adjuster, removal,
      inspection and installation, 2B-12
    timing belt, removal, installation and adjustment, 2B-7
    valve covers, removal and installation, 2B-2
    valve springs, retainers and seals, replacement, 2B-15
  3.3L and 3.8L V6 engines, 2C-1 through 2C-16
    crankshaft
      front oil seal, replacement, 2C-11
      pulley, removal and installation, 2C-8

    cylinder heads, removal and installation, 2C-13
    exhaust manifolds, removal and installation, 2C-6
    hydraulic roller lifters, removal, inspection and
      installation, 2C-12
    intake manifold, removal and installation, 2C-4
    mounts, check and replacement, 2C-16
    oil
      cooler, removal and installation, 2C-16
      pan, removal and installation, 2C-14
      pump, removal, inspection and installation, 2C-15
    rear main oil seal, replacement, 2C-16
    repair operations possible with the engine
      in the vehicle, 2C-3
    rocker arms and pushrods, removal, inspection and
      installation, 2C-11
    timing chain
      and sprockets, removal, inspection and
        installation, 2C-10
      cover, removal and installation, 2C-9
    valve covers, removal and installation, 2C-3
  four-cylinder, 2A-1 through 2A-20
    camshaft oil seal, replacement, 2A-9
    camshaft(s), removal, inspection and
      installation, 2A-11
    crankshaft front oil seal, replacement, 2A-9
    cylinder head, removal and installation, 2A-13
    driveplate, removal and installation, 2A-17
    exhaust manifold, removal, inspection
      and installation, 2A-6
    general information, 2A-2
    intake manifold, removal, inspection and installation, 2A-3
    mounts, check and replacement, 2A-18
    oil
      pan, removal and installation, 2A-14
      pump, removal, inspection and installation, 2A-15
    rear main oil seal, replacement, 2A-18
    repair operations possible with the engine
      in the vehicle, 2A-3
    rocker arm and hydraulic valve lash adjuster, removal,
      inspection and installation, 2A-10
    timing belt and covers, removal, inspection and
      installation, 2A-6
    valve cover, removal and installation, 2A-3
    valve springs, retainers and seals, replacement, 2A-12
  General engine overhaul procedures, 2D-1 through 2D-34
    balance shafts (four-cylinder engine only), removal,
      inspection and installation, 2D-18
    block
      cleaning, 2D-20
      inspection, 2D-22
    camshaft, installation, 2D-31
    camshaft and bearings, removal and inspection, 2D-16
    crankshaft
      inspection, 2D-25
      installation and main bearing oil clearance
        check, 2D-28
      removal, 2D-20
    cylinder compression check, 2D-8
    cylinder head, cleaning and inspection, 2D-13
    cylinder head, disassembly, 2D-12
    cylinder head, reassembly, 2D-15
    cylinder honing, 2D-23

engine
    disassembly sequence, 2D-11
    general information, 2D-6
    reassembly sequence, 2D-26
    removal, methods and precautions, 2D-9
    removal and installation, 2D-9
    initial start-up and break-in after overhaul, 2D-34
    main and connecting rod bearings, inspection, 2D-26
    piston rings, installation, 2D-27
    pistons and connecting rods, inspection, 2D-23
    pistons and connecting rods, installation and rod
        bearing oil clearance check, 2D-32
    pistons and connecting rods, removal, 2D-17
    rear main oil seal, installation, 2D-31
    rebuilding alternatives, 2D-10
    Top Dead Center (TDC) for number one piston,
        locating, 2D-6
    vacuum gauge diagnostic checks, 2D-8
    valves, servicing, 2D-15
Engine electrical systems, 5-1 through 5-10
    alternator, removal and installation, 5-8
    battery
        cables, check and replacement, 5-2
        emergency jump starting, 5-2
        removal and installation, 5-2
    charging system
        check, 5-6
        general information and precautions, 5-6
    distributor (3.0L V6 engine only), removal, inspection and
        installation, 5-6
    ignition
        coil, check and replacement, 5-4
        system
            check, 5-3
            general information, 5-2
    starter motor
        in-vehicle check, 5-9
        removal and installation, 5-10
    starting system, general information and precautions, 5-9
    voltage regulator, general information, 5-9
Evaporative emissions control (EVAP) system, 6-20
    check, 1-22
Exhaust
    manifold, removal, inspection and installation
        four-cylinder engine, 2A-6
        3.0L V6 engine, 2B-4
        3.3L and 3.8L V6 engine, 2C-6
    system
        check, 1-17
        servicing, general information, 4-16
Exhaust Gas Recirculation (EGR) system
    3.0L and 3.3L/3.8L only, 6-18
    test, 1-26

F

Fluid level checks, 1-8
Four-cylinder engine, 2A-1 through 2A-20
    camshaft oil seal, replacement, 2A-9

camshaft(s), removal, inspection and
        installation, 2A-11
    crankshaft front oil seal, replacement, 2A-9
    cylinder head, removal and installation, 2A-13
    driveplate, removal and installation, 2A-17
    exhaust manifold, removal, inspection and installation, 2A-6
    general information, 2A-2
    intake manifold, removal, inspection and
        installation, 2A-3
    mounts, check and replacement, 2A-18
    oil pan, removal and installation, 2A-14
    oil pump, removal, inspection and installation, 2A-15
    rear main oil seal, replacement, 2A-18
    rocker arm and hydraulic valve lash adjuster, removal,
        inspection and installation, 2A-10
    timing belt and covers, removal, inspection
        and installation, 2A-6
    valve cover, removal and installation, 2A-3
    valve springs, retainers and seals, replacement, 2A-12
Fraction, decimal and millimeter equivalents, 0-19
Front door
    removal and installation, 11-12
    window glass, removal and installation, 11-15
Front fender, removal and installation, 11-6
Fuel and exhaust systems, 4-1 through 4-16
    accelerator cable, replacement, 4-8
    air cleaner assembly, removal and installation, 4-7
    air intake plenum or upper intake manifold (V6 models),
        removal and installation, 4-13
    exhaust system servicing, general information, 4-16
    fuel
        injection system
            check, 4-9
            general information, 4-8
        level sending unit, check and replacement, 4-5
        lines and fittings, replacement, 4-3
        pressure relief procedure, 4-2
        pump/fuel pressure, check, 4-2
        pump, fuel pressure regulator and inlet strainer, removal
            and installation, 4-4
        rail and injectors, check, removal and installation, 4-10
        tank
            cleaning and repair, general information, 4-7
            removal and installation, 4-7
    Idle Air Control (IAC) valve, check and replacement, 4-12
    throttle body, check, removal and installation, 4-10
Fuel filter replacement, 1-25
Fuel system check, 1-18
Fuses, general information, 12-4
Fusible links, general information, 12-4

G

**General engine overhaul procedures,
    2D-1 through 2D-34**
    balance shafts (four-cylinder engine only), removal,
        inspection and installation, 2D-18
    block
        cleaning, 2D-20
        inspection, 2D-22
    camshaft, installation, 2D-31

camshaft and bearings, removal and inspection, 2D-16
crankshaft
　　inspection, 2D-25
　　installation and main bearing oil clearance check, 2D-28
　　removal, 2D-20
cylinder compression check, 2D-8
cylinder head, cleaning and inspection, 2D-13
cylinder head, disassembly, 2D-12
cylinder head, reassembly, 2D-15
cylinder honing, 2D-23
engine
　　disassembly sequence, 2D-11
　　general information, 2D-6
　　reassembly sequence, 2D-26
　　removal, methods and precautions, 2D-9
　　removal and installation, 2D-9
initial start-up and break-in after overhaul, 2D-34
main and connecting rod bearings, inspection, 2D-26
piston rings, installation, 2D-27
pistons and connecting rods, inspection, 2D-23
pistons and connecting rods, installation and rod bearing
　　oil clearance check, 2D-32
pistons and connecting rods, removal, 2D-17
rear main oil seal, installation, 2D-31
rebuilding alternatives, 2D-10
Top Dead Center (TDC) for number one piston, locating, 2D-6
vacuum gauge diagnostic checks, 2D-8
valves, servicing, 2D-15
Grille, removal and installation, 11-6

H

Headlights
　adjustment, 12-8
　bulb, replacement, 12-7
　housing, removal and installation, 12-8
　switch, check and replacement, 12-11
Heater core, replacement, 3-10
Heater/air conditioner
　blower motor (front), removal and installation, 3-8
　control assembly, removal and installation, 3-12
Hinges and locks, maintenance, 11-3
Hood
　latch and cable, removal and installation, 11-6
　removal, installation and adjustment, 11-3
Horn, check and replacement, 12-16
Hub and bearing assembly
　front, removal and installation, 10-9
　rear, removal and installation, 10-13
**Hydraulic roller lifters, removal, inspection
　and installation, 2C-12**

I

Idle Air Control (IAC) valve, check and replacement, 4-12
Ignition
　coil, check and replacement, 5-4

switch and lock cylinder, removal and installation, 12-6
system
　check, 5-3
　general information, 5-2
Instrument cluster
　bezel, removal and installation, 11-17
　removal and installation, 12-15
Intake air temperature sensor, 6-4
Intake manifold, removal, inspection and installation
　four-cylinder engine, 2A-3
　3.0L V6 engine, 2B-3
　3.3L and 3.8L V6 engines, 2C-4
Interior quarter trim panels, removal and installation, 11-21
**Introduction to the Dodge Caravan, Plymouth Voyager and
　Chrysler Town & Country, 0-5**

J

Jacking and towing, 0-16

L

Leaf spring
　mounts, removal and installation, 10-11
　removal and installation, 10-12
Liftgate
　removal installation and adjustment, 11-14
　strut replacement, 11-15
Lower console, removal and installation, 11-16

M

Main and connecting rod bearings, inspection, 2D-26
Maintenance schedule, 1-7
Maintenance techniques, tools and working facilities, 0-8
Major tune-up, 1-6
**Master cylinder, removal, installation and vacuum seal
　replacement, 9-12**
Minor tune-up, 1-6
Mirrors, removal and installation, 11-23
Multi-function switch, check and replacement, 12-6
**Multi-Port Electronic Fuel Injection (MPI) system and
　information sensors - description, 6-3**

N

**Neutral start/back-up light switch, check and
　replacement, 7-4**

O

Oil
  cooler, removal and installation, 2C-16
  pan, removal and installation
    four-cylinder engine, 2A-14
    3.0L V6 engine, 2B-15
    3.3L and 3.8L V6 engines, 2C-14
  pump, removal, inspection and installation
    four-cylinder engine, 2A-15
    3.0L V6 engine, 2B-16
    3.3L and 3.8L V6 engines, 2C-15
  seal, replacement, 7-3
On Board Diagnosis (OBD) system - description and trouble code access, 6-5
Overhead console, removal and installation, 11-17

P

Parking brake
  cables, replacement, 9-16
  pedal assembly, removal, installation and adjustment, 9-16
  shoes (models with rear disc brakes), replacement, 9-17
Piston rings, installation, 2D-27
Pistons and connecting rods
  inspection, 2D-23
  installation and rod bearing oil clearance check, 2D-32
  removal, 2D-17
Positive Crankcase Ventilation (PCV) system, 6-17
Positive Crankcase Ventilation (PCV) valve check and replacement, 1-22
Power brake booster, check, removal and installation, 9-15
Power door lock system, description and check, 12-18
Power seats, description and check, 12-20
Power steering
  fluid cooler, removal and installation, 10-18
  fluid level check, 1-12
  pump, removal and installation, 10-16
  system, bleeding, 10-18
Power window system, description and check, 12-19
Powertrain Control Module (PCM) - removal and installation, 6-4
Proportioning valves, check and replacement, 9-14

Q

Quarter window glass, removal and installation, 11-16

R

Radiator/transmission oil cooler, removal and installation, 3-4

Radio and speakers, removal and installation, 12-13
Rear main oil seal
  installation, 2D-31
  replacement
    four-cylinder engine, 2A-18
    3.0l V6 engine, 2B-18
    3.3L and 3.8L V6 engines, 2C-16
Rear window defogger
  switch, removal and installation, 12-15
  check and repair, 12-15
Relays, general information, 12-5
Repair operations possible with the engine in the vehicle, 2A-3, 2C-3
Rocker arm and hydraulic valve lash adjuster, removal, inspection and installation
  four-cylinder engine, 2A-10
  3.0L V6 engine, 2B-12
Rocker arms and pushrods, removal, inspection and installation, 2C-11

S

Safety first!, 0-20
Seat belt check, 1-25, 11-24
Seats, removal and installation, 11-24
Shift cable, check and adjustment, 7-4
Shock absorbers (rear), removal and installation, 10-12
Sliding door, removal and installation, 11-14
Spark plug
  check and replacement, 1-23
  wire check and replacement, 1-25
Stabilizer bar
  and bushings (front), removal, inspection, and installation, 10-4
  rear, removal, inspection, and installation, 10-10
Starter motor
  in-vehicle check, 5-9
  removal and installation, 5-10
Starting system, general information and precautions, 5-9
Steering
  gear, removal and installation, 10-15
  knuckle, removal and installation, 10-10
  system, general information, 10-12
  wheel, removal and installation, 10-13
Steering and suspension
  check, 1-16
  systems, general information, 10-3
Strut/coil spring, disassembly, inspection, and reassembly, 10-6
Struts (front), removal, inspection and installation, 10-5
Suspension and steering systems, 10-1 through 10-20
  axle assembly (rear), removal and installation, 10-12
  balljoints, check and replacement, 10-9
  control arm, removal, inspection and installation, 10-7
  hub and bearing assembly
    front, removal and installation, 10-9
    rear, removal and installation, 10-13
  leaf spring
    mounts, removal and installation, 10-11
    removal and installation, 10-12

power steering
 fluid cooler, removal and installation, 10-18
 pump, removal and installation, 10-16
 system, bleeding, 10-18
shock absorbers (rear), removal and installation, 10-12
stabilizer bar and bushings
 front, removal, inspection and installation, 10-4
 rear, removal, inspection and installation, 10-10
steering
 gear, removal and installation, 10-15
 knuckle, removal and installation, 10-10
 system, general information, 10-12
 wheel, removal and installation, 10-13
strut/coil spring, disassembly, inspection, reassembly, 10-6
struts (front), removal, inspection and installation, 10-5
tie-rod ends, removal and installation, 10-14
track bar and mount, removal and installation, 10-11
wheel alignment, general information, 10-19
wheels and tires, general information, 10-18

T

Thermostat, check and replacement, 3-2
Throttle body, check, removal and installation, 4-10
Tie-rod ends, removal and installation, 10-14
Timing belt
 and covers, removal, inspection and
  installation, 2A-6
 removal, installation and adjustment, 2B-7
Timing chain
 and sprockets, removal, inspection and installation, 2C-10
 cover, removal and installation, 2C-9
Tire and tire pressure checks, 1-10
Tire rotation, 1-16
Top Dead Center (TDC) for number one piston,
 locating, 2D-6
Towing the vehicle, 0-16
Track bar and mount, removal and installation, 10-11
Transaxle band adjustment (3-speed 31TH transaxle), 7-8
Transaxle throttle cable (3-speed 31TH transaxle), check
 and adjustment, 7-4

Troubleshooting, 0-21
Tune-up and routine maintenance, 1-1 through 1-26
Turn signal/hazard flasher, check and
 replacement, 12-5

U

Underhood hose check and replacement, 1-15
Upholstery and carpets, maintenance, 11-2

V

Vacuum gauge diagnostic checks, 2D-8
Valve covers, removal and installation, 2A-3, 2B-2 and 2C-3
Valve springs, retainers and seals, replacement,
 2A-12 and 2B-15
Valves, servicing, 2D-15
Vehicle identification numbers, 0-6
Vinyl trim, maintenance, 11-2
Voltage regulator, description and general information, 5-9

W

Water pump
 check, 3-6
 replacement, 3-6
Wheel
 alignment, general information, 10-19
 cylinder, removal and installation, 9-12
Wheelhouse splash shield, removal and installation, 11-23
Wheels and tires, general information, 10-18
Windshield
 and fixed glass, replacement, 11-3
 washer fluid, 1-9
 wiper motor, check and replacement, 12-14
Wiper blade inspection and replacement, 1-16
Wiring diagrams, general information, 12-23

Haynes Automotive Manuals

ACURA
12020 Integra '86 thru '89 & Legend '86 thru '90
12021 Integra '90 thru '93 & Legend '91 thru '95
Integra '94 thru '00 - see HONDA Civic (42025)
MDX '01 thru '07 - see HONDA Pilot (42037)
12050 Acura TL all models '99 thru '08

AMC
Jeep CJ - see JEEP (50020)
14020 Concord/Hornet/Gremlin/Spirit '70 thru '83
14025 (Renault) Alliance & Encore '83 thru '87

AUDI
15020 4000 all models '80 thru '87
15025 5000 all models '77 thru '83
15026 5000 all models '84 thru '88
Audi A4 '96 thru '01 - see VW Passat (96023)
15030 Audi A4 '02 thru '08

AUSTIN
Healey Sprite - see MG Midget (66015)

BMW
18020 3/5 Series '82 thru '92
18021 3 Series including Z3 models '92 thru '98
18022 3-Series Z4 models '99 thru '05
18023 3-Series '06 thru '10
18025 320i all 4 cyl models '75 thru '83
18050 1500 thru 2002 except Turbo '59 thru '77

BUICK
19010 Buick Century '97 thru '05
Century (front-wheel drive) - see GM (38005)
19020 Buick, Oldsmobile & Pontiac Full-size (Front wheel drive) '85 thru '05
19025 Buick, Oldsmobile & Pontiac Full-size (Rear wheel drive) '70 thru '90
19030 Mid-size Regal & Century '74 thru '87
Regal - see GENERAL MOTORS (38010)
Skyhawk - see GM (38030)
Skylark - see GM (38020, 38025)
Somerset - see GENERAL MOTORS (38025)

CADILLAC
21015 CTS & CTS-V '03 thru '12
21030 Cadillac Rear Wheel Drive '70 thru '93
Cimarron, Eldorado & Seville - see GM (38015, 38030, 38031)

CHEVROLET
10305 Chevrolet Engine Overhaul Manual
24010 Astro & GMC Safari Mini-vans '85 thru '05
24015 Camaro V8 all models '70 thru '81
24016 Camaro all models '82 thru '92
Cavalier - see GM (38015)
Celebrity - see GM (38005)
24017 Camaro & Firebird '93 thru '02
24020 Chevelle, Malibu, El Camino '69 thru '87
24024 Chevette & Pontiac T1000 '76 thru '87
Citation - see GENERAL MOTORS (38020)
24027 Colorado & GMC Canyon '04 thru '10
24032 Corsica/Beretta all models '87 thru '96
24040 Corvette all V8 models '68 thru '82
24041 Corvette all models '84 thru '96
24045 Full-size Sedans Caprice, Impala, Biscayne, Bel Air & Wagons '69 thru '90
24046 Impala SS & Caprice and Buick Roadmaster '91 thru '96
Impala '00 thru '05 - see LUMINA (24048)
24047 Impala & Monte Carlo all models '06 thru '11
Lumina '90 thru '94 - see GM (38010)
24048 Lumina & Monte Carlo '95 thru '05
Lumina APV - see GM (38035)
24050 Luv Pick-up all 2WD & 4WD '72 thru '82
Malibu - see GM (38026)
24055 Monte Carlo all models '70 thru '88
Monte Carlo '95 thru '01 - see LUMINA
24059 Nova all V8 models '69 thru '79
24060 Nova/Geo Prizm '85 thru '92
24064 Pick-ups '67 thru '87 - Chevrolet & GMC
24065 Pick-ups '88 thru '98 - Chevrolet & GMC
24066 Pick-ups '99 thru '06 - Chevrolet & GMC
24067 Chevy Silverado & GMC Sierra '07 thru '12
24070 S-10 & GMC S-15 Pick-ups '82 thru '93
24071 S-10, Sonoma & Jimmy '94 thru '04
24072 Chevrolet TrailBlazer, GMC Envoy & Oldsmobile Bravada '02 thru '09
24075 Sprint '85 thru '88, Geo Metro '89 thru '01
24080 Vans - Chevrolet & GMC '68 thru '96
24081 Full-size Vans '96 thru '10

CHRYSLER
10310 Chrysler Engine Overhaul Manual
25015 Chrysler Cirrus, Dodge Stratus, Plymouth Breeze, '95 thru '00
25020 Full-size Front-Wheel Drive '88 thru '93
K-Cars - see DODGE Aries (30008)
Laser - see DODGE Daytona (30030)
25025 Chrysler LHS, Concorde & New Yorker, Dodge Intrepid, Eagle Vision, '93 thru '97
25026 Chrysler LHS, Concorde, 300M, Dodge Intrepid '98 thru '04
25027 Chrysler 300, Dodge Charger & Magnum '05 thru '09
25030 Chrysler/Plym. Mid-size '82 thru '95
Rear-wheel Drive - see DODGE (30050)
25035 PT Cruiser all models '01 thru '10
25040 Chrysler Sebring '95 thru '06, Dodge Stratus '01 thru '06, Dodge Avenger '95 thru '00

DATSUN
28005 200SX all models '80 thru '83
28007 B-210 all models '73 thru '78
28009 210 all models '78 thru '82
28012 240Z, 260Z & 280Z Coupe '70 thru '78
28014 280ZX Coupe & 2+2 '79 thru '83
300ZX - see NISSAN (72010)
28018 510 & PL521 Pick-up '68 thru '73
28020 510 all models '78 thru '81
28022 620 Series Pick-up all models '73 thru '79
720 Series Pick-up - see NISSAN (72030)
28025 810/Maxima all gas models '77 thru '84

DODGE
400 & 600 - see CHRYSLER (25030)
30008 Aries & Plymouth Reliant '81 thru '89
30010 Caravan & Ply. Voyager '84 thru '95
30011 Caravan & Ply. Voyager '96 thru '02
30012 Challenger/Plymouth Saporro '78 thru '83
Challenger '67-'76 - see DART (30025)
30013 Caravan, Chrysler Voyager, Town & Country '03 thru '07
30016 Colt/Plymouth Champ '78 thru '87
30020 Dakota Pick-ups all models '87 thru '96
30021 Durango '98 & '99, Dakota '97 thru '99
30022 Durango '00 thru '03, Dakota '00 thru '04
30023 Durango '04 thru '09, Dakota '05 thru '11
30025 Dart, Challenger/Plymouth Barracuda & Valiant 6 cyl models '67 thru '76
30030 Daytona & Chrysler Laser '84 thru '89
Intrepid - see Chrysler (25025, 25026)
30034 Dodge & Plymouth Neon '95 thru '99
30035 Omni & Plymouth Horizon '78 thru '90
30036 Dodge and Plymouth Neon '00 thru '05
30040 Pick-ups all full-size models '74 thru '93
30041 Pick-ups all full-size models '94 thru '01
30042 Pick-ups full-size models '02 thru '08
30045 Ram 50/D50 Pick-ups & Raider and Plymouth Arrow Pick-ups '79 thru '93
30050 Dodge/Ply./Chrysler RWD '71 thru '89
30055 Shadow/Plymouth Sundance '87 thru '94
30060 Spirit & Plymouth Acclaim '89 thru '95
30065 Vans - Dodge & Plymouth '71 thru '03

EAGLE
Talon - see MITSUBISHI (68030, 68031)
Vision - see CHRYSLER (25025)

FIAT
34010 124 Sport Coupe & Spider '68 thru '78
34025 X1/9 all models '74 thru '80

FORD
10320 Ford Engine Overhaul Manual
10355 Ford Automatic Transmission Overhaul
11500 Mustang '64-1/2 thru '70 Restoration Guide
36004 Aerostar Mini-vans '86 thru '97
Aspire - see FORD Festiva (36030)
36006 Contour/Mercury Mystique '95 thru '00
36008 Courier Pick-up all models '72 thru '82
36012 Crown Victoria & Mercury Grand Marquis '88 thru '10
36016 Escort/Mercury Lynx '81 thru '90
36020 Escort/Mercury Tracer '91 thru '02
Expedition - see FORD Pick-up (36059)
36022 Escape & Mazda Tribute '01 thru '11
36024 Explorer & Mazda Navajo '91 thru '01
36025 Explorer/Mercury Mountaineer '02 thru '10
36028 Fairmont & Mercury Zephyr '78 thru '83
36030 Festiva & Aspire '88 thru '97
36032 Fiesta all models '77 thru '80
36034 Focus all models '00 thru '11
36036 Ford & Mercury Full-size '75 thru '87
36044 Ford & Mercury Mid-size '75 thru '86
36045 Ford Fusion & Mercury Milan '06 thru '10
36048 Mustang V8 all models '64-1/2 thru '73
36049 Mustang II 4 cyl, V6 & V8 '74 thru '78
36050 Mustang & Mercury Capri '79 thru '93
36051 Mustang all models '94 thru '04
36052 Mustang '05 thru '10
36054 Pick-ups and Bronco '73 thru '79
36058 Pick-ups and Bronco '80 thru '96
36059 Pick-ups & Expedition '97 thru '09
36060 Super Duty Pick-up, Excursion '99 thru '10
36061 F-150 full-size '04 thru '10
36062 Pinto & Mercury Bobcat '75 thru '80
36066 Probe all models '89 thru '92
Probe '93 thru '97 - see MAZDA 626 (61042)
36070 Ranger/Bronco II gas models '83 thru '92
36071 Ford Ranger '93 thru '10 & Mazda Pick-ups '94 thru '09
36074 Taurus & Mercury Sable '86 thru '95
36075 Taurus & Mercury Sable '96 thru '01
36078 Tempo & Mercury Topaz '84 thru '94
36082 Thunderbird/Mercury Cougar '83 thru '88
36086 Thunderbird/Mercury Cougar '89 thru '97
36090 Vans all V8 Econoline models '69 thru '91
36094 Vans full size '92 thru '10
36097 Windstar Mini-van '95 thru '07

GENERAL MOTORS
10360 GM Automatic Transmission Overhaul
38005 Buick Century, Chevrolet Celebrity, Olds Cutlass Ciera & Pontiac 6000 '82 thru '96
38010 Buick Regal, Chevrolet Lumina, Oldsmobile Cutlass Supreme & Pontiac Grand Prix front wheel drive '88 thru '07
38015 Buick Skyhawk, Cadillac Cimarron, Chevrolet Cavalier, Oldsmobile Firenza Pontiac J-2000 & Sunbird '82 thru '94
38016 Chevrolet Cavalier/Pontiac Sunfire '95 thru '05
38017 Chevrolet Cobalt & Pontiac G5 '05 thru '11
38020 Buick Skylark, Chevrolet Citation, Olds Omega, Pontiac Phoenix '80 thru '85
38025 Buick Skylark & Somerset, Olds Achieva, Calais & Pontiac Grand Am '85 thru '98
38026 Chevrolet Malibu, Olds Alero & Cutlass, Pontiac Grand Am '97 thru '03
38027 Chevrolet Malibu '04 thru '10
38030 Cadillac Eldorado & Oldsmobile Toronado '71 thru '85, Seville '80 thru '85, Buick Riviera '79 thru '85
38031 Cadillac Eldorado & Seville '86 thru '91, DeVille & Buick Riviera '86 thru '93, Fleetwood & Olds Toronado '86 thru '92
38032 DeVille '94 thru '05, Seville '92 thru '04 Cadillac DTS '06 thru '10
38035 Chevrolet Lumina APV, Olds Silhouette & Pontiac Trans Sport '90 thru '96
38036 Chevrolet Venture, Olds Silhouette, Pontiac Trans Sport & Montana '97 thru '05
GM Full-size RWD - see BUICK (19025)
38040 Chevrolet Equinox '05 thru '09 Pontiac Torrent '06 thru '09
38070 Chevrolet HHR '06 thru '11

GEO
Metro - see CHEVROLET Sprint (24075)
Prizm - see CHEVROLET (24060) or TOYOTA (92036)
40030 Storm all models '90 thru '93
Tracker - see SUZUKI Samurai (90010)

GMC
Vans & Pick-ups - see CHEVROLET

HONDA
42010 Accord CVCC all models '76 thru '83
42011 Accord all models '84 thru '89
42012 Accord all models '90 thru '93
42013 Accord all models '94 thru '97
42014 Accord all models '98 thru '02
42015 Accord '03 thru '07
42020 Civic 1200 all models '73 thru '79
42021 Civic 1300 & 1500 CVCC '80 thru '83
42022 Civic 1500 CVCC all models '75 thru '79
42023 Civic all models '84 thru '91
42024 Civic & del Sol '92 thru '95
42025 Civic '96 thru '00, CR-V '97 thru '01, Acura Integra '94 thru '00
42026 Civic '01 thru '10, CR-V '02 thru '09
42035 Odyssey models '99 thru '10
Passport - see ISUZU Rodeo (47017)

HYUNDAI
43010 Elantra all models '96 thru '10
43015 Excel & Accent all models '86 thru '09
43050 Santa Fe all models '01 thru '06
43055 Sonata all models '99 thru '08

INFINITI
G35 '03 thru '08 - see NISSAN 350Z (72011)

ISUZU
Hombre - see CHEVROLET S-10 (24071)
47017 Rodeo, Amigo & Honda Passport '89 thru '02
47020 Trooper '84 thru '91, Pick-up '81 thru '93

JAGUAR
49010 XJ6 all 6 cyl models '68 thru '86
49011 XJ6 all models '88 thru '94
49015 XJ12 & XJS all 12 cyl models '72 thru '85

JEEP
50010 Cherokee, Comanche & Wagoneer Limited all models '84 thru '01
50020 CJ all models '49 thru '86
50025 Grand Cherokee all models '93 thru '04
50026 Grand Cherokee '05 thru '09
50029 Grand Wagoneer & Pick-up '72 thru '91
50030 Wrangler all models '87 thru '11
50035 Liberty '02 thru '07

KIA
54050 Optima '01 thru '10
54070 Sephia '94 thru '01, Spectra '00 thru '09, Sportage '05 thru '10

LEXUS
ES 300/330 - see TOYOTA Camry (92007) (92008)
RX 330 - see TOYOTA Highlander (92095)

LINCOLN
Navigator - see FORD Pick-up (36059)
59010 Rear Wheel Drive all models '70 thru '10

MAZDA
61010 GLC (rear wheel drive) '77 thru '83
61011 GLC (front wheel drive) '81 thru '85
61012 Mazda3 '04 thru '11
61015 323 & Protegé '90 thru '03
61016 MX-5 Miata '90 thru '09
61020 MPV all models '89 thru '98
Navajo - see FORD Explorer (36024)
61030 Pick-ups '72 thru '93
Pick-ups '94 on - see Ford (36071)
61035 RX-7 all models '79 thru '85
61036 RX-7 all models '86 thru '91
61040 626 (rear wheel drive) '79 thru '82
61041 626 & MX-6 (front wheel drive) '83 thru '92
61042 626 '93 thru '01, & MX-6/Ford Probe '93 thru '02
61043 Mazda6 '03 thru '11

MERCEDES-BENZ
63012 123 Series Diesel '76 thru '85
63015 190 Series 4-cyl gas models, '84 thru '88
63020 230, 250 & 280 6 cyl sohc '68 thru '72
63025 280 123 Series gas models '77 thru '81
63030 350 & 450 all models '71 thru '80
63040 C-Class: C230/C240/C280/C320/C350 '01 thru '07

MERCURY
64200 Villager & Nissan Quest '93 thru '01
All other titles, see FORD listing.

MG
66010 MGB Roadster & GT Coupe '62 thru '80
66015 MG Midget & Austin Healey Sprite Roadster '58 thru '80

MINI
67020 Mini '02 thru '11

MITSUBISHI
68020 Cordia, Tredia, Galant, Precis & Mirage '83 thru '93
68030 Eclipse, Eagle Talon & Plymouth Laser '90 thru '94
68031 Eclipse '95 thru '05, Eagle Talon '95 thru '98
68035 Galant '94 thru '10
68040 Pick-up '83 thru '96, Montero '83 thru '93

NISSAN
72010 300ZX all models incl. Turbo '84 thru '89
72011 350Z & Infiniti G35 all models '03 thru '08
72015 Altima all models '93 thru '06
72016 Altima '07 thru '10
72020 Maxima all models '85 thru '92
72021 Maxima all models '93 thru '01
72025 Murano '03 thru '10
72030 Pick-ups '80 thru '97, Pathfinder '87 thru '95
72031 Frontier Pick-up, Xterra, Pathfinder '96 thru '04
72032 Frontier & Xterra '05 thru '11
72040 Pulsar all models '83 thru '86
72050 Sentra all models '82 thru '94
72051 Sentra & 200SX all models '95 thru '06
72060 Stanza all models '82 thru '90
72070 Titan pick-ups '04 thru '10, Armada '05 thru '10

OLDSMOBILE
73015 Cutlass '74 thru '88
For other OLDSMOBILE titles, see BUICK, CHEVROLET or GM listings.

PLYMOUTH
For PLYMOUTH titles, see DODGE.

PONTIAC
79008 Fiero all models '84 thru '88
79018 Firebird V8 models except Turbo '70 thru '81
79019 Firebird all models '82 thru '92
79025 G6 all models '05 thru '09
79040 Mid-size Rear-wheel Drive '70 thru '87
Vibe '03 thru '11 - see TOYOTA Matrix (92060)
For other PONTIAC titles, see BUICK, CHEVROLET or GM listings.

PORSCHE
80020 911 Coupe & Targa models '65 thru '89
80025 914 all 4 cyl models '69 thru '76
80030 924 all models incl. Turbo '76 thru '82
80035 944 all models incl. Turbo '83 thru '89

RENAULT
Alliance, Encore - see AMC (14020)

SAAB
84010 900 including Turbo '79 thru '88

SATURN
87010 Saturn all S-series models '91 thru '02
87011 Saturn Ion '03 thru '07

SATURN
87020 Saturn all L-series models '00 thru '04
87040 Saturn VUE '02 thru '07

SUBARU
89002 1100, 1300, 1400 & 1600 '71 thru '79
89003 1600 & 1800 2WD & 4WD '80 thru '94
89100 Legacy models '90 thru '99
89101 Legacy & Forester '00 thru '06

SUZUKI
90010 Samurai/Sidekick/Geo Tracker '86 thru '01

TOYOTA
92005 Camry all models '83 thru '91
92006 Camry all models '92 thru '96
92007 Camry/Avalon/Solara/Lexus ES 300 '97 thru '01
92008 Toyota Camry, Avalon and Solara & Lexus ES 300/330 all models '02 thru '06
92009 Camry '07 thru '11
92015 Celica Rear Wheel Drive '71 thru '85
92020 Celica Front Wheel Drive '86 thru '99
92025 Celica Supra all models '79 thru '92
92030 Corolla all models '75 thru '79
92032 Corolla rear wheel drive models '80 thru '87
92035 Corolla front wheel drive models '84 thru '92
92036 Corolla & Geo Prizm '93 thru '02
92037 Corolla models '03 thru '11
92040 Corolla Tercel all models '80 thru '82
92045 Corona all models '74 thru '82
92050 Cressida all models '78 thru '82
92055 Land Cruiser FJ40/43/45/55 '68 thru '82
92056 Land Cruiser FJ60/62/80/FZJ80 '80 thru '96
92060 Matrix & Pontiac Vibe '03 thru '11
92065 MR2 all models '85 thru '87
92070 Pick-up all models '69 thru '78
92075 Pick-up all models '79 thru '95
92076 Tacoma, 4Runner & T100 '93 thru '04
92077 Tacoma all models '05 thru '09
92078 Tundra '00 thru '06, Sequoia '01 thru '07
92079 4Runner all models '03 thru '09
92080 Previa all models '91 thru '95
92081 Prius '01 thru '08
92082 RAV4 all models '96 thru '10
92085 Tercel all models '87 thru '94
92090 Sienna all models '98 thru '09
92095 Highlander & Lexus RX-330 '99 thru '07

TRIUMPH
94007 Spitfire all models '62 thru '81
94010 TR7 all models '75 thru '81

VW
96008 Beetle & Karmann Ghia '54 thru '79
96009 New Beetle '98 thru '11
96016 Rabbit, Jetta, Scirocco, & Pick-up gas models '75 thru '92 & Convertible '80 thru '92
96017 Golf, GTI & Jetta '93 thru '98, Cabrio '95 thru 02
96018 Golf, GTI & Jetta '98 thru '05
96019 Jetta, Rabbit, GTI & Golf '05 thru '11
96020 Rabbit, Jetta, Pick-up diesel '77 thru '84
96023 Passat '98 thru '05, Audi A4 '96 thru '01
96030 Transporter 1600 all models '68 thru '79
96035 Transporter 1700, 1800, 2000 '72 thru '79
96040 Type 3 1500 & 1600 '63 thru '73
96045 Vanagon air-cooled models '80 thru '83

VOLVO
97010 120, 130 Series & 1800 Sports '61 thru '73
97015 140 Series all models '66 thru '74
97020 240 Series all models '76 thru '93
97040 740 & 760 Series all models '82 thru '88

TECHBOOK MANUALS
10205 Automotive Computer Codes
10206 OBD-II & Electronic Engine Management
10210 Automotive Emissions Control Manual
10215 Fuel Injection Manual, '78 thru '85
10220 Fuel Injection Manual, '86 thru '99
10225 Holley Carburetor Manual
10230 Rochester Carburetor Manual
10240 Weber/Zenith/Stromberg/SU Carburetor
10305 Chevrolet Engine Overhaul Manual
10310 Chrysler Engine Overhaul Manual
10320 Ford Engine Overhaul Manual
10330 GM and Ford Diesel Engine Repair
10333 Engine Performance Manual
10340 Small Engine Repair Manual
10345 Suspension, Steering & Driveline
10355 Ford Automatic Transmission Overhaul
10360 GM Automatic Transmission Overhaul
10405 Automotive Body Repair & Painting
10410 Automotive Brake Manual
10415 Automotive Detailing Manual
10420 Automotive Electrical Manual
10425 Automotive Heating & Air Conditioning
10430 Automotive Reference Dictionary
10435 Automotive Tools Manual
10440 Used Car Buying Guide
10445 Welding Manual
10450 ATV Basics
10452 Scooters 50cc to 250cc

SPANISH MANUALS
98903 Reparación de Carrocería & Pintura
98904 Manual de Carburador Modelos Holley & Rochester
98905 Códigos Automotrices de la Computadora
98906 OBD-II & Sistemas de Control Electrónico del Motor
98910 Frenos Automotriz
98913 Electricidad Automotriz
98915 Inyección de Combustible '86 al '99
99040 Chevrolet & GMC Camionetas '67 al '87
99041 Chevrolet & GMC Camionetas '88 al '98
99042 Chevrolet Camionetas Cerradas '68 al '95
99043 Chevrolet/GMC Camionetas '94 al '04
99048 Chevrolet/GMC Camionetas '99 al '06
99055 Dodge Caravan/Ply. Voyager '84 al '95
99075 Ford Camionetas y Bronco '80 al '94
99076 Ford F-150 '97 al '09
99077 Ford Camionetas Cerradas '69 al '91
99088 Ford Modelos de Tamaño Mediano '75 al '86
99089 Ford Camionetas Ranger '93 al '10
99091 Ford Taurus & Mercury Sable '86 al '95
99095 GM Modelos de Tamaño Grande '70 al '90
99100 GM Modelos de Tamaño Mediano '70 al '88
99106 Jeep Cherokee, Wagoneer & Comanche '84 al '00
99110 Nissan Camionetas & Pathfinder '80 al '96
99118 Nissan Sentra '82 al '94
99125 Toyota Camionetas y 4-Runner '79 al '95

Over 100 Haynes motorcycle manuals also available

7-12